W9-BSM-188

Special Edition
Using
SQL

Rafe Colburn

A Division of Macmillan USA
201 West 103rd Street
Indianapolis, Indiana 46290

SPECIAL EDITION USING SQL

Copyright © 2000 by Que

International Standard Book Number: 0-7897-1974-6

Library of Congress Catalog Card Number: 98-89290

Printed in the United States of America

First Printing: October 1999

01   00   99   4   3   2   1

TRADEMARKS

WARNING AND DISCLAIMER

Publisher
Dean Miller

Acquisitions Editor
Randy Haubner

Development Editor
Sean Dixon

Managing Editor
Lisa Wilson

Project Editor
Natalie Harris

Copy Editors
Kelly Talbot
Barbara Hacha

Indexer
Diane Brenner

Proofreader
Benjamin Berg

Technical Editor
Michael Ask

Team Coordinator
Cindy Teeters

Software Development Specialist
Jason Haines

Interior Design
Ruth Harvey

Cover Design
Dan Armstrong
Ruth Harvey

Layout Technicians
Tim Osborn
Staci Somers
Mark Walchle

Production Control
Dan Harris
Heather Moseman

TABLE OF CONTENTS

About the Author

Rafe Colburn is a consultant with Interpath Communications. His responsibilities include application and database design and development for large Internet-related projects. Rafe is also the author of *Teach Yourself CGI Programming in a Week*, for Sams.net, and is the co-author of *Teach Yourself Netscape Web Publishing in a Week*, also for Sams.net. Rafe makes his home in Apex, North Carolina. He can be reached via email at `rafe@rc3.org`, and his home page is `http://rc3.org`. More information about this book can be found at `http://rc3.org/sqlbook`.

DEDICATION

This book is dedicated to my family, the Colburns and Thorkelsons, who have lent me a lifetime of support.

ACKNOWLEDGMENTS

Writing a book is a momentous task, and it's impossible to thank all the people who helped to produce the book in this small space, not to mention all the people who helped out indirectly with their support and patience. First of all, I'd like to thank the people at Que who were with me all the way, Randy Haubner and Sean Dixon. I'd also like to thank my technical editor, Michael Ask.

Most importantly, I'd like to thank my wife for months of perseverance as I sequestered myself in the study to bring this book into existence. Without her patience and love, I never could have made it.

TELL US WHAT YOU THINK!

As the reader of this book, *you* are our most important critic and commentator. We value your opinion and want to know what we're doing right, what we could do better, what areas you'd like to see us publish in, and any other words of wisdom you're willing to pass our way.

As a publisher for Que, I welcome your comments. You can fax, email, or write me directly to let me know what you did or didn't like about this book—as well as what we can do to make our books stronger.

Please note that I cannot help you with technical problems related to the topic of this book, and that due to the high volume of mail I receive, I might not be able to reply to every message.

When you write, please be sure to include this book's title and author as well as your name and phone or fax number. I will carefully review your comments and share them with the author and editors who worked on the book.

Fax: 317.581.4666
Email: office_que@mcp.com
Mail: Publisher
            Que
            201 West 103rd Street
            Indianapolis, IN 46290 USA

INTRODUCTION

Relational databases are some of the most widely used and important computer applications available. They provide a powerful and flexible means for storing data of all kinds. Indeed, they work behind the scenes of many of the applications you probably use, directly or indirectly, every day. The relational model, which is described in detail in the first chapter of *Special Edition Using SQL*, is extremely scalable. In fact, relational databases are used for applications as small as home recipe files and as large as the data storage systems used by banks to keep track of all the transactions that they process.

SQL, the Structured Query Language, is the query language that enables database programmers to retrieve data from, to modify data in, and to manage most relational databases. Although there are some differences in the way SQL is supported among the various database vendors, the language is standard enough that after you've learned it for one database product, you'll be able to use it with any other database product that supports SQL. SQL consists of only a few types of statements, and it is easy to learn well enough to perform basic queries. As your needs become more complex and your confidence in your SQL querying abilities grows, so too will the complexity of the queries that you write.

One of the nicest things about SQL is that it encourages experimentation. The queries for retrieving data are completely separate from those used to modify data, so you can enter any type of data retrieval query you like without fear of damaging the data within your database. SQL also encourages experimentation because nearly all queries consist of a single statement, so they're easy to write. Most databases provide interactive programs that enable you to enter queries and immediately view the results, so you can rapidly write and modify your queries until they retrieve exactly the data you're looking for. When your queries are perfected, you can transfer them into your applications.

HOW THIS BOOK IS ORGANIZED

The first chapter of *Special Edition Using SQL*, "The Structured Query Language," provides a foundation on which to build your knowledge of SQL. It describes how relational databases work and some of the history behind relational databases. The basic syntax of SQL is also described. Chapter 2, "Database Design," is devoted to explaining the design of relational databases. It discusses topics such as entity-relationship modeling and database normalization to enable you to build well-designed databases that provide the highest possible level of database integrity without sacrificing performance.

Chapters 3, "Creating Databases," and 4, "Inserting, Updating, and Deleting Records," begin to get into the meat of SQL. They are devoted to discussing the creation of tables, the basic unit of storage in relational databases, and the SQL statements used to populate databases after they're created. Chapter 3 also contains a general, high-level discussion of the types of data that can be stored in a relational database. I also introduce the sample database, which is used to store information about movies, in Chapter 3. That database will provide a common thread through nearly all the examples in this book.

Chapters 5 through 9 are devoted to data retrieval. Believe it or not, all five chapters are devoted to the SELECT statement, which is the SQL statement used to retrieve data from databases. The discussion begins with a basic explanation of how to retrieve the data you want from a single table and moves on to describe more complex techniques, such as using aggregate functions on groups of rows, joining multiple tables in a single query, and using subqueries within other queries.

Chapter 10, "Using Views," describes the use of views to provide customized means of accessing the data in a database for particular users. Chapter 11, "The SQL Security Model," is devoted to an explanation of the SQL security model and explains how you can restrict access to certain database resources to specific users.

Chapters 12, "Handling Specific Types of Data," 13, "Database Performance and Integrity," and 14, "Transactions and Cursors," are devoted to real-world issues that database programmers run into every day. Chapter 12 expands on the discussion of data types in Chapter 3 by explaining in detail how all the data types in a relational database are used and manipulated. Chapter 13 takes on the issue of database performance and explains how queries are optimized by database servers before they are executed. It also discusses database integrity—how to ensure that your tables contain the data that you think they contain. Chapter 14 is devoted to two advanced tools used by database programmers: cursors and transactions. Cursors are used to deal with query results one at a time (as opposed to in a batch), and transactions are used to maintain database integrity and to ensure that a database can be fully recovered in case of a disaster.

Chapters 15, "Writing Stored Procedures," 16, "More on Transact-SQL Stored Procedures," and 17, "Writing Oracle PL/SQL Stored Procedures," are devoted to discussing how to write stored procedures. Stored procedures are programs that are written and stored within the database so that they can called by most external applications. Chapter 15 discusses stored procedures in general, with an emphasis on those written in Transact-SQL. Chapter 16 covers stored procedures written in Transact-SQL in detail. Chapter 17 explains stored procedures written in Oracle PL/SQL, which are completely different from stored procedures for any other database.

Chapters 18 through 21 are devoted to discussing particular databases. Chapter 18, "Oracle," discusses Oracle; Chapter 19, "Microsoft SQL Server and Sybase Adaptive Server," discusses Transact-SQL, encompassing both Sybase databases and Microsoft SQL Server. Chapter 20, "Microsoft Access," is all about Microsoft Access, and Chapter 21, "MSQL and MySQL," discusses Mini-SQL and MySQL, two simple databases that are popular on Linux.

Chapters 22 through 24 provide an introduction to Internet programming and, more importantly, how to build database-backed Web applications. They explain the basics of HTML, how to build forms for the Web, and various application development platforms for building Web applications.

Although the foremost objective of this book is to teach you the ins and outs of standard SQL, I've taken things a bit further than that. The secondary goal of this book is to provide you with the tools you need to build database-backed applications. Although this book won't teach you how to use your favorite application development environment to build a graphical front end for your applications, it does explain how databases fit into larger application designs and how to build applications so that they use relational databases appropriately. By marrying information on how to use SQL with information on application design and development, I hope to provide you with the tools that you need to not only query databases, but to fit databases into a larger application design.

In the last part of this book, I provide a basic discussion of how to build database-backed Web applications. As the Web grows in popularity, both as a means of delivering information to the public and as a full-fledged application development platform, the use of databases by Web programmers is growing by leaps and bounds. Nearly every major Web site that currently exists uses relational databases in some capacity. Some use them for data storage for their applications, just as a traditional application would; others use them for storing all the content that they publish on the Web.

As the Web world and database world converge, I think it's important to provide some middle ground between the two. This book should help Web programmers get up to speed in terms of programming databases, and at the same time, it should provide database programmers with an introduction to the techniques used to develop Web applications.

You can access more information on the Web at the following URL:

```
http://www.mcp.com/product_support
```

When you locate the URL, you'll be asked to enter the book's ISBN. Enter 0789719746, then click the Search button to go to the book's information page. There you will find one or more useful links to the code and other pieces of information.

SPECIAL FEATURES OF THIS BOOK

One of the main features of this book is the "In the Real World" section of each chapter. After I finish discussing the subject of each chapter, I provide some additional information that you might find useful when you attempt to apply material from the chapter in the real world. These sections consist of additional information, case studies, or other information that extends the discussion found in the chapter itself.

Also, throughout this book you will find Tips, Notes, Cautions, Sidebars, and Cross References. These elements provide a variety of information, ranging from warnings you shouldn't miss to ancillary information that will help you program SQL more easily and efficiently.

| Tip #1001 from *Rafe Colburn* | Tips are designed to point out tricks of the trade that will decrease the time you need to write efficient, useful SQL queries and increase the user-friendliness of your database applications. |

Note

Notes are designed to provide you with extra information about a topic without weighing you down. You can skip a Note if you don't have the time for it, but Notes do provide useful information above and beyond the main discussion.

Caution

Don't ignore Cautions! If you pay attention to what they have to say, you can save hours of work.

Cross References are designed to point you to other locations in this book that will provide supplemental or supporting information. Cross References appear as follows:

→ For a full discussion of the rules of normalization, **see** "Normalization," **p. 44**

This is a sidebar
Sidebars are designed to provide information that is ancillary to the topic at hand. Read these if you want to learn more about particular issues related to the current discussion.

CONVENTIONS USED IN THIS BOOK

The following typographical conventions are used in this book:

Type	Meaning
Italic	New terms or phrases when initially defined.
`Monospace`	Anything that is a part of SQL or other languages.
UPPERCASE	All SQL commands appear in uppercase.
Bold	Any part of code the reader must type.

PART I

DESIGNING AND CONSTRUCTING A DATABASE

CHAPTER 1

THE STRUCTURED QUERY LANGUAGE

In this chapter

The *Structured Query Language*, heretofore referred to as SQL, provides a set of commands used for entering, changing, and viewing the contents of relational databases. SQL is commonly pronounced "sequel," so if you hear someone referring to a programming language in that fashion, it's SQL that he is talking about. Some SQL programmers refer to it using that pronunciation; others refer to it by the letters in the abbreviation. The only reason I mention this is that when I write about SQL in this book, I'll refer to it as though the letters are pronounced distinctly. Thus, I'll say "an SQL statement," as opposed to "a SQL statement."

THE RELATIONAL MODEL

Today, the dominant paradigm in the world of databases is the relational model. The fundamental attribute of the relational model is that data is stored within tables. Each table consists of rows and columns; the rows each represent a single record, and the columns contain the data that makes up each record. The intersection of each column and row is referred to as a *field*. Fields contain what might be referred to as *atomic* values. By that I mean that a field should contain a value that represents the smallest useful unit possible. Perhaps you have a database that is used to store data about employees at a company. If you wanted, you could store multiple names in a single field, separating them with commas or some other delimiter; however, that would then leave you with no way to retrieve only one of those names with an SQL command. If each of the names were stored in a separate field, it could be retrieved individually. By the same token, if you needed to retrieve the last names of the employees without their first names or middle initials, you could break the parts up into separate fields as well. The important point here is that a field is the smallest discrete unit that can be retrieved or changed using SQL. I'll cover this topic in depth when I discuss database normalization in Chapter 2, "Database Design."

Note

The relational model requires only that the information stored in a database be presented to users in a tabular format. The data can be physically stored in the manner that is most efficient, tabular or not. The tabular format of relational databases is an abstraction that lies at the heart of the relational model. The purpose of the relational model is to separate the presentation and manipulation of data from the way it is stored physically. For example, even though data is viewed and manipulated through tables in Oracle, the data itself is actually stored in a complex binary data structure that allows it to be retrieved and altered quickly.

The relational theory, which was originally described by mathematician E. F. Codd in his paper "A Relational Model of Data for Large Shared Data Banks," does not use the terms table, column, and row. When he spoke of these elements, he referred to tables as *relations*, columns as *attributes*, and rows as *tuples*. However, in this book, I will refer to them as tables, columns, and rows because in the world of SQL, that is the terminology that is used.

Note

Codd's theory for database management was originally created in 1969 and 1970. In 1968, Dr. Codd realized that mathematics could be applied to the problem of database management, and thus, he came up with the relational model. No commercial databases implement the relational model in full accordance with Codd's theories, but nonetheless, his relational model serves as the foundation for the large majority of database management systems deployed today.

Table 1.1 contains an example of what a table (or relation) might look like. As you can see, each column contains a particular type of data, and each record comprises a single instance of the values stored in each of the columns. The rows each represent a single record.

TABLE 1.1   A SAMPLE TABLE

id	title	studio	budget
1	Mineral House	Giant	20
2	Prince Kong	MPM	3.25
3	The Code Warrior	MPM	10.3
4	Bill Durham	Delighted Artists	10.1

So, in Table 1.1, each row (or record) is made up of four columns, id, title, studio, and budget. To briefly return to the idea of atomic values being stored in fields, you should be able to see that the values in each of the fields in Table 1.1 are discrete in the sense that they each comprise one useful piece of information. Relational databases are made up of groups of tables like Table 1.1 that are linked together through relationships. For example, if there were another table in the database that contained information on each studio, you could look up information on the studio that produced each of the movies by cross-referencing the studio column in Table 1.1 and the column that contained the studio name in the table that contains studio data.

By taking advantage of relationships between tables, you can avoid duplicating data in several places in a database. For example, you might want to also store the city where each studio is located in your database. You could include studio_city as a column in Table 1.1, but then that information would be duplicated every time a new movie from an existing studio is created. (Movies 3 and 4 would both have the same value in the studio_city column because they are both from the same studio.) It's better to split the information into two tables and then cross-reference the two tables to obtain that information when you need it.

The practice of designing your databases so that information is not needlessly duplicated in more than one location is referred to as *normalization*. Normalizing your databases helps to prevent inconsistency in your data by minimizing the number of values you have to update when you want to make a change to a particular piece of information.

→ The rules of normalization are covered in Chapter 2, "Database Design," in the section "Normalization."

When I discuss the relational model, there are several rules to which a database system must conform to fit within the constraints of the model. There are three categories into which these rules fall; there are rules that concern *data structure*, rules that concern *data integrity*, and rules that concern *data manipulation*.

> **Note**
>
> This section really only glosses over the rules of the relational model. It provides enough information to understand how the relational model is practically applied to databases today, but it does not cover in detail the tenets of relational theory. For an extremely detailed discussion of the relational model, see *An Introduction to Database Systems*, by C. J. Date.

RULES CONCERNING DATA STRUCTURE

The cardinal rule of data structure within the relational model is that all data must be presented to the user within tables. As I already explained, this rule only relates to data presentation, not to the way the data is stored.

This is, in fact, one of the most powerful properties of the relational model. It provides a level of abstraction between data presentation and storage so that no matter which relational database product you're using, how the data physically stored, or what platform you're using it on, the data is viewed and manipulated in the same manner.

When you write programs that interact with relational databases, you are spared the necessity of learning how to manipulate data within a particular file structure or dealing with other storage issues of the kind that would plague you with a flat file database, or any other type of application-specific data file. For example, when you create databases based on flat files, you have to deal with creating delimiters between fields and then not violating those delimiters within your data. Alternatively, you can separate your data into fields by character, so the first 40 characters of each line hold the person's name, the next 60 characters hold her address, and the last 25 characters hold her job title. Relational databases shield the user from this type of data wrangling.

Another rule regarding data structure in a relational database is that the data in every field of the database is an *explicit value*. In other words, there are no values stored in the database that exist only as pointers to other data within a database. If a movie is connected to a particular studio, that connection is illustrated by the fact that there is a value in the table containing movies that corresponds to a value in the table containing studios, not by a pointer that indicates that the two tables are somehow linked.

RULES REGARDING DATA MANIPULATION

There are a number of operations that can be applied to the data within a relational database. Just as mathematical operators are used to manipulate numbers, relational operators are used to manipulate tables.

A query is used to apply one or more relational operators to a table or group of tables within a database. SQL is a language that enables programmers to apply relational operators to databases. Numbers are the products of mathematical formulas; tables are the products of SQL queries. No matter how data retrieved from a relational database is eventually represented, it was retrieved in the form of a table. Queries that return a single record return a table containing a number of columns and a single row. Queries that return the value contained in a single field actually return a table consisting of one column and one row. After the data has been retrieved, it does not have to be presented in a tabular format; it can be placed in a Web page or used to pre-fill a form.

The fact that relational databases demand that all query results are returned as tables enables you to nest queries within one another as *subqueries*. This is because certain SQL constructs can use data within a table as input, and as you already know, all queries return tables as output. For example, the IN construct is used to compare a value to each member of a group of values. You can enter the members of the group manually, like this:

```
SELECT *
FROM Movies
WHERE studio IN ('MPM', 'Giant')
```

In the preceding query, the values in the studio column are compared to the two values MPM and Giant. IN expects to receive a list of values, or if you think about this in tabular terms, a table with one column and some number of rows. A query that generates a table that returns data in a single column can be used to replace the list of values with IN, as shown in Listing 1.1.

LISTING 1.1   AN EXAMPLE OF A SUBQUERY

```
SELECT *
FROM Movies
WHERE studio IN (SELECT name FROM Studios)
```

The table returned by the inner SELECT statement provides the values to which the items in the studio column of Movies are compared.

→ Subqueries are covered in Chapter 9, "Subqueries."

RULES CONCERNING DATA INTEGRITY

When data is stored in a database, the relational model demands that it conform to certain rules regarding integrity. For example, every row must contain a value (or group of values) that identifies it uniquely. These values are referred to as the *primary key*. In Table 1.1, the id column was the primary key.

Tip 1 from *Rafe Colburn*	Most databases do not rigidly enforce the database integrity rules. Despite the fact that in order to comply with the rules of the relational model, each row in a database must contain a unique value in the primary key, by default most databases will enable you to violate this rule. However, databases also generally provide facilities that enable you to enforce these rules if you choose to do so.

A set of columns in a table that corresponds to the primary key in another table is referred to as a *foreign key*. For example, consider the relationship between Movies and Studios. In the Studios table, name is the primary key. The studio column in the Movies table is a foreign key that corresponds to the name column in the Studios table. Any values used in a foreign key column must point to an existing primary key within the table to which they refer. This concept is referred to as *referential integrity*.

Additional integrity rules can be imposed on certain columns; for example, you can create a rule that mandates that all the values in the salary column in an employee table be between 10000 and 90000. These rules are imposed using CHECK conditions, which are discussed in the "Column Constraints" section of Chapter 3.

Even though integrity rules are required by any system that conforms strictly to the relational model, most databases give you the option of not enforcing rules of integrity in your database. Generally, databases do not require you to specify which columns are being used as primary or foreign keys and do not enforce integrity constraints on you if you don't identify these keys. SQL (Structured Query Language)

THE SQL LANGUAGE

One requirement of the relational model is that a single language be used for all communications with a relational database. This language is required to take care of all tasks relating to the manipulation, definition, and administration of databases. For this reason, in nearly every case, all the configuration and administrative data for database management systems is actually stored within tables in the database itself.

For the vast majority of relational database systems, the Structured Query Language fulfills the language requirement of relational database systems. The full SQL standard is more than 600 pages long, and no commercial relational database system fully conforms to the standard. This book covers the details of the language that are most commonly implemented in commercial relational database products. There are a number of reasons why databases don't implement the full SQL standard, the most significant being that new features have been added to the standard more quickly than they can be added to the database products that attempt to adhere to the standard.

SQL is made up of statements used to accomplish three types of tasks—data manipulation, data definition, and database administration.

DATA MANIPULATION

Within the category of statements for data manipulation, there are two types of commands: commands that are used to retrieve data, and commands that modify data. There is a single statement that is used to retrieve data stored within a database: SELECT. Thanks to the rich capabilities of SQL, however, very precise conditions can be set up to retrieve complex sets of data using a single query. In fact, the five chapters in the second part of this book are dedicated to explaining the use of the SELECT statement alone. Listing 1.2 contains an example of a simple SELECT statement.

LISTING 1.2   A SELECT STATEMENT

```
SELECT *
FROM Studios

STUDIO_ID STUDIO_NAME          STUDIO_CITY          ST
--------- -------------------- -------------------- --
        1 Giant                Los Angeles          CA
        2 MPM                  Burbank              CA
        3 Delighted Artists    Austin               TX
        4 FKG                  Apex                 NC
        5 Metaversal Studios   Los Angeles          LA
```

Note

Statements that are used to retrieve data from a database using the SELECT statement are usually referred to as queries.

The statements available for manipulating data within a database are UPDATE, INSERT, and DELETE. As you can probably imagine, the UPDATE statement is used to make changes to records, the INSERT statement is used to create new records in a table, and the DELETE statement is used to remove records from a table. There are examples of these three types of statements in Listing 1.3.

LISTING 1.3   DATA MANIPULATION STATEMENTS

```
UPDATE Studios
SET studio_city = 'Houston'
WHERE studio_state = 'TX'

1 row updated.

DELETE FROM Studios
WHERE studio_name = 'Giant'

1 row deleted.

INSERT INTO Studios
(studio_id, studio_name, studio_city, studio_state)
```

continues

LISTING 1.3   CONTINUED

```
VALUES
(5, 'Big Pictures', 'Culver City', 'CA')

1 row created.
```

DATA DEFINITION

Statements used for data definition create or alter the structure of the database or allocate resources to a database. First among these statements is CREATE. The CREATE command can be used to create databases, views, and tables. Listing 1.4 contains an example of the CREATE statement, used to create a table.

LISTING 1.4   CREATING A TABLE USING THE CREATE STATEMENT

```
CREATE TABLE example
(name            VARCHAR2(60),
rank             CHAR(10),
serial_number    NUMBER)
Table created.
```

In some databases, after an element such as a table has been created, it can be changed using an ALTER statement. For example, if you had wanted to make the serial_number column in the table you just created into a character field instead of a number field, the ALTER command could be used to change the data type of the column, as shown in Listing 1.5.

LISTING 1.5   AN EXAMPLE OF THE USAGE OF ALTER

```
ALTER TABLE example
MODIFY serial_number CHAR(10)
```

```
Table altered.
```

Tip 2 from
Rafe Colburn

The ALTER statement does not enable you to indiscriminately make changes to the data type or size of a column. Usually, all the data in the column must comply with the new data type and fit within the new column size or the column must not contain any values.

DATABASE ADMINISTRATION

Database administration commands are used to grant and remove privileges from users and to perform other tasks related to general database operation, rather than specific manipulation of elements within the database.

In most cases, the configuration of the database is stored within tables in the database itself that are accessible only to the database administrator's account. When this is the case, you can use the standard data manipulation commands to configure the database.

Tip 3 from
Rafe Colburn

Most databases also provide tools that are used specifically to modify the configuration of the database. Those databases that do not store the configuration parameters in standard tables within the database require the use of these tools to make configuration changes.

SQL STANDARDS

Although the SQL language has some compelling features and is easy to use, the greatest advantage that it provides is its wide adoption among database vendors. SQL is the standard language for communicating with relational databases, and although the implementations of the language vary somewhat between vendors, the language generally remains the same no matter which database platform you choose. SQL standards are reviewed and approved internationally by the International Standards Organization (ISO). In the United States, they are approved by the National Institute of Standards and Testing (NIST).

The current SQL standard is SQL-92 (the standard that was approved in 1992). Unfortunately, no commercial databases are fully compliant with the SQL-92 standard. Most of them support a large percentage of the features in the standard, plus some proprietary extensions created by the vendor. This book will cover the features of SQL that are implemented in database applications, rather than hewing to the official standard, because some of the features in the standard will not work in any product. The standard previous to SQL-92 is SQL-89. Unlike SQL-92, the SQL-89 has been implemented in most commercial databases.

If you are interested in reviewing the SQL standard, it is available from the American National Standards Institute. There are also several books that cover the standard: *Understanding the New SQL: A Complete Guide*, by Jim Melton and Alan R. Simon, and *A Guide to the SQL Standard: 3rd Edition*, by C. J. Date and Hugh Darwen.

SQL SYNTAX

Before I can begin a detailed discussion of specific SQL commands, I should first discuss basic SQL syntax. SQL, like every other language from English to C++, has certain basic rules that dictate its structure and syntax. Before I can discuss how specific SQL commands are written, it's necessary to cover the general rules that apply to the language as a whole.

SQL, for the most part, is interpreted one statement at a time. Unlike procedural languages such as C or Perl, you don't write SQL programs (unless you're writing a stored procedure, which is written using extensions to SQL). Instead, you send statements to a database one at a time. These individual statements are interpreted by the database, which returns their results before the next statement is processed.

Some general rules that apply to SQL are that it is not case sensitive, it ignores white space, and it provides for nesting. It's also important to understand the basic constructs that are standard parts of SQL syntax, such as quoting strings and using parenthises.

CASE SENSITIVITY

Generally speaking, SQL is not case sensitive. In other words, the language interpreter does not distinguish between things written in uppercase and lowercase letters. As far as most databases are concerned, this statement

```
select *
from table
```

and this one

```
SELECT *
FROM TABLE
```

and for that matter, this one

```
Select *
FROM table
```

are all identical. You can write your SQL code in the manner that is most visually appealing to you; it won't make a difference one way or the other. You should note, however, that certain databases enable you to specify whether the names of elements within the database are case sensitive. So, even though keywords in the language are not case sensitive, everything else is. In Listing 1.6, the keywords in the statement are listed in boldface letters, so that you can distinguish them from the names of data elements.

LISTING 1.6   A QUERY WITH KEYWORDS HIGHLIGHTED

```
SELECT person_name, Person_Name
FROM People
WHERE Person_State = 'TX
```

If the database were set up so that case sensitivity for data elements was turned on, person_name and Person_Name would represent two different entities, whereas under normal circumstances they would both point at the same columns in the database. Certain software packages that work with databases require that the database distinguish between uppercase and lowercase letters when dealing with data entities.

Tip 4 from Rafe Colburn	In this book, I use the capitalization convention put forth by noted SQL expert Joe Celko. He suggests that language keywords use all capital letters, names of tables be capitalized, and column names be specified using lowercase letters. I find that SQL code written under this convention is easy to read, although you are not by any means required to use it yourself.

WHITE SPACE

Another feature of SQL is that it ignores white space. As long as independent elements of your queries are separated by some white space, they will be parsed by the database. There is no restriction that requires you to place all the elements of a statement on a single line, that you use tabs to indent sections of your code, or that you enter a line feed after every clause.

The following statements are all the same:

```
SELECT * FROM Table

SELECT *
FROM Table

SELECT
*
FROM
Table
```

SQL doesn't care how you split up your statements, as long as there's some white space between each element of the statement. Obviously a statement such as the following wouldn't work:

```
SELECT*FROMTable
```

In this book, the convention will be to place each clause of an SQL query on a line by itself, so a SELECT statement with several clauses looks like the following:

```
SELECT *
FROM Table
WHERE column_1 = 'value'
ORDER BY column1
```

NESTING

Another fundamental quality of SQL is that it provides for nesting of queries. What this means is that queries can be embedded within other queries, and the output will be used in place of the nested function call or query. Nesting is a capability that is fundamental to writing code in SQL; it enables you to write extremely powerful queries.

There are two types of elements that can be nested within an SQL query: other SQL queries and function calls. When a query is nested within another query, it's referred to as a subquery. Listing 1.1, which contains an example of a subquery, is an illustration of a nested query. The inner SELECT statement is nested within the IN expression of the outer SELECT statement. The principle of nesting also holds true for function calls. If two functions are going to be applied to a single expression, one of the function calls can be nested within the other. To trim the white space from the right side of a string and convert all the letters within it to uppercase, the query in Listing 1.7 could be used.

LISTING 1.7   NESTING FUNCTION CALLS IN A SELECT STATEMENT

```
SELECT RTRIM(UPPER('Example string    '))
FROM Dual

RTRIM(UPPER('E
--------------
EXAMPLE STRING
```

Tip 5 from
Rafe Colburn

Dual is a special table in an Oracle database. Put simply, Dual is a table that contains no rows and no columns. When you need to write a query that does not need to return any data stored within the database, you can specify Dual as the table to query.

The call to the UPPER() function is nested within the call to the RTRIM() function. The RTRIM() function is used to remove any white space from the end of the string, and the UPPER() function converts all the lowercase letters in the string to uppercase letters.

→ Functions are covered in Chapter 6, "Using the Where Clause," in the section "Useful Functions for WHERE Clauses."

QUOTING STRINGS

When strings are used in the SQL language, they are enclosed within single quotation marks. For example, if you want to compare a value in a column to a string as opposed to an integer or a value in another column, it should be enclosed within single quotation marks. Take a look at this example:

```
SELECT *
FROM People
WHERE name = 'Rafe'
```

The single quotation marks around the word Rafe indicate that the value in the name column should be compared to the word Rafe. If the expression were constructed like this

```
SELECT *
FROM People
WHERE name = Rafe
```

the values in the name column would be compared to the values in the Rafe column. If the column contains numbers, no quotation marks are used. For example, an expression that compares values in a column with a numeric data type to a number looks like this:

```
SELECT *
FROM People
WHERE salary = 100000
```

What happens when you want to use a string that contains a single quotation mark? You have to "escape" it so that it's not considered to be the end of the string. Take a look at this example:

```
SELECT *
FROM Businesses
WHERE business_name = 'Rafe's Place'
```

That construct won't work, because the SQL interpreter will assume that the string being compared is Rafe, and s Place is just a fragment of a string in limbo, and will return an error. Instead, you need to use two single quotes in a row (like this: ' ') to indicate that the single quote within the name is part of the string being compared and not the character that terminates the string. Here's the proper syntax for the previous comparison:

```
SELECT *
FROM Businesses
WHERE business_name = 'Rafe''s Place'
```

PARENTHESES

The standard grouping operator in SQL is the parentheses. They are used to establish precedence in mathematical expressions and complex comparisons and to set off subqueries from the rest of a query. Listing 1.8 contains an example of a subquery.

LISTING 1.8   A QUERY CONTAINING A SUBQUERY

```
SELECT movie_title
FROM Movies
WHERE studio IN
    (SELECT name
    FROM Studios)

MOVIE_TITLE
------------------------
Mineral House
Codependence Day
The Rear Windows
Prince Kong
The Linux Files
The Code Warrior
Bill Durham
SQL Strikes Back
The Programmer
Hard Code

10 rows selected.
```

As you can see, the parentheses are used to separate the subquery from the rest of the query. The subquery is evaluated first, and the results are used within the rest of the query. By the same token, parentheses can be used within a mathematical expression, and they have the same effect as they do in an algebraic equation, which is to ensure that one portion of an expression is evaluated before another. The order of evaluation for items in parentheses is the same in SQL as it is in algebra. Inner parentheses are evaluated before outer parentheses. When multiple sets of parentheses at the same level of precedence exist, the query optimizer built into the database determines the order in which the expressions will be evaluated.

Compare the results of the two following queries :

```
SELECT 8 + 2 * 5
FROM Dual

8+2*5
- - - - - - - - - -
        18

SELECT (8 + 2) * 5
FROM Dual

(8+2)*5
- - - - - - - - - -
        50
```

As you can see, in the first query, the expression 2 * 5 is evaluated first, and the results (10) are added to 8 to return a result of 18. In the second query, the parentheses establish the precedence so that 8 + 2 is evaluated first, and then the result (10) is multiplied by 5.

RELATIONAL OPERATIONS

There are a number of operations that are common to all relational databases. I glossed over some of them earlier in this chapter, and as you know from the description of the relational model, all of them return data in a tabular format. I'm going to describe the SQL commands that are used to implement these operations in detail later in this book, but before doing so, I'm going to describe the basic types of operations that are available.

SELECTION

Selection returns a particular set of rows from a table. It is also referred to as *restriction* because it restricts the set of rows returned based on some criteria. It doesn't necessarily have to use a filter to restrict the rows returned, it can return all the rows from a table. Restriction pertains only to which rows are returned, not to the columns that are included in the query results. The query in Listing 1.9 uses the restriction operation to limit the number of rows returned by a query.

LISTING 1.9 A QUERY THAT APPLIES THE RESTRICTION TO A TABLE

```
SELECT *
FROM Studios
WHERE studio_state = 'TX'


  STUDIO_ID STUDIO_NAME          STUDIO_CITY          ST
- - - - - - - - - - - - - - - - - - - - - - - - - - - - -  - -
          3 Delighted Artists    Austin               TX
```

PROJECTION

Projection limits the columns returned by a query. Rather than returning every column in the table like the query in Listing 1.9, projection enables you to return only a specific subset of the columns in a table. Projection is implemented by passing a specific list of columns to a SELECT statement, as demonstrated in Listing 1.10.

LISTING 1.10   USING PROJECTION TO RETURN SPECIFIC COLUMNS

```
SELECT studio_name, studio_state
FROM Studios

STUDIO_NAME          ST
-------------------- --
Giant                CA
MPM                  CA
FKG                  NC
Delighted Artists    TX
Metaversal Studios   CA
```

More often than not, both projection and selection are used together when writing database queries. Selection is used to limit the number of records returned, and projection is used to return specific fields from each record. Listing 1.11 combines selection from Listing 1.9 and projection from Listing 1.10.

LISTING 1.11   USING BOTH PROJECTION AND SELECTION IN ONE STATEMENT

```
SELECT studio_name, studio_state
FROM Studios
WHERE studio_state = 'TX'

STUDIO_NAME          ST
-------------------- --
Delighted Artists    TX
```

JOIN

A *join* is a relational operation that combines multiple tables and treats them as a single table for the purposes of a query. Joins are implemented by specifying more than one table in the FROM clause of a SELECT statement.

→ Joins are fully explained in Chapter 8, "Combining Tables Using Joins."

More often than not, join operations are also combined with selection and projection operations so that the query does not return an unmanageable set of results. Listing 1.12 contains an example of a join operation.

LISTING 1.12   A JOIN OPERATION

```
SELECT movie_title, studio_name
FROM Movies, Studios
WHERE Movies.studio_id = Studios.studio_id

MOVIE_TITLE              STUDIO_NAME
-------------------      -------------------
Mineral House            Giant
Codependence Day         Giant
The Rear Windows         Giant
Prince Kong              MPM
The Linux Files          MPM
The Code Warrior         MPM
Bill Durham              Delighted Artists
SQL Strikes Back         Delighted Artists
The Programmer           Delighted Artists
Hard Code                FKG

10 rows selected.
```

DATABASE APPLICATION DELIVERY

Before proceeding with my discussion of the SQL language in the chapters to come, I'd like to digress and discuss the larger context in which the SQL language is used. Although it is common to enter SQL queries directly into a database, in many cases your SQL statements will exist as components of larger applications. Through the history of the SQL language, the applications that incorporate database queries have changed radically.

As you know, SQL is used for communications with a relational database; however, it is very specialized. It doesn't contain the other features found in most programming languages that make them suitable for general application development. So, although SQL is perfectly suited for querying and manipulating the contents of databases, it must be used with other programming languages when you write database applications.

I'd like to discuss some of the platforms used for database application deployment as they've appeared throughout the history of the relational model, and then, I'd like to talk about the general SQL interfaces provided with most database products.

HOST-BASED APPLICATIONS

When relational databases were originally developed, computing was still in the Paleozoic era. Big iron ruled the earth. Applications were hosted on mainframes and were accessed via text-based interfaces. COBOL and batch processing were hallmarks of most business applications.

This host-based model of computing dominated until the rise of the PC in the 1980s. One advantage of this model was that it was easy to administer. Rather than dealing with hundreds and thousands of users, each with software installed on his desktop computer, system administrators simply made sure that the mainframe was well-fed and running properly, and for the most part, everything took care of itself.

This was also the era of the infamous "green screen" application. Dumb terminals (with green or amber monochrome screens), running either Digital's VT series of protocols or IBM's 3270 protocol, were most often used as the platform by which mainframe applications were delivered to users. Needless to say, these interfaces were complex, unsightly, and slow. This is not to say that they weren't efficient. When a user was intimately familiar with the "screens" in the application, he could rapidly enter data or retrieve the results he needed.

In any case, as I said previously, this era ended with the rise of the PC. As personal computers became affordable, users were no longer content with a dumb terminal running host-based applications. Despite the fact that the era of the green screen, dumb terminal, and mainframe has passed, there are still many systems based on this technology in use today.

THE CLIENT/SERVER ERA

As the cost of computing power plummeted in the 1980s, personal computers took over the role of the mainframe as the dominant computing paradigm. IBM and Digital, along with a host of lesser players, were replaced by companies like Microsoft, Intel, and Compaq at the top of the computer industry food chain.

Along with the PC revolution came *client/server architecture*. This model, also referred to as *n-tier architecture*, shifted much of the processing burden from the mainframe or other large system to the user's desktop PC. The database remained on a large system, and the user interface and much of the business logic was stored on the client. Oftentimes, a piece of software called an application server was installed on another server, which handled the communications between the database server and the client software.

This era was marked by the rise of rapid application development languages such as Microsoft's Visual Basic, Borland's Delphi, and Powerbuilder, among a host of others. A testament to the power of the client/server model is Visual Basic's title as the language that boasts the most programmers of any. All these application development tools enable you to write your user interfaces and business logic in your language of choice, whereas you write your database queries in SQL.

Users were no longer bound by the "green screen" applications that had once dominated. Instead, their client-side applications were implemented with graphical user interfaces. They were also often faster because much of the processing took place right on the PC, and only the final results of an operation were reported back to the database or application server.

This new model of application deployment was not without its flaws, however. Even as the client/server model improved the interface of applications and shifted much of the processing burden to the client, it created an immense administrative load for businesses. Because a large chunk of the applications are written for and deployed on the client machines, any time the applications are changed, the software has to be updated at the client. When thousands of users depend on an application, this can create a headache for administrators.

Another problem is that desktop PCs themselves require more administration than the dumb terminals of old. Current operating systems are composed of thousands of files, and removing or changing any one of them can possibly render a PC useless. Compare that to the ease of plugging a dumb terminal into a power outlet and network connector and then immediately logging in to the mainframe.

The client/server model enabled application developers to write database applications that provided a richer user experience than the old host-based applications, but at the same time, they begat significant maintenance problems.

DATABASE APPLICATION DELIVERY VIA THE WEB

Client/server computing is still the dominant paradigm under which most database-backed business applications are written. Microsoft Windows NT and most commercial UNIX derivatives have feasted on the new demand for mid-range servers brought on by the explosion of client/server applications.

In 1993, Tim Berners-Lee invented the World Wide Web at CERN, a research facility in Switzerland. He wrote both a Web browser and a Web server on his Next workstation. Little did he know then that the Web would enjoy an explosion in popularity that would make it ubiquitous by the end of the twentieth century.

The Web was originally used to distribute static text pages and images; in business, its future was to be as a platform for the delivery of relational database applications. One of the great problems facing client/server programmers is that every new application demanded a new executable program on the client side and an all-new interface, but at least the applications could be easy to use and visually appealing. On the other hand, host-based applications are delivered to any client that can communicate via the protocol that the terminal server speaks.

The most compelling feature of Web-based applications is that the Web browser can be used as a universal client for connecting to the application server (via the Web server). Using HTML forms, full-featured graphical interfaces to database applications can be built and deployed via the Web browser. Many rapid application development environments have been built specifically for the Web, and others have been updated so that they can be used to write Web applications in addition to client/server applications.

Like the host-based applications of old, changes to the application do not require software updates on each of the clients accessing the application. Web applications do not need to be ported to various platforms either; they will run on any platform that has a Web browser available. Contrast this against client/server applications, which must be ported to each operating system on which they will run.

Ironically, this new trend toward building Web applications for database connectivity is in some ways a return to the host-based model from which we began. IBM is advertising their mainframes as a server platform for Web applications, and most of the application logic has made its way back to the server.

Web applications are not the end-all and be-all of database application deployment, any more than host-based applications or client/server applications were. However, they are growing in popularity for good reasons. They are the latest evolutionary step in the world of large-scale computer applications, and there is little doubt that at some point in perhaps the not so distant future, they'll be replaced by the next greatest thing.

COMMAND-LINE INTERFACES

Although in their final form, most database applications are delivered through one of the methods described previously, most databases include a program that enables you to plug queries directly into the database engine and view the results. These programs are useful for creating ad hoc reports from the data within the database and for testing queries before you use them in your applications. Database administrators often use them to enter queries for administrative tasks as well.

When you enter the queries in this book, chances are that you'll be entering them through an interface such as this, rather than wrapping entire applications around them for testing and instructional purposes. If you're not aware of the existence of one of these programs for the database you plan on using as you read this book, you should probably do some research into this topic before you proceed further.

There's no consistency among databases in the naming of these types of programs. The command-line interface to Oracle is `sqlplus`; Sybase uses `isql`. Query tools are provided with Windows databases such as Microsoft Access and SQL Server and Sybase SQL Anywhere. In any case, these programs will make your life much easier as a database administrator or programmer.

IN THE REAL WORLD

One change that has been brought about in large part by the massive proliferation of Web-based applications is the use of relational databases for all sorts of nontraditional applications. For most of their history, relational databases were used largely for what one might think of as "traditional" database applications. One reason for their restriction to these types of roles has been the traditionally high cost of the servers that support relational databases. For most of their history, relational databases were restricted to large systems, such as mainframe and mini computers. It has only been relatively recently that a wide array of relational database products have become available for smaller scale servers and personal computers.

The traditional applications for databases lent themselves to tabular representation of data. Things such as transaction records, customer biographical information, and account histories all lend themselves to the relational model. However, relational databases provide advantages that all sorts of applications can capitalize on, and indeed, more and more applications have been making use of these advantages.

When relational databases first came into use on the Web, it was largely through Web interfaces to traditional applications or for electronic commerce. For example, companies began to Web-enable applications that enabled users to enter their weekly time cards or update their employee records. Similarly, the back-end storage for electronic commerce sites maps well to the relational model. Product catalogs are essentially tabular data, and online shopping carts, account information, and transaction histories all fall well within the traditional realm of relational database applications.

More recently, however, many Web sites have begun to store all their content within relational databases. For example, many newspaper Web sites store all their news stories as records in relational databases and then use Web application servers to retrieve the stories and present them by placing the values stored in the fields in templates. Whereas a transaction record might contain a transaction ID, the ID and quantity of the item ordered, the method of payment, and the customer ID of the purchaser, a news story can be broken into fields such as headline, byline, body, and date of publication. By storing their content in this manner, Web sites free themselves from the necessity of dealing with thousands of files each containing a single story, and parsing those files and combining them with templates.

The broadening reach of the relational database market is good news for database programmers. As the number of applications to which relational databases are commonly applied increases, skills in SQL programming become more and more valuable. The potential market for database applications has by no means been fully mined; as our society becomes more and more information intensive, the number of potential uses for relational databases grows constantly.

DATABASE DESIGN

In this chapter

The first step in creating any database application is to assess the data that you'll be working with. The second step is to design a database in which to store that data. This is an iterative process that involves figuring out what kinds of data you'll be storing, how all the data inter-relates, and how it should be organized.

After you've figured out how the data should be organized, you'll need to actually write the SQL statements that create the database; that's covered in Chapter 3. In the meantime, this chapter will discuss the principles of database design, and how you can apply these principles to solve your data-related problems.

Before I dive into the discussion of database design, let me first offer you a word of warning and encouragement. If you aren't a seasoned database designer don't expect to master it all quickly. In some ways, database design, like programming, is as much about art and magic as it is about simply eyeing a set of data and running it through a specific set of rules.

So, don't expect to create a perfect database on your first attempt; most designers are still finding ways they could have done things better long after they implement a design.

There are, however, a couple of methodologies that should be helpful as you try to create databases. *Entity-relationship modeling* is a process by which you examine your data to deter-mine how it can be represented in tables, or *entities*, and then determine how those entities relate to one another. *Normalization* is a method of organizing your data after it is arranged into tables so that it conforms to the rules of a *normal form*. These normal forms are time-tested standards for organizing data in a relational database, and are designed to eliminate specific data integrity problems.

> **Note**
>
> In many ways, the rules of database design are more like the rules of grammar than the rules of mathematics. In other words, they are guidelines, rather than inflexible laws. While the rules have a good reason for existing, there are also situations in which you'll need to break even what seem to be the most fundamental rules. The secret is knowing when to break these rules, and unfortunately, that knowledge comes only with experience. This book will cover the common pitfalls you can run into when designing databases, and hope-fully enable you to avoid them.

But, before I get into these design methodologies, I'd like to return to a subject that I intro-duced in Chapter 1, database structure.

DATABASE STRUCTURE

If there was one important point in Chapter 1, it was that relational databases are all about tables. All queries return their results as tables, and all the data in the database is stored in tables. Obviously, when you're thinking about how your data will be organized, it's impor-tant to think about how your data should be grouped together within a structure based on tables.

In Chapter 1, I discussed the basic fact that tables form the foundation of the relational model, but I didn't talk too much about how these tables are organized, other than the fact that they're made up of rows and columns. Before I discuss some of the additional attributes of tables, let me quickly review the rules of the relational model, which I discussed in the previous chapter.

- All data must be presented to users in a tabular format.
- Table cells must contain a single value. Table cells are the atomic unit of relational databases. The contents of cells are treated as single values by relational databases.
- For the purposes of data integrity, every row must contain a value (or group of values) that uniquely identifies that row.
- When there is a relationship between two tables within the database, all the data in the column that expresses the relationship must be represented in the related table. Basically, what this means is that if data in a column in one table represents a relationship with data in another table, all the values in that column must appear in the corresponding column in the second table.

Strangely enough, the default behavior of most databases is to make the third and fourth rules optional. Not all the rows in your tables must be unique, and there need not be a formal link between related tables. However, if you do choose to enforce these rules, in the long run the integrity of your data will be higher.

The value (or group of values) that uniquely identifies each row is referred to as the *primary key*. When the primary key from one table corresponds to a column in another table, it expresses a relationship between the two tables, and the column (or columns) in the other table are referred to as a *foreign key*. I will return to the topic of these keys when I start discussing the nuts and bolts of database design in this chapter.

Before delving further into the topic of design, let me introduce a new term that I'll use throughout the rest of the book. When I talk about the overall design of a group of tables, I will refer to it as the *schema*. The schema of a database is a list of all the tables in the database, along with the keys and columns in each of those tables. The schema of a table includes the table name, a list of the columns in the table, and an indication of the keys.

The notation used to portray the schema for a database contains the name of the table, followed by the names of the columns within parentheses. The primary key column (or columns) in the table should be underlined with two lines. Here's an example:

```
some_table (primary_key, column1, column2, column3)
```

DATABASES GOOD AND BAD

Before I get into design methodology, I'd like to first discuss some of the qualities that mark good databases and bad databases. Hopefully, you'll learn to recognize these qualities in databases you use and design, and in the process, learn to create databases that exhibit more of the good qualities and fewer of the bad ones.

CHARACTERISTICS OF GOOD DATABASES

When you think about it, the characteristics of well-designed databases are self-evident. Good databases make it easy to retrieve the data you need, exhibit high integrity so that the data remains consistent after updates, and perform as well as possible.

Naturally, while a good database exhibits all three of those qualities, there are tradeoffs among them. For example, it might make it easy to retrieve data if you store it all in a single table; however this can lead to poor performance, and can lead to needless duplication of data that lowers the integrity of your database. On the other hand, splitting your data up into many tables can ensure that you never run into problems with data integrity, but can make it tiresome to write queries that return the data you need, and can also be detrimental to performance. Designing a database that is solely focused on good performance over concerns of organization and integrity is probably likely to be unsatisfactory as well.

It's up to you to create the proper recipe for your database. You should be mindful of all three of the qualities—performance, integrity, and organization—when you design your database, balancing each of them as appropriate for your application. In the end, the ultimate positive characteristic of any database is that it provides high levels of user satisfaction, and that it reliably meets its requirements.

SYMPTOMS OF BAD DATABASES

All too often, it's easier to point out the wrong way to do things than to explain how to do them correctly. Not surprisingly, the symptoms of a bad database are more or less the opposites of the good qualities described previously. It's quite possible to design a confusing database with bad performance and poor integrity. Hopefully this chapter will help you to avoid doing so. Symptoms of a badly designed database include

- Columns or tables with confusing or unclear names.
- Requiring users to enter the same data more than once, or to change the value of the same piece of data in multiple locations in an update.
- Allowing data in the database to get out of sync, so that multiple queries seeking the same piece of information return different results.
- Poor performance. Improperly designed databases simply return the results of queries more slowly than they should, and thus make database applications more difficult to use. Chapter 12 includes an extensive discussion of database performance issues.
- Difficulty in determining the relationship between pieces of data.
- Duplicate rows within a single table.

THE DESIGN PROCESS

In order to explain how database design works, I'm going to quickly discuss each step involved in designing a database, followed by an in-depth discussion of each of the tasks.

Throughout the detailed discussion, I'll introduce you to the film industry database that will be used as the context of most of the examples in this book.

Let's take a look at each of the steps involved in database design:

1. Information gathering. Obviously, before you can design a database, you need to know exactly what will be stored in the database.

2. Taking inventory. After you've found all the information you'll store in the database, you need to create a laundry list of all the types of data you've found, and the attributes of those types.

3. Entity-relationship modeling. Arrange the data into individual entities and attributes of those entities. Determine how the entities are related.

4. Determine which level of normalization is required for your database. Apply the normalization rules to your data until it conforms to the normal form you chose.

5. Write the SQL code necessary to create the database, and then create the database in your relational database system.

6. Determine which users should have access to your data, and then grant the appropriate levels of access to the users.

7. Populate your database with data.

These are general steps that can be taken in the process of designing a database. They are by no means set in stone, and if another method works better for you, that is the method you should follow. In the end, it is the result that matters, not necessarily the route by which you arrived at that result.

THE PRE-DESIGN PHASE OF DESIGN

Before you can write any code, or even start designing the architecture of your database, you must first determine which data will be stored within your database. Most databases are created to replace an existing record keeping system, or to serve as data repositories for a particular application.

Tip 6 from
Rafe Colburn

One of the most important steps in designing a new database is interviewing users. Before you can even begin to design a database, it is necessary to determine what data should be stored within the database, and how it should be accessed. The only way to make these determinations is to talk with the people who will actually use the application, and ascertain exactly what their requirements are.

For example, let's take an early look at the movie database that I'm going to discuss throughout this book. If you were going to keep records on all the movies that are released each year in a relational database, the first step would be to determine exactly which data should be incorporated into that database. Obviously, there is an incredible amount of data associated with the production of a single movie, much less all the movies released each year. Sifting through it and determining what is useful is a difficult job. Furthermore, you must determine whether the system is replacing an existing system or providing entirely new functionality, and then make sure that it will successfully replicate the existing system. Finally, you must gather all the requirements for the database from the designers of the applications that will use the database, and perhaps the end users as well.

Note

> Equally important, as you research what will go into the database, is what you expect to get out of it. In the end, the most important product of a database application is the query results and reports that can be retrieved. Indeed, your application will most likely be judged by most users on this criterion alone.

Let's take a look at the example for this book. In this case, the application I'm designing will serve as a repository for information about the film industry. It could include information on studios, movies, cast and crew, shooting locations, financial results for movies and studios, and plenty of other things. Obviously, the scope of such an application is very large; in this book, I'm going to select specific aspects of the movie industry and include them in the sample database.

After examining the problem, I decided that this database would store information on movies, studios, locations, directors, cast members, and the roles that they play. In the real world, I'd need to survey the potential users of the application and determine which information they required. After this decision has been made, I can start to focus on exactly which information will need to be stored in the database, and how it should be structured.

ORGANIZING YOUR DATA

After you've researched the application you're about to tackle, and have a general idea about the data you need to store in the database as well as the reports you'd like to get out of it, you're ready to start thinking about the structure of your database.

The first step is to create a taxonomy of the information in your database. Which higher level objects can stand alone, and what are the properties associated with those higher level objects? The first step is to discover what the high level objects in your database are, and then build your database around them.

Note

> Several of the terms that I used in the previous paragraph have specific technical meanings, but here I am using them in a more generic sense. In the context of this discussion, objects are just items that are important enough to the design of the database that they can stand alone. Properties are just pieces of information used to describe each object. These general concepts will be applied specifically to the relational model later in the chapter.

Most of the time, the data that you have will almost arrange itself into logical categories without too much effort on your part. Turn to the sample database. The database centers around movies. So, it seems evident that you'd want a record in the database for each movie. Some of the properties of each movie are:

- title
- cast
- director
- studio
- budget
- date of release
- location
- gross receipts

PART

I

CH

2

There are, of course, many other potential attributes of a movie. There's the rest of the movie crew, the name of the caterer on the set, and endless other technical details, which we're leaving out of this application.

You probably also notice that some of the items in the list of attributes of the movie also have some attributes themselves, for example, each cast member has attributes such as the following:

- first name
- last name
- role
- payment
- telephone number
- zip code
- social security number
- union membership
- city and state of residence

Again, those are just some of the potential attributes for a cast member. The attributes for a director are similar, although they would not include role. There is also a long list of potential attributes for each studio.

In any case, these are the types of lists you need to create after you've determined which data will be included in your database. Having a list of all the entities in your database and the attributes that correspond to them will make it easier to start modeling how the database itself will be designed.

FUNCTIONAL DEPENDENCY AND CANDIDATE KEYS

After your data is broken down into discrete objects, the next step is to figure out how the data will be structured within the database. You've already taken the first step, which was to break down the objects and figure out what their properties are. Now, you need to take it a step further. Determine which tables need to be created, which columns will go into those tables, and how the tables will be related. There's also the problem of finding a unique identifier, or primary key, for each table. So, before I can explain the entity-relationship modeling process, I need to explain some important concepts that underpin database design.

How do you determine which columns make up the primary key for a table, and which attributes belong with which entities? In order to do this, you need to understand a concept referred to as functional dependency, which basically amounts to figuring out which values in tables are determined (or identified) by others.

FUNCTIONAL DEPENDENCY

Before I write a solid definition of functional dependency, I'd like to first introduce the concept through an example. The table I'm using for this example is called `things`; in this table, we have three columns; `name`, `price`, and `color`. Every item in the table has a single price, but they each come in several colors. Table 2.1 contains a few rows from `things`.

TABLE 2.1   A SUBSECTION OF THE things TABLE

name	price	color
marble	.99	white
marble	.99	blue
marble	.99	red
toothbrush	2.99	green
toothbrush	2.99	white
shovel	10.99	brown
candle	1.99	pink
candle	1.99	blue

In the table, the price for each of the marbles is 99 cents, no matter what the color. What this means is that `price` is functionally dependent on `name`, and, for that matter, `name` is functionally dependent on `price`. The price of each marble is the same, just as the price of each toothbrush is the same, and the price of each candle is the same. This is the definition of *functional dependency*. One group of values is functionally dependent on another if, for every possible set of values in the first group, there is one and only one possible set of values for the items in the second group.

This is the case in Table 2.1. There is one `price` that corresponds to each `name`. In Table 2.1, there is also only one `name` that corresponds to each `price`; but this purely happenstance. What would happen if I added another record to `things` named `fork`, with a color of `silver` and a price of `2.99`? There would still be a single `price` for every `name`, but multiple items with the same name would exist, so `name` would no longer be dependent on `price`.

Tip 7 from	
Rafe Colburn	The most important concept that underpins functional dependency is that for one item to be functionally dependent on another, the dependency must hold true for every possible value of the item, not just the values that currently exist. This is why you must give careful consideration to the data in your database, over and above the actual values that are in your possession when you originally create the design. This is what occurred when I added `fork` to Table 2.1. The fact that fork and toothbrush have the same price means that the name column can no longer functionally depend on the price column.

There is a specific notation for indicating functional dependency. An arrow operator is used to indicate that one item (or group of items) is functionally dependent on another. For example, to note that price is functionally dependent on name, the following notation is used:

```
{name} -> {price}
```

Take functional dependency a bit further. Where does `color` fit into this scheme? You already know that `color` is not functionally dependent on either `price` nor `name`. Multiple color values exist for both. You can also see that neither `price` nor `name` are functionally dependent on `color`. So, where does that leave us? Remember that values can be functionally dependent on groups of values in addition to single values. Take a look at this notation:

```
{name, color} -> {price}
```

Just as `price` is functionally dependent on `name` alone, it is also dependent on combinations of `name` and `color`. For each combination of `name` and `color` there is a single `price`. The following functional dependencies also exist, but are referred to as being *trivial* because the dependent item is simply a subset of the set of values on which it depends:

```
{name, color} -> {name}
{name, color} -> {color}
```

Naturally, each of the three values is functionally dependent on the set composed of all three columns, but those dependencies are also trivial. What happens if suddenly blue marbles become very scarce, and thus, the price for them goes up relative to other marbles? Take a look at Table 2.2.

TABLE 2.2 A NEW VERSION OF THE things TABLE

name	price	color
marble	.99	white
marble	5.99	blue

continues

TABLE 2.2   CONTINUED

name	price	color
marble	.99	red
toothbrush	2.99	green
toothbrush	2.99	white
shovel	10.99	brown
candle	1.99	pink
candle	1.99	blue

As you can see, blue marbles are $5.99; other marbles still cost 99 cents. What this tells you immediately is that `price` is no longer functionally dependent on `name` alone. It's possible to have more than one price on items with the same name. Instead, the dependency on which you must rely is

`{name, color} -> {price}`

When you start thinking about how to determine which values should appear within particular tables when designing databases, you should always have functional dependency in mind. After you've designed a few databases, it will be easy to figure out functional dependencies most of the time, but at first, it might be difficult.

One of the key questions that can be answered by systematically evaluating data to find functional dependencies is which column (or columns) should be used as the primary key for a table.

CANDIDATE KEYS AND PRIMARY KEYS

You already know what a primary key is. It's a set of columns (remember that a set can contain one value) which uniquely identifies every record (or potential record) stored within a table. A *candidate key* is any column or group of columns that contains values that uniquely identify each row in the database. The primary key is just one of the candidate keys. Some tables yield only a single candidate key; others have many candidate keys. When there are multiple candidate keys within a table, one of them must be chosen as the primary key. The remaining candidate keys are referred to as *alternate keys*.

There are two hard and fast rules that are used to qualify any set of values as a candidate key. The first is the *uniqueness property*, with which you're already familiar. Here's the rule:

> No two records in a table have the same value for the set of columns comprised by the candidate key.

The second rule is the *irreducability property*. This rule is stated as follows:

> No subset of columns from the set of columns being considered as a candidate key exhibits the uniqueness property.

Let me turn one last time to Table 2.2 in order to explain these two properties. There are two sets of columns that exhibit the uniqueness property: {name, price, color}, and {name, color}. Both sets uniquely identify each row in the table, but looking at the irreducability property, you can see that only one of the two sets is a candidate key. {name, color} is clearly a subset of {name, price, color}, so {name, color} is the only candidate key for the things table. Choosing {name, color} as the primary key for things is easy because it's the only candidate key available.

Now, let's return quickly to the topic of functional dependency. All the columns in a table that are not part of a candidate key must be functionally dependent on the candidate key. If a column isn't functionally dependent on the candidate key, the candidate key won't uniquely identify each row under all possible circumstances, and thus isn't a candidate key at all.

CHEATING

Now that I've treated you to a fairly detailed discussion of candidate keys and functional dependency, let me tell you how many database designers cheat. If you don't feel like putting a lot of effort into finding candidate keys and evaluating values based on functional dependency, even though you probably should, you can simply create a column that will contain a unique identifier for each row. The easiest way to do this is to simply add a numeric column to your table that will be incremented every time a new row is added to the database. Each row will then automatically contain a value that is unique to it alone. Many databases allow you to create auto-incrementing fields expressly for this purpose.

There are some arguments against this tactic, however. One is that despite the fact that each row will be technically unique, if the values in all the columns other than the index column you created are identical, your database probably has an integrity problem that is masked by the ID column.

There are also plenty of arguments in favor of using ID columns as well, the strongest being that it makes it easier to use foreign keys and to perform join operations if you use a single column as the primary key for a table. The side I take in this argument is that using these columns can make your life much easier, but you shouldn't use them as a crutch to enable you to forget about functional dependency and the properties that define candidate keys. You should probably design your database as though you weren't going to use ID columns, and then add them to the design before you create the tables.

| Tip 8 from
Rafe Colburn | Creating an auto-incrementing column to serve as the primary key for your tables can also improve the performance of your database applications, particularly if you would otherwise have to use a compound primary key. By using the specialized primary key fields as a foreign key in other tables, you can join the two tables using a single comparison in the where clause of your queries, thus improving the performance of your joins. It also reduces the size of tables that would otherwise have to include multiple columns to create a relationship with tables with compound candidate keys. |

Practically speaking, most tables that do not already have a single column that can easily be used as the primary key are assigned an auto-incrementing ID column to make working with the tables easier. In the examples in this book, I'm going to use an ID column for the tables because it is what you will most commonly find in the real world, and because ID columns make it easier to explain how joins work.

ENTITY-RELATIONSHIP MODELING

Now that I've explained those concepts, I can return to the design of the sample database for this book to explain the next phase of database design. The issue at hand is deciding what each table in the database should contain. A solid understanding of candidate keys and functional dependency are crucial to these decisions.

Entity-relationship modeling is an established methodology for determining the structure of databases. Along with it come entity-relationship diagrams, which are used to illustrate the hierarchy of entities and properties within a database. Before I dive into an explanation of how the entity-relationship model would be applied to the sample database, I'm going to provide a high level overview of the steps in the entity-relationship model:

1. Identify discrete entities
2. Identify the properties of those entities
3. Identify the relationships between the entities

Let's take a look at how these steps are applied to a real-world case.

IDENTIFYING ENTITIES

The first step in the entity-relationship design process is to identify the entities that you'll be dealing with. These entities will correspond roughly with the tables in your database, when you're all finished. Let me go back and pull out a list of the possible entities in the sample database that I talked about earlier.

- `movies`
- `studios`
- `locations`
- `actors`
- `directors`

That seems like a good list of the entities that exist within the database of movie information that I envisioned. However, although some actors might disagree, both directors and actors are people. We will need to store the same basic types of information about both of them within the database. In fact, some people, like Clint Eastwood, are both actors and directors. It doesn't seem to make much sense to split them into two arbitrary tables, so I winnowed the list of entities to four for the time being.

So, the new list of entities is:

- movies
- studios
- locations
- people

A distinction can be drawn between *weak* and *strong* entities. Weak entities exist only while a particular regular entity exists. In the sample database, studios, movies, and people are strong entities. The values in these tables don't rely on another entity for meaning. On the other hand, locations is a weak entity, because without the movie that was shot at the location, the location itself is of no significance.

When you're drawing an E-R diagram, entities appear in rectangles. Regular entities appear in a single rectangle; weak entities are represented by a double rectangle (see Figure 2.1).

Figure 2.1
An E-R diagram showing the entities in a database.

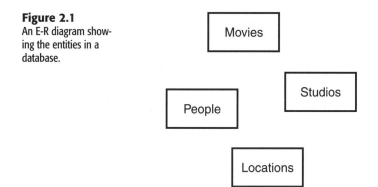

After the list of entities is created, it's time to identify the properties of each of the entities.

IDENTIFYING PROPERTIES

After the entities have been identified, it is necessary to identify the properties of each of those entities. Earlier in this chapter, I made a list of some of the properties associated with each of the entities in the database, so that list can be refined for use here. Let's look at each of the entities individually.

First, let's look at the movies entity. What are the properties of this entity? For each movie, there is a release date, budget, and amount of gross receipts (shortened to gross). For the purpose of this database, the budget and gross will be given in millions. Each movie also has a director and studio; these are included as properties of movies as well. Each movie also has a cast, which includes both the names of the actors as well as the roles they played, but this information can't be included as a property of movies because movies can contain more than one cast member. I'll discuss how these values are described a bit later. Each movie can also have a number of locations; these aren't included as properties of the `movies` entity either, again because multiple locations can exist for each movie. So, here's the list we're left with for movies:

- `release date`
- `budget`
- `gross`
- `director`
- `studio`

The properties of the studio entity are much simpler. Only the city and state where each studio is located are stored in the database.

- `studio name`
- `studio city`
- `studio state`

Now, let's turn our attention to the people entity. The following properties are included for the people entity:

- `name`
- `address`
- `phone`
- `social security number`
- `union membership status`

The `name` and `address` properties are actually composite properties that consist of several fields. The name property is a composite of the `first` and `last` name, and the address property actually consists of the `street address`, `city`, `state`, and `zip code` fields.

The `location` entity has as its properties the `movie` that was shot at the location, as well as the `city`, `state`, and `country` where the shooting occurred.

In an entity-relationship diagram, properties are enclosed within ellipses, and are connected to the entities with which they are associated by single lines, as shown in Figure 2.2. Composite properties are also connected to their parts using single lines.

Note

Before I actually create tables to represent these entities in the database, I'm going to add an ID field to each of them, mainly to make it easier to perform join operations on the tables later. The point I wanted to make earlier about ID fields was that you should never rely on them to provide uniqueness for rows in your tables; the other values in the table should stand alone without the ID field that you create.

Figure 2.2
An E-R diagram that
includes properties.

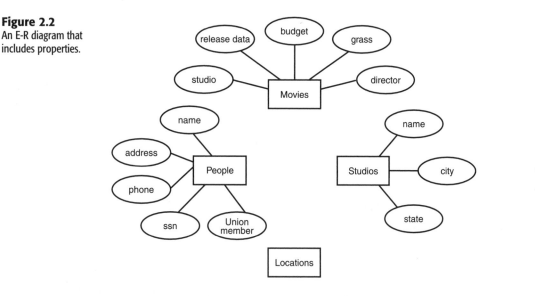

IDENTIFY RELATIONSHIPS

The next step is to identify relationships among the entities you've listed. There are three types of data relationships that can exist, *one-to-one*, *one-to-many*, and *many-to-many*. I'll discuss each of them individually.

ONE-TO-ONE RELATIONSHIPS

A one-to-one relationship exists when one item is functionally dependent on another. Usually, when a one-to-one relationship exists between two entities, it's easier just to include them both in the same table. For example, in theory, you could consider the release date for each movie to be an entity separate from the movie itself, and create a table of dates that contained movie titles as properties of those dates, but there's no point in doing so. The release date for each movie is functionally dependent on the movie itself, so it's easier just to make it a property of the movie.

MANY-TO-ONE RELATIONSHIPS

Many-to-one relationships occur when one entity can correspond to several occurrences of the other entity. There are a number of these types of relationships in the sample database. Let's take a look at them.

There is a many-to-one relationship from movies to studios and from movies to directors. Each studio can produce multiple movies, and each director can direct multiple movies. This is why the primary key from the people table exists as a property of the movie entity. In the database, the director column is a foreign key corresponding to the people table. The same is true of the studio property of the movie entity; the studio property of a movie is a foreign key from the studio entity.

There is also a many-to-one relationship between movies and locations. movie is a property of locations because each movie can be shot at any number of locations. movie will be a foreign key within the locations table. The notation for describing each of these relationships is as follows:

```
director (from movies to people)
studio (from movies to studios)
location (from locations to movies)
```

MANY-TO-MANY RELATIONSHIPS

Implementing many-to-many relationships is a bit more complex than many-to-one relationships because they can't be handled through a simple foreign key. Instead, a special table, called a *connecting table*, must be created specifically to express the relationship between the two entities.

Tip 9 from *Rafe Colburn*	Unless you are absolutely certain that a relationship between two things is a many-to-one or one-to-one relationship, you should err on the side of assuming that the relationship is many-to-many, and create a connecting table to express that relationship. Going back into your applications later and changing the code to reflect a many-to-many relationship instead of a one-to-many relationship can be painful.

Remember back when I was talking about properties, and I said that I wouldn't explain where cast members and roles would be placed just yet? That's because the cast of a movie actually involves a many-to-many relationship between the movie and person entities.

Each person can act in any number of movies, but at the same time, most movies feature more than one actor. Because each field in a relational database can contain only a single, atomic value, there's no way to include the entire cast of a movie within the record for a single movie. There's also no way to include the list of movies in which each person has appeared within one record in the database.

So, a new entity that contains the casts for all the movies in the database is created. It represents two many-to-one relationships; the relationship from cast to movies, and the relationship from cast to people. Two additional properties also exist within the connecting table; the name of the role, and the amount that was paid for the performance. The primary key for this table is the combination of the movie to which the role is assigned and the cast member that played the role. You would think that the role name itself could be used as the primary key until you think about the number of movies with roles like "Policeman" and "Bystander #1".

The new cast entity is added to the entity-relationship diagram, connected to the person entity and the movie entity through many-to-one relationships.

> **Note**
>
> There are two types of participants in relationships, *total* and *partial*. If a table is a total participant in a relationship, every record in the table must participate within the relationship. `movie` is a total participant in the relationship with both `studios` and `directors`; every movie comes from a studio, and every movie has a director. If a table is a partial participant in a relationship, the records in that table do not necessarily have to participate in the relationship, although in some cases, all of them may, in fact, be participants. Person is a partial participant in the relationship with movies; some people are directors, others are actors, perhaps others are neither actors nor directors in the movie.

DIAGRAMMING RELATIONSHIPS

Figure 2.3 contains an entity-relationship diagram with the new cast entity, and the many-to-one and many-to-many relationships I've discussed. This is the final entity-relationship model for the database.

Figure 2.3
An E-R diagram that
includes relationships.

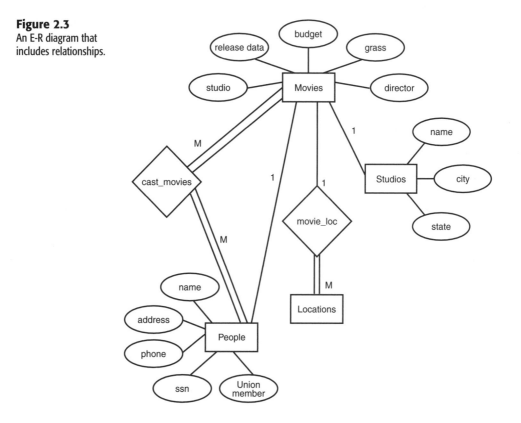

Relationships are portrayed in entity-relationship diagrams as follows:

- Relationships appear as diamonds, with lines connecting to the tables on each side of the relationship, and the name of the relationship in the diamond. For example, the relationship from movies to studios is labeled as `movie_studio`.

- The diamond has a double border if the relationship links a weak entity to the regular entity upon which it depends. The relationship between weak entity location and strong entity movie, `location_movie`, appears within a doubled diamond.

- The lines linking relationships to entities are labeled with a '1' or an 'M', depending on the nature of the relationship. Many-to-one relationships are labeled with a '1'; many-to-many relationships are linked with an 'M'.

- Partial participants in a relationship are indicated with a single line, total participants are indicated with a double line. Contrast the line connecting person to the director relationship, and the double line connecting movie to the director relationship.

As you can see, the foreign keys discussed earlier in the chapter as properties of entities, like the `director` for each movie, are now correctly diagrammed as relationships between the tables.

After the entity-relationship modeling is complete, you're one step away from creating tables within the database. The entity-relationship diagram should provide you with a good blueprint for your database. The final step in the design process is to get a handle on the integrity of your database using normalization. But first, I want to quickly cover another type of notation used to describe tables.

To quickly summarize the design of the table, the name of the table is listed, followed by a list of the columns in the table, enclosed in parentheses. The primary key of the table should be underlined with a double line. Here's an example:

```
studios (name, city, state)
```

NORMALIZATION

Normalization is a process by which you winnow out redundant data within your database. The entity-relationship model, when properly applied, should enable you to avoid redundancy for the most part. Before you deploy a database, you still want to be sure that your database conforms to the appropriate normal forms.

Note

The term *normalization* actually refers to bringing a database into compliance with the first normal form, but is often misused to describe the process of bringing a database into compliance with any of the normal forms. This section of the book actually covers the first, second, third, and Boyce-Codd normal forms, and thus goes beyond the basic concept of normalization.

There are lots of normal forms to which your data can subscribe. In this chapter, I'll describe the first normal form (1NF), second normal form (2NF), third normal form (3NF), and Boyce-Codd normal form (BCNF). These will be sufficient for the great majority of databases. After I cover these normal forms, I'll include some cases under which it makes sense to "denormalize" your tables.

Each higher normal form must also meet the criteria of all the lower normal forms. For example, any database that is 3NF is, by definition, also in 1NF and 2NF. The *normalization process* is the process by which a group of tables is restructured to successively meet high and higher forms of normalization. Again, most databases should meet the criteria of 3NF (or BCNF) in order to avoid problems when adding, updating, or removing data from the database. These problems are referred to as *anomalies*, and the anomalies that are eliminated with each normal form are explained with those forms. In any case, before I discuss the normal forms themselves, I want to cover one of the main principles required for the normalization process, nonloss decomposition.

NONLOSS DECOMPOSITION

Nonloss decomposition, sometimes referred to as lossless decomposition, is the process of breaking down a single table into multiple tables, without losing any of the data stored within the table. Any changes to a table or group of tables using nonloss decomposition are reversible because all the data is retained through the decomposition process.

I'll demonstrate how we could divide the studios table into two tables using nonloss decomposition, and also how it could be divided improperly using *lossy decomposition*. First, remember that the studios table contains the city and state where the studios are located; they are functionally dependent on the studio ID, which serves as the primary key. Take a look at the four tables in Figure 2.4.

Figure 2.4
Two alternatives for splitting a table.

alternative 1:

Studios_City	
name	**city**
Giant	Las Angleles
MPM	Burbank

Studios_State	
name	**city**
Giant	CA
MPM	CA

alternative 2:

Studios_City	
name	**city**
Giant	MPM
Las Angleles	Burbank

Studios_State	
city	**state**
Burbank	Los Angeles
CA	CA

As you can see, in the first case, the studios table is split into two tables, and both of them contain the primary key from studios. The second case splits the studios table, and the primary key is retained only in the first table. The second table contains only the city and state. Only the first case was split using nonloss decomposition, so why was data lost in the second case?

To understand why, recall the discussion of functional dependence earlier in the chapter. In order for a set of columns to serve as a candidate key, all the other columns in the table must be functionally dependent on that set of values. The relationships between the non-key columns and the key are important information. If that information is lost when a table is split, the table was not divided based on the principle of nonloss decomposition.

Both Studios_City and Studios_State maintain the relationship between the city and state attributes and the name, which was the primary key in the Studios table, and is the primary key of both Studios_City and Studios_State. On the other hand, while the city and name relationship is maintained in Studios_City_2, the City_State contains only the city and state, thus eliminating the meaningful relationship between the studio name and state. Because more than one studio can exist within the same city and state, and cities with the same name can exist in more than one state, there's no reliable way to link the studio to its state with Studios_City_2 and City_State.

A simple test to determine whether a table was divided properly is to ask whether the two tables can be joined together to create the table from which they were derived. In the first case, the answer is yes, in the second, the answer is no. Now that the concept of nonloss decomposition has been explained, I can proceed with an explanation of the normal forms.

THE FIRST NORMAL FORM

A table is considered to be in the first normal form, or 1NF, if all the fields contain only scalar values (as opposed to lists of values). As you might remember, this is a fundamental rule of the relational model.

While the idea of what constitutes 1NF should be pretty evident, now that you understand data relationships, I can explain it in detail. If all your tables are in 1NF, many-to-one relationships must be expressed using multiple tables, whereas one-to-one relationships can be expressed within a single table. If one column is functionally dependent on a key, the values in that column have a one-to-one relationship with the corresponding value of the key. Non-normalized tables can express a many-to-one relationship within a single table.

Let's look at an example. Not long ago, I was working with a database that contained two tables, members and divisions. Each division could have more than one member, and each member could be associated with more than one division. As I discussed in the section of this chapter that covered many-to-many relationships, these two tables should have been joined using a connecting table, which would allow you to use a join operation to list all the members of a particular division, or to list all the divisions associated with a particular member.

Unfortunately, this database was designed poorly. A one-letter abbreviation was designated for each division, and the division memberships for each person were listed in a single field in each member record, with each division signified by a single letter in the division field. For example, the divisions field for a member might include the string 'HCD', which meant that the user was a member of the 'hardware', 'software', and 'CGI programming' divisions. There are a number of reasons why this design was bad:

- Even though this is a many-to-many relationship, the data was structured so that the relationship could be evaluated in terms of the divisions for each member, and not the members for each division. This made the relationship half as useful as it could be, at best.
- There was no way to express the relationship using a single join operation because the list of divisions had to be extracted from the field, broken up, and then cross referenced to the divisions table.
- In order to update or insert a member's division list, the list of divisions had to be created and inserted into the single field, which again requires code outside a single SQL statement.

It's important at this point to understand that there is no technical reason why the design I just described does not conform to the first normal form. Aside from its meaning, 'HCD' is a valid string. The problem is caused by the fact that HCD is a pointer to three rows in another table. In that sense, the divisions field contains multiple values, rather than a single value as dictated by the first normal form.

SECOND NORMAL FORM

For a table to be in the second normal form, or 2NF, there are two requirements:

- The database must also be in 1NF.
- All the nonkey columns in the table must be functionally dependent on the entire primary key.

I'll explain 2NF through another example of poor database design. Let's pretend for a moment that we didn't go through the entity-relationship modeling process, and we came up with a table called movies with the following columns:

```
movies (studio, movie, budget, studio_city, avg_temp)
```

The avg_temp column contains the average annual temperature for the city in the studio_city column. The primary key for the column consists of the studio and movie columns. Table 2.3 contains some sample content from that table.

TABLE 2.3   SAMPLE CONTENT FROM THE MOVIES TABLE

studio	movie	budget	studio_city	avg_temp
Giant	The Big Picture	180	Milpitas	73
Giant	Diehard 38	50	Milpitas	73
Whetstone	Cry With Me	12	Vancouver	60
MPM	Gone Fishing	32	Austin	82
MPM	Butter Knife	72	Austin	82

Let's break down the functional dependencies in the table. The budget column is functionally dependent on the entire primary key, which identifies each movie. The studio_city column is functionally dependent upon only the studio column; the city where the studio is located does not change based on the value in the movie column. The avg_temp column is functionally dependent on only the studio_city column. The average temperature for a city is derived only from the name of the city, not from the studio or movie. In short, this table is a mess; it's in gross violation of 2NF.

The main problem with the lack of normalization here is that it causes *update anomalies*, or problems with SQL operations that update the values in the table. Let's take a close look at the types of problems it causes:

- INSERT operations require unnecessary information. New values cannot be inserted into the database without inserting data that you may not even have. For example, what if you want to store the fact that the average annual temperature in Fargo, North Dakota is 12 degrees, but there are no movie studios in Fargo? Say that you want to enter a new studio called Snoreworks, which is located in Los Angeles, but they haven't yet released any movies? This database architecture puts you in a position where you must have lots of unrelated data to make any insertions into the table.

- DELETE operations remove more information than is necessary. If you wanted to delete the movie "Cry With Me" from the database, not only would the movie be removed, but the location of the studio Whetstone and the average temperature in Vancouver would also be lost.

- UPDATE operations must deal with redundant information. The average temperature in Austin and Milpitas appear in the table more than once, as do the locations of the studios Giant and MPM. In order to change either of them, you must search the database and replace every occurrence at once, or risk returning inconsistent information from queries.

How do you fix these problems? The solution is to break up the table into multiple tables, while obeying the rules of nonloss decomposition. The projection operation is used to divide a table into smaller tables; each of the new tables contains a subset of the rows from the original table. So, how should the movies table that I described earlier be projected into separate tables that satisfy the second normal form?

First, because the `avg_temp` column is functionally dependent on only the `studio_city` column; a new table should be created that contains only the `avg_temp` and `studio_city` columns. The second problem with the table is that {`studio`, `movie`} is the primary key for the movies table, but `studio_city` is functionally dependent on `studio`, but not `movie`. To solve this problem, the `studio_city` column must be removed from the `movies` table, and a new table containing only the `studio` and `studio_city` columns must be created. This leaves us with three tables:

cities (<u>city</u>, avg_temp)

studios (<u>studio</u>, city)

<u>movies</u> (<u>movie</u>, studio, budget)

Each of these tables fits within the constraints of the second normal form. You can see the values stored in the new table in Figure 2.5. You should also note that these tables were projected from the original `movies` table so that none of the functional dependencies were lost, and thus, all the information stored in the original table is retained. At the same time, the update anomaly is eliminated.

Figure 2.5
The `movies` table reduced to 2NF.

Movies		
movie	**studio**	**budget**
SQL Strikes Back	Delighted Artist	5.0
Codependence Day	Giant	15.0
Hard Code	FKG	77.0

Studios	
studio	**city**
Delighted Artists	Austin
Giant	Los Angeles
FKG	Apex

Cities	
city	**avg_temp**
Austin	78
Los Angeles	72
Apex	80

THE THIRD NORMAL FORM

The third normal form, or 3NF, dictates that all the nonkey columns in a table must be functionally dependent on a candidate key. There can be no interdependencies among nonkey columns. Consider a projection of the old `movies` table used in the previous section that contains the `studio`, `studio_city`, and `avg_temp` columns.

```
studios (studio, studio_city, avg_temp)
```

Technically, this table conforms to 2NF. The `avg_temp` column is functionally dependent on `studio`, through the *transitive* property. The transitive property states that if the `studio_city` column is functionally dependent on the `studio` column, and the `avg_temp` column is functionally dependent on the `studio_city` column, `avg_temp` is functionally dependent on the `studio` column.

Transitive dependency causes the update anomaly to once again rear its ugly head. Let's take a look at what happens when you try to make a change to the `studios` table given its current design:

- A new city and temperature cannot be inserted unless a new studio is inserted as well.
- When updating the database, you once again have to deal with redundancy in the table. If there is more than one city in a particular state, and you want to update the average temperature for that city, you must update it in each of the rows to avoid inconsistency.
- Because more information is tied together than is necessary, when you delete rows from the database, you might delete information that you wanted to keep as a result of deleting the information you wanted to get rid of. If there's only one studio in Los Angeles, and you want to delete it, the average temperature for Los Angeles is also lost.

So, the solution is once again to create multiple tables by taking projections from the original `studios` table. In this case, the `studios` table would be divided into two tables, with the following schema:

```
studios (studio, studio_city)
```

```
cities (city, avg_temp)
```

These two tables eliminate the problems inherent in the single `studios` table. No longer must you enter a new studio to enter a new city, nor will you lose the average temperature for a city when you delete a studio. Each value in the database will only occur in a single location, reducing the potential for errors in updates.

Note

One might be tempted to think that the `locations` entity also contains a case of transitive identity, and thus should be projected into multiple tables to comply with 3NF. However, this is not the case. There are three properties in the `locations` table: `movie`, `city`, and `state`. It may seem that the `state` column is functionally dependent on `city`, however, it is actually functionally dependent only on `movie`, just like the `city` column. Consider the case where one movie is filmed in Springfield, Illinois, and another is filmed in Springfield,

Missouri. The value of the `state` column is not determined by the `city`, but by the movie with which it is associated. In fact, all three columns in the table are the only candidate key, and are thus the primary key. The movie column alone cannot be the primary key because movies can be filmed in multiple locations, and obviously, more than one movie can be filmed in the same city and state. So, the schema of the table looks like:

```
locations (movie, city, state)
```

BOYCE-CODD NORMAL FORM

The Boyce-Codd Normal form, or BCNF, is a refinement of 3NF. For most tables, 3NF and BCNF are the same, but 3NF does not cover a specific case where more normalization is required, so BCNF was created to address that case. Even though it is almost identical to 3NF, it did not simply replace 3NF because it is slightly more restrictive.

The rule for BCNF is that all the functional determinations in the table have a candidate key as their *determinant*. Using the functional dependency notation I described earlier in the chapter, the determinant is the left side of the functional dependency (the right side of a functional dependency is referred to as the *dependent*). Take a look at the functional determination:

```
{name} -> {price}
```

`name` is the determinant, and `price` is the dependent.

How do 3NF and BCNF differ? Under 3NF, all *nonkey* columns must be functionally dependent on a candidate key. Under BCNF, even columns that are part of a candidate key must be functionally dependent upon another candidate key, if they have any functional dependencies at all. BCNF and 3NF are exactly the same, except under a single condition, which is:

- The table has two or more candidate keys.
- At least two of the candidate keys are composed of more than one column.
- The composite candidate keys share a column.

Now, let's look at an example under which BCNF and 3NF differ. I'm going to return to something I talked about earlier, ID columns. An ID column is a column inserted into a table for the sole purpose of serving as a primary key. Let's say that the cast table contains both the movie title and a movie ID, along with the person's name from the people table, are the combined primary key of the cast table. Thus, the schema is as follows:

```
cast (movie_title, movie_id, person_name, role, payment)
```

There are two candidate keys for this table, {`movie_id, person_name`}, and {`movie_title, person_name`}. Both `role` and `payment` are functionally dependent on both of the candidate keys, as they should be to fit within the constraints of both 3NF and BCNF. The problem here is mutual dependency. `movie_title` is functionally dependent on `movie_id`, and vice versa. Under 3NF, this would be acceptable, as both of those columns are parts of a candidate key, however, under BCNF, this is not acceptable. Take a look at a few rows from the cast table, contained in Table 2.4.

TABLE 2.4   ROWS FROM THE cast TABLE

movie_title	movie_id	person_name	role	payment
Hard Code	9	Paul Monk	Handyman	10000
Hard Code	9	Brian Smith	Bystander	500
Bill Durham	4	Carol Delano	Nurse	7500

As you can see, an update anomaly exists in this table, although it is not as egregious as some we've seen earlier. The redundancy problem occurs between movie_title and movie_id. The easiest solution to the problem is to replace this table with two projections, cast and movies.

```
movies (movie_id, movie_title)

cast (movie_id, person_name, role, payment)
```

HIGHER NORMAL FORMS

There are even higher normal forms available. The *fourth normal form* (4NF) eliminates independent many-to-one relationships between columns. It would seem that it is concerned with entities similar to the location entity that I discussed earlier, which contains three columns, all which are part of the key. Here is the schema:

```
locations (movie, city, state)
```

However, city and state are not independent. Not only does the movie both determine the city and the state, but the city also determines the state. On the other hand, if we replaced the state column with an independent value, like genre, this table could be normalized under 4NF. (I'll rename the table movie_info to avoid confusion.) Here's the schema:

```
movie_info (movie, city, genre)
```

This table conforms to BCNF because all the columns are part of the only candidate key. Take a look at a few rows from the movie_info table in Table 2.5. As you can see, there's plenty of redundancy.

TABLE 2.5   THE movie_info TABLE

movie	city	genre
Hard Code	Los Angeles	comedy
Hard Code	New York	comedy
Bill Durham	Santa Cruz	drama
Bill Durham	Durham	drama
The Code Warrior	New York	horror

4NF basically states that, because `city` and `genre` are independent of one another, this table can be replaced by these two projections:

```
movie_city_info (movie, city)
movie_genre_info (movie, genre)
```

No data is lost in that transformation, and the redundancy is eliminated.

The *fifth normal form* is satisfied when all tables are projected into as many tables as possible in order to avoid redundancy. It takes normalization via projections to its furthest logical conclusion. Consider the location entity yet again. Even though all its columns are part of the candidate key, it is still subject to nonloss decomposition. Here's the schema:

```
locations (movie, city, state)
```

This table can actually be broken down into three tables:

```
movie_city (movie, city)
movie_state (movie, state)
city_state (city, state)
```

If all three of those tables are combined using a join operation, the original table is reconstituted. When all tables in the database have been broken down such that any further decomposition would result in their being unable to be reconstituted using joins, the database is considered to be in 5NF.

Tip 10 from
Rafe Colburn

The problem with higher normal forms, like 5NF, is that they require many joins to gather a relatively small amount of data from the database. From a performance perspective, it is oftentimes a better idea to stick with the lowest normal form that still enables you to avoid update anomalies.

DENORMALIZATION

Most often, databases are normalized to 3NF or BCNF. Further normalization is considered to be optional. However, the extent to which you normalize a database is in many cases determined by performance. You can, of course, normalize all your databases to 5NF, but in many cases, joins are slow, and creating useful views of the data will require using several joins.

When you put your database to use, you should always consider performance when normalizing, and, if the performance is unacceptable, consider denormalizing the database to a lower normal form to reduce the number of joins required in your queries. Just remember that you will have to account for update anomalies that result from denormalization.

IN THE REAL WORLD

When you visit the Amazon.com Web site to order a book and you place an order, all the information that makes up your order is entered in an online transaction processing (OLTP) system. OLTP systems are designed so that many applications can enter and retrieve information concurrently without sacrificing the integrity of the data in the database. The order entry system, order fulfillment system, inventory system, and a few others probably all use the same database, coming at it from different angles. The key to successfully building such a system is the ability of all the systems that rely on the database to query and update tables within it concurrently without breaking it, losing information, or causing records to get out of sync.

These systems demand the use of the higher normal forms in the database design in order to avoid data redundancy and the anomalies that come with it. They are also designed around the idea that records will be inserted, deleted, or updated a few at a time, and that most of the transactions will be short. Systems designed for this purpose are well suited to the specific task for which they were designed. Unfortunately, there are other uses for databases that are mostly incompatible with the OLTP model.

When you have a system that is accepting and processing thousands (or millions) of transactions every day, interesting trends can be extrapolated from the data. Jeff Bezos, the CEO of Amazon.com, probably wants to know whether customers who purchase books are also purchasing movies, and whether there is any correlation between the books people buy and the movies that they buy. For example, if many customers are purchasing Stephen King novels, and then seeking out the movie adaptations of those novels and purchasing them at the same time, Amazon.com may want to start promoting movie versions of books directly on the Web pages for those books, and vice versa.

If customers who live in Los Angeles tend to purchase self-help books, then perhaps Amazon.com should try determine where customers are located, and then market the types of books to them that they might find interesting. Amazon.com has implemented all sorts of recommendations features that theoretically make it easier for customers to find items that they will like.

Unfortunately, these types of large scale functions are basically incompatible with the OLTP design model. As you've already read in this chapter, bringing database designs into compliance with higher normal forms generally means splitting large tables into smaller tables and binding them together with foreign key relationships. For example, when an order is placed at Amazon.com, a list of tables like the one that follows might all be referenced:

- Customer, which contains basic biographical information for each customer who has ever purchased an item.
- Order, a table that contains a row for each order, including the payment method, shipping type, total cost, shipping cost, a foreign key from the addresses table that points to the shipping address, a foreign key from the customer table that points to the purchaser, and perhaps many others.

- `Address`, a table with all the addresses entered in the Web site, either as shipping or billing addresses.

- `Payment`, a table that contains the payment information for each order.

- `Items_Ordered`, a table that contains a row for each item in every order, referencing the `Order` table through a foreign key, and the `Inventory` table through another foreign key.

- `Inventory`, a table that contains a list of items for sale and how many of each item are currently in stock.

To extrapolate trend and decision support (DSS) information from this system, massive joining queries are required. `Amazon.com` adds thousands of rows to most of these tables every day, and some queries that create reports might literally require you to join all six of these tables. Performing such a complex query on an OLTP system could bring all the applications that rely on it to a screeching halt, thus preventing it from fulfilling the task for which it was designed.

For this reason, an alternative theory of database design was created for data warehousing. Data warehouses are built to allow users to analyze massive amounts of transactional data at once to extrapolate trends. The most famous tired anecdote of the data warehousing world is the one where the large retail chain (whose name changes depending on who's telling the story) used data warehousing to figure out that men who came to the store in the evening to purchase diapers also purchased beer at the same time, and thus made tons of money by placing the diapers and beer closer together in the store. The point being that only by tossing all your transactional data into one giant system and analyzing it to find out what trends will emerge can you make the best use of your database systems.

Because data warehouses are designed to enable executives to throw incredible amounts of data together and extrapolate high level information from them, the validity of the lower level data is not as important as system performance and the ability to find the results that are required. So, instead of concentrating on normalizing the tables and providing the highest level of data integrity possible, data warehouses denormalize the data in a way that expedites the particular queries that interest the people generating the reports, and focus on providing good performance on large queries.

In a data warehouse, `Amazon.com` might not bother with separate `Order` and `Items_Ordered` tables. Instead of joining the two, the system might just throw all the data together in one large table. Perhaps the `Inventory` table might also be included in that one table in order to speed performance of the system. It's hard to make assumptions, because the way that the tables are denormalized depends entirely upon the type of information that the users want to retrieve from the data warehouse.

Unsurprisingly, data warehousing is a topic that has inspired a number of books unto itself. One of the best of these is Ralph Kimball's *The Data Warehouse Toolkit*.

CHAPTER **3**

CREATING DATABASES

In this chapter

After the design of your database is complete, the next task is to implement the design by creating the tables within a relational database. Most databases provide you with plenty of latitude in terms of how tables are implemented. You can create as few or as many rules as you like.

At the most basic level, you can just set up the tables and columns and begin entering data. However, in many databases, you can implement a much richer database architecture than that. You can specify which columns are keys, create rules to enforce database integrity, and set up default values for certain columns. You can also delineate the relationships between tables.

By building these rules into your database when it is created, you can avoid writing extra data validation code into the programs that you use to access the database, and you can ensure that no matter how data is entered, it complies with the guidelines that you specify.

There is one statement used to define tables within a database, CREATE TABLE. In SQL, the CREATE statement is used to create all database objects, whether they are tables, indexes, or new database users. The keyword following CREATE is used to specify what type of object the statement should create.

In the previous chapter, I explained the procedures used to design a relational database. Although I discussed how tables should be organized and how properties should be assigned to various tables, I didn't discuss the structure of those tables, other than to indicate which columns were keys. In this chapter, I'm going to discuss how to use the CREATE TABLE statement to add new tables and how the CREATE INDEX statement is used to build indexes for columns and groups of columns. I'm also going to provide a detailed example that explains how the movie database is created.

CREATING A DATABASE

In some databases, before you can create individual tables within a database, it's necessary to create a new database and allocate space for storing the records. In most databases, the CRE- ATE DATABASE command is used to initialize a new database. Many database packages also provide graphical tools that can be used to create new databases, and in fact, some low-end databases leave out the CREATE DATABASE command and require you to create databases through a graphical interface. In its most basic incarnation, the CREATE DATABASE statement looks like this:

```
CREATE DATABASE database_name
```

Oracle requires that database names be less than eight characters long. In Oracle, a database named FI can be created using the following statements:

```
CREATE DATABASE FI
```

There are lots of additional arguments that can be passed to a CREATE DATABASE statement that specify the physical location where the database will be stored, log file information, and other information relating to the operation of the database. These options vary significantly among various database implementations, so I'll cover them later when I talk about specific databases.

There are a number of other CREATE statements that can be used to specify various other internal settings for a database. For example, using the CREATE TABLESPACE command in Oracle, you can allocate more physical drive space for tables. The CREATE SCHEMA command can be used to create more than one table in a single statement. I'll discuss some of these CREATE statements in various places throughout the book. For the purposes of this chapter, the most important statement by far is the CREATE TABLE statement.

CHOOSING WHICH DATABASE TO ACCESS

When you've created more than one database, you need to specify the database in which to find tables in your SQL statements. In most databases, you can prepend a table name with the database name to indicate that the table is in a database other than the one that is currently active. For example, in Microsoft SQL Server, if you're currently using a database called DB_ONE, but you want to retrieve data from a table within DB_TWO, you could use the following SELECT statements:

```
SELECT *
FROM DB_TWO..Some_Table
```

Tip 11 from *Rafe Colburn*	Using two periods between the database name and the table name is actually shorthand. If the name of the user who owns the database can be inferred, the . . notation can be used. The full notation includes the ID of the user who owns the table, along with the database name and table name, like this: `DB_TWO.sa.Some_Table`

If you want to switch to a totally different database for your queries, most databases provide the USE or DATABASE command. If you wanted to switch from DB_ONE to DB_TWO for a series of queries, you could just use the following to make DB_TWO active:

```
USE DB_TWO
```

CREATING A TABLE

To define a new table within a database, the CREATE TABLE statement is used. The CREATE statement can be used to create more than just tables, so you have to specify that you're creating a table when you use it. The basic structure of a CREATE TABLE statement is as follows:

```
CREATE TABLE Table_Name
(column_name    datatype[(size)],
column_name    datatype[(size)],
...)
```

The table specified by Table_Name will be created with the columns specified in the column listing. Each column name must be followed by a data type for that column. Most data types require that you specify a size for the field. I'll explain the details of the data types that are available soon.

Take a look at a real table definition very quickly, before I get into the explanations of the individual data types. Listing 3.1 contains a CREATE TABLE statement that could be used to create a table in Oracle to store information about movie studios. Users of most other databases will want to look at Listing 3.2, which creates the same table using Transact SQL (which is supported by Sybase and Microsoft SQL server).

LISTING 3.1 A STATEMENT TO CREATE THE Studios TABLE

```
CREATE TABLE Studios
(name        CHAR(20),
city         VARCHAR2(50),
state        CHAR(2),
revenue      NUMBER)
```

LISTING 3.2 A STATEMENT THAT CREATES THE Studios TABLE IN TRANSACT SQL

```
CREATE TABLE Studios
(name        CHAR(20),
city         VARCHAR(50),
state        CHAR(2),
revenue      FLOAT)
```

For now, don't worry about the data types listed in the table; I'll explain what they are in the next section, so just look at the structure of the statement. This statement creates a table called Studios with four columns: name, city, state, and revenue. There are a lot more options available when a table is created; I could have specified the primary key, set up relationships with other tables, or placed constraints on the values that could be entered in the columns. I'll explain how to do all those things later in this chapter.

RELATIONAL DATA TYPES

Relational databases enable you to choose from a variety of data types for each column when you create your tables. These data types not only affect how data is stored on disk, but more importantly, how data is. For example, if you are comparing two numbers or two dates, you don't want to compare them alphabetically. Storage requirements are important as well. You don't want to reserve 255 bytes of space for a field that requires only 2 bytes of space to hold the abbreviation for a state. Similarly, you don't want to reserve only 5 bytes of space for a telephone number that can be up to 10 digits long.

Fortunately, relational databases provide you with a wide array of data types that you can assign to columns within your databases. There are data types for text strings, numbers, dates, and other objects, such as binary data and large text objects. Unfortunately, each relational database product has its own distinct set of data types. All the products support the same basic data types, but they are often referred to by different names depending on which product you're using.

Some databases offer a variety of subtypes for some of the types; for example, in addition to a basic numeric type, they might offer specific types for integers, floating point numbers, and money. I'd like to cover the general types of data that are offered by nearly every database.

Note

> Despite the fact that most database vendors support a large part of the SQL-89 standard and some of the SQL-92 standard, they haven't reached as much agreement when it comes to data types. Most databases support the same basic data types, but the details of those types differ between databases, and most databases also support a number of nonstandard data types. I'm going to discuss data types in general terms, but you will probably need to review the documentation specific to your database when you create tables. I've also covered some vendor-specific information in this book, in Part VI, "Specific Databases."

Relational data types fall into four different categories: string data, numeric data, temporal data, and large objects. String data types can hold basically any type of data, but that data is treated as nothing more than a string of characters. Numeric and temporal data types, on the other hand, receive special treatment by the database. They can be used in mathematical expressions, and there are generally special functions available for manipulating data of these types. The final category includes large objects, which are used to store large quantities of information. Generally, these are handled differently internally by the database than the other data types. For example, most databases do not enable you to compare the values within large objects to one another.

One important difference between data types is how data for those types is handled within SQL statements. String data, temporal data, and large objects must all be enclosed within single quotation marks when they are used within SQL statements; on the other hand, numeric data must not be enclosed within single quotes, or it will be treated as a string instead.

STRING DATA

Most databases offer two string data types, fixed length and variable length. The difference is that fixed length fields always occupy the same amount of space in memory, no matter how much data you actually place in them, whereas variable length strings only occupy the amount of memory consumed by their contents, no matter what their maximum size is.

The data type for fixed length strings is usually CHAR. When you create a fixed length string, you must specify the length of the string. For example, in Listing 3.1, I created a column called state, of the type CHAR(2). This column always uses two bytes of disk space, even if it is actually empty or contains only one character. Similarly, the name field is a fixed length field that can hold up to 20 characters. CHAR fields are automatically padded with spaces to fill out any space that is not consumed by the data placed in them.

Strings can also be stored in variable length fields. These fields are generally specified using the identifier VARCHAR or in the case of Oracle, VARCHAR2. Like fixed length fields, variable length fields must be specified with a maximum length. For example, the city field in Listing 3.1 can contain up to 50 characters, since it is specified as VARCHAR2(50). The difference between it and a field specified using CHAR(50) is that although it can hold up to 50 characters, it will be resized to fit its contents. So, if a city name is 10 characters long, it will take up 10 bytes of space in memory instead of the 50 that a CHAR(50) field would consume.

The maximum sizes for character fields vary widely between databases. Oracle provides for CHAR fields up to 2000 bytes in length and VARCHAR2 fields up to 4000 bytes in length. Some databases restrict you to 255 bytes in both types. In some cases, you might need to store more data in a character field than either of the two data types I've already discussed provide for.

Most databases provide a data type for large character objects. Oracle provides the CLOB (character large object) data type for text that won't fit within a VARCHAR2 field. It will hold up to four gigabytes of data. Microsoft SQL Server provides the TEXT data type for large strings.

NUMERIC DATA

The large majority of commercial databases differentiate between numeric and character data. Unlike character data, numeric data does not have to be enclosed in single quotation marks. You can also include numeric data in mathematical expressions. Whereas character data is stored within CHAR and VARCHAR fields, numeric data has types of its own.

Even so, you can store numeric data within character fields, and in fact, sometimes it makes more sense to put numeric data in a character field. For example, things such as zip codes and phone numbers should probably be stored in character fields, even though they're made up of numbers. Many numeric data types remove leading zeros from the data, and sometimes these numeric strings also contain non-numeric data. Unless you're going to use a number in a mathematical context, you might as well put it in a character field.

Most databases provide at least two numeric data types—one for integers and another for floating point numbers. Some others provide more distinct numeric types, such as MONEY, which always allots two numeric places after the decimal point. Table 3.1 contains a list of common numeric data types. Some of them might not be supported by your database, and your database might include some that aren't in the table.

The number of digits supported by numeric fields in databases varies. In many databases, you can specify how many digits a number supports, just as you can specify how many characters a CHAR field holds.

Table 3.1 Numeric Data Types in SQL

Type	Definition
DECIMAL	A floating point number.
FLOAT	A floating point number.
INTEGER(size)	An integer of specified length.
MONEY	A number that contains exactly two digits after the decimal.
NUMBER	A standard number field that can hold a floating point number.

Temporal Data Types

Another distinct data type supported by most relational databases is temporal data: dates and times. Databases vary widely in the ways that they handle temporal data. The way dates are stored and displayed differs, and some databases support more temporal data types than others.

Basically, the three types of temporal data supported by relational databases are dates, times, and date-time combinations. Some databases support only a single temporal data type that combines both a date and time. Others support all three.

> **Note**
>
> I'd like to take a moment to discuss the year 2000 problem and year 2000 compliance. The roots of the Y2K problem, as it's commonly called, lie within a false assumption made by programmers, which was that their programs would be replaced before the turn of the century. Unfortunately, because of this, much of the code written until very recently only allocated two characters for the year portion of a date, and programs operated under the assumption that all years began with 19. So, at the turn of the century, these programs will assume that the year is 1900 instead of 2000. The date data types in most modern databases are Y2K compliant, but you can write applications that aren't Y2K compliant. If you opt not to use a standard date field and you use two digits to store the year, you can run into the Y2K problem, just as programmers going all the way back to the sixties have. All commercial software publishers provide Y2K compliance statements for their products, so you should verify that the database product you choose is Y2K compliant. If it isn't, take the steps necessary to rectify the problem.

There are some other data types that are supported by some databases, but you don't need to understand them yet. In Chapter 12, "Handling Specific Types of Data," I'll cover all the data types in more detail. In the meantime, you can apply what I've explained about data types thus far to the sample database and start nailing down the schema for each table I'll use in the book.

SPECIFYING KEYS

Most databases don't require you to indicate which columns in a database are keys. However, it's a good idea to identify them anyway to ensure that duplicate rows aren't created in your database by mistake. When you create a table, you can specify both candidate keys and the primary key for the table. The UNIQUE keyword is used to indicate that a column (or group of columns) must not be duplicated anywhere else in the table. After values have been entered in a set of columns with a UNIQUE constraint, any values entered in the future that duplicate an existing set of values will be rejected by the database. Listing 3.3 contains an example in which the UNIQUE keyword is used at the table level to specify a candidate key.

LISTING 3.3   CREATING THE Studios TABLE WITH KEYS

```
CREATE TABLE Studios
(studio_id        NUMBER,
name             CHAR(20),
city             VARCHAR2(50),
state            CHAR(2),
UNIQUE (name))
```

In Listing 3.3, the UNIQUE clause indicates that each value in the name column must be unique. To specify that a combination of columns must be unique, include more than one column in the UNIQUE clause. To specify multiple candidate keys, you can include more than one UNIQUE clause in a statement, as demonstrated in Listing 3.4.

LISTING 3.4   MULTIPLE CANDIDATE KEYS IN A SINGLE TABLE

```
CREATE TABLE Studios
(studio_id        NUMBER,
name             CHAR(20),
city             VARCHAR2(50),
state            CHAR(2),
UNIQUE (name),
UNIQUE (city, state))
```

Both the name column and the combined city and state columns are candidate keys. This configuration would be useful if there were a bizarre federal law prohibiting the establishment of more than one movie studio in the same town. To specify a primary key instead of a candidate key, the PRIMARY KEY clause is used. It can be used in the same CREATE TABLE statement with UNIQUE clauses, but only one primary key can be specified per table. In Listing 3.5, a table is created with both a primary key and a candidate key.

LISTING 3.5   A TABLE WITH BOTH A PRIMARY AND A CANDIDATE KEY

```
CREATE TABLE Studios
(studio_id        NUMBER,
name            CHAR(20),
city            VARCHAR2(50),
state            CHAR(2),
PRIMARY KEY (studio_id),
UNIQUE (name))
```

You can also specify both candidate and primary keys when a column is defined instead of creating the keys in a separate clause at the end of the CREATE TABLE statement. If you want to define multicolumn keys, you need to specify them at the table level, not at the column level. Listing 3.6 contains keys defined at the column level.

LISTING 3.6   A TABLE WITH KEYS DEFINED IN THE COLUMN DEFINITIONS

```
CREATE TABLE Studios
(studio_id        NUMBER PRIMARY KEY,
name            CHAR(20) UNIQUE,
city            VARCHAR2(50),
state            CHAR(2))
```

PART
I
CH
3

Unfortunately, not all databases enable you to specify keys in this manner, and you have to use a unique index, which will be discussed later in this chapter, or enforce data integrity by comparing inserted values to all the rows in the database before they are inserted. These particular examples are from an Oracle database.

FOREIGN KEYS

Oracle, along with many other databases, enables you to indicate that a column is a foreign key that references a column in some other table. The REFERENCES clause is used to create a relationship between a set of columns in one table and a candidate key in the table that is being referenced. Listing 3.7 demonstrates how a relationship from the Movies table to the Studios table can be established using the REFERENCES clause at the column level.

LISTING 3.7   SETTING UP A FOREIGN KEY RELATIONSHIP

```
CREATE TABLE Movies
(movie_title     VARCHAR2(40),
studio_id         NUMBER REFERENCES Studios(studio_id))
```

You can also use REFERENCES in the table form if the key being referenced contains more than one column. For example, if movie_title and studio_id make up the primary key of the Movies table, and you want to create a relationship between a table containing a list of the movies that are currently showing and the Movies table, you could use the statement in Listing 3.8.

LISTING 3.8   THE Showtimes TABLE

```
CREATE TABLE Showtimes
(theater_name    VARCHAR2(50),
screen           NUMBER,
showing          DATE,
movie_title      VARCHAR2(40),
studio_id        NUMBER,
PRIMARY KEY (theater_name, screen, showing),
(movie_title, studio_id) REFERENCES Movies(movie_title, studio_id))
```

The movie_title and studio_id columns in the Showtimes table reference the columns with the same names in the Movies table.

In Listing 3.7, the REFERENCES clause creates a dependent relationship between the studio_id column in Movies and the studio_id column in Studios. In Oracle, you can use the ON CASCADE DELETE clause along with the REFERENCES clause to automatically delete the corresponding row in the Studios table if you delete the row that references it in the Movies table. Under many circumstances, you probably wouldn't want to use that clause because the row in the dependent table is oftentimes useful even if the row that references it is gone, especially if it's referenced by more than one row. For example, if you used the ON CASCADE DELETE clause in Listing 3.8, whenever you deleted a movie, its studio would also be deleted, even if other movies referenced it.

COLUMN CONSTRAINTS

In addition to enabling you to specify which columns are keys, most databases also enable you to constrain the values that can appear in a particular column. For example, some databases enable you to set up column constraints that would either check to ensure that no employee had a higher salary than her boss or prevent users from entering dates in the future on their expense reports.

DISALLOWING NULL VALUES

The most basic and commonly supported column constraint is one that prevents null values from being entered in a particular column. A field in which no data has been inserted contains the null value. Basically, a null value indicates that the contents of the field are unknown. There are a lot of issues involved in dealing with nulls, and these issues are described in Chapter 12, "Handling Specific Types of Data." You might want to prevent null values from being entered in columns that are part of a candidate key or part of the primary key. In fact, because of the problems nulls can cause, you might want to bar users from leaving them in any field in your tables. Using the PRIMARY KEY clause automatically precludes the insertion of nulls in the primary key columns.

When specifying columns, adding the phrase NOT NULL to the column definition will require that a value is entered in that column whenever a new row is inserted. It will also prevent users from setting a value in that column to null when the table is updated. Listing 3.9 demonstrates how NOT NULL could be used in the creation of the Studios table.

LISTING 3.9 DEFINING THE Studios TABLE WITHOUT NULLS

```
CREATE TABLE Studios
(studio_id       NUMBER PRIMARY KEY,
name            CHAR(20) NOT NULL,
city            VARCHAR2(50) NOT NULL,
state           CHAR(2) NOT NULL)
```

In Listing 3.9, none of the columns can contain null values. The NOT NULL phrases in the definitions of name, city, and state prevent nulls, as does the PRIMARY KEY phrase with studio_id.

You can also explicitly allow null values for a column by including the word NULL after the column definition. This is the default for most databases and is not necessary, but you can still include it if you want to be explicit.

→ To find out more about nulls, **see** "Inserting Null or Default Values," **p. 82**, "Dealing with Null Values," **p. 114**, and "Nulls and Numbers," **p. 283**

OTHER CONSTRAINTS

Many databases also enable other constraints on the data that can be entered in a particular column. These constraints use the relational operators discussed in detail in Chapter 6, "Using the WHERE Clause." Basically, when a constraint is placed on a column, the value that will be inserted through an INSERT or UPDATE statement is evaluated against the condition in the column constraint. The statement will only succeed if the data meets the constraint.

The CHECK keyword is used to create a constraint for a column. For example, say your movie database doesn't include any movies with a budget of less than $50,000. You could use the constraint in Listing 3.10 to reject any movies with a budget lower than $50,000.

LISTING 3.10 A Movies TABLE WITH A COLUMN CONSTRAINT

```
CREATE TABLE Movies
(movie_title    VARCHAR2(40) PRIMARY KEY,
studio_id       NUMBER,
budget          NUMBER CHECK (budget > 50000))
```

The expression budget > 50000 tests each value entered for the budget column, and rejects any that are less than or equal to 50000. You can also define constraints at the table level, using the CONSTRAINT keyword. The advantage of table-level constraints is that you can name the constraints and that you can create constraints that affect multiple columns. The PRIMARY KEY and UNIQUE constraints that I already discussed can both be used as table-level constraints. Listing 3.11 contains an example of a table-level constraint that has a name.

PART

I

CH

3

LISTING 3.11 A CREATE STATEMENT WITH A NAMED, TABLE-LEVEL CONSTRAINT

```
CREATE TABLE Movies
(movie_title    VARCHAR2(40),
studio_id       NUMBER,
release_date    DATE,
CONSTRAINT release_date_constraint
CHECK (release_date BETWEEN '01-JAN-1980' AND '31-DEC-1989'))
```

The CREATE statement in Listing 3.11 contains a constraint named release_date_constraint that enables only movies with release dates within the 1980s to be inserted into the database. By naming your constraints in such a manner, they can be addressed later. That way, you can activate or deactivate them as necessary.

Tip 12 from
Rafe Colburn

The types of constraints that you can place on columns using the CHECK clause are somewhat primitive. You can use a special type of stored procedure, called a *trigger*, to perform more advanced tests on data in a particular field before it is inserted or modified. Using triggers, you can also manipulate the data being inserted prior to its insertion.

→ To find detailed information on triggers, **see** "Triggers," **p. 379**

DEFAULT VALUES

Another option available when you're defining a table is to include default values for columns in the table. For example, if you'd like to tag each record with the date and time at which it was inserted, you can do so by using the DEFAULT keyword. Consider the CREATE statement in Listing 3.12.

LISTING 3.12 A CREATE STATEMENT WITH DEFAULT VALUES

```
CREATE TABLE Movies
(movie_title     VARCHAR2(40) NOT NULL,
release_date     DATE DEFAULT SYSDATE NULL,
genre            VARCHAR2(20)
                        DEFAULT 'Comedy'
CHECK genre IN ('Horror', 'Comedy', 'Drama'))
```

Both the release_date and genre columns in Listing 3.12 have default values. In the case of release_date, the value of the release date defaults to the current date and time (remember that in Oracle, there are no separate date and time data types), but null values are enabled in the column. If you wanted to insert a null value in the release_date column, you'd have to use it specifically because the column already has another default value. The genre column defaults to 'Comedy', and there is a constraint on the column that verifies that one of the values in the IN clause is being inserted.

Tip 13 from	You can use any valid expression you like as the default value for a particular column in a table. For example, if you wanted to make the date a week from the current date the default value for a column, you could use SYSDATE + 7 as the value in the DEFAULT clause for a particular column.
Rafe Colburn	

DESIGN OF THE MOVIE INFO DATABASE

In the previous chapter, I described the process of designing a relational database, and at the same time, I introduced the sample database that will be used throughout this book. The general layout of each table was defined back in Chapter 2. Now, I want to describe the design of each table in detail, and introduce the actual CREATE TABLE statements used to create the tables.

THE Movies TABLE

All the data in the movie information database hinges on the Movies table. Even though all the other tables are not directly dependent on Movies, the primary function of the database is to provide information about various movies, and thus, all the other tables are secondary to it from that perspective. In any case, because the information on the movies themselves is of the most importance, I'm going to explain the design of the Movies table first.

I've used all sorts of layouts for the Movies table in examples up until this point. Now, I'm going to narrow down the list of columns that I actually want to include in the table. I've decided that the information that should be included is the movie title, the ID of the studio that produced the movie, the ID of the director who directed the movie, the release date of the movie, the gross revenues for the movie, and the movie's budget. I've also decided to include a movie id field in the table to make it simpler to join the Movies table with other tables in the database. Basically, joins require that values in a column from each of the tables match in order to join cleanly. Adding a single numeric column to every table to serve as the primary key makes it easier to share the primary keys as foreign keys and then join the tables later.

The ID column serves as the primary key for the table and the movie title-studio ID combination is a candidate key. The studio ID column is also a foreign key which references the Studios table. This is also true for the People table and the director_id column; director_id is a foreign key from People. I'll discuss its layout next.

Rather than requiring specificity in the budget and gross columns, I've decided that the values in these columns should be in millions, so a movie with a budget of 10 really cost 10 million dollars to make. Naturally, the release date column is a date. Listing 3.13 contains the SQL statement that is used to create the table.

LISTING 3.13 THE CREATE STATEMENT FOR THE Movies TABLE

```
CREATE TABLE Movies
(movie_id        NUMBER,
movie_title     VARCHAR2(20),
studio_id        NUMBER REFERENCES Studios (studio_id),
director_id     NUMBER REFERENCES People (person_id),
gross           NUMBER,
budget         NUMBER,
release_date    DATE,
PRIMARY KEY (movie_id),
UNIQUE (movie_title, studio_id))
```

The previous statement would create the Movies table in an Oracle database. If you're using another database package, the statement might differ from the one in Listing 3.13 somewhat. As you can see, the statement sets up the columns as well as the keys and relationships with other tables. In an Oracle database, you are not required to supply anything other than the column names and data types, so the CREATE statement in Listing 3.14 would work as well.

Now, examine the data types briefly. I use the generic number type for both of the IDs as well as the budget and gross numbers. The number data type provides for both integers and floating point numbers, so it works fine for both of these columns. The generic date data type also works fine for release_date. For the movie title, I used VARCHAR2(20), which limits the length of movie titles to 20 characters or less. Under ordinary circumstances, I'd probably make this limit more liberal and set up the movie title with a limit of 80 characters, but in this book, I need to fit all of the columns in the table within a single screen 80 characters wide, so I'm using smaller fields.

LISTING 3.14 A BASIC CREATE STATEMENT

```
CREATE TABLE Movies
(movie_id        NUMBER,
movie_title     VARCHAR2(20),
studio_id        NUMBER,
director_id     NUMBER,
gross           NUMBER,
budget         NUMBER,
release_date    DATE)
```

The CREATE statement in Listing 3.14 will work, but it doesn't place any of the integrity constraints found in Listing 3.13 on the contents of the database. Nothing will prevent users from entering duplicate rows or inserting values in the studio_id column that don't match studios in the Studios table.

So, in the interest of ensuring that you have data integrity, you'll use the first of the two examples to create the real table. The question at this point is whether you want to impose any constraints on the table or include any default values for the columns. As you already know, the UNIQUE and PRIMARY KEY clauses prevent users from inserting null values into the `movie_id`, `studio_id`, or `movie_title` fields. If you want to enter movies into the database before they are released, it makes sense to enable null values in the `gross` and `release_date` columns. If you allow movies to be entered before they go into production, it further makes sense to allow null values in the `director_id` and `budget` columns.

The final question is whether any constraints or default values should be included. In this case, it really doesn't make much sense to use any default values in the database definition. There is no expectation of consistency among values in any of the columns as there would be if there were a column to store the creation date of the record. On the other hand, I am going to create constraints for the `budget` and `gross` columns to ensure that people entering data in the database understand that the columns are enumerated in millions. I just have to figure out a reasonable maximum for these fields and then constrain the fields so that they fall within that limit. I think that 200 for the budget and 1000 for the gross seem like safe limits; at least, they were safe limits until the movie Titanic hit the box office. This leads me to reiterate a very important point, which is that you should always plan your databases with an eye on the data you expect it to contain in the future, not just the data you have when you create the tables. A `CREATE` statement that builds the table with the constraints is in Listing 3.15.

LISTING 3.15   BUILDING A `Movies` TABLE WITH CONSTRAINTS ON THE GROSS AND BUDGET COLUMNS

```
CREATE TABLE Movies
(movie_id          NUMBER,
movie_title       VARCHAR2(20),
studio_id          NUMBER REFERENCES Studios (studio_id),
director_id       NUMBER REFERENCES People (person_id),
gross             NUMBER,
budget        NUMBER,
release_date     DATE,
PRIMARY KEY (movie_id),
UNIQUE (movie_title, studio_id),
CONSTRAINT gross_constraint
CHECK (gross < 1000),
CONSTRAINT budget_constraint
CHECK (budget < 200))
Table created.
```

THE `Studios` TABLE

If you choose to use the `CREATE TABLE` statement with the `REFERENCES` clause to create the `Movies` table, you need to create the `Studios` table first so that the column being referenced exists. The `Studios` table is a bit simpler than the `Movies` table; it contains columns for the studio ID, the studio name, and the city and state in which the studio is located. In this table, I'm following the same small field convention that I used in the `Movies` table to ensure that all the columns can fit on a single screen without wrapping. Listing 3.16 contains a `CREATE` statement for the `Studios` table.

LISTING 3.16   THE CREATE STATEMENT FOR THE Studios TABLE

```
CREATE TABLE Studios
(studio_id          NUMBER PRIMARY KEY,
studio_name      VARCHAR2(20) UNIQUE,
studio_city      VARCHAR2(20) NOT NULL,
studio_state     CHAR(2) NOT NULL)

Table created.
```

As you can see from the query in Listing 3.16, I included the column constraints at the column level rather than specifying them at the table level. studio_id is the primary key, and studio_name is a candidate key. No null values are provided for in this table.

The REFERENCES clause in the Movies table refers to the studio_id column in this table. As you can see, they both use the NUMBER data type.

THE People TABLE

The People table contains the most fields of any table in the film industry database. One of the more interesting things about the design of the People table is that it contains several fields that will normally contain numbers but will be defined with string data types. String data types are used because the data in the fields will be used in string comparisons rather than in mathematical operations.

Like the other tables in the database, the People table contains an ID field, both for use as a foreign key and to make it easier to join People with other tables. It also contains separate fields for the person's first and last names, as well as address, city, state, zip, and phone fields. Also included are fields to store the person's social security number and union membership status. Listing 3.17 contains a CREATE TABLE statement that would set up this table.

LISTING 3.17   THE CREATE TABLE STATEMENT FOR THE People TABLE

```
CREATE TABLE People
(person_id          NUMBER PRIMARY KEY,
person_fname     VARCHAR2(10) NOT NULL,
person_lname     VARCHAR2(10) NOT NULL,
person_address    VARCHAR2(30),
person_city      VARCHAR2(20),
person_state     CHAR(2),
person_zip        CHAR(10),
person_phone     CHAR(10),
person_ssn        CHAR(9) UNIQUE,
person_union     CHAR(1) DEFAULT 'y')
Table created.
```

Take a look at the attributes of this table. First of all, readers should note that it is really only useful for storing information about people who live in the United States. My apologies to international readers, but this was done for simplicity's sake in the sample database. If this table were designed for people from all countries, a country field would be added, accommodations would be made to store state or province information other than United States' two letter state codes, and the social security number column would provide for null values. The person_zip field would also accommodate postal codes from all countries.

For the most part, null values are provided for in this table, although a first name, last name, person ID, and social security number are required. This might pose problems if you wanted to add Cher or Prince to the database, but it's fine for this example. Note that the fields for the zip code, phone number, and social security number are fixed length fields. This is because each of these types of data has a standard length. The length of 10 for the zip code fields provides space for the five digit zip code, and the four digit +4 code. The phone field provides for exactly ten characters of information: the three digit area code, the three digit exchange, and the four digit extension. Providing for no more than ten characters prevents users from entering extraneous formatting that will only serve to confuse you later. The social security number field is a CHAR(9) field because all social security numbers are 9 digits long. The UNIQUE qualifier prevents users from entering duplicate SSNs.

The last field in the database is a flag that specifies whether a given person is a member of the Screen Actors Guild (SAG), a union for actors. In this case, I use a one character field to store the flag and give it a default value of 'y' because nearly all working actors are SAG members. In SQL Server, I could have created this field using the BIT data type, which holds a single bit of information that signifies whether a flag is on or off.

THE Cast_Movies TABLE

The Cast_Movies table is a connecting table that connects the Movies table with the People table to store the casts for the movies in the database. The primary key of this table consists of foreign keys from the Movies and People tables. Two columns that are significant to the relationship between the two tables are also part of this table, role and payment. The role column is used to store the name of the character the person played in the movie, and the payment column contains the amount that he was paid to play the role. Listing 3.18 contains the CREATE statement used to generate this table.

LISTING 3.18   THE CREATE STATEMENT FOR THE Cast_Movies TABLE

```
CREATE TABLE Cast_Movies
(movie_id          NUMBER REFERENCES Movies (movie_id),
person_id         NUMBER REFERENCES People (person_id),
role            VARCHAR2(20),
payment         NUMBER,
PRIMARY KEY (movie_id, person_id),
CONSTRAINT minimum_pay
CHECK (payment > 500))
Table created.
```

The two foreign key relationships in the table are clearly noted in the column definitions for `movie_id` and `person_id`, and the combination primary key is specified at the table level. There is also a constraint on the payment column that prevents users from entering a payment below the imaginary Screen Actors Guild minimum (there really is a Screen Actors Guild minimum, but I don't think it's $500).

THE Locations TABLE

The `Locations` table stores a list of locations where movies were shot. It contains three columns that are all part of the primary key. The movie id column is a foreign key from the `Movies` table. This table is also only useful for locations within the United States. The `CREATE` statement for this table is in Listing 3.19.

LISTING 3.19   THE CREATE STATEMENT FOR THE Locations TABLE

```
CREATE TABLE Locations
(movie_id        NUMBER REFERENCES Movies (movie_id),
city             VARCHAR2(20),
state            CHAR(2),
PRIMARY KEY (movie_id, city, state))

Table created.
```

INDEXES

Obviously, performance is a prime concern when you're creating databases. As I already discussed in the previous chapter in the section on data normalization, performance concerns can override other valid concerns when it comes to database design. Indexes enable you to gain some speed when retrieving data from a database in exchange for losing some speed when you insert or update data within a database.

Indexes for tables are comparable to indexes in books. In an index, a sorted list of the data from the table is kept along with pointers to the places where the data is found in the table. This is analogous to the sorted list of subjects in a book that is found in a book's index. When a query is run and an indexed field is referenced in the WHERE clause, the values are looked up in the index rather than in the table itself, and then the database jumps immediately to the location in the table where the data is stored.

Indexes themselves are stored in a data structure called a B-tree, which provides fast information retrieval if you know the data you're looking for. When an index is created, all the data in the column (or columns) being indexed is stored within the B-tree structure. When data is inserted into the table, updated within the table, or deleted from the table, the B-tree is updated to include the new information. The performance tradeoff caused by indexes comes into play when the data in the table is changed, as that change has to be applied to the index as well as the table.

The structure of a CREATE INDEX statement is as follows:

```
CREATE [UNIQUE] INDEX index_name ON table (column)
```

To create an index for a column, the following code is used:

```
CREATE INDEX movie_title_index ON Movies (movie_title)
```

After the index is created, any time the movie_title column is referenced within the WHERE clause of a statement, the movie's title will be looked up in the index before it is found within the table. You can also create indexes for multiple columns simultaneously. When these indexes are created, search times can improve greatly for queries in which all the columns in the index appear in the WHERE clause. Take a look at an index that uses a combination of columns. In this case, I'm going to create a single index for a person's first and last names.

```
CREATE INDEX person_full_name ON People (person_fname, person_lname)
```

CREATING UNIQUE INDEXES

As described earlier in the chapter, you can place a constraint on a column (or set of columns) within a table so the contents of those columns must be unique for each row. You can also create unique indexes that ensure that every value in a particular column or group of columns is unique. These indexes also improve the performance of queries that search these columns, of course.

To create a unique index for the movie_title and studio_id columns of the Movies table, you would use the following SQL statements:

```
CREATE UNIQUE INDEX movie_index ON Movies (movie_title, studio_id)
```

When you create a unique index for a column that already contains data, the data is tested to ensure that there are no duplicate values before the index is created. Whenever a value is added to a column with a unique index or changed within a column with a unique index, the value is compared to the other values in the column, and if there is a duplicate, the operation will fail.

CLUSTERED INDEXES

A clustered index not only creates an index for a table, but also reorders the rows in the table so that they match the order of the rows in the index. Whenever a row is added to the table, the table itself is rearranged so that the new row is in the proper location. A clustered index can slow down statements that modify the table even more than a standard index because the operations not only have to update the index, but they also have to place the rows in the table itself in the correct order. On the other hand, a table with a clustered index can be even faster to query than a table with a standard index.

PART

I

CH

3

Tip 14 from
Rafe Colburn

Only one clustered index can be created per table because the rows in the table will be sorted according to the values in that index.

REASONS TO INDEX A COLUMN

There are a number of criteria that make data within one column more suitable for indexing than another. Here's a list of qualities data should have in order to best take advantage of indexes:

- A variety of values. Indexes work better if there is a large variety of values in the column, just as is the case with a book's index. If a table has 300 rows, but there are only three possible values for an indexed column, the index will be nearly useless (because there will be lots of duplicate entries in the index pointing to different locations). The movie_title column in Movies and the combination of the first and last name columns in the People table are both ideal candidates for indexing because the values will be different in almost every row.

- Frequent use in queries. The more values in an indexed column are used within the WHERE clause of queries, the more useful the index is. If you never filter query results based on the value in a particular column, there's really no point in creating an index for that column.

- Frequent use in joining operations. Joining two tables using indexed columns in each table can be much faster than joining based on non-indexed columns. Because the values in an index are ordered, it is faster to match up values from two indexes than it is to match up values from two raw columns.

WHEN NOT TO INDEX

Because indexes improve the performance of queries, you'd think that it might make sense just to index every column in every table. By thinking about the converses of the reasons why, it's good to index particular columns. You can immediately deduce some reasons why it's better not to create indexes for some other columns. You shouldn't index columns that contain few different values nor columns that you never plan on using in join operations or within the WHERE clause.

There are some other situations where it doesn't make sense to create indexes, either. It doesn't make sense to create indexes when a table is updated more often than it is queried because indexes slow down table updates. You should also be selective when it comes to the number of indexes you create because each index takes up drive space. Small tables also don't benefit all that much from indexes.

It is difficult to make up general rules of thumb for indexing because query optimizers differ greatly from database to database. The best suggestion I can offer is to create indexes if the performance of queries on a particular column is slow. If the performance improves with the index, keep it; if not, remove it.

IN THE REAL WORLD

If you created the sample tables in this chapter in the order in which they were presented, you probably ran into a problem. Because there are columns in the Movies table that reference the People and Studios tables, those tables must be created before the Movies table is created (if you use REFERENCES). Because foreign key relationships can make it difficult to create tables in the appropriate order, it is often easier to apply constraints and create relationships after all your tables are created initially.

Similarly, after you have placed constraints on your tables, it can be difficult to drop or truncate tables because the integrity constraints in the database prevent such activities. It is often necessary to remove these restrictions before you perform bulk operations for them to work at all.

There are two ways this can be accomplished. You can either turn off constraints temporarily so that you can perform the operations; or you can use the ALTER TABLE statement to remove the constraints altogether.

Removing these constraints can also be necessary due to performance considerations. When you link tables together using REFERENCES clauses, every time you want to insert, modify, or delete a record, the database must check to ensure that the constraints placed on the database through REFERENCES clauses are satisfied. As your tables grow larger and the number of transactions your database processes rises, relationships created using REFERENCES can have a significant effect on the performance of your database.

In Oracle, you can turn off existing constraints using the DISABLE clause of the ALTER TABLE command. As you know, you can name constraints within the CREATE statement if you want. If you know the name of a constraint, you can disable it using the following command:

```
ALTER TABLE table_name
DISABLE_CONSTRAINT constraint_name
```

If you don't know the name of the constraint you're trying to remove (or it doesn't have a user-defined name), you can find it in the Oracle system table User_Constraints.

To add constraints after a table has been created, the ALTER TABLE command is also used, in this case, with the ADD subcommand. To add a constraint that prevents users from entering budgets less than 5 to the Movies table, the following command would be used:

```
ALTER TABLE Movies
ADD CONSTRAINT release_date_in_future
CHECK (budget >= 5)
```

When you add a constraint, all the existing data must meet the criteria specified by the constraint. Most databases provide graphic tools that enable you to manage your tables, making it easy to create all your tables and then add foreign keys later.

CHAPTER 4

CREATING, CHANGING, AND REMOVING RECORDS

In this chapter

After you have created the tables that make up a database, the next step is to populate your database with data. First, you need to gather the data that will be placed in the database. Then, you must condition the data so that it is accurate and consistent. Finally, you must use the INSERT statement to add the data to the database.

In addition to the INSERT statement, there are two other SQL statements used to alter the contents of a table: UPDATE and DELETE. In this chapter, I'm going to discuss all three of these statements. I'm also going to explain three other statements used for database maintenance: TRUNCATE, DROP, and ALTER.

PREPARING YOUR DATA

When you insert data into a database, it is vital to be sure that it conforms to whatever convention has been established for data of that type. For example, if you have a column that indicates whether a particular option is on or off, you should make a decision up front about which two values will be used to describe the current state of the field. You could use 'true' and 'false', 'yes' and 'no', or even 1 and 0; the most important thing is that the values are consistent throughout the column. This is one advantage of the BIT data type that I touched on in the previous chapter; because it provides for only two possible values, you can be certain that all the values follow the same convention. Retrieving the appropriate data from the database when you write queries will become difficult if you fail to enforce consistency in your data, as will interpreting the data after it has been retrieved.

To further illustrate my point, consider telephone numbers as a type of value which is inserted into a database. In some cases, people divide parts of a phone number using periods, like this: 919.555.1212. Others use the American notation: (919) 555-1212. In truth, it is best to enter telephone numbers in a database with no punctuation at all because the punctuation does not provide any useful information in the telephone number. However, the most important thing is that you follow the same convention regardless of the one you choose. If you do not ensure that telephone numbers are all entered into a database using the same format, two values that contain the same telephone number might not be identical within the database.

The point is that it's not enough to gather some data and stick it in tables in a database; the more consistently you can format the data before you insert it, the more useful that data will be. Be sure that your capitalization is consistent in character data and that you remove things such as leading and trailing spaces that don't add any information to your data. When you've conditioned your data as best you can, you're ready to actually add records to your tables.

THE INSERT STATEMENT

The INSERT statement is the only SQL statement that enables you to add new records to an existing table. (The SELECT ... INTO statement can be used to create a new table and populate it with rows at the same time.) You can use the INSERT statement to add records to a table one at a time, or through the use of subqueries (which are discussed at length in Chapter 9), you can copy any amount of data from one table to another.

The basic structure of the INSERT statement is as follows:

```
INSERT INTO table_name
[(column_list)]
VALUES
(value_list)
```

The table_name is the name of the table into which you want the record (or records) inserted. If you want to insert values into a subset of the columns within a table and allow the default values to populate the rest of the columns, you can include the list of columns to be populated in your INSERT statement. If you omit the column list, the INSERT statement assumes that you will supply a value for every column in the table.

Take a look at an example of an INSERT statement that creates a new row in the Studios table. If you don't supply a column list in your INSERT statement, a value must exist in the VALUES clause for every column in the table, and the values must appear in the order in which the columns appear in the table.

Tip 15 from
Rafe Colburn

In most databases, the columns in tables appear in the order in which they were created. When you create a new table with the CREATE TABLE statement, the columns retain the order in which they were specified in that original statement. New columns that are added later using the ALTER TABLE statement are appended to the list of columns.

An INSERT statement for a new record in the Studios table is provided in Listing 4.1.

LISTING 4.1   AN INSERT STATEMENT FOR THE Studios TABLE

```
INSERT INTO Studios
VALUES (1, 'Giant', 'Los Angeles', 'CA')

1 row created.
```

The columns in the Studios table are studio_id, studio_name, studio_city, and studio_state. Because the values are included in the VALUES clause in that order, the INSERT statement works properly. If I were unsure of the order, I could include the list of columns as well as the list of values, as shown in Listing 4.2.

LISTING 4.2   AN INSERT STATEMENT THAT INCLUDES COLUMN NAMES

```
INSERT INTO Studios
(studio_city, studio_state, studio_name, studio_id)
VALUES ('Burbank', 'CA', 'MPM', 2)

1 row created.
```

As you can see from the example, when you specify the list of columns for which values will appear in the VALUES clause, the order of those columns is not important.

Tip 16 from	Generally speaking, it is better style to go ahead and include the column list in all your
Rafe Colburn	INSERT statements so that your code is easier to go back and understand later. If you have tables that contain many columns, it might be difficult to remember which values map to which columns if you leave out the column list.

INSERTING NULL OR DEFAULT VALUES

There are two methods that can be used to insert a null value into a field in a record. If the field has a default value of null, you can use an INSERT statement that includes a column list and ignore that column both in the list of columns and in the list of values. Consider a situation where you want to enter a new person in the People table, but you only know her name and social security number. By simply leaving out the other columns from the column list, you can leave null values in the other fields. Listing 4.3 contains an INSERT statement that demonstrates how to insert this new record into the database.

LISTING 4.3   ENTERING A NEW RECORD WITH NULL FIELDS

```
INSERT INTO People
(person_id, person_fname, person_lname, person_ssn)
VALUES (1, 'Jeff', 'Price', '543890123')

1 row created.
```

Jeff Price has been entered into the database, but most of the fields in the record are null. Listing 4.4 contains a SELECT statement that retrieves this record from the database.

LISTING 4.4   A SELECT STATEMENT THAT RETRIEVES THE RECORD THAT WAS JUST CREATED

```
SELECT *
FROM People
WHERE person_id = 1

PERSON_ID PERSON_FNAME          PERSON_LNAME
--------- -------------------- --------------------
PERSON_ADDRESS
----------------------------------------------------------
PERSON_CITY                   PE PERSO PERSON_PHO PERSON_SS P
----------------------------- -- ----- ---------- --------- -
        1 Jeff                 Price

                                                543890123 y
```

As you can see, the record is composed of mostly null fields because no values for those fields were supplied in the INSERT statement. However, you should note that the person_union field contains a value of y. This is because there is a default value other than null set for that field. To insert a null value into that field, the column name and null value must be explicitly specified, as demonstrated in Listing 4.5.

LISTING 4.5   SPECIFYING NULL VALUES WITHIN AN INSERT STATEMENT

```
INSERT INTO People
(person_id, person_fname, person_lname, person_ssn, person_union)
VALUES (1, 'Jeff', 'Price', '543890123', NULL)

1 row created.
```

The INSERT statement in Listing 4.5 places a null value in the person_union field instead of the default value of y. If a column provides for null values, you can insert a null into that field no matter what the data type of the field is.

As demonstrated indirectly in Listing 4.3, if you want to keep the default value for a particular column when you create a new record, you should leave out both the column name from the column list and the value from the value list. The query will assume that the default value is to be inserted.

USING SELECT AND INSERT TOGETHER

Now I'm going to talk about subqueries. Subqueries involve nesting one query inside another. In this case, I'm going to discuss how a SELECT statement can be used within an INSERT statement to provide values to be inserted in a table. This concept is discussed in detail in Chapter 9, which is dedicated to a discussion of subqueries. The use of the SELECT statement itself starts in Chapter 5 and continues all the way through Chapter 9.

PART

I

CH

4

Tip 17 from
Rafe Colburn

Using a subquery within an INSERT statement is particularly useful if you are using a database that does not enable you to make changes to tables after they've been created. To change a table, you must copy all the values into a second table, drop the original table, and then create a new table that reflects the changes. Using a subquery within an INSERT makes it easy to copy all the values from the original table into the temporary table and then back into the new table after it has been created.

Despite the fact that the meaty discussions of SELECT and subqueries have not yet taken place, I think it's important to discuss subqueries as they relate to the INSERT statement here. As you've already seen, an INSERT statement has three basic components, one of which is optional.

The first component is the `INSERT INTO` *table* part of the statement, which indicates that the statement is, in fact, an `INSERT` statement and specifies the table into which the record will be inserted. The second component is the list of columns for which values will be included. If values will be included for every column, this component is optional. The third component, the one that I'm going to talk about here, is the `VALUES` clause, which is used to supply the list of values that will be included in the new record.

Instead of entering a list of values in the `VALUES` clause, you can include a `SELECT` statement that will supply those values. For example, say that I created a new table in which to store a list of cities and states using the `CREATE` statement in Listing 4.6.

LISTING 4.6 A NEW TABLE IN WHICH TO STORE CITIES AND STATES

```
CREATE TABLE City_State
(city            VARCHAR2(20),
state           CHAR(2));

Table created.
```

I can populate this table with all the cities and states stored in the `Studios` table using a subquery within an `INSERT` statement, as demonstrated in Listing 4.7.

LISTING 4.7 POPULATING THE City_State TABLE USING A SUBQUERY

```
INSERT INTO City_State
SELECT studio_city, studio_state FROM Studios

5 rows created.
```

Take a quick look at how this actually works. First, look at the results of the subquery in Listing 4.8.

LISTING 4.8 THE RESULTS OF THE SUBQUERY IN LISTING 4.7

```
SELECT studio_city, studio_state
FROM Studios

STUDIO_CITY          ST
-------------------- --
Los Angeles          CA
Burbank              CA
Apex                 NC
Austin               TX
Los Angeles          LA
```

Each of the rows returned by the query in Listing 4.8 is used to create a new row in `City_State` in Listing 4.7. As you can see, using a subquery to create rows enables you to create more than one record at a time. Take a look at the contents of the `City_State` table, shown in Listing 4.9, after I run the query in Listing 4.7.

LISTING 4.9   THE CONTENTS OF THE City_State TABLE

```
SELECT *
FROM City_State

CITY                    ST
-------------------- --
Los Angeles          CA
Burbank              CA
Apex                 NC
Austin               TX
Los Angeles          LA
```

As you can see, the query results from Listing 4.8 and Listing 4.9 are the same. The further intricacies of using subqueries within INSERT statements are described in Chapter 9.

COPYING TABLES AND ELIMINATING DUPLICATE ROWS

One particularly useful application for subqueries within the INSERT statements is to copy the contents of one table to another. Some databases do not enable you to make changes to tables after they have been created, so if you want to resize a column, change a data type, or make some other change to the structure of a table, you must create a new table and move the values from the old table to the new one. Subqueries make it very easy to copy values from one table to another.

First, as shown in Listing 4.10, I'm going to create a copy of the Studios table, except without the column constraints.

LISTING 4.10   A STATEMENT THAT CREATES A DUPLICATE OF THE Studios TABLE

```
CREATE TABLE Studios_Copy
(studio_id          NUMBER,
studio_name        VARCHAR2(20),
studio_city        VARCHAR2(20),
studio_state       CHAR(2))

Table created.
```

After the duplicate table has been created, I can use an INSERT statement with a subquery to copy the values from the original table to the copy, as shown in Listing 4.11.

LISTING 4.11   COPYING THE VALUES FROM THE Studios TABLE TO Studios_Copy

```
INSERT INTO Studios_Copy
SELECT * FROM Studios

5 rows created.
```

Now, the SELECT statement in Listing 4.12 retrieves the new contents of Studios_Copy.

LISTING 4.12   THE CONTENTS OF THE Studios_Copy TABLE

```
SELECT *
FROM Studios_Copy

STUDIO_ID STUDIO_NAME              STUDIO_CITY          ST
---------- --------------------    --------------------  --
        1 Giant                    Los Angeles          CA
        2 MPM                      Burbank              CA
        4 FKG                      Apex                 NC
        3 Delighted Artists        Austin               TX
        5 Metaversal Studios       Los Angeles          LA
```

As you can see, the contents of Studios are now in Studios_Copy as well. The most important rule here is that the data types in the new table can be different from those in the old table. As long as the data returned by the subquery can be inserted into the new table without error, the records will be copied successfully. In other words, if you're copying data from a column of type VARCHAR(255) to a VARCHAR(25) column, the query will work fine as long as the values being inserted are 25 characters or less. Of course, you should only attempt this if you know that all the values in that VARCHAR(255) column are less than 25 characters long. This is useful because most databases will not enable you to change the data types of columns while there is data in the table, so you must copy the data to another table, make the change, and then copy the data back into the table.

You can also use these data copying techniques to eliminate duplicate rows in a table. As you already know, every row in a table in a relational database should be unique. Sometimes, if a database is improperly designed, there can be multiple rows that have all the values in each column in common. For example, what if I added all the cities and states from the People table to the City_State table? The query in Listing 4.13 does just that, and leaves you with the collection of rows shown in Listing 4.14.

LISTING 4.13   AN INSERT STATEMENT THAT ADDS ALL THE CITIES AND STATES IN THE People TABLE TO THE City_State TABLE

```
INSERT INTO City_State
SELECT person_city, person_state FROM People

11 rows created.
```

LISTING 4.14   THE CONTENTS OF THE City_State TABLE

```
SELECT *
FROM City_State

CITY                  ST
-------------------- --
Los Angeles          CA
Burbank              CA
Apex                 NC
Austin               TX
Los Angeles          LA
```

```
Cary                NC
Cary                NC
Buffalo             NY
Dallas              TX
Houston             TX
Bellaire            TX

CITY                ST
-------------------  --
Knoxville           TN
New Orleans         LA
Madison             WI
Houston             TX
Cary                NC

16 rows selected.
```

As you can see from the query results in Listing 4.14, there are now some duplicate rows in the City_State table. Under the relational model, duplicate rows are taboo, so the question becomes "How should they be removed?" Under normal circumstances, when you want to remove rows from a table, you use the DELETE statement, which will be discussed later in this chapter. Unfortunately, because these rows are identical, there's no way to delete one without deleting the other.

The DISTINCT operator can be used with the SELECT statement to return only unique values. The use of this operator is discussed in Chapter 7, but I'd like to show you how it works here. Take a look at the query in Listing 4.15, which is identical to the query in Listing 4.14, except that it includes DISTINCT.

LISTING 4.15   A STATEMENT THAT SELECTS THE UNIQUE ROWS FROM City_State

```
SELECT DISTINCT *
FROM City_State

CITY                ST
-------------------  --
Apex                NC
Austin              TX
Bellaire            TX
Buffalo             NY
Burbank             CA
Cary                NC
Dallas              TX
Houston             TX
Knoxville           TN
Los Angeles         CA
Los Angeles         LA

CITY                ST
-------------------  --
Madison             WI
New Orleans         LA

13 rows selected.
```

As you can see, only the unique rows in the City_State table are retained in the results in Listing 4.15. So, to remove the duplicate rows from the table, you can copy the distinct values from City_State to a duplicate table, delete all the rows in City_State, and then copy the rows back to City_State, as shown in Listing 4.16.

LISTING 4.16   A SEQUENCE OF QUERIES THAT REMOVES DUPLICATE ROWS FROM THE City_State TABLE

```
CREATE TABLE City_State_Copy
(city              VARCHAR2(20),
state              CHAR(2))

Table created.

INSERT INTO City_State_Copy
SELECT DISTINCT * FROM City_State

13 rows created.

DELETE FROM City_State

16 rows deleted.

INSERT INTO City_State
SELECT * FROM City_State_Copy

13 rows created.

DROP TABLE City_State_Copy

Table dropped.
```

The queries in Listing 4.16 remove all the duplicate rows from the City_State table. Go over the steps in the example quickly. First, a copy of the City_State table named City_State_Copy is created. Next, all the unique rows in City_State are inserted in the City_State_Copy table; this removes all the duplicates from the results that are entered into City_State_Copy—though none of the records in City_State have been removed at this point. After the duplicates have been removed, I use the DELETE statement to remove all the records in City_State. Then, all the records in City_State_Copy are copied back into City_State. Finally, the DROP TABLE command (which is discussed later in this chapter) is used to delete the duplicate table.

THE DELETE STATEMENT

Just as the INSERT statement is used to add records to a table, the DELETE statement is used to remove records from a table. The structure of the DELETE statement is very simple:

```
DELETE FROM table
[WHERE condition]
```

The optional WHERE clause is used to limit the number of rows that are removed by the DELETE statement. If you leave the WHERE clause out, all the rows in the table will be deleted, as was the case in Listing 4.16. Using the WHERE clause, you can specify conditions that each row must satisfy in order to be removed. For example, the query in Listing 4.17 would remove all the rows in the City_States table in which the state is TX.

LISTING 4.17 A DELETE STATEMENT THAT DELETES ROWS THAT HAVE TX IN THE STATE FIELD

```
DELETE FROM City_State
WHERE state = 'TX'

4 rows deleted.

SELECT *
FROM City_State

CITY                    ST
--------------------    --
Apex                    NC
Buffalo                 NY
Burbank                 CA
Cary                    NC
Knoxville               TN
Los Angeles             CA
Los Angeles             LA
Madison                 WI
New Orleans             LA

9 rows selected.
```

Use of the WHERE clause to filter the rows in a table is described in Chapter 6.

THE UPDATE STATEMENT

The UPDATE statement is used to make changes to existing rows in a table. The structure of the UPDATE statement is as follows:

```
UPDATE table
SET column = value, ...
[WHERE condition]
```

The UPDATE statement has three parts. First, you must specify which table is going to be updated. The second part of the statement is the SET clause, in which you should specify the columns that will be updated as well as the values that will be inserted. Finally, the WHERE clause is used to specify which rows in the table will be updated.

Now, take a look at an example. If the studio Giant moved from Los Angeles, CA, to New York, NY, you would need to update its row in the Studios table, using the query in Listing 4.18.

LISTING 4.18   AN UPDATE STATEMENT THAT CHANGES THE CITY AND STATE FOR A STUDIO

```
UPDATE Studios
SET studio_city = 'New York', studio_state = 'NY'
WHERE studio_id = 1

1 row updated.
```

As you can see, in the SET clause, I change both the city and state fields. The WHERE clause indicates that only the row with a studio ID of 1 should be updated. When you're writing UPDATE statements that should only affect one row in a table, it's always a good idea to use the primary key in the WHERE clause to ensure that only a single row will be affected by the changes.

The UPDATE statement in Listing 4.18 can also be rewritten with all the column names to the left of the = sign in the SET clause and all the values to the right of the = sign. The UPDATE statement in Listing 4.19 is identical to the one in Listing 4.18, except that it takes this format.

LISTING 4.19   AN ALTERNATIVE NOTATION FOR AN UPDATE STATEMENT

```
UPDATE Studios
SET (studio_city, studio_state)= ('New York', 'NY')
WHERE studio_id = 1
```

If you leave out the WHERE clause in an UPDATE statement, all the rows in the table being updated will be affected by that statement. Take a look at the query and results in Listing 4.20.

LISTING 4.20   A STATEMENT THAT USES UPDATE TO CHANGE ALL THE ROWS IN A TABLE

```
UPDATE Studios
SET studio_state = 'AK'

5 rows updated.

SELECT *
FROM Studios

STUDIO_ID STUDIO_NAME          STUDIO_CITY           ST
--------- -------------------- --------------------- --
        1 Giant                Los Angeles           AK
        2 MPM                  Burbank               AK
        4 FKG                  Apex                  AK
        3 Delighted Artists    Austin                AK
        5 Metaversal Studios   Los Angeles           AK
```

The query results in Listing 4.20 show that the state for every row in the database has the same state now.

THE TRUNCATE STATEMENT

If you want to remove all the rows from a table, you can use the TRUNCATE (or TRUNC, for short) statement instead of the DELETE statement. The two statements in Listing 4.21 have the same effect.

LISTING 4.21   A COMPARISON OF TRUNCATE AND DELETE

```
DELETE FROM Studios

5 rows deleted.

TRUNCATE TABLE Studios

Table truncated.
```

The only difference is that the DELETE statement actually performs a delete operation on each row in the table, and the database performs all attendant tasks along the way. On the other hand, the TRUNCATE statement simply throws away all the rows at once and can be much quicker than using DELETE for that reason. Using either statement leaves you with an empty table at the end.

The main problem that you can run into when you use the TRUNCATE statement is that integrity constraints are not checked before each row in the truncated table is removed. If you have cascading turned on so that dependent items will be removed when the row that references those items is removed, the settings will be ignored if you use TRUNCATE. If your tables are not set up with interdependencies such as these, using TRUNCATE and a DELETE statement that deletes all the rows in a table will have the same effect.

Tip 18 from
Rafe Colburn

> Some programmers write special stored procedures called triggers, which are called whenever a particular event occurs. One event that can call a trigger is the deletion of a row. The TRUNCATE statement ignores triggers; if you use them, you should stick with the DELETE statement for removing records.

PART

I

CH

4

THE DROP STATEMENT

When you want to remove elements from a database, such as tables, indexes, or even users and databases, you use the DROP statement. The DROP statement is somewhat similar to the CREATE statement in that there are a number of distinct uses for the DROP statement that depend on the keyword it is used with. Just as the CREATE TABLE and CREATE INDEX commands don't have much in common other than the fact that they're used to create new elements within the database, the DROP TABLE and DROP INDEX commands are used to remove these individual elements.

DROP TABLE

The DROP TABLE statement can be used to remove a table from a database. When a table is deleted, all the data in it is deleted as well, as are all the indexes for the table. If constraints have been placed on other tables that refer to the table being dropped, they are also removed. Listing 4.22 demonstrates how the DROP TABLE statement is used.

LISTING 4.22   A STATEMENT THAT REMOVES THE Studios TABLE FROM A DATABASE

```
DROP TABLE Studios

Table dropped.
```

DROP INDEX

To turn off indexing for a particular column or group of columns in a database, use the DROP INDEX command. Because indexes, like tables, are named, you just enter DROP INDEX, followed by the index name, as shown in Listing 4.23.

LISTING 4.23   THE DROP INDEX STATEMENT IS USED TO REMOVE AN INDEX FROM A COLUMN

```
DROP INDEX movie_index

Index dropped.
```

THE ALTER STATEMENT

If the CREATE statement at the table level is analogous to the INSERT statement at the row level and the DROP statement is analogous to the DELETE statement, the ALTER statement is analogous to the UPDATE statement. ALTER is used to make changes to existing elements within a database.

Whereas DROP and CREATE are both available in nearly every database, many databases do not provide the ALTER statement. Instead, you must delete the existing element and re-create it if you want to make any changes to it. In the part of this book that discusses specific database packages, I'll indicate which databases support ALTER statements.

ALTER TABLE

The ALTER TABLE statement is used to make changes to the schema of a table. Columns can be added, and the data types for columns can be changed as long as the data within the column conforms to the new data type. Depending on the database you're using, you can also use the ALTER TABLE statement to make changes to the way that the data itself is stored on disk. One thing you'll notice is that columns cannot be removed using the ALTER TABLE statement. If you want to remove a column from a table, you must drop the table and re-create it without the column you want to discard.

Tip 19 from
Rafe Colburn

> Many databases do not support the ALTER TABLE statement. To make changes to the schema of tables in those databases, you must drop the tables and re-create them with the changes applied.

The syntax of the ALTER TABLE statement is a bit more complex than some other queries, so I'll talk about it in the abstract before providing examples. Basically, the statement can take one of two forms: It can either be used to add a column (or columns) to a table, or it can be used to modify a table. Take a look at the syntax for each.

Here's the syntax for an ALTER TABLE statement used to add a column to an existing table:

```
ALTER TABLE table
ADD (column datatype [DEFAULT expression]
[REFERENCES table (column)]
[CHECK condition])
```

As you can see, all the attributes that can be assigned to a column when it is created can be applied to a new column added to an existing table. An example of an ALTER TABLE statement that adds new columns to a table is included in Listing 4.24.

LISTING 4.24   A STATEMENT THAT ADDS A NEW COLUMN TO AN EXISTING TABLE

```
ALTER TABLE Studios
ADD (revenue NUMBER DEFAULT 0)

Table altered.
```

PART

I

CH

4

One constraint that cannot be added to a table that already has rows is the NOT NULL constraint. This constraint cannot be added because when you create a new column in a table with existing rows, by default all the values in that column will be null. There's no way to populate those fields at the same time that the column is created; thus it's infeasible to use the NOT NULL constraint in this circumstance. This also applies to the UNIQUE constraint. If the table already has rows, there is no way to add a column containing all unique values.

An ALTER TABLE statement can also be used to add table-level constraints to a table. The syntax for such a statement is as follows:

```
ALTER TABLE table
ADD ([CONSTRAINT name CHECK comparison]
[(column(s) REFERENCES table (columns)]
```

Just as you can add table-level constraints when you create new tables using the CREATE TABLE statement, you can add constraints at the table level using the ALTER TABLE statement. An example of the use of ALTER TABLE is in Listing 4.25.

LISTING 4.25   USE OF THE ALTER TABLE STATEMENT TO ADD CONSTRAINTS TO A TABLE

```
ALTER TABLE Studios
ADD (CONSTRAINT check_state CHECK (studio_state IN ('TX', 'CA', 'WA')))

Table altered.
```

Now, look at the usage of the ALTER TABLE statement to modify columns within an existing table. Take a look at the syntax of an ALTER TABLE statement that makes changes to existing columns:

```
ALTER TABLE table
MODIFY column [data type]
[DEFAULT expression]
[REFERENCES table (column)]
[CHECK constraint]
```

The MODIFY statement is similar to the ADD statement, except that changes are made to an existing column in a table, rather than adding a new column. The fundamental rule that applies to modifying a column is that all the data within the column being modified must meet the column's criteria after the modification. For example, if you tried to transform a VARCHAR field into a NUMBER field, the transformation wouldn't work. Similarly, if you tried to reduce the size of a VARCHAR column, but some of the values in the column were longer than the new size, the modification wouldn't work either.

Listing 4.26 contains an example of an ALTER TABLE statement that modifies an existing column. In this case, a constraint is added, and the size of the field is changed.

LISTING 4.26   A STATEMENT THAT MODIFIES A COLUMN IN A TABLE

```
ALTER TABLE People
MODIFY person_union VARCHAR2(10)

Table altered.
```

IN THE REAL WORLD

One task you'll probably face when you create a relational database is importing data from other sources into the database. Some applications don't require any data to be inserted in the database before the application can be used, but most programmers find themselves dealing with so-called legacy data when they plan their databases.

Naturally, the primary concern when dealing with legacy data is being sure that the design of the database incorporates all the fields and relationships required to model that data in a relational database. However, an important secondary concern is the means by which the legacy data will be transferred into the new database.

In this chapter, I described how data can be inserted in a table using the INSERT statement, but when you are dealing with large amounts of legacy data, creating individual INSERT statements to enter all the data in your tables is time consuming and repetitive. Fortunately, there are a number of options available when you need to insert large amounts of data into your tables at once.

If the data you want to insert in a particular table is formatted properly and stored in a structured text file, it can usually be inserted into the database using a program called a *loader*. Most database products come with their own loader programs, which each work somewhat differently.

Each database comes with its own data-loading program, and unfortunately, there is no real standardization among them. Some databases use loaders that emulate the Oracle loader because of Oracle's high market share.

Another option for loading data into a database, which might not be as fast, is to write a loader of your own. Depending on your competency with other programming languages and your knowledge of database loaders, this might be the best option for you. For example, when I have data stored in a formatted flat file, I write a Perl program that uses the DBI/DBD libraries to connect to the database and issue INSERT statements for each row in the data file. This is because I know Perl and the commands related to the Perl database interface (DBI) better than I know the loader for any individual database, and I use different relational databases for different projects.

Getting back to the loaders that are packaged with various databases, let me provide an example of how the Oracle loader is used. The Oracle loader uses a single file that contains both the instructions for loading the data into the database and the actual data that will be loaded. The program itself is named sqlldr, and it is called using the following syntax:

```
sqlldr user/password control=loadfile.ctl
```

L The control file contains both the data that will be loaded into the database and the instructions for processing that data. An example of a control file that loads data delimited by the pipe (¦) character into the Studios table is included in Listing 4.27.

LISTING 4.27   AN SQL*LOADER CONTROL FILE

```
LOAD DATA
INFILE *
INTO TABLE Studios
FIELDS TERMINATED BY "¦" OPTIONALLY ENCLOSED BY '"'
TRAILING NULLCOLS
(studio_id, studio_name, studio_city, studio_state)
BEGINDATA
5¦"Dreamworks SQL"¦"Culver City"¦CA
6¦"Perfect Pictures"¦Houston¦TX
7¦O'Ryan¦Huntsville¦AB
```

Let me explain briefly how the control file works. The table into which the data will be inserted is specified using the INTO TABLE clause. Then, the character (or group of characters) used as the delimiter is specified, along with the quotation character. The quotation

PART

I

CH

4

character is included so that the delimiter can be used within quotation marks and not be interpreted as the field delimiter. In this example, a pipe enclosed within double quotes would be inserted into the database and would not indicate that the field is ending and another is beginning. Next is the column list, which maps to the fields in the data file. Each column in the column list corresponds to a field in the input data. The TRAILING NULLCOLS statement indicates that any columns in the column list for which data is not included in the data will be assumed to be null. The BEGINDATA keyword indicates that the rest of the file will consist of records to be inserted into the database.

This is just one method that can be used with SQL*Loader. You can also break data up into fields based on the number of columns of text it occupies, or insert records consisting of more than one line in the data file. You can also make changes to the data before you insert it in the database using some of the functions built into Oracle.

Other databases use different loader programs. For example, the Microsoft SQL Server loader (and unloader) is called bcp. If you need to insert bulk amounts of data into your database, you should investigate the loader application for your database and use it.

PART II

RETRIEVING DATA FROM A DATABASE

CHAPTER 5

THE **SELECT** STATEMENT

In this chapter

After you've designed, created, and populated your database, the next step is to access the data stored inside. SQL provides a single statement used to retrieve data that is stored in a database—SELECT. The basic syntax of the SELECT statement is deceptively simple, but as I proceed through this section of the book, you'll learn powerful techniques that will enable you to pinpoint the records that you want to retrieve.

SELECT statements are made up of a number of clauses, some of which are optional. Before I can discuss advanced data retrieval techniques, I need to explain the basic clauses that are used to build SELECT statements. In this chapter, I'm going to introduce the SELECT statement and explain how to retrieve records from a table. In the chapters that follow this one, I'll explain how you can narrow the scope of your SELECT statements to return only the data you want.

ANATOMY OF A SELECT STATEMENT

Before I discuss the SELECT statement in detail, let me first present an example of a typical SELECT statement and explain it quickly. Listing 5.1 contains a SELECT statement and the output from the database produced by that statement.

LISTING 5.1   A BASIC SELECT STATEMENT

```
SELECT movie_title, studio_id
FROM Movies
WHERE movie_title = 'The Code Warrior'

MOVIE_TITLE            STUDIO_ID
-------------------- ----------
The Code Warrior              4
```

As you can see from the results of the query, this particular SELECT statement has returned the contents of two fields in one row of the database. When the database engine received the query, it searched the values in the title field until it located the value for "The Code Warrior", and then it retrieved the values from the movie_title and studio_id fields and printed them for the user, along with the column headings.

Here's the syntax of a simple SELECT statement:

```
SELECT select_list
FROM table [, table, ... ]
[ WHERE condition ]
```

Note

This is the syntax for a SELECT statement that contains only the essential clauses shared by nearly every SELECT statement. There are a number of additional clauses that can be added; they will be discussed as I progress through Part II of the book.

The *select_list* element of the query enables you to specify a list of columns that will be returned by a query. The *table* element specifies from which table (or tables, in the case of joins, which are covered in Chapter 8, "Combining Tables Using Joins") the data should be retrieved. The WHERE clause enables you to compare values and filter the results of the query based on those comparisons. If you want to retrieve every row from a database, the WHERE clause is not required.

Tip 20 from *Rafe Colburn*	It is my habit to place the FROM clause and the WHERE clause on separate lines from the SELECT statement and select list. As I stated back in Chapter 1, "The Structured Query Language," SQL is very permissive in terms of its tolerance for white space, so you can include as much white space as you like to make your code more readable. As your SELECT statements increase in complexity, the number of clauses in your statements will increase, and the size of each clause will increase. Placing them all on separate lines makes it easier to determine where each clause begins and ends, in turn making your code easier to read.

SPECIFYING COLUMNS TO RETRIEVE

The SELECT statement in Listing 5.1 included a WHERE clause, which is an optional element that constrains the set of rows that are returned by a query. As you will see in Listing 5.2, the WHERE clause is optional. Listing 5.2 includes only the list of columns to be retrieved and the table from which the rows are selected.

LISTING 5.2   A SELECT STATEMENT THAT RETRIEVES ALL THE ROWS IN THE Movies TABLE

```
SELECT movie_title
FROM Movies

MOVIE_TITLE
-------------------
Vegetable House
Prince Kong
The Code Warrior
Bill Durham
Codependence Day
The Linux Files
SQL Strikes Back
The Programmer
Hard Code
The Rear Windows

10 rows selected.
```

PART

II

CH

5

Take this minimalist SQL query apart. The first element of the query is the SELECT command. The next element, movie_title, contains a list of columns to display (in this case, only a single column is displayed). The third element, FROM, is used to separate the columns to be selected from the name of the table from which the data should be retrieved. The final element in this query is the name of the table that is being queried, which in this case is Movies. Multiple tables can also be queried using a single SELECT statement. The method for doing so is described in Chapter 8.

Consider the list of columns a bit more fully. You can specify a list of columns in any order that you like, and the columns will be displayed in that order. The queries in Listings 5.3 and 5.4 are examples of queries that retrieve the contents of multiple columns.

LISTING 5.3 A QUERY THAT RETRIEVES MULTIPLE COLUMNS

```
SELECT movie_title, studio_id
FROM Movies

MOVIE_TITLE             STUDIO_ID
-------------------- ----------
Vegetable House             1
Prince Kong                 2
The Code Warrior            4
Bill Durham                 3
Codependence Day            1
The Linux Files             2
SQL Strikes Back            3
The Programmer              3
Hard Code                   4
The Rear Windows            1

10 rows selected.
```

LISTING 5.4 A QUERY THAT RETRIEVES THE SAME COLUMNS IN A DIFFERENT ORDER

```
SELECT studio_id, movie_title
FROM Movies

STUDIO_ID MOVIE_TITLE
---------- --------------------
        1 Vegetable House
        2 Prince Kong
        4 The Code Warrior
        3 Bill Durham
        1 Codependence Day
        2 The Linux Files
        3 SQL Strikes Back
        3 The Programmer
        4 Hard Code
        1 The Rear Windows

10 rows selected.
```

As you can see from the query results, changing the order in which you specify the columns changes the order in which the columns are displayed. This is one of the ways you can customize the appearance of the reports you generate using the SELECT statement.

SELECTING ALL COLUMNS USING *

To select all the columns in a particular table, you can simply enter * in place of the list of columns you want to select. So, rather than entering

```
SELECT studio_name, studio_city, studio_state, studio_id
FROM Studios
```

you could simply enter

```
SELECT *
FROM Studios
```

You would think that these two queries would produce the same output, but first, take a look at Listings 5.5 and 5.6.

LISTING 5.5 A QUERY THAT SELECTS ALL THE COLUMNS IN THE Studios TABLE

```
SELECT studio_name, studio_city, studio_state, studio_id
FROM Studios

STUDIO_NAME          STUDIO_CITY          ST  STUDIO_ID
-------------------  -------------------  --  ----------
Giant                Los Angeles          CA           1
MPM                  Burbank              CA           2
FKG                  Apex                 NC           4
Delighted Artists    Austin               TX           3
Metaversal Studios   Los Angeles          CA           5
```

LISTING 5.6 A QUERY THAT SELECTS ALL THE COLUMNS IN Studios USING *

```
SELECT *
FROM Studios

STUDIO_ID STUDIO_NAME          STUDIO_CITY          ST
--------- -------------------  -------------------  --
        1 Giant                Los Angeles          CA
        2 MPM                  Burbank              CA
        4 FKG                  Apex                 NC
        3 Delighted Artists    Austin               TX
        5 Metaversal Studios   Los Angeles          CA
```

PART

II

CH

5

As you can see, the columns are not listed in the same order in the results of both queries. The results of the query that uses SELECT * lists the columns in the order in which they were originally entered in the CREATE TABLE statement. On the other hand, naming each column individually enables you to specify the order in which the columns appear.

There are two problems with using the SELECT * construct within applications. The first has to do with maintainability. When you use SELECT * within your query, no indication of what columns are actually being used is provided within the syntax of the statement, thus making it harder to know how your code will have to change if the schema of the database that is being queried changes. From this standpoint, explicitly specifying the columns within the query that will be used makes your code easier to read and maintain. The second problem is performance. It is always faster, in terms of processing time, to run a query that has a list of columns in the select list instead of a *. This is true even if the select list contains every column in the table, like the query in Listing 5.5.

Tip 21 from
Rafe Colburn

SELECT * is often used to quickly view the contents of a database, rather than as a tool to produce structured reports. When you don't remember exactly what the structure of a table is or you need to view all the records before you write a query to extract the specific data you're looking for, SELECT * is a handy shortcut.

PERFORMING CALCULATIONS ON SELECTED DATA

Using SQL, you can easily perform calculations on the data in your database and include the results of the calculations in the query output. To do so, you can simply replace a standard entry in the list of columns you want to select with a mathematical expression that contains numbers, column names, or both.

INCLUDING EXPRESSIONS IN A SELECT STATEMENT

The expressions that you include in a query don't necessarily have to include a column at all. Numbers, mathematical expressions, and strings can all be included in SELECT statements and will be printed along with the rest of the results of the query, as shown in Listing 5.7.

LISTING 5.7 A QUERY THAT CONTAINS A MATHEMATICAL EXPRESSION

```
SELECT 'Random text', movie_title, 2 + 2
FROM Movies

'RANDOMTEXT MOVIE_TITLE                    2+2
---------- -------------------- ----------
Random text Vegetable House              4
Random text Prince Kong                  4
Random text The Code Warrior             4
Random text Bill Durham                  4
Random text Codependence Day             4
Random text The Linux Files              4
Random text SQL Strikes Back             4
Random text The Programmer               4
Random text Hard Code                    4
Random text The Rear Windows             4

10 rows selected.
```

The query in Listing 5.7 was totally worthless, except as an example. The string Random text and the number 4 are printed as columns in the query results, along with the movie_title field from the Movies table. The string is set apart from the rest of the columns being selected by single quotation marks. The mathematical expression is evaluated before it is included in the results. If you enclosed the expression within single quotation marks, it would be evaluated as a string, and 2 + 2 would be inserted in the results instead of 4, the results currently shown in Listing 5.8. The same holds true for column names as well.

LISTING 5.8   ITEMS INSIDE QUOTATION MARKS IN THE SELECT LIST ARE TREATED AS STRINGS AND ARE NOT EVALUATED

```
SELECT 'Random text', 'movie_title', 2 + 2
FROM Movies

'RANDOMTEXT 'MOVIE_TITL         2+2
---------- ----------- ----------
Random text movie_title          4
Random text movie_title          4
Random text movie_title          4
Random text movie_title          4
Random text movie_title          4
Random text movie_title          4
Random text movie_title          4
Random text movie_title          4
Random text movie_title          4
Random text movie_title          4

10 rows selected.
```

USING COLUMN NAMES IN EXPRESSIONS

You can include column names as part of the expressions that you use within the SELECT statement. Just as you can include calculations such as 2 + 2 in your query, you can also include calculations that incorporate columns from the table being queried, such as 2 * budget, which would return the movie's budget multiplied by 2. You can also use multiple column names in a single expression if you want.

Say that you wanted to determine what the gross for a particular movies was in UK pounds instead of dollars. Keeping two separate columns in the database for movie grosses in US dollars and UK pounds wouldn't make a whole lot of sense. For one thing, every time the exchange rate changed, the pounds column would no longer be correct. Another problem is that every time you updated the value in one column, you would have to update the other accordingly.

To make a long story short, it makes more sense to simply multiply the value in the column that stores the US gross in dollars by the current exchange rate to determine the gross in UK pounds. (Remember that in the sample database, the budget and gross columns are denominated in millions, so this actually returns the results millions of pounds.) Fortunately, you can do this within your select statement, as shown in Listing 5.9.

LISTING 5.9   A QUERY THAT INCLUDES A CALCULATION USING DATA FROM A COLUMN

```
SELECT movie_title, gross, gross * 1.5
FROM Movies
```

MOVIE_TITLE	GROSS	GROSS*1.5
Vegetable House	30	45
Prince Kong	51.5	77.25
The Code Warrior	17.8	26.7
Bill Durham	15.6	23.4
Codependence Day	30	45
The Linux Files	17.5	26.25
SQL Strikes Back	10	15
The Programmer	45.3	67.95
Hard Code	30	45
The Rear Windows	17.5	26.25

10 rows selected.

As you can see, the output contains three columns: the title of each movie, the gross revenue of the movie as it is stored in the database, and the gross multiplied by 1.5. Assuming the exchange rate between the United States and Britain is 1.5 pounds per dollar, this output would contain the gross revenue totals in each currency. To get up-to-date numbers, all you must do is replace 1.5 with the current exchange rate.

It's just as easy to create expressions that utilize the data from more than one column. To calculate how profitable (or unprofitable) a movie was, all you need to do is subtract the movie's budget from the movie's gross box office receipts. Listing 5.10 contains a query that does just this for all the movies in the database.

LISTING 5.10   A QUERY THAT CALCULATES THE PROFITS FOR MOVIES

```
SELECT movie_title, gross, budget, gross - budget
FROM Movies
```

MOVIE_TITLE	GROSS	BUDGET	GROSS-BUDGET
Vegetable House	30	20	10
Prince Kong	51.5	3.25	48.25
The Code Warrior	17.8	10.3	7.5
Bill Durham	15.6	10.1	5.5
Codependence Day	30	15	15
The Linux Files	17.5	22.2	-4.7
SQL Strikes Back	10	5	5
The Programmer	45.3	50	-4.7
Hard Code	30	77	-47
The Rear Windows	17.5	50	-32.5

10 rows selected.

The fourth column of the query results show just how profitable each movie was. Negative numbers indicate that the movie reported a loss rather than a profit.

These are just a few simple examples of the types of data transformations that can be achieved from within a SQL statement. Not only can you perform arithmetic calculations on the data returned by a query, but you can also run specific aggregate functions on that data, as I will discuss in Chapter 7, "Aggregating Query Results." These functions make it easy to find out the average, maximum, minimum, or count of a particular set of values.

Most databases also ship with a library of functions that can be used to modify data returned by queries. Some of these functions will be introduced in Chapter 6, "Using The WHERE Clause." The use of these functions will be discussed in detail in Chapter 12, "Handling Specific Types of Data."

ARITHMETIC OPERATORS SUPPORTED BY SQL

Now seems like a good time to explain the variety of arithmetic operators available in SQL. Not only can these be used to transform the data returned by queries, but they can also be used as parts of filters used to constrain the number of rows returned by queries, as you will discover later in this chapter. Table 5.1 contains a list of arithmetic operators supported by SQL.

TABLE 5.1   ARITHMETIC OPERATORS SUPPORTED BY SQL, LISTED BY ORDER OF OPERATIONS

Operator	Usage
()	Parentheses
/	Division
*	Multiplication
-	Subtraction
+	Addition

In some systems including algebra, multiplication, division, addition, and subtraction all have a different ranking when it comes to precedence. Multiplication is evaluated before division, which is in turn evaluated before addition. Subtraction brings up the rear. In SQL, multiplication and division have the same precedence, and addition and subtraction have the same precedence. So, when either multiplication and division or addition and subtraction are used in the same expression, the operators with like precedence are evaluated from right to left.

As explained in Chapter 1, parentheses can be used to group expressions and affect their precedence or to simply organize them so that they're more readable. Parentheses can be used within the select list of a SELECT statement to transform data in complex ways. Say that you have a database that contains the average annual temperature in July in popular

European travel destinations. You'd like to share this data with some Americans making travel plans, but it's stored in Celsius, and they don't know how to convert Celsius temperatures to Farenheit. Fortunately, you can easily convert the temperature from Celsius to Farenheit in your SQL query, as shown in Listing 5.11:

LISTING 5.11   A QUERY THAT CONVERTS TEMPERATURES FROM CELSIUS TO FAHRENHEIT

```
SELECT city, ((1.8 * avg_temp) + 32)
FROM Temperatures
```

CITY	((1.8*AVG_TEMP)+32)
London	61.7
Berlin	64.4
Paris	66.2

As you can see, using parentheses, it was easy to set the temperature calculation apart from the rest of the query. It also made it clear what the order of operations was, even though it would have worked properly had I left out the parentheses.

Tip 22 from Rafe Colburn	Parentheses can often be used to improve the readability of your code, even when they aren't required in order to make a particular expression work properly. By grouping elements of an expression within parentheses, you can illustrate clearly the order in which the expression is evaluated and what elements are related.

USING AS TO NAME COLUMNS AND EXPRESSIONS

You can use the AS keyword to assign names to columns and expressions in your queries. These names can be used to improve the appearance of the output of your queries and to assign names to expressions that under ordinary circumstances could not be referred to by name. Here's a SQL statement that includes an AS clause:

```
SELECT expr [ AS alias ], expr2 [ AS alias ] [, ...]
FROM table [, table, ...]
[ WHERE condition ]
```

As you can see from the output in Listing 5.11, when you use mathematical expressions within your SELECT statements, the column headings can look a bit strange. Ordinarily, the name of the field that is displayed in a particular column makes a good enough column heading, but in cases like the previous example, the column heading just doesn't make much sense.

It's bad enough to have to deal with these strange-looking column headings when you're trying to format the output of a query for presentation, but this problem is even more significant when you're writing programs that include SQL queries. If the contents of each column are referenced by the column name, how do you reference a column called `((1.8 * TEMP) + 32)`?

Fortunately, SQL provides us with the AS clause to avoid these sorts of nasty problems. The AS clause enables you to assign an alias to a column returned by a SELECT statement. Listing 5.12 contains the SELECT statement used in the previous example with an AS clause to make the output more readable.

LISTING 5.12   RENAMING AN EXPRESSION USING AS

```
SELECT city, ((1.8 * avg_temp) + 32) AS temperature
FROM Temperatures
```

```
CITY                                               TEMPERATURE
-------------------------------------------------  -----------
London                                                    61.7
Berlin                                                    64.4
Paris                                                     66.2
```

As you can see from the output of the query, the values of the data ar the same, but the heading of the second column is now TEMPERATURE. Although the AS construct is useful in beautifying the output of a SELECT statement, it is even more useful when used in conjunction with a programming environment that lets you address to the results of queries by the column name. By assigning a name using AS, you can easily refer to these columns, which under other circumstances you would not be able to address because they wouldn't have standard, single-word names. The AS construct is especially handy when used in conjunction with aggregate functions, which are discussed in Chapter 7, "Aggregating Query Results."

You can also assign a multiword heading to a column by enclosing the alias using double quotes, as shown in Listing 5.13.

PART

II

CH

5

LISTING 5.13   USING A MULTIWORD COLUMN ALIAS

```
SELECT city, ((1.8 * temp) + 32) AS "Average Temperature"
FROM Temperatures
```

```
CITY                     Average Temperature
------------------------  --------------------
London                           61.7
Berlin                           64.4
Paris                            66.2
```

Caution

Using multi-word aliases for columns was introduced with the SQL-92 standard and is not supported by all databases.

Tip 23 from
Rafe Colburn

Some databases enable you to rename expressions in the select list by specifying a name for the column and connecting to the expression using an = sign, like this:

```
SELECT total = 2 + 2
FROM Some_Table
```

However, this technique does not provide any advantages over using AS and does not work in many databases. So, if the database you're using supports both of these styles for renaming columns, I recommend that you use AS to make your code more portable and understandable to programmers who are unfamiliar with the = notation.

FILTERING QUERY RESULTS USING THE WHERE CLAUSE

Most of the queries you've seen thus far simply return all the rows in a particular table; if you want to constrain the results of a query, the WHERE clause is used. The WHERE clause reduces the number of rows returned by a particular query by retaining rows based on the contents of a particular field or group of fields. Listing 5.14 contains an example of a query that uses a WHERE clause.

LISTING 5.14   A QUERY THAT USES A WHERE CLAUSE

```
SELECT movie_title, studio_id
FROM Movies
WHERE movie_title = 'Codependence Day'


MOVIE_TITLE              STUDIO_ID
-------------------- ----------
Codependence Day             1
```

As you can see, the only row returned by the query was the one containing the movie "Codependence Day". The WHERE clause tests the value of in the movie_title field in each row of the Movies table to see whether it is equal to "Codependence Day." If it is, the row is included in the results of the query; if it is not, the row is discarded. Testing a field against a value for equality is just one of many options available for filtering data using a WHERE clause. These options are covered in greater detail in the Chapter 6, "Using the WHERE Clause."

Before I move on, however, I'd like to show you the other operators available when you are writing statements that use the WHERE clause. In the next chapter, I will demonstrate how you can combine expressions that use these operators to create compound WHERE clauses and select data based on the contents of more than one column. By comparing the results of the queries with the unabridged contents of the Movies table, you can easily see how the WHERE clause filters data.

Note

All the operators can be used to compare numeric data, string data, and data of other types, including dates. One thing these operators do not work with is null values. I'll explain why these operators don't work with nulls and what you can do to perform queries that filter data based on null values in the next section of this chapter.

OPERATORS FOR PERFORMING COMPARISONS

Now, take a quick inventory of the operators that can be used to create expressions inside a WHERE clause. You've already seen the = operator. The = operator evaluates as true if the two values being compared are identical. It can be used to test numbers, strings, and dates. Unlike Perl and some other languages, in SQL separate operators are not used to compare strings and numbers. Table 5.2 contains a list of the comparison operators available in SQL.

TABLE 5.2 COMPARISON OPERATORS SUPPORTED BY THE SQL STANDARD

Operator	True if
=	equal
<>, !=	unequal
>	greater than
<	less than
>=	at least
<=	no more than

One thing to note (and this is true for all operators, not just =) is that when you're testing numeric data, you don't need to use the single quotation marks around the data being compared. Listing 5.15 contains an example.

LISTING 5.15 A QUERY THAT SELECTS RECORDS BASED ON A NUMERIC COMPARISON

```
SELECT movie_title, gross
FROM Movies
WHERE gross < 20

MOVIE_TITLE           GROSS
------------------- ----------
The Code Warrior         17.8
Bill Durham              15.6
The Linux Files          17.5
SQL Strikes Back           10
The Rear Windows         17.5
```

PART

II

CH

5

As you can see from the query results, movies that grossed less than $20 million are listed in the query results. Take a look at a query that's almost the same, except that the number is enclosed in single quotation marks. Listing 5.16 contains a query that encloses the number in single quotation marks.

LISTING 5.16   QUERYING AGAINST A NUMBER USED AS A STRING

```
SELECT movie_title, gross
FROM Movies
WHERE gross < '20'

MOVIE_TITLE                GROSS
-------------------   ----------
The Code Warrior            17.8
Bill Durham                 15.6
The Linux Files             17.5
SQL Strikes Back              10
The Rear Windows            17.5
```

As you can see, the results of the queries in Listings 5.15 and 5.16 are the same. When you're comparing numeric data, single quotation marks are not required.

To test whether two values are not equal, you can use either of the following two operators: <> or !=. Each of them has the same effect, which is to determine whether two values being compared are identical, and if they are not, the expression evaluates as being true.

To select every movie other than "Codependence Day", you could use either of the following two queries, as shown in Listing 5.17.

LISTING 5.17   A WHERE CLAUSE THAT TESTS FOR INEQUALITY

```
SELECT movie_title, studio_id
FROM Movies
WHERE movie_title != 'Codependence Day'

SELECT movie_title, studio_id
FROM Movies
WHERE title <> 'Codependence Day'

MOVIE_TITLE                STUDIO_ID
-------------------   ----------
Vegetable House             1
Prince Kong                 2
The Code Warrior            4
Bill Durham                 3
The Linux Files             2
SQL Strikes Back            3
The Programmer              3
Hard Code                   4
The Rear Windows            1

9 rows selected.
```

> **Caution**
>
> Only the <> operator is valid according to the SQL standard; the != operator has been adopted by many database vendors but is nonstandard. For reasons of portability, you should use <> especially because there is no good reason not to.

The other four operators are less than (<), greater than (>), less than or equal to (<=), and greater than or equal to (>=). The less than operator evaluates as true if the value to the left of the operator is less than the value to its right. The greater than operator evaluates to true if the value on the left of the operator is larger than the value on the right. You can probably figure out the purpose of the remaining two operators on your own.

Strings are compared based on the rules discussed at the end of this chapter under the heading "How the Equality of Strings Is Determined."

Values in columns can be compared to values in other columns if you prefer. For example, in Listing 5.18, movies that have a higher budget than gross are displayed.

LISTING 5.18   A QUERY THAT COMPARES TWO COLUMNS

```
SELECT movie_title, gross, budget
FROM Movies
WHERE gross < budget

MOVIE_TITLE              GROSS      BUDGET
--------------------  ----------  ----------
The Linux Files             17.5        22.2
The Programmer              45.3          50
Hard Code                     30          77
The Rear Windows            17.5          50
```

The previous query compares the values in the budget column to the values in the gross column. Each row is checked, and if the value of budget is greater than the value of gross, that row is included in the query results.

Despite the fact that in the previous query, both the gross and the budget columns were included in the select list, it is not necessary to select the columns that you use in the WHERE clause. Any column in the table can be used as a basis for comparison, regardless of whether it is selected.

CASE SENSITIVITY IN STRING COMPARISONS

Some databases compare strings in a case-sensitive manner; others do not. In other words, depending on your database platform and settings, 'sql' might be equal to 'SQL'. Usually, this option can be set when the database is initially created. If your database is case sensitive, you can use the UPPER() and LOWER() functions to make sure the cases in both the strings match. As you might imagine, the UPPER() function converts all the letters in a string to uppercase, and the LOWER() function converts all the characters in a string to lowercase.

PART

II

CH

5

Listing 5.19 contains an example that demonstrates how the LOWER() function can be used to avoid case-sensitivity problems.

LISTING 5.19   USING LOWER() TO AVOID CASE-SENSITIVITY PROBLEMS

```
SELECT studio_name
FROM Studios
WHERE LOWER(studio_state) = 'ca'

STUDIO_NAME
- - - - - - - - - - - - - - - - - - - -
Giant
MPM
Metaversal Studios
```

If you were using a case-sensitive database and you were unsure of how state abbreviations were capitalized, the LOWER() function could be used as shown in Listing 5.19 to convert the values in the studio_state column to lowercase.

PERFORMING CALCULATIONS IN THE WHERE CLAUSE

Just as you can perform calculations on the data that you select from a database, you can also perform calculations within a WHERE clause to assist you in filtering records.

Take a look at an example in Listing 5.20 that uses a calculation within the WHERE clause.

LISTING 5.20   USING AN EXPRESSION IN A WHERE CLAUSE

```
SELECT movie_title, gross, budget
FROM Movies
WHERE gross > (2 * budget)

MOVIE_TITLE            GROSS     BUDGET
- - - - - - - - - - - - - - - - - - -  - - - - - - - - - -  - - - - - - - - - -
Prince Kong            51.5      3.25
```

The previous query searches for movies that were extremely successful; it returns all records in which the value of the gross column is more than twice that of the budget column.

DEALING WITH NULL VALUES

Null values were originally introduced back in Chapter 3, "Creating Databases," when their impact on database design was discussed. Null values can be somewhat aggravating when you are selecting data from a database because they cannot be tested against using any of the standard comparison operators. Comparison operators do not work with null values because the value of null is considered to be unknown, and thus, nulls are not considered to be equal to anything, even other nulls.

Note

For the purposes of this section, I updated the records for the movies "Bill Durham" and "Prince Kong" so that GROSS is null.

TESTING FOR NULL VALUES

Fortunately, SQL provides special keywords for testing whether a field contains a null value. In the WHERE clause, the phrase IS NULL is used to determine whether that field contains a null value or any other value. Testing to see whether a field contains a null value is straightforward, as demonstrated in Listing 5.21.

LISTING 5.21   SELECTING RECORDS BASED ON NULL VALUES

```
SELECT movie_title
FROM Movies
WHERE gross IS NULL

MOVIE_TITLE
------------------------------
Prince Kong
Bill Durham
```

There are two important things to notice in the previous SQL query. One is that instead of using a standard comparison operator, the keyword IS is used when you are checking to see if a field is null. The second thing you should notice is that the word "null" is not enclosed in single quotation marks. The string 'NULL' and the keyword NULL are two entirely different things.

You can also negate the IS NULL phrase by using its counterpart, IS NOT NULL, which evaluates as being true if the field contains any value other than the null value. Listing 5.22 demonstrates how to use IS NOT NULL.

LISTING 5.22   USING THE IS NOT NULL CLAUSE

```
SELECT movie_title
FROM Movies
WHERE gross IS NOT NULL

TITLE
------------------------------
Mineral House
Codependence Day
The Linux Files
SQL Strikes Back
The Programmer
The Code Warrior

6 rows selected.
```

PART

II

CH

5

ACCOUNTING FOR NULL VALUES IN OTHER QUERIES

As you already know, nulls are considered to be unknown values. This differentiates them from empty values, such as `' '`, which is an empty string, or `0`. These values are known, but they are empty. Null is a value that might or might not be empty and is unknown.

Let me stop for a second and explain this more clearly. Because a null value is considered to be unknown, there is no basis for determining, or even assuming, that it is equal to, greater than, or less than any other value. In fact, relational databases do not even assume that nulls are not equal to other expressions. Nulls are also not considered to be equal to each other—hence the need for the special `IS NULL` and `IS NOT NULL` clauses.

Listings 5.23 and 5.24 contain a couple of queries that demonstrate what I'm talking about. First, look at some of the contents of the `Movies` table.

LISTING 5.23   THE MOVIE TITLES AND GROSSES FROM THE `Movies` TABLE

```
SELECT movie_title, gross
FROM Movies

MOVIE_TITLE              GROSS
-------------------- ----------
Vegetable House             30
Prince Kong
The Code Warrior          17.8
Bill Durham
Codependence Day            30
The Linux Files           17.5
SQL Strikes Back            10
The Programmer            45.3
Hard Code                   30
The Rear Windows          17.5

10 rows selected.
```

As you can see, the movies "Prince Kong" and "Bill Durham" have a null value in the gross column. This indicates that the gross for the movie is unknown, probably because the movie hasn't yet been released. If the movie was just spectacularly unpopular, it would have a `0` in the gross column instead.

The results of the following queries will include neither "Prince Kong" nor "Bill Durham."

LISTING 5.24   SELECTING RECORDS USING STANDARD COMPARISON OPERATORS

```
SELECT movie_title, gross
FROM Movies
WHERE gross < 20

MOVIE_TITLE              GROSS
-------------------- ----------
The Code Warrior          17.8
The Linux Files           17.5
SQL Strikes Back            10
```

```
The Rear Windows           17.5


SELECT movie_title, gross
FROM Movies
WHERE gross >= 20


MOVIE_TITLE             GROSS
------------------- ----------
Vegetable House            30
Codependence Day           30
The Programmer           45.3
Hard Code                  30
```

If you were hoping to catch all the rows in the Movies table, you'd have to add a third query that used an IS NULL clause to retrieve the rest of the movies, such as the one in Listing 5.25.

LISTING 5.25   USING THE IS NULL CLAUSE

```
SELECT movie_title, gross
FROM Movies
WHERE gross IS NULL

MOVIE_TITLE             GROSS
------------------- ----------
Prince Kong
Bill Durham
```

Here's a sneak preview of Chapter 6, "Using the WHERE Clause." Rather than including the IS NULL phrase in a third query, you could use the logical OR operator to include an IS NULL in one of the other two queries, as shown in Listing 5.26.

LISTING 5.26   A QUERY WITH A COMPOUND WHERE CLAUSE

```
SELECT movie_title, gross
FROM Movies
WHERE gross >= 20 OR gross IS NULL


MOVIE_TITLE             GROSS
------------------- ----------
Vegetable House            30
Prince Kong
Bill Durham
Codependence Day           30
The Programmer           45.3
Hard Code                  30

6 rows selected.
```

Logical operators will be covered thoroughly in the next chapter.

SORTING QUERY RESULTS

One characteristic of relational databases is that the order of columns and rows in a table is not important. Neither rows nor columns are required to be accessed, and they are not treated sequentially by the database. This is one of the characteristics that differentiates them from flat files and spreadsheets.

This means that it's easy to retrieve records from the database in any order that you prefer. Ordinarily, query results are returned in the order in which they were originally inserted. When you are viewing the results of a query, you might prefer to see those results sorted according to the contents of a particular column. The ORDER BY clause is used to sort query results.

USING ORDER BY

The syntax for SELECT statements that use the ORDER BY clause follows this format:

```
SELECT select_list
FROM table[ , table ... ]
[ WHERE condition ]
[ ORDER BY { column ¦ alias ¦ position } [ ASC ¦ DESC ] ]
```

The query output will be sorted based on the contents of the column (or columns) that you specify in the ORDER BY clause. Listing 5.27 contains an example.

LISTING 5.27   USING THE ORDER BY CLAUSE

```
SELECT movie_title, studio_id, budget, release_date
FROM Movies
ORDER BY movie_title

MOVIE_TITLE           STUDIO_ID     BUDGET RELEASE_D
-------------------   ----------   -------- ---------
Bill Durham                   3       10.1 15-JUL-88
Codependence Day              1         15 01-JUL-97
Hard Code                     4         77 18-APR-95
Prince Kong                   2       3.25 01-MAY-79
SQL Strikes Back              3          5 01-NOV-98
The Code Warrior              4       10.3 01-SEP-91
The Linux Files               2       22.2 22-AUG-93
The Programmer                3         50 17-APR-93
The Rear Windows              1         50 11-JUL-87
Vegetable House               1         20 01-JAN-75

10 rows selected.
```

As you can see, the list of movies is sorted alphabetically by the title. You can also sort query results based on the values in numeric fields, which is demonstrated in Listing 5.28.

LISTING 5.28   SORTING QUERY RESULTS BASED ON NUMERIC DATA

```
SELECT movie_title, studio_id, budget, release_date
FROM Movies
ORDER BY budget


MOVIE_TITLE           STUDIO_ID     BUDGET RELEASE_D
--------------------  ----------  ---------- ---------
Prince Kong                   2       3.25 01-MAY-79
SQL Strikes Back              3          5 01-NOV-98
Bill Durham                   3       10.1 15-JUL-88
The Code Warrior              4       10.3 01-SEP-91
Codependence Day              1         15 01-JUL-97
Vegetable House               1         20 01-JAN-75
The Linux Files               2       22.2 22-AUG-93
The Programmer                3         50 17-APR-93
The Rear Windows              1         50 11-JUL-87
Hard Code                     4         77 18-APR-95

10 rows selected.
```

The order of the columns is not affected by the column you use to sort the query results; they're presented in the same order no matter which column you order the results by. ORDER BY can also be used to sort records according to the values in a date field. Listing 5.29 shows the results of a query that is sorted on the contents of the release_date field, which is a DATE field.

LISTING 5.29   SORTING QUERY RESULTS BASED ON DATE VALUES

```
SELECT movie_title, studio_id, budget, release_date
FROM Movies
ORDER BY release_date

MOVIE_TITLE           STUDIO_ID     BUDGET RELEASE_D
--------------------  ----------  ---------- ---------
Vegetable House               1         20 01-JAN-75
Prince Kong                   2       3.25 01-MAY-79
The Rear Windows              1         50 11-JUL-87
Bill Durham                   3       10.1 15-JUL-88
The Code Warrior              4       10.3 01-SEP-91
The Programmer                3         50 17-APR-93
The Linux Files               2       22.2 22-AUG-93
Hard Code                     4         77 18-APR-95
Codependence Day              1         15 01-JUL-97
SQL Strikes Back              3          5 01-NOV-98

10 rows selected.
```

PART

II

CH

5

SORTING RECORDS IN DESCENDING ORDER

Query results can be sorted in descending order as well as ascending order. To list query results in descending order, append DESC to the ORDER BY clause in the query. Listing 5.30 contains an example of a query that contains date data sorted in descending order.

LISTING 5.30   QUERY RESULTS IN DESCENDING ORDER

```
SELECT movie_title, studio_id, budget, release_date
FROM Movies
ORDER BY release_date DESC

MOVIE_TITLE          STUDIO_ID     BUDGET RELEASE_D
-------------------- ---------- ---------- ---------
SQL Strikes Back             3          5 01-NOV-98
Codependence Day             1         15 01-JUL-97
Hard Code                    4         77 18-APR-95
The Linux Files              2       22.2 22-AUG-93
The Programmer               3         50 17-APR-93
The Code Warrior             4       10.3 01-SEP-91
Bill Durham                  3       10.1 15-JUL-88
The Rear Windows             1         50 11-JUL-87
Prince Kong                  2       3.25 01-MAY-79
Vegetable House              1         20 01-JAN-75

10 rows selected.
```

The keyword ASC is also available to sort query results in ascending order; however, ascending sorts are the default, so that keyword is rarely used.

SORTING BY EXPRESSIONS

Not only can you sort query results by the values in a particular column, you can also use the ORDER BY clause to sort the results of expressions. There are two different methods that you can use to apply the ORDER BY clause to an expression. You can select the expression by its position in the SELECT list, or you can rename the expression using AS and use that name in the ORDER BY clause. Some databases also enable you to enter the entire expression in the ORDER BY clause, but this method isn't as reliable as the other two that I mentioned.

Here is an example that demonstrates both methods. Look at the code from Listing 5.31, which determined the profits of the movies in the database with a small enhancement. In Listing 5.32, I show how you could rewrite the SELECT statement so that it's sorted using the AS construct by the expression that determines the profits. In Listing 5.33, I show how the SELECT statement could be rewritten so that it references the expression by its position in the select list.

LISTING 5.31   SORTING DATA ON AN EXPRESSION USING AS

```
SELECT movie_title, gross, budget, gross - budget AS profits
FROM Movies
ORDER BY profits
```

```
MOVIE_TITLE              GROSS     BUDGET    PROFITS
....................   ..........  ..........  ..........
Hard Code                   30        77        -47
The Rear Windows          17.5        50      -32.5
The Linux Files           17.5      22.2       -4.7
The Programmer            45.3        50       -4.7
SQL Strikes Back            10         5          5
The Code Warrior          17.8      10.3        7.5
Vegetable House             30        20         10
Codependence Day            30        15         15
Prince Kong                         3.25
Bill Durham                         10.1

10 rows selected.
```

LISTING 5.32   SORTING DATA ON AN EXPRESSION USING ITS POSITION

```
SELECT movie_title, gross, budget, gross - budget
FROM Movies
ORDER BY 4

MOVIE_TITLE              GROSS     BUDGET  GROSS-BUDGET
....................   ..........  ..........  ............
Hard Code                   30        77        -47
The Rear Windows          17.5        50      -32.5
The Linux Files           17.5      22.2       -4.7
The Programmer            45.3        50       -4.7
SQL Strikes Back            10         5          5
The Code Warrior          17.8      10.3        7.5
Vegetable House             30        20         10
Codependence Day            30        15         15
Prince Kong                         3.25
Bill Durham                         10.1

10 rows selected.
```

PART

II

CH

5

Comparing the two examples, you can see that the query in Listing 5.31 is significantly more readable than the one in Listing 5.32. Renaming expressions using AS and then sorting using the new name is generally the preferred method.

You might also find it interesting that because the GROSS column for two of the records is null, the arithmetic expression doesn't work on them. In this database, null values are appended to the end of a sorted column. Later in this chapter, I'm going to discuss sort order and how items are ranked in sorted data.

SECONDARY SORTS

You can specify more than one column on which data should be sorted. It might be easiest to think about the first sort as categorizing the data and sorting it and the second sort as sorting the data in each of the categories. To use a secondary sort, you simply need to add a second select item to the ORDER BY clause in the SELECT statement. As is the case with most SQL queries, it might be easiest to explain this through an example. In Listing 5.33, the movies are sorted first by studio and second by title.

LISTING 5.33   USING TWO SORTS TO CATEGORIZE AND SORT DATA

```
SELECT movie_title, studio_id
FROM Movies
ORDER BY studio_id, movie_title

MOVIE_TITLE          STUDIO_ID
-------------------- ----------
Codependence Day             1
The Rear Windows             1
Vegetable House              1
Prince Kong                  2
The Linux Files              2
Bill Durham                  3
SQL Strikes Back             3
The Programmer               3
Hard Code                    4
The Code Warrior             4

10 rows selected.
```

You can use all the same techniques in multi-item sorts that you can use in single-item sorts. Renamed expressions, ASC, and DESC are all supported. Listing 5.34 illustrates how you can use both an ascending and descending sort in the same query.

LISTING 5.34   USING ASCENDING AND DESCENDING SORTS IN THE SAME QUERY

```
SELECT movie_title, studio_id, gross - budget AS profits
FROM Movies
ORDER BY studio_id, profits DESC

MOVIE_TITLE          STUDIO_ID    PROFITS
-------------------- ---------- ----------
Codependence Day             1         15
Vegetable House              1         10
The Rear Windows             1      -32.5
Prince Kong                  2
The Linux Files              2       -4.7
Bill Durham                  3
SQL Strikes Back             3          5
The Programmer               3       -4.7
The Code Warrior             4        7.5
Hard Code                    4        -47

10 rows selected.
```

As you can see from the query results, the studio names are sorted in ascending order, but the profits are listed in descending order within each studio. You can also see from the query results that because the secondary sort was a descending sort, the records with null values were listed first instead of last.

How the Equality of Strings Is Determined

In most cases, the order in which sorted items are ranked is somewhat intuitive. For example, if a column contains numbers, an ascending sort ranks those numbers in order from smallest to largest. Similarly, if a column contains dates and they are sorted in descending order, they are listed from the most recent to the furthest in the past.

Unfortunately, things get a bit trickier with strings. Is the string 'AAA' greater than 'aaa', or are they equal? What about 'BBB'—is it greater than 'aaa'? Are strings that begin with numbers greater or less than strings that begin with letters? These are the types of questions to which the answers can vary based on which database you're using. Part VI, "Specific Databases," which covers the databases available from the major vendors, will answer these questions for those databases, but you should also be able to find the answers in the documentation for your database.

The rules that apply to sorts based on strings also apply when strings are compared using comparison operators. Because sorts basically just use comparison operators to rank values, you can apply all these rules when you're determining whether one string is greater than the other in expressions in a WHERE clause.

Listing 5.35 contains the contents of a small table I created expressly for the purpose of testing how sorts based on the value of strings works (note that I'm using Oracle8 in these particular examples). The table I'm using is called Sortme, and it contains a single column, named test, of the type VARCHAR2(3).

LISTING 5.35 THE Sortme TABLE IN NO PARTICULAR ORDER

```
SELECT *
FROM Sortme

TES
---
aaa
001
AAA
Aaa
...
BBB
a
B

8 rows selected.
```

First, to get an idea of how strings are sorted, sort the Sortme table. The results are in Listing 5.36.

PART
II

CH
5

LISTING 5.36   THE SORTED VERSION OF THE Sortme TABLE

```
SELECT *
FROM Sortme
ORDER BY test

TES
---
...
001
AAA
Aaa
B
BBB
a
aaa

8 rows selected.
```

As you can see from the query results, the basic order of sorted strings seems to be punctuation, numbers, uppercase letters, and then lowercase letters. There are actually specific rules that define how strings are compared.

HOW STRINGS ARE COMPARED

There is actually a very specific method for comparing strings in SQL. Strings are compared character by character. The first character that differs between the two strings determines which string is "greater" than the other. The method for determining which of the two different characters is greater is to look up both of them in the database's collation sequence or character set and to figure out which one is larger. The subsection at the end of this section on character sets describes exactly how the precedence of each character is determined.

Because of the character-by-character methodology, the length of the strings being compared is largely irrelevant. The only way that the length matters is if the two strings are identical through the length of the shorter string, in which case the longer string is considered to be greater. In other words, if the two strings are 'Smith' and 'Smithsonian', the string 'Smithsonian' is greater because the s in the sixth position of 'Smithsonian' is greater than nothing.

SORTING STRINGS IGNORING CASE

If you want to sort a list of strings in a manner that is not case sensitive, you can use the LOWER() function in the ORDER BY clause, just as you can use it in a WHERE clause. Listing 5.37 demonstrates the usage of the LOWER() function in an ORDER BY clause.

LISTING 5.37   USING LOWER() IN AN ORDER BY CLAUSE

```
SELECT *
FROM Sortme
ORDER BY LOWER(test)
```

```
TES
---
...
001
a
aaa
AAA
Aaa
B
BBB

8 rows selected.
```

As you can see from the results of Listing 5.37, the rows are sorted as though all the letters were lowercase. Thus, the strings `'aaa'`, `'Aaa'`, and `'AAA'`, are all equivalent for the purposes of this query, and `'a'` is less than `'B'`.

CHARACTER SETS

The reason that the string sorts I described previously worked the way that they do is because the database I was querying uses the ASCII character set. The ASCII character set has assigned a number between 0 and 255 to all the printable characters that are available. The characters between 0 and 127 are standardized among all ASCII users; the ones between 128 and 255 can vary between computer platform, application, and country.

When a database uses the ASCII character set, the characters in strings are ranked based on their position in the character set. The character `'a'` has a value of 97, whereas the character `'B'` has a value of 66, thus `'B'` is ranked before `'a'` in sorts.

However, ASCII is not the only character set that exists. For example, IBM mainframes use the EBCDIC character set, which lists the characters in a different order from ASCII and thus sorts strings in a different order.

IN THE REAL WORLD

One of the most important real world issues you'll face is minimizing the number of queries that you use. Generally speaking, the fewer queries your applications must make, the better the performance will be. This is not necessarily always the case; some complex queries take a very long time to run, and splitting them into multiple, simpler queries might make sense.

However, if your queries are simple and straightforward, using more queries will have a negative impact on the performance of your applications. The purpose of this section is to explain when some advanced techniques can be used to save programming time and processing time in your applications.

In this chapter, I really only covered the most basic types of SELECT statements. These statements consisted of a list of columns, a table from which to retrieve the values in those columns, and simple, single comparison WHERE clauses. Unfortunately, novice and even intermediate SQL programmers tend to use more queries than are necessary to achieve particular tasks. The next three chapters will discuss various techniques that can be used with SELECT statements to limit the records returned by queries more precisely.

There are two different areas where queries can be conserved when you are writing applications. The first area involves situations where data from more than one table is required. For example, consider a query that retrieves a list of the locations for all the movies in the database. Using a join, as described in Chapter 8, these results can be retrieved using a single query. Novice programmers might be tempted to write a query that retrieves a list of all the movie IDs and titles from the Movies table, then use a loop to iterate over those results, and use queries to retrieve a list of locations for each of those movies.

The other area where programmers might be tempted to split a task into multiple queries when it really only requires one query is when data within a table will be compared to other data within the same table. For example, consider a situation where you want to find a list of states where more than one person in the People table live. One might retrieve a list of the states and person names from the People table and then use a loop to issue a query for each of the people to determine if other people live in the same state. This is the slow and unwieldy way to accomplish this task. There are two ways to retrieve such a list: You can use a self-join (described in Chapter 8) or a subquery (described in Chapter 9).

CHAPTER **6**

USING THE WHERE CLAUSE

In this chapter

In Chapter 5, "The SELECT Statement," I covered the SELECT statement, which is used to retrieve data from tables in a database. I also introduced the WHERE clause, which is used to determine which rows should be included in the results of a query. The WHERE clause acts as a filter, discarding rows that do not match the criteria and keeping those that do.

In this chapter, I'll explain more techniques that you can use within the WHERE clause to increase the precision of your queries so they return the set of rows you require. In the preceding chapter, I discussed using comparison operators within the WHERE clause. Now, I'm going to cover some other methods that will enable you to write more powerful queries. I'll also discuss how you can create compound queries using logical operators.

Of course, it's important to remember that the WHERE clause isn't just used with the SELECT statement; it's also used to select rows that will be affected by UPDATE and DELETE statements. Use of the WHERE clause is the same no matter which of these three statements you're using.

THE WHERE CLAUSE, A RECAP

Before I start introducing additional capabilities of the WHERE clause, allow me to very briefly review the characteristics of the WHERE clause that I discussed in the previous chapter. Listing 6.1 contains prototypes of the WHERE clause in the UPDATE, DELETE, and SELECT statements.

LISTING 6.1 THE WHERE CLAUSE IN UPDATE, DELETE, AND SELECT STATEMENTS

```
UPDATE table
SET ( column = value, ... )
[ WHERE expression ]

DELETE FROM table
[ WHERE expression ]

SELECT select_list FROM table
[ WHERE expression ]
```

I've already discussed some topics related to the WHERE clause in previous chapters. It might be helpful to you to refer back to them as you read this chapter.

→ To find a table of valid comparison operators, **see** "Operators for Performing Comparisons," **p. 111**

→ For techniques for comparing strings, **see** "Sorting Strings Ignoring Case," **p. 124**

→ For an explanation of how to match null values using the WHERE clause, **see** "Dealing with Null Values," **p. 114**

USING LOGICAL OPERATORS IN THE WHERE CLAUSE

In many cases, using a single comparison in your WHERE clause will not enable you to specify exactly which data you want to extract from a table. Take a look at examples of queries that require multiple comparisons to isolate particular data that apply to the movie database. Perhaps you'd like to find all the movies from the studio Delighted Artists that grossed more than $50 million. Maybe you'd like to find all the movies with budgets between $10 and $20 million dollars. Neither of these requirements can be satisfied using any single expression that you've yet seen.

SQL provides three logical operators that enable you to include multiple expressions in the WHERE clause. Actually, two of them are specifically for including multiple expressions in the WHERE clause, and the other is used to negate the results of an expression (or group of expressions). These three operators are AND, OR, and NOT.

PROGRAMMING LOGIC

The operation of the WHERE clause is dictated by Boolean logic; in other words, its expressions always evaluate to one of two values: true or false. If the outcome of the WHERE clause is true, the row will be selected; if the outcome is false, the row will not be selected.

Look at a simple example. Assume that a particular field in a database table contains the number 5. If the expression being evaluated is field > 3, the expression will evaluate as true. On the other hand, if the expression is field < 3, the expression will evaluate as false. If the first expression appeared within a WHERE clause, the row would be included in the data that was selected; the latter expression would indicate that the row should not be selected.

Logical operators enable you to string multiple expressions together to create compound expressions that evaluate to a single value of true or false.

THE AND OPERATOR

The AND operator evaluates as true if the expressions on each side of the operator evaluate as true. If either one of them is false, then the entire expression returns a value of false. For example, if you wanted to find movies from the studio Delighted Artists (which has a studio_id of 3) with a null value in the gross column, it would be necessary to use the AND operator, as I do in Listing 6.2.

LISTING 6.2   A QUERY THAT USES THE AND OPERATOR

```
SELECT movie_title, studio_id, gross
FROM Movies
WHERE studio_id = 3 AND gross IS NULL

MOVIE_TITLE                                  STUDIO_ID    GROSS
-------------------------------------------- ----------  ----------
Bill Durham                                          3
```

PART

II

CH

6

In Listing 6.2, you can see that the query matched the only record for which both of the stated criteria were true. There are multiple rows in which the value in the GROSS column is null, and there are multiple rows from the studio Delighted Artists, but only the row which matches both criteria is returned by this query.

THE OR OPERATOR

The OR operator evaluates as true if either the expression to the right or the expression to the left of OR is true. If both the expressions surrounding the OR operator are true, OR will evaluate to true as well. The SELECT statement in Listing 6.3 is identical to the statement in Listing 6.2, except that it uses OR instead of AND. Notice the difference in the results.

LISTING 6.3 A QUERY THAT USES THE OR OPERATOR

```
SELECT movie_title, studio_id, gross
FROM Movies
WHERE studio_id = 3 OR gross IS NULL

MOVIE_TITLE                                 STUDIO_ID      GROSS
-------------------------------------       ----------  ----------
Prince Kong                                     2
Bill Durham                                     3
SQL Strikes Back                                3            10
The Programmer                                  3          45.3
```

Not only was the row that matched both criteria included, but so were all the rows from the studio Delighted Artists and all the rows in which the gross was null. When either of the expressions in the WHERE clause was true, the row was included in the query results.

THE NOT OPERATOR

The NOT operator is used to reverse the Boolean value of a particular expression. For example, in the numerical universe, the expression 2 = 2 is true. If you add a NOT to the expression, making it NOT 2 = 2, the expression becomes false. The NOT operator is ordinarily used when you know which data you want to exclude from the results.

For example, say that you want to see a list of all the movies that come from studios other than Delighted Artists. Listing 6.4 shows how to write such a query using the NOT operator.

LISTING 6.4 USING THE NOT OPERATOR TO EXCLUDE ROWS

```
SELECT movie_title, studio_id
FROM Movies
WHERE NOT studio_id = 3


MOVIE_TITLE                                 STUDIO_ID
-------------------------------------       ----------
Mineral House                                   1
Prince Kong                                     2
The Code Warrior                                2
Codependence Day                                1
The Linux Files                                 2
Hard Code                                       4
The Rear Windows                                1

7 rows selected.
```

As you can see, all the movies except those from Delighted Artists are included. You could also use the OR operator to write the statement as shown in Listing 6.5.

LISTING 6.5 USING THE OR OPERATOR TO EXCLUDE ROWS

```
SELECT movie_title, studio_id
FROM Movies
WHERE studio_id = 1
OR studio_id = 2
OR studio_id = 3

MOVIE_TITLE                                 STUDIO_ID
------------------------------------------- ----------
Mineral House                                      1
Prince Kong                                        2
The Code Warrior                                   2
Bill Durham                                        3
Codependence Day                                   1
The Linux Files                                    2
SQL Strikes Back                                   3
The Programmer                                     3
The Rear Windows                                   1

9 rows selected.
```

The results of the two queries are identical, and in this case, writing the statement using the OR operator isn't much more trouble than using the NOT operator. However, if there were 100 rows in this table and 10 different studios, writing the statement using the OR method would be significantly more painful than the NOT method, which would remain the same. Now imagine that there were 1000 different studios in a large table or that you had no idea which studios were in the table, only that you didn't want the movies from Delighted Artists. If you want to exclude particular data, NOT is the proper choice.

When you're using comparison operators, you can duplicate the functionality of the NOT operator using a different comparison operator. For example, the WHERE clause used in Listing 6.4

```
WHERE NOT studio = 'Delighted Artists'
```

is identical to

```
WHERE studio <> 'Delighted Artists'
```

However, there are certain other comparisons, which I will discuss soon, that require the use of the NOT operator to negate their results. One example of these comparisons that you've already seen is the IS NULL comparison. To determine whether a column contains a value other than null, the NOT operator must be used, changing the comparison to IS NOT NULL.

PART

II

CH

6

USING MULTIPLE BOOLEAN OPERATORS

Multiple Boolean operators can be used to create complex WHERE clauses that can evaluate more than two expressions. Say that I wanted to write a query that looks for items that have no gross revenues and are from either the studio MPM or Delighted Artists. Such a query can be written using multiple Boolean operators, as shown in Listing 6.6.

LISTING 6.6   A QUERY THAT USES MULTIPLE BOOLEAN OPERATORS

```
SELECT movie_title, studio_id, gross
FROM Movies
WHERE studio_id = 2
OR studio_id = 3
AND gross IS NULL

MOVIE_TITLE                                STUDIO_ID    GROSS
-----------------------------------------  ----------   ----------
Prince Kong                                    2
The Code Warrior                               2         17.8
Bill Durham                                    3
The Linux Files                                2         17.5
```

As you can see from the query results, I failed to accomplish my goal. Not only did the query results include the two items that have no gross, I also got some extra items from MPM that have values in the gross column. This is because the AND operator is evaluated before the OR operator. Examine this closely before moving on. The OR operator, by virtue of being evaluated last, divides this SELECT statement into two queries. Only one of the two expressions that surround the OR operator must be true for a row to be selected. So, any rows that are from the studio MPM are selected. The query also selects all the rows that have a null value in the gross column and are from the studio Delighted Artists. This means that the extra rows from MPM are included along with the two rows I wanted.

As the complexity of your queries increases, it can be difficult to keep track of the order in which these operators are evaluated. Fortunately, parentheses can be used to group expressions within your WHERE clause, just as they can be used to group individual elements with mathematical expressions used in the SELECT list. Listing 6.7 uses parentheses to establish a specific order of evaluation for the query in Listing 6.6 and enables me to select only the rows that I actually wanted.

LISTING 6.7   A QUERY THAT USES MULTIPLE BOOLEAN OPERATORS AND PARENTHESES

```
SELECT movie_title, studio_id, gross FROM Movies
WHERE (studio_id = 2
OR studio_id = 3)
AND gross IS NULL

MOVIE_TITLE                                STUDIO_ID    GROSS
-----------------------------------------  ----------   ----------
Prince Kong                                    2
Bill Durham                                    3
```

As you can see, the parentheses set up the statement so that the OR expression is evaluated first, and the resulting value is used in the AND expression. In the query in Listing 6.7, the query checks to see if the studio for each row is MPM or Delighted Artists, and it then checks to see if the gross is null. If both of the conditions are true, the AND statement evaluates as true, and the row is selected—which is how I originally intended the query to work.

Tip 24 from	
Rafe Colburn	Generally speaking, it's always better to err on the side of using too many sets of parentheses over not using enough. Even if parentheses are not required to establish the proper order of operations in a query, you should still set each comparison apart individually to improve the readability of your code.

OPERATOR PRECEDENCE

Back in Chapter 5, I listed the order of operations for mathematical operators. The boolean operators also fit into this chain of precedence. Table 6.1 shows the precedence for all of the mathematical operators and boolean operators on a single chart.

TABLE 6.1 BOOLEAN AND MATHEMATICAL OPERATORS SUPPORTED BY SQL, LISTED IN ORDER OF OPERATIONS HIGHEST PRECEDENCE TO LEAST.

Operator	Usage
()	Parentheses
%, /, *	Multiplicative operators
+, -, &, |	Other operators
AND, NOT, OR	Boolean operators
+	Addition

As you can see from the chart, parentheses are always evaluated before the other operators. Following the parentheses are the mathematical operators, which are then followed by the Boolean operators.

THE IN CLAUSE

There are some additional clauses in the SQL language that can be used to simplify queries that would otherwise use multiple Boolean operators. The first example of these is the IN clause, which takes the place of multiple OR operators that are used to check whether one of a group of values appears in a particular column. The IN operator determines whether the value being tested is equal to one of the values in a set. Listing 6.8 shows the structure of the IN clause.

PART

II

CH

6

LISTING 6.8   THE IN CLAUSE

```
SELECT select_list
FROM table
WHERE column [NOT] IN ( value_list )
```

Now, look at an example. I want to find out if a movie is from either MPM or Delighted Artists. This was accomplished in Listing 6.7 using an OR operator. Listing 6.9 demonstrates how the IN clause can be used to compare the value in the studio_id column to each of the members of a list.

LISTING 6.9   USING THE IN CLAUSE

```
SELECT movie_title, studio_id
FROM Movies
WHERE studio_id = 2
OR studio_id = 3

SELECT movie_title, studio_id
FROM Movies
WHERE studio_id IN (2, 3)

MOVIE_TITLE                              STUDIO_ID
---------------------------------------- ----------
Prince Kong                                      2
The Code Warrior                                 2
Bill Durham                                      3
The Linux Files                                  2
SQL Strikes Back                                 3
The Programmer                                   3

6 rows selected.
```

IN AND SUBQUERIES

Another use of the IN clause is to compare the values in a column with the results of a SELECT statement. You can replace the list of values used by the IN clause with a SELECT statement, and the results of that SELECT statement will be used as the comparison list for the IN clause. Subqueries are covered in detail in Chapter 9, "Subqueries," but I'm going to include an example of a subquery in Listing 6.10.

I would like to find all the movies in the database that were directed by directors from Texas. The directors for each movie are listed in the Movies table, but the locations where those directors live are stored in the People table. Using a subquery within the IN clause enables me to get a list of all the directors from Texas and then use that list to find movies by those directors.

LISTING 6.10   USE OF A SUBQUERY WITHIN AN IN CLAUSE

```
SELECT movie_title, studio_id
FROM Movies
WHERE director_id IN (
   SELECT person_id
   FROM People
   WHERE person_state = 'TX'
)
MOVIE_TITLE                                STUDIO_ID
-----------------------------------------  ----------
Prince Kong                                        2
Hard Code                                          4
```

The results of the query inside the IN clause provide the list of values for the IN clause. This enables you to select the records in one table based on the contents of another. Again, this topic will be discussed in exhaustive detail in Chapter 9, but I wanted to introduce it here because it's a very important function of the IN clause.

IN VERSUS OR

The main efficiencies to be gained from the IN clause can be realized when you need to select data that meets any of a large number of options. Saving one OR operator using the IN clause, as I did in Listing 6.9, doesn't simplify the query very much. However, if the list of values being compared contained 5 or 10 items, the query would be more readable if an IN clause were used instead of multiple occurrences of OR.

Another advantage of using IN instead of multiple OR operators is that IN usually provides better performance. OR operators do not take advantage of indexing on the columns being searched, but IN does; if you're filtering data based on the contents of an indexed column, the IN clause can offer performance advantages.

Tip 25 from
Rafe Colburn

You should use IN comparisons instead of multiple comparisons linked using OR whenever possible in order to improve the maintainability of your queries. Adding an additional value to an IN clause is much easier than including another OR and comparison in your query. It also makes your code easier to read later.

PART

II

CH

6

NOT IN

The Boolean value of an IN expression can be reversed using the NOT operator. Although the NOT operator was not particularly useful when coupled with the standard comparison operators, it is indispensable when used with special comparisons within the WHERE clause, such as IN.

IN selects all the rows in which the value being tested matches one of the values in the list provided. NOT IN selects all the rows in which the value being tested does not match any of the values in the list. Listing 6.11 shows the results of a query that is the opposite of the one in Listing 6.9.

LISTING 6.11   USING NOT TO NEGATE AN IN CLAUSE

```
SELECT movie_title, studio_id
FROM Movies
WHERE studio_id NOT IN (2, 3)

MOVIE_TITLE                              STUDIO_ID
---------------------------------------- ----------
Mineral House                                    1
Codependence Day                                 1
Hard Code                                        4
The Rear Windows                                 1
```

The functionality of NOT IN can be duplicated using the AND operator. For NOT IN to work, the value being tested cannot be the equal to any of the items in the list. Listing 6.12 demonstrates how you would duplicate the functionality of NOT IN using the AND operator.

LISTING 6.12   DUPLICATING THE FUNCTIONALITY OF NOT IN USING AND

```
SELECT movie_title, studio_id
FROM Movies
WHERE studio_id <> 2 AND studio_id <> 3

MOVIE_TITLE                              STUDIO_ID
---------------------------------------- ----------
Mineral House                                    1
Codependence Day                                 1
Hard Code                                        4
The Rear Windows                                 1
```

THE BETWEEN CLAUSE

The BETWEEN clause and its opposite, NOT BETWEEN, are used to check whether a value falls within a specified range of values. Here's an example of how a BETWEEN clause is written:

```
SELECT select_list
FROM table
WHERE column [NOT] BETWEEN lower_value AND upper_value
```

The BETWEEN clause is inclusive; the values used to specify the bounds of the range being tested are included in the range. To demonstrate what I mean, let me first explain that you can create the equivalent of a BETWEEN clause using two comparison operators and the AND operator. All a BETWEEN clause really does is check to see whether a value is greater than or equal to the lower value, and less than or equal to the higher value. Allow me to demonstrate what I mean by "inclusive" through the queries in Listings 6.13 and 6.14.

LISTING 6.13   USING THE AND OPERATOR TO TEST AGAINST A RANGE OF NUMBERS

```
SELECT movie_title, budget
FROM Movies
WHERE budget > 10 AND budget < 50
```

```
MOVIE_TITLE                                   BUDGET
---------------------------------------     ----------
Mineral House                                     20
The Code Warrior                                10.3
Bill Durham                                     10.1
Codependence Day                                  15
The Linux Files                                 22.2
```

LISTING 6.14   USING THE BETWEEN CLAUSE

```
SELECT movie_title, budget
FROM Movies
WHERE budget BETWEEN 10 AND 50

MOVIE_TITLE                                   BUDGET
---------------------------------------     ----------
Mineral House                                     20
The Code Warrior                                10.3
Bill Durham                                     10.1
Codependence Day                                  15
The Linux Files                                 22.2
The Programmer                                    50
The Rear Windows                                  50

7 rows selected.
```

As you can see from the results of the two queries, the results from Listing 6.13 do not include the movies "The Programmer" and "The Rear Windows," whereas the results in Listing 6.14 do. This is because the greater than operator does not evaluate as true if the number to the left of the operator is equal to the number on the right of the operator. On the other hand, a BETWEEN clause is considered to be true if the number being tested is equal to the higher or lower boundary of the range. To write the query from Listing 6.13 so that it returns the same results as Listing 6.14, you can use the alternative shown in Listing 6.15.

LISTING 6.15   DUPLICATING THE FUNCTIONALITY OF BETWEEN USING AND

```
SELECT movie_title, budget
FROM Movies
WHERE budget >= 10 AND budget <= 50

MOVIE_TITLE                                   BUDGET
---------------------------------------     ----------
Mineral House                                     20
The Code Warrior                                10.3
Bill Durham                                     10.1
Codependence Day                                  15
The Linux Files                                 22.2
The Programmer                                    50
The Rear Windows                                  50

7 rows selected.
```

NOT BETWEEN

NOT BETWEEN is used to determine whether a value is outside a specified range. NOT BETWEEN is the opposite of BETWEEN. It considers the boundries of the range to be contained within that range and thus does not consider an expression to be true if the value being tested is equal to either of the boundary values.

The functionality of the NOT BETWEEN operator can be duplicated using the OR operator. When you're checking to make sure a number is between two other numbers, it logically follows that the number should both be greater than the smaller number and less than the larger number. On the other hand, it would be difficult for a number to be both greater than the larger number and less than the smaller number. Therefore, the OR operator is required. Take a look at Listings 6.16 and 6.17 to see how NOT BETWEEN and two expressions combined using an OR compare.

LISTING 6.16 USING THE OR OPERATOR TO TEST AGAINST A RANGE OF NUMBERS

```
SELECT movie_title, budget
FROM Movies
WHERE budget < 10 OR budget > 50

MOVIE_TITLE                                 BUDGET
-----------------------------------------   ----------
Prince Kong                                      3.25
SQL Strikes Back                                 5
Hard Code                                        77
```

LISTING 6.17 USING THE NOT BETWEEN CLAUSE

```
SELECT movie_title, budget
FROM Movies
WHERE budget NOT BETWEEN 10 AND 50

MOVIE_TITLE                                 BUDGET
-----------------------------------------   ----------
Prince Kong                                      3.25
SQL Strikes Back                                 5
Hard Code                                        77
```

As you can see, the results in Listings 6.16 and 6.17 are identical. If you wanted to include the boundary values for the range in the test, the easiest choice would be to use the <= and >= operators along with the OR operator, especially if the column contains floating point numbers rather than integers.

BETWEEN AND TEMPORAL DATA

The BETWEEN clause is also useful for checking to see whether a particular date and time falls within a range of dates and times. Listing 6.18 contains an example of this functionality.

LISTING 6.18   FINDING DATES WITHIN A PARTICULAR RANGE

```
SELECT movie_title, release_date
FROM Movies
WHERE release_date BETWEEN '01-JAN-91' AND '31-DEC-95'

MOVIE_TITLE                                RELEASE_D
---------------------------------------    ---------
The Code Warrior                           01-SEP-91
The Linux Files                            22-AUG-93
The Programmer                             17-APR-93
Hard Code                                  18-APR-95
```

As you can see from the query results, all the movies with release dates between the first of January of 1991 and the last day of December of 1995 are returned.

BETWEEN AND STRINGS

The BETWEEN operator can also be used with strings, just as regular comparison operators can be used with strings. For example, to find all of the people whose last names start with letters between "A" and "M," the query in Listing 6.19 would be used.

LISTING 6.19   USING BETWEEN WITH STRINGS

```
SELECT person_fname, person_lname
FROM People
WHERE person_lname BETWEEN 'A' AND 'M'

PERSON_FNAME            PERSON_LNAME
--------------------    --------------------
Brandon                 Brooks
Peter                   Jong
Maggie                  Davis
Carol                   Delano
```

The string comparison rules discussed at the end of Chapter 5 apply to the BETWEEN clause, just as they do to standard comparison operators.

MATCHING PARTS OF STRINGS USING LIKE

The LIKE clause is used to create simple expressions that match patterns within a string. It is used to solve problems where you want to find strings that have some of their contents in common or where you know what part of a string is, but you don't know the entire thing. For example, you can use it to find names starting with the letter S, or strings that contain the word "brown". It can also be used to solve "fill in the blank" types of problems—for example, to find a string that begins with "The bomb is hidden in" and ends with "and is about to explode."

Users accustomed to UNIX regular expressions will find this pattern-matching system simplistic, but it is still very useful when you know part of a string that you're looking for or when you know a group of characters that several strings you want to select have in common. The LIKE clause can also be negated by using the NOT operator.

The LIKE operator is used as follows:

```
SELECT select_list
FROM table
WHERE column [NOT] LIKE 'pattern' [ESCAPE char]
```

Unlike the BETWEEN and IN operators, the functionality of the LIKE clause cannot be duplicated using comparison operators and Boolean operators.

Take a look at a simple sample query that uses a LIKE clause. For pattern-matching expressions, the SQL standard provides two wildcard characters: %, which matches any group of characters (including a group that contains no characters), and _, which matches any single character. The query in Listing 6.20 returns all the movies that have a title beginning with "The".

LISTING 6.20   MATCHING STRINGS USING THE LIKE CLAUSE

```
SELECT movie_title
FROM Movies
WHERE movie_title LIKE 'The %'

MOVIE_TITLE
-----------------------------------------
The Code Warrior
The Linux Files
The Programmer
The Rear Windows
```

CONSTRUCTING PATTERNS

When constructing patterns, you should substitute wildcard characters for the unknown parts of the string. If you know how many characters are in the missing part of the string, you should use one or more _ characters; otherwise, the % character is appropriate. Table 6.2 lists the two wildcard characters.

TABLE 6.2   WILDCARD CHARACTERS USED WITH THE LIKE CLAUSE

Wildcard	Matches
_	Any single character
%	Any group of 0 or more characters

Certain database products support more wildcard characters than the two in Table 6.2, but if you're concerned with portability, you should stick with the two standard wildcards.

Back in Listing 6.20, I demonstrated how strings that begin with a particular substring can be matched using a LIKE clause. You can just as easily use LIKE to match strings that contain a particular substring anywhere within them or to match strings ending with a particular substring. You can also use LIKE to match individual characters if you know what the length of the string you're searching for should be or if you want to match minor variations on a particular string.

Listing 6.21 contains a query that searches for strings ending in the letter r, and Listing 6.22 contains a query that searches for the string "Code" anywhere within a particular string.

LISTING 6.21 A QUERY THAT SEARCHES FOR STRINGS BASED ON THE ENDING

```
SELECT movie_title
FROM Movies
WHERE movie_title LIKE '%r'

MOVIE_TITLE
----------------------------------------
The Code Warrior
The Programmer
```

LISTING 6.22 A QUERY THAT SEARCHES FOR SUBSTRINGS ANY WHERE WITHIN ANOTHER STRING

```
SELECT movie_title
FROM Movies
WHERE movie_title LIKE '%Code%'

MOVIE_TITLE
----------------------------------------
The Code Warrior
Codependence Day
Hard Code
```

As you can see from the results of Listing 6.22, the movie "Codependence Day" was selected, even though it actually begins with the string "Code". The % operator matches any string, even one that contains no characters, so strings beginning or ending with "Code" are selected. A statement that contained the following WHERE clause would match any string, even an empty one:

```
WHERE column LIKE '%'
```

Patterns for use with LIKE can also be constructed using the _ wildcard, which matches any single character. For example, say that you wanted to find any people with a four-letter first name. The query in Listing 6.23 could be used.

LISTING 6.23   FINDING STRINGS WITH A FIXED NUMBER OF CHARACTERS

```
SELECT person_fname, person_lname
FROM People
WHERE person_fname LIKE '____'

PERSON_FNAME        PERSON_LNAME
-------------------- --------------------
Jeff                Price
Paul                Monk
```

If there were a movie director named "Terri" but you were unsure whether her name ended with a "y" or an "I," you could use the single character wildcard to cover both contingencies, as shown in Listing 6.24. This pattern would also match other strings like "Terro" or "Terre."

LISTING 6.24   FINDING STRINGS WITH A ONE-CHARACTER VARIATION

```
SELECT director_fname, director_lname
FROM Directors
WHERE director_fname LIKE 'Terr_'
```

COMPOUND WHERE CLAUSES USING LIKE

Multiple LIKE expressions can also be tied together using Boolean operators in a single WHERE clause. For example, to find all the movies with titles containing the word "Linux" or the word "Programmer," two LIKE comparisons and a Boolean operator are required. Listing 6.25 uses both tests in a single query that uses the OR operator.

LISTING 6.25   A COMPOUND WHERE CLAUSE USING LIKE

```
SELECT movie_title
FROM Movies
WHERE mvie_title LIKE '%Linux%'
OR movie_title LIKE '%Programmer%'

MOVIE_TITLE
----------------------------------------
The Linux Files
The Programmer
```

It's rarer to use the AND operator to tie together multiple patterns that test the same column unless you're not sure in which order the strings will appear.

For example, if you expect that both "Linux" and "Files" appear within the same string, you'd probably write the WHERE clause like this

```
WHERE title LIKE '%Linux%Files%'
```

unless you didn't know whether "Linux" or "Files" comes first in the column. If you know that they both appear, but not the order in which they appear, you would write the WHERE clause as shown in Listing 6.26.

LISTING 6.26 TYING MULTIPLE PATTERNS TOGETHER USING AND

```
SELECT movie_title
FROM Movies
WHERE movie_title LIKE '%Linux%'
AND movie_title LIKE '%Files%'
```

ESCAPING WILDCARD CHARACTERS

At some point, you might want to use a LIKE expression to locate one of the wildcard characters within a string. For example, if you want to match a string that contains the string "50%", the following pattern won't work because the percent sign is interpreted as a string that matches any character or group of characters:

```
WHERE column LIKE '% 50% %'
```

The string above would match "available for 50% off," but it would also match "for 500 years" or "a 1 in 50 chance" as well. For this reason, SQL enables you to specify a character that is used to escape wildcard characters. In other words, it indicates that the wildcard character should be interpreted literally rather that being translated so that it matches patterns.

Unlike some programming languages, SQL does not provide a default escape character, nor does repeating the wildcard character twice in a row indicate that it should be escaped. Rather, you can specify the character you want to use as the escape character using the ESCAPE clause. For example, if you're feeling nostalgic about C or Perl programming, you can use the backslash (\) character to escape wildcard characters, as demonstrated in Listing 6.27.

LISTING 6.27 USING THE ESCAPE CLAUSE TO ESCAPE WILDCARD CHARACTERS

```
SELECT movie_title
FROM Movies
WHERE movie_title LIKE '%50\%%' ESCAPE \
```

The query in Listing 6.27 will select any row in which the string in the column being checked contains the substring "50%." The benefit of being able to select your own escape character is that you can be sure that the character used to escape wildcard characters won't be included in the data being tested.

LIKE AND PERFORMANCE

One disadvantage of using LIKE clauses is that they can hinder the performance of your queries. The % wildcard is slower than the _ wildcard, and the position of the % wildcard within the pattern can also have a significant effect on performance.

Depending on the size of the table that you're querying, this might be an issue. For example, right now the Movies table contains 8 rows. Because the table is so small, any impact that using wildcards has will probably seem negligible. On the other hand, if there were 8,000 or 80,000 movies in the table, using % could significantly slow down a query.

PART

II

CH

6

Using % at the beginning of a matching pattern is particularly slow. So the performance of a WHERE clause like the following will in all likelihood be poor:

```
WHERE title LIKE '%Files'
```

If you can avoid such a construct, even by using multiple expressions that use the _ wildcard (combined using the OR operator), you should probably do so.

For example, if the title column was created with a maximum size of 8 characters instead of 80, you could write the previous WHERE clause like the following and achieve the same results as the query that used the % wildcard:

```
WHERE (title LIKE '_Files')
OR (title LIKE '__Files')
OR (title LIKE '___Files')
```

That WHERE clause works because only three expressions are required to cover all of the possible values in the title field. In most cases, it would perform much better as well. In most cases, you can write your queries using %, and if the performance is unacceptable, you can rewrite them using _ to see if the speed improves.

Matching One or More Characters

With UNIX regular expressions, there are two different wildcards, one that is used to match zero or more characters (*) and one that matches one or more characters (+). In SQL, the % character matches zero more more characters, and there is no wildcard character that matches one or more characters. Fortunately, you can match any string of one or more characters using the _% construct. Here's an example:

```
WHERE column LIKE 'Something_%'
```

Useful Functions for WHERE Clauses

There are a number of functions that can be used within WHERE clauses that make it easier to find the records that you're looking for. I've already discussed the UPPER() and LOWER() functions, which are used to avoid problems with case sensitivity. There are several other functions that can be used within the WHERE clause to find specific information.

This section will cover types of functions that are found in most popular databases. The implementations and function names vary from vendor to vendor, but functions that fall into these categories are generally available. Most database vendors include functions that are not part of the SQL standard in their database implementations that can be used to manipulate the data within a WHERE clause to help match particular data. There is a more complete discussion of built-in functions in Chapter 12, "Handling Specific Types of Data."

All these functions can be used both in the select list and the WHERE clause, although I imagine that you'll find most of them more useful in the WHERE clause. In most of the examples in this section, I'm going to use literal strings to explain how these functions work, but when you use these functions, you'll most likely use column names instead.

REMOVING EXCESS SPACES

The TRIM() function is used to strip leading and trailing spaces from a string. This function can be used to format data for output or to convert a string for purposes of comparison. Assume that there's a movie with the title 'The Deadly MIME   '. As you can see, four spaces have been appended to the end of the title. The TRIM() function will remove the spaces from the end of the string so that a WHERE clause like the one in Listing 6.28 will evaluate as true.

LISTING 6.28   USING TRIM() WITHIN A QUERY

```
SELECT title
FROM Movies
WHERE TRIM(title) = 'The Deadly MIME'
```

The movie title 'The Deadly MIME   ' is equal to the string in Listing 6.28 after the extra spaces have been removed using TRIM().

In some databases, the RTRIM() and LTRIM() functions are available to remove white space from the right and left ends of a string, respectively.

Tip 26 from
Rafe Colburn

When you compare values in CHAR fields to values in VARCHAR fields, it is sometimes necessary to use RTRIM on the CHAR value to remove the spaces that are used as padding in order for the values to match.

STRING LENGTH

The LENGTH() function is used to determine the length of a string. It returns an integer containing the number of characters in the string to which it is applied. Remember the WHERE clause back in Listing 6.23 that found all of the people with four-letter first names using LIKE? It would be better written like this:

```
WHERE LENGTH(person_fname) = 4
```

TYPE CONVERSION FUNCTIONS

Most databases have a number of functions that can convert data between data types for the purposes of comparison. Unfortunately, the names and implementations of these functions vary from product to product. The functions specific to most of the popular database packages will be discussed in Part VI, "Specific Databases." However, I want to cover the topic generally here.

The CONVERT() function is generally used to convert data from one type to another. Unfortunately, it is not implemented in all databases. The use of the CONVERT() function is as follows:

```
CONVERT(datatype[(length)], expression)
```

PART

II

CH

6

The first argument is the datatype to which the data will be converted. If the datatype requires the specification of the size of the field, it should be included in parentheses after the datatype. The second argument is the expression (or column name) that will be converted. If your database implements the CONVERT() function, it will convert between datatypes as best it can. For example, it can convert strings containing numeric data to a numeric data type:

```
CONVERT(NUMBER, '100')
```

Here's an example of how data conversions are implemented in Oracle databases. Say that you have a string such as 'January 1, 1999'. You know this is a date, but Oracle expects a date in the format '01-JAN-99'. Oracle provides the TO_DATE() function to perform these types of conversions. The following function call would convert the date string to a proper Oracle date:

```
TO_DATE('January 1, 1999', 'MONTH DD, YYYY')
```

There are a number of other data type conversion functions available in Oracle and in other database products. For example, Sybase makes the DATE function available to convert strings to dates. Conversion of fields from one type to another is discussed in depth in Chapter 12.

NESTING FUNCTIONS

The SQL language enables you to nest functions so that you can use multiple functions to modify the value in a single expression. For example, say that you have a column in an Oracle database that contains a series of values such as 'The date is 1/18/99   ', and you want to extract the date from them. You could nest the SUBSTR(), RTRIM(), and TO_DATE() functions to return the data in the date format, as shown in Listing 6.29.

LISTING 6.29 NESTED FUNCTION CALLS

```
SELECT TO_DATE(RTRIM(SUBSTR('The date is 1/18/99     ', 13)), 'MM/DD/YY')
FROM Dual

TO_DATE(R
---------
18-JAN-99
```

The most important thing to remember when nesting functions is that they are evaluated in order from innermost to outermost. In the previous example, the SUBSTR() function is evaluated first, followed by the RTRIM() function, followed by the TO_DATE() function. in Listing 6.29.

AGGREGATE FUNCTIONS

There are also a number of aggregate functions that are to provide reports based on all the values within a particular column. These functions are covered in detail in Chapter 7.

IN THE REAL WORLD

When you write applications that interface with relational databases, one of the most important tasks you face is gathering data that will be used in the WHERE clause of your queries. Generally speaking, applications that interface with databases do not have fully hard-coded queries. In most cases, the select list and tables in the FROM clause are known when the program is written, but the criteria for which rows to select are oftentimes not present.

Take, for example, an application that enables users to search the Movies table for a particular movie. The application might enable the user to search based on the movie title, the director, or the release date. However the search interface is implemented in the application, the information gathered from the user must be plugged in to the WHERE clause of the query during the program's execution.

Look at a number of query interfaces and see their effect on how queries are written within a program. The most basic query interface within an application might involve listing all the entries in a table or perhaps all the movies that were created within the past 60 days. These queries tend to be hard-coded within the calling application. In the first case, no WHERE clause would be used. In Oracle, the second case would be written as the following:

```
SELECT movie_title
FROM Movies
WHERE release_date BETWEEN (SYSDATE - 60) AND SYSDATE
```

The second type of query interface enables users to search on the contents of a particular field. For example, perhaps users are enabled to search the movie database based on the titles of the movies. A single field is provided in which users can enter part of a movie's title, and the application will return a list of movies that match that title. In this case, the application must insert the title segment that the user enters in a LIKE comparison in the WHERE clause of the search query, as follows:

```
SELECT movie_title
FROM Movies
WHERE movie_title LIKE '%title_segment%'
```

The calling program would replace *title_segment* with the actual text that the user entered. This is just one example of this sort of query; you could also enable users to enter a date and locate all the movies released after that date or select a director from a pull-down list and return all the movies directed by that person. In all these cases, the fields in the WHERE clause remain the same; only the values to which they are compared are populated dynamically by the calling application.

In some cases, the program that uses the SQL call must build the entire WHERE clause dynamically. Consider a search interface that enables users to search for a cast member based on any of a number of criteria. The form might contain fields for the person's city, state, and first and last names. When the form input is processed by the application, it must determine which fields contain user input and, therefore, which conditions must be included in the WHERE clause of the query that retrieves the search results.

Conditions must be added dynamically based on user input because including conditions that do not conform to fields that contain user input will constrain the result set unnecessarily or hinder application performance. If the application contains first name, last name, city, and state fields, you might consider building a WHERE clause such as the one in this query:

```
SELECT person_fname, person_lname
FROM People
WHERE person_fname LIKE '%first_name%'
AND person_lname LIKE '%last_name%'
AND person_city LIKE '%city%'
AND person_state = 'state'
```

What if the person only entered Smith in the last name field and left the rest of the fields blank? The LIKE comparisons for the first name and city will match every row because the space between the two percent signs is empty. This might hurt performance, however, if the conditions are evaluated despite the fact that they match every row. Another problem is that the state comparison uses =, not LIKE, perhaps because the states are available in a pull-down list. If no state is selected, the state field is empty, and no records will be matched. For these reasons, it is necessary to start your queries with an empty WHERE clause and add fields dynamically based on the input provided by the user.

When you write database applications, it's important to consider how the WHERE clauses in your queries are constructed and which elements they must contain. You should be sure to design your applications so that they contain the appropriate WHERE clauses to match the user interface elements that you provide.

CHAPTER **7**

AGGREGATING QUERY RESULTS

In this chapter

The features of the SELECT statement that you've seen so far are useful for extracting specific data from a database, such as the gross revenue from a particular movie or all the directors who live in a particular state. However, the SELECT statement also provides powerful reporting capabilities that you can use to take a more holistic view of the data in your database.

You can retrieve the average or sum of all the values in a particular column, or you can categorize all the values in a column and count all the values in each category, summarizing them in the results of a single query. For example, using the aggregate functions that I discuss in this chapter and the grouping clause, you can easily calculate the average budget of all the movies produced by a particular studio or the sum of the revenues of all the movies released in a particular year.

This chapter will cover the aggregate functions that enable you to perform calculations on values in a particular column. It will also cover the GROUP BY clause, which enables you to categorize the results of an aggregate query.

SELECTING UNIQUE VALUES USING DISTINCT

The Movies table contains several movies from each studio. If you wanted a simple list of all the studios in the database, a query like the one in Listing 7.1 wouldn't work.

LISTING 7.1   RETRIEVING ALL OF THE STUDIOS IN THE DATABASE

```
SELECT studio_id
FROM Movies

STUDIO_ID
----------
         1
         2
         4
         3
         1
         2
         3
         3
         4
         1

10 rows selected.
```

As you can see, all the studios are represented on the list, but there are multiple occurrences of each of them. SQL provides the DISTINCT operator to winnow out duplicates from a list of values. Listing 7.2 uses the DISTINCT operator to remove the duplicates from the results in Listing 7.1.

LISTING 7.2   SELECTING UNIQUE STUDIOS FROM THE MOVIES TABLE

```
SELECT DISTINCT studio_id
FROM Movies

STUDIO_ID
----------
         1
         2
         3
         4
```

As you can see from the query results in Listing 7.2, when the DISTINCT operator is used, only a single occurrence of each value in the studio column is returned.

Generally speaking, the use of the DISTINCT operator is as follows:

```
SELECT [DISTINCT] select_list
FROM table[ , table, ... ]
[WHERE expression]
[ORDER BY expression]
```

SELECTING DISTINCT COMBINATIONS OF VALUES

If more than one column is supplied in the select list, each unique combination of the values in the columns is selected. Listing 7.3 contains a list of all the studios, director IDs, and movie titles in the database. Listing 7.4 contains a list of the studios and director IDs with duplicates eliminated using DISTINCT.

LISTING 7.3   TITLES, STUDIOS, AND DIRECTOR IDs IN THE MOVIES TABLE

```
SELECT movie_title, studio_id, director_id
FROM Movies

MOVIE_TITLE          STUDIO_ID DIRECTOR_ID
-------------------- ---------- -----------
Vegetable House              1           1
Prince Kong                  2          10
The Code Warrior             4           2
Bill Durham                  3           9
Codependence Day             1           1
The Linux Files              2           2
SQL Strikes Back             3           9
The Programmer               3           1
Hard Code                    4          10
The Rear Windows             1           1

10 rows selected.
```

PART

II

CH

7

LISTING 7.4   DISTINCT COMBINATIONS OF STUDIO AND DIRECTOR ID

```
SELECT DISTINCT studio_id, director_id
FROM Movies

STUDIO_ID DIRECTOR_ID
---------- -----------
        1           1
        2           2
        2          10
        3           1
        3           9
        4           2
        4          10

7 rows selected.
```

Seven rows were selected in Listing 7.4 because both The Programmer and Bill Durham have the same director and studio, as shown in Listing 7.3. If three columns were included in the select list of Listing 7.4, the unique combinations of all three of those columns would be included in the query results.

Take a look at the query in Listing 7.5. It's a valid query.

LISTING 7.5   SELECTING ALL THE DISTINCT ROWS FROM THE DATABASE

```
SELECT DISTINCT *
FROM Movies
```

The query in Listing 7.5 returned all the rows from the Movies table. If it returned less, it would indicate that there are rows in the table that are identical. As you know, if your database fulfills the requirements of the relational model, there are no duplicate rows in any table. The primary key should be unique for every row in your database, which would ensure that there are always as many DISTINCT rows in your tables as there are rows.

DISTINCT AND NULLS

As you know from the discussions of null values earlier in the book, nulls cannot be considered to be equal to each other because null values are unknown. Well, the DISTINCT operator breaks this rule. For the purposes of the DISTINCT operator, all nulls are considered to be equal to each other.

Selecting the DISTINCT values in the gross column of the Movies table demonstrates this principle, as shown in Listing 7.6.

LISTING 7.6   DISTINCT VALUES FROM THE GROSS COLUMN

```
SELECT DISTINCT gross
FROM Movies
```

```
GROSS
```

```
----------
        10
      17.5
      17.8
        30
      45.3
```

```
6 rows selected.
```

As you already know, there are two rows in the Movies table that have a null value in the gross column. As you can see from these query results, one of the two nulls has been discarded.

Aggregate Functions

There are a number of aggregate functions available for use within SQL. Instead of acting on the contents of a single field in a database, they act on a set of values returned by a query. For example, they enable you to count the number of rows in a table that match a particular set of criteria, or they enable you to take the average of the values in a particular column in a table.

These functions can act on all the rows in a table, a subset of the rows in a table selected using a WHERE clause, or groups of the selected data organized using the GROUP BY clause. Aggregate functions are used as follows:

```
SELECT function(column)
FROM table [ , table ... ]
[ WHERE condition ]
```

When these functions are used, generally the select list consists of a single column (the one from which the aggregate value will be computed) and a single "row" of data is returned (the one that contains the aggregate that you were computing). Listing 7.7 contains a query that uses an aggregate function, in this case COUNT().

LISTING 7.7 USING AN AGGREGATE FUNCTION

```
SELECT COUNT(*)
FROM Movies

COUNT(*)
----------
        10
```

As you can see from the query results, only one row is returned, and it contains the total number of rows in the Movies table, which was calculated using COUNT(). If you include a nonaggregate expression in the select list, an error message is generated. For an example, look at the output in Listing 7.8.

LISTING 7.8 MIXING STANDARD COLUMNS AND AGGREGATE FUNCTIONS IN ONE QUERY

```
SELECT title, COUNT(*)
FROM Movies

SELECT title, COUNT(*) FROM Movies
       *
ERROR at line 1:
ORA-00937: not a single-group group function
```

On the other hand, you can include mathematical and string expressions in the select list with no problems, as shown in Listing 7.9.

LISTING 7.9 USING STRING EXPRESSIONS WITH AGGREGATE FUNCTIONS

```
SELECT 'There are', COUNT(*), 'movies in the database'
FROM Movies;

'THEREARE   COUNT(*) 'MOVIESINTHEDATABASE'
---------- ---------- --------------------
There are           8 movies in the database
```

The GROUP BY clause, which will be covered in depth later, enables you to divide the query results into subgroups based on the values in some columns and then run the aggregate function on each of those groups.

Tip 27 from *Rafe Colburn*	You can use multiple aggregate functions within a single select list. For example, to retrieve the sum of both the budget and gross columns within the same query, the following SQL code is used:
	
	```SELECT SUM(budget), SUM(gross)```
	```FROM Movies```

AGGREGATE FUNCTIONS AND THE WHERE CLAUSE

The WHERE clause can be used with queries that use aggregate functions to specify a set of rows that will be included in the function's calculation. For example, a query that counts the number of movies that opened during the 1980s appears in Listing 7.10.

LISTING 7.10 THE NUMBER OF MOVIES THAT OPENED DURING THE '80S

```
SELECT COUNT(*)
FROM Movies
WHERE release_date BETWEEN '01-JAN-1980' AND '31-DEC-1989'


  COUNT(*)
----------
        2
```

In my database, only two movies opened in that time frame. Any WHERE clause that can be used with standard SELECT statements can be used with SELECT statements that contain aggregate functions.

RENAMING AGGREGATE RESULTS

The AS keyword can be used to rename the results of aggregate functions, just as it can be used to rename any other expression in a select list. Listing 7.11 contains an example of the use of the AS keyword in an aggregate query.

LISTING 7.11   USING AS IN AN AGGREGATE QUERY

```
SELECT COUNT(*) AS total
FROM Movies

     TOTAL
----------
         8
```

Tip 28 from
Rafe Colburn

If you are going to refer to columns returned by a query by their names in a programming environment that enables you to embed SQL queries in your code, it's important to use the AS keyword to rename columns that use aggregate functions. The combination of function names and punctuation that make up aggregate query calls cannot be referenced from within most programming languages.

THE COUNT() FUNCTION

The first aggregate function I'm going to cover is the COUNT() function, mainly because I already introduced you to it in the first few listings in this chapter. As you've probably already gathered, the COUNT() function simply counts all the occurrences of a particular column in the result set of a query.

If you just want to count the number of rows returned by a query, the easiest thing to do is use the COUNT(*) expression, as I did in the examples earlier in this chapter. There are two reasons for this; one is that it enables the query optimizer to decide which column to actually use for the count, perhaps providing some small performance increase; the second is that you don't have to worry about whether the column you're counting contains nulls or whether it exists. A query that counts all the People from Texas appears in Listing 7.12.

LISTING 7.12   COUNTING ALL THE ROWS IN THE MOVIES TABLE

```
SELECT COUNT(*)
FROM People
WHERE person_state = 'TX'
```

continues

LISTING 7.12   CONTINUED

```
COUNT(*)
----------
         4
```

COUNT() AND NULLS

The COUNT(*column_name*) function does not include columns containing a null value in the total. If you use COUNT(*), this is a non-issue because it counts all the rows regardless of their contents. The fact that null values are not included can be useful, however, if nulls are used to indicate something in particular in your database.

For example, in the Movies table, if the value in the gross column is null, it indicates that the movie has not opened in theaters and thus has not earned any income. By counting the number of entries in the gross column, you can tell how many movies have opened, as shown in Listing 7.13.

LISTING 7.13   COUNTING VALUES IN A COLUMN THAT CONTAINS NULLS

```
SELECT COUNT(gross)
FROM Movies

COUNT(GROSS)
------------
           8
```

The two rows with null values in the gross column are not included in the query results.

COUNT() AND DISTINCT

The DISTINCT operator can be used along with COUNT() to return a list of unique values in a particular set of rows, rather than a count of all the values in the row. The DISTINCT operator should appear within the parentheses in the function call. Here's the structure of a SELECT statement that uses COUNT() and DISTINCT:

```
SELECT COUNT(DISTINCT column)
FROM table
```

The query in Listing 7.14 counts the number of unique studios in the Movies database.

LISTING 7.14   COUNTING THE NUMBER OF UNIQUE VALUES IN A COLUMN

```
SELECT COUNT(DISTINCT studio_id)
FROM Movies


COUNT(DISTINCTSTUDIO_ID)
------------------------
                       4
```

THE SUM( ) AND AVG( ) FUNCTIONS

The SUM( ) function simply adds up all the values in a set of rows and returns the result. The AVG( ) function calculates the average (or in statistical terms, the mean) of a set of values. Unlike the COUNT( ) function, which can count the values in any type of column, the SUM( ) and AVG( ) functions only work on columns containing numeric data. Listing 7.15 contains a query that adds up the budgets for all the movies in the database. Listing 7.16 contains a query that calculates the mean of the budgets of all the movies in the Movies table.

LISTING 7.15 USING SUM( ) TO ADD UP THE VALUES IN A COLUMN

```
SELECT SUM(budget)
FROM Movies



SUM(BUDGET)
-----------
    262.85
```

LISTING 7.16 USING AVG( ) TO CALCULATE THE AVERAGE OF A GROUP OF VALUES

```
SELECT AVG(budget)
FROM Movies

AVG(BUDGET)
-----------
    26.285
```

Tip 29 from
Rafe Colburn

When null values are included in a column to which either the AVG( ) or the SUM( ) function is applied, the nulls are ignored. With the AVG( ) function, the null values are not included in the sum or in the number of values by which the sum of the values is divided.

Both the AVG( ) and the SUM( ) functions can be used with the DISTINCT operator, just like the COUNT( ) function. With the DISTINCT function, the average or sum of the unique values in the result set will be taken. Compare the query results in Listings 7.16 and 7.17 to the results in Listings 7.18 and 7.19.

LISTING 7.17 USING SUM( ) TO ADD UP THE VALUES IN A COLUMN

```
SELECT SUM(DISTINCT budget)
FROM Movies



SUM(DISTINCTBUDGET)
-------------------
              65.1
```

LISTING 7.18 USING AVG() TO CALCULATE THE AVERAGE OF A GROUP OF VALUES

```
SELECT AVG(DISTINCT budget)
FROM Movies

AVG(DISTINCTBUDGET)
-------------------
          23.65
```

THE MIN() AND MAX() FUNCTIONS

The MIN() function is used to locate the smallest value in a set of values, and the MAX() function is used to locate the largest value in a set. Both of these functions can be used with any data type. The MAX() function will happily find the greatest string (based on the string comparison rules discussed back in chapter 5), the most recent date (or the date furthest in the future), or the largest number in a set. The MIN() function will do just the opposite.

Tip 30 from
Rafe Colburn

Neither the MIN() and nor the MAX() functions return null values if other values are available in the column. Null values are treated as unknown and thus cannot be considered to be greater than or less than any other values.

Both of these functions can be used with the DISTINCT operator, but there's really no reason to use it because these functions return a single value from a set, rather than performing an aggregate operation on all the values in a set.

Listing 7.19 contains an example of the use of the MIN() function that finds the earliest release date of all the movies in the Movies table.

LISTING 7.19 SELECTING THE EARLIEST RELEASE DATE FROM THE Movies TABLE

```
SELECT MIN(release_date)
FROM Movies


MIN(RELEA
---------
01-JAN-75
```

DIVIDING AGGREGATES INTO CATEGORIES

If you wanted to create a report that listed the combined budget of all the movies from each studio, you could create a query for each studio that used the SUM() function to get the total budget for all the movies from that studio. You'd have several queries like the one in Listing 7.20, one for each studio.

LISTING 7.20   A QUERY THAT CALCULATES THE COMBINED BUDGET OF ALL THE MOVIES FROM THE STUDIO DELIGHTED ARTISTS

```
SELECT SUM(budget)
FROM Movies
WHERE studio_id = 3

SUM(BUDGET)
-----------
      65.1
```

This poses two problems, however. One is that you'd have to create a separate query for each of the studios in the list; the other is that you'd have to know the name of every studio in the database. These problems make it very impractical to use this method to generate such a report.

Rather than using separate queries, however, you can use the GROUP BY clause in your SQL statement to automatically categorize your query results and run your aggregate functions on the rows in each of the categories as opposed to the entire result set.

THE GROUP BY CLAUSE

The GROUP BY clause categorizes your query results according to the contents of one of the columns in the database. In this way, it is somewhat similar to DISTINCT in that it returns a row for a unique value in the column that you are using to group the data. Unlike DISTINCT, however, if you use an aggregate function on another column in the table, GROUP BY will apply that function to groups of rows based on the value in the grouped column. The syntax of a statement using the GROUP BY clause looks like this:

```
SELECT select_list
FROM table [ , table, ... ]
[ WHERE condition ]
[ GROUP BY group_by_list ]
[ ORDER BY order_by_list ]
```

The number of groups created by the query is the same as the number of rows returned if you used the DISTINCT operator on the grouping column in a SELECT statement.

In Listing 7.21, I use the SUM() function to figure out the combined budgets of all the movies in the Movies table. In Listing 7.22, I use the GROUP BY clause to calculate the sum of the budgets for each studio in the Movies table.

LISTING 7.21   THE SUM() OF ALL THE BUDGETS IN THE Movies TABLE

```
SELECT SUM(budget) FROM Movies

SUM(BUDGET)
-----------
    277.85
```

LISTING 7.22   THE SUM() OF THE BUDGETS FOR EACH STUDIO IN THE MOVIES TABLE

```
SELECT studio_id, SUM(budget)
FROM Movies
GROUP BY studio_id

STUDIO_ID SUM(BUDGET)
---------- -----------
        1          85
        2       25.45
        3        65.1
        4        87.3
```

As you can see from the query results, the query in Listing 7.22 returns a list of all the studios in the database and the sum of the budgets for the movies from that studio.

LISTING 7.23   USING DISTINCT TO RETURN ONE ROW FOR EACH UNIQUE VALUE IN A COLUMN

```
SELECT DISTINCT studio_id
FROM Movies
STUDIO_ID
----------
        1
        2
        3
        4
```

In fact, if you use the GROUP BY clause without an aggregate function, the results of the query are identical to those of a query that uses the DISTINCT operator, as shown in Listing 7.24.

LISTING 7.24   USING GROUP BY WITHOUT AN AGGREGATE FUNCTION

```
SELECT studio_id
FROM Movies
GROUP BY studio_id

STUDIO_ID
----------
        1
        2
        3
        4
```

Another way that the GROUP BY clause is similar to the DISTINCT operator is that it considers all null values to be the same in terms of grouping. All the items with a value of null in the grouped column are placed in the same group.

The most important rule you must remember when using GROUP BY to generate categorized query results is that the column you want to use to categorize the results must appear in the group list. A query like this would not work because studio is not in the select list:

```
SELECT SUM(budget)
FROM Movies
GROUP BY studio_id
```

The GROUP BY clause will work with any of the aggregate functions; COUNT(), SUM(), AVG(), MIN(), and MAX() all work as you would expect.

GROUPS AND SUBGROUPS

Just as the ORDER BY clause can sort query results within categories, the GROUP BY clause can create groups and subgroups if more than one column is specified. Listing 7.25 contains an example that counts the number of movies each director has directed within each studio. The ORDER BY clause must appear after the GROUP BY clause; the order is not optional.

LISTING 7.25   USING GROUP BY TO CREATE SUBGROUPS

```
SELECT studio_id, director_id, COUNT(*)
FROM Movies
GROUP BY studio_id, director_id


  STUDIO_ID DIRECTOR_ID   COUNT(*)
  --------- -----------  ---------
          1           1          3
          2           2          1
          2          10          1
          3           1          1
          3           9          2
          4           2          1
          4          10          1

7 rows selected.
```

As you can see, the results are first categorized by the studio, and then by the director_id. If the GROUP BY clause were GROUP BY director_id, studio_id, the query results would show how many movies for each studio all the directors had directed, as shown in Listing 7.26. As it is, it shows the breakdown of how many movies each director has directed for each studio.

LISTING 7.26   ANOTHER QUERY THAT USES GROUP BY TO CREATE SUBGROUPS

```
SELECT studio_id, director_id, COUNT(*)
FROM Movies
GROUP BY director_id, studio_id

STUDIO_ID DIRECTOR_ID   COUNT(*)
--------- -----------  ---------
        1           1          3
        3           1          1
        2           2          1
        4           2          1
```

PART

II

CH

7

continues

LISTING 7.26 CONTINUED

```
        3           9           2
        2          10           1
        4          10           1
```

7 rows selected.

GROUP BY AND ORDER BY

The ORDER BY clause can be used along with the GROUP BY clause to sort the results of the grouped query. To sort query results when using a GROUP BY clause, simply append the ORDER BY clause to the SQL statement, as shown in Listing 7.27.

LISTING 7.27   USING ORDER BY AND GROUP BY IN THE SAME QUERY

```
SELECT studio_id, COUNT(*)
FROM Movies
GROUP BY studio_id
ORDER BY studio_id

STUDIO_ID   COUNT(*)
---------- ----------
        1           3
        2           2
        3           3
        4           2
```

Just as the GROUP BY clause cannot contain a column name that is not part of the select list, the ORDER BY clause cannot contain a column name that's not part of the GROUP BY clause. Attempting to include a column name in the ORDER BY clause that's not in the GROUP BY clause will produce a syntax error.

You can also include multiple columns in the ORDER BY clause, as long as they also appear in the GROUP BY clause. Take a look at Listing 7.28 for an example.

LISTING 7.28   USING MULTIPLE COLUMN NAMES IN BOTH THE ORDER BY AND GROUP BY CLAUSES

```
SELECT studio_id, director_id, COUNT(*)
FROM Movies
GROUP BY studio_id, director_id
ORDER BY studio_id, director_id

STUDIO_ID DIRECTOR_ID   COUNT(*)
---------- ----------- ----------
        1           1           3
        2           2           1
        2          10           1
        3           1           1
        3           9           2
```

```
       4           2           1
       4          10           1
```

7 rows selected.

The order of the columns in the ORDER BY clause does not have to match the order of the columns in the GROUP BY clause. The query will sort on the secondary grouping before sorting on the primary grouping if you want. The results of such a query are shown in Listing 7.29, although the query results in Listing 7.30 might look more sensible to you.

LISTING 7.29   SORTING ON THE SECONDARY GROUPING CRITERIA BEFORE THE PRIMARY CRITERIA

```
SELECT studio_id, director_id, COUNT(*)
FROM Movies
GROUP BY studio_id, director_id
ORDER BY director_id, studio_id

STUDIO_ID DIRECTOR_ID   COUNT(*)
---------- ----------- ----------
         1           1          3
         3           1          1
         2           2          1
         4           2          1
         3           9          2
         2          10          1
         4          10          1
```

7 rows selected.

LISTING 7.30   ANOTHER QUERY THAT SORTS ON THE SECONDARY CRITERIA BEFORE THE PRIMARY CRITERIA

```
SELECT director_id, studio_id, COUNT(*)
FROM Movies
GROUP BY studio_id, director_id
ORDER BY director_id, studio_id

DIRECTOR_ID STUDIO_ID   COUNT(*)
----------- ---------- ----------
          1          1          3
          1          3          1
          2          2          1
          2          4          1
          9          3          2
         10          2          1
         10          4          1
```

7 rows selected.

Also note that using multiple columns in the GROUP BY clause does not compel you to use the same number of columns in the ORDER BY clause. Listing 7.31 contains a query that sorts

PART
II

CH

7

based only on the primary criteria, and Listing 7.32 contains a query that sorts based only on the secondary criterion.

LISTING 7.31 A GROUPED QUERY THAT ONLY SORTS BASED ON THE PRIMARY GROUPING COLUMN

```
SELECT studio_id, director_id, COUNT(*)
FROM Movies
GROUP BY studio_id, director_id
ORDER BY studio
```

```
STUDIO_ID DIRECTOR_ID   COUNT(*)
--------- -----------  ----------
        1           1           3
        2           2           1
        2          10           1
        3           1           1
        3           9           2
        4           2           1
        4          10           1

7 rows selected.
```

LISTING 7.32 A GROUPED QUERY THAT ONLY SORTS BASED ON THE SECONDARY CRITERION

```
SELECT studio_id, director_id, COUNT(*)
FROM Movies
GROUP BY studio_id, director_id
ORDER BY director_id
```

```
STUDIO_ID DIRECTOR_ID   COUNT(*)
--------- -----------  ----------
        1           1           3
        3           1           1
        2           2           1
        4           2           1
        3           9           2
        2          10           1
        4          10           1

7 rows selected.
```

USING GROUP BY WITH THE WHERE CLAUSE

The WHERE clause can be used within statements that use a GROUP BY clause in order to restrict which rows are included in the query results before they are grouped together. For example, you can include only the movies released between two specified dates in the query results or only those movies not from a particular studio.

When you use a WHERE clause in a SELECT statement that uses GROUP BY, the WHERE clause is first applied to the data to determine what rows should be included in the query results. Then, the rows that are selected using the WHERE clause are grouped, and the actual query results are generated. Listing 7.33 counts the number of movies for each studio that were released in the 1980s by using BETWEEN in the WHERE clause.

LISTING 7.33 COMBINING GROUP BY AND THE WHERE CLAUSE

```
SELECT studio_id, COUNT(*)
FROM Movies
WHERE release_date BETWEEN '01-JAN-80' AND '31-DEC-89'
GROUP BY studio_id


  STUDIO_ID   COUNT(*)
---------- ----------
         1          1
         3          1
```

FILTERING QUERY RESULTS USING HAVING

SQL provides another method of filtering query results when the GROUP BY statement is used. Whereas the WHERE clause filters query results before the results are grouped, the HAVING clause filters the results afterward. Expressions in the HAVING clause are applied to each group as a whole rather than to individual rows.

For example, say that you want to find all the studios that have combined movie budgets of greater than $60 million. Using the WHERE clause, there would be no easy way to filter individual rows so that the correct result was generated. However, using HAVING, you can calculate the sum of the budgets for each studio and return only those groups with a sum greater than $60 million, as demonstrated in the Listing 7.34.

LISTING 7.34 USING HAVING TO FILTER GROUPS IN THE QUERY RESULTS

```
SELECT studio_id, SUM(budget)
FROM Movies
GROUP BY studio_id
HAVING SUM(budget) > 60

STUDIO_ID SUM(BUDGET)
---------- -----------
         1          85
         3        65.1
         4        87.3
```

As you can see, the aggregate function in Listing 7.34 is used both in the select list and the HAVING clause. A common mistake is to use the column name alone in the HAVING clause, but this will generally produce an error. The expression must be the same in both the select list and the HAVING clause.

Column names that do not appear in the select list cannot be used by the HAVING clause at all. The HAVING clause appears before the ORDER BY clause, but after the GROUP BY clause. See Listing 7.35 for the proper order of these clauses.

LISTING 7.35   A STATEMENT THAT USES HAVING, GROUP BY, AND ORDER BY

```
SELECT studio_id, SUM(budget) FROM Movies
GROUP BY studio_id
HAVING SUM(budget) > 60
ORDER BY studio_id

STUDIO_ID SUM(BUDGET)
---------- -----------
        1          85
        3        65.1
        4        87.3
```

COMPOUND EXPRESSIONS AND THE HAVING CLAUSE

There's no reason why you can't use compound expressions in the HAVING clause, just as you would in the WHERE clause. The only restriction is that on some systems, all the expressions in the HAVING clause must correspond to like expressions within the SELECT list. A query such as the one in Listing 7.36 would not work in some databases (although it works in Oracle8, as shown in the listing).

LISTING 7.36   A QUERY THAT USES A COLUMN NOT IN THE SELECT LIST IN THE HAVING CLAUSE

```
SELECT studio_id, SUM(budget)
FROM Movies GROUP BY studio_id
HAVING SUM(budget) > 60
AND MAX(release_date) > '90-DEC-31'

STUDIO_ID SUM(BUDGET)
---------- -----------
        1          85
        3        65.1
        4        87.3
```

HAVING AND WHERE

HAVING and WHERE clauses can be utilized within the same query. Sometimes it makes sense to filter the results of a query using both of the two methods. For example, say that you wanted to find all the movies from directors whose average gross is greater than $10 million, but to avoid skewing results, you want to exclude movies that have a null gross because they are not yet released. Listing 7.37 shows how this type of task can be accomplished using a combination of the HAVING and WHERE clauses.

LISTING 7.37   USING WHERE AND HAVING IN A SINGLE QUERY

```
SELECT director_id, AVG(gross)
FROM Movies
WHERE gross IS NOT NULL
GROUP BY director_id
HAVING AVG(gross) > 10
```

```
ORDER BY AVG(gross)

DIRECTOR_ID AVG(GROSS)
----------- ----------
          2      17.65
         10         30
          1       30.7
```

As you can see from Listing 7.37, the order of clauses in a SELECT statement goes WHERE ...
GROUP BY ... HAVING ... ORDER BY. You can also see that both the GROUP BY and HAVING
clauses contribute to the results of the statement. Waiting to throw out null values until the
HAVING clause would remove other useful data from the query, as it would lead to the discard
of an entire group rather than just a single row. By the same token, I could not have filtered
based on the results of an aggregate had I opted to use only the WHERE clause.

IN THE REAL WORLD

Transact SQL which is supported by Microsoft SQL Server and Sybase Adaptive Server,
provides an additional means through which you can use aggregate functions. Using the
COMPUTE BY clause, you can apply aggregate functions to query results within the same
queries that retrieve the results themselves. If you are creating reports using SQL (as
opposed to retrieving the data using SQL and formatting the reports using some other language), the COMPUTE BY clause can save a lot of work in terms of programming. For example,
Listing 7.38 returns the title, gross, and budget for each of the movies in the database, as
well as the average gross and budget for all the movies in the table.

LISTING 7.38   USING THE COMPUTE BY CLAUSE TO CREATE A REPORT

```
SELECT movie_title, budget, gross
FROM Movies
COMPUTE AVG(budget), AVG(gross)

movie_title              budget                  gross
-----------------------  ----------------------  ----------------------
Mineral House            20                      30
Prince Kong              3                       52
The Code Warrior         10                      18
Bill Durham              10                      16
Codependence Day         15                      30
The Linux Files          22                      18
SQL Strikes Back         5                       10
The Programmer           50                      45
Hard Code                77                      30
The Rear Windows         50                      18
                         avg                     avg
                         ======================  ======================
                         26.200000               26.700000

(11 row(s) affected)
```

As you can see, the report includes not only the individual budget and gross values for each movie, it also includes the average budget and gross values for all the movies in the database. If you didn't use the COMPUTE clause, you would need two queries to obtain these results: one that retrieved the individual budget and gross values and another that retrieved the averages. You can also combine the functionality of a query that returns individual values and the GROUP BY clause using COMPUTE BY. To use COMPUTE BY, you must use an ORDER BY clause to group the rows returned by the query so that the aggregate functions can be applied to each group. Take a look at the example in Listing 7.39.

LISTING 7.39 USING COMPUTE BY TO APPLY AGGREGATE FUNCTIONS TO GROUPS OF ROWS

```
SELECT movie_title, studio_id, budget, gross
FROM Movies
ORDER BY studio_id
COMPUTE SUM(budget), SUM(gross) BY studio_id

movie_title            studio_id    budget              gross
--------------------   ----------   -----------------   ------------------
Mineral House          1            20                  30
Codependence Day       1            15                  30
The Rear Windows       1            50                  18

                                    sum                 sum
                                    =================   ==================
                                    85                  78


movie_title            studio_id    budget              gross
--------------------   ----------   -----------------   ------------------
Prince Kong            2            3                   52
The Code Warrior       2            10                  18
The Linux Files        2            22                  18

                                    sum                 sum
                                    =================   ==================
                                    35                  88


movie_title            studio_id    budget              gross
--------------------   ----------   -----------------   ------------------
Bill Durham            3            10                  16
SQL Strikes Back       3            5                   10
The Programmer         3            50                  45

                                    sum                 sum
                                    =================   ==================
                                    65                  71


movie_title            studio_id    budget              gross
--------------------   ----------   -----------------   ------------------
Hard Code              4            77                  30

                                    sum                 sum
                                    =================   ==================
                                    77                  30

(14 row(s) affected)
```

The ORDER BY clause is used to group the rows in the query results based on the value in the studio_id column, and the aggregate functions are applied to the rows in each of the groups. Although all the results of this query could be retrieved with only two queries to format the results in this manner (without using an external program), eight queries without the COMPUTE BY clause would be required.

CHAPTER **8**

COMBINING TABLES USING JOINS

In this chapter

In many cases, when you query a database, not all the data you require is stored within a single table. Even if all the data you need is stored within single table, you might need to compare it to data stored within another table to retrieve the correct set of rows. Much of the time, data is distributed through many tables by design to eliminate redundancy in your data.

To return data from more than one table using a single query, a join is required. To compare data in one table to data in another, you can use a join or a subquery (subqueries are discussed in Chapter 9, "Subqueries"). In this chapter, I will discuss the various types of joining queries that are available and why the relational model makes them necessary.

The data selection techniques that I have discussed thus far were applied to single tables. In this chapter, I'll explain how to extend those techniques to query multiple tables using a single SELECT statement.

JOINS AND NORMALIZATION

When you design a database, it is important to normalize your tables so the same piece of information doesn't appear in multiple tables, causing problems when you need to update that information later. Unfortunately, what this means is that to get all the information you need when you're querying the database, you often need to access more than one table.

By using joins, you can retrieve information from multiple tables using a single SELECT statement. This enables you to recombine information that has been spread throughout multiple tables through normalization.

WHAT IS A JOIN?

A *join* is a query that combines data from multiple tables. Take a look at the structure of a standard SELECT statement:

```
SELECT column_list
FROM table [ , table, ... ]
[ WHERE condition ]
```

The main difference (in syntax) between the SELECT statements in the previous three chapters and a SELECT statement that uses a join is that multiple tables are specified in the FROM clause of a join statement. A typical, non-joining SELECT statement looks like the following:

```
SELECT *
FROM Movies
```

On the other hand, a SELECT statement that joins two tables contains multiple references to tables in the table list:

```
SELECT *
FROM Movies, Studios
```

The problem with that SELECT statement is that it will return every possible combination of the two tables. If the Movies table contains 8 rows and the Studios table contains 10 rows, the query will return 80 rows of data. This is almost never a desirable outcome.

To write joins that make sense, you need two things: columns in each of the tables that are join-compatible, and a condition upon which to join the tables. Look at each of these two requirements closely.

JOIN-COMPATIBLE COLUMNS

For two tables to be joined in a sensible manner, they need to have some data in common. Take a look at Listings 8.1 and 8.2, which contain some of the columns from the Movies table and the People table.

LISTING 8.1 THE title AND director_id COLUMNS FROM THE Movies TABLE

```
SELECT movie_title, director_id
FROM Movies
ORDER BY director_id

MOVIE_TITLE                                    DIRECTOR_ID
--------------------------------------------   -----------
Mineral House                                            1
Codependence Day                                         1
The Programmer                                           1
The Rear Windows                                         1
The Code Warrior                                         2
The Linux Files                                          2
Bill Durham                                              9
SQL Strikes Back                                         9
Prince Kong                                             10
Hard Code                                               10
aws
10 rows selected.
```

LISTING 8.2 THE person id, person fname, AND person lname COLUMNS FROM THE People TABLE

```
SELECT person_id, person_fname, person_lname
FROM People
ORDER BY person_id

PERSON_ID PERSON_FNAME         PERSON_LNAME
--------- -------------------- --------------------
        1 Jeff                 Price
        2 Chuck                Peterson
        3 Brandon              Brooks
        4 Brian                Smith
        5 Paul                 Monk
        6 Reece                Randall
        7 Peter                Jong
```

continues

LISTING 8.2   CONTINUED

```
         8 Maggie                Davis
         9 Becky                 Orvis
        10 Carol                 Delano

10 rows selected.
```

The `director_id` column from the `Movies` table corresponds with the `person_id` column from the `People` table. In fact, as you might remember from the discussion of database design back in Chapter 3, "Creating Databases," `director_id` is a foreign key from the `People` table. Because these two columns correlate, you can use them to form a join.

In the larger sense, columns from different tables can be considered to be "join-compatible" if they contain data that holds the same meaning. Containing data of the same type isn't enough. Just because two columns contain integers or are of type `VARCHAR(20)`, that doesn't mean that there is any meaningful relationship between the data in the columns.

For example, compare the `person_id` column in the `People` table to the `gross` column in the `Movies` table. Both of the columns contain numbers, but there is no relationship between the two columns. Even if some of the values in the columns matched, writing a query that joined the two tables based on the contents of those columns would not produce useful results.

On the other hand, the two columns that I mentioned initially, the `director_id` column in `Movies` and the `person_id` column in `People`, can be used to retrieve the name of the director for each of the movies listed in the Movies table, as demonstrated in Listing 8.3.

LISTING 8.3   A JOIN QUERY

```
SELECT movie_title, person_fname, person_lname
FROM Movies, People
WHERE director_id = person_id


MOVIE_TITLE              PERSON_FNAME          PERSON_LNAME
-----------------------  --------------------  ------------------
Mineral House            Jeff                  Price
Codependence Day         Jeff                  Price
The Programmer           Jeff                  Price
The Rear Windows         Jeff                  Price
The Code Warrior         Chuck                 Peterson
The Linux Files          Chuck                 Peterson
Bill Durham              Becky                 Orvis
SQL Strikes Back         Becky                 Orvis
Prince Kong              Carol                 Delano
Hard Code                Carol                 Delano

10 rows selected.
```

As you can see from the query results, the `title` column from the `Movies` table and the `person_fname` and `person_lname` columns from the `Directors` tables are included in the query results. The `WHERE` clause in the query brings me to the second requirement of any `SELECT` statement which performs a join.

Usually, the columns that make the best joins are keys, either primary or foreign. For example, you can always join two tables if the primary key in one of the tables appears as a foreign key in the other.

Tip 31 from *Rafe Colburn*	When you use a table that has a compound primary key within a join, you must use all the columns in the primary key in the joining condition to select particular rows based on the primary key. This means that multiple joining conditions must be used within the `WHERE` clause to create a successful join.

THE JOINING CONDITION

To write a useful `SELECT` statement that uses a join, a joining condition is required. Basically, a *joining condition* is a condition within the `WHERE` clause that expresses the relationship between the tables being joined. In cases where there are more than two tables being joined, multiple joining conditions are required.

In the `SELECT` statement in Listing 8.3, the joining condition is `director_id = person_id`. That condition indicates that of all the rows generated when two tables are joined, only the ones in which the `person_id` field in the `People` table and the `director_id` field in the `Movies` table match will be included in the query results.

In terms of both join compatibility and a joining condition, it's important to remember that tables need not explicitly be designed to join together. The columns you used to join the two tables in Listing 8.3 happen to have a foreign key relationship, but that's definitely not a requirement. Often, more interesting views of data can result from relationships that are discovered only after the database has been designed and created. For example, Listing 8.4 contains a query that would find any people who live in the same town as a movie studio.

LISTING 8.4 A JOINING QUERY TO FIND PEOPLE WHO LIVE IN THE SAME CITY AS A MOVIE STUDIO

```
SELECT person_fname, person_lname, studio_name
FROM People, Studios
WHERE person_state = studio_state
AND person_city = studio_city
```

Null values never evaluate as true in a joining condition. If either of the columns in the joining condition contains a null value, that row will be discarded, even if they both are null. Null values in this case are treated as though they contain an unknown value and thus cannot be considered equal to one another (or greater or less than one another).

USING JOINS

There are a number of syntactical rules and other techniques that are associated with joins. Many of these are derived from practical issues that crop up when you have to deal with columns in multiple tables in a single query.

For example, when you're joining two tables and they both contain columns with the same name, you should prepend the column name with the table name and a period. Listing 8.5 restates the query from Listing 8.3 with this notation.

LISTING 8.5   A JOIN QUERY THAT SPECIFIES THE TABLE WITH COLUMN NAMES

```
SELECT Movies.movie_title,
People.person_fname, People.person_lname
FROM Movies, People
WHERE Movies.director_id = People.person_id

MOVIE_TITLE                 PERSON_FNAME            PERSON_LNAME
------------------------    -------------------     -------------------
Mineral House               Jeff                    Price
Codependence Day            Jeff                    Price
The Programmer              Jeff                    Price
The Rear Windows            Jeff                    Price
The Code Warrior            Chuck                   Peterson
The Linux Files             Chuck                   Peterson
Bill Durham                 Becky                   Orvis
SQL Strikes Back            Becky                   Orvis
Prince Kong                 Carol                   Delano
Hard Code                   Carol                   Delano

10 rows selected.
```

As you can see, the only difference between the two queries is that the names of the tables in which each column appears are included in the second query. This use is optional unless the columns in each table have the same name; however, when you're writing complex queries, it's smart to use this notation even if you don't have to.

DETERMINING WHAT COLUMNS TO SELECT

When you're writing a SELECT statement that joins multiple tables, rarely do you want to select all the columns available using *. When you use * in a join, all the columns in all the tables in the select list are included in the query results. As you might imagine, this can reduce the readability of your query results. Listing 8.6 contains the output of a query that returns data that includes all the columns available in a join.

LISTING 8.6   A JOIN QUERY THAT SELECTS ALL THE COLUMNS AVAILABLE

```
SELECT *
FROM Movies, People
WHERE Movies.director_id = People.person_id
AND Movies.movie_title = 'The Code Warrior'
```

```
MOVIE_ID MOVIE_TITLE                                      STUDIO_ID     BUDGET
-------- ---------------------------------------------- ---------- ----------
     GROSS RELEASE_D DIRECTOR_ID  PERSON_ID PERSON_FNAME
-------- --------- ----------- ---------- --------------------
PERSON_LNAME
--------------------
PERSON_ADDRESS
---------------------------------------------------------
PERSON_CITY                       PE PERSO PERSON_PHO PERSON_SS
----------------------------- -- ----- ---------- ----------
        3 The Code Warrior                                  2        10.3
     17.8 01-SEP-91          2           2 Chuck
Peterson

  MOVIE_ID MOVIE_TITLE                                      STUDIO_ID     BUDGET
-------- ---------------------------------------------- ---------- ----------
     GROSS RELEASE_D DIRECTOR_ID  PERSON_ID PERSON_FNAME
-------- --------- ----------- ---------- --------------------
PERSON_LNAME
--------------------
PERSON_ADDRESS
---------------------------------------------------------
PERSON_CITY                       PE PERSO PERSON_PHO PERSON_SS
----------------------------- -- ----- ---------- ----------
150 Saddleburr Trail
Cary                          NC 27511 9195553891 881023737
```

As you can see from the output of the query, the results are nearly unreadable. Looking at the query results, you can see that the person_id column and the director_id column contain the same values. When two tables are joined using an equality comparison, the two columns used in the comparison are always redundant. It's not necessary to include both of them in the query results.

In fact, it's generally a good idea to only include those columns of data that you are actually going to use. For example, if you're really only interested in the name of the movies and directors you're selecting, you should include only those columns in your query results, as demonstrated in Listing 8.5.

SHORTENING TABLE NAMES

Rather than using the full name to indicate from which table each column in the select list or WHERE clause is taken, you can specify aliases for table names in the table list. To specify an alias for a table name, simply include it after the table name. For example, if you are using the People table but you want to abbreviate People as P, you would write the table list as FROM People P. Of course, using abbreviations that are too short can eliminate the readability gained by adding the table name to the column name in the first place, so be careful. The use of table aliases is demonstrated in Listing 8.7.

LISTING 8.7   CREATING TABLE ALIASES

```
SELECT M.movie_title, P.person_fname, P.person_lname
FROM Movies M, People P
WHERE M.director_id = P.person_id

MOVIE_TITLE               PERSON_FNAME          PERSON_LNAME
-----------------------   --------------------  -------------------
Mineral House             Jeff                  Price
Codependence Day          Jeff                  Price
The Programmer            Jeff                  Price
The Rear Windows          Jeff                  Price
The Code Warrior          Chuck                 Peterson
The Linux Files           Chuck                 Peterson
Bill Durham               Becky                 Orvis
SQL Strikes Back          Becky                 Orvis
Prince Kong               Carol                 Delano
Hard Code                 Carol                 Delano

10 rows selected.
```

As you can see, when you create aliases for tables, you can prepend the table alias onto the column name to identify the table in lieu of the entire table name.

JOINS AND RELATIONSHIPS

When I discussed data relationships back in Chapter 2, "Database Design," I talked about three kinds of relationships: *one-to-one*, *one-to-many*, and *many-to-many*.

One-to-one relationships are represented within a single table. Each movie has a single value for its gross revenue, and each value in the gross revenue column is assigned to a particular movie. To find the gross revenue for a particular movie, you simply find the gross revenue value in the row for that movie (see Listing 8.8).

LISTING 8.8   A ONE-TO-ONE RELATIONSHIP

```
SELECT gross
FROM Movies
WHERE movie_title = 'The Code Warrior'

GROSS
----------
      17.8
```

A one-to-many relationship occurs when one of the two entities in a relationship corresponds to multiple instances of the other entity but each instance of the second entity corresponds to only one instance of the first entity. For example, each studio produces many movies, but each movie is produced by a single studio. Studios are stored in one table and movies in another. Thus, you would say that there is a one-to-many relationship between studios and movies. A join, such as the one in Listing 8.9, is used when you want to express the relationship.

LISTING 8.9   A ONE-TO-MANY RELATIONSHIP

```
SELECT movie_title, studio_name
FROM Movies, Studios
WHERE movie_title = 'The Code Warrior'
AND Movies.studio_id = Studios.studio_id


MOVIE_TITLE                                 STUDIO_NAME
------------------------------------------- -------------------------
The Code Warrior                            MPM
```

Many-to-many relationships are created when entities on either side of a relationship are related to multiple occurrences of the entities on the other side of the relationship. In the sample database, the relationship between cast members and movies is a many-to-many relationship. Expression of many-to-many relationships is discussed later in this chapter in the section "Using Joining Tables."

HOW JOINS ARE PROCESSED

There are several steps in processing any query and producing the results. These steps are particularly important when it comes to joins because they can help to illustrate performance problems that can arise when complex join queries are executed. Looking at the order in which these steps are undertaken should clarify why queries produce the results that they do and why some queries work and others don't.

First, the Cartesian product of the tables being joined is generated. The Cartesian product is the combination of all the rows in each table with all the rows in the others. If each table contains one row, the Cartesian product consists of a single row. If each table contains 8 rows, the Cartesian product is 64 rows. The number of rows in the Cartesian product is calculated by multiplying the row count for all the tables in the join together. So a three-table join with tables of 50, 100, and 10 rows would generate a Cartesian product of 50,000 rows. It's not difficult to figure out why the performance of SELECT statements degrades rapidly as you add tables to a join.

The Cartesian product of the joined tables is then used as a single table for the purposes of the query. The new working table preserves the order of the rows in the joined tables. The next step is to apply the WHERE clause to all the rows in the working table. All the rows for which the WHERE clause is true are retained. Because the select list has not yet been applied to the working table, the WHERE clause can contain references to any columns in the working table. If there are subqueries (which are discussed in the next chapter) in the WHERE clause, they're evaluated so that the results can be used in the WHERE clause.

Next, if a GROUP BY clause is present, the remaining rows in the working table are sorted according to common values in the columns specified in the GROUP BY clause.

If aggregate functions are present in the select list, they are then applied, and the working table is replaced by one that contains the aggregate values (in groups, if a GROUP BY clause was used).

If there's a HAVING clause in the query, it is applied to the groups created using the GROUP BY clause. Rows that do not conform to the HAVING clause are discarded.

Finally, the select list is applied to the table that remains; expressions are evaluated and columns that aren't in the select list are removed, thereby leaving the final query results.

TYPES OF JOINS

There are several types of joining queries. The joins that I've used so far fall under the category of *equijoins*, which are joins that combine tables based on equal values in each of the two tables being joined. However, there are a number of other types of joins that can be used to select data based on different relationships other than simple equality.

NATURAL JOINS

A natural join is a particular type of equijoin. Basically, a *natural join* is one in which only one column appears in the query results to represent the two join-compatible columns that were used in the joining condition. Some databases handle this automatically. Take Listing 8.5 for example. In some databases, the director_id field would only be included once in the query results, even though it occurs in both the Movies and the Directors tables. Because the data will be identical in the two columns, one of the columns can be left out of the query results. Listing 8.10 contains a demonstration of a natural join in action.

LISTING 8.10   A NATURAL JOIN

```
SELECT M.studio_id, movie_title,
Studio_name
FROM Movies M, Studios S
WHERE M.studio_id = S.studio_id

STUDIO_ID MOVIE_TITLE              STUDIO_NAME
---------- -------------------      --------------------------
        1 Mineral House            Giant
        1 Codependence Day         Giant
        1 The Rear Windows         Giant
        2 Prince Kong              MPM
        2 The Linux Files          MPM
        2 The Code Warrior         MPM
        3 Bill Durham              Delighted Artists
        3 SQL Strikes Back         Delighted Artists
        3 The Programmer           Delighted Artists
        4 Hard Code                FKG

10 rows selected.
```

In Listing 8.10, I manually selected only one of the two studio ID columns, but in many cases, the database will automatically discard one of the two columns in the query results.

Natural joins work because they involve the primary key in one table and the same values stored as a foreign key in another table. Because the database is aware of this relationship, it expects that data would be joined on those columns.

JOINS BASED ON OTHER CONDITIONS

Data in each table can be compared based on conditions other than equality. You can create "less-than" joins and "greater-than" joins, which utilize compare values split between the tables in the join based on criteria other than equality. These joins still include the basic joining condition that equijoins do, but they also include at least one additional inter-table comparison.

As is the case with most of the concepts in the SQL language, these types of queries are best explained using an example. Here's a query that finds movies that were truly colossal failures; a single cast member was paid more than the gross revenues of the movie. Perhaps the president of the studio is looking for producers she should fire in a budget-cutting move. Listing 8.11 contains the query.

LISTING 8.11   A GREATER-THAN JOIN

```
SELECT M.movie_title, C.person_id,
(M.gross * 1000000), C.payment
FROM Movies M, Cast_Movies C
WHERE M.movie_id = C.movie_id
AND C.payment > (M.gross * 1000000)


MOVIE_TITLE             PERSON_ID (M.GROSS*1000000)     PAYMENT
------------------      ---------- -----------------    ----------
The Rear Windows                1          17500000     18500000
```

Looking at the query, you can see that the requirement for a joining condition is met in the WHERE clause by the comparison that finds the rows in the Movies and Cast_Movies tables, which share the same movie_id. However, you can also see the comparison that discards all the combined rows except for those that contain a cast member who earned more for making the movie than the movie grossed in the theaters. By virtue of this additional expression in the WHERE clause, the query contains a greater-than join. You should also note that because the gross column is enumerated in millions, whereas the payment column contains the actual amount of payment, I had to insert mathematical expressions into the select list and WHERE clause to compare the values in the two columns.

Joins can also be based on inequality. Whereas a standard join condition is always required, the inequality operators (<> or !=) can be used with the join condition to filter the results of a query. Listing 8.12 contains a query that returns a list of people who are in the same state as a studio but not in the same city.

LISTING 8.12   A JOIN THAT USES A CONDITION OF INEQUALITY

```
SELECT person_fname, person_lname, studio_name
FROM People, Studios
WHERE person_state = studio_state
AND person_city <> studio_city
```

PERSON_FNAME	PERSON_LNAME	STUDIO_NAME
Jeff	Price	FKG
Chuck	Peterson	FKG
Brian	Smith	Delighted Artists
Paul	Monk	Delighted Artists
Reece	Randall	Delighted Artists
Carol	Delano	Delighted Artists

6 rows selected.

SELF-JOINS

Another interesting join variant is the *self-join*, which, as strange as it might sound, joins a table with itself. Obviously, the joining condition is very important here. Take a look at this query:

```
SELECT *
FROM Movies, Movies
```

If you're wondering what it would return, simply multiply the number of rows in the Movies table by itself and double the number of columns in the table, and you'll get the idea (because the query would return 100 very wide rows, I've opted not to include the results here). To pare down the list of rows that are returned, the joining condition is critical. It is also important to remove all unnecessary rows from the query results because by default, there will be two copies of each column in the self-joined query.

Tip 32 from
Rafe Colburn

When you use self-joins, you must create aliases for at least one of the tables included in the FROM clause. Because both tables have the same name, without an alias, it is impossible to compare values from one instance of the table to values from the other. Usually, aliases are created for both occurrences of the table being self-joined, for the sake of readability. For example, the query that I used as an example previously would probably be written as follows to clearly demonstrate which columns used in the SELECT list and WHERE clause come from which occurrence of the table:

```
SELECT *
FROM Movies M1, Movies M2
```

Self-joins are used to compare values within a single column to each other. For example, you might want to find out whether any actors live in the same state. The query in Listing 8.13 finds all actors who share the same state, no matter what that state is.

LISTING 8.13   A SEARCH USING A STANDARD WHERE CLAUSE

```
SELECT DISTINCT P1.person_id, P1.person_fname,
P1.person_lname, P1.person_state
FROM People P1, People P2
WHERE P1.person_state = P2.person_state
AND P1.person_id != P2.person_id

PERSON_ID PERSON_FNAME          PERSON_LNAME          PE
--------- -------------------   -------------------   --
        2 Chuck                 Peterson              NC
        1 Jeff                  Price                 NC
        4 Brian                 Smith                 TX
       10 Carol                 Delano                TX
        5 Paul                  Monk                  TX
        6 Reece                 Randall               TX

6 rows selected.
```

There's no way to retrieve these results if you use a standard single-table query with a WHERE clause, although it could be accomplished using a correlated subquery (subqueries are discussed in Chapter 9). There are some interesting things to note regarding this query. First, you should see how it meets the two requirements of every useful join. The join-compatible columns are the two instances of the person_state column and the joining condition is P1.person_state = P2.person_state.

The next thing you should notice is the condition P1.person_id != P2.person_id. This eliminates the problem with every row being selected because each state matches itself. Only rows in which the state matches and the person_id fields do not are considered.

Tip 33 from
Rafe Colburn

Eliminating rows where the primary key matches itself is a standard part of any self-join. When you write queries that use self-joins, the goal is to find two rows within the same table that have a particular relationship to each other. In Listing 8.12, the goal was to find all the states that have more than one person from the People table in them and the names of those people. When a table is self-joined, a row is created that joins each record with itself. Obviously, all the values in each of those records will be the same, and the row will match the equality criteria in the WHERE clause. However, because the row is joined to itself, the results are not relevant to the query and should be discarded by throwing out all rows for which the primary keys in the first and second tables are equal.

Finally, unless the DISTINCT operator is used, if there are more than two people from any state, each person will appear as many times as there are other people from that state. So, because there are four people in the database from Texas, each person from Texas would appear three times in the query results if I didn't use DISTINCT.

The DISTINCT operator is crucial when you're using self-joins. When you're writing non-joining queries, using the DISTINCT operator with a table's primary key doesn't make any sense because each value in that column must be unique. However, when you're using a self-join (or any join for that matter), many rows containing each primary key are produced. Often, you need only one row for each value of the primary key, and the DISTINCT operator is required.

JOINING MORE THAN TWO TABLES

You can join more than two tables at a time simply by adding their names to the list of tables being joined. Unfortunately, creating meaningful joins of more than two tables is not quite so simple.

Just as a join of two tables produces a number of combined rows equal to the number of rows in each of the tables multiplied together, adding an additional table multiplies the previous total by the number of rows in the table that was added. So a join of three tables, each containing only 100 rows, would generate a combined table of one million rows. Needless to say, adding additional tables to your queries can have an adverse effect on the performance of your queries. It takes a lot longer to process one million rows of data than it does to process ten thousand (generally speaking).

The criteria for creating a useful joining query with more than two tables are the same as those for two-table joins; both join-compatible columns and joining criteria are required. Before I go any further, allow me to present you with an example. Listing 8.14 retrieves the title, name of the director, studio, and city where the studio is located for all the movies in the database. By looking at the database schema, you can see that the title and studio for each movie are stored in the Movies table. The name of the director can be retrieved from the People table, and the city where the studio is located can be retrieved from the Studios table.

LISTING 8.14   A QUERY THAT JOINS THREE TABLES

```
SELECT M.movie_title, M.studio_id, P.person_fname,
P.person_lname, S.studio_city
FROM Movies M, People P, Studios S
WHERE M.director_id = P.person_id
AND M.studio_id = S.studio_id

MOVIE_TITLE              STUDIO_ID PERSON_FNAME          PERSON_LNAME
-------------------      --------- --------------------- --------------------
STUDIO_CITY
-------------------
Mineral House                   1 Jeff                  Price
Los Angeles

Codependence Day                1 Jeff                  Price
Los Angeles

The Rear Windows                1 Jeff                  Price
Los Angeles


MOVIE_TITLE              STUDIO_ID PERSON_FNAME          PERSON_LNAME
```

```
------------------- ---------- -------------------- --------------------
STUDIO_CITY
--------------------
The Programmer                 3 Jeff               Price
Austin

The Linux Files                2 Chuck              Peterson
Burbank

The Code Warrior               2 Chuck              Peterson
Burbank


MOVIE_TITLE             STUDIO_ID PERSON_FNAME        PERSON_LNAME
------------------- ---------- -------------------- --------------------
STUDIO_CITY
--------------------
Bill Durham                    3 Becky              Orvis
Austin

SQL Strikes Back               3 Becky              Orvis
Austin

Prince Kong                    2 Carol              Delano
Burbank


MOVIE_TITLE             STUDIO_ID PERSON_FNAME        PERSON_LNAME
------------------- ---------- -------------------- --------------------
STUDIO_CITY
--------------------
Hard Code                      4 Carol              Delano
Apex


10 rows selected.
```

Because there are three tables used in the query, two join-compatible sets of columns and joining comparisons are required to express the relationships of the three tables. In this case, the join-compatible columns are `director_id` in the `Movies` table, `person_id` in the `People` table, and `studio_id` in both the `Studios` and `Movies` tables. One thing you should notice is that not all the join-compatible columns have to maintain join compatibility with each other. By this, I mean that the `studio_id` columns need not be compatible in any way with the join-compatible columns that express the other relationship, the `person_id` and `director_id` columns.

USING JOINING TABLES

As I discussed back in Chapter 2, *joining tables* are used as glue to create many-to-many data relationships. Take, for example, the relationship between cast members and movies. Most actors appear in more than one movie, and all movies have more than one actor. The `Cast_Movies` table was created to indicate what actors have appeared in which movies. It also stores additional information: the role the actor played in the movie and how much he was paid.

Because the constraints inherent in the relational model require that a joining table be used to implement many-to-many relationships, a three-table join is required to reunite data split between the data on each side of the relationship. Listing 8.14 contains a query that returns the cast members and the roles that they played in the movie "The Code Warrior."

LISTING 8.15   RETRIEVING DATA IN A MANY-TO-MANY RELATIONSHIP

```
SELECT P.person_fname, P.person_lname,
CM.role
FROM Movies M, People P, Cast_Movies CM
WHERE M.movie_id = CM.movie_id
AND CM.person_id = P.person_id
AND M.movie_title = 'The Code Warrior'

PERSON_FNA PERSON_LNA ROLE
---------- ---------- -------------------

Jeff       Price      Thomas Black
Brian      Smith      Robert Maxwell
Paul       Monk       Malcolm Richards
Maggie     Davis      Nina Smith
Carol      Delano     Pam Green
```

There are three separate conditions within the WHERE clause of the SELECT statement in Listing 8.14. The first joins the Movies table to the Cast_Movies table, the second joins the People table with the Cast_Movies table, and the third discards cast members from all the movies other than "The Code Warrior." The first two conditions are necessary to link the data from the People table to the data from the Movies table, as there is no way to directly link the data in the two tables.

Contrast this with a joining query used to find the director of a particular movie, such as the one in Listing 8.15.

LISTING 8.16   A STANDARD JOINING QUERY

```
SELECT M.movie_title, P.person_fname, P.person_lname
FROM Movies M, People P
WHERE M.director_id = P.person_id
AND M.movie_title = 'The Code Warrior'

MOVIE_TITLE              PERSON_FNAME          PERSON_LNAME
----------------------   -------------------   -------------------

The Code Warrior         Chuck                 Peterson
```

Because there is only one director per movie, a separate joining table to manage a many-to-many relationship is not needed. The ID of the director appears as a foreign key within the Movies table itself.

OUTER JOINS

All the joining queries discussed thus far return only those rows that satisfy the join condition. *Outer joins* return all the rows that satisfy the join condition, as well as all the other rows from one of the two tables in the table list.

For example, Listing 8.16 contains a query that lists all the people who have directed a movie.

LISTING 8.17   A LISTING OF PEOPLE WHO HAVE DIRECTED A MOVIE

```
SELECT person_fname, person_lname, movie_title
FROM People, Movies
WHERE person_id = director_id
```

PERSON_FNAME	PERSON_LNAME	MOVIE_TITLE
Jeff	Price	Mineral House
Jeff	Price	Codependence Day
Jeff	Price	The Programmer
Jeff	Price	The Rear Windows
Chuck	Peterson	The Code Warrior
Chuck	Peterson	The Linux Files
Becky	Orvis	Bill Durham
Becky	Orvis	SQL Strikes Back
Carol	Delano	Prince Kong
Carol	Delano	Hard Code

By using an outer join, you can include all the people who haven't directed a movie in the query results as well. Listing 8.17 contains such an outer join using the Oracle join syntax.

LISTING 8.18   AN OUTER JOIN

```
SELECT person_fname, person_lname, movie_title
FROM People, Movies
WHERE person_id = director_id(+)
```

PERSON_FNAME	PERSON_LNAME	MOVIE_TITLE
Jeff	Price	Mineral House
Jeff	Price	Codependence Day
Jeff	Price	The Programmer
Jeff	Price	The Rear Windows
Chuck	Peterson	The Code Warrior
Chuck	Peterson	The Linux Files
Brandon	Brooks	
Brian	Smith	
Paul	Monk	
Reece	Randall	
Peter	Jong	

PERSON_FNAME	PERSON_LNAME	MOVIE_TITLE

continues

LISTING 8.18   CONTINUED

```
Maggie          Davis
Becky           Orvis               Bill Durham
Becky           Orvis               SQL Strikes Back
Carol           Delano              Prince Kong
Carol           Delano              Hard Code
```

16 rows selected.

The query in Listing 8.18 creates an outer join using Oracle's notation. If you compare the queries in Listing 8.17 and Listing 8.18, you'll see that the only difference between the two is the (+) behind the name of the director_id field in the second query. This notation indicates to Oracle that it should add a row that contains nulls that matches the person_id in the People table for any rows that do not match a director_id in the Movies table.

This type of query is referred to as a left outer join because all the rows in the table on the left side of the join comparison are included in the query results. The converse is the right outer join, which includes all the rows in the table to the right of the comparison operator.

The implementation of outer join syntax varies wildly among different databases that support SQL. Transact SQL, which is supported by Sybase and Microsoft SQL Server, provides special operators that are used strictly for outer joins. They're listed in Table 8.1. These operators are used in the WHERE clause that specifies the join condition in place of a the = operator that would normally be used in an equijoin.

TABLE 8.1   OPERATORS FOR CREATING OUTER JOINS

Operator	Effect
*=	Include all rows from the first table specified in results
=*	Include all rows from the second table specified in results

UNION JOINS

A UNION isn't a join as you've come to understand them through this chapter. Rather than including multiple tables in the FROM clause of a SELECT statement, UNION enables you to tie multiple queries together in a single result set. The results of a UNION query appear as though they were selected from a single table, when in fact they're selected from multiple tables. The structure of a UNION statement is as follows:

```
SELECT select_list
FROM table [ , table ... ]
[WHERE condition]
UNION [ALL]
SELECT select_list
FROM table [ , table ... ]
 [WHERE condition]
```

There are various vendor-specific rules on the compatibility of the select lists between the two queries used in a UNION. For example, the query in Listing 8.19 will work, but the query in Listing 8.20 will not (at least in an Oracle database).

LISTING 8.19   A VALID UNION QUERY

```
SELECT person_id, person_city, person_state
FROM People
UNION
SELECT studio_id, studio_city, studio_state
FROM Studios

PERSON_ID PERSON_CITY                                       PE
--------- ---------------------------------------------- --
        1 Cary                                             NC
        1 Los Angeles                                      CA
        2 Burbank                                          CA
        2 Cary                                             NC
        3 Austin                                           TX
        3 Buffalo                                          NY
        4 Apex                                             NC
        4 Dallas                                           TX
        5 Houston                                          TX
        6 Bellaire                                         TX
        7 Knoxville                                        TN

PERSON_ID PERSON_CITY                                       PE
--------- ---------------------------------------------- --
        8 New Orleans                                      LA
        9 Madison                                          WI
       10 Houston                                          TX

14 rows selected.
```

LISTING 8.20   AN INVALID UNION QUERY

```
SELECT person_id, person_city
FROM People
UNION
SELECT studio_id, studio_city, studio_state
FROM Studios

SELECT person_id, person_city
*
ERROR at line 1:
ORA-01789: query block has incorrect number of result columns
```

As you can see from the query results in Listing 8.19, all ten rows from the People table and all four rows from the Studios table were included in the query results. The query results are automatically sorted by the columns in the select list from left to right.

Just because two queries are compatible for a UNION doesn't mean that the query results will make sense. Take the query in Listing 8.21 for example.

LISTING 8.21 A NONSENSICAL UNION QUERY

```
SELECT person_id, person_city, person_fname
FROM People
UNION
SELECT studio_id, studio_city, studio_state
FROM Studios
```

```
PERSON_ID PERSON_CITY                               PERSON_FNAME
--------- ---------------------------------------- --------------------
        1 Cary                                     Jeff
        1 Los Angeles                              CA
        2 Burbank                                  CA
        2 Cary                                     Chuck
        3 Austin                                   TX
        3 Buffalo                                  Brandon
        4 Apex                                     NC
        4 Dallas                                   Brian
        5 Houston                                  Paul
        6 Bellaire                                 Reece
        7 Knoxville                                Peter

PERSON_ID PERSON_CITY                               PERSON_FNAME
--------- ---------------------------------------- --------------------
        8 New Orleans                              Maggie
        9 Madison                                  Becky
       10 Houston                                  Carol

14 rows selected.
```

The query worked, but the results don't make a lot of sense. The states from the Studios table are mixed with the first names from the People table. When you're choosing queries to join using the UNION keyword, it's necessary to make sure that the columns mesh properly.

THE ALL OPTION

When you use the UNION operator to combine multiple queries, any duplicate rows are discarded, and the results are automatically sorted based on the columns in the select list from left to right. For example, Listing 8.22 contains the results of a UNION query that selects all the states from the Studios and People tables.

LISTING 8.22 A QUERY THAT DEMONSTRATES PROPERTIES OF THE UNION OPERATOR

```
SELECT person_state
FROM People
UNION
SELECT studio_state
FROM Studios
```

```
PE
--
CA
LA
```

```
NC
NY
TN
TX
WI
```

7 rows selected.

As you can see, only the unique rows are retained in the query results, and the results are sorted based on the contents of the only column in the query results. The ALL operator causes the UNION operator to return every row of the combined queries, not just the unique rows, as demonstrated in Listing 8.23.

LISTING 8.23   RETAINING DUPLICATE ROWS USING THE ALL OPERATOR

```
SELECT person_state
FROM People
UNION ALL
SELECT studio_state
FROM Studios

PE
--
NC
NC
NY
TX
TX
TX
TN
LA
WI
TX
NC

PE
--
CA
CA
NC
TX
CA
```

16 rows selected.

All the rows in the preceding query were retained because the ALL operator was used.

COMBINING UNION AND ORDER BY

There are special rules that govern the use of the ORDER BY clause with queries that use the UNION operator. If there is only one column in the UNION query and the ALL operator is not used, the ORDER BY clause is disallowed because the query results are automatically sorted when the duplicate rows are discarded. If multiple columns are included in the select list, the results are automatically sorted based on the contents of all the columns, from left to right, as shown in Listing 8.24.

LISTING 8.24   AUTOMATIC SORTING IN A UNION QUERY

```
SELECT studio_id, studio_state
FROM Studios
UNION
SELECT person_id, person_state
FROM People

STUDIO_ID ST
---------- --
        1 CA
        1 NC
        2 CA
        2 NC
        3 NY
        3 TX
        4 NC
        4 TX
        5 CA
        5 TX
        6 TX

STUDIO_ID ST
---------- --
        7 TN
        8 LA
        9 WI
       10 TX
       11 NC
```

The query results are first grouped and sorted by the IDs in the studio_id/person_id column, and then each of those groups is sorted based on the values in the state column. The ORDER BY clause can be used to change the precedence of the columns when it comes to sorting, as shown in Listing 8.25.

LISTING 8.25   USING ORDER BY WITH A UNION QUERY

```
SELECT studio_id, studio_state
FROM Studios
UNION
SELECT person_id, person_state
FROM People
ORDER BY studio_state

STUDIO_ID ST
---------- --
        1 CA
        2 CA
        5 CA
```

```
        8 LA
        1 NC
        2 NC
        4 NC
       11 NC
        3 NY
        7 TN
        3 TX

STUDIO_ID ST
---------- --
        4 TX
        5 TX
        6 TX
       10 TX
        9 WI

16 rows selected.
```

The results of the query are sorted by the states and then by the IDs.

INTERSECT

An INTERSECT query is very similar to a UNION query, except that only data that is common to the results of both queries is included in the results. If multiple columns are specified in the select list, the values in all the columns must match for the rows to intersect. Listing 8.25 returns the states that the People and Studios tables have in common.

LISTING 8.26 A QUERY THAT FINDS DATA COMMON TO TWO TABLES USING INTERSECT

```
SELECT person_state
FROM People
INTERSECT
SELECT studio_state
FROM Studios

PE
--
NC
TX
```

North Carolina and Texas appear in the state fields in both of the tables and thus are the only rows returned by the database.

MINUS

A MINUS query returns all the rows that appear in the first query but do not appear in the second query. It does not return any rows from the second query; it simply subtracts the result set of the second query from the first and returns the remaining rows. Take a look at Listings 8.27 and 8.28.

LISTING 8.27   A QUERY THAT USES MINUS TO KEEP ONLY UNIQUE ROWS FROM THE
People TABLE

```
SELECT person_state
FROM People
MINUS
SELECT studio_state
FROM Studios

PE
--
LA
NY
TN
WI
```

LISTING 8.28   ANOTHER MINUS QUERY THAT KEEPS THE UNIQUE ROWS FROM Studios

```
SELECT studio_state
FROM Studios
MINUS
SELECT person_state
FROM People

ST
--
CA
```

Neither North Carolina nor Texas appear in the query results in either Listing 8.27 or
Listing 8.28 because they appear in both of the tables. In Listing 8.27, all the values unique
to the People table are included, and in Listing 8.28, all the values unique to the Studios
table are included.

SQL-92 JOIN SYNTAX

Some databases support the join syntax proposed in the SQL-92 standard. Instead of adding
comparisons to the WHERE clause to express the join, additional code describing the join is
included in the FROM clause. This method of creating joins is more verbose than the method
that I've described throughout this chapter, and some programmers prefer it. In any case, I
would be remiss if I left out this syntax because it is commonly used, particularly with
Microsoft Access.

INNER JOINS

Inner joins are the most common type of joins. They compare values from each of the tables
included in the FROM clause and return the rows that satisfy the conditions established for the
join. The queries in Listings 8.29 and 8.30 both return the same set of results.

LISTING 8.29   A JOINING QUERY THAT USES THE TRADITIONAL SYNTAX

```
SELECT movie_title, person_fname, person_lname
FROM Movies, People
WHERE director_id = person_id
```

movie_title	person_fname	person_lname
Mineral House	Jeff	Price
Prince Kong	Carol	Delano
The Code Warrior	Chuck	Peterson
Bill Durham	Becky	Orvis
Codependence Day	Jeff	Price
The Linux Files	Chuck	Peterson
SQL Strikes Back	Becky	Orvis
The Programmer	Jeff	Price
Hard Code	Carol	Delano
The Rear Windows	Jeff	Price

(10 row(s) affected)

LISTING 8.30   A JOINING QUERY THAT USES SQL-92 SYNTAX

```
SELECT movie_title, person_fname, person_lname
FROM Movies INNER JOIN People
ON director_id = person_id
```

movie_title	person_fname	person_lname
Mineral House	Jeff	Price
Prince Kong	Carol	Delano
The Code Warrior	Chuck	Peterson
Bill Durham	Becky	Orvis
Codependence Day	Jeff	Price
The Linux Files	Chuck	Peterson
SQL Strikes Back	Becky	Orvis
The Programmer	Jeff	Price
Hard Code	Carol	Delano
The Rear Windows	Jeff	Price

(10 row(s) affected)

The comparison that ordinarily appears in the WHERE clause is included in the FROM clause of the query in Listing 8.30, along with the INNER JOIN keywords, which join the Movies and People table. A WHERE clause could be included with the query as well, as shown in Listing 8.31.

LISTING 8.31   A JOINING QUERY THAT USES SQL-92 SYNTAX AND A WHERE CLAUSE

```
SELECT movie_title, person_fname, person_lname
FROM Movies INNER JOIN People
ON director_id = person_id
```

continues

LISTING 8.31   CONTINUED

```
WHERE movie_id = 1

movie_title             person_fname            person_lname
-----------------------  ---------------------   --------------------
Mineral House           Jeff                    Price

(1 row(s) affected)
```

As you can see, both the WHERE clause and the ON clause coexist peacefully. This illustrates the main advantage of using the SQL-92 syntax instead of the traditional join syntax. It separates the conditions that are used to join tables from those that are used to filter the results of the query.

To join more than two tables, INNER JOIN constructs can be nested within one another, as shown in Listing 8.32.

LISTING 8.32   USING INNER JOIN TO JOIN MORE THAN TWO TABLES

```
SELECT person_fname, person_lname, movie_title
FROM Movies INNER JOIN
(Cast_Movies INNER JOIN People
ON Cast_Movies.person_id = People.person_id)
ON Movies.movie_id = Cast_Movies.movie_id

person_fname            person_lname            movie_title
-----------------------  ---------------------   -----------------------
Jeff                    Price                   The Code Warrior
Brian                   Smith                   The Code Warrior
Paul                    Monk                    The Code Warrior
Maggie                  Davis                   The Code Warrior
Carol                   Delano                  The Code Warrior
Chuck                   Peterson                SQL Strikes Back
Brandon                 Brooks                  SQL Strikes Back
Reece                   Randall                 SQL Strikes Back
Peter                   Jong                    SQL Strikes Back
Becky                   Orvis                   SQL Strikes Back
Jeff                    Price                   The Rear Windows

(11 row(s) affected)
```

The nested INNER JOIN constructs enable the programmer to express the many-to-many relationship between movies and their respective casts. Multiple comparisons can also be used in the ON clause to join tables that have compound primary keys with tables that contain foreign keys pointing to them.

OUTER JOINS

There are two operators used to build outer joins with the SQL-92 syntax, LEFT JOIN and RIGHT JOIN. The LEFT JOIN operator includes all the records from the table to the left of the operator; the RIGHT JOIN operator includes all the records to the right of the operator. Take the two queries in Listing 8.33 and 8.34 for example.

LISTING 8.33   THE LEFT JOIN OPERATOR

```
SELECT movie_title, city, state
FROM Movies LEFT JOIN Locations
ON Movies.movie_id = Locations.movie_id
```

movie_title	city	state
Mineral House	Los Angeles	CA
Mineral House	Portland	ME
Prince Kong	Portland	OR
The Code Warrior	(null)	(null)
Bill Durham	(null)	(null)
Codependence Day	Houston	TX
The Linux Files	(null)	(null)
SQL Strikes Back	(null)	(null)
The Programmer	Philadelphia	PA
Hard Code	(null)	(null)
The Rear Windows	(null)	(null)

(11 row(s) affected)

LISTING 8.34   THE RIGHT JOIN OPERATOR

```
SELECT movie_title, person_fname, person_lname
FROM Movies RIGHT JOIN People
ON Movies.director_id = People.person_id
```

movie_title	person_fname	person_lname
Mineral House	Jeff	Price
Codependence Day	Jeff	Price
The Programmer	Jeff	Price
The Rear Windows	Jeff	Price
The Code Warrior	Chuck	Peterson
The Linux Files	Chuck	Peterson
(null)	Brandon	Brooks
(null)	Brian	Smith
(null)	Paul	Monk
(null)	Reece	Randall
(null)	Peter	Jong
(null)	Maggie	Davis
Bill Durham	Becky	Orvis
SQL Strikes Back	Becky	Orvis
Prince Kong	Carol	Delano
Hard Code	Carol	Delano
(null)	Fran	Friend

(17 row(s) affected)

The query in Listing 8.33 returns all the rows in the Movies table, which was listed first. In the second listing, 8.34, all the rows in the second table listed, People, are included. You can also combine the inner join operator with the outer join operators by nesting the outer join within an inner join, as shown in Listing 8.35.

LISTING 8.35   COMBINING INNER AND OUTER JOINS

```
SELECT movie_title, studio_name, city, state
FROM Studios INNER JOIN
(Movies LEFT JOIN Locations
ON Movies.movie_id = Locations.movie_id)
ON Studios.studio_id = Movies.movie_id


movie_title               studio_name           city                state
-----------------------   -------------------   -----------------   -----
Mineral House             Giant                 Los Angeles         CA
Mineral House             Giant                 Portland            ME
Prince Kong               MPM                   Portland            OR
The Code Warrior          Delighted Artists     (null)              (null)
Bill Durham               FKG                   (null)              (null)
Codependence Day          Metaversal Studios    Houston             TX

(6 row(s) affected)
```

Nesting inner joins within outer joins is disallowed, but nesting an outer join within an inner join is perfectly acceptable, as demonstrated in Listing 8.35.

Tip 34 from
Rafe Colburn

When deciding whether to use SQL-92 join syntax or the traditional join syntax demonstrated throughout this chapter, the number one concern is portability. Not all databases support the SQL-92 syntax, so if there is some concern that the data will be moved to another database platform, you should stick to the traditional syntax, which is supported by almost every database.

IN THE REAL WORLD

Now that I've covered joins, it's time to return briefly to the topic of database normalization. Database normalization and joins go hand in hand. As you learned back in Chapter 2, the process of applying normal forms to your data generally involves splitting up tables by taking projections of the data within the table and creating new tables based on those projections.

Joins enable you to view tables that have been normalized in a denormalized manner that might be more convenient. Although normalization enables you to avoid potential traps when you're inserting, updating, and deleting records in a table, it does nothing for the general usefulness to humans of that data. The rules of normalization dictated that I split the data specific to studios into a table separate from the table containing information about movies.

Unfortunately, it might be the case that I never want to view movies without seeing the studio name, city, and state with them. This is where joins come in. You can see a denormalized view of the two tables using the query in Listing 8.36.

LISTING 8.36   A QUERY THAT PRESENTS A DENORMALIZED VIEW OF TWO TABLES

```
SELECT movie_title, studio_name, studio_city, studio_state
FROM Movies, Studios
WHERE Movies.studio_id = Studios.studio_id

movie_title              studio_name            studio_city            studio_state
----------------------   --------------------   --------------------   ------------
Mineral House            Giant                  Los Angeles            CA
Codependence Day         Giant                  Los Angeles            CA
The Rear Windows         Giant                  Los Angeles            CA
Prince Kong              MPM                    Burbank                CA
The Code Warrior         MPM                    Burbank                CA
The Linux Files          MPM                    Burbank                CA
Bill Durham              Delighted Artists      Austin                 TX
SQL Strikes Back         Delighted Artists      Austin                 TX
The Programmer           Delighted Artists      Austin                 TX
Hard Code                FKG                    Apex                   NC

(10 row(s) affected)
```

Without joins, it would be extremely impractical to normalize database designs because it would be impossible to present data from the database in the most useful manner using a single query.

CHAPTER

9

SUBQUERIES

In this chapter

Sometimes, the easiest way to accomplish a particular objective within a SQL query is to use the output of one query within another. These nested queries, referred to as subqueries, can be used within a WHERE clause to help filter data or within an INSERT statement to copy data from one table to another.

Subqueries are used when data that is stored within a particular table needs to be used somewhere within another query, and they are basically an exercise in nesting. Just as you can nest function calls within other function calls, you can nest queries inside other queries. Using subqueries, you can accomplish the same types of things that would require variables in a procedural language. Rather than executing a statement and storing the results in a variable that will be used in a second statement, the first statement is simply nested within the second.

Subqueries are a complex issue for a number of reasons. The first is that there are two fundamentally different types of subqueries. The second is that subqueries can be used within several types of SQL statements, and third, the usage of subqueries differs depending on the type of data that the subquery returns. Before diving into subqueries, I should point out that much of the functionality provided by subqueries can be duplicated using joining queries. Whenever I introduce a new type of subquery in this chapter, I'll explain how the functionality can be duplicated using a join (if possible). If the functionality of a particular subquery can't be duplicated with a join, I'll point that out as well (after all, the most important functionality is the kind that you can't get any other way).

Note

Due to the simplicity of the sample database, the data will not always enable me to necessarily demonstrate subqueries in such a way that the examples make it obvious why using a subquery is superior to another method of retrieving the same data (or the only way to retrieve that data). Nonetheless, I will explain the situations where subqueries are the appropriate technique for retrieving a particular slice of data.

What Is a Subquery?

In the simplest sense, a *subquery* is a SELECT statement that is nested within another SQL statement and provides data used by the statement in which it is nested. When discussing subqueries, I will refer to the outer query, the one in which the subquery is nested, as the *enclosing query*. The subquery is the *nested query*. A query can be both a subquery and an enclosing query, due to the fact that SQL does not place any limitations on the nesting of queries. If a query is a subquery, another query can appear within the WHERE clause of that query as well.

Tip 35 from
Rafe Colburn

Some people refer to the enclosing query as the *outer query* and the nested query as the *inner query*.

Let me start out with an example. Listing 9.1 contains the same example that appeared back in Chapter 6, "Using the WHERE Clause," when I touched on the fact that subqueries are commonly used with IN expressions.

LISTING 9.1   A SUBQUERY WITHIN AN IN EXPRESSION

```
SELECT movie_title, studio_id
FROM Movies
WHERE director_id IN (
    SELECT person_id
    FROM People
    WHERE person_state = 'TX'
)

MOVIE_TITLE                                STUDIO_ID
----------------------------------- ----------
Prince Kong                                        2
Hard Code                                          4
```

PART
II
CH
9

The inner query in Listing 9.1 provides a list of values from the person_id field to the IN expression in the enclosing query. If subqueries did not exist, this query would have taken the form of two separate queries, shown in Listings 9.2 and 9.3.

LISTING 9.2   RETRIEVING A LIST OF PEOPLE FROM TEXAS

```
SELECT person_id
FROM People
WHERE person_state = 'TX'

PERSON_ID
----------
         4
         5
         6
        10
```

LISTING 9.3   RETRIEVING A LIST OF MOVIES WITH A DIRECTOR FROM TEXAS

```
SELECT movie_title, studio_id
FROM Movies
WHERE director_id IN (4, 5, 6, 10)

MOVIE_TITLE               STUDIO_ID
----------------------- ----------
Prince Kong                       2
Hard Code                         4
```

The data returned by the query in Listing 9.2 would have to be plugged into Listing 9.3 if a subquery was not used. As you can see, the nesting capabilities of SQL make it much easier to gather the information that was actually required (the list of movies with directors from Texas) using a single query containing a subquery.

REPLACING A SUBQUERY WITH A JOIN

The query in Listing 9.1 can also be rewritten as a join rather than a query and subquery, as shown in Listing 9.4.

LISTING 9.4   A JOIN THAT DUPLICATES THE FUNCTIONALITY OF A SUBQUERY

```
SELECT movie_title, studio_id
FROM Movies, People
WHERE director_id = person_id
AND person_state = 'TX'

MOVIE_TITLE              STUDIO_ID
------------------------ ----------
Prince Kong                      2
Hard Code                        4
```

The results of the queries in Listing 9.4 and Listing 9.1 are identical. There's no reason why one of these queries is better than the other. They are equivalent from a performance standpoint, and as you can see, the results of the queries are the same. You should use the technique with which you are more comfortable.

TYPES OF SUBQUERIES

There are two types of subqueries, correlated and noncorrelated. A *correlated subquery* requires data returned by the enclosing query before it can be executed. The subquery is then executed using data received from the enclosing query, and the data returned by the subquery is plugged back into the enclosing query for comparison.

A *noncorrelated subquery* is evaluated before the enclosing query, and the data returned by the subquery is used by the enclosing query. Noncorrelated subqueries are the simpler of the two, but they are not necessarily more commonly used.

Subqueries can also be used in INSERT statements to supply rows of VALUES to be inserted into a table. Finally, subqueries can be used within UPDATE and DELETE statements to create complex WHERE conditions when joins aren't enabled.

NONCORRELATED SUBQUERIES

A query that uses a noncorrelated subquery executes the nested query, plugs the value (or values) returned into the enclosing query, and processes the enclosing query. You can spot a noncorrelated subquery because the nested query does not contain any references to the enclosing query. Listing 9.1 contains an example of a noncorrelated subquery, and the general syntax of such a query is as follows:

```
SELECT select_list
FROM table [ , table, ...]
WHERE column_name IN
(SELECT [DISTINCT] column FROM table
[WHERE condition])
```

There are a number of ways noncorrelated subqueries can be written, but the most common probably uses the IN clause.

In Listing 9.1, the subquery selects a list of IDs from the People table, which is then used as the list of values for the IN clause. This query is referred to as a noncorrelated subquery because the subquery is in no way dependent on the enclosing query. The subquery is executed, and the results of the subquery are compared to each row in the table being accessed by the enclosing query. As you'll soon see, a correlated subquery utilizes data selected by the enclosing query and then provides results based partly on that data.

CORRELATED SUBQUERIES

A correlated subquery differs from a noncorrelated subquery in that items from the select list of the enclosing query are used within the WHERE clause of the subquery. It is easiest to explain a correlated subquery with an example.

A correlated subquery will remind you of a join in that the contents of a table in the subquery will be compared to the contents of a table in the enclosing query, much as the contents of two tables are compared when you use a join. The difference is that instead of using a joining condition, a correlated subquery references the contents of the table in the outer query within the WHERE clause of the inner query, as demonstrated in Listing 9.5.

LISTING 9.5   A CORRELATED SUBQUERY

```
SELECT person_fname, person_lname
FROM People P1
WHERE 'Pam Green' IN (
        SELECT role
        FROM Cast_Movies
        WHERE P1.person_id = cast_member_id
)

PERSON_FNAME          PERSON_LNAME
-------------------   -------------------
Carol                 Delano
```

The preceding query processes each row in the People table as follows:

1. The contents of the row are read from the database.
2. The subquery is executed, and the value from the row currently being processed by the enclosing query is used in the WHERE clause of the subquery.
3. The results of the subquery are passed to the WHERE clause.
4. If the WHERE clause is true, the row is added to the result set; if not, the row is ignored.

The query in Listing 9.5 can be duplicated using a join as shown in Listing 9.6.

LISTING 9.6   THE QUERY IN LISTING 9.5 AS A JOIN

```
SELECT person_fname, person_lname
FROM People, Cast_Movies
WHERE cast_member_id = person_id
AND role = 'Pam Green'


PERSON_FNAME          PERSON_LNAME
--------------------  --------------------
Carol                 Delano
```

However, as you will see later, there are certain tasks that can be accomplished using a sub-query that cannot be accomplished in any other way.

SUBQUERIES THAT RETURN A LIST OF VALUES

Subqueries can be used in two different contexts: a context where a single value is required and a context where a list of values is required. When a list of values is required, a subquery can return any number of values (including 0) and still work correctly within the query.

Caution

> A subquery that is used within a WHERE clause must always return values from a single column. Specifying multiple columns in the select list of the subquery will generally produce an error.

Subqueries that return lists can be used with expressions that you've already seen, such as IN and NOT IN, as well as with special keywords, such as EXISTS, ANY, and ALL.

USING SUBQUERIES WITH IN

As I discussed in Chapter 6, an IN expression is used to test whether a value matches one of a set of values. A subquery can be used to provide that set of values. You've already seen several queries that use a subquery within an IN comparison, so I won't belabor the point by including another here.

When using a subquery in an IN clause, it's important to note that the subquery is not required to return multiple values. When you enter the values in an IN clause manually, there's no reason to use IN if you want to compare a column to a single value (or to include no values at all). When you use a query to fill the clause, there's no guarantee that the query will return a particular number of results, so the query will work properly even if the result set is empty, although it will evaluate as false for every row in the database.

The query in Listing 9.7 retrieves a list of people who have both acted in a movie and directed a movie. It compares all the director IDs in the Movies table to a list of all the people who have acted in a movie (from the Cast_Movies table).

LISTING 9.7   A QUERY THAT USES A SUBQUERY IN THE IN CLAUSE

```
SELECT person_fname, person_lname
FROM People
WHERE person_id IN (
        SELECT director_id
    FROM Movies
)
AND person_id IN (
        SELECT DISTINCT cast_member_id
    FROM Cast_Movies
)

PERSON_FNAME          PERSON_LNAME
-------------------   -------------------
Jeff                  Price
Chuck                 Peterson
Becky                 Orvis
Carol                 Delano
```

The inner queries return a list of the unique cast members from the cast_movies table and a list of director IDs from the movies table; each value in the person_id field is compared to that list, and all the matching rows are returned by the query. One thing you might notice about this query is that it uses not one, but two subqueries. As you can see, multiple clauses that use subqueries can be stitched together in a single enclosing query with Boolean operators.

Tip 36 from
Rafe Colburn

As you can see, in Listing 9.7 I used the DISTINCT operator in the second subquery. When you're using a subquery in an IN clause, use of the DISTINCT operator is optional. In some cases, it might be faster to throw away the duplicates from the result set before making a comparison against the list. If you encounter performance problems, you should experiment to determine whether using DISTINCT improves performance.

The same query can be written as a join, as shown in Listing 9.8.

LISTING 9.8   REWRITING LISTING 9.7 AS A JOIN

```
SELECT DISTINCT person_fname, person_lname
FROM Movies, Cast_Movies, People
WHERE person_id = cast_member_id
AND person_id = director_id


PERSON_FNAME          PERSON_LNAME
-------------------   -------------------
Becky                 Orvis
Carol                 Delano
Chuck                 Peterson
Jeff                  Price
```

USING IN WITH CORRELATED SUBQUERIES

The subqueries used with IN clauses can be either correlated or noncorrelated. A correlated subquery is useful if you want to compare data from each row to a value selected using the data from the row currently being evaluated. For example, I'd like to find all the people who directed a movie for Delighted Artists, which has a studio ID of 3. Listing 9.9 demonstrates how this can be accomplished using a correlated subquery.

LISTING 9.9 USING A CORRELATED SUBQUERY WITH IN

```
SELECT person_fname, person_lname
FROM People P1
WHERE 3 IN (
      SELECT studio_id
    FROM Movies
    WHERE director_id = P1.person_id
)

PERSON_FNAME          PERSON_LNAME
-------------------   -------------------
Jeff                  Price
Becky                 Orvis
```

Using a correlated subquery in that situation provides a somewhat convoluted route to the results I was looking for. In Listing 9.10, you'll see that I could have obtained the same results using either a noncorrelated subquery or a join.

LISTING 9.10 DUPLICATING A CORRELATED SUBQUERY WITH A NONCORRELATED SUBQUERY AND A JOIN

```
SELECT person_fname, person_lname
FROM People
WHERE person_id IN (
      SELECT director_id
    FROM Movies
    WHERE studio_id = 3
)

SELECT DISTINCT person_fname, person_lname
FROM People, Movies
WHERE person_id = director_id
AND studio_id = 3

PERSON_FNAME          PERSON_LNAME
-------------------   -------------------
Jeff                  Price
Becky                 Orvis
```

REPLACING A SELF JOIN WITH A SUBQUERY

Back in Chapter 8, "Combining Tables Using Joins," I demonstrated the use of self joins by finding all the people who live in the same state. I've copied the query into Listing 9.11 so that you don't have to flip back.

LISTING 9.11   A SELF JOIN THAT FINDS ALL THE PEOPLE WHO LIVE IN THE SAME STATE

```
SELECT DISTINCT P1.person_fname,
P1.person_lname, P1.person_state
FROM People P1, People P2
WHERE P1.person_state = P2.person_state
AND P1.person_id != P2.person_id

PERSON_FNA PERSON_LNA PE
---------- ---------- --
Fran       Friend     NC
Chuck      Peterson   NC
Jeff       Price      NC
Carol      Delano     TX
Paul       Monk       TX
Reece      Randall    TX
Brian      Smith      TX

7 rows selected.
```

The same results can be obtained through the use of a correlated subquery, as shown in Listing 9.12.

LISTING 9.12   A CORRELATED SUBQUERY THAT DUPLICATES A SELF JOIN

```
SELECT person_fname, person_lname, person_state
FROM People P1
WHERE person_state IN
    (SELECT person_state
    FROM People P2
    WHERE P1.person_state = P2.person_state
AND P1.person_id != P2.person_id)
PERSON_FNAME            PERSON_LNAME            PE
--------------------    --------------------    --
Jeff                    Price                   NC
Chuck                   Peterson                NC
Brian                   Smith                   TX
Paul                    Monk                    TX
Reece                   Randall                 TX
Carol                   Delano                  TX
Fran                    Friend                  NC

7 rows selected.
```

Although the results of the two queries are identical, in this case the correlated subquery might be more readable than the self join. Either method will work; you can use the technique with which you're most comfortable.

SUBQUERIES AND NOT IN

Subqueries can also be used to generate the list of values for a NOT IN clause, which will return true if the value being tested does not match any of the values in the list. For example, to find all the people who have not directed a movie, the query in Listing 9.13 could be used.

LISTING 9.13   A SUBQUERY USED IN A NOT IN CLAUSE

```
SELECT person_fname, person_lname
FROM People
WHERE person_id NOT IN
      (SELECT director_id
       FROM Movies)
```

```
PERSON_FNAME          PERSON_LNAME
--------------------  --------------------
Brandon               Brooks
Brian                 Smith
Paul                  Monk
Reece                 Randall
Peter                 Jong
Maggie                Davis

6 rows selected.
```

The query in Listing 9.13 is a good example of a query that cannot be duplicated exactly using a join. Consider the joining query in Listing 9.14.

LISTING 9.14   A JOIN TO FIND PEOPLE WHO HAVE NOT DIRECTED A MOVIE

```
SELECT DISTINCT person_fname, person_lname
FROM People, Movies
WHERE person_id != director_id
```

```
PERSON_FNAME          PERSON_LNAME
--------------------  --------------------
Becky                 Orvis
Brandon               Brooks
Brian                 Smith
Carol                 Delano
Chuck                 Peterson
```

```
Jeff            Price
Maggie          Davis
Paul            Monk
Peter           Jong
Reece           Randall

10 rows selected.
```

The problem is that there's no way, using a regular join, to compare each of the IDs in the People table to the entire set of director IDs in the Movies table. Because none of the people in the People table match all the director IDs in the Movies table, all of them are returned by the query. (This query would actually return 90 rows for all the person/movie combinations that didn't have the same person_id and director_id had I not used the DISTINCT operator.)

However, NOT IN queries are notoriously slow. Fortunately, an outer join can be used to duplicate the query results of a query that would ordinarily use a subquery within a NOT IN clause. The outer join in Listing 9.15 is an example of how an outer join could be used to duplicate the results shown in Listing 9.13. I will go ahead and include the movie_title field in the query results so that you can get a better idea of how the query works.

LISTING 9.15   DUPLICATING A NOT IN SUBQUERY WITH AN OUTER JOIN

```
SELECT DISTINCT person_fname, person_lname, movie_title
FROM People, Movies
WHERE People.person_id = Movies.director_id(+)
AND Movies.movie_title IS NULL

PERSON_FNAME           PERSON_LNAME           MOVIE_TITLE
------------------     ------------------     -----------------------
Brandon                Brooks
Brian                  Smith
Maggie                 Davis
Paul                   Monk
Peter                  Jong
Reece                  Randall

6 rows selected.
```

The query in Listing 9.15 is an outer join that selects all the names of the directors for all the movies in the movie database, along with all the rest of the rows in the People table. All the people who haven't directed a movie do not appear in a director_id field in the Movies table; thus, their value in the movie_title field is null. By throwing out all the rows with a value in the movie_title field, only the people who have not directed a movie are retained.

Tip 38 from
Rafe Colburn

Under most circumstances, using the subquery in Listing 9.13 would be adequate to solve this problem; you only need resort to the outer join solution when performance becomes an issue.

USING EXISTS

The EXISTS keyword was designed specifically for use with subqueries. The syntax of a statement that uses the EXISTS keyword is as follows:

```
SELECT select_list
FROM table
WHERE EXISTS (subquery)
```

If the subquery returns any values, the EXISTS clause returns true; if not, it returns false.

> **Note**
>
> Static values could be used as the expression passed to the EXISTS clause, as with IN, but then the statement would always return true and wouldn't be very useful.

Although an EXISTS clause can be used with a noncorrelated subquery, there's not much point in doing so. When used with a noncorrelated subquery, if the subquery returns any rows, the EXISTS clause will be true for every row in the query; if it returns no, the EXISTS clause will be false for every row in the query.

On the other hand, EXISTS is very useful when used with a correlated subquery. As you know, when you use a correlated subquery, the subquery itself is run one time for every row in the database, and a value from the row currently being processed is used by the WHERE clause of the subquery. Using an EXISTS clause, you can compare data from each row of the database against data stored in other tables. This enables you to locate all the people who have directed a movie using yet another method. Listing 9.16 lists all the people who have directed a movie, this time using a correlated subquery.

LISTING 9.16   USING A CORRELATED SUBQUERY AND AN EXISTS CLAUSE

```
SELECT person_fname, person_lname
FROM People
WHERE EXISTS
    (SELECT movie_title
     FROM Movies
     WHERE director_id = People.person_id)

PERSON_FNAME          PERSON_LNAME
--------------------  --------------------
Jeff                  Price
Chuck                 Peterson
Becky                 Orvis
Carol                 Delano
```

As you've seen, this type of task can also be accomplished using a noncorrelated subquery or a join; choose the method that seems most readable to you.

Finding Empty Sets Using NOT EXISTS

The NOT EXISTS clause is used to find rows that do not return matches from a correlated subquery. It's used to find rows that do not contain a related piece of data in another table. For example, the query in Listing 9.17 returns any studios from which no movies have been released.

LISTING 9.17   A QUERY THAT USES NOT EXISTS WITH A CORRELATED SUBQUERY

```
SELECT studio_name
FROM Studios S1
WHERE NOT EXISTS
    (SELECT movie_title
    FROM Movies
    WHERE studio_id = S1.studio_id)


STUDIO_NAME
--------------------
Metaversal Studios
```

Notice that this method provides another way to accomplish the tasks that I laid out in Listings 9.14 and 9.15.

Using Comparison Operators with ANY and ALL

The ANY and ALL clauses enable you to use comparison operators to test multiple subquery results for conditions other than equality or inequality. When I discuss subqueries that return a single value, you'll see other methods for using comparison operators, but they choke on queries that return multiple values.

IN and NOT IN enable you to test for the equality or inequality of a value when compared to a list of values returned by a subquery. The ANY and ALL operators provide the same capability with all the other comparison operators. The basic syntax of a query using ANY or ALL is as follows:

```
[SELECT or INSERT or DELETE statement]
WHERE expression comparison_operator (ANY¦ALL)
      (subquery)
```

Using ANY

When the ANY clause is used, a value from the current row is compared to each value in the result set of the subquery using the specified comparison operator; if any of the comparisons are true, the entire comparison is considered to be true. The functionality of an IN clause can be duplicated using a query such as the one in Listing 9.18.

LISTING 9.18   USING ANY TO DUPLICATE THE FUNCTIONALITY OF IN

```
SELECT movie_title, studio_id
FROM Movies
WHERE director_id = ANY
        (SELECT person_id
    FROM People
    WHERE person_state = 'TX')
```

Obviously, using ANY to duplicate the functionality of IN is not particularly useful. The capability to use different comparison operators with an ANY clause is where it gains its utility. For example, if you wanted to find the names of all the actors who had earned more than $100,000 for appearing in a movie, the query in Listing 9.19 could be used.

LISTING 9.19   A SUBQUERY THAT USES AN ANY CLAUSE

```
SELECT person_fname, person_lname
FROM People P1
WHERE 100000 <= ANY
    (SELECT payment
    FROM Cast_Movies
    WHERE P1.person_id = cast_member_id)
```

PERSON_FNAME	PERSON_LNAME
Jeff	Price
Brandon	Brooks
Brian	Smith
Paul	Monk
Reece	Randall
Peter	Jong
Maggie	Davis
Becky	Orvis

8 rows selected.

Any people who were paid more than $100,000 for an appearance in a movie are listed in the query results. This type of query can be duplicated using an EXISTS clause and a correlated subquery as shown in Listing 9.20.

LISTING 9.20   DUPLICATING THE FUNCTIONALITY OF ANY USING EXISTS

```
SELECT person_fname, person_lname
FROM People
WHERE EXISTS
    (SELECT cast_member_id
    FROM Cast_Movies
    WHERE payment >= 100000
    AND person_id = cast_member_id)
```

```
PERSON_FNAME          PERSON_LNAME
--------------------  --------------------
Jeff                  Price
Brandon               Brooks
Brian                 Smith
Paul                  Monk
Reece                 Randall
Peter                 Jong
Maggie                Davis
Becky                 Orvis

8 rows selected.
```

Believe it or not, Listing 9.21 demonstrates how this type of query can also be duplicated using a join.

LISTING 9.21   DUPLICATING THE FUNCTIONALITY OF ANY USING A JOIN

```
SELECT DISTINCT person_fname, person_lname
FROM People, Cast_Movies
WHERE payment > 100000
AND person_id = cast_member_id

PERSON_FNAME          PERSON_LNAME
--------------------  --------------------
Becky                 Orvis
Brandon               Brooks
Brian                 Smith
Jeff                  Price
Maggie                Davis
Paul                  Monk
Peter                 Jong
Reece                 Randall

8 rows selected.
```

USING ALL

ALL clauses are similar to ANY clauses except that after the value is compared to all the items returned by the subquery, if any of the comparisons are false, the entire clause is false. In other words, if there's a comparison based on equality, the value on the left of the comparison must be equal to every item in the result set for the ALL clause to evaluate as true. Listing 9.22 is identical to Listing 9.19 except that ALL is used instead of ANY. It finds all the people who have been paid $100,000 or more for every movie in which they've appeared.

LISTING 9.22   A QUERY THAT USES AN ALL COMPARISON

```
SELECT person_fname, person_lname
FROM People P1
WHERE 100000 >= ALL
    (SELECT payment
    FROM Cast_Movies
```

continues

LISTING 9.22 CONTINUED

```
    WHERE P1.person_id = cast_member_id)

PERSON_FNAME          PERSON_LNAME
--------------------  -------------------
Chuck                 Peterson
Carol                 Delano
Fran                  Friend
```

To duplicate the outcome of an ALL clause, NOT EXISTS must be used instead of EXISTS, and the opposite comparison operator must be used in the WHERE clause of the subquery.

The functionality of an ALL clause can be mimicked using aggregate functions in subqueries, which I will discuss in the next section.

SUBQUERIES THAT RETURN A SINGLE VALUE

Subqueries that return multiple values must be used with clauses that can deal with a list of values. That's why standard comparison operators cannot be used without the ANY or ALL clauses, and most of the subqueries use IN and EXISTS to deal with the results of queries.

On the other hand, subqueries that return a single value can be used with the standard comparison operators. They can also be used as elements within a BETWEEN clause.

Caution

When a WHERE condition expects a single value and you use a subquery to generate that value, the subquery must return exactly one value. There's no leeway, as there is with multivalue subqueries.

In Listing 9.23, I find all the movies that were produced by a studio based in North Carolina using a subquery.

LISTING 9.23 A STATEMENT THAT USES A SUBQUERY THAT RETURNS A SINGLE VALUE

```
SELECT movie_title
FROM Movies
WHERE studio_id =
    (SELECT studio_id
        FROM Studios
        WHERE studio_state = 'NC')

MOVIE_TITLE
-----------------------------------------
Hard Code
```

The reason I wrote this query was to demonstrate a situation where you might not actually want to use a comparison operator and subquery that returns a single value. As you can see, the query works as expected because only one studio is in North Carolina. Listing 9.24 demonstrates what would happen if the state in question were California instead.

LISTING 9.24   A STATEMENT IN WHICH A SINGLE VALUE IS EXPECTED BUT MULTIPLE VALUES ARE RETURNED BY A SUBQUERY

```
SELECT movie_title
FROM Movies
WHERE studio_id =
    (SELECT studio_id
        FROM Studios
        WHERE studio_state = 'CA')

ERROR at line 4:
ORA-01427: single-row subquery returns more than one row
```

I would have been better served by using either an IN clause with a subquery or a join to find the solution to this query. Using the ANY and ALL clauses, you can even use comparison operators with lists of values. Those methods ensure that your query will return the values you expect rather than an error message.

SUBQUERIES AND AGGREGATE FUNCTIONS

A query that uses an aggregate function always returns a single value (as long as you don't use a GROUP BY clause). Thus, by using aggregate functions, you can use standard comparison operators along with subqueries.

For example, the query in Listing 9.25 uses the AVG() aggregate function to find all the movies with a budget above the average budget for all movies.

LISTING 9.25   USING AN AGGREGATE FUNCTION IN A SUBQUERY

```
SELECT movie_title, budget
FROM Movies
WHERE budget >
    (SELECT AVG(budget)
    FROM Movies)

MOVIE_TITLE               BUDGET
------------------------- ----------
The Programmer                50
Hard Code                     77
The Rear Windows              50
```

The inner query returns a value of 26.285. As you can see from the query results, all the movies with a budget greater than 26.285 are returned by the query. This query cannot be duplicated using a join or a subquery that returns multiple values because it requires the average of all the values in the budget column.

The query in Listing 9.25 was a noncorrelated subquery. You can also use correlated subqueries that return a single value. For example, instead of checking each movie to see if its budget is higher than the average for all movies, I can check to see if its budget is higher that the average for the studio that produced it, as shown in Listing 9.26.

LISTING 9.26   A CORRELATED SUBQUERY USING AN AGGREGATE FUNCTION

```
SELECT movie_title, budget
FROM Movies M1
WHERE budget >
    (SELECT AVG(budget)
    FROM Movies M2
        WHERE M1.studio_id = M2.studio_id)

MOVIE_TITLE                   BUDGET
------------------------ ----------
The Linux Files               22.2
The Programmer                  50
The Rear Windows                50
```

The correlated subquery in Listing 9.26 retrieves the average budget for all the movies from the same studio as the movie in the row currently being evaluated by the query. That average is then compared to the budget in the current row. This is the sort of functionality that is only available through a correlated subquery. As you saw in Listing 9.26, the noncorrelated subquery could compare each row to a value that was constant for all the rows; using a correlated subquery, you can generate a value specific to the row being tested (such as the average budget I used) and compare against that.

Any of the aggregate functions can be used within subqueries. The MIN() and MAX() functions are particularly useful. For example, if I wanted to find out whether the studio Giant has released any movies that grossed more than all the movies released by MPM, I could use the query in Listing 9.27.

LISTING 9.27   USING A SUBQUERY WITH THE MAX() FUNCTION

```
SELECT movie_title, budget
FROM Movies
WHERE studio_id = 1
AND budget >
       (SELECT MAX(budget)
       FROM Movies
       WHERE studio_id = 2)

MOVIE_TITLE                   BUDGET
------------------------ ----------
The Rear Windows                50
```

"The Rear Windows," with a budget of $50 million, is the only movie from Giant that cost more than the highest budget movie from MPM to make. As I discussed earlier, aggregate functions can be used to duplicate the functionality of ALL clauses. Listing 9.28 shows how the query in Listing 9.27 could be written using ALL.

LISTING 9.28   USING ALL INSTEAD OF AN AGGREGATE FUNCTION

```
SELECT movie_title, budget
FROM Movies
```

```
WHERE studio_id = 1
AND budget > ALL
        (SELECT budget
        FROM Movies
        WHERE studio_id = 2)


MOVIE_TITLE                    BUDGET
------------------------    ----------
The Rear Windows                   50
```

As you can see, the decision whether to use an aggregate function or ALL is really one of personal preference. If you were using a < or <= comparison, you'd just have to use MIN() instead of MAX().

WRITING COMPLEX QUERIES

I've now discussed all the building blocks that are available for writing queries that retrieve data from a database. Before continuing onward, I'd like to discuss how some of these techniques can be used together to use subqueries to retrieve data using more complex techniques.

NESTING SUBQUERIES

Subqueries provide for infinite nesting. Just as a subquery can be nested within a standard query, a subquery can be nested within another subquery. The only constraint on the level of nesting provided for is performance. As you nest subqueries further and further, the performance of your queries will decrease, just as adding tables to joins will negatively impact performance.

For example, how would you find the studios that have made movies that paid more money to cast members than they grossed in the box office? Listing 9.29 uses a subquery nested within another subquery to solve this problem.

LISTING 9.29   A QUERY THAT USES A SUBQUERY AND NESTED SUBQUERY

```
SELECT studio_name
FROM Studios
WHERE studio_id IN
    (SELECT studio_id
    FROM Movies M1
    WHERE (gross * 1000000) <
        (SELECT SUM(payment)
        FROM Cast_Movies
        WHERE M1.movie_id = movie_id)
    )

STUDIO_NAME
-------------------
Giant
```

Look at the query in Listing 9.29 from the inside out. First, look at the innermost subquery, a correlated subquery that calculates the sum of the payments to all the actors in each movie in the Movies table. That value is then compared to the gross of each movie (multiplied by one million because grosses and budgets are listed in millions of dollars and payments are listed in dollars). The outer subquery returns a list of values to the enclosing query, which contains the studio ID for each movie that paid more to actors than it grossed. That list is evaluated within an IN clause to extract the list of studio names for those studios.

From the example, you can see that it is possible not only to nest one subquery within another but to mix correlated and noncorrelated subqueries in the same statement. Anywhere a value or list of values can be inserted in a WHERE clause, a subquery can be used instead.

COMBINING SUBQUERIES AND JOINS

Perhaps I would like to extract more information from the database than just the name of the studios that have produced movies that had cast payments exceeding their gross receipts, such as the title of the movie and the gross receipts as well. Because that information is distributed among three different tables, I need to use a join to combine it all in a single result set, as shown in Listing 9.30.

LISTING 9.30 A SUBQUERY AND JOIN WITHIN THE SAME STATEMENT

```
SELECT S.studio_name, M.movie_title, (1000000 * M.gross) AS RECEIPTS
FROM Movies M, Studios S
WHERE S.studio_id = M.studio_id
AND (M.gross * 1000000) <
    (SELECT SUM(payment)
    FROM Cast_Movies CM
    WHERE M.movie_id = CM.movie_id)
```

STUDIO_NAME	MOVIE_TITLE	RECEIPTS
Giant	The Rear Windows	17500000

By combining a join and a subquery, I'm able to use the sum of the cast payments for each of the movies in the Movies table, but at the same time, I can extract information from both the Studios table and Movies table to include in the results. I used the table aliases in the column notation in Listing 9.30 to enhance the readability of the query.

What happens if I want to include the cast payments in the query results as well as the other columns included in Listing 9.30? In this case because fields from all three tables involved in the query will have columns included in the results, no subquery is used. Instead, a three table join is required. In Listing 9.31, I use a three table join along with the GROUP BY clause, so that I can use an aggregate function.

LISTING 9.31   A THREE TABLE JOIN WITH A GROUP BY CLAUSE

```
SELECT S.studio_name, M.movie_title,
(1000000 * M.gross) AS RECEIPTS, SUM(CM.payment) AS PAYMENT
FROM Studios S, Movies M, Cast_Movies CM
WHERE S.studio_id = M.studio_id
AND CM.movie_id = M.movie_id
GROUP BY S.studio_name, M.movie_title, M.gross
HAVING (M.gross * 1000000) < SUM(CM.payment)


STUDIO_NAME           MOVIE_TITLE                 RECEIPTS    PAYMENT
-------------------   -----------------------     ---------   ---------
Giant                 The Rear Windows            17500000    18500000
```

Dissect that query. First, look at the columns that are returned by the query. The studio_name and movie_title fields are returned with an expression that multiplies the gross for the movie by one million and renames it RECEIPTS and the sum of the payments for all the cast members for the movie, renamed PAYMENT. The three tables used in the query are listed in the FROM clause. Two joining conditions are listed in the WHERE clause; the Movies and Studios tables are joined based on the studio_id field, and the Movies and Cast_Movies tables are joined based on the movie_id field.

The rest of the query is more interesting. The GROUP BY clause is used because you don't want the sum of the payments for all the movies together; rather, you want the sum of the payments for each movie that meets the criteria. Therefore, the studio name and movie title are included in the GROUP BY clause. The gross is also included in the GROUP BY clause so that I can use it in the HAVING clause. The HAVING clause itself is used to discard any movies for which the sum of the payments paid to cast members is not larger than the movie's gross receipts.

USING A SUBQUERY IN A HAVING CLAUSE

Just as subqueries can be used in the WHERE clause, they can also be used in the HAVING clause. Listing 9.32 contains an example of a query that uses a subquery in a HAVING clause.

LISTING 9.32   A SUBQUERY WITHIN A HAVING CLAUSE

```
SELECT movie_id, SUM(payment)
FROM Cast_Movies CM
GROUP BY movie_id
HAVING SUM(payment) >
    (SELECT gross * 1000000
    FROM movies
    WHERE movie_id = CM.movie_id)


MOVIE_ID SUM(PAYMENT)
---------- ------------
        10     18500000
```

USING SUBQUERIES IN UPDATE AND DELETE STATEMENTS

As you already know, when you write UPDATE and DELETE statements, a WHERE clause is used to specify what rows will be affected. If you need to evaluate data from more than one table in the WHERE clause, you need to use a subquery instead of a join because many databases don't support multiple tables in the UPDATE statement or the DELETE statement.

USING SUBQUERIES WITH DELETE

The DELETE statement has a FROM clause, but unlike the SELECT statement, multiple tables cannot be included in that clause. For example, a normal DELETE statement might look like this:

```
DELETE FROM Movies
WHERE studio_id = 1
```

If you didn't know what the studio ID for the studio Giant was, you might be tempted to use a join to retrieve the studio ID for that studio from the database, as you would do if this were a SELECT statement. Unfortunately, this often won't work in a DELETE statement. Instead, a subquery is required, such as this:

```
DELETE FROM Movies
WHERE studio_id IN
    (SELECT studio_id
    FROM Studios
    WHERE studio_name = 'Giant')
```

Correlated subqueries are also enabled within a DELETE statement, like this:

```
DELETE FROM Movies
WHERE gross <
    (SELECT SUM(payment)
    FROM Cast_Movies
    WHERE Movies.movie_id = movie_id)
```

USING SUBQUERIES WITH UPDATE

The same conditions that necessitate the use of subqueries with DELETE statements also necessitate their use with UPDATE. The structure of a normal UPDATE statement is as follows:

```
UPDATE table_name
SET column = value
[WHERE condition]
```

There are two places where a column name can be used within an UPDATE statement. It can be used within the WHERE clause to specify what rows should be updated, and it can be used within the SET clause to supply new values for columns.

Subqueries that appear within the WHERE clause of an UPDATE statement work in the same way that they do in the WHERE clauses of SELECT and DELETE statements. Here's an example:

```
UPDATE Movies
SET gross = gross * 2
WHERE studio_id IN
    (SELECT studio_id
    FROM Studios
    WHERE studio_state = 'CA')
```

You can also update the values in fields with values obtained via a subquery. This is one of the rare cases where a subquery can retrieve values from more than one column. Rather than using basic column = value pairs in your UPDATE statement, you provide a list of columns and set them equal to a subquery. Here's an example of a query that uses a subquery to determine a single value:

```
UPDATE Movies M1
SET budget =
    (SELECT SUM(payment)
    FROM Cast_Movies
    WHERE M1.movie_id = movie_id)
```

The previous query updates every row in the Movies table by replacing the current budget with the sum of the payments made to all the actors in the movie. Note that it's a correlated subquery. Here's another example, which works in Oracle databases:

```
UPDATE People
SET (person_city, person_state) =
    (SELECT studio_city, studio_state
    FROM Studios
    WHERE studio_name = 'Giant')
WHERE person_id = 1
```

That query replaces the city and state for the person with an ID of 1 with the city and state where the studio Giant is located. Naturally, you can include a subquery in both the SET clause and WHERE clause of an UPDATE statement if you choose to do so. The next listing contains an example of such a query.

LISTING 9.33   A SUBQUERY IN BOTH THE SET AND WHERE CLAUSES OF AN UPDATE STATEMENT

```
UPDATE Cast_Movies
SET payment =
    (SELECT (.5 * AVG(budget)) * 1000000
FROM Movies)
WHERE cast_member_id =
    (SELECT person_id
    FROM People
    WHERE person_fname = 'Jeff'
AND person_lname = 'Price')
AND movie_id =
    (SELECT movie_id
    FROM Movies
    WHERE movie_title = 'The Code Warrior')
```

The previous query contains three subqueries. In the SET clause, the subquery takes the average budget of all the movies, cuts it in half, and returns the dollar amount by multiplying it by one million. The subqueries in the WHERE clause are used to derive the movie ID and person ID from the names, which are known.

USING SUBQUERIES WITH INSERT

As you know, INSERT statements have no WHERE clause, but they can still be used with subqueries. Just as subqueries can be used to provide the values in the SET clause of an UPDATE statement, they can provide the values in an INSERT statement as well.

A subquery can be used to provide some or all of the values in the VALUES clause of an insert statement. The structure of an INSERT statement is as follows:

```
INSERT INTO table
(column_list)
VALUES
(expression or subquery list)
```

Now, take a look at how you might use subqueries within an INSERT statement. First, a subquery can simply provide all the values for an INSERT statement. For example, say that I created a new table called Directors (with the same schema as the People table) and I wanted to populate it with all the people who have directed a movie. I could use the query in Listing 9.34.

LISTING 9.34 AN INSERT STATEMENT WITH A NESTED SUBQUERY

```
INSERT INTO Directors
VALUES
    (SELECT *
    FROM People
    WHERE person_id IN
        (SELECT director_id
        FROM Movies)
    )
```

The subquery uses a nested subquery to obtain a list of all the people who have directed a movie; then, all the rows returned by the subquery are inserted into the table.

Tip 39 from
Rafe Colburn

If you want to copy the contents of a table into another table, this is the easiest method by which to do it. Just create a new table with the same schema as the old one, and use a statement like the following:

```
INSERT INTO New_Table
VALUES
    (SELECT *
    FROM Old_Table)
```

You can substitute a subquery for a column or group of columns in an insert statement as well, as demonstrated in Listing 9.35.

LISTING 9.35   USING A SUBQUERY WITHIN A LARGER LIST OF VALUES

```
INSERT INTO Studios
(studio_id, studio_name, studio_city, studio_state)
VALUES (1, 'New Studio',
    (SELECT person_city, person_state
    FROM People
    WHERE person_id = 1))
```

IN THE REAL WORLD

One decision faced by SQL programmers is whether to use a join or a subquery in a particular situation. Although there are a few situations where only a join or a subquery is suitable, in most situations, the two techniques are completely interchangeable. There are two criteria that must be weighed when you are making such a determination: application performance and maintainability of your code.

If two queries always return the same results, you should decide by measuring the performance of the queries and choosing the one that provides the best results. Database performance is discussed in depth in Chapter 13, "Database Performance and Integrity," but I'd like to talk about it briefly here.

Most databases provide tools that enable you to determine how long particular queries take to execute. These profiling tools enable you to make exact determinations of what queries perform better and thus what techniques you should choose. As your databases grow, indistinguishable differences in performance can magnify, so you should measure the performance of your queries periodically to determine whether the various techniques continue to compare as well as they did when your databases were smaller.

Assuming performance is equivalent, the other factor in determining what technique to use is the readability and maintainability of the code. The main factor here is, of course, personal preference. If queries that use subqueries make more sense to you, you should use them. On the other hand, if you prefer using joins for everything if you can, then that's what you should use.

You should remember that the most important difference between joins and subqueries is that joins can include columns from all the tables in the query in the result set, whereas subqueries can contain only columns from the table (or tables) in the FROM clause of the enclosing query. If you have trouble keeping track of how both joins and subqueries work, you should consider sticking with joins wherever possible because they are applicable in a wider variety of situations.

The rule that I follow personally is to use subqueries whenever I am only going to select rows from one table but need to use data in another table in the WHERE clause, even if I could use a join in that situation. For me, it's more readable to include only tables from which columns will be selected in the FROM clause of a query.

Another consideration you might want to think about is coding standards for a group of programmers. Many organizations have multiple programmers working on the same project, and it is necessary for coding standards to be established so that programmers can read and modify each other's code without breaking things. In these types of situations, it's important to create rules that govern what programming techniques will be used and stick to them.

In some cases, consistency and adherence to established coding standards can override performance considerations or at least move them to the back burner. The rule might be that coding standards should be followed until performance reaches some level that is deemed unacceptable. At that point, optimization for performance is exchanged for readability or standards compliance.

The rules and considerations for programming will vary depending on the type of application that you're working on, the size of the team, and many other factors. My advice, even if you're working on a project alone, is to establish some standards or at least rules of thumb so that you can write your code more quickly and so that you can understand it when you go back to edit it somewhere down the road.

PART III

DATABASE MANAGEMENT

USING VIEWS

In this chapter

In some cases, you might find yourself entering the same database query repeatedly. By using *views*, you can store the criteria that made up a particular query and then revisit that query any time you want without retyping it. In essence, views are virtual tables that treat the output of a select statement as if it were a table unto itself.

In the ANSI SQL standard, views are referred to as viewed tables, and the actual tables upon which they are built are referred to as base tables. Viewed tables, or views, are useful for presenting data in different ways to different users, and in saving common queries so that it's not necessary to recreate them continually. They can also provide a useful layer of abstraction between base tables and the view of the data that the user sees.

The most important thing to understand about views is that they are not snapshots of data returned by a particular query, but rather that they are a copy of the SELECT statement itself. Every time you access a view, the query on which the view is based is run, and the data that is currently in the base tables is returned.

CREATING VIEWS

Using views, you can apply relational operations such as projection, restriction, and join to create pseudotables that contain only the data that is most useful to people querying the database. Consider the SQL statement in Listing 10.1.

LISTING 10.1   A STANDARD SELECT STATEMENT

```
SELECT movie_title, director_id
FROM Movies

MOVIE_TITLE              DIRECTOR_ID
-------------------- ----------
Mineral House                  1
Prince Kong                   10
The Code Warrior               2
Bill Durham                    9
Codependence Day               1
The Linux Files                2
SQL Strikes Back               9
The Programmer                 1
Hard Code                     10
The Rear Windows               1

10 rows selected.
```

The results in Listing 10.1 are a simple projection of the Movies table. If I wanted to preserve that projection for future use, I could create a view instead, as shown in Listing 10.2.

LISTING 10.2   THE CREATE VIEW STATEMENT

```
CREATE VIEW Movie_Director
AS
SELECT movie_title, director_id
```

```
FROM Movies

View created.
```

After the view is created, you can then select data from the view instead of from the table, as demonstrated in Listing 10.3

LISTING 10.3 A QUERY THAT RETRIEVES DATA FROM A VIEW

```
SELECT *
FROM Movie_Director

MOVIE_TITLE          DIRECTOR_ID
-------------------- -----------
Mineral House                  1
Prince Kong                   10
The Code Warrior               2
Bill Durham                    9
Codependence Day               1
The Linux Files                2
SQL Strikes Back               9
The Programmer                 1
Hard Code                     10
The Rear Windows               1

10 rows selected.
```

The most important attribute of views is that they don't store a snapshot of the data returned by a SELECT statement; instead, they create a pseudotable based on the output of the SELECT statement in the view. In other words, if you make changes to the table that underlies the view and then select data from the view, the changes will be reflected, as shown in Listing 10.4

LISTING 10.4 VIEWS REFLECT CHANGES TO THE UNDERLYING TABLES

```
UPDATE Movies
SET movie_title = 'Vegetable House'
WHERE movie_title = 'Mineral House'

1 row updated.

SELECT *
FROM Movie_Director
WHERE movie_title = 'Vegetable House'

MOVIE_TITLE          DIRECTOR_ID
-------------------- -----------
Vegetable House                1
```

The query results in Listing 10.4 reflect the change made to the Movies table. When views are queried, the underlying tables are always referenced so that the current data is retrieved by the query. In some cases, you can also update underlying tables through a view, but I'll discuss this later in the chapter.

PART
III

CH
10

Another important point to take away from Listing 10.4 is that you can include WHERE clauses in SELECT statements that query views. The WHERE clause inside the view is executed first, and the WHERE clause in your query is then applied to the virtual table returned by the view.

ADVANTAGES OF USING VIEWS

In the introduction to this chapter, I glossed over a few advantages provided by views. Although views are certainly optional, there are a number of ways they can make it easier to perform certain tasks. The following sections outline some of the advantages of incorporating views into your databases.

CONVENIENCE

The greatest advantage provided by views is convenience. Views enable you to present your data in the manner that is most comfortable for your users, regardless of the layout of your physical tables. It's much easier for a users to type SELECT * from a view that contains only the columns they regularly use than it is for them to select particular columns from a base table (users can also select particular columns from a view, if they prefer). If users are repeatedly performing the same joins or subqueries, capturing those queries in views can make their lives much easier.

HIDING THE EFFECTS OF NORMALIZATION

As I discussed at length in Chapter 2, "Database Design," for your tables to exhibit integrity when it comes to updates, deletions, and insertions, you must normalize your data. Usually, this involves breaking down large tables into smaller tables based on functional dependency. Unfortunately, once data has been normalized and split into multiple tables, joins are required to reunite the data and view it as the output of a single query.

Using views, you can store these queries so that the information can be accessed without writing the necessary joining query. The view itself contains the joining query, and the queries you write will act on the results of the join. I'm going to discuss views that use joining queries later in the chapter in the section titled "Views that Use Joins," but I'd like to go ahead and provide an example to explain this point. The normalization process ensures that information related to studios stays in the Studios table and that information related to movies stays in the Movies table. However, using a view, you can list studios by name instead of by ID and keep the studio location with the movie information, as shown in Listing 10.5.

LISTING 10.5   A VIEW THAT COMBINES THE Movies AND Studios TABLES

```
CREATE VIEW Movie_With_Studio
AS
SELECT movie_title, budget, gross, studio_name,
studio_city, studio_state
FROM Movies, Studios
WHERE Movies.studio_id = Studios.studio_id
```

```
SELECT movie_title, studio_name
FROM Movie_With_Studio

MOVIE_TITLE          STUDIO_NAME
-------------------- --------------------
Vegetable House      Giant
Prince Kong          MPM
The Code Warrior     MPM
Bill Durham          Delighted Artists
Codependence Day     Giant
The Linux Files      MPM
SQL Strikes Back     Delighted Artists
The Programmer       Delighted Artists
Hard Code            FKG
The Rear Windows     Giant

10 rows selected.
```

RESTRICTING DATA AVAILABLE TO USERS

In some cases, you might want to provide access to some data stored within a table to particular users without making the contents of the entire table available to them. For example, perhaps you don't want certain users to be able to see the budget and gross for movies stored in the database. If they can see the Movies table, they'll have access to that information. By creating a view of the Movies table that leaves out the budget and gross and allowing them access only to that view, you can prevent them from seeing information to which they're not entitled, as is demonstrated by the example in Listing 10.6.

LISTING 10.6 A VIEW THAT PRESENTS ONLY A SUBSECTION OF COLUMNS FROM Movies

```
CREATE VIEW Movies_Minus_Financials
AS
SELECT movie_id, movie_title, studio_id, release_date, director_id
FROM Movies

SELECT *
FROM Movies_Minus_Financials

MOVIE_ID MOVIE_TITLE          STUDIO_ID RELEASE_D DIRECTOR_ID
---------- -------------------- ---------- --------- -----------
         1 Vegetable House              1 01-JAN-75           1
         2 Prince Kong                  2 01-MAY-79          10
         3 The Code Warrior             2 01-SEP-91           2
         4 Bill Durham                  3 15-JUL-88           9
         5 Codependence Day             1 01-JUL-97           1
         6 The Linux Files              2 22-AUG-93           2
         7 SQL Strikes Back             3 01-NOV-98           9
         8 The Programmer               3 17-APR-93           1
         9 Hard Code                    4 18-APR-95          10
        10 The Rear Windows             1 11-JUL-87           1

10 rows selected.
```

Of course, up to this point, I haven't discussed how you would actually specify whether users have access to particular resources such as tables and views. Database access is controlled using the GRANT and REVOKE statements, which I will cover in Chapter 11, "The SQL Security Model."

Creating a Layer of Abstraction

A general principle of system design is that abstraction is a good thing. By inserting a layer of abstraction in a system, you can shield the user accessing the data from the underlying structure of the data itself. Your database engine provides a layer of abstraction between your data, which is stored in a particular data structure on a hard drive, and you. When you execute a SQL statement, the database engine translates it into the instructions necessary to retrieve the data you require. Similarly, you can use views to insert a layer between the user and the base tables upon which your views are built. This has the effect of shielding users from changes to the base tables. When you make a change to the schema of a base table, you can update your views to reflect the change without disrupting the structure of the data that users see. To take advantage of this capability, it's necessary to create your views in such a manner that changes to base tables won't cause changes to the views. One way to make sure that this is the case is to use column aliases, as I'm about to describe.

Creating Column Aliases

If you want, you can create names for the columns in your views within the CREATE statement for the view itself. The list of column names is specified in a comma-separated list in the CREATE statement immediately after the name of the view. Listing 10.7 contains an example.

Listing 10.7 A View that Includes Column Aliases

```
CREATE VIEW Movie_Financials (title, budget, gross)
AS
SELECT movie_title, budget, gross
FROM Movies

View created.

SELECT *
FROM Movie_Financials


TITLE                  BUDGET     GROSS
--------------------   --------   --------
Vegetable House            20        30
Prince Kong              3.25      51.5
The Code Warrior         10.3      17.8
Bill Durham              10.1      15.6
Codependence Day           15        30
The Linux Files          22.2      17.5
SQL Strikes Back            5        10
The Programmer             50      45.3
```

```
Hard Code              77        30
The Rear Windows       50        17.5

10 rows selected.
```

As you can see, the column name for the `movie_title` field has been changed to `title` for the purposes of the view. In this view, creating aliases for the column names doesn't seem to be very useful. The columns already have clear, explanatory names. The alias functionality is really provided for views in which expressions are included in the select list of the embedded query or views where joins are used and columns are specified in the select list using the table.column notation.

Some databases also enable you to use the `AS` keyword within the query to create aliases for columns, but the standard method is to provide a list of column names with the view name in the `CREATE VIEW` statement.

SINGLE-TABLE VIEWS

The view that I created in Listing 10.2 was a single-table view. It was based on a projection of columns from within the `Movies` table alone. Single table views are often used when a table contains many columns and rows, and allowing users to run queries against subsets of the table makes things easier than allowing them to view the entire table. If you find that users are often running queries with the same set of comparisons in the `WHERE` clause or with the same select list, it might be easier to set up a view based on the commonly used `SELECT` statement.

A single table view can also be useful if only particular rows or columns in a table are relevant to a user. Giving them access to a view instead of the entire table can restrict them from seeing information that they should not see or are not interested in seeing.

In creating views, you can use both projection and restriction operations. So, if you wanted to create a view that contained only the names and telephone numbers for people from Texas, you would use a `CREATE VIEW` statement like the one in Listing 10.8.

LISTING 10.8 A VIEW THAT CONTAINS THE NAMES AND PHONE NUMBERS FOR PEOPLE FROM TEXAS

```
CREATE VIEW Texas_Phone_List
AS
SELECT person_fname, person_lname, person_phone
FROM People
WHERE person_state = 'TX'

View created.

SELECT *
FROM Texas_Phone_List
```

continues

LISTING 10.8   CONTINUED

```
PERSON_FNA PERSON_LNA PERSON_PHO
---------- ---------- ----------
Brian      Smith      2185551335
Paul       Monk       7135558193
Reece      Randall    7135550143
Carol      Delano     2818691355
```

VIEWS WITH EXPRESSIONS AND FUNCTIONS

As you already know, you can include function calls and mathematical expressions in the select lists of your queries along with column names. These types of expressions can also be used in views. For example, in the Movies table, I decided to abbreviate the budget and gross columns by listing them in millions. By using a mathematical expression in the select statement that creates the view, I can multiply the gross and budget numbers by one million before they are displayed, as shown in Listing 10.9

LISTING 10.9   A VIEW THAT USES MATHEMATICAL EXPRESSIONS IN THE SELECT LIST

```
CREATE VIEW Movie_Financials
AS
SELECT movie_title, gross * 1000000, budget * 1000000
FROM Movies

ERROR at line 3:
ORA-00998: must name this expression with a column alias
```

If you try to create a view using this statement, you'll find that many databases will return an error because the column names are invalid. If you use mathematical expressions within the SELECT statement of a view, you must include column aliases as well. The reason most databases won't let you create a view like the one in Listing 10.9 is because it leaves you without a way to specify columns when you write queries that access the view.

As I discussed a bit earlier, to get around this problem, you can use column aliases. In Listing 10.10, I demonstrate how the view in Listing 10.9 can be created to take advantage of column aliases.

LISTING 10.10   A VIEW THAT USES MATHEMATICAL EXPRESSIONS AND COLUMN ALIASES

```
CREATE VIEW Movie_Financials  (title, actual_gross, actual_budget)
AS
SELECT movie_title, gross * 1000000, budget * 1000000
FROM Movies

View created.

SELECT title, actual_gross, actual_budget
FROM Movie_Financials
```

```
TITLE                ACTUAL_GROSS ACTUAL_BUDGET
-------------------- ------------ -------------
Vegetable House          30000000      20000000
Prince Kong              51500000       3250000
The Code Warrior         17800000      10300000
Bill Durham              15600000      10100000
Codependence Day         30000000      15000000
The Linux Files          17500000      22200000
SQL Strikes Back         10000000       5000000
The Programmer           45300000      50000000
Hard Code                30000000      77000000
The Rear Windows         17500000      50000000

10 rows selected.
```

As you can see, the columns in the view now have proper names. Using aliases for column names when you use expressions in the select list of a view is especially important if you want to select columns from a view by name. If you wanted to retrieve only the actual gross from the view in Listing 10.9, you would be unable to do so because the column did not have a usable name. On the other hand, the column aliases in the CREATE VIEW statement of Listing 10.10 enable you to create SELECT statements such as the one in Listing 10.11.

PART III

CH

10

LISTING 10.11   A SELECT STATEMENT THAT RETRIEVES A SINGLE COLUMN FROM A VIEW

```
SELECT actual_gross
FROM Movie_Financials
WHERE title = 'The Code Warrior'


ACTUAL_GROSS
------------
    17800000
```

As I stated earlier, you can also use functions within the select list of a view. For example, if I were creating a view for use only in a manner that wasn't case sensitive, I could use the UPPER() function in the select list and create aliases for the columns in the CREATE VIEW statement, as shown in Listing 10.12.

LISTING 10.12   A VIEW THAT USES A FUNCTION CALL IN THE SELECT LIST

```
CREATE VIEW Movies_Upper (title)
AS
SELECT UPPER(movie_title)
FROM Movies

View created.

SELECT title
FROM Movies_Upper
```

continues

LISTING 10.12   CONTINUED

```
TITLE
--------------------
VEGETABLE HOUSE
PRINCE KONG
THE CODE WARRIOR
BILL DURHAM
CODEPENDENCE DAY
THE LINUX FILES
SQL STRIKES BACK
THE PROGRAMMER
HARD CODE
THE REAR WINDOWS

10 rows selected.
```

USING AGGREGATE FUNCTIONS IN VIEWS

You can also create views with SELECT statements that use aggregate functions. Consider the example in Listing 10.13.

LISTING 10.13   A VIEW THAT USES AN AGGREGATE FUNCTION

```
CREATE VIEW Total_Movie_Revenue (total_revenue)AS
SELECT SUM(gross)
FROM Movies

View created.

SELECT *
FROM Total_Movie_Revenue

TOTAL_REVENUE
------------
       213.1
```

As you can see from the query results, that view is probably not particularly useful because it returns a table containing only a single row and column. However, using the GROUP BY clause, you can create views that return larger and more useful sets of results. For example, in Listing 10.14, I created a view that returns the sum and average of the budgets for each studio.

LISTING 10.14   A VIEW THAT USES AGGREGATE FUNCTIONS AND THE GROUP BY CLAUSE

```
CREATE VIEW* Budget_By_Studio (studio, total_budget, avg_budget)
AS
SELECT studio_id, SUM(budget), AVG(budget)
FROM Movies
GROUP BY studio_id

SELECT * FROM Budget_By_Studio
```

```
STUDIO TOTAL_BUDGET AVG_BUDGET
---------- ------------ ----------
         1           85 28.3333333
         2        35.75 11.9166667
         3         65.1       21.7
         4           77         77
```

Just as you should use aliases for the column names in a view when you use mathematical expressions in your select list, you should also use them when you create views with aggregate functions. Even if your database supports the creation of views that don't have "queryable" names, leaving such names in place makes the results difficult to read.

One potential point of confusion surrounding the use of aggregate functions in views is over the HAVING clause. As you know, when you write a SELECT statement that filters the results based on the outcome of an aggregate function, the HAVING clause is used. After aggregate results have been captured within a view, when you write SELECT statements that return rows from that view, the WHERE clause is used to filter the results instead of the HAVING clause. Consider the examples in Listings 10.15 and 10.16.

PART III CH 10

LISTING 10.15   FILTERING AGGREGATE RESULTS USING A HAVING CLAUSE

```
SELECT studio_id, AVG(budget) AS avg_budget
FROM Movies
GROUP BY studio_id
HAVING AVG(budget) > 50
```

```
STUDIO_ID AVG_BUDGET
---------- ----------
         4         77
```

LISTING 10.16   FILTERING AGGREGATE RESULTS ACCESSED THROUGH A VIEW

```
SELECT studio, avg_budget
FROM Budget_By_Studio
WHERE avg_budget > 50
```

```
STUDIO AVG_BUDGET
---------- ----------
         4         77
```

As you can see, the results of the queries in Listing 10.15 and Listing 10.16 are the same. The aggregate query results in the view are treated as though they are a regular table, so the WHERE clause is used when you want to restrict the rows returned by the view.

Interestingly, you can use aggregate functions in queries that return data from views built using aggregate functions. Take, for example, the query in Listing 10.17. It takes the sum of the average budgets for each of the studios in the Movies table.

LISTING 10.17 A QUERY THAT APPLIES AN AGGREGATE FUNCTION TO A VIEW

```
SELECT SUM(avg_budget)
FROM Budget_By_Studio


SUM(AVG_BUDGET)
- - - - - - - - - - - - - - -
          138.95
```

VIEWS THAT USE JOINS

In addition to views that are built using a query that selects data from a single table, you can create views that are made up of parts of joined tables. This enables you to get around the normalization rules that require you to distribute data among multiple tables to avoid integrity problems. For example, as you know, neither one-to-many nor many-to-many relationships can be expressed within a single table if your data is to be normalized to any degree.

Because views are simply representations of data that is actually stored in another manner, you can create views that do not obey the rules of normalization. In Listing 10.18, you can see a view that contains the names of people who live in the same state as where a movie studio is located.

LISTING 10.18 PEOPLE WHO LIVE IN A STATE WHERE A MOVIE STUDIO IS LOCATED

```
CREATE VIEW People_In_Studio_State
AS
SELECT person_fname, person_lname, studio_name, person_state
FROM People, Studios
WHERE person_state = studio_state


View created.

SELECT * FROM People_In_Studio_State

PERSON_FNA PERSON_LNA STUDIO_NAME          PE
- - - - - - - - - - - - - - - - - - - - - - - - - - - - -  - -
Maggie     Davis      Metaversal Studios   LA
Jeff       Price      FKG                  NC
Chuck      Peterson   FKG                  NC
Fran       Friend     FKG                  NC
Brian      Smith      Delighted Artists    TX
Paul       Monk       Delighted Artists    TX
Reece      Randall    Delighted Artists    TX
Carol      Delano     Delighted Artists    TX

 8 rows selected.
```

When you create views using joins, the alias list can be important if there are shared column names among the tables that you are joining. Just as aliases are required when you use functions or expressions in the select list of a view's SELECT statement, they are required when you specify the table name in the select list of a join that is used to create a view. Listing 10.19 contains an example of a view that uses column aliases because table identifiers are used in the select list.

LISTING 10.19   A VIEW THAT USES COLUMN ALIASES AND A JOIN

```
CREATE VIEW Local_Actors (movie, person, state)
AS
SELECT Loc.movie_id, P.person_id, Loc.state
FROM Locations Loc, People P, Cast_Movies CM
WHERE Loc.state = P.person_state
AND Loc.movie_id = CM.movie_id
AND P.person_id = CM.person_id

View created.

SELECT *
FROM Local_Actors

MOVIE      PERSON ST
---------- ---------- --
         3          1 NC
```

The view in Listing 10.19 contains a list of actors who appeared in movies that were filmed in the state where they live. This enables studio executives to see which films used local actors. Column aliases are used to make the columns in the view accessible.

CREATING VIEWS WITH SUBQUERIES

You can also use queries that contain subqueries to create views. These subqueries are used just as they would be in an ordinary SELECT statement. Listing 10.20 is an example of a view that contains a subquery.

LISTING 10.20   A VIEW THAT USES A SUBQUERY IN ITS SELECT STATEMENT

```
CREATE VIEW Movies_From_Big_Budget_Studios
AS
SELECT movie_title, budget, gross
FROM Movies
WHERE studio_id IN
   (SELECT studio_id
   FROM Movies
   GROUP BY studio_id
   HAVING AVG(budget) > 50)

View created.
```

continues

LISTING 10.20   CONTINUED

```
SELECT *
FROM Movies_From_Big_Budget_Studios

MOVIE_TITLE              BUDGET      GROSS
--------------------     ----------  ----------
Hard Code                    77          30
```

The query used to create the view contains a subquery that returns a list of all the studios with an average budget greater than $50 million. The results of that query are passed to the IN clause in the outer query, which is, in turn, used to create the view. These types of views are useful because they can hide the complexity of certain queries from database users who don't know how to program in SQL. It's much easier to point a user to a particular view than it is to explain to them how to write a query which uses an aggregate function within a subquery.

USING OTHER JOIN OPERATIONS IN VIEWS

Join operations such as UNION, MINUS, and INTERSECT can also be used to create views. Indeed, UNION can be especially useful when you want to treat two tables as though they were a single table using a view. For example, assume you want to create a view that contains a list of all the cities and states that are used in the database. In most databases, duplicates generated through a UNION query are thrown out, so the view in Listing 10.21 will provide a list of all the unique city and state combinations that exist within the database.

LISTING 10.21   A VIEW BASED ON A UNION QUERY

```
CREATE VIEW Cities_And_States (city, state)
AS
SELECT studio_city, studio_state
FROM Studios
UNION
SELECT person_city, person_state
FROM People
UNION
SELECT city, state
FROM Locations

View created.

SELECT *
FROM Cities_And_States

CITY                     ST
--------------------     --
Apex                     NC
Austin                   TX
Bellaire                 TX
Buffalo                  NY
Burbank                  CA
```

```
Cary                NC
Dallas              TX
Houston             TX
Knoxville           TN
Los Angeles         CA
Madison             WI

CITY                ST
------------------- --
New Orleans         LA

12 rows selected.
```

As you can see, the query gathers all the cities and states from the three tables and returns the unique values from that set.

NESTING VIEWS

There is no rule that says views cannot be nested. In other words, in addition to building views based on queries of base tables, you can also build views based on queries of other views. Thus, if you created a view that used mathematical expressions, aggregate functions, or some other data-manipulation code for columns in the view, you could create a new view that joined that view with a base table or with another view.

Consider the view Movie_Financials that I created back in Listing 10.10. I can create a view that includes the actual budget for a movie and the payment made to each of the actors in the movie relatively easily, as shown in Listing 10.22.

LISTING 10.22 A VIEW CREATED FROM BASE TABLES AND ANOTHER VIEW

```
CREATE VIEW Movie_Cast (id, title, budget, role, payment)
AS
SELECT Movies.movie_id, Movie_Financials.title,
Movie_Financials.actual_budget, Cast_Movies.role, Cast_Movies.payment
FROM Movies, Movie_Financials, Cast_Movies
WHERE Movies.movie_id = Cast_Movies.movie_id
AND Movies.movie_title = Movie_Financials.title

View created.

SELECT title, budget, role, payment
FROM Movie_Cast

TITLE                   BUDGET ROLE                      PAYMENT
------------------- ---------- --------------------- ----------
The Code Warrior      10300000 Thomas Black                50000
The Code Warrior      10300000 Robert Maxwell             653000
The Code Warrior      10300000 Malcolm Richards           137000
The Code Warrior      10300000 Nina Smith                 822000
The Code Warrior      10300000 Pam Green                   28500
SQL Strikes Back       5000000 George Blake               332100
```

continues

LISTING 10.22   CONTINUED

```
SQL Strikes Back      5000000 Mitch Crane          155000
SQL Strikes Back      5000000 Chris Parker         809000
SQL Strikes Back      5000000 Paul Nero            513200
SQL Strikes Back      5000000 Sheila Slade        1580000
The Rear Windows     50000000 Manfred Powell     18500000

11 rows selected.
```

Calling the `Movie_Financials` view from within the `Movie_Cast` view works as expected; the `actual_budget` column is included in the query results. In this case, using the `Movie_Financials` view saved me from having to recreate the expression that is used to derive the `actual_budget` from the budget listed in the `Movies` table. By nesting the views, I insulate myself from any changes made to the formula used to determine the actual budget. If the budget is no longer stored as the movie's budget in millions of dollars, I can make a change to the `Movie_Financials` view and `Movie_Cast` will still work as expected. This concept is what I was referring to when I talked about using views for abstraction.

UPDATING VIEWS

Up to this point, I've explained how data can be retrieved from a database through views. What I haven't yet explained is how data can be updated through a view. Records can be updated, inserted, and deleted through views, although there are several restrictions on how these commands can be used. Views against which `INSERT`, `DELETE`, and `UPDATE` statements can be used are referred to as *updatable views*.

The long and short of it is that these commands only work with a specific subset of views. Furthermore, any `INSERT`, `DELETE`, or `UPDATE` statements that are applied to a view must meet any conditions enforced by the base tables for the view as well. For example, if a view does not include a column that is defined as `NOT NULL` in the base table, records cannot be inserted using that view.

Tip 40 from
Rafe Colburn

> The rules applying to which views can be updated vary widely among databases. Some databases only disallow statements that modify views for those views that are, logically speaking, non-updatable, whereas others place broader restrictions on the types of views that allow updates. You should always consult the documentation for your database before you assume that an update against a view will work or test the update with dummy data before using it within an application.

The first and most fundamental rule regarding updatability of views is that each row in the view must map to a single row in the base table (or tables) that are used in the view. The following constructs break this rule and prevent a view from being updatable:

- Aggregate functions in the select list
- The `DISTINCT` operator

- Use of GROUP BY and HAVING in the view
- Mathematical expressions in the select list

Under no circumstances should updates to these types of views work because there is no logical manner through which the SQL statement that modifies the view can determine which records in the base table to update. The ANSI standard is a bit stricter about what types of views are updatable, although as you already know, not all databases comply with the ANSI standard. The ANSI rules disallow modification of data in any view that uses one of the following constructs:

- References to multiple tables through subqueries, any type of join, including those that use the FROM close, or operators like UNION
- Function calls, mathematical expressions, and aggregates in the select list
- References to a non-updatable view anywhere in the view
- Use of DISTINCT in the select list

PART

III

CH

10

In any case, after you've determined that the view you have created can be modified, you can issue UPDATE, DELETE, and INSERT statements against the view, just as you can against base tables. First, look at an insert statement that adds a record to a table through a view. The first step is to create an updatable view, as shown in Listing 10.23.

LISTING 10.23   AN UPDATABLE VIEW

```
CREATE VIEW Basic_Movies
AS
SELECT movie_id, movie_title, studio_id, director_id, release_date
FROM Movies

View created.
```

After the view has been created, I can insert a new record into the Movies table through the view, as demonstrated in Listing 10.24.

LISTING 10.24   A STATEMENT THAT INSERTS A RECORD THROUGH A VIEW

```
INSERT INTO Basic_Movies
VALUES
(11, 'Star Wares', 1, 5, '01-JAN-1999')

1 row created.

SELECT *
FROM Basic_Movies
WHERE movie_id = 11

MOVIE_ID MOVIE_TITLE             STUDIO_ID DIRECTOR_ID RELEASE_D
-------- -------------------- ---------- ----------- ---------
      11 Star Wares                    1           5 01-JAN-99
```

As you can see, the new record was inserted into the Movies table, and the data in the new record can be accessed through the view. In Listing 10.25, you'll see that the values in the two columns from Movies that are not included in the view are null.

LISTING 10.25   A LOOK AT A RECORD IN A BASE TABLE THAT WAS INSERTED VIA A VIEW

```
SELECT movie_id, movie_title, gross, budget
FROM Movies
WHERE movie_id = 11


  MOVIE_ID MOVIE_TITLE                    GROSS     BUDGET
---------- -------------------- ---------- ----------
        11 Star Wares
```

Take a look at what happens when I try to update fields in a base table through a view when the view does not include those fields. In Listing 10.26, I'm going to try to update the gross field in Movies through the Basic_Movies view.

LISTING 10.26   UPDATING NONEXISTENT FIELDS IN A VIEW

```
UPDATE Basic_Movies
SET gross = 50
WHERE movie_id = 11

ERROR at line 2:
ORA-00904: invalid column name
```

As you'd expect, you can't update columns that are not explicitly included in the view, even if they are part of a base table that is used in a view. For all intents and purposes, the view is a table itself; it's just that the data in the view is taken from other tables. Listing 10.27 contains a statement that really will update the Basic_Movies view.

LISTING 10.27   AN UPDATE STATEMENT APPLIED TO A VIEW

```
UPDATE Basic_Movies
SET movie_title = 'Stare Wares'
WHERE movie_id = 11

1 row updated.

SELECT *
FROM Basic_Movies
WHERE movie_id = 11

  MOVIE_ID MOVIE_TITLE          STUDIO_ID DIRECTOR_ID RELEASE_D
---------- -------------------- ---------- ----------- ---------
        11 Star Wares                   1           5 01-JAN-99
```

You can also use DELETE statements on updatable views; the rows that are affected will be deleted from the base table (or tables) that are used in the view, as demonstrated in Listing 10.28.

LISTING 10.28   A STATEMENT THAT DELETES A RECORD THROUGH A VIEW

```
DELETE FROM Basic_Movies
WHERE movie_id = 11

1 row deleted.

SELECT *
FROM Basic_Movies
WHERE movie_id = 11

no rows selected

SELECT movie_id, movie_title
FROM Movies
WHERE movie_id = 11

no rows selected
```

TASKS YOU CAN ACCOMPLISH WITH VIEWS

As you've already seen, there are lots of applications of views that can make your life as a database programmer easier by making things more convenient for your users. However, there are also some things that you can do by using views that can't be done in any other way.

As you know, there are no variables in SQL proper. For that matter, there is no method available for stringing statements together in groups; each query stands alone. Subqueries remove some of the need to carry data from one SQL statement to the next; they can be inserted where you would normally insert a variable in standard programming languages. The stored procedure languages that are available for most databases provide conditional statements, variables, and the other pieces found with most procedural languages, but SQL itself does not provide them.

One way you can look at views is as variables of sorts that can be used to provide query results from one statement to another. You can create views that contain results calculated using aggregate functions and mathematical functions and then join those views with other tables as though they were real tables.

Tip 41 from
Rafe Colburn

> If you're using a database that supports Transact-SQL, you can use temporary tables to store the results of queries and use that data in other queries, which would eliminate the need for these specialized views. Similarly, in Oracle PL/SQL, you can create PL/SQL tables to store query results in memory so that you can manipulate them.

Probably the easiest way to explain the application of views in this manner is to use a real-world example that takes advantage of this functionality. I worked on a project that presented magazine articles over the Web based on keywords assigned to the articles by the authors and profiles created by registered users.

THE TABLES IN THE EXAMPLE

First, let me briefly go over the base tables used in the example. For my purposes, there are four base tables that were part of this project. The first table contains the actual article content, including the headline, byline, and body of the article. The statement to create the table is included in Listing 10.29.

LISTING 10.29   THE CREATE STATEMENT FOR THE Articles TABLE

```
CREATE TABLE Articles
(id              INT PRIMARY KEY,
headline   VARCHAR2(255),
byline     VARCHAR2(80),
body             TEXT,
pub_date   DATE)

Table created.
```

The second table contains a list of "keywords" that are used for both the articles and the profiles. This table is used to assign the keywords to particular categories and to store the descriptions of each of the keywords. The schema for this table is outlined in Listing 10.30.

LISTING 10.30   THE CREATE STATEMENT FOR THE Keywords TABLE

```
CREATE TABLE Keywords
(id              INT PRIMARY KEY,
category   VARCHAR2(12),
descript   VARCHAR2(40))

Table created.
```

The remaining two tables map the keywords to users and articles. These tables are both joining tables used to implement many-to-many relationships from Articles to Keywords and from Users to Keywords. The Users table is not discussed here because it is not actually used by the system. The CREATE statements for the two joining tables are provided in Listings 10.31 and 10.32.

LISTING 10.31   THE CREATE STATEMENT FOR Article_Keywords

```
CREATE TABLE Article_Keywords
(article_id     INT,
keyword_id      INT)

Table created.
```

LISTING 10.32 **THE CREATE STATEMENT FOR** User_Keywords

```
CREATE TABLE User_Keywords
(user_id         INT,
keyword_id       INT)

Table created.
```

In the real system, these tables have more fields than the ones listed here, but for purposes of simplicity, I've only included the fields that are relevant to the example.

HOW THE SYSTEM WORKS

Now that you've seen the underlying tables, let me explain how the system works. Whenever a user views a list of articles, the articles are sorted according to the values assigned to them by the weighting system. There are two categories of keywords: For each keyword that matches between the article and user in the first category, two points are assigned, and for each match in the second category, one point is assigned. Furthermore, more points are assigned based on the article's currency. If the article was published less than a week ago, five points are assigned, and articles published between one and two weeks ago are assigned four points.

The goal for this system was to enable the person writing the program that displays the list of articles on a Web page to obtain a weighted list of articles using a single database query. Unfortunately, because the system uses lots of aggregate functions and other mathematical expressions, there's no way to write one SELECT statement that returns a weighted list of articles. One option would be to write queries, read the results into arrays when they are returned, and then plug values from the arrays back into more queries to obtain the necessary results, but obviously this violates the rule of retrieving the list through one query.

So, I created views that contained each part of the weighting formula, then created another view that added them all together, and joined them with the actual data in the Articles table.

THE VIEWS IN THE SYSTEM

Now, take a look at the views used in the system. This system uses four views, three of which are used to store the components of the article weight and the fourth of which is used to combine the total weight for the article with the actual fields that are used to store the article data. First, look at the two views that are used to weight the articles based on keywords. These views are basically identical, except that one tallies the keyword matches for the interest category, and the other tallies the keyword matches for the non-interest category.

The role of each of these views is to join the Article_Keywords and User_Keywords tables on the keyword_id field and to count the number of rows in which the keywords match and are in the appropriate categories. The results are grouped by both the user_id field and the article_id field. Listings 10.33 and 10.34 contain the statements that are used to create the views.

LISTING 10.33 THE `Interest_Weight` VIEW

```
CREATE VIEW Interest_Weight (user_id, article_id, weight)
AS
SELECT user_id, article_id, COUNT(Article_Keywords.keyword_id)
FROM User_Keywords, Article_Keywords
WHERE Article_Keywords.keyword_id = User_Keywords.keyword_id
AND Article_Keywords.keyword_id IN
    (SELECT id
FROM Keywords
WHERE category = 'interest')
GROUP BY user_id, article_id

View created.

SELECT *
FROM Interest_Weight


   USER_ID ARTICLE_ID    WEIGHT
---------- ---------- ----------
         1          1          1
         1          2          2
         1          3          3
         2          2          1
         2          3          2
```

LISTING 10.34 THE `Non_Interest_Weight` VIEW

```
CREATE VIEW Non_Interest_Weight (user_id, article_id, weight)
AS
SELECT user_id, article_id, COUNT(Article_Keywords.keyword_id)
FROM User_Keywords, Article_Keywords
WHERE Article_Keywords.keyword_id = User_Keywords.keyword_id
AND Article_Keywords.keyword_id IN
    (SELECT id
FROM Keywords
WHERE category = 'non-interest')
GROUP BY user_id, article_id

View created.

SELECT *
FROM Non_Interest_Weight

USER_ID ARTICLE_ID    WEIGHT
---------- ---------- ----------
       1          1          2
       1          2          1
       2          1          1
       2          2          1
```

If these views were real tables, the combination of the user_id and article_id fields would serve as the primary key for the table. These views contain the respective weight for each article and user combination in the database. When a user requests a list of articles, the rows that are associated with their user ID are retrieved from these views to determine which articles they might be interested in.

The other view that must be created contains the weights for each article based on how recently the article was published. This view uses the UNION operator to join multiple queries that select articles based on the value in the pub_date field. In this case, UNION is used as an if construct. Basically, I want to assign a particular value to each article based on when it was published. To assign values that vary depending on the contents of the pub_date field, multiple queries must be strung together using the UNION operator. If the UNION operator were not used, I would have to write individual queries for each range of dates required by the weighting system, and it would be impossible to capture this information in a view. In any case, Listing 10.35 contains the statement that creates this view.

LISTING 10.35 THE Time_Weight VIEW

```
CREATE VIEW Time_Weight (article_id, weight)
AS
SELECT id, 5
FROM Articles
WHERE pub_date BETWEEN (SYSDATE - 2) AND SYSDATE
UNION
SELECT id, 3
FROM Articles
WHERE pub_date BETWEEN (SYSDATE - 7) AND (SYSDATE - 2)
UNION
SELECT id, 0
FROM Articles
WHERE pub_date < (SYSDATE - 7)

View created.

SELECT *
FROM Time_Weight


ARTICLE_ID      WEIGHT
----------   ----------
         1            3
         2            5
         3            0
```

The expressions in the BETWEEN clauses in the view simply subtract days from the current date, so SYSDATE - 2 means "two days ago," and SYSDATE - 7 means "seven days ago." Basically, what this means is that stories that were published within the past two days are assigned a weight of five, and stories published between two and seven days ago are assigned a weight of three. Stories older than that are assigned a weight of zero.

After the Time_Weight view has been created, I can create the view that contains the total weight for each of the articles. This view combines the weights generated in the other three views to create a total weight for each article. The weight calculation formula is captured in a single expression in the select list of the query, and like the first two views I created, this one is keyed on the combination of the `article_id` and the `user_id` fields. The view is implemented by joining the three views I've already created; the statement that creates the view is in Listing 10.36.

LISTING 10.36 THE `Article_Weight` VIEW CONTAINS THE AGGREGATE WEIGHT FOR EACH USER AND ARTICLE COMBINATION

```
CREATE VIEW Article_Weight (article_id, user_id, weight)
AS
SELECT IW.article_id, IW.user_id,
(IW.weight * 2) + NIW.weight + TW.weight
FROM Time_Weight TW, Interest_Weight IW, Non_Interest_Weight NIW
WHERE IW.user_id = NIW.user_id
AND IW.article_id = NIW.article_id
AND IW.article_id = TW.article_id

View created.

SELECT user_id, article_id, weight
FROM Article_Weight
ORDER BY user_id, article_id

USER_ID ARTICLE_ID    WEIGHT
---------- ---------- ----------
         1          1          7
         1          2         10
         2          2          8
```

As you can see, in the view the three weighting tables are joined, and the weights are added up to calculate the total weight for each article for all the registered users. Thus, the view contains a row for each user and article combination for which there is a keyword match. Any article and user pairings that do not have any keywords that match are considered to have a weight of zero and are not listed in the `Article_Weight` view.

THE ARTICLE RETRIEVAL QUERY

After that view has been created, all that's left to do is to write the query that retrieves the actual articles from the database. This query will join the `Article_Weight` table with the `Articles` table and return only the rows that pertain to the user who is currently retrieving the articles. An example of a query that is used to retrieve these articles is shown in Listing 10.37.

LISTING 10.37 A QUERY THAT RETRIEVES WEIGHTED ARTICLES

```
SELECT weight, id, headline
FROM Article_Weight, Articles
WHERE id = article_id
AND user_id = 1
ORDER BY weight DESC
```

```
WEIGHT          ID HEADLINE
----------  ----------  -------------------------------------------
      10           2 Linux Overtakes Windows in Market Share
       7           1 Y2K Problem Causes Headaches
```

The number 1 is just an example of a potential value of user_id. This query will return only the articles for which there is a keyword match between the article and the current user in both categories (interest and non-interest).

IN THE REAL WORLD

When you create the physical design of your database, the way the data will be used is important, but the real relationships between the data are even more important. You must make sure that your data is normalized and that both integrity and performance are acceptable. Unfortunately, this leaves you in a position where the data might not be organized for presentation to users. This problem grows when you have users of different types accessing the same database.

Consider the movies database. It contains all sorts of information, some of which might not be of interest to all the different types of users who will be accessing the database. For example, the typical users of the movies database are people in the accounting department, studio executives, and people who work in casting. Each of them have different needs when it comes to querying the database. I'm going to explain how one might create views that make it easy for users to get the information they need from the database without writing lots of complex queries themselves.

First, look at the executives. In this case, high-level views of the data will be most useful to them, so for their use, I'd create breakdowns of the financial numbers for each studio, as shown in Listing 10.38.

LISTING 10.38 A VIEW THAT CONTAINS HIGH LEVEL FINANCIAL DATA FOR EXECUTIVES

```
CREATE VIEW Executive_Studio_Breakdown
(name, avg_budget, avg_gross, avg_profit,
total_budget, total_gross, total_profit)
AS
SELECT Studios.studio_name, AVG(budget), AVG(gross), AVG(gross - budget),
SUM(budget), SUM(gross), SUM(gross - budget)
FROM Studios, Movies
WHERE Studios.studio_id = Movies.studio_id
GROUP BY Studios.studio_name
```

Accounting users are interested in financial data, but at a more granular level than the executives. For example, the accountants might want to see how the budget for each movie compares to the amount of money spent to hire the cast of the movie and the average cost for cast members in a movie. I can capture that information in a single view, as shown in Listing 10.39.

LISTING 10.39 A VIEW FOR ACCOUNTANTS THAT ANALYZES THE MONEY SPENT ON A MOVIE CAST

```
CREATE VIEW Movie_Cast_Cost
(movie_id, budget, total_cast_payment, avg_cast_payment, num_cast)
AS
SELECT Cast_Movies.movie_id,
Movies.budget,
SUM(Cast_Movies.payment),
AVG(Cast_Movies.payment),
COUNT(Cast_Movies.payment)
FROM Cast_Movies, Movies
WHERE Cast_Movies.movie_id = Movies.movie_id
GROUP BY Cast_Movies.movie_id, Movies.budget
```

The view `Movie_Cast_Cost` retrieves each movie with cast members from the database and lists the budget for the movie, the total amount paid to cast members, the average amount paid to cast members, and the number of paid cast members in the movie. This enables the accountants to track the amount paid to cast members for each movie.

Finally, look at a report that might interest people who work in casting. In this case, they're just interested in a list of cast members and roles for each movie in the database. This view makes it easy to see which people have appeared in which movies, how much they were paid, and what roles they played. The view for people who work in casting appears in Listing 10.40.

LISTING 10.40 A VIEW CONTAINING CAST INFORMATION

```
CREATE VIEW Movie_Cast_Info
AS
SELECT Movies.movie_title, People.person_fname,
People.person_lname, Cast_Movies.role, Cast_Movies.payment
FROM Movies, People, Cast_Movies
WHERE Movies.movie_id = Cast_Movies.movie_id
AND People.person_id = Cast_Movies.movie_id
```

These are just some examples of views that might be useful to various types of users who have access to a database. Encapsulating these complex queries in views makes things a lot easier for individual users who might be interested in accessing a database.

CHAPTER **11**

THE SQL SECURITY MODEL

In this chapter

SQL uses a layered security model that provides database administrators with fine-grained control of access to database resources. The SQL security model is made up of *privileges*, *users*, and *resources*. Basically, users are given the privilege to perform a variety of operations on resources. For example, you can give a user the right to select data from a table, but not to issue UPDATE, DELETE, or INSERT statements against that table.

There are two statements that are used to control database access, GRANT and REVOKE. Unsurprisingly, the GRANT statement is used to grant privileges to users, and the REVOKE statement is used to remove privileges from users. Before I discuss the assignment of privileges, however, I'd like to discuss users and how to create them.

AN OVERVIEW OF DATABASE SECURITY

In any type of multiuser environment, information security is very important. Whenever sensitive data can potentially be accessed by people who are not part of its intended audience, steps must be taken to ensure that the data will only be seen by the people who should have the right to see it. Most businesses wouldn't leave their confidential financial reports in plain view when they leave at night. By the same token, it is important to secure your confidential information when it is stored electronically.

Consider, for a moment, file permissions. Most operating systems give users the right to control access to files so that other users can't see or change the original copies unless the owner of the files explicitly allows them to do so. By the same token, access to objects within a relational database can generally be controlled so that only certain users have the right to view or change information in the database. Generally, access to database objects is managed by assigning IDs to database users and restricting their access based on their IDs.

Database products vary widely in how they implement their user models. Many databases have their own user management systems built in. Users are created explicitly for use within the database and have nothing to do with the underlying operating system on which the database resides. Most of the popular databases, including Oracle, Sybase, and Microsoft SQL Server, use this approach to user management. Databases also often share user information with the operating system itself.

In any case, you should be sure to manage the security of your databases carefully so that unauthorized users do not have access to private information.

THE DATABASE ADMINISTRATOR ACCOUNT

There is one account that is created when you create your database, the database administrator account. If you are using a single-user database application, this is really the only account that exists. Basically, the database administrator, or DBA, has the authority to perform any operation she wants on the database that she administers. The DBA account can be used to create databases and users or even to specify that other users have DBA privileges in the database.

The DBA is the ultimate owner of all the objects in the database. No matter who owns them, the DBA can go in and add, change, or remove records, or even full tables, at a whim. The DBA account is extremely powerful. Because the user logged in with the DBA account has the power to do whatever he wishes in the database, you should only use it when it is necessary.

It is safer to create individual user accounts for most tasks and only use the DBA account when it is specifically required for an administrative task. Most databases break up the privileges possessed by the DBA account and enable you to assign them to users individually. You can assign these privileges to users and allow them to perform the DBA tasks as required. This helps to prevent destructive mistakes, which are easier to make when the user has the authority to alter or remove any part of the database.

Even if you do need to use the DBA account, if more than one person requires administrative privileges, you can create accounts for them that have DBA privileges; that way, that they each log in under a unique ID, and you can track their activities through the database logs.

DATABASE OWNERS

A bit later in this chapter, I am going to explain the hierarchy of objects within a typical relational database. At the top of the hierarchy is the master database, which is owned by the DBA account. Below that are individual databases that can be owned by other users. The database owner (DBO) has special rights to the database that she owns. Some of these rights can be granted to other users.

PART

III

CH

11

For example, when a database is created, only the owner of the database has the right to create and drop objects within the database. The database owner can grant these rights to other users if the DBO chooses to do so, or the DBO can retain exclusive rights to create and drop these objects.

CREATING DATABASE USERS

The user model of databases can vary significantly from product to product. Some databases provide very robust user models, including roles-based privilege assignment. Others provide only the barest implementation of multiuser capabilities or do not provide any multiuser capabilities at all.

This chapter covers databases that implement the standard SQL security model. Some databases enable administrators to add and delete accounts through a graphical interface rather than through SQL statements. Unfortunately, these types of administrative interfaces are specific to the products for which they were designed. Your database must provide for users to be created and modified using SQL statements to take advantage of the information in this chapter.

Users are created with the CREATE USER statement. Creating a user is as simple as entering CREATE USER and the username to be created, as follows:

```
CREATE USER some_user
```

```
User created.
```

Usually, users are assigned passwords to prevent people from logging in and modifying their databases freely, and some databases require that passwords be assigned when users are created. The method for assigning passwords to users varies from database to database. When you create a user in Oracle, a password can be specified using the keywords IDENTIFY BY:

```
CREATE USER some_user IDENTIFY BY password
```

```
User created.
```

You should take a look at the documentation for your database before you create users or investigate any of the security-related features to make sure that you're using the appropriate syntax. Most databases offer a number of other options that can be set when a user is created. For example, in some cases you can specify what database items that the user creates will be stored in. Certain databases enable you to set quotas for the amount of space the user can consume. Again, you should refer to the documentation for your database product to find out more about these options.

Tip 42 from	In Oracle, to switch to a new user, you can use the CONNECT statement. The CONNECT statement ends your current session and creates a new session as the user that you log in as. For example, if you are logged in as system and you create the new account somebody, you can switch to that account using the following command:
Rafe Colburn	`CONNECT somebody`

Modifying Users

 is the case with most database elements that can be created using a CREATE statement, users can also be modified using an ALTER statement. The ALTER USER statement enables you to change the user attributes that can be set initially within the CREATE USER statement. For example, you can change a user's password in Oracle using the ALTER USER statement like this:

```
ALTER USER some_user IDENTIFY BY newpassword
```

```
User altered.
```

Removing Users

Users can be removed using the DROP USER command. Generally, only users with DBA privileges are allowed to drop users. (Other users can have the capability to drop users if that right is granted to them by the DBA.) To remove a user from a database, the following SQL statement is used:

```
DROP USER user
```

DATABASE ELEMENTS

For the purpose of database security, there is a hierarchy of elements for which settings can be adjusted. They range from the database at the top level to a column at the lowest level. It perhaps makes the most sense to think of these elements as a group of concentric circles, as shown in Figure 11.1.

Figure 11.1
Elements in the SQL
Security model.

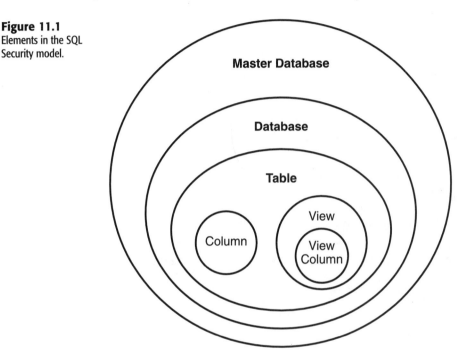

Let me explain each element in the figure, from the outside to the inside. In most cases, the element that encompasses all the other elements is the master database. The master database is owned by the system manager account (often called sa or system) and holds all the information related to the database within it, including the tables that contain the information about the users themselves and the definitions of the other tables and elements stored in the database.

DATABASES

Below the master database are the other individual databases. Each user is often assigned his own database, or a database is created for a particular application or project. When you're programming, chances are that you'll be storing your data in one of these subdatabases below the master database. For example, the movie-related sample tables that I've used throughout this book would probably all be stored in a database called `moviedb` or something similar. These subdatabases all run within the context of the master database's instance. They are not distinct processes, and usually, they all use the storage allocated to the master database. They simply provide distinct ownership settings and name spaces to the user. For example, I could create two databases, `development` and `moviedb`, and include the same tables within both of them without ever running into problems with name collisions.

Generally speaking, you can select which database you want to issue queries against with the `use` command. For example, if I were querying the `development` database and I wanted to run some queries against `moviedb`, I could just enter the following SQL command:

```
use moviedb
```

From that point forward, until I issue another `use` command, all my queries are applied to that database.

You can also specify a table from another database from within a query using the same dot notation that is used to indicate from which table a particular column is taken. You can specify this additional detail at any point, but it is only required when you want to query a table from a database other than the one currently being used. For example, if, after typing `use moviedb`, I wanted to select a list of movies in the `Movies` table in the `development` database, I could use the query in listing 11.1 to retrieve it without switching back to `development`.

LISTING 11.1 A QUERY THAT RETRIEVES DATA FROM A DATABASE OTHER THAN THE ONE CURRENTLY BEING USED

```
SELECT studio_name
FROM development.Studios

STUDIO_NAME
-------------------
Giant
MPM
FKG
Delighted Artists
Metaversal Studios
```

You can also mix calls to multiple databases within a single query. You can place tables in different databases within the FROM clause to join them, or you can reference a table in one database in a subquery and reference a table in the current database in the outer query. The only rules that affect the joining of multiple tables in such a manner are those imposed using GRANT and REVOKE statements. As an example of a query that uses tables in multiple databases, Listing 11.2 contains a query that compares the `Movies` tables in the `moviedb` and `development` databases.

LISTING 11.2   A QUERY THAT RETRIEVES DATA FROM MULTIPLE DATABASES

```
SELECT moviedb.Movies.movie_id, development.Movies.movie_title
FROM development.Movies, moviedb.Movies
WHERE development.Movies.movie_id = moviedb.Movies.movie_id

MOVIE_ID MOVIE_TITLE
---------- --------------------
         1 Vegetable House
         2 Prince Kong
         3 The Code Warrior
         4 Bill Durham
         5 Codependence Day
         6 The Linux Files
         7 SQL Strikes Back
         8 The Programmer
         9 Hard Code
        10 The Rear Windows
        16 SQL Planet

  MOVIE_ID MOVIE_TITLE
---------- --------------------
        17 The Maltese Tuple
12 rows selected.
```

TABLES

The next level down in the security model contains database tables. As you already saw, each table exists within a specific database, and tables with the same name in more than one database do not necessarily have anything in common. For example, a table called People in a database called magazines might not have anything at all in common with the People table in the moviedb database.

Generally speaking, tables are owned by the user who creates them, and the user can control the security settings for those tables. Security settings can also be specified for columns in tables and views based on tables, providing fine-grained access to data within the database. However, tables are probably the most common level at which security settings are modified. I'll discuss them further when I begin to discuss the actual security privileges that can be manipulated.

VIEWS

By using views and the access control capabilities built in to most databases, you can restrict users' access to exactly the data you want them to see. For example, say you want to let a certain group of users see people from Texas, but not from any other states. You could create a view like the one in Listing 11.3.

LISTING 11.3   A SIMPLE EXAMPLE OF A VIEW

```
CREATE VIEW People_From_Texas
AS
SELECT *
FROM People
WHERE person_state = 'TX'
```

Then, you could restrict those users' access to the People table and grant them access to the People_From_Texas view. You can also restrict access to columns in a similar manner. You might want to allow certain people to view everything but the financial information about movies, so you could create a view like this:

```
CREATE VIEW Movie_Info
AS
SELECT movie_id, movie_title, director_id, studio_id
FROM Movies
```

Then, you could allow the users to access the view instead of the base table Movies. It is through uses like these that views are a powerful means by which you can manage access to a particular set of data.

COLUMNS AND VIEW COLUMNS

As you've already seen, you can manage the capability of users to access certain data within a table by creating views that contain a subset of the data in the table, and by then providing access to the view instead of the base table. You can grant the update privilege to users, which enables them to make changes to all the columns in the view or table. However, in some cases, you might want to restrict changes to a subset of the columns within a particular view or table. For example, if you are using a view to provide restricted access to a table, it will probably include the primary key for the table. You might not want to let users actually change the values in that column. SQL provides the capability to restrict updates by column, as well as by table or view, so that you can allow users to only update values in certain columns.

USING GRANT AND REVOKE

Now that I've explained the types of objects that you can restrict access to, I'm going to explain how the GRANT and REVOKE statements can be used to set or remove specific privileges for resources. The basic syntax of a GRANT statement is this:

GRANT *privilege* ON *object* TO *user*

Similarly, the syntax for REVOKE is as follows:

REVOKE *privilege* ON *object* FROM *user*

There is a specific set of privileges that can be applied to resources within a database. These privileges vary among database products, but the same basic themes hold true from product to product. Table 11.1 contains the security privileges for tables, views, and columns that are available in Oracle 8.

TABLE 11.1   ORACLE SECURITY PRIVILEGES

Statements	Privileges
Tables Only	
ALTER	User can issue ALTER statements against the table.
REFERENCES	User can create foreign key relationships that reference columns within this table.
INDEX	User can create indexes on columns within this table.
ALL	Users can perform all three preceding functions.
Tables and Views	
SELECT	User can issue SELECT statements against table.
INSERT	User can insert records into table.
UPDATE	User can modify records in table.
DELETE	User can delete records in table.

So, to provide an example of how the GRANT statement might be used, if the user development owns the entire movie database and another user named patricia exists, development can allow patricia to retrieve records from the Movies table as follows:

```
GRANT SELECT ON Movies TO patricia
```

Assuming patricia had no access to the table before, she can now write SELECT statements that retrieve rows from Movies. If the database administrator changes his mind, he can revoke Patricia's access to the Movies table using the following REVOKE statement:

```
REVOKE SELECT ON Movies FROM patricia
```

You can also revoke or grant all the permissions relevant to a particular object simultaneously using the ALL keyword. For example, if the database administrator wanted to provide Patricia with full access to the Movies table, he could use the following statement:

```
GRANT ALL ON Movies TO patricia
```

Then, if he wanted to remove those privileges, he could just as easily revoke them all at once:

```
REVOKE ALL ON Movies FROM patricia
```

You can also specify lists of objects in GRANT and REVOKE statements to make multiple adjustments at one time. For example, say there's another user with the login karen that Rafe wants to prevent from accessing all the data in the database. He could make changes to both Patricia and Karen's access to the database at the same time, like this:

```
REVOKE ALL ON Movies FROM patricia, karen
GRANT UPDATE ON Movies, Studios TO patricia, karen
```

Note that I included a list of objects in the GRANT statement. The GRANT and REVOKE statements enable you to use lists to change the privileges for multiple users or on multiple objects at one time.

Tip 43 from
Rafe Colburn

> In Oracle, before a user can log in and query any tables, she must have the CREATE SES-
> SION privilege. The CREATE SESSION privilege enables users to create a new database
> session, or in other words, to connect to the database. You can add this privilege with the
> GRANT statement:
>
> GRANT CREATE SESSION TO *user*

THE PUBLIC USER

In addition to setting the permissions for individual database users, some databases also enable you to adjust the permissions for all users at one time. In Oracle, the user public acts as a proxy for all users who do not have specific privileges set for an object.

For example, I have granted specific privileges to karen and patricia for the Movies table. However, I haven't granted them or anyone else any privileges related to the Studios table. I can allow or deny everyone access to Studios by adjusting the privileges of the user public. Take a look at this query:

```
GRANT ALL ON Studios TO public
```

It enables any user who can log in to the database to make any changes he likes to the contents of the Studios table. Naturally, I can rein in users by granting only the privileges that they actually need:

```
REVOKE ALL ON Studios FROM public
GRANT SELECT ON Studios TO public
```

By making adjustments to the privileges of the public user, you can avoid the necessity of creating security settings for each of the users with access to a database.

ALLOWING USERS TO GRANT PRIVILEGES

By default, when you grant privileges to a user, she is not allowed to in turn grant those privileges to someone else. However, you can use the WITH GRANT OPTION clause to enable users to grant any privileges that they possess to other users. For example, if I grant the select privilege to patricia for the table Movies, she can view all the records in the table, but she cannot enable anyone else to view those records. If I grant her privileges with the WITH GRANT OPTION clause turned on, she can grant the SELECT option to other users.

The syntax of a GRANT statement that uses WITH GRANT OPTION is as follows:

```
GRANT SELECT ON Movies TO patricia WITH GRANT OPTION
```

Patricia then has the right to grant the SELECT privilege for the Movies table to other users. Patricia could log in to the database and issue enter the following statement, which would allow Peter and Paul to select data from the Movies table:

```
CONNECT patricia
Connected.

GRANT SELECT ON Movies TO peter, paul
```

Note that Patricia did not specify WITH GRANT OPTION when she allowed Peter and Paul to access the Movies database, so Peter and Paul are prevented from giving the SELECT privilege to other users. Peter would fail if he logged in and tried to grant the SELECT privilege to another user like this:

```
CONNECT peter
Connected.

GRANT SELECT ON Movies TO jeff
```

On the other hand, Patricia could include the WITH GRANT OPTION clause when she grants access to the Movies table to Peter and Paul, granting them the right to include other users in the list of people allowed to access the Movies table.

Tip 44 from *Rafe Colburn*	You should be careful with the WITH GRANT OPTION clause because when you give that option to a user, he can in turn give that option to other users, and you can quickly lose control of the list of people who have access to your data. When you give the grant option to users, you should make sure that you can trust them not to pass that option on to other users who shouldn't provide other users with access to the data that was originally protected.

ORDER OF GRANTS AND REVOKES

The order in which grant and revoke statements are executed is important. The most recent statement that adds or removes a privilege for a user is the one that takes effect. After the following two statements are executed, patricia no longer has access to write select statements that query the People table:

```
GRANT SELECT ON People TO patricia
REVOKE ALL ON People FROM patricia
```

Even though the SELECT privilege is more specific than the privilege ALL, revoking all privileges to the People table from patricia removes her capability to select rows from that table. The fact that she was granted the select privilege on that table explicitly doesn't matter.

SECURITY ROLES

Some databases enable administrators to create a layer of abstraction between database objects and database users through *roles*. Basically, roles are just bundles of security settings. You can associate any number of security settings to a particular role and then assign users to that role to give them the role's privileges. Then, if you create a new user, you can just assign them to the appropriate roles instead of granting them each privilege that they require individually. If for some reason a new table is created or the access available to all the members of the role should change, the role can be updated and all the privileges associated with members of the role will automatically reflect that change.

CREATING AND DROPPING ROLES

In one sense, roles are a lot like users. You create a role using the CREATE ROLE statement, and then you edit the privileges available to that role using GRANT and REVOKE statements. The CREATE ROLE statement is used as follows:

```
CREATE ROLE accounting
```

After the role has been created, you can assign privileges to that role, as though it were a user:

```
GRANT UPDATE (budget, gross) ON Movies TO accounting
GRANT SELECT ON Movies TO accounting
```

You can also remove existing roles using the DROP ROLE command as follows:

```
DROP ROLE accounting
```

ASSIGNING USERS TO ROLES

After you have created a role and have assigned the appropriate privileges to it, you can associate users with that role. Users are added to roles using the GRANT statement, and they are removed from roles using the REVOKE statement. The syntax to grant a role to a user is the same as the syntax for granting him a privilege:

```
GRANT role TO user
```

If paul, who currently has no privileges assigned to him for the Movies table, attempts to retrieve a list of movies from that table, an error will be returned, as shown in Listing 11.4.

LISTING 11.4   THE RESULTS OF AN UNPRIVILEGED QUERY

```
CONNECT paul
Connected.

SELECT movie_title
FROM development.Movies

ERROR at line 2:
ORA-00942: table or view does not exist
```

Note that the error message returned when paul tries to access the Movies table with a query indicates that the table does not exist. This is a security measure designed to prevent users from being able to discover tables that they don't have the necessary privileges to access. To assign the accounting role to paul, giving him access to select rows from the Movies table, the following command is used:

```
CONNECT development
Connected.

GRANT accounting TO paul

Grant succeeded.
```

Then, you can connect back again as paul and see that he can retrieve records from the Movies table, as shown in listing 11.5.

```
CONNECT paul
Connected.

SELECT MOVIE_TITLE
FROM development.Movies

MOVIE_TITLE
-------------------
Vegetable House
Prince Kong
The Code Warrior
Bill Durham
Codependence Day
The Linux Files
SQL Strikes Back
The Programmer
Hard Code
The Rear Windows
SQL Planet

MOVIE_TITLE
-------------------
The Maltese Tuple

12 rows selected.
```

Users who have been granted the accounting role are able to update the budget and gross columns in the Movies table, but not any of the others. With that in mind, take a look at the three SQL statements in Listing 11.6.

```
CONNECT paul
Connected.

UPDATE development.Movies
SET movie_title = 'Walks Like a Duck'
WHERE movie_id = 17

UPDATE development.Movies
                   *
ERROR at line 1:
ORA-01031: insufficient privileges

UPDATE development.Movies
```

continues

LISTING 11.6   CONTINUED

```
SET budget = 20
WHERE movie_id = 17

1 row updated.

UPDATE development.Movies
SET budget = 20, movie_title = 'Walks Like a Duck'
WHERE movie_id = 17

UPDATE development.Movies
                 *
ERROR at line 1:
ORA-01031: insufficient privileges
```

The first query in Listing 11.6 fails because Paul has not been granted the UPDATE privilege on the movie_title column of the Movies table. The second query succeeds because Paul is allowed to update the budget column of Movies, due to his being granted membership in the accounting role. The third query fails completely. Even though Paul is allowed to make changes to the budget column, he must have the right to update every column in the SET clause for the UPDATE statement to succeed.

When a user is granted membership in a role, she can also be granted the right to include other users in that role. This option is similar to WITH GRANT OPTION, except that it applies to roles instead of privileges. To empower a user to add other users to a role, the following statement is used:

```
GRANT role TO user WITH ADMIN OPTION
```

ASSIGNING ROLES TO OTHER ROLES

One interesting attribute of roles is that they can be assigned to one another. When one role is assigned to another, the second of the two roles has all the privileges associated with the first role, plus all the second role's privileges as well. This flexible model of assigning and managing roles makes it easy to construct complex security models for your databases without sacrificing maintainability.

Consider the following two roles:

```
CREATE ROLE casting
GRANT INSERT ON Cast_Movies TO casting
GRANT SELECT ON Cast_Movies TO casting
GRANT UPDATE ON Cast_Movies TO casting
CREATE ROLE director
GRANT DELETE ON Cast_Movies TO director
```

In this case, members of the casting role are able to view, add, or change entries in the cast information for movies, but they are not able to remove cast members from a movie.

Members of the director role are only allowed to delete cast members from a movie; they are not allowed to make any other changes to the cast. Look at how to create a role with all these privileges at the same time:

```
CREATE ROLE executive_producer
GRANT casting TO executive_producer
GRANT director TO executive_producer
```

The new role, executive_producer, has the ability to select, insert, update, and delete rows in the Cast_Movies table by virtue of the fact that all the capabilities of the other two roles are assigned to it. So, if I grant the executive_producer role to Paul, he will be able to make any changes he wants to the Cast_Movies table. For example, he can insert a new row in Cast_Movies, as shown in Listing 11.7.

LISTING 11.7   A MEMBER OF THE executive_producer ROLE INSERTS A RECORD INTO THE Cast_Movies TABLE

```
INSERT INTO development.Cast_Movies
VALUES
(1, 5, 'John James', 50000);

1 row created.
```

If I revoke the insert privilege from the casting role, Paul will no longer be able to insert rows into the Cast_Movies table, as demonstrated in Listing 11.8.

LISTING 11.8   AN INSERT STATEMENT THAT WILL FAIL BECAUSE THE USER DOES NOT HAVE INSERT PRIVILEGES FOR THE TABLE

```
REVOKE INSERT ON Cast_Movies FROM casting

Revoke succeeded.


CONNECT paul
Connected.

INSERT INTO development.Cast_Movies
VALUES
(2, 5, 'John James', 50000);

ERROR at line 1:
ORA-01031: insufficient privileges
```

If the privileges assigned to one of the roles changes, all the roles that are assigned to that role also reflect the changes. In that sense, changes to roles cascade to users and roles that derive their privileges from the role that was changed.

VIEWS AND DATABASE SECURITY

Next to the ability to differentiate between users through their login accounts, the most useful security-related feature of relational databases is views. As I've already demonstrated in this chapter and in the section "Restricting Data Available to Users" in Chapter 10, "Using Views," you can prevent users from accessing particular information by creating views that do not contain that information.

The key to using views successfully is making sure that the proper information is being captured within the views and that the security privileges for the users or roles that access the views and the tables upon which they are based are managed correctly. Generally speaking, this means that the users or roles should have no access to the tables themselves and that they should be making all their queries against views.

As you've seen throughout this chapter, when a user wants to issue SQL queries against a table that they do not own, they have to prepend the username of the owner to the table name to access the table. Views can be created that enable users to eliminate the necessity of prepending the table name with the owner's username in every query. For example, the view in Listing 11.9 enables Paul to access the Movies table without prepending development to the name every time.

Tip 45 from
Rafe Colburn

In Oracle, for a user to be able to create tables, views, and other database objects, the DBA must grant her the resource role.

LISTING 11.9 A VIEW THAT IMPORTS A TABLE INTO ANOTHER USER'S NAME SPACE

```
CONNECT paul
Connected.

CREATE VIEW Movies
AS
SELECT *
FROM development.Movies

View created.

SELECT movie_id
FROM Movies

MOVIE_ID
----------
         1
         2
         3
         4
         5
         6
         7
         8
```

```
         9
        10
        16

    MOVIE_ID
    ----------
        17

12 rows selected.
```

As you can see from the listing, after creating the `Movies` view in his personal name space, Paul can access the contents of `development.Movies` without actually entering the prefix `development`.

<table>
<tr><td>Tip 46 from
Rafe Colburn</td><td>In Oracle databases, you can get around creating views to import other tables into your name space by using synonyms. Basically, synonyms are used to assign alternative names to views or tables. So, to create a synonym from <code>development.Movies</code> to <code>Movies</code>, the following statement is used:

<code>CREATE SYNONYM Movies FOR development.Movies</code>

You could just as easily create a synonym for an object that already resides within your name space. Given that you've already created a view called <code>Movies</code>, you could create a synonym to it with a shorter name, like this:

<code>CREATE SYNONYM Mov FOR Movies</code></td></tr>
</table>

CUSTOMIZING ACCESS THROUGH VIEWS

I've already discussed how views and database privileges can be combined to manage what data users are able to access. I'd like to actually demonstrate through examples how you might go about setting up their database to ensure that users are only able to see and modify the data to which they should have access.

Say you've created a user who only needs to view the list of movies that currently appear within the database. Under no circumstances will this user be allowed to make any changes to the data, and he should not need to use joins to obtain the information that he needs. In this case, the easiest thing to do is first to revoke all the user's access to the base tables, then to create a view that joins the tables with information pertinent to the user, and then to present them as a view. This process is illustrated in Listing 11.10.

LISTING 11.10   SETTING UP A VIEW FOR A USER WHO ONLY NEEDS TO VIEW A MOVIE LISTING

```
CREATE USER guest
IDENTIFIED BY guest

User created.

REVOKE ALL ON Movies FROM guest
```

continues

LISTING 11.10   CONTINUED

```
Revoke succeeded.

REVOKE ALL ON People FROM guest

Revoke succeeded.

REVOKE ALL ON Studios FROM guest

Revoke succeeded.

CREATE VIEW Movie_List (title, studio, director_fname,
director_lname, release_date)
AS
SELECT movie_title, studio_name, person_fname,
person_lname, release_date
FROM Movies, Studios, People
WHERE director_id = person_id
AND Movies.studio_id = Studios.studio_id

View created.

GRANT SELECT ON Movie_List TO guest

Grant succeeded.

GRANT connect TO guest

Grant succeeded.

CONNECT guest/guest
Connected.

SELECT *
FROM development.Movie_List
```

TITLE	STUDIO	DIRECTOR_F	DIRECTOR_L	RELEASE_D
Vegetable House	Giant	Jeff	Price	01-JAN-75
Prince Kong	MPM	Carol	Delano	01-MAY-79
The Code Warrior	FKG	Chuck	Peterson	01-SEP-91
Bill Durham	Delighted Artists	Becky	Orvis	15-JUL-88
Codependence Day	Giant	Jeff	Price	01-JUL-97
The Linux Files	MPM	Chuck	Peterson	22-AUG-93
SQL Strikes Back	Delighted Artists	Becky	Orvis	01-NOV-98
The Programmer	Delighted Artists	Jeff	Price	17-APR-93
Hard Code	FKG	Carol	Delano	18-APR-95
The Rear Windows	Giant	Jeff	Price	11-JUL-87
SQL Planet	Giant	Becky	Orvis	06-JAN-95
TITLE	STUDIO	DIRECTOR_F	DIRECTOR_L	RELEASE_D

```
-------------------- -------------------- ---------- ---------- ----------
The Maltese Tuple    MPM                  Chuck      Peterson   08-AUG-91

12 rows selected.

SELECT *
FROM development.Movies

ERROR at line 1:
ORA-00942: table or view does not exist
```

Let me quickly walk you through the sequence of events in Listing 11.10. First, I create a new user with the username and password of guest. Then, I proceed to revoke all his privileges for the Studios, Movies, and People tables. In all likelihood, this is unnecessary because the user shouldn't have access to those tables anyway. However, I include those statements to be comprehensive.

After revoking access to the tables that guest shouldn't see, I create the view that guest is allowed to see. The Movie_List view joins the Movies, Studios, and People tables to provide information for the guest user in one location. After the view is created, I grant the SELECT privilege to guest for the view so that he can query against it. Then, because this account is new (and because I'm using an Oracle database), I grant guest the connect role so that he can actually connect to the database.

After all the guest user's privileges are set up appropriately, I use the CONNECT statement to log in as guest. At that point, I select all the data in the Movie_List view to show that it works, and I attempt to select all the data in the Movies table to show that it doesn't work.

Views can also be used to restrict what rows in a table users are allowed to retrieve. For example, a view can be used to restrict the guest user from selecting any users who aren't from Texas. I have already revoked all the guest account's privileges to the People table; in Listing 11.11, I create a new view that contains only people from Texas and grant the guest user all privileges on that view.

PART

III

CH

11

LISTING 11.11   A VIEW THAT CONTAINS ONLY PEOPLE FROM TEXAS

```
CREATE VIEW People_From_Texas
AS
SELECT *
FROM People
WHERE person_state = 'TX'

GRANT ALL ON People_From_Texas TO guest
```

When the guest user writes statements that affect the People_From_Texas view, only those rows in the base table that are visible though the view are affected. Take a look at the queries in Listing 11.12.

LISTING 11.12   QUERIES POSTED AGAINST A VIEW CONTAINING A WHERE CLAUSE

```
CONNECT guest/guest
Connected.

SELECT person_fname, person_lname, person_state
FROM development.People_From_Texas

PERSON_FNA PERSON_LNA PE
---------- ---------- --
Brian      Smith      TX
Paul       Monk       TX
Reece      Randall    TX
Carol      Delano     TX

INSERT INTO development.People_From_Texas
(person_id, person_fname, person_lname, person_address, person_city,
person_state, person_zip, person_phone, person_ssn)
VALUES
(15, 'Some', 'Person', 'Address', 'City', 'NY',
'12345', '8185551212', '012345678')

1 row created.

UPDATE development.People_From_Texas
SET person_state = 'NC'
WHERE person_state = 'NY'

0 rows updated.

DELETE FROM development.People_From_Texas
WHERE person_id = 15

0 rows deleted.
```

The first query in listing 11.12 is a SELECT statement. As you can see, there are only four rows in the view because it includes only those people who are from Texas. The next query inserts a new row into the view and thus into the base table, People. As you can see from the results of this statement, if a view to which a user has access is updatable and the insert privilege has been granted to the user for that view, the user can insert new rows into the base table even if the data in the row is outside the constraints provided in the WHERE clause of the view.

Next, the guest user attempts to change all the users with NY in the state field to NC. As you can see from the query results, this does not affect any of the rows in the database, even though there are at least two rows that match the WHERE clause in the query in the People base table. The query affects only those rows that are included in the view, not the base table itself. The same is true for the DELETE statement; the ID specified in the WHERE clause does not correspond with a row in the view, so no rows are deleted. This puts users in the interesting situation where they can insert rows into a base table without being able to delete them, without the privileges explicitly being stated that way.

IN THE REAL WORLD

Database security settings often do not come into play with real-world applications because there is a client/server or Web application between the actual user and the database. Most Web applications use a single database user for all transactions, and the security is implemented within the application itself. This is also the case for many client/server applications. The application security is built in to the application and is applied before the queries are ever built and executed against the database.

For small applications, the application often simply logs in through the system administrator account and executes all its queries with DBA privileges. If the database is larger, the DBA will create a special account for the application to use that does not have all the privileges granted to the DBA user. There is no need for the application to be able to create new users, to grant privileges to other users, or to perform DBA functions such as backing up or restoring the database.

In cases where the same data must be accessed by more than one application or by more than one user who logs in to the database directly, it is important to carefully manage the privileges those users are granted. For example, consider a human resources database for a corporation. One application might be written to enable employees to enter their time each week. The privileges assigned to the database user for that application would allow him to enter hours worked for each employee and retrieve hours-worked data as well. The application itself would provide the security that prevents employees from entering, updating, or viewing time cards for their colleagues.

The payroll application used to create paychecks and handle other accounting tasks for each employee of the company would probably connect to the database through a different user ID. This ID would have the privileges necessary to obtain the hourly pay or salary of each employee, as well as the various payroll deductions required. The user would probably not have the privileges necessary to update or delete data entered by the employees, although he might be allowed to enter alternative records if changes needed to be made. Dividing access to the database among users assigned to each application makes sense to prevent users from gaining access to information that they should not be allowed to see and to ensure that applications are not miscoded, providing access to the wrong data.

PART IV

REAL-WORLD ISSUES

CHAPTER 12

HANDLING SPECIFIC TYPES OF DATA

In this chapter

One of the most difficult tasks in working with databases is dealing with all the different types of data that can be stored within a database. There are complexities specific to each type of data that you'll need to know about when programming. This chapter is dedicated to providing some instruction on how to best store and manipulate information so that it is most useful.

Relational databases provide *strong data typing*; you can set up fields in your databases so that they can hold only a particular type of data. These data types enable you to make assumptions about data stored within particular fields. You don't have to wonder whether you can subtract the value in a numeric field from the value in another numeric field; the values in those fields must be numbers. Any value in a date field can be compared to the current date based on time without using a meaningless means of comparison such as a string comparison. Some languages, including many languages used to write applications that communicate with databases, provide *weak data typing*. These languages generally do not distinguish between different types of data; you can easily store a date, a number, or a string within the same variable. Things such as arithmetic operations are not restricted to particular types of values; if you try to use an improper type in an operation, an error will be generated or the results will come out strangely.

By the same token, you can manage how large the values in various fields can be by setting the field size when you create your tables. If you make the data type for a certain column CHAR(10), then you know that the value in that field will always be 10 characters long. If a value less than 10 characters long is placed in the field, the field will pad the string with spaces until it consumes 10 characters of space.

It's up to you to take advantage of these features when you design your databases. There's no rule, other than the rule of common sense, that says you must place your data in fields with the appropriate data type. You can easily just specify all the fields you create as VARCHAR(255) if you want. However, the cards are stacked against you if you choose to design your databases this way. To incorporate fields in mathematical expressions or sort them numerically (as opposed to alphabetically), they must be created as numeric fields. By the same token, there is no reasonable means to compare dates unless you place them within date fields.

Given that you are going to carefully decide which data type to use for each column in your database, the question of how to best make use of the data in your queries remains. In this chapter, I'll describe how data can be converted from one type to another, explain how you can format data to insert it in a column of a particular data type, and discuss some of the limitations of various data types. I will also discuss how to format data for presentation and explain how data is compared and sorted.

NUMERIC DATA TYPES

Even though all numeric fields hold the same basic type of information, numbers, most databases provide several numeric data types that you can choose from for your database fields. Some of these fields are legitimately different from one other, such as integers and floating point numbers. Other data types, such as the MONEY data type, are just included for the convenience of programmers. A MONEY field is really just a floating point field that always makes sure the contents of the field are displayed with exactly two digits after the decimal point.

Consider the following list of numeric data types:

- DECIMAL
- FLOAT
- INTEGER
- NUMBER
- SMALLINT

The list contains the list of numeric data types supported by Oracle databases. In truth, all the fields are either synonyms for NUMBER or slight variations on the basic NUMBER data type. Other databases support their own numeric data types with different names and capacities from those in the preceding list.

SORTING NUMBERS

When you sort the results of a query based on the values in a column containing numbers, the records are sorted in basic numerical order. For example, take a look at the query results in Listing 12.1. The query simply returns a list of movies, with the results ordered by the values in the budget column.

LISTING 12.1   QUERY RESULTS SORTED BY THE VALUES IN A NUMERIC FIELD

```
SELECT movie_title, budget
FROM Movies
ORDER BY budget


MOVIE_TITLE              BUDGET
-------------------- ----------
Prince Kong               3.25
SQL Strikes Back             5
Bill Durham               10.1
The Code Warrior          10.3
Codependence Day            15
Vegetable House             20
The Linux Files           22.2
The Programmer              50
The Rear Windows            50
Hard Code                   77

10 rows selected.
```

PART
IV
CH
12

The results are clearly sorted in numerical order based on the values in the budget column. Consider how a list of numbers would be sorted if they appeared in a character field, such as

VARCHAR. The ORDER BY clause would sort them alphabetically, not numerically. A list of numbers sorted alphabetically follows:

```
1
10
11
2
3
35
4
```

All the numbers beginning with the same digit are grouped together, just as all words that begin with the same letter are grouped together when they are alphabetized. This creates an interesting problem when numbers appear in strings that also contain characters. For example, if they continued to make *Rocky* movies until the year 2025, the list of movies might look like this when alphabetized:

```
Rocky
Rocky 10
Rocky 11
Rocky 12
Rocky 2
Rocky 3
Rocky 4
```

For this reason, it is sometimes judicious to create a separate sort by field for records that contain combinations of letters and numbers. Numbers can be placed in this field to establish the appropriate sort order for the records in the table. These sort by fields can be particularly useful when numbers are used before and after a decimal for counting. Consider the figure numbers in this book. Each figure is numbered primarily by the chapter number and secondarily by the figure number within the chapter. These numbers cannot be sorted properly alphabetically or numerically. Sorted alphabetically, the numbers look like this:

```
12.1
12.10
12.2
12.20
12.21
12.3
12.4
```

Sorted numerically, the numbers look the same because 14.21 is greater than 12.2 but less than 12.3. To be sorted as they should be, the numbers actually have to appear in a database like this, which means that they probably have to be stored in a separate column:

```
12.01
12.02
12.03
12.04
12.10
12.20
```

NULLS AND NUMBERS

As you already know, nulls represent unknown values. Because of this, they "corrupt" mathematical expressions. Any time a null crops up within a mathematical expression, the result of that expression becomes null itself because there is no way to include an unknown value within a calculation unless you are solving for it. Null values are explained in Chapter 5, "The SELECT Statement," in the section "Dealing with Null Values."

Sometimes, you might want to make an assumption about what the value represented by a null will be when your query executes so that your mathematical expressions return a real value. Various databases enable you to substitute real values for nulls in different ways. The SQL-92 standard specifies that nulls can be replaced using the COALESCE() function. COALESCE() accepts two arguments, the field that might contain a null and the value that should be substituted for the null. The NVL() function is Oracle's version of COALESCE(). It accepts the same two arguments and works the same way, but it has a different name.

Look at a practical example where NVL() or COALESCE() might be used. Before a movie has been released, the gross revenues for the movie are null. To obtain the average revenue for the movies in the database, the query in Listing 12.2 would have to be used.

LISTING 12.2   A QUERY THAT AVERAGES THE GROSS REVENUES FOR RELEASED MOVIES

```
SELECT AVG(gross)
FROM Movies
WHERE gross IS NOT NULL

AVG(GROSS)
- - - - - - - - - -
    24.7625
```

Unfortunately, this query might not be suitable in every situation because only released movies are counted in the average. If you want to include the number of unreleased movies against the average as well, you must use one of the null substitution functions, as shown in Listing 12.3.

LISTING 12.3   A QUERY THAT USES NULL SUBSTITUTION TO RETURN A VALUE FROM AN AGGREGATE FUNCTION

```
SELECT AVG(NVL(gross,0))
FROM Movies

AVG(NVL(GROSS,0))
- - - - - - - - - - - - - - - -
            19.81
```

As you can see, the results of the two queries are different. The sum of the gross revenues in the first query is divided by 8, whereas the sum of the gross revenues in the second query is divided by 10. The null substitution enables you to include every movie in the aggregate function without causing a null value to be returned.

PART

IV

CH

12

MATHEMATICAL EXPRESSIONS

In Chapter 5, "The SELECT Statement," I explained how basic arithmetic expressions can be used within the select list and WHERE clauses of queries. I also covered aggregate functions in Chapter 7, "Aggregating Query Results." As you might have imagined at the time, SQL has much broader mathematical capabilities than were illustrated in those two chapters. In addition to the four basic mathematical operators provided by SQL, there are also a number of functions for use in your mathematical expressions. The availability of these functions varies from database to database, but generally speaking, SQL implementations provide a large number of mathematical functions.

Mathematical functions are called in the same way that other functions are called from within SQL statements. The function is placed in the SELECT list or WHERE clause, and the argument to the function is entered within parentheses after the function name. For example, to take the square root of the gross revenues of each movie within a query, the SQRT() function is used as shown in Listing 12.4.

LISTING 12.4 A STATEMENT THAT INCLUDES A MATHEMATICAL FUNCTION WITHIN THE SELECT LIST

```
SELECT movie_title, SQRT(gross)
FROM Movies
WHERE studio_id = 1

MOVIE_TITLE          SQRT(GROSS)
-------------------- -----------
Vegetable House       5.47722558
Codependence Day      5.47722558
The Rear Windows       4.18330013
```

There's no logical reason why you would need the square root of the movie revenues, but the purpose of the previous example was to show how function calls in queries work. Mathematical functions can also be nested, and multiple function calls can be used within a single expression. Consider the query in Listing 12.5.

LISTING 12.5 A QUERY THAT CONTAINS NESTED MATHEMATICAL FUNCTION CALLS

```
SELECT movie_title, SQRT(POWER(gross, 2))
FROM Movies
WHERE studio_id = 1

MOVIE_TITLE          SQRT(POWER(GROSS,2))
-------------------- --------------------
Vegetable House                        30
Codependence Day                       30
The Rear Windows                     17.5
```

In the preceding query, I nested a call to the POWER() function within the call to the SQRT() function. First, note that the POWER() function actually requires two arguments, the value and the exponent. As you can see from the query results, the mathematical expression just squares the movie gross and then takes the square root of that number. When functions are nested, they are evaluated in order from inner to outer. So, first the number is squared, and then the square root is taken.

You can also include multiple function calls within a single expression and mix them with standard mathematical operators. If you had a table that contained two columns, each containing the length of one of the shorter sides of a right triangle, you could calculate the length of the longest side using the query in Listing 12.6 (which simply applies the Pythagorean theorem to the other two numbers).

LISTING 12.6   A QUERY THAT APPLIES THE PYTHAGOREAN THEOREM TO SIDES OF A RIGHT TRIANGLE

```
SELECT side_one, side_two,
SQRT(POWER(side_one, 2) + POWER(side_two, 2)) AS length
FROM triangles

   SIDE_ONE   SIDE_TWO     LENGTH
----------  ----------  ----------
        10          15  18.0277564
         4           6  7.21110255
         5           3  5.83095189
```

COMMON MATHEMATICAL FUNCTIONS

I've already demonstrated the use of two mathematical functions, SQRT() and POWER(). Most SQL implementations offer many other mathematical functions as well. Other mathematical functions with which you are already familiar are the aggregate functions introduced back in Chapter 7, MIN(), MAX(), SUM(), AVG(), and COUNT(). Table 12.1 contains a reference for some of the mathematical functions. Not every database supports all these functions. You should consult the documentation for your database to determine which of these functions are supported.

TABLE 12.1   MATHEMATICAL FUNCTIONS SUPPORTED BY SQL

Function	Purpose
ABS(*expr*)	Returns the absolute value of *expr*. Both ABS(5) and ABS(-5) return 5.
CEIL(*expr*)	Returns the smallest integer greater than or equal to *expr*. CEIL(1.1) returns 2, whereas CEIL(1) returns 1. CEIL(-1.1) returns -1. (In databases that use Transact-SQL, this function is CEILING().)
COS(*expr*)	Trigonometric function that returns the cosine of *expr* in radians.
COSH(*expr*)	Trigonometric function that returns the hyperbolic cosine of the angle represented by *expr*.

continues

TABLE 12.1 CONTINUED

Function	Purpose
EXP([expr])	EXP() returns the value of the special number *e* (2.71828 ...). When *expr* is specified, *e* raised to the power of *expr* is returned.
FLOOR(expr)	Returns the largest integer less than or equal to *expr*. FLOOR(1.1) returns 1, FLOOR(-1.1) returns -2, and FLOOR(1) returns 1.
LN(expr)	VReturns the natural log of *expr*. LN(5) returns 1.60943791.
LOG(base, expr)	Returns the log of base *base* of *expr*. LOG(10, 5) returns .698970004.
MOD(expr, divisor)	The modulus function. Returns the remainder when *expr* is divided by *divisor*. MOD(5,3) returns 2.
PI()	The value of pi with 16 digits following the decimal.
POWER(expr, exponent)	The exponential function; raises *expr* to the power of *exponent*. POWER(2,3) returns 8.
SIGN(expr)	Reverses the sign of *expr*.
SIN(expr)	Trigonometric function that returns the sine of *expr* in radians.
SINH(expr)	Trigonometric function that returns the hyperbolic tangent of the angle represented by *expr*.
SQRT(expr)	Returns the square root of *expr*.
TAN(expr)	Trigonometric function that returns the tangent of *expr* in radians.
TANH(expr)	Trigonometric function that returns the hyperbolic tangent of the angle represented by *expr*.

FORMATTING NUMBERS

Sometimes numbers in a database contain more significant digits than you want to display when you are generating reports from the database. To make sure calculations are accurate, most databases support very long numbers. For example, the NUMBER data type in Oracle 8 supports numbers up to 40 digits long.

Most databases support the ROUND() function, which enables you to decrease the precision of numbers for presentation. Oracle also provides the TRUNC() function, which simply removes digits from a number without rounding them. Both functions are used in the same manner. The only difference is in how they manipulate the numbers before they are presented. The syntax for both is as follows:

```
ROUND(val, precision)
TRUNC(val, precision)
```

These functions operate differently depending on whether *precision* is a positive or negative number. If *precision* is positive, the number is rounded so that no more than *precision* digits remain to the right of the decimal point in the number. Take the query in Listing 12.7, for example.

LISTING 12.7   A QUERY THAT USES ROUND() TO ELIMINATE DIGITS AFTER THE DECIMAL

```
SELECT ROUND(4.5, 2), ROUND(4.568137, 2)
FROM DUAL

ROUND(4.5,2) ROUND(4.568137,2)
----------- ----------------------
        4.5                  4.57
```

The number with six digits to the right of the decimal is rounded so that only two digits after the decimal remain. The first item in the select list, 4.5, is untouched because it already contained less than two digits after the decimal. Note that 4.568137 is rounded up, as it should be. Contrast this with the query in Listing 12.8, which uses the TRUNC() function.

LISTING 12.8   A QUERY THAT USES TRUNC() TO REMOVE DIGITS FOLLOWING THE DECIMAL

```
SELECT TRUNC(4.568137, 2)
FROM DUAL

TRUNC(4.568137,2)
----------------
           4.56
```

The TRUNC() function simply slices off all the digits beyond the *precision* specified in the function call.

Tip 47 from
Rafe Colburn

Oracle follows the American standard and rounds up numbers in which the value to be rounded ends in 5 or .5. In other words, ROUND(5.5, 0) returns 6, not 5.

PART
IV
CH
12

When the precision supplied to ROUND() or TRUNC() is a negative number, all the digits to the right of the decimal in the number are removed, along with number of digits specified as the precision to the right of the decimal. Take a look at the queries in Listing 12.9.

LISTING 12.9   USING ROUND() AND TRUNC() TO REMOVE PRECISION TO THE LEFT OF THE DECIMAL

```
SELECT ROUND(175, -2), TRUNC(175, -2)
FROM DUAL

ROUND(175,-2) TRUNC(175,-2)
------------- -------------
          200           100

SELECT ROUND(15.1, -1), TRUNC(15.1, -1)
FROM DUAL;

ROUND(15.1,-1) TRUNC(15.1,-1)
-------------- --------------
            20             10
```

As you can see from the second query in Listing 12.9, when a negative precision is specified, all the digits to the right of the decimal are eliminated, along with the digits to the left of the decimal. When TRUNC() is used, the number of digits specified as the precision are simply replaced by zeroes. ROUND() rounds the digits that are eliminated appropriately.

STRING DATA TYPES

There are two string data types in SQL, VARCHAR and CHAR. The difference between the two is that VARCHAR fields only consume as much space on disk and in memory as is actually used by the characters in the field. On the other hand, a CHAR field always consumes the number of bytes specified when the field is created. When strings are compared and manipulated, both types of fields work identically. There are also specialized data types that can hold extremely large strings, such as CLOB in Oracle and TEXT in Microsoft SQL Server; I'll discuss these data types later in the chapter because they have little in common with CHAR and VARCHAR.

CONCATENATING STRINGS

All databases provide a string concatenation operator that is used to treat multiple strings as though they are a single string. Oracle supports ¦¦ as the string concatenation operator, whereas Transact-SQL (used by Sybase databases and Microsoft SQL Server) uses + to concatenate strings. Both the operators work identically. The concatenation operator is used to create a mailing label name in Listing 12.10.

LISTING 12.10   STRING CONCATENATION

```
SELECT person_fname ¦¦ ' ' ¦¦ person_lname AS mail_name
FROM People

MAIL_NAME
- - - - - - - - - - - - - - - - - - - -
Jeff Price
Chuck Peterson
Brandon Brooks
Brian Smith
Paul Monk
Reece Randall
Peter Jong
Maggie Davis
Becky Orvis
Carol Delano
Fran Friend

11 rows selected.
```

In the query in Listing 12.10, person_fname and person_lname are concatenated with a string containing a single space in the middle. You can use string concatenation in any expression that contains strings. For example, you can use concatenated strings to create comparisons in the WHERE clause of a query, as shown in Listing 12.11.

LISTING 12.11   USING STRING CONCATENATION IN THE WHERE CLAUSE

```
SELECT person_id, person_fname, person_lname
FROM people
WHERE person_fname || ' ' || person_lname = 'Jeff Price'

PERSON_ID PERSON_FNA PERSON_LNA
--------- ---------- ----------
        1 Jeff       Price
```

STRING FUNCTIONS

Relational databases support a number of functions that enable users to manipulate strings for use within comparisons and to format them for input and output. Unfortunately, the names of these functions can differ significantly from one database to the next. Fortunately, these differences are, for the most part, superficial. For example, most databases provide a function for returning the length of a string in characters. In Oracle, the function is LENGTH(). In Transact-SQL, the function is CHAR_LENGTH(). Other than the difference in names, the functions both work identically. They accept a string or an expression that evaluates to a string as the argument, and they return an integer containing the number of bytes in that string.

SEARCHING STRINGS

Most relational databases provide some method for checking whether a particular string contains another string. For example, you can search the string Rafe Colburn to determine whether the string Col appears within it. In Oracle, the INSTR() function is used to search a string; it is used as follows:

```
INSTR(string1, string2 [, start [, occurrence]])
```

string1 is the string to be searched, and string2 is the string to search for. The start argument is the position in the string where the search should begin, and the location of the occurrence instance of string2 is returned by the function. This can probably be explained more easily using examples. The following function call returns 5 because the letter c occurs at the fifth position in the string to be searched:

```
INSTR('a b c b a', 'c')
```

In this function call, the search starts at position 4 in the string, so the function returns 7:

```
INSTR('a b c b a', 'b', 4)
```

The first b occurs before the search begins; the position of the second b is returned. Now take a look at this function call:

```
INSTR('a b c b a', 'a', 1, 2)
```

This query returns 9. The search starts at the first position in the string, but because the occurrence argument contains the number 2, the first occurrence of a is skipped, and the position of the second a is returned. The following query returns 0 because no matches that meet the parameters of the function call exist:

```
INSTR('a b c b a', 'a', 5, 2)
```

Listing 12.12 demonstrates how INSTR can be used within a query without using a LIKE comparison.

LISTING 12.12   A QUERY THAT FINDS ALL THE MOVIES WITH 'LINUX' IN THE TITLE

```
SELECT movie_title, INSTR(movie_title, 'Linux')
FROM Movies
WHERE INSTR(movie_title, 'Linux') <> 0

MOVIE_TITLE            INSTR(MOVIE_TITLE,'LINUX')
-------------------    --------------------------
The Linux Files                             5
```

Transact-SQL uses the CHARINDEX() function instead of the INSTR() function. It does not enable users to specify the starting position of the search or the occurrence whose location should be returned, so the query in Listing 12.12 would be restated in Transact-SQL as shown in Listing 12.13.

LISTING 12.13   USING THE CHARINDEX() FUNCTION FROM TRANSACT-SQL

```
SELECT movie_title, CHARINDEX('Linux', movie_title)
FROM Movies
WHERE CHARINDEX('Linux', movie_title) <> 0

movie_title
------------------------ -----------
The Linux Files             5

(1 row(s) affected)
```

SUBSTRINGS

Substring functions enable programmers to extract a specified range of characters from a larger string. Transact-SQL provides the SUBSTRING() function for taking substrings; the Oracle equivalent is SUBSTR(). The two functions are identical, except that the third argument to SUBSTR() is optional in Oracle; all three arguments are required in Transact-SQL. The syntax for calling the two functions is as follows:

```
SUBSTRING(string, start, length)
SUBSTR(string, start [, length])
```

The first argument is the string or expression that evaluates to a string from which the substring should be taken. The second argument is the position in the string where the substring begins, and the third argument is the length of the substring. If you are using the SUBSTR() function in Oracle and you leave out the third argument, all the characters between the starting position and the end of the string will be returned by the function.

Here are some examples of the substring function and its results (these aren't real queries—
the string returned by the function appears to the right of the equals sign):

```
SUBSTRING ('Rafe Colburn', 6, 3) = 'Col'
SUBSTR ('Rafe Colburn', 1, 4) = 'Rafe'
SUBSTR ('Rafe Colburn', 6) = 'Colburn'
```

COMBINING SEARCHES AND SUBSTRINGS

You can combine the INSTR() or CHARINDEX() functions with SUBSTR() or SUBSTRING() to
find and extract strings within larger strings. If you have strings that contain a delimiter of
some kind and you want to extract the text from either side of that delimiter, you can use a
combination of the INSTR() and SUBSTR() functions. For example, say that you have a database that includes both first and last names within a single field, and you want to retrieve the
last names from the table. The code in Listing 12.14 would accomplish this task in Oracle,
and the code in Listing 12.15 would work in Sybase or Microsoft SQL Server. The sample
table is displayed in Listing 12.16.

LISTING 12.14   EXTRACTING THE LAST NAMES FROM THE role FIELD IN Cast_Movies

```
SELECT role
FROM Cast_Movies


ROLE
----------------------------------------
Thomas Black
Robert Maxwell
Malcolm Richards
Nina Smith
Pam Green
George Blake
Mitch Crane
Chris Parker
Paul Nero
Sheila Slade
Manfred Powell
```

**LISTING 12.15   EXTRACTING THE LAST NAMES FROM THE name FIELD IN Some_Names IN AN
ORACLE DATABASE**

```
SELECT SUBSTR(role, INSTR(role, ' ') + 1)
FROM Cast_Movies


SUBSTR(ROLE,INSTR(ROLE,''))+1)
----------------------------------------
Black
Maxwell
Richards
Smith
```

continues

PART

IV

CH

12

LISTING 12.15   CONTINUED

```
Green
Blake
Crane
Parker
Nero
Slade
Powell

11 rows selected.
```

LISTING 12.16   EXTRACTING THE LAST NAMES FROM THE name FIELD IN Some_Names IN A SYBASE DATABASE

```
SELECT SUBSTRING(role, CHARINDEX(' ', role) + 1, 40)
AS last_name
FROM Cast_Movies


last_name
----------------------------------------
Black
Maxwell
Richards
Smith
Green
Blake
Crane
Parker
Nero
Slade
Powell

(11 row(s) affected)
```

Tip 48 from
Rafe Colburn

When you use the SUBSTR function in Transact-SQL, you can use the size of the column from which you're taking the substring as the length argument if you want to return all the characters between the starting position and the end of the string. The fact that the length is longer than the number of remaining characters will not break the function call.

SOUNDEX

Soundex is an algorithm that is used to compare strings based on their pronunciation. The SOUNDEX() function breaks down words phonetically that they can be compared based on how they sound rather than by the actual characters in the word. Both Transact-SQL and Oracle support the SOUNDEX() function. When a word is fed to the function, the SOUNDEX() version of the word is returned. Take a look at the example in Listing 12.17.

LISTING 12.17   USING THE SOUNDEX() FUNCTION

```
SELECT SOUNDEX('Colburn')
FROM Dual

SOUN
----
C416
```

Obviously the value returned, C416, is unreadable. The word is broken down by the Soundex algorithm for the purposes of comparison. For example, compare the results in Listing 12.17 to the results in Listing 12.18.

LISTING 12.18   ANOTHER SOUNDEX() EXAMPLE

```
SELECT SOUNDEX('Cohlberne')
FROM Dual

SOUN
----
C416
```

Even though the spelling in the two queries isn't even close to being identical, Soundex determines that the words do, in fact, have the same pronunciation. The SOUNDEX() function is useful when you have a directory of names or other proper nouns that users will be searching. You can search for matches based on the SOUNDEX() derivations of the words and hopefully find the appropriate records even if the user can't spell the name of whatever she's looking for. Consider the example in Listing 12.19, which queries the People table.

LISTING 12.19   SEARCHING THE People TABLE WITH SOUNDEX()

```
SELECT person_fname, person_lname
FROM People
WHERE SOUNDEX('Pedersen') = SOUNDEX(person_lname)

PERSON_FNA PERSON_LNA
---------- ----------
Chuck      Peterson
```

I'll explain briefly how SOUNDEX() works. First, it capitalizes all the letters in the word and pads the word with spaces as needed. The first letter of the word is retained as the first character in the Soundex representation of the word. (Observant readers will note at this point that the Soundex representations of strings never match if the first letters of the words don't match.) Next, letters in a certain group are dropped from the word if they aren't in the first position. Then, each letter is assigned a value between 1 and 6 (certain numbers are associated with particular letters). All consecutive pairs of duplicate digits are removed, and the string is padded with zeros if it is less than four characters long. If the string is longer than four characters, all the numbers after the fourth position are dropped.

DEALING WITH DATES

Dates are a somewhat more complex topic than strings or numbers when it comes to data manipulation in SQL. The problem with dates is that even though they are standardized, there are many ways to represent them visually. This becomes a problem when you enable users to enter dates and you either need to format them so that they can be inserted into a date field or need to retrieve the date from the database and format it in a way that is understandable to the user.

Another problem with dates is that they are handled by different databases in different ways. For example, Transact-SQL provides a number of data types to represent dates, whereas Oracle provides only the DATE type.

Finally, the functions used to format and manipulate dates vary between databases. Indeed, from one database to the next, these functions are generally completely different. So, other than in the most general sense, knowledge of how to handle dates in one database is not transferable to others. Take, for example, the functions used to retrieve the current date, which are listed in Table 12.2.

TABLE 12.2   FUNCTIONS FROM VARIOUS DATABASES THAT RETURN THE CURRENT TIME

Function	Database	Result
SYSDATE	Oracle	14-APR-99
GETDATE()	Sybase	1999-07-20 11:08:18.276
GETDATE()	MS SQL Server	1999-07-20 11:16:20
NOW()	MySQL	1999-07-20 11:14:26

As you can see, each database formats dates differently. Most relational databases store dates to a remarkable level of precision. Even though Oracle dates are presented in the day-month-year format by default, the dates stored within date fields are actually accurate down to fractions of seconds.

Another issue handled differently by various databases is date arithmetic. Most databases provide functions that enable users to add and subtract dates, however, these functions differ radically from one database to the next.

FORMATTING DATES FOR OUTPUT

When you have dates stored within a database that you want to place within a report, you usually have to perform some formatting on those dates before presenting them to the user. Rarely do users want to see dates that are precise out to the millisecond, and in many cases they don't want to see the dates in the default format provided by the database anyway. Oracle provides the TO_CHAR() function for presenting dates in a particular format. TO_CHAR() enables you to specify a date and a format, and TO_CHAR() will return the date in that format, as shown in the example in Listing 12.20.

LISTING 12.20   FORMATTING MOVIE RELEASE DATES WITH TO_CHAR()

```
SELECT TO_CHAR(release_date, 'MONTH DD, YYYY')
FROM Movies

TO_CHAR(RELEASE_DA
------------------
JANUARY   01, 1975
MAY       01, 1979
SEPTEMBER 01, 1991
JULY      15, 1988
JULY      01, 1997
AUGUST    22, 1993
NOVEMBER  01, 1998
APRIL     17, 1993
APRIL     18, 1995
JULY      11, 1987
JANUARY   06, 1995

TO_CHAR(RELEASE_DA
------------------
AUGUST    08, 1991

12 rows selected.
```

The format 'MONTH DD, YYYY' indicates that the date should be presented using the full month, the day of the month, and the year in four-digit format. MONTH, DD, and YYYY are all tokens that are replaced by the actual parts of the date being presented. There are a number of other tokens that can be plugged into the TO_CHAR() function to customize the output of dates in your reports. I'll provide a list of these tokens later in the chapter with the discussion of the TO_CHAR() and TO_DATE() functions.

Other databases provide similar functions for transforming dates into the appropriate formats for output. For example, in Transact-SQL, the general-purpose, data-conversion function CONVERT() is used to format dates for output. Unlike TO_CHAR(), however, there are predefined date styles that can be used with CONVERT() instead of various date parts that can be used to create styles from scratch. The use of the CONVERT() function will be discussed later in this chapter.

PART
IV
CH
12

FORMATTING DATES FOR INPUT

Before dates can be inserted into databases, they must be formatted so that the database recognizes the inserted value as a date. Databases vary in the amount of flexibility they provide in this area. Some databases read dates entered in a wide variety of formats properly; others have strict requirements that govern how a date must be formatted before it can be inserted in a particular field.

Generally speaking, there are two ways to prepare a date value for insertion into a database field. The first is to determine what the recognized date format is for the database you're using, to include code in the program that you're writing that formats dates appropriately, and then to include the formatted date in the SQL statement. The second is to use the data type conversion functions to manipulate the data so that it conforms to the format the database can recognize.

Ordinarily, the data that will be inserted into a date field in the database is string data, so the data conversion function must change the format of the string into one that the database recognizes as a valid date. In Oracle, the TO_DATE() function is used to convert strings to dates; the SQL standard (and Transact-SQL) uses the CONVERT() function. Both of these functions will be discussed in the section on data conversion later in this chapter.

Transact-SQL handles the conversion of date data in a character string to a date implicitly. If you use character data in a date context, it will attempt to convert that data into a date. If it fails to do so, the SQL statement will fail with an error.

DATE ARITHMETIC

Again, it is hard to generalize about date arithmetic because the methods for adding and subtracting dates vary so greatly from database to database. For example, Oracle enables you to add days to a date using a simple arithmetic expression, as shown in Listing 12.21.

LISTING 12.21 ADDING DAYS TO A DATE IN ORACLE

```
SELECT SYSDATE, SYSDATE + 3
FROM Dual

SYSDATE    SYSDATE+3
--------- ---------
14-APR-99 17-APR-99
```

One area of difficulty with Oracle is that it doesn't provide a function for performing date arithmetic with arbitrary units of time. In Transact-SQL, to add an hour to the current date, the following function call is used:

```
DATEADD (hour, 1, GETDATE())
```

The arguments to the DATEADD() function are the unit of time being added to the date, the number of that unit to add to the date, and the date to which those numbers will be added. To subtract units of time from a date, the DATEADD() function is used with a negative number of units. To subtract a week from the current date, the following function call would be used:

```
DATEADD (week, -1, GETDATE())
```

Table 12.3 contains a list of units that can be used with the DATEADD() function, as well as some other Transact-SQL date-related functions.

TABLE 12.3 DATE UNITS AND ABBREVIATIONS FOR USE WITH TRANSACT-SQL

Unit	Abbreviation	Range of values
millisecond	mm	0–999
second	ss	0–59

Unit	Abbreviation	Range of values
minute	mm	0–59
hour	hh	0–23
day	dd	1–31
weekday	dw	1–7
dayofyear	dy	1–366
week	wk	1–54
month	mm	1–12
quarter	qq	1–4
year	yy	1753–9999

There is no equivalent functionality in Oracle. Instead, you have to calculate the decimal value of an hour, and subtract that from the date to decrement it by an hour, as shown in Listing 12.22.

LISTING 12.22   DATE ARITHMETIC IN ORACLE

```
SELECT TO_CHAR(SYSDATE, 'HH:MI:SS'),
TO_CHAR(SYSDATE - (1/24), 'HH:MI:SS')
FROM Dual

TO_CHAR( TO_CHAR(
-------- --------
07:17:02 06:17:02
```

By using division expressions in your queries, you can perform date calculations within Oracle. The first item in the select list in Listing 12.22 returns the current time; the second subtracts 1/24 (or one hour) from the current time and returns that value.

Tip 49 from
Rafe Colburn

> Calculating various units of time in Oracle is easy when you consider the fact that a day is the base unit of time for Oracle. To calculate a minute, you just multiply 24 by 60 to determine the number of minutes in a day and then divide one by that value, as shown:
>
> `(1/(24 * 60))`
>
> To add one day and one minute to the current date, the following expression can be used:
>
> `SYSDATE + (1 + (1/(24 * 60)))`

Because the number of days in each month varies, Oracle supports a separate ADD_MONTHS() function that can be used to increment a date by a number of months. To use the ADD_MONTHS() function, simply pass a date and a number of months (positive or negative) to the function, as shown in Listing 12.23.

PART

IV

CH

12

LISTING 12.23   USING ADD_MONTHS() IN ORACLE

```
SELECT SYSDATE, ADD_MONTHS(SYSDATE, 6)
FROM Dual

SYSDATE     ADD_MONTH
--------- ---------
02-MAY-99 02-NOV-99
```

COMPARING DATES

As you've already seen, you can add or subtract specified amounts of time from dates using simple arithmetic in Oracle and DATEADD() in Transact-SQL. You also know that you can compare dates within the WHERE clause of a query. What you've not yet seen, however, is a method by which you can find the difference between two dates.

In Oracle, the MONTHS_BETWEEN() function is used to determine how many months have passed between two dates. Needless to say, it returns the number of months between the two dates specified as arguments; the time remaining after the number of months has been derived is returned as a decimal number. The query in Listing 12.24 will return how long ago each movie in the Movies table was released. The number that results from the function call is divided by 12 to return the time that has elapsed in years instead of months.

LISTING 12.24   USING THE MONTHS_BETWEEN() FUNCTION TO DETERMINE HOW LONG AGO SOMETHING HAPPENED

```
SELECT movie_title, (MONTHS_BETWEEN(SYSDATE, release_date)/12)
FROM Movies
WHERE release_date IS NOT NULL

MOVIE_TITLE             (MONTHS_BETWEEN(SYSDATE,RELEASE_DATE)/12)
------------------- -----------------------------------------
Vegetable House                          24.3382251
Prince Kong                              20.0048917
The Code Warrior                          7.67155839
Bill Durham                              10.8005907
Codependence Day                          1.83822506
The Linux Files                           5.69844011
SQL Strikes Back                           .504891726
The Programmer                            6.04521431
Hard Code                                 4.04252614
The Rear Windows                         11.8113433

10 rows selected.
```

In Transact-SQL, the DATEDIFF() function is used to return the time differential between two dates. The method by which the DATEDIFF() function is called is similar to that of the DATEADD() function; it accepts three arguments: the unit to be used and the two dates for which the differential will be calculated. The list of units supported by the DATEDIFF() function is in Table 12.3. It's the same as the list for DATEADD(). The DATEDIFF() function could be used as shown in Listing 12.25 to derive the number of years since each movie has been released.

LISTING 12.25 USING THE DATEDIFF() FUNCTION TO DETERMINE THE NUMBER OF YEARS SINCE A MOVIE'S RELEASE

```
SELECT movie_title, DATEDIFF(YEAR, release_date, getdate())
FROM Movies

movie_title
------------------------ -----------
Mineral House              24
Prince Kong                20
The Code Warrior            8
Bill Durham                11
Codependence Day            2
The Linux Files             6
SQL Strikes Back            1
The Programmer              6
Hard Code                   4
The Rear Windows           12

(10 row(s) affected)
```

ROUNDING TEMPORAL VALUES

As you know, the DATE data type in Oracle can support very precise date and time values. This is also true of DATETIME fields in Transact-SQL and of the date and time data types in all relational databases. Unfortunately, aside from formatting issues, comparing times that are kept to such a high level of precision can be difficult. If a time is precise to the millisecond, comparing it to another time to see whether they occurred in the same hour is fruitless. Unless they are identical down to the millisecond, the result of the comparison will be false.

Any time you're comparing dates, it's necessary to make sure that both dates are precise only to the level that the comparison is meaningful. If you want to find out if two dates fall within the same year, you only want to compare the year values, not the entire dates. You can create such comparisons by using TO_DATE() to format the dates as strings and then perform the comparison in Oracle, or you can use a function like DATEPART() in Transact-SQL to compare the meaningful parts of both dates to one another to confirm that they are equal.

In Oracle, the ROUND() and TRUNC() can also be used to reduce the precision of the values in date fields. The ROUND() function returns the date with a time of 12 a.m. if the current time is before 12 p.m. or the next day's date (relative to the date passed to the ROUND() function) with a time of 12 a.m. if the current time is after noon. The TRUNC() function simply returns the date passed to it with a time of 12 a.m. If you want to determine whether the date in a record is the same as the current date, you should use TRUNC() as shown in Listing 12.26.

LISTING 12.26 USING TRUNC() TO REDUCE THE PRECISION OF A DATE

```
SELECT movie_title
FROM Movies
WHERE release_date = TRUNC(SYSDATE)
```

```
no rows selected
```

In Transact-SQL, you can return the date from a date-and-time data field using the CON-VERT() function. Use of the CONVERT() function in this manner is discussed in the section "The CONVERT() Function" later in this chapter.

CONVERTING DATA BETWEEN TYPES

Most expressions and functions in SQL require that data be supplied in a particular context, and most comparisons require that the data being compared be of the same type. For example, the UPPER() function only works if the function's argument is a string. Similarly, a comparison such as the following will not work because '500' is enclosed within single quotation marks and is treated as a string rather than as a number:

```
'500' > 600
```

To compare the two values, which are both obviously numbers, one of the two values must be converted so that both of them are of the same data type.

Fields generally do not have to contain data of exactly the same type to be compared; some conversions are handled implicitly. Generally speaking, data types that are in the same category can be compared without being converted from one data type to the other. You can generally compare character and variable character fields without matching the data types exactly. This also holds true for numeric and date types.

If a database differentiates between fields that hold integers and floating point numbers, values in those types of fields can be compared freely with each other without conversion. Some databases provide many different date data types. As long as you make comparisons between one date data type and another, the database will implicitly handle any conversion necessary.

Many databases will also implicitly convert between categories of data if doing so makes sense in the context in which the data is used. For example, if you supply a number as the argument to the RTRIM() function in Oracle, the number will automatically be converted to a string for use by the function. Similarly, Transact-SQL automatically attempts to convert strings to dates if the strings are used in contexts where dates are expected.

THE CONVERT() FUNCTION

Databases that support Transact-SQL use the general purpose CONVERT() function to convert data between data types. The CONVERT() function uses three arguments to perform the conversion; the destination data type, the expression to be converted, and if a date is being converted to a string type, the output style of the date. Usage of the CONVERT() function is as follows:

```
CONVERT(data_type, expression[, style])
```

So, to convert a numeric field to a data field, the CONVERT() function could be used as shown in Listing 12.27.

LISTING 12.27   USING THE CONVERT() FUNCTION WITHIN A QUERY

```
SELECT budget
FROM Movies
WHERE CONVERT(CHAR(10), budget) = '50'

budget
--------------------
50
50

(2 row(s) affected)
```

The query in Listing 12.27 isn't very useful because the comparison could have just as easily been written WHERE budget = 50, but it does a fine job of illustrating its purpose, which was to show how CONVERT() is used. The CONVERT() function tells the database to treat the contents of the budget field as though they were stored in a field of type CHAR(10) instead of the numeric field that is really specified.

There are generally no restrictions on converting numeric data types to strings; as long as the number will fit within the field specification in the CONVERT() function, the data should be converted without a hitch. Converting strings to numbers is a bit more tricky because there are plenty of string characters and formats that are not translatable into numeric data. There are several conditions that will prevent data from being converted successfully:

- Commas in data to be converted to an integer or money.
- Decimal points in data to be converted to an integer.
- Letters in data to be converted to a numeric data type.
- Misspelled or invalid month names in data to be converted to a date and time.

The CONVERT() data type can be used to convert dates to and from other data types. Unlike Oracle, Transact-SQL does not enable you to simply specify a date format and then use it to convert a date to that format or to retrieve a date from a string presented in that format. Instead, there are several formats built in to Transact-SQL (they're listed in Table 12.4), and you must specify one of them when calling the CONVERT() function.

PART
IV
CH
12

Tip 50 from
Rafe Colburn

If you're working in multiple databases, it's important to remember that Oracle also supplies a CONVERT() function, but it is completely different from Transact-SQL's CONVERT() function. In Oracle, CONVERT() is a string function that translates string data from one character set to another. Like the Transact-SQL CONVERT() function, it accepts three arguments, but they are used to specify the string to be converted, the destination character set, and the source character set.

Not only is CONVERT() used to convert string values to dates, it's also used to present dates in formats other than the default, as shown in Table 12.4. It is in this role that the style attribute of the CONVERT() function comes into play. Transact-SQL provides a number of alternative formats for date presentation that can be supplied to alter the presentation of a date. Each format can be presented in one of two ways: with the two digits indicating the century or without them. A list of the formats and their appearance is provided in Table 12.4. An example that demonstrates the use of CONVERT() to format dates and times appears in Listing 12.28. In Table 12.4, the ID column shows the ID used to specify that format with a two digit year. The ID with Century column contains the ID for formats with a four digit year specified. The Standard column specifies which standard that format conforms to, and the Output column contains an example of what that format looks like.

LISTING 12.28   USING CONVERT() TO FORMAT A DATE

```
SELECT CONVERT(varchar, GETDATE(), 107)

- - - - - - - - - - - - - - - - - - - - - - - - - - - -
May 23, 1999

(1 row(s) affected)
```

TABLE 12.4   TRANSACT-SQL DATE FORMATS

ID	ID with Century	Standard	Output
-	0 or 100	default	May 23 1999 12:54PM
1	101	USA	05/23/99
2	2	SQL standard	99.05.23
3	103	English/French	23/05/99
4	104	German	23.05.99
5	105		23-05-99
6	106		23 May 99
7	107		May 23, 99
8	108		12:56:59
-	9 or 109	default + ms	May 23 1999 12:57:09:056PM
10	110	USA	05-23-99
11	111	Japan	99/05/23
12	112	ISO	990523

CONVERTING DATA TYPES IN ORACLE

There are three functions available in Oracle for converting values from one data type to another: TO_CHAR(), TO_DATE(), and TO_NUMBER(). I already discussed the use of the TO_CHAR() function with regard to formatting dates for output, but I didn't go into the fact that TO_CHAR() is the general-purpose function in Oracle for converting various data types to character types.

The TO_CHAR() function is used to convert numbers and dates into character strings. Most conversions from numbers to strings are handled implicitly. Say, for example, that you have a table called Test with this schema:

```
Name                            Null?    Type
------------------------------- -------- ----
TEST                                     VARCHAR2(20)
```

An INSERT statement such as the one that follows will work, even though the data in the list of values is numeric (it has no single quotes):

```
INSERT INTO Test
VALUES (500)
```

Oracle converts the number 500, into a string containing the number 500 automatically before it is inserted. Because implicit data conversion converts numbers to strings automatically, the main usage of the TO_CHAR() function is to format dates. Dates are implicitly converted into strings, but only into the default format (DD-MMM-YY). To convert a date to a string using a different format, both the date (or column name containing a date) and format must be provided to the TO_CHAR() function.

As I discussed earlier, formats are defined using tokens that represent various components of a date. These tokens are provided in Table 12.5 and Table 12.6. These tokens are grouped within single quotation marks to create date formats, as demonstrated in Listing 12.29.

LISTING 12.29   A DATE FORMAT CONTAINING BOTH TEXT AND TOKENS

```
SELECT TO_CHAR(SYSDATE, 'DAY, MONTH DD')
FROM Dual

TO_CHAR(SYSDATE,'DAY,MO
-----------------------
MONDAY   , MAY      03
```

PART

IV

CH

12

Tip 51 from
Rafe Colburn

You can include text expressions in the select list if you want to combine text with the date formats that you create. Take the following query, for example:

```
SELECT 'Today is', TO_CHAR(SYSDATE, 'DAY')
FROM Dual


'TODAYIS TO_CHAR(S
-------- ---------
Today is MONDAY
```

TABLE 12.5   TOKENS USED TO CREATE ORACLE DATE FORMATS FOR INPUT AND OUTPUT

Token	Represents
YYYY	Four-digit year
SYYYY	Signed year (includes B.C. years)
YYY	Last three digits of year
YY	Last two digits of year
Y	Last digit of year
IYYY	Four-digit year from ISO standard
IYY	Three-digit year from ISO standard
IY	Two-digit year from ISO standard
I	One-digit year from ISO standard
YEAR	The year spelled out
RR	Last two digits of year relative to current date
Q	Number of the quarter
MM	Number of month
RM	Roman numeral month
MON	Three letter abbreviation for month
MONTH	Full month name
WW	Number of weeks since the beginning of the year
DDD	Day of year
DD	Day of month
D	Day of week (numerical)
Y	Day of week (three-letter abbreviation)
DAY	Full day of week
HH	Hour (12-hour scale)
HH12	Hour (12-hour scale)
HH24	Hour (24-hour scale)
MI	Minute
SS	Seconds
SSSSS	Seconds since midnight
A.M.	Display A.M. or P.M. for time selected
P.M.	Same as A.M.
AM, PM	Display AM or PM (without periods)
J	Julian date

Token	Represents
A.D.	Display A.D. or B.C. depending on date
B.C.	Same as A.D.
AD, BC	Display AD or BC (without periods)
/,-:.	Date punctuation

TABLE 12.6   TOKENS USED IN DATE OUTPUT WITH TO_CHAR()

Token	Represents
"string"	A string to be inserted in the date format
fm	When used to preface the MONTH or DAY tokens, removes spaces padding the month or day (normally, month and day names are padded with spaces so that they all occupy as many spaces as the longest month and day names)
TH	Appends the appropriate TH suffix onto the token to which it is attached
SP	Causes the number to which it is attached to be spelled out
SPTH	Spells out the number to which it is attached and includes the appropriate TH suffix on the number
THSP	Same as SPTH

When the TO_CHAR() function is used, the capitalization of the tokens within the date format affects the output of the format. Basically, words generated by the TO_CHAR() function follow the same pattern of capitalization as the tokens to which they correspond. For example, consider the query results in Listing 12.30.

LISTING 12.30   HOW TOKEN CAPITALIZATION AFFECTS CAPITALIZATION OF OUTPUT

```
SELECT TO_CHAR(SYSDATE, 'Month'), TO_CHAR(SYSDATE, 'ddTHSP'),
TO_CHAR (SYSDATE, 'YEAR ad')
FROM Dual

TO_CHAR(S TO_CHAR(SYSDAT TO_CHAR(SYSDATE,'YEARAD')
--------- -------------- --------------------------------------------
May       fourth         NINETEEN NINETY-NINE ad
```

PART

IV

CH

12

Notice how the capitalization of the dates in the query results follows the capitalization of the tokens in the TO_CHAR() function calls. The fact that the first character of Month is capitalized indicates that only the first letter in the actual name of the month should be capitalized. You should also note that you can mix capitalization styles within a single call to TO_CHAR(). In the last select item, the name of the current year is capitalized, but the epoch is listed in lowercase letters.

The TO_DATE() function is used to convert character strings into Oracle dates. When a string and a format are provided to the TO_DATE() function, the string is compared to the format, and then, if possible, a date is extracted from the string that is supplied. The tokens used with the TO_DATE() function are the same as those used with the TO_CHAR() function. The use of the TO_DATE() function is demonstrated in Listing 12.31.

LISTING 12.31   USING TO_DATE() TO CONVERT A STRING TO A DATE

```
SELECT TO_DATE('March 1, 1999', 'Month DD, YYYY')
FROM Dual


TO_DATE('
---------
01-MAR-99
```

IN THE REAL WORLD

Another type of data that I haven't discussed yet in this chapter is *large objects*. Most databases support a data type that can hold large amounts of binary or character data. Some databases store the data within the database. Others write the data stored in these fields to files in the file system and just store pointers to the data in the database itself.

There are a number of restrictions on large objects that do not apply to other data types, due to the fact that handling such large amounts of data is unwieldy. Large objects cannot be indexed, and in some cases, they can't be searched using LIKE comparisons. Some databases also disallow the comparison of large objects using the standard comparison operators.

Limitations on the uses of large objects have become less painful as the capacity of the standard data types has increased. For example, in Microsoft SQL Server 6.5, the maximum size of a VARCHAR field was 255 characters. In version 7.0, the limit was raised to 4000 characters. Similarly, Oracle 8 supports up to 2000-character CHAR fields and 4000-character VARCHAR2 fields. As the capacity of these fields increases, the limitations on how large objects can be used become less important.

Obviously, large objects are still necessary for storing binary data and larger chunks of ASCII data, but the standard fields become applicable to more and more tasks. Most databases support a large object data type for storing character data and a large object data type for storing binary data. Oracle actually supports four large object data types. The CLOB (character large object) data type is used to store character data up to four gigabytes, and the BLOB data type can store up to four gigabytes of binary data in the field. There's also NCLOB, which is like CLOB, except that it supports multibyte character sets. The final large object type supported by Oracle is the BFILE type, which is actually a pointer to a file stored in the file system.

Transact-SQL supports the TEXT data type for storing up to two gigabytes of character data, and the IMAGE data type, which can store up to two gigabytes of binary data. Neither IMAGE nor TEXT fields can be used in the following instances:

- As arguments to stored procedures
- As arguments in RPC calls

- In UNION, ORDER BY, GROUP BY, or COMPUTE clauses
- In an index
- In joining comparisons or subqueries
- Anywhere in the WHERE clause, except in a LIKE comparison
- With the + string concatenation operator
- In a trigger that uses IN UPDATE

As you can see, there are plenty of restrictions placed on large objects by Transact-SQL. The list of restrictions is similar in most databases because dealing with such large amounts of data is difficult.

Unfortunately, the ways in which large objects can be utilized and manipulated within databases varies widely from platform to platform. For detailed information on how your database manufacturer implements large objects, you should see the documentation specific to the database.

CHAPTER 13

Database Performance and Integrity

In this chapter

Two issues that are fundamental to good database application design are performance and integrity. When you deploy an application, performance is obviously very important. If the performance of your application is unsatisfactory, the chances that it will be useful to its users are low. By the same token, data integrity is fundamental to any database. If you cannot be sure that the data you're dealing with is not corrupt, it's impossible to rely on the database for anything important.

Unfortunately, these two necessary attributes of any database application are set against one another in some ways. Many of the measures taken to ensure the integrity of a database tend to hinder performance. For most applications, these tradeoffs are insignificant because the demand placed on the database is not enough that performance becomes an issue. Even so, you should be aware of the techniques that can be used to improve database performance and of the tradeoffs between performance and integrity so that you can make informed decisions about how to design your database so that it meets your performance requirements without sacrificing integrity.

IMPROVING DATABASE PERFORMANCE

The first thing you should know about database performance is that it can be measured in multiple ways. Some optimizations will enhance performance across the board, but others will improve some aspects of performance but hinder others. Database performance can be measured by the following metrics:

- Response time
- Concurrent users supported
- Transactions per day

Obviously, any application will have a minimum requirement for each of these performance metrics, but in some cases, you might need to make tradeoffs between these types of performance.

PERFORMANCE CONSIDERATIONS IN DATABASE DESIGN

Before you put any thought toward writing your queries so that they provide the best possible performance, you should first make sure that your databases themselves are designed for optimal performance. As I discussed at the end of Chapter 2, "Database Design," there are several philosophies of database design. When you design your database, you should base the schema on the type of application you're building: decision support or online transaction processing. For more information on these types of applications, consult the "In the Real World" section of Chapter 2.

As a rule, the smaller the data type you can use to accomplish a task, the better. This is due to the simple logic that the less space is consumed by your data, the less overhead there is in searching the data in memory or reading it from disk. You should be mindful of the small amounts of overhead associated with various data types and column settings. For example, there is some overhead associated with variable character fields because a few bytes are needed to determine how much space is being consumed by the data within the field. However, if the data stored in the field does vary widely from field to field, the savings over plain character fields makes the overhead worthwhile.

There is also some savings associated with using NOT NULL fields instead of NULL fields. Fields that can hold NULL values use a few bytes of storage to indicate whether the value in the field is null or not.

Some databases support the BIT data type, which consumes only a single bit of storage, for storing Boolean values. There are a couple of advantages associated with BIT. The first is the miniscule amount of storage it consumes. The second advantage is that BIT fields eliminate the need to keep track of which values indicate whether the contents of the field are true (or on) or false (or off). For example, if you use a CHAR(1) field to store Boolean values, you're saddled with the burden of remembering whether true values use T and false values use F or true values use Y and false values use N or whatever. With the BIT data type, 1 is true and 0 is false.

PERFORMANCE MEASUREMENT TOOLS

Every time you execute a query, an *execution plan* is created for that query, and the database performs the operations in the execution plan. In a sense, queries are like math problems. Simple math problems only require a single operation to perform; when you add two and two, you perform one addition operation and come out with four. If you're multiplying multi-digit numbers by hand, you generally use one multiplication operation for each digit in one of the numbers, and then you add all the resulting numbers. There are even more operations involved in solving complex algebraic equations. An execution plan is similar; it is a list of all the individual operations used to obtain the results of the larger query.

In mathematics and in querying a database, there are generally many ways to solve a complex problem. If you're solving the problem, you choose the method that's easiest for you. In a database, the *query optimizer* chooses the execution plan that it believes is most efficient for performing the query. You can use database-performance measurement tools to see the actual operations that the query optimizer uses in the execution path that it chooses for a query.

Most databases contain some tools that enable you to view the execution plan for the queries that you execute and use them to determine whether you should use any optimizer hints to improve the performance of your queries. You can also write different queries and then compare how they are executed to determine which will provide your application with the best performance.

Databases that use Transact-SQL (Microsoft SQL Server, and all Sybase's products) use the SHOWPLAN setting to provide users with an analysis of how their queries are executed. Oracle uses the autotrace setting to provide the same functionality. These tools are used to break down your queries into the individual operations that are performed to fulfill them. I'm going to take a look at each of them in turn.

ORACLE AUTOTRACE

There are actually two methods you can use to see the execution plan for a particular query. If you want to view the execution plan for a query before you actually run the query, you can use the EXPLAIN PLAN command. If you just want to see the execution plans for queries after they are executed, you can use SET AUTOTRACE ON. When you don't care to see execution plans any more, you can turn off the autotrace setting by using SET AUTOTRACE OFF.

Tip 52 from
Rafe Colburn

If you're analyzing SELECT statements, using the AUTOTRACE setting to view the execution plans for queries is probably fine. However, if you're entering data manipulation statements, EXPLAIN PLAN provides a safe way to view execution plans for those queries without actually modifying the data in your tables.

Let me go ahead and provide an example of how the EXPLAIN PLAN command works. To use it, you just enter EXPLAIN PLAN FOR and then enter your query. The execution plan for a simple query is provided in Listing 13.1.

LISTING 13.1 THE EXECUTION PLAN FOR A SIMPLE QUERY

```
EXPLAIN PLAN FOR
SELECT *
FROM Movies;

Explained.
```

For EXPLAIN PLAN to work, you must have created a table that will hold the plans for the queries that are explained. There's a script called utlxplan.sql that comes with Oracle that will create a table called PLAN_TABLE so that you can use EXPLAIN_PLAN. If you create another table for plans, you have to specify the name of that table in your EXPLAIN PLAN statement, and the table must conform to the format of PLAN_TABLE. To identify distinct plans in your plan table, you can include a STATEMENT ID in your EXPLAIN PLAN statement, as shown in Listing 13.2.

LISTING 13.2 SAVING THE PLAN FOR A QUERY WITH A STATEMENT ID

```
EXPLAIN PLAN
SET STATEMENT_ID = 'foo'
FOR
SELECT movie_title
FROM Movies

Explained.
```

To retrieve the data from the plan table after you've explained the plan for a query, you can use a simple query like the one shown in Listing 13.3. These results include two columns, but there are many other columns of data available in the execution plans stored in the plan table.

LISTING 13.3   RETRIEVING EXPLAIN PLANS FROM A PLAN TABLE

```
SELECT operation, object_name
FROM Plan_Table
WHERE statement_id = 'foo'

OPERATION                        OBJECT_NAME
------------------------------   ----------------------------
SELECT STATEMENT
TABLE ACCESS                     MOVIES
```

The autotrace setting is a bit easier to use than EXPLAIN PLAN. The results of a query with autotrace turned on are displayed in Listing 13.4.

LISTING 13.4   EXAMINING AN EXECUTION PLAN USING THE AUTOTRACE SETTING

```
SET AUTOTRACE ON;

SELECT studio_name
FROM Studios;

STUDIO_NAME
--------------------
Giant
MPM
FKG
Delighted Artists
Metaversal Studios
Some Studio

6 rows selected.


Execution Plan
----------------------------------------------------------
   0      SELECT STATEMENT Optimizer=CHOOSE
   1    0   TABLE ACCESS (FULL) OF 'STUDIOS'




Statistics
----------------------------------------------------------
       219  recursive calls
         4  db block gets
        44  consistent gets
         3  physical reads
         0  redo size
       662  bytes sent via SQL*Net to client
       659  bytes received via SQL*Net from client
         4  SQL*Net roundtrips to/from client
         4  sorts (memory)
         0  sorts (disk)
         6  rows processed
```

As you can see, when autotrace is turned on, a lot of results are generated. The statistics table consists of information about the utilization of database and system resources by the query. More interesting to you is the execution plan.

There are three entries in the execution plan. The first column in the output contains the ID of the operation in the execution plan. The IDs are assigned sequentially (starting at 0) for each query. The second column displays the parent operation for the current operation, assuming there is one (the first operation in an execution plan does not have a parent), and finally, the third column contains the actual operation that was performed.

When you're familiar with the relative costs of the various operations supported by Oracle, it's easy to see where performance bottlenecks can be introduced when you view execution plans. For example, any time you see a FULL TABLE SCAN when you're using an indexed column in the WHERE clause of a query, you should investigate to determine whether you can replace that condition with one that takes advantage of the index.

Take a look at the execution plan for a more complex query. Listing 13.5 contains the plan for a three-table join.

LISTING 13.5 THE EXECUTION PLAN FOR A THREE-TABLE JOIN

```
SELECT movie_title, role, person_fname, person_lname
FROM Movies, Cast_Movies, People
WHERE Movies.movie_id = Cast_Movies.movie_id
AND People.person_id = Cast_Movies.person_id


Execution Plan
- - - - - - - - - - - - - - - - - - - - - - - - - - - - - - - - - - - - - - - - - - - -
  0        SELECT STATEMENT Optimizer=CHOOSE
  1     0    NESTED LOOPS
  2     1      NESTED LOOPS
  3     2        TABLE ACCESS (FULL) OF 'CAST_MOVIES'
  4     2        TABLE ACCESS (BY INDEX ROWID) OF 'PEOPLE'
  5     4          INDEX (UNIQUE SCAN) OF 'SYS_C00665' (UNIQUE)
  6     1      TABLE ACCESS (BY INDEX ROWID) OF 'MOVIES'
  7     6        INDEX (UNIQUE SCAN) OF 'SYS_C00667' (UNIQUE)
```

I'll discuss the operations used in the join in Listing 13.5 and the other operations used by an Oracle database in the section of this chapter that discusses query optimizers.

TRANSACT-SQL SHOWPLAN

Transact-SQL supports the SHOWPLAN setting for displaying execution plans when you run queries. To turn on SHOWPLAN, use the following command:

```
SET SHOWPLAN ON
```

Note

Microsoft SQL Server 7.0 replaces SET SHOWPLAN with two variations, SET SHOWPLAN_ALL and SET SHOWPLAN_TEXT. The SHOWPLAN_ALL setting provides an extremely detailed report on the execution plan for a query. SHOWPLAN_TEXT provies a simpler version of the report.

If you want to duplicate the functionality of Oracle's EXPLAIN PLAN command, you can turn on the NOEXEC setting like this:

```
SET NOEXEC ON
```

When both of those settings are on, when you enter queries, the execution plan will be displayed, and the query itself will not be executed. Listing 13.6 contains an example of a sequence of commands that will display the execution plan for the SELECT statement without actually executing that statement.

LISTING 13.6   USING SHOWPLAN AND NOEXEC TOGETHER

```
SET SHOWPLAN ON
SET NOEXEC ON

SELECT movie_title
FROM Movies

StmtText
-----------------------------------------------------------------------------
SELECT Movies.movie_title, Studios.studio_name
FROM Movies, Studios
WHERE Studios.studio_id = Movies.movie_id

(1 row(s) affected)

StmtText
-----------------------------------------------------------------------------
  |--Hash Match(Inner Join, HASH:([Studios].[studio_id])=([Movies].[movie_id]),
RESIDUAL:([Movies].[movie_id]=[Studios].[studio_id]))
       |--Table Scan(OBJECT:([rafeco].[dbo].[Studios]))
       |--Table Scan(OBJECT:([rafeco].[dbo].[Movies]))

(3 row(s) affected)


SET NOEXEC OFF
SET SHOWPLAN_TEXT OFF
```

Note

The SET SHOWPLAN_TEXT statements must be executed separately from the other queries in the listing.

PART

IV

Cн

13

Tip 53 from *Rafe Colburn*	There are two advantages of using NOEXEC (or, if you're an Oracle developer, EXPLAIN PLAN). The first is that you can see the execution plan for a complex query without waiting for the query to execute or viewing the results. You probably won't be interested in seeing the execution plan for a simple query that returns all the rows from a 10-row table. You probably will be interested in a query that contains a four-table join and returns 17,000 records. Viewing the plan without looking at the 17,000 records or waiting for the query to finish can make your life a lot easier. The second advantage is that you can view the execution plans for data manipulation statements without actually modifying the data in your database. If, to check out the execution plan for a DELETE statement, you actually had to delete records, the performance measurement tools wouldn't be nearly as useful.

INDEXES

Indexes are probably the single most important tool for improving the performance of database applications. A properly indexed database can be orders of magnitude faster than a non-indexed database for evaluating the same queries. The mechanics of creating indexes were discussed in Chapter 3, "Creating Databases." This section discusses how best to apply indexes to maximize the performance of your database.

How best to use indexes on a table depends entirely on how that table will be used. As I explained in Chapter 3, indexes improve the performance of SELECT statements, but they hinder the performance of UPDATE, INSERT, and DELETE statements. When the values in an indexed column change, the indexes must be updated along with the values in the column. The performance of transaction-processing systems, which tend to use as many data-modification queries as data retrieval queries, can be slowed by indexes.

Some queries benefit more from indexes than others, and in fact, some queries do not take advantage of indexes at all. After you index your tables properly, it's important to take advantage of those indexes by writing the proper queries.

The best way to take advantage of indexes is to use indexed columns in the WHERE, ORDER BY, and GROUP BY clauses of your queries. As a general rule, when you modify the value in an indexed column that is used in the WHERE clause, the index on that column will be ignored.

CLUSTERED INDEXES

Transact-SQL supports a particular type of index, the *clustered index*, which physically orders the records in a table according to the contents of a particular column.

As you know, a standard index keeps an ordered data structure representing the contents of a column (or group of columns). The performance advantage afforded by a clustered index is even greater. Because the table itself is ordered based on the values in a column, queries structured to take advantage of the clustered index can gain immense performance benefits.

The queries that best take advantage of clustered indexes are those that that order the values in a column as part of the query. For example, any query that uses the column with the clustered index in the ORDER BY or GROUP BY clause will gain large performance benefits.

QUERIES THAT UTILIZE INDEXES

Some queries completely ignore indexes and perform operations against the column in the table itself instead of the index on a column. Obviously, if you can, it's best to avoid these types of queries because they will perform worse than queries that do take advantage of indexing. You'll need to investigate the database you're using to determine exactly which queries do and don't take advantage of indexing. I'm going to go over some of the conditions that determine whether indexes are used in Oracle databases; they probably hold true for most other databases as well.

LIKE comparisons in which the beginning of the string being compared is specified do take advantage of indexes; LIKE comparisons that begin with a wildcard do not. Take a look at the following two examples. This query takes advantage of an index on the movie_title column:

```
SELECT movie_title
FROM Movies
WHERE movie_title LIKE 'The %'
```

However, this one does not:

```
SELECT movie_title
FROM Movies
WHERE movie_title LIKE '% Code %'
```

When you apply a function to a column in the WHERE clause, indexes will be ignored as well. Instead of looking up the value in the index, the query has to retrieve the value from the table, apply the function in question to it, and then compare that string to the string used within the WHERE clause. For example, the following query does not take advantage of indexes:

```
SELECT movie_title
FROM Movies
WHERE TRIM(movie_title) = 'Mineral House'
```

Tip 54 from
Rafe Colburn

The fact that applying functions to columns in the WHERE clause precludes the use of indexes means that you shouldn't be lazy and write queries like this:

```
SELECT movie_title
FROM Movies
WHERE UPPER(movie) = 'THE CODE WARRIOR'
```

If you can determine the actual capitalization for the values in a particular column, you should use that instead of relying on the UPPER or LOWER functions to enable you to perform a search that is not case sensitive.

PART
IV

CH
13

The same rule holds true for string concatenation in the WHERE clause. If you concatenate any strings with the columns used in a condition in the WHERE clause, indexes will again be ignored. For example, this query will not take advantage of indexes:

```
SELECT person_fname, person_lname
FROM People
WHERE person_fname || ' ' || person_lname = 'Rafe Colburn'
```

You'd be better off with this query:

```
SELECT person_fname, person_lname
FROM People
WHERE person_fname = 'Rafe' AND person_lname = 'Colburn'
```

Indexes are not used when the WHERE clause contains an IS NULL or IS NOT NULL comparison. Nulls are not included in indexes, so there's no way to find out which records contain null values from the index. Indexes are not used with IS NOT NULL queries because it's easier just to scan the entire table and discard records with null values in the column being searched.

In fact, any time you write a query that uses a condition of inequality to search a column, indexes are ignored. Consider this query:

```
SELECT movie_title
FROM Movies
WHERE movie_title <> 'The Code Warrior'
```

Each record must be processed individually to determine whether the movie_title is equal to 'The Code Warrior'. If it isn't, the row is discarded. Because there's no test of equality for the query, there's no way to look up the value in an index. This problem holds for any test of inequality, including NOT IN.

As you know, you can create indexes on multiple columns as well as on single columns. For a multicolumn index to be applied in a query, the first column in the index must be used in the WHERE clause. The way indexes are organized, the index values are read from left to right. If the initial column in the index isn't included in the WHERE clause, the database has no way to look up values in the index.

THE QUERY OPTIMIZER

To really get a handle on query performance, you have to understand how the query optimizer in the database that you use works. The query optimizer breaks down queries before they are executed and determines how best to execute them. An understanding of the query optimizer enables you to write queries in such a way as to take advantage of the biases of the optimizer.

For example, in Chapters 8, "Combining Tables Using Joins," and 9, "Subqueries," I discussed joins and subqueries. Query optimizers handle joins and subqueries differently, and two queries that produce the same results might take different amounts of time to produce those results, depending on how the query optimizer breaks them down.

Another advantage of understanding how the query optimizer works is that some databases enable programmers to embed optimizer hints within their queries that alter the behavior of the optimizer. If the query optimizer does not, by default, execute your query in the most efficient manner, you can use hints to alter the execution and improve the performance of the query.

HOW QUERY OPTIMIZERS WORK

It's difficult to generalize too greatly about how query optimizers work because every database's optimizer works differently. In fact, one of the main areas of competition in the database market is database performance. In large part, database performance is determined by the ability of the query optimizer to execute queries efficiently. Every database company has its own philosophy about the best way to optimize queries. If you find it necessary to go the extra mile in optimizing your queries for performance, you should research the query optimizer built into the database that you use.

In this chapter, I'm going to explain how the Oracle query optimizer works. Actually, I'm going to discuss how one of the three Oracle query optimizers works. To make their database perform best in a wide range of applications, Oracle actually enables database administrators to configure their Oracle installations so that they use one of three query optimizers.

The three optimizers are RULE, COST, and CHOOSE. The RULE optimizer calculates the execution plans available for a particular query and then applies a set of rules to determine which of the execution plans will provide the best performance. The COST optimizer works with the Oracle analyze command. The analyze command calculates statistics on all the objects in the database, and the COST optimizer then calculates the cost of various execution plans based on those statistics. The execution plan with the lowest cost is chosen. The final optimizer is the CHOOSE optimizer, which uses the RULE optimizer for unanalyzed tables and the COST optimizer for analyzed tables. Occasionally, it can hurt performance if an analyzed table and an unanalyzed table are used in the same query.

In Oracle databases, there are two different ways the database can access a table. It will perform a full table scan, or it will access the table by RowID.

> **Note**
>
> RowID is a hidden column in every table in Oracle that contains the physical location where the record is stored. Indexes correlate data with the RowIDs of records that contain that data, which is how they improve the performance of queries.

Whenever a query with no WHERE clause is executed, a full table scan is performed. The larger the table used in the query is, the longer a full table scan will take. Other queries look up records by RowID. When you search an indexed column, the piece of data you're looking for is located in the index, and the data is fetched from the record with the RowID stored in the index.

PART
IV
CH
13

Using Hints

When a query retrieves data from a table, one of two methods can be used—either a full table scan, or a lookup by RowID. This is just one example of the type of decision that the query optimizer in Oracle makes as it ascertains the best way to execute a query. Generally speaking, the optimizer does a good job of determining which execution plan to use when it runs a query. However, you can sometimes improve the performance of your queries by providing a "hint" to the compiler indicating which of the alternative methods that it can choose from is best.

continues

continued

In Oracle, hints are enclosed within a comment and a plus sign, immediately following the SQL command that they apply to. For example, to indicate that a SELECT statement should use a full table scan to retrieve data from the table, the following syntax is used:

```
SELECT /*+ FULL(Movies) */ movie_title
FROM Movies
```

The + inside the open comment operator indicates that a hint is enclosed within the comment. The hint itself, FULL(Movies), tells the query optimizer to use a full table scan on the Movies table to retrieve the rows.

You should only use hints if you know for a fact that the query will perform better with the hint you supply than it will by using the execution plan chosen by the query optimizer.

In this chapter, as I explain how the query optimizer works, I'll provide some other hints that you can use with the Oracle database to control execution of queries.

INDEXES AND THE OPTIMIZER

When the optimizer plans the execution plan for a query, it takes the indexes available into account. There are a couple of index operations available, INDEX UNIQUE SCAN and INDEX RANGE SCAN. An indexed column is referenced within the WHERE clause of a query, depending on the comparison used in the WHERE clause.

INDEX UNIQUE SCAN is used when the comparison in the WHERE clause is a single value, and the column in the WHERE clause is indexed with a unique index. Listing 13.7 includes a query and execution plan where the INDEX UNIQUE SCAN operation is used.

LISTING 13.7 A SELECT STATEMENT THAT USES INDEX UNIQUE SCAN AND ITS EXECUTION PLAN

```
SELECT movie_title
FROM Movies
WHERE movie_title = 'The Code Warrior'

Execution Plan
- - - - - - - - - - - - - - - - - - - - - - - - - - - - - - - - - - - - - - - - - -
  0        SELECT STATEMENT Optimizer=CHOOSE
  1     0    INDEX (UNIQUE SCAN) OF 'MOVIE_TITLE_INDEX' (UNIQUE)
```

The optimizer uses the INDEX UNIQUE SCAN operation to find the value in the index equal to the string in the WHERE clause, and then, because the movie_title column is the only item in the select list, the value returned by the query is pulled right from the index. If another column or multiple columns were specified in the select list, the RowID returned from the index would be passed to a lookup by RowID operation to retrieve the actual record.

A query with the primary key in both the select list and the WHERE clause that is compared to a single value is the most efficient query available. Because the value returned by the query is included in the index itself, no records need to be retrieved from the actual table, and an INDEX UNIQUE SCAN is a very efficient operation.

The second type of index operation is INDEX RANGE SCAN, which is used when the column in the WHERE clause is indexed with a nonunique index or when the expression in the comparison applies to multiple values. An INDEX RANGE SCAN reads multiple values from the index, unlike the INDEX UNIQUE SCAN, which reads only the value being sought. For example, the query in Listing 13.8 uses an indexed column in the WHERE clause, but because the index is not unique, INDEX RANGE SCAN is used.

LISTING 13.8   A QUERY AND EXECUTION PLAN THAT USE INDEX RANGE SCAN

```
SELECT person_fname, person_lname
FROM People
WHERE person_lname = 'Jong';

Execution Plan
-----------------------------------------------------------
    0      SELECT STATEMENT Optimizer=CHOOSE
    1    0    TABLE ACCESS (BY INDEX ROWID) OF 'PEOPLE'
    2    1      INDEX (RANGE SCAN) OF 'LNAME_INDEX' (NON-UNIQUE)
```

HANDLING MULTIPLE INDEXES IN ONE QUERY

The query optimizer can take advantage of multiple indexes within the same WHERE clause, assuming that there are multiple indexed columns (or an indexed column is used more than once) and that the conditions containing indexed columns can utilize indexes. Even if only some of the conditions in a WHERE clause can use indexes, you'll still see some performance improvement over WHERE clauses that contain no indexed columns or no conditions that can take advantage of indexes.

The People table has two indexes, fname_index and lname_index. (It also has a unique index on the person_id column because person_id is the primary key.) Listing 13.9 contains an example that I used earlier.

LISTING 13.9   A QUERY THAT USES TWO EQUALITY COMPARISONS COMBINED WITH AN AND OPERATOR

```
SELECT person_fname, person_lname
FROM People
WHERE person_fname = 'Rafe' AND person_lname = 'Colburn'

Execution Plan
-----------------------------------------------------------
    0      SELECT STATEMENT Optimizer=CHOOSE
    1    0    AND-EQUAL
    2    1      INDEX (RANGE SCAN) OF 'FNAME_INDEX' (NON-UNIQUE)
    3    1      INDEX (RANGE SCAN) OF 'LNAME_INDEX' (NON-UNIQUE)
```

Two INDEX RANGE SCAN operations are used to find all the RowIDs for people with the first name Rafe and to find the RowIDs for people with the last name Colburn. The two sets of

RowIDs are compared, and any that match are included in the query results. This is what's known as an AND-EQUAL operation.

Now, take a look at the query in Listing 13.10.

LISTING 13.10   A QUERY THAT USES TWO EQUALITY COMPARISONS COMBINED WITH AN OR OPERATOR

```
SELECT person_fname, person_lname
FROM People
WHERE person_fname = 'Rafe' OR person_lname = 'Colburn'

Execution Plan
----------------------------------------------------------
    0       SELECT STATEMENT Optimizer=CHOOSE
    1   0     CONCATENATION
    2   1       TABLE ACCESS (BY INDEX ROWID) OF 'PEOPLE'
    3   2         INDEX (RANGE SCAN) OF 'LNAME_INDEX' (NON-UNIQUE)
    4   1       TABLE ACCESS (BY INDEX ROWID) OF 'PEOPLE'
    5   4         INDEX (RANGE SCAN) OF 'FNAME_INDEX' (NON-UNIQUE)
```

The OR comparison is not as clean, from an optimization standpoint, as the AND operation, which uses an AND-EQUAL operation and two range scans. The OR operation uses the CONCATENATION operation, which takes all the rows matched by either of the conditions, strips out the duplicates, and returns the remaining records. The CONCATENATION operation is still relatively efficient, just not as efficient as the AND-EQUAL.

There is a specific hint used with indexes. To tell the optimizer specifically to use the indexes on a particular table, you should use the INDEX hint, as shown in Listing 13.11.

LISTING 13.11   USING THE INDEX HINT

```
SELECT /*+ INDEX(Movies) */ movie_title
FROM Movies
WHERE movie_title = 'The Code Warrior'

Execution Plan
----------------------------------------------------------
    0       SELECT STATEMENT Optimizer=CHOOSE (Cost=1 Card=1 Bytes=24)
    1   0     INDEX (UNIQUE SCAN) OF 'MOVIE_TITLE_INDEX' (UNIQUE) (Cost=
            1 Card=1 Bytes=24)
```

The condition in the WHERE clause is a standard comparison based on equality, so under normal circumstances, the index would be used. However, in certain cases, the cost-based optimizer might determine that ignoring the index would provide better performance. If you're sure this isn't the case, using the INDEX hint will force the database to take the index into account during the query.

DATA SET OPERATIONS

The operations used to manipulate data sets differ from those used to handle data one row at a time. All the operations discussed so far handle data row by row. When you use one of the TABLE ACCESS or INDEX SCAN operations, it can simply evaluate each row against the WHERE clause and then return it if the WHERE clause evaluates as true, without regard for how the row relates to the rest of the records in the table.

On the other hand, there are many SQL constructs that must examine all the rows returned by a query before they can return any rows at all. Consider, for example, an ORDER BY clause. The proper order of the rows returned by a query can't be determined until all the rows in the result set have been examined. The first two set operations you need to look at are SORT ORDER BY and SORT UNIQUE. As you might imagine, the SORT ORDER BY operation is used to reorder a result set so that it is ordered based on the values in the fields specified in the ORDER BY clause. SORT UNIQUE is used with DISTINCT to examine a set of rows and eliminate any duplicates.

As you know, when you use the MINUS, UNION, and INTERSECT operators, duplicate rows between the results in the queries are discarded (unless the database is explicitly instructed to do otherwise). The SORT UNIQUE operator is used with these queries as well.

Other data set operations include SORT AGGREGATE and SORT GROUP BY. You can probably imagine what these two operations do. The SORT AGGREGATE operator follows a TABLE ACCESS FULL and applies the aggregate function specified in the query to the results returned by the TABLE ACCESS FULL operation. When you use GROUP BY in a query, the database uses a TABLE ACCESS FULL to retrieve the results, SORT GROUP BY to break the rows down into groups, and then SORT AGGREGATE on each of the groups to calculate the results of the query.

THE QUERY OPTIMIZER AND VIEWS

As you know from Chapter 10, a view is basically just a saved query. For example, you might create a view for movies with revenue over $50 million, like this:

```
CREATE VIEW Movies_Over_50
AS
SELECT *
FROM Movies
WHERE gross > 50
```

After the view has been created, you can use a SELECT statement to query the view. Instead of running the conditions of the query against the results of the query stored in the view, the optimizer attempts to merge the two queries. Take a look at this query:

```
SELECT movie_title, gross
FROM Movies_Over_50
WHERE budget > 0
```

PART

IV

CH

13

The query optimizer will merge the two queries, turning them into one larger SELECT statement like this one:

```
SELECT movie_title, gross
FROM Movies
WHERE budget > 0
AND gross > 50
```

If the query in the view is constructed in such a way that it cannot be merged with the SELECT statement, the SELECT statement is applied to the results of the query in the view.

THE QUERY OPTIMIZER AND SUBQUERIES

Interestingly, the Oracle query optimizer will turn queries that contain subqueries into joins if it can do so. If the query can be evaluated in fewer steps using a join operation than it can be evaluating first the subquery and then the query containing the subquery, the query will be transformed into a join.

If the subquery cannot be turned into a join, the subquery will be processed, and the results of the subquery will be plugged into the outer query at the appropriate location. At that point, the outer query will be executed.

JOIN OPERATIONS

Oracle uses three join operations: MERGE JOIN operations, NESTED LOOPS operations, and HASH JOIN operations. The optimizer chooses the join operation to use depending on a number of factors, including the indexes available, the conditions in the query, and, if you've used the ANALYZE command, the statistics available for the operations. When you join more than two tables, the optimizer breaks down the query into a number of separate joins. For example, if you write a query that joins four tables, two of the tables will be joined and then the results of that join will be joined with the third table. Finally, the results of the join of the first two tables and the third table will be joined again to get the final results of the query. This is why multitable joins can be very slow; each additional table adds an entirely new join operation.

MERGE JOINs simply take the columns that are used in the joining condition of the query, sort them, and join them. This is the simplest form of a join operation and is generally used when there are no indexes available to speed up the query. There are several operations that precede the use of a MERGE JOIN. First, all the values used in the query are retrieved using a TABLE ACCESS FULL and sorted using a SORT JOIN operation. The two resulting lists of values are combined using a MERGE JOIN.

Both of the SORT JOIN operations are SET operations, so until they are complete, no rows can be returned to users. As soon as the results of the two SORT JOINs are passed to the MERGE JOIN operation, it begins returning rows.

The NESTED LOOPS operation simply takes a list of values from one column, reads them one at a time, and then searches all the values in the other column until it finds one that matches. This seems as if it would be slow, and it is if there are no indexes available. In a NESTED LOOPS operation, there are two tables. The first is the *driving table*, which contains the values that will only be evaluated once. The second table will be queried repeatedly to determine if there are matches between it and the first table.

To perform a NESTED LOOPS operation, a FULL TABLE SCAN is used against the dining table. Then, if the column used in the join comparison is the primary key of the secondary table, an INDEX UNIQUE SCAN is used against that table to determine whether it contains a value that matches the current value in the driving table. Performance problems become more acute the larger the driving table is. You should write your queries so that the driving table is as small as possible, and thus, the query needs to retrieve data from the secondary table as little as possible.

The third type of joining operation is the HASH JOIN. In a HASH JOIN, the database uses two TABLE ACCESS FULL operations to retrieve all the values in both columns in the join comparison and store them in memory. It then performs some hashing operations on the data to improve the performance of comparisons between the two sets and matches up the like values between the two tables. HASH JOIN operations do not take advantage of indexes. They don't perform set operations, so they begin returning rows to the user as soon as matches are found.

JOIN-RELATED HINTS

Naturally, because there are multiple ways to process joins, there are hints that can be used to specify which method should be used. There are two hints, ALL_ROWS and FIRST_ROWS, that are used to specify whether the optimizer favors execution plans that will return all the rows from the query as quickly as possible or those that will favor returning the first results as quickly as possible.

You can also use hints to specify exactly which operation should be used to create a join. There are three hints available, which correspond to the three join operations, USE_NL, USE_MERGE, and USE_HASH. If your query has more than two tables in the FROM clause, you should specify the table associated with the operation in parentheses after the hint itself. For example, if you're joining the Movies, Cast_Movies, and People tables and you want to use the Movies table as the driving table in a NESTED LOOPS operation, you would write the query as shown in Listing 13.12.

PART

IV

CH

13

LISTING 13.12   USING A HINT TO SPECIFY THE OPERATION AND INITIAL TABLE USED FOR A JOIN

```
SELECT /*+ USE_NL(Movies) */
movie_title, role, person_fname, person_lname
FROM Movies, Cast_Movies, People
WHERE Movies.movie_id = Cast_Movies.movie_id
AND People.person_id = Cast_Movies.person_id
```

DATA INTEGRITY

Data integrity is a completely different issue from database performance, but it is no less important. Many databases are used to store information that is absolutely critical to the success of a business, a Web site, or whatever else the owner is using them for. To rely on a database, you must be completely sure, or as close to completely as sure as possible, that the contents of the database have not undergone unauthorized modification and that they haven't been corrupted.

Perhaps more important is the requirement that the data conform to the rules set forth by the owners of the database. There are a number of methods by which you can ensure that the data in a database both meets the integrity requirements of the relational model and that it meets the business requirements for any applications that will use the database. The most common methods for enforcing integrity requirements are unique indexes, check constraints, foreign key constraints, and triggers.

All these concepts have already been covered in this book or will be covered a bit later (triggers are discussed in parts of Chapters 15, 16, and 17). Of interest to you in this chapter is the effect that these methods of enforcing data integrity have on the performance of a database. If performance is not a consideration, you can place as many integrity constraints on columns in your tables as you want and be sure that all your data is correct. Unfortunately, rare is the case where performance is simply not a consideration. At some point, performance will slow to an unacceptable level, and you'll need to make decisions about which integrity constraints can be removed.

In some cases, you can move the enforcement of database integrity rules into the applications that are interacting with the database and out of the database. This is suboptimal for a number of reasons, but in times where extra performance is needed, it might be an acceptable workaround to placing all the integrity constraints you would like on the tables themselves. It's often a good idea to enforce data integrity with your application and with the database because it can save performance; the issues come into play when you try to enforce integrity with the application instead of with the database.

Enforcing Integrity in a Database Application

When you write an application that modifies data within a database, you should include code that enforces some of the integrity rules for your database within the application itself. For example, if you have a column in your database that is specified as NOT NULL, you should check the user's input for that field to make sure that she has entered a value. Similarly, if a column has a check constraint placed on it that says that a value must be within a certain range, you should also test user input for that field within your application.

Even though the database will still test the values before they are inserted or updated, you can improve the performance of the database simply by conserving transactions that you knew wouldn't work anyway. Every time you trap invalid user input within your application, you conserve a database transaction that would have failed. Depending on your users, this can really improve the performance of your database.

There are some types of integrity constraints that make less sense to test before the application attempts to execute a data manipulation statement. Take a foreign key constraint for example. To test it within your application, you would have to issue a SELECT statement to determine whether a value being modified corresponded to a value within the column referenced by the foreign key constraint. This really wouldn't provide much improvement over just attempting to insert or update the record and finding out whether the value satisfied the constraint.

As you add integrity constraints to your tables, you should think about how they can be expressed in the applications that issue statements that modify records in the table. Not only can it improve performance by saving bad transactions, but if performance needs to be improved even more, you can remove constraints in your database and rely on the constraints enforced by the application.

There are a few issues that crop up when you attempt to replace integrity constraints in the database with input validating code in your applications. The first is that if a user can accidentally (or intentionally) get around the constraints in the application, she can enter bad data in your database with impunity. The second, and more important, is that for most databases, there is no guarantee that data will only be entered with the application that has the input checking code built into it. If the validation code in your PowerBuilder application works great but someone comes in and enters bad data using SQL*Plus, your efforts were all for naught. It's usually best to keep the integrity constraints at the database level so that there is no way users can enter invalid data in the database without manually disabling those constraints.

INTEGRITY VERSUS PERFORMANCE

Now that I've discussed the general issues of integrity constraints and performance, I'd like to cover some of the specific database integrity constraints and how their use affects database performance. There are performance issues associated with all integrity constraints, simply due to the fact that every constraint you add causes additional processing to be performed whenever the operation with which it is associated is executed.

Take a trigger for example. When you execute a data modification statement against a particular table, the database first has to determine whether any triggers exist for that table. Obviously, this step has to be performed regardless of whether triggers exist. If there are triggers defined for the table, the database must determine whether the triggers apply to the statement that is being executed. For example, if there is an update trigger for the table and the statement is an INSERT statement, the trigger is ignored. If the trigger does apply to the current statement, the trigger must be executed. Obviously, all these steps require some processing time. If your tables simply have no triggers defined, your data modification statements will execute more quickly.

PART
IV

CH
13

→ To learn more about triggers, see "Triggers" p. 379

The same is true for any integrity constraint. Whether the constraint is as simple as NOT NULL or as complex as a trigger that queries other tables to determine whether a value is valid, all constraints affect performance. As a database programmer, you must determine whether the benefits in terms of integrity that come with setting up constraints of various types outweigh the performance implications of using them. Generally, a good rule of thumb is to include any constraints you require to ensure the integrity of your data and then remove them in order of importance if performance is unacceptable.

IN THE REAL WORLD

In this book, I've already discussed how you can use the database to enforce integrity constraints on tables in detail. However, for most applications, it makes sense to write your applications so that they validate the data entered by users before the data manipulation statements are even executed. I'd like to describe some techniques that you can use in your applications to ensure the validity of data entered by users and that can improve the overall performance of your applications by reducing the load on your database.

There are two main advantages of performing data validation at higher levels of your application. The first is that it distributes the burden of performing the validation tasks among several components of your application, improving performance. The second is that you can provide feedback to your users earlier, making it easier for them to correct mistakes.

Consider the levels of a typical application. If the application is a client/server application, there's the client application that runs on the user's computer, perhaps an application server, and there's the database server. In addition to the constraints and triggers enforced at the database level, you can perform additional data validation at both the application-server level and at the client level. The same holds true for Web applications. You can use JavaScript to validate user input in the Web browser (the client level), at the application server level, and at the database level.

The two main methods of ensuring data integrity at the client level are to check user input as it is entered and to constrain the number of input choices available to users to valid values. I'd like to talk about the second method first. Most application-development environments support multiple types of user-interface widgets. Generally, basic text-input fields are provided that enable users to enter whatever they like in them. Unfortunately, when you provide users with this much flexibility, you're forced to make sure that the data they entered fits the format that's required.

Better options for many fields include check boxes, pull-down lists, and radio buttons. For example, if you want to allow users to select which state they live in, you can provide them with a twenty-letter character field where they can enter whatever they want, a two-letter character field where they can enter a state abbreviation (or any other two letters), or a select list that allows them to choose from 1 of 50 states. If you use the select list, you don't need to worry about whether the user entered the name or abbreviation for a valid state at all. Any time there is a fixed number of options available to the users, you should consider whether it's easier to provide them with a structured data input field than it is to allow them to enter information in a free-form manner.

One issue that arises is the population of these fields. There are several options available here, and choice of one of them is generally predicated by the performance of the application. One method is to simply hard-code the values available for your structured fields into the application. The advantage is that there's no performance hit taken when the field is populated; the disadvantage is that if the options change, you have to make a change to the application itself. If your application is a client/server application used by many users, redistributing the application could be painful.

The second option is to store the data in the database and query the database to populate the fields every time a user views the form. This is convenient because it enables you to change the options by simply updating a table in the database. The disadvantage is that if your database's performance is already taxed, you will increase the overhead by including queries in your forms.

The third option is to cache the data for the fields somehow so that it isn't part of the application but also doesn't require a database query to retrieve. This is often a good tradeoff if you want flexibility but are also constrained by performance considerations.

When determining how to populate these fields, you should take two factors into account. The first is how often the options will change, and the second is the performance of your application. I've already discussed performance a bit, so I'm going to talk about the volatility of your data. If the field you're populating simply allows users to choose Yes or No, it can probably be hard-coded into the application. It's unlikely that the these values will change with any frequency. A less extreme example is a pull-down list of states; chances are that the names of the states in the United States will not change often enough to warrant generating the list dynamically every time the form is displayed.

On the other hand, there might be cases where the items on a form are tailored to each user or change very frequently. In those cases, storing the potential options in the database and allowing users to select from them is the only viable programming option.

The other method of constraining user input before it gets to the database is to perform data validation at the various layers of your application. Obviously, the best option when it comes to data validation is to check as much data as possible at the client level. Any performance overhead from data validation at the client level only affects that user and isn't passed on to other users who are using the same system. This isn't the case at the application-server level or at the database level. It's also better for users to receive immediate feedback when they make a mistake in input than to require them to submit the form and receive a list of errors pointing out any mistakes in the input that they made.

Even if performance doesn't dictate that you place your data validation at the client level, you should include client-side validation in your applications along with validation at the application-server and database levels. Performance is improved by client-side validation even if validation at the other levels is implemented because fewer database transactions are needed when errors are trapped before data is ever submitted.

CHAPTER 14

TRANSACTIONS AND CURSORS

In this chapter

One thing you might have noticed in the process of reading this book is that SQL lacks many of the features that are mainstays of most programming languages. There are no variables, no loops or conditional statements, and no user-defined functions or subroutines. Because SQL was originally designed to enable users to write statements that retrieve records from databases or to modify the data stored within databases, these constructs were not necessary.

To process the results of queries or apply business logic to data stored within a database, programmers were required to retrieve the data using some other application, process the data, and then update the contents of the database. Companies that sell relational databases eventually extended SQL so that programmers could embed programs in their databases along with their data. These programs are called *stored procedures*.

With stored procedures, data manipulation can occur entirely within the database. The SQL extensions for writing stored procedures also add many of the constructs provided in other languages to SQL itself. I am going to discuss stored procedures in detail in Chapters 15, "Writing Stored Procedures," 16, "More on Transact-SQL Stored Procedures," and 17, "Writing Oracle PL/SQL Stored Procedures," but I wanted to go ahead and explain what they are so that I can explain how they relate to the topics in this chapter—transactions and cursors.

Both transactions and cursors are useful outside the context of stored procedures, but their use often goes hand in hand with stored procedures, so it is important to discuss how the two concepts relate.

TRANSACTIONS

Through this book, I've treated each SQL statement as an individual unit—an entity unto itself. Now, I'm going to switch gears a bit and talk about transactions. Basically, *transactions* are SQL statement groups that are treated as single units for the purposes of processing. A transaction can consist of a single statement, if that's all that's necessary to perform a particular task, or it can include multiple statements. The important characteristic of transactions is that unless all the statements within a transaction are executed, none of the changes made in the transaction are applied to the database.

This is important because it guarantees database consistency in case the system fails in the middle of performing the transaction. Think about a database system used to manage checkouts and inventory at a grocery store. When a customer buys some items and checks out, the amount that she paid is posted to an accounting database, and all the items purchased are removed from the inventory through that database. The store orders new groceries when the items in inventory drop down to a certain level. When the order arrives, the new items are added to the inventory totals in the database.

When a business has all its data stored in a database in such a manner, a log of every change to the database must be kept. If there were no transactions, each change to the database would have to be tracked separately, and more importantly, there would be no way to group statements to determine which ones were part of the same group. For example, a shopper might purchase 80 items; if each of the items being purchased were entered in the database as a separate transaction, it would be difficult to determine which of those transactions should be reversed if it were necessary to do so.

For example, if the database crashed or the system lost power in the middle of scanning the shopper's items, her purchase would be left half complete. It would be necessary to reverse her transaction, but doing so could be difficult without a list of the items that had already been scanned. This is where SQL transactions come in. Using transactions, you could bundle all the shopper's items in a single transaction, along with any other SQL statements used to process the purchase. Then, if the queries associated with that purchase needed to be reversed for some reason, the transaction could be aborted and the changes would be discarded.

HOW TRANSACTIONS WORK

Basically, there are three actions associated with transactions. The first of the three actions initiates the transaction. When the transaction has been initiated, all the subsequent SQL statements are treated as part of that transaction until the transaction is terminated. The second action associated with transactions is the commit action. When a transaction is committed, the transaction ends, and all the modifications to the database made during the transaction are applied to the database. The third action is used to end the transaction and discard any changes made up to that point.

Generally speaking, until a transaction has been committed, the changes made in that transaction are not visible to other people who are using the database. Only after those changes have been committed will other users see the changes.

USING TRANSACTIONS IN ORACLE

Databases that support transactions provide specific commands for starting, committing, and rolling back transactions. In SQL*PLUS (the command line interface to Oracle), the COMMIT keyword is used to commit transactions, and the ROLLBACK keyword is used to roll them back.

There is no command to begin transactions. When one transaction ends (through either a rollback or a commit), a new transaction is initiated automatically. There are a number of actions that automatically commit changes to the database: Creating or dropping tables or views, or using alter, connect, disconnect, or one of several other commands all automatically commit any changes in the current transaction to the database. Exiting SQL*PLUS also automatically commits any changes to the database. On the other hand, if your session is somehow terminated spontaneously (say your computer loses its network connection to the database), the current transaction will be rolled back automatically.

Take a look at an example of how transactions work in SQL*PLUS. First, I'll select some rows from the Movies table in Listing 14.1.

Listing 14.1   A select Statement

```
SELECT movie_id, movie_title
FROM Movies

MOVIE_ID MOVIE_TITLE
---------- --------------------
         1 Vegetable House
         2 Prince Kong
         3 The Code Warrior
         4 Bill Durham
         5 Codependence Day
         6 The Linux Files
         7 SQL Strikes Back
         8 The Programmer
         9 Hard Code
        10 The Rear Windows

10 rows selected.
```

If I issue a DELETE statement, for the purposes of my database session, the rows will be treated as though they were removed, as demonstrated in Listing 14.2.

Listing 14.2   Deleting Rows from the Movies Table

```
DELETE FROM Movies
WHERE movie_id IN (1, 3, 5, 7)

4 rows deleted.

SELECT movie_id, movie_title
FROM Movies


   MOVIE_ID MOVIE_TITLE
---------- --------------------
         2 Prince Kong
         4 Bill Durham
         6 The Linux Files
         8 The Programmer
         9 Hard Code
        10 The Rear Windows

6 rows selected.
```

After the rows have been removed, they are no longer visible from this user session, but other users who log in will still see the rows as though they have not been deleted. The ROLLBACK command can be used to abort the transaction, as shown in Listing 14.3.

LISTING 14.3   USING ROLLBACK TO REVERSE A TRANSACTION

```
ROLLBACK

Rollback complete.

SELECT movie_id, movie_title
FROM Movies

MOVIE_ID MOVIE_TITLE
---------- --------------------
         1 Vegetable House
         2 Prince Kong
         3 The Code Warrior
         4 Bill Durham
         5 Codependence Day
         6 The Linux Files
         7 SQL Strikes Back
         8 The Programmer
         9 Hard Code
        10 The Rear Windows
10 rows selected.
```

After the ROLLBACK command, the Movies table is restored to its original state. The COMMIT command finalizes the current transaction and writes any changes made during that transaction to the database. In Oracle, when a transaction has been committed, a new transaction begins, and when the ROLLBACK command is issued, the new current transaction is rolled back.

AUTOCOMMIT

Most database tools include a special mode called *autocommit mode*, which automatically commits the transaction to the database when a SQL statement is executed. In Oracle SQL*PLUS, you can turn on autocommit mode using the following command:

```
SET AUTOCOMMIT ON
```

If you prefer, you can have SQL*PLUS commit changes to the database after a set number of commands by using a number for the autocommit setting, like this:

```
SET AUTOCOMMIT 5
```

The previous setting would issue a commit after every five SQL statements executed. To turn off autocommit mode and return to manually committing transactions, change the autocommit setting to off:

```
SET AUTOCOMMIT OFF
```

To view the current autocommit setting, the following command is used:

```
SHOW AUTOCOMMIT
```

PART

IV

CH

14

USING TRANSACTIONS IN TRANSACT-SQL

Unlike Oracle databases, databases that use Transact-SQL treat each SQL statement as an individual transaction unless explicitly instructed to do otherwise. Because you must declare transactions in Transact-SQL explicitly, there are four transaction-related SQL statements: BEGIN, SAVE, COMMIT, and ROLLBACK. Transact-SQL also supports named transactions and savepoints, which offer a lot of flexibility when it comes to rolling back transactions to a specific point.

The first transaction-related statement is BEGIN TRANSACTION:

```
BEGIN {TRAN | TRANSACTION} [transaction_name]
```

The BEGIN TRANSACTION statement initiates a new transaction (TRAN is just an abbreviation for TRANSACTION). You can specify a name for a transaction and then commit or roll back the transaction by name at a later point. This is useful when you use savepoints or nest transactions within an initial transaction.

Tip 55 from
Rafe Colburn

> When using transaction names, you can only name savepoints and the outer transaction in a set of nested transactions. Transactions that are initiated from within another transaction cannot be named.

The SAVE statement is similar to BEGIN, except that it preserves the state of a transaction at a particular point within an existing transaction. By using savepoints in a particularly complex transaction, you can roll back subsets of the statements within the transaction by specifying the name of the savepoint instead of the name of the transaction (or by leaving the name off). The syntax of the SAVE command is as follows:

```
SAVE { TRANSACTION | TRAN } savepoint_name
```

Unlike the BEGIN command, the SAVE command requires that a name be specified. The name is used to distinguish the savepoint from the transaction within which it appears.

The COMMIT statement is used to end a transaction and apply the changes made during that transaction to the database. When the transaction has been committed, the statements within the transaction are applied to the database, and the database returns to autocommit mode until another transaction is begun. The syntax of the COMMIT statement is as follows:

```
COMMIT [ TRANSACTION | TRAN | WORK ] [transaction_name]
```

TRANSACTION, TRAN, and WORK are all synonyms and are optional. The transaction name is also optional. It is useful if you are using nested transactions and want to commit the outer named transaction instead of the innermost transaction, which will be committed by default.

The last transaction-related statement is ROLLBACK, which discards any changes made since the transaction was begun or up until the last savepoint was set:

```
ROLLBACK [ TRANSACTION | TRAN | WORK ]
[ transaction_name | savepoint_name ]
```

Again, the TRANSACTION keyword is optional. If a savepoint or transaction name is specified, the transaction is rolled back to that transaction. If not, the transaction is rolled back to its state before the current transaction. If you are using nested transactions, the transaction will be rolled back to the state before the innermost transaction. Figure 14.1 demonstrates how transactions are used in Transact-SQL.

Figure 14.1
Usage of transactions in Transact-SQL

```
begin tran example (A new transaction named example is opened)

data modification query 1

save tran savepoint_1

data modification query 2

rollback savepoint_1
    (data modification query 2 is rolled back)

data modification query 3

commit tran
    (data modification queries 1 and 3 are committed)
```

DATABASE LOCKS

One problem that all computer systems run into is dealing with concurrent access to shared resources. If one program is accessing a particular file, it will be unavailable to any other programs. Similarly, if one program is using a particular slice of a computer's memory, no other programs should be able to write data to it. (Operating systems that don't prevent programs from overwriting memory used by other programmers tend to crash a lot.)

Databases also use locks to manage concurrent access to resources within the database. Most relational databases are a part of multiuser systems. When one user is updating an existing record or creating a new record, other users should not be able to see the records which are being updated until the update is complete.

The problem of multiple users accessing the same data is defined in computer science as the *lost update problem*. The lost update problem is best described using an example. Revisit the example I used earlier in the chapter, in which I talked about a transaction processing system for a grocery store. Most grocery stores have multiple checkout lines, with checkers ringing up purchases for customers all at once. Each of the cash registers is linked to a database on the back end that not only provides the prices and descriptions for the items as they're scanned, but also stores the information from each customer transaction.

After each customer transaction is completed, the total for the transaction is added to the cumulative total for all the transactions that day. This is where the lost update error comes into play. What happens when two customers complete their transactions at almost exactly the same time? The first customer, at checkout counter A, finishes his transaction, so the cash register retrieves the current total for the day's transactions from the database, adds the total for the transaction that just finished to that amount, and then stores that number in place of the number it originally retrieved.

At the same time (or almost the same time), the customer at register B completes her transaction. That register retrieves the current daily total from the database, adds the amount of the current transaction to that number, and then updates the daily total in the database with the new sum. Unfortunately, if the transactions are timed just right, cash register A will retrieve the sum from the database, cash register B will retrieve the same number database, register A will save the new sum, and then register B will save the sum again, overwriting the change made by register A. This sequence of events is illustrated in Figure 14.2.

Figure 14.2
An illustration of the lost update problem.

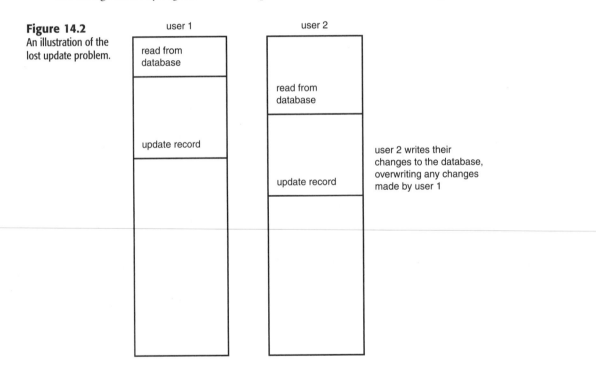

Locks eliminate the lost update problem by blocking access to a particular resource for all other users when a particular user is making a change to it. So, if the database supported locking, when register A completed its transaction, it would obtain a lock on the total receipts for the day, read the value, update it, and then release the lock. Register B would be forced to wait until register A released the lock before it could update the daily total with the receipts for its transaction. Locks eliminate the lost update problem by ensuring that a resource can only be involved in one transaction at a time. Figure 14.3 shows how locks are used to eliminate the lost update problem illustrated in Figure 14.2.

Figure 14.3
How locks protect data in transactions.

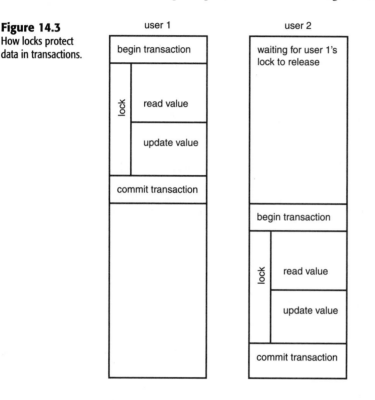

TYPES OF LOCKS

Relational databases support two types of locks: *row-level* locks and *table-level* locks. Generally speaking, table-level locks are supported by all databases, whereas row-level locks are only supported by higher-end databases. Basically, the level of locking that a database provides determines the granularity of the locks that are created.

If a database supports only table-level locking, the entire table is locked when a user is posting a transaction that utilizes a row from that table. Needless to say, this can lead to performance problems if there are lots of users who are trying to update data in the table at the same time.

Row-level locking is more flexible. Databases that support row-level locking only lock those records that are being utilized by a transaction. Row-level locking enables databases to perform much better when accessed by many users because performing a transaction that updates only a single row locks only that row and not the table within which it resides.

TRANSACTIONS AND STORED PROCEDURES

Often, a stored procedure will encapsulate all the SQL statements necessary to complete a transaction. Consider the example I used earlier involving the grocery store. The developer of the system could write a stored procedure that retrieves the total for the day's transactions and adds the current transaction to it.

Because multiple SQL statements can be encapsulated within a single stored procedure, it often makes sense to capture common transactions in this manner and then call the stored procedure from an external program instead of executing each SQL statement individually. This provides two advantages. The first is that it abstracts the purpose of the transaction from what the transaction actually does. The second is that it allows the transaction to be called in multiple ways.

Look at the advantages in terms of abstraction first. When you encapsulate your transactions within stored procedures, the calling program does not need to know anything about how the procedure works internally. The calling program calls a procedure such as increment_daily_total, and the SQL statements within that procedure do the actual updating. If the way that the daily total is derived or the place where it is stored changes, you need only to make the change to the stored procedure. As long as it accepts the same values as input and returns the same results, none of the calling programs will need to be changed. This layer of abstraction is incredibly useful when you have common transactions that can be called in a number of different ways.

The second advantage is the fact that encapsulating your transactions within stored procedures makes it easier to call them in more than one way. When you write a stored procedure, you can call it from a Web application written in Cold Fusion, a client/server application written in PowerBuilder, and from the database command-line interface itself easily. Instead of porting the code necessary to complete the transaction from one technology to the next, you can write it once as a stored procedure and call it from almost any application. Again, when you make changes to that stored procedure, you won't need to change the calling applications in any way (unless the inputs or outputs change).

Tip 56 from *Rafe Colburn*	Despite the fact that it's often wise to encapsulate all the SQL statements from a transaction within a stored procedure, it's generally a good idea to begin and commit the transaction from outside the stored procedure. Rather than enabling the stored procedure to commit the changes before the application has received the results, it's safer to call the stored procedure, verify that it executed correctly, and then commit the changes.

THE TRANSACTION LOG

Not only are you able to reverse the effects of a transaction by rolling it back before it is committed, but you can also roll back transactions that have already been committed using the transaction log. Database transaction logs are used to keep a record of every transaction committed since a certain point in time, generally since the database was backed up.

Say that you most recently made a backup of your database two weeks ago, and your database server's hard drive failed today, requiring you to restore the database from a backup. Restoring the database would actually be a two-step process. The first step is to restore the database backup itself, and the second step is to replay the transaction log entries from the time of the backup to the time of the failure. Because the transaction log records every transaction, this returns the database to the state it was in at the time of its failure.

CURSORS

hroughout this book, you've seen queries that return all their data in the form of a single table. When you perform an update or a delete, it affects every one of the rows that meet the criteria set in the WHERE clause. Similarly, when you write a SELECT statement to retrieve records from a database, all the rows that are returned by the query are displayed at once.

However, at times, you might need to perform different operations on various records in the database based on the contents of those records. Obviously, one way to do that is to write many SQL statements with WHERE clauses that isolate each group of rows that require a specific operation. However, sometimes it's just easier to write a single query and deal with each of the rows returned one at a time.

In many cases, when database applications are written, the entire results of the query are retrieved by the application, and the results are processed record by record by the calling program. To provide the same functionality within a database, *cursors* are used.

Consider how a normal query works. You send a query to a database, and each row is evaluated based on the contents of the WHERE clause. The rows that satisfy the criteria in the WHERE clause are returned, and the others are discarded. If an ORDER BY clause is provided, the results are sorted before being returned.

A cursor sends the query to the database, but it then returns the rows one at a time as they are requested instead of returning them in one large batch. As the rows are returned, you can manipulate their contents with an external program or with a stored procedure inside the database. In this chapter, I'm going to explain how cursors are used in Transact-SQL and PL/SQL. Even if you're not using a database that supports Transact-SQL, you should read that section because it explains the general functionality of cursors. The section on cursors in PL/SQL explains how cursors are used within an Oracle database and is not as generally applicable to other databases because of the eccentricities of Oracle.

USING CURSORS IN TRANSACT-SQL

Using cursors is a multistep process. First, the cursor must be declared, which creates the cursor and associates it with a SELECT statement. When you are ready to use the cursor you created, it must be opened. After the cursor is open, you can retrieve the rows using the cursor and act on those rows. Using the cursor, you can fetch, update, or delete each row individually. Finally, when you're done with the cursor, it must be closed. I'm going to take you through each of the steps required to use a cursor in the following sections.

DECLARING A CURSOR

To use a cursor, it must first be declared. The declaration is used to initialize a cursor and to tie a SELECT statement to that cursor. The declaration is used to identify the cursor, but the query is not actually evaluated until the cursor is opened. The cursor declaration is equivalent to a variable declaration in programming languages. The general syntax for a DECLARE CURSOR statement is as follows:

```
DECLARE cursor_name CURSOR
FOR select_statement
[ FOR [ READ ONLY ¦ UPDATE [ OF column_list ] ] ]
```

An example of a cursor declaration is provided in Listing 14.4.

LISTING 14.4   A CURSOR DECLARATION IN TRANSACT-SQL

```
DECLARE get_movies CURSOR
FOR SELECT movie_id, movie_title, studio_id
FROM Movies
```

In the example in Listing 14.4, the cursor named get_movies is tied to a select statement that retrieves the movie ID, title, and studio for all the movies in the database. When a cursor is declared, you can specify whether rows can be updated through the cursor and, if so, which columns can be updated specifically.

Take a look at the options available after the SELECT statement in the cursor syntax. There are two options for a cursor that can be used, FOR READ ONLY and FOR UPDATE. If a cursor is declared as FOR READ ONLY, only fetch operations can be performed against the cursor. If the FOR UPDATE option is specified, rows can be updated and deleted through the cursor, as well as read. The OF construct is used to restrict which columns can be updated through the cursor. To declare the cursor in Listing 14.4 so that only the movie_title and studio_id columns could be updated, the declaration in Listing 14.5 would be used.

LISTING 14.5   RESTRICTING WHICH COLUMNS CAN BE UPDATED THROUGH A CURSOR

```
DECLARE get_movies CURSOR
FOR SELECT movie_id, movie_title, studio_id
FROM Movies
FOR UPDATE OF movie_title, studio_id
```

Tip 57 from
Rafe Colburn

If you do not specify whether a cursor is FOR UPDATE or FOR READ ONLY, the database server will determine from the query itself whether the cursor should be updatable and declare it accordingly (basically, if a view created with the query would be updatable, the cursor will be updatable). However, you should make these declarations explicitly so that it's clear later how the cursor can and should be used.

OPENING A CURSOR

After a cursor has been declared, it can be opened. Opening a cursor executes the query tied to the cursor and prepares for the commands used to retrieve or update the rows returned by the query. The code used to open the `get_movies` cursor is demonstrated in Listing 14.6.

LISTING 14.6   OPENING THE `get_movies` CURSOR

```
OPEN get_movies
```

FETCHING ROWS FROM A CURSOR

One of the actions that can be taken on a cursor is fetching rows from the cursor. The default behavior is to fetch rows one at a time, but you can fetch more than one at once if you prefer to do so. When the cursor is opened, it is placed at the first row of the result set. Each fetch then retrieves a row from the result set and moves the cursor down to the next row. When all the rows have been fetched from the cursor, a return code is passed back indicating that no rows remain.

The statement to fetch a row from a cursor is simple:

```
FETCH cursor_name
```

In Listing 14.7, I demonstrate how cursors work by fetching a couple of rows from the `get_movies` cursor.

LISTING 14.7   FETCHING ROWS FROM THE `get_movies` CURSOR

```
FETCH get_movies
movie_id    movie_title                studio_id
----------- -------------------------- -----------
1           Mineral House              1

(1 row(s) affected)

FETCH get_movies

movie_id    movie_title                studio_id
----------- -------------------------- -----------
2           Prince Kong                2

(1 row(s) affected)
```

In Transact-SQL, when a cursor is empty, the result code 2 is passed back through the `@@sqlstatus` variable. This is useful when you write stored procedures that iterate over the rows retrieved using a cursor. The stored procedure uses a loop that fetches rows until the `@@sqlstatus` variable is set to 2 and then exits.

When you write stored procedures, it is also useful to place the values from each row that you fetch into variables automatically so that you can manipulate them within your program. You can store the results of a fetch in variables using the INTO clause of the FETCH statement, as shown in Listing 14.8.

LISTING 14.8   STORING THE RESULTS OF A FETCH INTO VARIABLES

```
FETCH get_movies INTO @id, @title, @studio
```

To fetch rows from a cursor into variables, you must first declare those variables in a DECLARE statement. The method for declaring these variables is provided in Chapter 15 in the section "Working with Variables."

I'll discuss the use of cursors within stored procedures further in Chapter 15.

If you prefer, you can fetch more than one row at a time from a cursor using the SET CURSOR ROWS command. The number of rows to be returned by every fetch is set on a cursor-by-cursor basis, as shown here:

```
SET CURSOR ROWS number_of_rows FOR cursor_name
```

The SET CURSOR ROWS command is only available in Sybase Adaptive Server, not Microsoft SQL Server.

UPDATING OR DELETING WITH CURSORS

There is not a special command for updating or deleting with cursors as there is for fetching rows. Instead, a special WHERE clause is used with the existing UPDATE and DELETE statements. The CURRENT OF construct is used to indicate that the current row (or group of rows) in the cursor should be the target of the UPDATE or DELETE statement. In Listing 14.9, I demonstrate how CURRENT OF is used in a WHERE clause.

LISTING 14.9   USING CURRENT OF WITH AN UPDATE STATEMENT

```
UPDATE Movies
SET movie_title = 'The Phantom Guinness'
WHERE CURRENT OF get_movies
```

```
(1 row(s) affected)
```

The CURRENT OF construct indicates that the movie_title field of the record where the get_movies cursor is currently located should be updated. To remove the row that the cursor is currently pointing to, CURRENT OF is used within a DELETE statement, as in Listing 14.10.

LISTING 14.10   USING CURRENT OF WITH A DELETE STATEMENT

```
DELETE FROM Movies
WHERE CURRENT OF get_movies
```

```
(1 row(s) affected)
```

After CURRENT OF is used within an UPDATE or DELETE statement, the cursor is moved to the next row (group of rows) automatically.

> **Note**
>
> If the cursor is attached to a query that contains a join, you cannot delete from that cursor. You also can't use the cursor with an UPDATE statement if the query is nonupdatable.

> **Tip 58 from**
> *Rafe Colburn*
>
> If you execute a DELETE or UPDATE statement while a cursor is open, the remaining records in the result set to which the cursor is attached will reflect the changes made by the UPDATE or DELETE statement that you executed. As such, it's not necessary to use the CURRENT OF construct to delete or update rows while you are iterating over a cursor. You can retrieve the primary key of the table from the cursor and then use that value within the WHERE clause of the UPDATE or DELETE statement to modify that record.

CLOSING AND DEALLOCATING CURSORS

There are two commands used to tie up the loose ends of a cursor. The CLOSE statement is used to close a cursor (disallowing any fetches, updates, or deletes) previously opened with an OPEN statement. You can no longer address rows within the cursor, but it remains declared. The DEALLOCATE statement not only closes the cursor, but it also revokes its declaration.

The main difference between the two statements is that after you close a cursor, you can use the OPEN statement to reopen the cursor, and the cursor will point to the first row in the results again. On the other hand, after a cursor has been deallocated, you have to declare the cursor again to use it.

The syntax of the two statements consist of the command and the cursor name, as follows:

```
CLOSE cursor_name
```

```
DEALLOCATE cursor_name
```

Listing 14.11 contains an example that demonstrates how both CLOSE and DEALLOCATE statements are used.

LISTING 14.11   USING CLOSE AND DEALLOCATE

```
DECLARE get_movies CURSOR
FOR SELECT movie_id, movie_title, studio_id
FROM Movies

OPEN get_movies

FETCH get_movies

movie_id    movie_title                studio_id
---------   ------------------------   -----------
1           Mineral House              1

(1 row(s) affected)

CLOSE get_movies

OPEN get_movies

FETCH get_movies

movie_id    movie_title                studio_id
---------   ------------------------   -----------
1           Mineral House              1

(1 row(s) affected)

DEALLOCATE get_movies

OPEN get_movies

Msg 16916, Level 16, State 1
A cursor with the name 'get_movies' does not exist
```

As you can see, when a cursor is closed and reopened, it returns to the first row in the query results. You can also see that when a query has been deallocated, it is no longer accessible with the OPEN command.

Tip 59 from
Rafe Colburn

When you close a cursor, the rows setting for that cursor is not affected. If you have changed that setting, the change will still be in effect when you reopen the cursor. Deallocating a cursor removes the rows setting as well.

USING CURSORS IN ORACLE PL/SQL

Unlike Transact-SQL, Oracle requires that you use cursors within the context of stored procedures written in PL/SQL. For that reason, I'm going to jump ahead a little bit and talk about PL/SQL stored procedures. A stored procedure written in PL/SQL contains three sections, the declarations section, the executable commands section, and the exception-handling section.

When you use a cursor within a PL/SQL stored procedure, the cursor must be declared in the declarations section, and the rows can be fetched using the cursor from within the executable commands section. In this chapter, I'm going to describe briefly how cursors are declared and used within a PL/SQL stored procedure. More information on PL/SQL itself can be found in Chapter 17.

DECLARING CURSORS

Every PL/SQL program contains a declarations section in which all the variables (and constant values) to be used within the executable commands section of the program are identified. The syntax used to declare a cursor is as follows:

```
CURSOR cursor_name IS
select_statement;
```

Generally, a variable is declared that will contain the rows fetched using the cursor. PL/SQL provides the %ROWTYPE construct for use with these variables. Basically, declaring a variable with the row type of a cursor allows the variable to inherit all the column names and datatypes from the records retrieved using the cursor. So, the following command is used to create a variable to hold the records from a declared cursor:

```
some_row cursor_name%ROWTYPE;
```

some_row is the variable that will hold the results of each record fetched using cursor_name. Listing 14.12 contains the declarations section of a PL/SQL program that uses a cursor.

LISTING 14.12   THE DECLARATIONS SECTION OF A PL/SQL PROGRAM

```
DECLARE
CURSOR get_movies IS
SELECT movie_id, movie_title, studio_id
FROM Movies;
movie_record get_movies%ROWTYPE;
```

The declarations section of a PL/SQL program begins with the keyword DECLARE. As you can see, the variable movie_record is assigned the row type of the cursor get_movies. The declarations section ends when the executable commands section is initiated using the BEGIN keyword.

USING CURSORS WITHIN PL/SQL PROGRAMS

After a cursor has been created in the declarations section of a PL/SQL program, it can be used within the executable commands section of the program. Listing 14.13 contains a PL/SQL program that uses the get_movies cursor, although it doesn't do anything other than open the cursor, fetch a record, and close the cursor.

PART

IV

CH

14

LISTING 14.13   USING A CURSOR WITHIN A PL/SQL PROGRAM

```
DECLARE
CURSOR get_movies IS
SELECT movie_id, movie_title, studio_id
FROM Movies;
movie_record get_movies%ROWTYPE;
BEGIN
OPEN get_movies;
FETCH get_movies INTO movie_record;
CLOSE get_movies;
END;
.
/

PL/SQL procedure successfully completed.
```

In the body of the stored procedure, I open the stored procedure, fetch a row (assigning its contents to the movie_record variable), and then close the stored procedure. Unlike Transact-SQL, PL/SQL requires that the results of the fetch operation be assigned to a variable (or variables). Transact-SQL prints the results if they are not assigned elsewhere, but PL/SQL does not duplicate this behavior.

The executable commands section of the program is terminated by the END keyword. The period on a line by itself terminates the larger PL/SQL block, and the / command runs the program.

Tip 60 from	In SQL*PLUS, the / command can be used to repeat the last query that you entered. More extensive information on how to use SQL*PLUS is provided in Chapter 18, which covers Oracle specifically.
Rafe Colburn	

CURSOR ATTRIBUTES

There are a number of attributes associated with cursors in PL/SQL that can be used within PL/SQL programs. These attributes are used to indicate the current status of the cursor, and they all return Boolean values except %ROWCOUNT. These attributes are listed in Table 14.1.

TABLE 14.1   CURSOR ATTRIBUTES IN PL/SQL

Attribute	Status
%FOUND	True if another record can be fetched from the cursor
%NOTFOUND	True if no more records can be fetched from the cursor
%ISOPEN	True if the cursor has been opened
%ROWCOUNT	The number of records fetched from the cursor so far

LOOPING OVER A CURSOR

The PL/SQL program back in Listing 14.13 fetched only the first record from the get_movies cursor. To fetch all the rows returned by the cursor, a loop is required. Using the LOOP command and the %NOTFOUND attribute, you can write a loop that fetches all the records returned by the query assigned to get_movies. Listing 14.14 shows how such a loop is constructed.

LISTING 14.14   LOOPING OVER A CURSOR

```
DECLARE
CURSOR get_movies IS
SELECT movie_id, movie_title, studio_id
FROM Movies;
movie_record get_movies%ROWTYPE;
BEGIN
OPEN get_movies;
LOOP
FETCH get_movies INTO movie_record;
EXIT WHEN get_movies%NOTFOUND;
END LOOP;
CLOSE get_movies;
END;
.
/
```

In this program, the LOOP statement is used to initiate the loop. The exit condition for the loop is established using the EXIT WHEN construct. The loop exits when the get_movies%NOTFOUND attribute is true (the "is true" is implied). The END LOOP statement marks the end of the statements to be executed within the loop. Again, this PL/SQL program doesn't do anything. In Listing 14.16, I include some SQL statements in the program to add some real functionality. First, I'm going to create a new table to use in the example in Listing 14.15.

LISTING 14.15   A TABLE TO HOLD THE RESULTS OF STATEMENTS IN A PL/SQL PROGRAM

```
CREATE TABLE Movies_Example
(example_id      NUMBER,
example_title    VARCHAR(25),
example_s_id     NUMBER)
```

LISTING 14.16   A PL/SQL PROGRAM THAT INSERTS ROWS INTO A TABLE

```
DECLARE
CURSOR get_movies IS
SELECT movie_id, movie_title, studio_id
FROM Movies;
movie_record get_movies%ROWTYPE;
BEGIN
```

PART

IV

CH

14

continues

LISTING 14.16 CONTINUED

```
OPEN get_movies;
LOOP
FETCH get_movies INTO movie_record;
EXIT WHEN get_movies%NOTFOUND;
INSERT INTO Movies_Example
VALUES (movie_record.movie_id, movie_record.movie_title,
movie_record.studio_id);
END LOOP;
CLOSE get_movies;
END;
.
/
```

This program inserts all the records retrieved using the get_movies cursor into the
Movies_Example table. You can also iterate over the records in a cursor using a FOR loop, as
demonstrated in Listing 14.17.

LISTING 14.17 LOOPING OVER A CURSOR USING A FOR LOOP

```
DECLARE
CURSOR get_movies IS
SELECT movie_id, movie_title, studio_id
FROM Movies;
movie_record get_movies%ROWTYPE;
BEGIN
OPEN get_movies;
FOR movie_record IN get_movies
LOOP
FETCH get_movies INTO movie_record;
INSERT INTO Movies_Example
VALUES (movie_record.movie_id, movie_record.movie_title,
movie_record.studio_id);
END LOOP;
CLOSE get_movies;
END;
.
/
```

The FOR ... IN statement is an alternative to the EXIT WHEN statement. It has the same
result, however; it retrieves each of the rows in get_movies and then exits. The final method
by which you can loop over a cursor, shown in Listing 14.18, uses a WHILE loop.

LISTING 14.18 A WHILE LOOP THAT LOOPS OVER A CURSOR

```
DECLARE
CURSOR get_movies IS
SELECT movie_id, movie_title, studio_id
FROM Movies;
movie_record get_movies%ROWTYPE;
BEGIN
OPEN get_movies;
```

```
    WHILE get_movies%FOUND
LOOP
FETCH get_movies INTO movie_record;
INSERT INTO Movies_Example
VALUES (movie_record.movie_id, movie_record.movie_title,
movie_record.studio_id);
END LOOP;
CLOSE get_movies;
END;
.
/
```

When there are no more records left to retrieve from the cursor, get_movies%FOUND returns false instead of true, which causes the loop to exit. The stored procedures in Listings 14.16, 14.7, and 14.18 all populate the Movies_Example table with the records displayed in Listing 14.19.

LISTING 14.19   THE CONTENTS OF THE Movies_Example TABLE AFTER THE PL/SQL PROGRAMS ARE RUN

```
SELECT *
FROM Movies_Example

EXAMPLE_ID EXAMPLE_TITLE             EXAMPLE_S_ID
---------- ------------------------- ------------
         1 Vegetable House                      1
         2 Prince Kong                          2
         3 The Code Warrior                     4
         4 Bill Durham                          3
         5 Codependence Day                     1
         6 The Linux Files                      2
         7 SQL Strikes Back                     3
         8 The Programmer                       3
         9 Hard Code                            4
        10 The Rear Windows                     1

10 rows selected.
```

IN THE REAL WORLD

I'd like to discuss some of the real world issues related to locks. I already explained what locks are in this chapter and detailed how they solve the lost update problem. I'd now like to plumb deeper into the issue and talk about how database locking can affect database applications when they're deployed.

Problems surrounding concurrent use of a shared resource are nothing new. Whether the resource happens to be a table in a relational database, a file on a hard drive, or just an address in a computer's RAM is irrelevant. At some point, a software developer has to deal with the fact that unless access to that resource is managed correctly, data is going to be overwritten. That, of course, is where locks come in.

However, locks themselves can cause problems. At least two questions must be asked. How restrictive should a lock be? Under what conditions should a lock be released? When programs that create locks don't behave themselves or when the locks themselves don't behave, systems will come to a grinding halt.

I was building an electronic commerce site that enabled users to visit a Web site and purchase downloadable products when I ran into some problems involving locks. The session management system on the site, which was used to keep track of users on the site and associate them with the contents of their shopping cart, inserted a row into a table every time they loaded a page. This feature was used to keep track of user activity for the purpose of judging the effectiveness of the site. It also updated the session table itself to move up the expiration date for the session as long as the user was actively using the site.

The application server locked the entire sessions table every time it updated the session record for the user. To handle the large audience of users who would be visiting the site concurrently, the application server opened multiple connections to the database to allow queries to be executed simultaneously. The interface to the user sessions table was written using stored procedures. The stored procedure to verify the user's session accepted the session ID, verified that it was valid, and then refreshed the expiration date for the session. It also added a row to the logging table to indicate that the user had visited another page.

This stored procedure did not contain a commit instruction; instead, it left it up to the calling program to issue a commit or rollback depending on the return code returned by the stored procedure. Unfortunately, the calling program didn't commit transactions either, so the order of events that occurred was that a user would move to a new page, and the sessions table would be locked and updated. After the update, the session would return, but no commit would be issued. So, if another user moved to another page and her session validation procedure call was issued over a different connection, the procedure would see that the table was locked by the other database connection and would wait for the lock to be released. Because the procedure call that originally created the lock was long gone, the call would simply wait indefinitely. Eventually, all the database connections belonging to the application server would be consumed, and users would be denied access to the site because no more database connections would be available.

Fortunately, this problem was easy to fix. As soon as the Web application developers discovered that they had to commit their changes after calling queries, the new commit code was added to every dynamic page on the site (for insurance), and the locking problem was solved, but only temporarily. Unfortunately, as the site was constructed, the locking problem still occurred occasionally. A transaction would be left uncommitted, and eventually all the sessions would hang waiting for that lock to be released, preventing users from accessing the site.

When the commit code was added to the dynamic pages, it was included in a single call at the very bottom of every page so that all the changes made through stored procedure calls on that page would be committed immediately before execution of the page finished. This worked fine almost all the time, but it would still crop up occasionally, seemingly at random.

Eventually it was discovered that the event that triggered this problem involved users calling pages that contained runtime errors. If a runtime error occurred on a page (as often happened during development) and the page had already opened a transaction, the runtime error would halt execution of the page before the commit could be issued, and the transaction would be left open indefinitely. The lesson learned here was that no time should be wasted between the point at which a transaction is known to be successful and the commission of that transaction.

A different problem that cropped up on the site highlighted a another issue involving resource contention, and this one had nothing to do with user-initiated locks. As I said earlier, the applications on this site used stored procedures to communicate with the database. The site used an Oracle database, and the stored procedures were written in PL/SQL.

Oracle packages (containers for multiple stored procedures) are compiled, and when an item on which they depend changes, they become invalid and must be recompiled before they can be executed. After a long bout of dealing with the locking problems that I described previously, the site locked up again. When we started drilling into the system views to figure out what was locked and what the database connections were waiting on, we discovered that the packages were waiting to compile.

As it turns out, the database administrators had made some changes to a table, which forced all the packages that referenced that table to become invalid and recompile on the next execution. In Oracle, all compilation jobs wait until any currently executing jobs that reference something related to that package are complete before compilation begins. A package on which all the packages waiting to compile depended was being executed and thus held up access to the entire site.

As it turned out, the program that created the dynamic downloadable products was associated with a package and was simply holding the package open waiting for requests to create products. Because the external program was holding the package open indefinitely, none of the packages that depended on it could compile, and so all users were prevented from accessing the site. When the program was killed, all the packages waiting to compile compiled, and we were off and running again.

This illustrates the complex issue of resource contention in databases. Database systems, particularly systems with lots of users and components, can get into extremely complex locking scenarios that are difficult to debug. Even though transactions are an absolutely essential component of any database that supports multiple users, they can make life painful at times.

PART V

STORED PROCEDURES

CHAPTER **15**

WRITING STORED PROCEDURES

In this chapter

I already presented a sneak preview of stored procedures in the previous chapter in the course of my discussion of cursors. In this chapter, I'm going to provide an overview of the types of tasks you can accomplish with stored procedures and explain how stored procedures are written.

Despite the fact that many databases support stored procedures, they are really outside the scope of the SQL query language. Oracle stored procedures are not written in SQL, but in PL/SQL. Sybase databases and Microsoft SQL Server enable you to write stored procedures in Transact-SQL. Because the SQL standard does not cover stored procedures, the implementation of stored procedures varies widely from database to database. A stored procedure written to work in an Oracle database must be completely rewritten to run in Sybase Adaptive Server or IBM DB/2.

Even so, the philosophy behind stored procedures is pretty similar no matter which database you use. The purpose of stored procedures is to enable database developers to write more complex programs within a database than can be written using a single query. Rather than forcing developers to write all their "business logic" outside the database and simply use the database as a repository for data, databases with stored procedures provide a full procedural programming language within the database.

Stored procedures provide several advantages. The first is that they enable you to make the logic associated with your data as portable as the data itself. For example, say that you run a bookstore, and you track all your inventory in a relational database. Every time a customer purchases a book and the transaction is entered at the register, the inventory is updated. The real-time tracking of the inventory enables you to keep track of when books need to be ordered, and you don't have to worry about running out of popular titles.

Furthermore, assume that the program running at the register is a client/server application written using PowerBuilder. If the cash register system is the only application that uses the inventory database, you can just write the inventory control code in PowerBuilder. When a person buys a book, the PowerBuilder application will execute an UPDATE statement that decrements the number of copies of that book in inventory by one.

Later, however, your bookstore opens an online store that is powered by Java servlets. It must interface with your inventory system so that books ordered online are properly removed from inventory after they are purchased. Because your inventory management code is embedded in your client/server application, you must rewrite it in your Java servlet. This leaves you with two copies of the code to maintain, both written in different languages.

The better option is to write the inventory management code as a package of stored procedures and let every application that needs to interact with the system call those stored procedures rather than manipulating the tables themselves. There are a number of advantages to using this approach:

■ It enables you to write and maintain a single set of code that is utilized by all current and future applications that utilize the database.

■ It insulates the application developers from the structure of your database. Rather than forcing them to manipulate your tables directly, they call an application-programming interface expressed through a stored procedure. If changes to the data model occur, the stored procedure is updated to reflect those changes, but the applications calling that stored procedure will work without changes.

■ It can provide better performance because the programming logic and the SQL queries themselves within the stored procedures are stored in the database in a compiled format so that they do not need to be parsed every time they are called.

Unfortunately, discussing how to write stored procedures in a general way is difficult because the construction of stored procedures differs greatly depending on the brand of database you are using. In the course of this discussion of stored procedures, I'm going to explain in this chapter and in Chapter 16, "More on Transact-SQL Stored Procedures," how each concept is expressed in Transact-SQL, and then, in Chapter 17, "Writing Oracle PL/SQL Stored Procedures," I'm going to explain the concept in terms of Oracle PL/SQL.

One particular type of stored procedure I'm going to discuss in this chapter is the trigger. *Triggers* are stored procedures that are executed automatically whenever a particular event occurs. For example, you can write a trigger that is executed whenever a row is inserted in a specific table. Triggers are often used as an alternative means by which you can validate values before they are inserted into fields, in lieu of table constraints.

WRITING A STORED PROCEDURE

Stored procedures are created using the `CREATE PROCEDURE` statement. `CREATE PROCEDURE` simply wraps an identifier around some Transact-SQL or PL/SQL code and saves it for future use. You can write all the commands that appear in stored procedures without a `CREATE PROCEDURE` statement; they'll be executed like any other query and won't be stored anywhere.

The structure of a `CREATE PROCEDURE` statement is as follows:

```
CREATE PROCEDURE procedure_name
[@parameter_name datatype[(length)], ...]
AS
SQL statements
```

The `CREATE PROCEDURE` statement is used to identify the stored procedure and to define any parameters that are passed to the stored procedure when it is called. In its simplest form, a stored procedure is a saved query. For example, Listing 15.1 contains a stored procedure that selects the `movie_title` for all the movies in the `Movies` table.

LISTING 15.1 A SIMPLE STORED PROCEDURE

```
CREATE PROCEDURE get_movie_titles
AS
SELECT movie_title
```

continues

LISTING 15.1   CONTINUED

```
FROM Movies

GO
```

There are a number of methods you can use to call the stored procedure after it has been created. The easiest way is to simply enter the procedure name by itself as a query, as shown in Listing 15.2.

LISTING 15.2   CALLING A STORED PROCEDURE

```
get_movies_titles

movie_title
-----------------------
Mineral House
The Code Warrior
Bill Durham
Codependence Day
The Linux Files
SQL Strikes Back
The Programmer
Hard Code
The Rear Windows

(9 row(s) affected)
```

PASSING PARAMETERS TO A STORED PROCEDURE

Simply encapsulating a static query within a stored procedure isn't very useful; after all, you could use a view, a more flexible alternative, for that. You can pass values to a stored procedure when it is called and then use those values within the queries in the stored procedure. When you create the stored procedure, you must list the parameters that the procedure accepts. When the stored procedure is called, you are required to include all those parameters in the code that calls the procedure.

For example, you could rewrite the stored procedure in Listing 15.1 so that it accepts a studio ID as a parameter and returns all the movies from that studio. The new CREATE PROCEDURE statement that creates the stored procedure is included in Listing 15.4.

Before I present the new stored procedure, however, I need to explain a property of stored procedures in general. There is no way to edit a stored procedure. To make a change to a stored procedure, you have to discard the existing version and create a new one in its place. Many database tools take care of this for you by transparently retrieving the existing stored procedure from the database and then replacing it when you save any changes. However, when you're editing a stored procedure using a direct interface to the database, you must drop an existing stored procedure manually before you can create another with the same name. The code for doing so appears in Listing 15.3.

LISTING 15.3 **CODE TO DROP THE STORED PROCEDURE** get_movie_titles **IN** **TRANSACT-SQL**

```
IF object_id('get_movie_titles') IS NOT NULL
BEGIN
    DROP PROCEDURE get_movie_titles
END

GO
```

This command did not return data, and it did not return any rows

When you are updating existing stored procedures, you can include that code (substituting the name of your stored procedure for get_movie_titles, of course) before the CREATE PROCEDURE statement to clean up the existing procedure before creating the new one. Oracle eliminates this problem by providing the OR REPLACE clause in stored procedures, which automatically discards stored procedures with the name of the one being created.

Getting back to the get_movie_titles procedure, when the existing procedure has been dropped, the new one, which accepts a studio ID, can be created. That procedure is in Listing 15.4.

LISTING 15.4 **A NEW** get_movie_titles **PROCEDURE, WHICH ACCEPTS A PARAMETER**

```
CREATE PROCEDURE get_movie_titles @studio_id INTEGER
AS
SELECT movie_title
FROM Movies
WHERE studio_id = @studio_id

GO
```

The list of parameters for the stored procedure are included after the procedure name. In this case, the stored procedure accepts one parameter, @studio_id, which is an integer. Inside the stored procedure, the @studio_id parameter is replaced with the value passed to the stored procedure, and that value is used within the WHERE clause. The @ character is used to indicate that a particular identifier is a reference to a variable and not a column name, table name, or other identifier.

The following methods can be used to call a stored procedure:

```
execute get_movie_titles 1

exec get_movie_titles 1

execute get_movie_titles @studio_id = 1

execute movies.dbo.get_movie_titles 1

get_movie_titles 1
```

In Listing 15.5, you can see the results of the stored procedure call. The results would be the same no matter how it was called (assuming that the parameter was the same).

LISTING 15.5 CALLING A STORED PROCEDURE WITH A PARAMETER

```
get_movie_titles 1

movie_title
-----------------------
Mineral House
Codependence Day
The Rear Windows

(3 row(s) affected)
```

Using multiple parameters is trivial; you simply include them in a comma-separated list, as shown in Listing 15.6.

LISTING 15.6 WRITING A STORED PROCEDURE WITH MULTIPLE PARAMETERS

```
IF object_id('get_movie_titles') IS NOT NULL
BEGIN
    DROP PROCEDURE get_movie_titles
END

GO

CREATE PROCEDURE get_movie_titles @studio_id INTEGER,
@director_id INTEGER
AS
SELECT movie_title
FROM Movies
WHERE studio_id = @studio_id
AND director_id = @director_id

GO

get_movie_titles 3, 9

movie_title
-----------------------
Bill Durham
SQL Strikes Back

(2 row(s) affected)
```

Tip 61 from
Rafe Colburn

You can set the default values for parameters passed to a stored procedure in the CREATE PROCEDURE statement. If you wanted the @studio_id parameter to default to 1 in the stored procedure in Listing 15.4, you could declare it like this:

```
CREATE PROCEDURE get_movie_titles
@studio_id INT = 1
AS
```

```
SELECT movie_title
FROM Movies
WHERE studio_id = @studio_id
```

WORKING WITH VARIABLES

Passing a parameter to a stored procedure is one way to set a variable. In Transact-SQL, variables are indicated by prepending an @ (at) sign to the name of the variable, which differentiates them from column and table identifiers (both names and aliases). As is the case with almost every query language, variables are used to store data for the duration of the program's execution. So, when you pass a movie ID to the get_movie_titles stored procedure, the value is available through the variable @studio_id as long as get_movie_titles is running. In this case, the stored procedure consists of only a single query, so the variable is used in the WHERE clause in that query and then discarded when the program's execution ends.

If you want to use a variable without specifying it as a parameter of the stored procedure, it must be created using the DECLARE statement. Just as each column in a table must have a data type, each variable used in a Transact-SQL stored procedure must be cast using a specific data type as well. Coincidentally, the data types for variables and columns in tables are the same, except that variables cannot be declared using either the TEXT or IMAGE types.

Use the following syntax to declare variables:

```
DECLARE variable_name DATATYPE(size)
```

So, if you wanted to declare the two parameters used in the get_movie_titles procedure as variables within the program, you would use the following code:

```
DECLARE studio_id INTEGER
DECLARE director_id INTEGER
```

The two variables could also be created in a single line of code, saving one DECLARE statement and improving performance minimally:

```
DECLARE studio_id INTEGER, director_id INTEGER
```

In Transact-SQL, variable names can be no longer than 29 characters and must follow the rules for naming identifiers, which are listed in Chapter 19, "Microsoft SQL Server and Sybase Adaptive Server."

Tip 62 from
Rafe Colburn

Most stored procedures are written in sections, with the first section being the declarations section. All of the DECLARE statements for the program should appear in the declarations section of the program. Not only does this prevent you from using variables before they are initialized, but it also enables you to quickly see a list of all the variables that are used within a stored procedure.

SETTING VARIABLES

After you've declared your variables, you can set them with values. As you've already seen, one common method for setting variables is to pass the values to the stored procedure as parameters. The parameters passed to a stored procedure are automatically placed in the parameters that were specified when the procedure was initially created.

Variables are set using SELECT statements. To set a variable to a particular value, it must be placed in the select list and set equal to an expression. No FROM clause is required in Transact-SQL SELECT statements, so you can set a variable to a static value, to the results of a subquery, or to the value contained in a particular column. It is simplest to set a variable to a static value. You can set a variable to a static value using the code in Listing 15.7.

LISTING 15.7 ASSIGNING A STATIC VALUE TO A VARIABLE

```
DECLARE @studio_id VARCHAR(25)

SELECT @studio_id = '3'

PRINT @studio_id
(1 row(s) affected)

3
```

Tip 63 from
Rafe Colburn

The PRINT statement can only print values that are of type CHAR or VARCHAR. Implicit type conversions are not provided for. To print numbers or dates, you must use the CONVERT function to change the value to the appropriate data type before you use the PRINT function.

You can also set a variable to a value within the context of a standard SQL query. For example, consider the stored procedure in Listing 15.8.

LISTING 15.8 SETTING A VARIABLE WITHIN A QUERY

```
DECLARE @cnt INT

SELECT @cnt = COUNT(*)
FROM Movies

PRINT CONVERT(VARCHAR(25), @cnt)

GO

(1 row(s) affected)

9
```

Values can be assigned to variables using a subquery in the select list of a SELECT statement, as demonstrated in Listing 15.9.

LISTING 15.9 SETTING A VARIABLE USING A SUBQUERY

```
DECLARE @average VARCHAR(25)

SELECT @average = CONVERT(VARCHAR(25), (SELECT AVG(budget) FROM Movies))

PRINT @average

GO

(1 row(s) affected)

28.777777
```

The subquery returns only one value because it uses an aggregate function, and that value is assigned to the @average variable. What happens if a query returns more than one value and you assign it to a variable? Take a look at Listing 15.10.

LISTING 15.10 USING A VARIABLE ASSIGNMENT IN A QUERY THAT RETURNS MULTIPLE ROWS

```
DECLARE @title VARCHAR(25)

SELECT @title = movie_title
FROM Movies

PRINT @title

GO

(9 row(s) affected)

The Rear Windows
```

Only the last row from the query results is printed when the code is executed. This is because the movie title of the current row is assigned to the variable @title every time a row is retrieved by the query. When the query finishes executing, the value of movie_title in the last row returned by the query remains in the @title variable. All the values of movie_title were assigned to the @title variable during the course of the query's execution, but the value was replaced every time the query fetched a new row.

One thing you have to watch out for is queries that return null. If you try to assign a null value to a variable, an error will occur, so you have to ensure either that none of your queries return nulls or that you use the ISNULL function to handle this condition. ISNULL enables you to specify a default value that will be assigned to a variable if the value that was supposed to be assigned to the variable turned out to be null. So the query in Listing 15.11 throws an error, whereas the query in Listing 15.12 prints the word Null, which was specified using the ISNULL function.

LISTING 15.11   A QUERY THAT RETURNS A NULL VALUE

```
DECLARE @var VARCHAR(25)

SELECT @var = CONVERT(VARCHAR(25), AVG(budget))
FROM Movies
WHERE budget < 0

PRINT @var

GO

(1 row(s) affected)
```

LISTING 15.12   A QUERY THAT USES ISNULL TO TRAP ASSIGNMENT ERRORS RELATED TO NULL VALUES

```
DECLARE @var DEC
SEELCT @var = ISNULL(AVG(budget), 0)
FROM Movies
WHERE budget < 0

PRINT @var

GO

(1 row(s) affected)

0.000000
```

DEFINING BLOCKS OF CODE

In SQL, a block of statements is defined using BEGIN and END statements. The BEGIN and END statements serve the same purpose as braces do in some other languages: They enable a group of statements to be used where a single statement is ordinarily required.

For example, when you write conditional constructs using IF statements, the statement that immediately follows the IF statement is executed if the condition is true. If a block of code follows the IF statement, all the code in the block will be executed. You can place SQL statements within blocks wherever you like in your stored procedures to organize your code.

The syntax for a block of statements is as follows:

```
BEGIN
    SQL statements
END
```

You can also nest BEGIN ... END blocks within other blocks. This is important because it enables you to nest conditional statements to create complex conditional structures. For example, you can nest blocks of SQL as follows:

```
BEGIN
    SQL statements
    BEGIN
        SQL statements
    END
    SQL statements
    BEGIN
        SQL statements
        BEGIN
            SQL statements
        END
        SQL statements
    END
    SQL statements
END
```

CONDITIONAL STATEMENTS USING IF

The IF keyword is used to create conditional constructs in stored procedure extensions to SQL. IF statements evaluate a Boolean expression to determine whether the statement (or block of code) tied to the IF statement should be executed. If the Boolean condition is true, the code will be executed; if not, it will be skipped. The ELSE keyword can be added to provide alternative code that will be executed if the expression is false.

The Boolean conditions themselves are evaluated identically to those used in the WHERE clause of a normal query. A comparison operator can be used to return a value of true or false, or a query can be used. Queries that return results are considered to be true; queries that return null are considered to be false.

Listing 15.13 contains an example of an IF statement that tests the value of a variable and then executes a query if the value is true.

LISTING 15.13 AN IF STATEMENT IN SQL

```
DECLARE @thing INT
SELECT @thing = 10
IF @thing > 5
    UPDATE Movies
    SET release_date = GETDATE()
    WHERE movie_id = @thing
GO

(1 row(s) affected)
```

Because @thing is greater than 5, the Movies table is updated. Just as WHERE clauses in queries support compound expressions using Boolean operators, so, too, does the IF statement. Take a look at the query in Listing 15.14. It uses a compound expression in the IF statement.

LISTING 15.14   A COMPOUND EXPRESSION IN AN IF STATEMENT

```
DECLARE @thing INT
SELECT @thing = 10
IF @thing > 5 AND @thing < 10
    UPDATE Movies
    SET release_date = GETDATE()
    WHERE movie_id = @thing
GO

(1 row(s) affected)
```

In Listing 15.14, the UPDATE statement is not executed because the value of thing is not between 5 and 10. The @thing < 10 expression is false, so the whole expression is considered to be false. One thing you can't do in an IF statement is use the special comparison operators that work in the WHERE clause. IF does not support BETWEEN, LIKE, IN, and the other special WHERE operators.

USING QUERIES IN IF EXPRESSIONS

There are two ways you can use a query in an IF expression. If the query returns a single value, you can plug the query into a normal expression, and the result of the query will be used in the comparison. You can also include a query as the entire expression if you use the EXISTS keyword. The expression will evaluate as true if the query returns any results at all. Null values return false.

Take a look at an IF statement that uses the value returned by a query in an expression. To be used in a normal expression, a query must return a single value. In Listing 15.15, the stored procedure runs a select statement if the Movies table contains fewer than 15 rows.

LISTING 15.15   SQL CODE THAT USES THE VALUE RETURNED BY A QUERY IN AN IF STATEMENT

```
IF (SELECT COUNT(*) FROM Movies) < 15
    SELECT movie_title
    FROM Movies

movie_title
------------------------
Mineral House
The Code Warrior
Bill Durham
Codependence Day
The Linux Files
SQL Strikes Back
The Programmer
Hard Code
The Rear Windows

(9 row(s) affected)
```

In Listing 15.16, I've written some SQL code that uses a query within an IF statement without a comparison operator. Instead, the EXISTS keyword is used to create a true/false condition. In the listing, the SELECT statement associated with the IF statement is not executed because the query used in the IF condition does not return any results.

LISTING 15.16   USING A QUERY AS THE CONDITION OF AN IF STATEMENT

```
IF EXISTS (SELECT movie_id FROM Movies WHERE studio_id = 10)
    SELECT DISTINCT studio_id
    FROM Movies

This command did not return data, and it did not return any rows
```

USING BLOCKS OF CODE WITH IF STATEMENTS

Rather than using a single statement with an IF statement, you can use a block of code defined using BEGIN and END. Using a block of code is easy, you simply insert the BEGIN statement immediately after the IF statement, then include the body of the code block, and then close the block with END. For an example, see Listing 15.17.

LISTING 15.17   EXECUTING A BLOCK OF CODE WITHIN AN IF STATEMENT

```
DECLARE @new_revenue DEC

IF EXISTS (SELECT movie_id FROM Movies WHERE studio_id = 1)
    BEGIN
        SELECT @new_revenue = 50

        UPDATE Movies
        SET gross = @new_revenue
        WHERE studio_id = 1
    END

(1 row(s) affected)


(3 row(s) affected)
```

USING IF ... ELSE

Ordinarily, an IF statement is used to execute a specific statement or block when a Boolean condition is true. Using the ELSE keyword, you can also include a statement or block that will be executed if the test condition of the IF statement is false. The structure of an IF ... ELSE construct is as follows:

```
IF condition
    SQL statement
ELSE
    SQL statement
```

If the condition in the IF statement is true, the SQL statement (or block) that follows is executed. If the condition is false, the statement (or block) that follows the ELSE keyword is executed. Listing 15.18 contains an example of an IF ... ELSE construct.

LISTING 15.18   AN IF ... ELSE CONSTRUCT

```
IF EXISTS (SELECT * FROM Movies WHERE studio_id = 8)
    SELECT COUNT(*) FROM Movies
WHERE studio_id = 8
ELSE
    PRINT "No movies found."

No movies found.
```

NESTING IF STATEMENTS AND BLOCKS

You can build complex conditional structures by nesting IF statements within one another. An IF statement, even if it includes an ELSE clause, is considered to be a single statement when used within another IF statement. This means that you can nest IF statements without using blocks, although you can certainly enclose the statements within blocks if you prefer to do so. Listing 15.19 contains an example of a nested IF statement.

LISTING 15.19   A NESTED IF STATEMENT

```
DECLARE @thing INT
SELECT @thing = 7
IF @thing > 5
    IF @thing > 10
        PRINT "The variable is greater than 10."
    ELSE
        PRINT "The variable is greater than 5."
ELSE
    PRINT "The variable is less than or equal to 5."

(1 row(s) affected)

The variable is greater than 5.
```

As you can see, there is an IF ... ELSE statement nested within the outer IF statement in Listing 15.19. Because the @thing variable contains a value greater than 5, the inner IF statement is evaluated. The value is less than 10, so the ELSE branch of the inner IF statement is executed. Nested IF statements are really only useful if you're going to include ELSE clauses as well; without ELSE clauses, it's just as easy to use Boolean operators to create compound IF statements instead of using nesting. Consider the examples in Listing 15.20 and 15.21.

LISTING 15.20   A NESTED IF STATEMENT WITHOUT AN ELSE CLAUSE

```
DECLARE @crow INT
DECLARE @bar INT
```

```
SELECT @crow = 1
SELECT @bar = 2
IF @crow = 1
    IF @bar = 2
        PRINT "Both conditions were true."

(1 row(s) affected)


(1 row(s) affected)

Both conditions were true.
```

LISTING 15.21   AN IF STATEMENT THAT USES A COMPOUND CONDITION

```
DECLARE @crow INT
DECLARE @bar INT
SELECT @crow = 1
SELECT @bar = 2
IF @crow = 1 AND @bar = 2
    PRINT "Both conditions were true."

(1 row(s) affected)


(1 row(s) affected)

Both conditions were true.
```

As you can see, the code in both of the listings produces the same results. Either is acceptable, but generally speaking, it's preferable to use the code in Listing 15.21. It's less complex and easier to read than the code in Listing 15.20.

Most of the time, you'll need to use blocks within nested IF statements. Blocks of code are used within nested IF statements the same way they are used in any other IF statement. An example of a nested IF statement that uses blocks appears in Listing 15.22.

LISTING 15.22   A NESTED IF STATEMENT WITH BLOCKS

```
DECLARE @crow INT
DECLARE @bar INT
DECLARE @display VARCHAR(25)
SELECT @crow = 1
SELECT @bar = 2

IF @crow > 10
    BEGIN
        SELECT @display = CONVERT(VARCHAR(25), @crow - @bar)
        PRINT @display
    END
ELSE
    BEGIN
```

continues

LISTING 15.22   CONTINUED

```
        SELECT @display = CONVERT(VARCHAR(25), @crow + @bar)
        PRINT @display
    END

(1 row(s) affected)


(1 row(s) affected)


(1 row(s) affected)

3
```

USING LOOPS

Loops provide a means by which you can execute the same statements repeatedly until a particular condition is satisfied. In some ways, a SELECT statement behaves as a loop. In most cases, the SELECT statement evaluates every row in a table (or every row in a joined set of tables); the condition that ends the execution of the SELECT statement is the lack of any rows to process. In the process of looping over all the rows in the tables specified in the FROM clause of the query, the SELECT statement evaluates each of them as specified in the query and prints the appropriate results.

SELECT statements do in a single statement what would generally require many statements in a regular programming language. Because SQL is highly specialized for manipulating and handling tabular sets of data, much of the functionality in a standard programming language is implied in SQL when it comes to iterating over sets of rows in a table.

In some cases, however, there is a need to create generic looping structures in SQL because the SELECT (or UPDATE or DELETE) statements do not provide all the functionality necessary to accomplish a particular task. As I said before, a loop just executes repeatedly until a specified condition is satisfied. In SQL, that can be until a particular variable is set to a particular value, until all the rows have been fetched from a cursor, or until any other Boolean condition evaluates as false.

Transact-SQL provides only a single type of loop, the WHILE loop. Most programming languages provide a number of different looping constructs, which I'll discuss a bit later. The WHILE loop is the most flexible of looping structures. It can be used to accomplish anything that the other looping constructs can; however, the others might be more readable in certain cases.

WHILE LOOPS

The structure of a WHILE loop is very similar to that of an IF statement. Instead of executing a statement or block once if the condition supplied is true, it executes the statement or block repeatedly until the condition is false or until the loop is explicitly ended using the BREAK statement. The structure of a WHILE loop is as follows:

```
WHILE condition
    statement
```

If you want to use a block as the body of the WHILE loop, the following structure is used:

```
WHILE condition
    BEGIN
        statements
    END
```

An example of a WHILE loop appears in Listing 15.23. It illustrates the most important point to make about WHILE loops, which is that the body of the WHILE loop must contain some code that will eventually make the condition over which the WHILE loop is iterating evaluate as false. If there is no such code in the body of the WHILE loop, you will be left with an infinite loop, and your program will never continue execution past the loop statement (it will run forever). In a bit, I'll discuss another method by which you can avoid infinite loops and, indeed, how you can use them to your advantage.

LISTING 15.23 AN EXAMPLE OF A WHILE LOOP

```
DECLARE @crow INT
DECLARE @display VARCHAR(25)
SELECT @crow = 1
WHILE @crow < 5
    BEGIN
        SELECT @display = CONVERT(VARCHAR(25), @crow)
        PRINT @display
        SELECT @crow = @crow + 1
    END

(1 row(s) affected)


(1 row(s) affected)

1

(1 row(s) affected)


(1 row(s) affected)

2

(1 row(s) affected)


(1 row(s) affected)

3
```

continues

LISTING 15.23 CONTINUED

```
(1 row(s) affected)


(1 row(s) affected)

4

(1 row(s) affected)
```

This loop is executed until the value of @crow is greater than 5. When the loop begins, the value of @crow is 1, and the loop contains a statement that increments the value of @crow by 1 every time the loop is executed. As you can see from the results of the program, the loop is executed five times. Execution ceases when the value of @crow is 5 and the condition is no longer true.

INFINITE LOOPS

Creating an infinite loop is simple. For example, this code will execute until you manually halt the execution of the program using some external means (either by killing the process or by hitting the key sequence to break execution):

```
WHILE 1 = 1
    PRINT "Still going ..."
```

It's sometimes easy to create infinite loops unintentionally. Consider the modification of the program in Listing 15.23 found in Listing 15.24.

LISTING 15.24 AN INFINITE WHILE LOOP

```
DECLARE @crow INT
SELECT @crow = 1
WHILE @crow <> 10
    BEGIN
        PRINT @crow
        SELECT @crow = @crow + 2
    END
```

The loop will never stop executing because @crow will never be equal to 10. Had I left the condition unchanged, the loop would exit after the value of @crow became 11, but because I'm incrementing @crow by 2 each time, the number 10 is skipped. It's easy to find yourself in these situations, so you should think carefully about the condition you're using to set up the WHILE loop and how you're manipulating the values in the condition within the WHILE loop as well.

The Another means by which you can stop the execution of a WHILE loop is to use the BREAK statement. BREAK simply stops the execution of the loop at that point (skipping any statements that follow in the body of the loop), and continues execution of the program with the first statement immediately following the loop.

If you want to end a loop using a condition other than the one that you used to create the loop in the first place, you can include an IF statement within the body of the loop that executes a BREAK statement. For example, if you have a lot of code in the body of your loop, you might want to stop the execution of the loop at some point before all the code inside the loop is executed and the looping condition is evaluated again. You can insert a IF statement with a BREAK into the code at that point so that the loop exits immediately if a certain condition is met.

Generally, constructing loops so that the loop is an infinite loop and the exit condition actually appears within the loop in an IF statement is not necessary. However, an example of a case where this technique might be useful appears in Listing 15.25.

LISTING 15.25   AN INFINITE LOOP THAT IS TERMINATED BY A BREAK STATEMENT

```
DECLARE @total INT
WHILE 1 = 1
    BEGIN
        SELECT @total = COUNT(*) FROM A_Table
        IF @total > 100
            BREAK
        INSERT INTO A_Table
        (primary_key)
        VALUES (@total + 1)
    END

(1 row(s) affected)
```

The loop condition, 1 = 1, obviously always evaluates as true, so the loop is infinite. The condition that terminates the loop appears in the IF statement within the loop body. Every time the loop is executed, the variable @total is set to the number of rows in the table A_Table. If there are more than 100 rows in the table, the loop execution stops. Otherwise, a new row is inserted in A_Table.

RESTARTING A LOOP USING CONTINUE

The CONTINUE statement is used to suspend the execution of one iteration of a loop and restart at the loop condition. In some loops, you might want to only execute the entire body of the loop if a certain condition is true; however, you don't want to exit the loop entirely. That's what the CONTINUE statement is designed to do. If the loop encounters a CONTINUE statement, none of the remaining statements in the body of the loop are executed, and the program returns to the condition that initiated the loop in the first place.

Listing 15.26 contains an example of an SQL program that uses the CONTINUE statement to print only movies from studios that have produced movies totaling over $100 million.

LISTING 15.26   A LOOP THAT USES THE CONTINUE STATEMENT

```
DECLARE @total_studios INT
DECLARE @cnt INT
DECLARE @rev INT
SELECT @studios = MAX(studio_id)
FROM Movies
WHILE @cnt <= @total_studios
    BEGIN
        SELECT @rev = SUM(gross)
        FROM Movies
        WHERE studio_id = @cnt
        IF @rev < 100
            CONTINUE
        SELECT movie_title
        FROM Movies
        WHERE studio_id = @cnt
    END

(1 row(s) affected)

...

(1 row(s) affected)

movie_title
-------------------------
Mineral House       .
Codependence Day
The Rear Windows

(3 row(s) affected)

(1 row(s) affected)

...

(1 row(s) affected)

movie_title
-------------------------

(0 row(s) affected
```

The loop obtains the sum of the grosses for each of the studios and then stops executing if the sum is less than 100. If the sum is greater than 100, it prints out a list of movies from that studio.

NESTED LOOPS

Just as you can nest IF statements, you can also nest loops. When you nest loops, the inner loop is executed until the loop condition is satisfied, and the execution then returns to the outer loop. Listing 15.27 contains nested loops that iterate over all the days in a week and then over the hours in each day.

LISTING 15.27   NESTED FOR LOOPS

```
DECLARE @day INT
DECLARE @hour INT
DECLARE @display VARCHAR(25)
SELECT @day = 1
WHILE @day <= 7
    BEGIN
    SELECT @display = CONVERT(VARCHAR(25), @day)
    PRINT @display
    SELECT @hour = 1
    WHILE @hour <= 24
        BEGIN
        SELECT @display = CONVERT(VARCHAR(25), @hour)
        PRINT @display
        SELECT @hour = @hour + 1
        END
    SELECT @day = @day + 1
    END
```

The output of the listing is truncated because it prints the number for each of the hours in a week for every day of the week, producing well over 100 lines of output. The CONTINUE and BREAK statements apply to the innermost loop in which they appear. If the hours loop in Listing 15.27 contained a BREAK statement, execution of the hours loop would cease and would return to the days loop. Similarly, if a CONTINUE statement appeared in the hours loop, execution would return to the WHILE condition for that loop, not the outer days loop.

LOOPING OVER A CURSOR

In SQL programming, one of the most common uses for loops is to fetch rows from a cursor and process them. Because a cursor retrieves rows from a result set incrementally instead of processing them all as a batch, loops are required when you don't know how many rows are fetched by the query that sets up a cursor. For example, if you write a cursor that you know will return five rows, you can just write a program that contains five FETCH statements that will process all the rows. If something changes and the cursor returns six rows, unless you change your program, one of the rows returned by the cursor will go unprocessed.

Even if the number of rows returned by the cursor never changes, unless you want to do something completely different with every one of the rows in the cursor, it makes sense to write loops to handle cursors. Generally speaking, loops make maintenance of code easier because they prevent you from having to change the same piece of code in more than one place. If you're going to perform the same operation on multiple pieces of data, it's easier to put that code in a loop and then iterate over all the data you want to process.

Databases that support cursors provide special variables that indicate the status of the last cursor operation. You can use this variable within the condition that sets up a WHILE loop to fetch all the rows in a cursor. For example, in Transact-SQL, Sybase uses the @@sqlstatus variable to store the result of the previous FETCH operation; Microsoft uses the

@@fetch_status variable. In both cases, a value of 0 indicates that the fetch was successful, so to iterate over all the rows in a cursor, you can begin a WHILE loop like this:

```
WHILE @@sqlstatus = 0
```

Listing 15.28 contains a program that opens a cursor on the Movies table, loops over all the rows in the cursor, and prints the title of the movie in each of the rows. As an example of why you might use a cursor to process a set of rows instead of just using a SELECT statement, the program prints the titles of all the profitable movies in uppercase letters and the titles of all the unprofitable movies in lowercase.

LISTING 15.28   A SQL QUERY THAT LOOPS OVER A CURSOR

```
DECLARE get_movies CURSOR
FOR SELECT movie_title, gross, budget
FROM Movies
OPEN get_movies
-- Fetch the first row from the cursor
FETCH get_movies INTO @title, @gross, @budget
-- Loop over the remaining rows
WHILE @@fetch_status = 0
    BEGIN
    IF @gross >= @budget
        PRINT UPPER(@title)
    ELSE
        PRINT LOWER(@title)
FETCH get_movies INTO @title, @gross, @budget
    END

(1 row(s) affected)


(1 row(s) affected)

MINERAL HOUSE

(1 row(s) affected)


(1 row(s) affected)

THE CODE WARRIOR

(1 row(s) affected)


(1 row(s) affected)

BILL DURHAM

(1 row(s) affected)


(1 row(s) affected)
```

```
CODEPENDENCE DAY

(1 row(s) affected)


(1 row(s) affected)

the linux files

(1 row(s) affected)


(1 row(s) affected)

SQL STRIKES BACK

(1 row(s) affected)


(1 row(s) affected)

the programmer

(1 row(s) affected)


(1 row(s) affected)

hard code

(1 row(s) affected)


(1 row(s) affected)

THE REAR WINDOWS

(0 row(s) affected)
```

The first row is fetched from the cursor before the loop begins. If there are no rows in the cursor, the loop never begins (because the value of @@fetch_status is not equal to 0). Additional rows are fetched at the end of the loop, but there's no reason why that has to be the case. I could just as easily perform the fetch at the beginning of the body of the loop; the rest of the code in the body of the loop would still be executed. For the purposes of read-ability, however, it makes sense to fetch the row as the last thing before the status of the fetch is evaluated. As you can see, the contents of the @title, @gross, and @budget variables are replaced every time the loop is executed.

TRIGGERS

Triggers are specialized stored procedures that are executed automatically when a particular event occurs and are used to enforce data integrity. They are similar to constraints (which were discussed in Chapter 3, "Creating Databases") in that they are used to ensure that the data in a table conforms to rules determined by the database designer. Triggers can be written using the full array of SQL statements that are available to writers of stored procedures, whereas constraints are used to enforce specific conditions, such as foreign key relationships, uniqueness, or conformance to a particular comparison operator.

CREATING TRIGGERS

Just as stored procedures are created using the CREATE PROCEDURE command, triggers are created using CREATE TRIGGER. The types of triggers that you can create vary depending on the database that you're using. For example, Oracle enables you to create triggers that run before, after, or instead of an update, delete, or insert. On the other hand, Transact-SQL enables you to write triggers that are executed before delete, insert, or update operations. The options for creating a trigger in Oracle PL/SQL are discussed in Chapter 17.

The syntax for creating Transact-SQL triggers in Microsoft SQL Server is as follows:

```
CREATE TRIGGER [owner_name].trigger_name
ON [owner_name].table_name
FOR (INSERT, UPDATE, DELETE)
AS
      trigger code
```

You must provide each trigger with a name so that it can be referenced later. You must also indicate what table the trigger will act on. The FOR clause is used to specify what table operations will fire the trigger. It can contain any combination of INSERT, UPDATE, and DELETE. The actual SQL code follows the AS keyword.

REMOVING TRIGGERS

The DROP TRIGGER command is used to remove a trigger. You can remove triggers using the following command:

```
DROP TRIGGER trigger_name
```

In Transact-SQL, triggers are automatically dropped if a new trigger is created for the table that applies to the same operations.

WRITING TRIGGERS

The code inside a trigger is generally used to verify that the operation being performed is valid in terms of the integrity of the database. Because triggers can include conditional logic and queries of other tables, they are much more powerful than simple check constraints. Generally, triggers are used with transaction-related commands to accept or reject changes to the database.

For example, if you didn't want to allow any rows with a budget of over 100 to be inserted into the Movies table, you could use the trigger in Listing 15.29.

LISTING 15.29   A TRIGGER THAT PREVENTS INSERTIONS INTO A TABLE

```
CREATE TRIGGER movies_insert
ON Movies
FOR INSERT
AS
BEGIN
    IF budget > 100
        BEGIN
    ROLLBACK TRANSACTION
            PRINT "Insertions into Movies with a budget over 100 are not allowed."
        END
END
```

When I attempt to insert a record into the Movies table, the trigger runs, and the insertion is refused, as shown in Listing 15.30.

LISTING 15.30   THE movies_insert TRIGGER PREVENTS INSERTIONS INTO Movies

```
INSERT INTO Movies
(movie_id, movie_title, studio_id, director_id, gross,
budget, release_date)
VALUES
(15, 'Test Movie', 3, 5, 50, 101, GetDate())

Insertions into Movies are not allowed.
```

The trigger is fired after the execution of the statement is finished; all the constraints associated with the table will be evaluated before the trigger runs. If I left a column null that had a NOT NULL constraint, the insertion would be refused based on the violation of the constraint, and the trigger would not execute.

CONSTRAINING TRIGGERS BASED ON COLUMN

As you know, the INSERT and DELETE commands affect entire rows, not specific columns. However, you can use the UPDATE command to change the values in only some of the columns in a table. Using the UPDATE(column) condition, you can constrain your triggers so that they only take action if an update affects a particular column (or set of columns).

The UPDATE(column) condition evaluates as true if the UPDATE statement that fired the trigger affects the column in the condition. If it only affects other columns, the UPDATE(column) condition returns false. These conditions can be included in compound expressions with other conditions, or they can be used by themselves. Listing 15.31 contains an update trigger that uses the UPDATE condition to roll back the transaction when the movie_title column is updated.

LISTING 15.31   A TRIGGER THAT USES THE UPDATE CONDITION

```
CREATE TRIGGER movie_update
ON Movies
FOR UPDATE
AS
BEGIN
    IF UPDATE(movie_title)
        BEGIN
            ROLLBACK TRANSACTION
            PRINT "The movie title cannot be changed."
        END
END
```

In Listing 15.32, you'll see that updates to other columns in the Movies table are allowed, but updates to the movie_title column are prevented.

LISTING 15.32   TESTING UPDATES AFTER AN UPDATE TRIGGER IS IN PLACE

```
UPDATE Movies
SET movie_title = 'New Title'
WHERE movie_id = 1

The movie title cannot be changed.

UPDATE Movies
SET budget = 25
WHERE movie_id = 1

(1 row(s) affected)
```

IN THE REAL WORLD

One of the most powerful features of stored procedures is that they enable application designers to include a layer of abstraction between the database and the application they're writing. Instead of writing lots of SQL queries to retrieve information from the database and manipulate data within the database, they can write calls to stored procedures that do the actual work of dealing with the contents of the database.

I worked on an electronic commerce site where we abstracted all the calls to the database using stored procedures. The site itself contained no SQL queries, only calls to stored procedures. All of the business logic for the site was encapsulated within the stored procedures; in fact, the stored procedures even called external programs to handle the tasks that couldn't be written in SQL.

The main advantage provided by building the stored-procedure–based API was that it abstracted all the complexity of the database from the Web application. In this case, the database architecture was very complex, and it made sense to encapsulate all the queries within stored procedures so that the database programmers could simply present a static interface to the application programmers and handle all the optimization and performance tuning themselves.

When you build SQL queries into your applications, database programmers often have to dig into the program code to aid the application developers in writing queries that are optimized for performance. Using stored procedures can remove this responsibility from the application developers.

Another advantage the stored-procedure API provided was flexibility for the future. As you know from the chapter covering database design, data relationships are implemented differently depending on whether they are one-to-one, one-to-many, or many-to-many. If the relationship between two pieces of data changes, the queries used to manipulate that data have to be changed as well. If a table is split into multiple tables because a data relationship changes from one-to-one to one-to-many, multiple UPDATE, INSERT, and DELETE statements must be used where only one was used before. If all the queries used in an application are embedded within the application itself, any time a change to the database schema such as the one I described is made, those queries have to be updated throughout the application. Encapsulating the queries within a stored procedure enables you to update the queries within the stored procedure and leave the actual application that uses the database unchanged.

We also gained a lot of advantages in reusability by using stored procedures. Rather than duplicating a particular query in multiple places within the application, we simply inserted a call to the procedure that was wrapped around the query. This type of reusability can also generally be accomplished on the application-development side by encapsulating the queries within functions, but it doesn't provide the added advantage of segregating database code from the application code.

When you create database-backed applications, whether they are written for the Web or a client/server environment, you can often gain lots of efficiency by encapsulating as much of the database code as possible within stored procedures. A final advantage is that if you wind up porting your application from one development environment to another, the more business logic you have running on the database side, the less application code you have to port. Oftentimes, it's much more difficult to migrate to a different database than it is to migrate to a different application environment, so building your business logic into database code makes sense.

CHAPTER 16

MORE ON TRANSACT-SQL STORED PROCEDURES

In this chapter

In the previous chapter, I described some of the basic techniques used in programming stored procedures, including conditional statements with IF and repeating structures using WHILE loops. I also explained how stored procedures themselves are created, how to create variables, and how to pass values to stored procedures using parameters.

This chapter will discuss some advanced techniques used in creating stored procedures, mainly related to Transact-SQL. In the next chapter, I'm going to explain how to write stored procedures using PL/SQL, the procedural language built in to Oracle databases. In this chapter, I'm going to cover the use of temporary objects for storing data used by stored procedures, how to write error-handling code for Transact-SQL stored procedures, and some advanced techniques for writing triggers.

GENERAL TRANSACT-SQL PROGRAMMING INFORMATION

When you write blocks of code in Transact-SQL, statements are executed, and output is sent to the user whenever a GO keyword is encountered. This is why you often see a GO statement after each statement in a block of Transact-SQL code. Stored procedures don't use the GO statement because all the output from a stored procedure is held until execution of that stored procedure is complete.

GLOBAL VARIABLES

In the preceding chapter, I explained how variables work in Transact-SQL. You can create them using the DECLARE statement, change the values using SELECT, and substitute variables in your expressions in places you would ordinarily place a literal value or a reference to a column. There is a special set of variables that is maintained by the database server itself; these variables are collectively known as global variables. In some cases, you can set the value of these variables, but you cannot create them. The values stored in global variables are available to all users, and they are differentiated from normal variables because the names are preceded by two @ signs, not one.

> **Note**
>
> Users can create variables beginning with two @ signs, such as @@foo, but that won't make them global variables. They're just local variables named in a confusing manner.

Table 16.1 contains a list of some of the more important global variables and specifies whether the variable is specific to Sybase or Microsoft databases. You can find the full list of global variables with the documentation for your database.

TABLE 16.1   GLOBAL VARIABLES IN TRANSACT-SQL DATABASES

Variable	Supported by	Contains
@@connections	MS, Syb	The number of connections attempted since the most recent time the database was started.

Variable	Supported by	Contains
@@cursor_rows	MS	The number of rows returned by the cursor most recently opened by the user (the value of this variable varies depending on the user retrieving it). If no cursor has been opened or the cursor most recently opened has been deallocated, this variable contains 0.
@@error	MS, Syb	The result code for the most recent statement issued by the user. The value of the variable is specific to the user retrieving it. If the user's most recent command was successful, the value of this variable is 0.
@@fetch_status	MS	The result of the most recent FETCH performed against the cursor. A value of 0 indicates that the FETCH was successful, -1 means that the FETCH failed or no rows remain in the cursor, and -2 indicates that the row was not found.
@@identity	MS, Syb	Specific to each user; the most recent value inserted into an identity column. If the most recent INSERT statement was performed on a table with no identity column, the value of this variable is null. This is useful if you want to retrieve the primary key for the most recent row inserted in a table with an identity column.
@@max_connections	MS, Syb	The number of simultaneous connections supported by the computer running the database.
@@max_precision	MS	The number of digits of precision to the right of the decimal supported for DECIMAL and NUMERIC data types. The default is 28.
@@nestlevel	MS, Syb	Begins with 0. Incremented by 1 when a stored procedure is called from within another stored procedure. So, if a stored procedure calls a stored procedure, which in turn calls another stored procedure, the value is 2. The maximum value of this variable is 16. If it rises above 16, the transaction is terminated to prevent infinite recursion.
@@options	MS	The value of SET options for query processing for the current session.
@@rowcount	MS, Sybase	The number of rows affected by the most recent query. If the statement affected no rows (such as CREATE TABLE), the value is 0.
@@servername	MS, Sybase	The name of the server on which the database is installed.
@@spid	MS, Sybase	The process ID of the database server process.
@@sqlstatus	Sybase	Returns the status of the current cursor; 0 indicates that the most recent fetch was successful, 1 indicates that an error occurred, and 2 indicates that there are no more rows left in the cursor.
@@version	MS, Sybase	The date, version number, and processor type for the database.

PART

V

CH

16

Global variables can be used anywhere that local variables can be used. To print the current database version, simply use @@version within a PRINT statement, as shown in Listing 16.1.

LISTING 16.1 USING A GLOBAL VARIABLE

```
PRINT @@version

Microsoft SQL Server  7.00 - 7.00.623 (Intel X86)
    Nov 27 1998 22:20:07
    Copyright (c) 1988-1998 Microsoft Corporation
    Standard Edition on Windows NT 4.0 (Build 1381: Service Pack 4)
```

The most important distinction to be drawn is between global variables that have values specific to every session and those that contain the same value for every session. For example, @@error contains the return code for the most recent statement executed by the current user. Whenever a user retrieves the value of this variable, that value contains the result code from her most recent statement, even if other users have executed statements between the end of her most recent statement and the time when the value is retrieved. On the other hand, variables such as @@version and @@servername contain truly global values; the same value is returned regardless of which session is using the variables.

USING RETURN TO LEAVE STORED PROCEDURES

The RETURN statement is used to immediately cease the processing of a PL/SQL block or a stored procedure. When it is called within a stored procedure, it halts the execution of that procedure and shifts the control of the program back to the caller.

HANDLING ERRORS

One issue that crops up whenever you design programs is how to handle errors. You have to determine when your program should check for errors and how the errors should be acted on. Most programs handle errors by testing conditions during the execution of the program and exiting with an error message when the condition indicates that a condition is outside the acceptable norm.

The simplest way to provide a user with feedback that an error has occurred is to simply print the error with a PRINT statement. Unfortunately, this isn't a particularly useful way to indicate that some exception has occurred. For one thing, if the error is fatal, it won't cease execution of the code block, nor will it indicate to the database itself that an error has occurred. Generally speaking, PRINT statements are more useful for generating diagnostics during the execution of a program to let the user know what's happening.

USING RAISERROR

RAISERROR is a specialized command used to exit programs and report a certain error condition. The command is flexible; it can raise a user-defined error with a custom error message, or it can reference a system error message if you prefer. There are some differences in the way RAISERROR is implemented on the Microsoft and Sybase platforms. Not only is the syntax a bit different, but the range of error codes for system errors and user-defined errors differs from one implementation to the other. The syntax for the Microsoft version of RAISERROR follows:

```
RAISERROR ( { error_number ¦ 'error message' } , severity, state
        [, argument_list] )
    [ NOWAIT ] [WITH LOG] [SETERROR]
```

The syntax for the Sybase implementation of RAISERROR is as follows:

```
RAISERROR error_number [ { 'error message' ¦ @@variable_name } ]
    [ , arguments ]
    [ WITH { error_data ¦ extended_select_list } ]
```

The syntax for RAISERROR is somewhat complex in both implementations. Fortunately, most of it is optional. If you want to write your RAISERROR commands so that they work in both Sybase and Microsoft SQL Server, you must use the following syntax:

```
RAISERROR error_number 'error message'
```

A safe value for cross-platform error messages is 50,000. Now, take a look at the options available for returning error messages for Sybase and Microsoft SQL Server specifically.

USING RAISERROR WITH MICROSOFT SQL SERVER

Normally, when you use RAISERROR with Microsoft SQL Server, you specify an error number or an error message. The cutoff between system-defined error messages and user-defined error messages is 50,000. If you don't specify an error number, the system assigns the 50,000 as the error message for your error by default. (Errors that include an error message instead of an error number are referred to as *ad hoc errors*.) The second argument supported by Microsoft SQL Server is the severity of the error. The severity setting indicates what type of error occurred and what action the program should take. A list of severity levels supported by SQL Server appears in Table 16.2.

TABLE 16.2   SEVERITY LEVELS OF EXCEPTIONS IN TRANSACT-SQL.

Code	Vendor Description	Description
00-01	Miscellaneous System Information	A general informational message that indicates that an event occurred, not that an error occurred.
02-06	Reserved	These severity levels are not used yet.
07	Notification: Status Information	An informational message that reports the status of an event.
08	Notification: User Intervention Required	Indicates that an event has occurred that requires some action by the user.

continues

TABLE 16.2 CONTINUED

Code	Vendor Description	Description
09	User Defined	This level is reserved for user-defined messages in the sysmessages table or that are created on an ad hoc basis. Generally, when you create error messages, you should give them a severity level of 09.
10	Information	An informational message related to DBA activities.
11	Specified Database Object Not Found	An item specified in a query was not found.
12	Unused.	
13	User Transaction Syntax Errors	The SQL code for a transaction was not used properly. This occurs when the closing statements for a transaction (COMMIT or ROLLBACK) are not properly matched to BEGIN TRAN statements.
14	Insufficient Permissions	The user does not have permission to perform the operation he attempted, for some reason. Reasons can include lack of access to a specified object and constraint violations.
15	Syntax Error in SQL Statement	The database is unable to parse the SQL statement you've entered. Hopefully, after reading this book, you'll never see one of these error messages.
16	Miscellaneous User Error	A common severity level for developer-created errors. It can also be raised when a datatype conversion fails or an object is used improperly.
17	Insufficient Resources	This severity level accompanies errors that are thrown when some database resource is exhausted. For example, if the database runs out of locks, allocation units, or space in tempdb, an error with this severity will be thrown, and the process that exhausted those resources will be terminated.
18	Nonfatal Internal Error	Another severity level that is commonly used by developers. Errors with this severity level are often the result of problems with remote database connections.
19	SQL Server Fatal Error in Resource	This error is raised when some limit within SQL Server is reached.
20	SQL Server Fatal Error in Current Process	A particular statement has encountered a problem that does not affect the current database or the server overall.
21	SQL Server Fatal Error in Database (dbid) Processes	An error has occurred that affects all the processes currently using the database, but not the database itself.
22	SQL Server Fatal Error Table Integrity Suspect	The table or index returned by the error message is damaged and probably needs to be dropped and rebuilt.
23	SQL Server Fatal Error: Database Integrity Suspect	The entire contents of the database are possibly corrupt. Restarting the database or DBCC checks might clear up the problem.

Code	Vendor Description	Description
24	Hardware Error	There is some problem with the server's hardware, generally involving the media where the database is stored.
25	Internal System Error	A problem internal to SQL Server has arisen.

Through the severity level, you can specify whether the procedure or block of code will continue to execute after the error is encountered and whether the user's session will be terminated. Depending on the severity that is assigned to the error message, the error will be logged in the Windows NT error log as well.

The state argument can generally be specified as 1; it only needs to be changed if a particular error message requires that a state be specified. The values of state can range from 1 to 127.

The argument_list is a list of variables that will be substituted for tokens listed within the error message. You can include tokens in ad hoc errors or in user-defined error messages that you create. Certain system error messages also include tokens into which values in the argument list are placed. Placeholders are denoted in your error messages with tokens that represent particular data types, which follow the format %data_type. Listing 16.2 contains an example of how arguments and placeholders are used; in the listing, the token %s (which is for strings) is replaced by the value of @foo.

LISTING 16.2   A RAISERROR STATEMENT THAT USES ARGUMENTS

```
DECLARE @foo VARCHAR(50)
SELECT @foo = 'foo'
RAISERROR ('This message contains a placeholder: %s', 18, 1, @foo)
```

```
Server: Msg 50000, Level 18, State 1, Line 3
This message contains a placeholder: foo
```

A complete list of the placeholders for various data types is included in Table 16.3.

TABLE 16.3   DATA TYPE PLACEHOLDERS FOR THE RAISERROR COMMAND

Placeholder	Type
d or i	Signed integer
o	Unsigned octal
p	Pointer
s	String
u	Unsigned integer
x or X	Unsigned hexadecimal

PART
V

CH
16

There three flags that can be set for the RAISERROR command with SQL Server. The first is the WITH LOG flag, which is used to indicate that an entry should be placed in the Windows NT Event Log when the statement is executed. Only the SA account can use the WITH LOG flag, and it is mandatory for errors with a severity of 19 or greater. The second flag is the NOWAIT flag, which indicates that the error message should be sent to the client immediately. The SETERROR flag sets the @@error variable to the error number of the current error (50,000 if you throw an ad hoc error). Under normal circumstances, only errors with a severity of 19 or higher set the @@error variable.

USING RAISERROR WITH SYBASE

The syntax of RAISERROR with Sybase is similar to the syntax supported by Microsoft SQL Server, but there are some important differences. Unlike SQL Server, Sybase accepts both an error number and an error message. Error numbers 17,000 through 19,999 are assigned to system errors, the messages for which can be found in the master..sysmessages table. User error messages should have values of 20,000 or higher. For error codes above 20,000, if an error message is not specified in the RAISERROR statement, the sysmessages table in the local database is searched for the error.

The error message itself can take the form of a literal string, a literal string with placeholders for arguments, or a variable. For example, if you construct an error message and store it in a variable called @error_message, you can place that value in a RAISERROR statement as follows:

```
RAISERROR 20001 @error_message
```

You can use placeholders within your error messages with Sybase as you can with SQL Server. When you include arguments to be substituted for placeholders, you can include literal values as well as variable names. Obviously, this isn't useful when you're writing the error message yourself, but if you're using a user-defined or system error message that contains placeholders, it can make sense to use literal values. Here's an example that does use a literal error string:

```
RAISERROR 200001 'Hey, %1 broke the database!', 'Rafe'
```

TRAPPING ERRORS

After you know how to report errors from within a Transact-SQL program, you have to learn how to trap those errors during the course of execution of the program. The most common method for trapping errors is the use of the @@error global variable. As I stated earlier in the chapter, when a statement executes normally, @@error is set to 0. If some error is encountered in the process of running the command, @@error is set to the return code for the error. You can include conditional statements in your programs that test the value of @@error and then raise an error if the return code contains an unexpected value.

Another option is to use the @@rowcount variable to trap errors. If you are certain that a query should affect a specified number of rows, you test the value of @@rowcount after the query runs to make sure that the query executed properly. If it didn't, you can use RAISERROR to report the mistake.

Take a look at some examples. In the first example, in Listing 16.3, I'm writing some code that attempts to update some rows in the Movies table. After the UPDATE statement is executed, I test the @@error variable to see if the UPDATE statement worked. If it didn't, I raise an error. I'm also wrapping the UPDATE statement and error checking in a transaction so that a partial update isn't applied to the table.

LISTING 16.3 A TRANSACT-SQL BLOCK THAT USES @@error FOR ERROR TRAPPING

```
BEGIN TRAN T1

UPDATE Movies
SET movie_title = NULL
WHERE movie_id > 5

IF @@error <> 0
    BEGIN
        ROLLBACK TRAN
        RAISERROR ('Update of movies table failed.', 18, 1)
    END
ELSE
    COMMIT TRAN

Server: Msg 515, Level 16, State 2, Line 0
Cannot insert the value NULL into column 'movie_title', table
➥'rafeco.dbo.Movies'; column does not allow nulls. UPDATE fails.
The statement has been terminated.
Server: Msg 50000, Level 18, State 1, Line 10
Update of movies table failed.
```

Using @@rowcount, I can raise an error if a statement does not have the effect I thought it would. For example, if I expect a DELETE statement to remove some rows from a table, I can check the value of @@rowcount after the statement is complete to make sure that it worked. In this case, using a transaction is unnecessary because the error only occurs if no rows are deleted. If no rows are deleted, there's nothing to roll back! The example is in Listing 16.4.

LISTING 16.4 TRIGGERING AN ERROR CONDITION ON THE CONTENTS OF @@rowcount

```
DELETE FROM Movies
WHERE movie_id > 10

IF @@rowcount = 0
    RAISERROR ('No rows were deleted', 18, 7)

Server: Msg 50000, Level 18, State 7, Line 5
No rows were deleted
```

USING THE RETURN STATEMENT

The RETURN statement provides another option for error handling within stored procedures. Whenever a RETURN statement is encountered within a Transact-SQL program, the program ceases execution at that point and returns control to the caller (whether it's the database client or a program calling a stored procedure). When used within a stored procedure, RETURN can also include a return code, which the calling program can then use to determine the outcome of the procedure. The syntax for a RETURN statement is as follows:

```
RETURN [(return_code)]
```

The return code itself is just an integer. The purpose of the RETURN statement is to abort the processing of a Transact-SQL block or procedure without raising an error. Generally, RETURN is used when you write a stored procedure (or Transact-SQL block) where more than one query is issued. If the results of the first query indicate that the second query shouldn't be executed, you can use the RETURN statement to shift processing back to the caller.

Of course, you can also just put the other statements in the program inside a conditional construct so that execution skips past them if the condition is not met, but there are a couple of reasons why using RETURN is better. The first is that if you're using a stored procedure, you can pass a return code to the caller indicating what actually happened when the procedure was executed. The second is that if your program is complex, it's a lot easier to write an IF statement that executes a RETURN statement than it is to wrap the remainder of the program within a block inside the IF statement.

Take a look at how you might use the RETURN command within a stored procedure. As I said previously, RETURN is really only useful if you're performing more than one task inside a stored procedure. In this case, the stored procedure raises by 25 percent the gross of all movies with a gross under a specified amount. If the query affects any rows, those records are selected from the database; otherwise, the procedure returns 1. The stored procedure is in Listing 16.5.

LISTING 16.5 A STORED PROCEDURE THAT USES THE RETURN COMMAND

```
CREATE PROCEDURE update_movie_gross @gross_limit DEC = NULL
AS
UPDATE Movies
SET gross = gross * 1.25
WHERE gross < @gross_limit

IF @@rowcount = 0
    RETURN 1

SELECT movie_title, gross
FROM Movies
WHERE gross < @gross_limit * 1.25

The command(s) completed successfully.
```

CREATING USER-DEFINED ERROR MESSAGES

The sp_addmessage system stored procedure is provided to enable users to create custom error messages in the master..sysmessages table. The syntax for sp_addmessage is as follows:

```
sp_addmessage message_id, severity, 'error message'
    [, language] [, {true ¦ false}] [, REPLACE]
```

To create a simple error message with a severity of 7 (warning), the following command is used:

```
sp_addmessage 50010, 7, 'This is an error message.'
```

If an error message with a message ID of 50,010 already existed, I would need to include the REPLACE keyword with the sp_addmessage call. The length of error messages is limited to 255 characters. To call the error I created, I could just use the RAISERROR command, as follows:

```
RAISERROR 50010
```

USING TEMPORARY OBJECTS

In some cases, when you write stored procedures, you can't accomplish everything you want to with a single query, and it's necessary to store the data retrieved by a query temporarily so that you can perform multiple operations on it during the procedure. Chances are that if you're manipulating the data to make it easier to present, you don't want to modify the existing data within the table where it is stored, so you need some temporary storage space to hold the modified data. Many relational database systems support complex data structures such as arrays, and arrays of records; Transact-SQL does not. It does, however, allocate special storage space for storing temporary items.

You already know about two means by which you can store information when you're executing a Transact-SQL program. You can store it in a variable, where it will persist until execution of the procedure is complete, or you can store it within one of the tables in your database, where it will reside until it is deleted. For temporary storage, tempdb provides a work area where you can store data for manipulation or later retrieval.

There are a number of types of temporary objects that can be created; they differ based on how long they persist and who is allowed to access them. The most common temporary structure is the variable, which I covered in the preceding chapter and which does not use tempdb (the contents of variables are stored in memory).

How tempdb WORKS

tempdb is a special database that is created with every SQL Server installation. The main difference between tempdb and other databases is that all users can create objects in tempdb, and the contents of tempdb are erased every time the database server is restarted. In fact, no items stored in tempdb persist past the next restart of the database, and many items do not persist that long. Depending on how an item was created, it can persist only for the duration of the session in which it was created or even only for the execution of the procedure in which it was created.

`tempdb` is also used by the database to store temporary tables created during the execution of complex queries. Problems can arise if all the space allocated to `tempdb` is consumed; when `tempdb` is full, queries that need to use `tempdb` simply wait until enough space to continue execution is freed.

CREATING A TEMPORARY TABLE

There are a number of different ways to create tables in `tempdb`, depending on whom you want to have permission to view and modify the table and how long you want the table to persist. One way to create a table within `tempdb` is to prepend the table name with a # (pound sign). When a table is created in this manner, it is stored in `tempdb`, and it is automatically removed when the current session ends or, if it was created in a stored procedure, when execution of the procedure is complete. In Listing 16.6, I create a table in `tempdb`.

LISTING 16.6   CREATING A COPY OF THE Movies TABLE IN tempdb

```
CREATE TABLE #Movies
(movie_id       int,
movie_title   varchar(25),
studio_id     int,
budget        dec,
gross         dec,
release_date  datetime,
director_id   int)

The command(s) completed successfully.
```

After the temporary table is created, I can issue INSERT, UPDATE, DELETE, and SELECT statements against the temporary table, just as I can against any other table in the database. I'm also free to use the temporary table in joins with other temporary tables or with tables in other databases.

CLASSES OF TEMPORARY OBJECTS

Temporary objects are classified based on the type of access allowed to an object. There are two classes, local and global. Local objects can only be accessed by the user who created them, and global objects can be accessed by any user with access to the database. Generally speaking, local objects only persist for the duration of the session or procedure that created them, whereas global objects persist until the database is restarted. Obviously, creating global objects that only persist for the duration of a session or procedure would be useless because there's really no way that other users would have time to access them in the short time that they exist.

As I discussed previously, you can create temporary objects using the # qualifier before the name. In fact, the # qualifier is used to create local temporary objects. Table 16.4 contains a list of classes of temporary objects available in Transact-SQL.

TABLE 16.4   CLASSES OF TEMPORARY OBJECTS

Class	Platform	Prefix	Access	Exists Until
Local tables	both	#	Local	Current session or stored procedure ends
Local stored procedure	MS	#	Local	Current session or stored procedure ends
Global table, stored procedure, view	MS	#	Global	Current session ends
Persistent temporary objects	both	none	Global	Database restarted
Model objects	both	none	Global	Created when database starts, removed when database shut down
Worktables	both	none	internal	Created by database itself, persist until query which created them ends

PART

V

CH

16

PERSISTENT TEMPORARY OBJECTS

Persistent temporary objects are just standard database objects that are created in `tempdb` instead of standard temporary tables. When you create a standard object in `tempdb`, that object will persist until the database is shut down or, like any object in any database, until it is explicitly dropped. Unlike temporary objects, persistent objects created in `tempdb` are accessible by any database user. If the information you want to store is sensitive, you should store it in another database and delete it when necessary rather than risking exposure to other users by storing it in `tempdb`.

WAITFOR

A `WAITFOR` statement is simply used to include a time delay in a block of Transact-SQL statements. There are two separate forms of the `WAITFOR` command. `WAITFOR DELAY` simply waits until a specified period of time elapses and then continues execution. `WAITFOR TIME` waits for the specified time to arrive and continues execution at that point. As you might imagine, you can create scheduled tasks using the `WAITFOR TIME` command. For example, if you want to run a large batch job at a time when the database has few users, you can use `WAITFOR TIME` to schedule the task for a time in the middle of the night. If you want to set up a command so that it will run in 30 minutes after you go to lunch, `WAITFOR DELAY` is the better choice.

The `WAITFOR DELAY` command accepts an argument in the form of a time in hours, minutes, and seconds, like this:

```
WAITFOR DELAY hours:minutes:seconds
```

So, if you want execution to pause for five minutes in the middle of a program, you can use the following statements:

```
WAITFOR DELAY 00:05:00
```

You can also use WAITFOR DELAY in combination with a WHILE loop to repeatedly check for a particular condition. For example, if you want to write a program that checks for new movies once an hour until one is inserted, you can use the following statements:

```
WHILE (SELECT COUNT(*) FROM Movies = 10)
    WAITFOR DELAY 01:00:00
```

The syntax for WAITFOR TIME is similar to WAITFOR DELAY:

```
WAITFOR TIME hour:minute:second:millisecond
```

Tip 64 from
Rafe Colburn

The items in a time string are read from largest to smallest, so leaving off elements removes smaller units from the specification. For example, 10:05 means 10 hours and 5 minutes, not 10 seconds and 5 milliseconds.

ADVANCED TRIGGER-WRITING TECHNIQUES

In the preceding chapter, I introduced triggers and explained some techniques for creating triggers in Transact-SQL databases. At this point, I'd like to cover some of the more advanced trigger-related topics for Transact-SQL.

ROLLBACK TRIGGER

In Chapter 13, "Database Performance and Integrity," in the section "Using Transactions in Transact-SQL," I explained how the ROLLBACK command is used to reverse any changes made since a transaction was initiated. When you are writing Transact-SQL triggers for a Sybase database, you can use a rollback command specific to triggers, ROLLBACK TRIGGER. This command is used to roll back any changes made in the course of executing the trigger and the statement that initially fired the trigger in the first place. It also ceases execution of the trigger at that point. If you want to raise an error when the ROLLBACK TRIGGER statement is encountered, you can use the WITH RAISERROR clause with the ROLLBACK TRIGGER statement.

You can write a trigger that uses the @@rowcount variable to determine whether an operation succeeded. For example, you might want to write a trigger that rolls back any statement that affects more than five rows in the database. The source code for such a trigger is in Listing 16.7, and a statement that fires the trigger is in Listing 16.8.

LISTING 16.7 A TRIGGER THAT ROLLS BACK THE CURRENT STATEMENT IF TOO MANY ROWS ARE AFFECTED

```
CREATE TRIGGER movies_modify_trigger
ON Movies
```

```
FOR INSERT, UPDATE, DELETE
AS
IF @@rowcount > 5
    ROLLBACK TRIGGER WITH RAISERROR 'Too many rows affected.'
PRINT 'See how that works?'
```

LISTING 16.8   A STATEMENT THAT FIRES movies_modify_trigger

PART

V

CH

16

```
UPDATE Movies
SET movie_title = 'Whatever'

Too many rows affected.
```

The trigger is fired when the query in Listing 16.8 is executed because it updates more than five rows in the Movies table. When the trigger fires, the IF statement is executed because the @@rowcount variable is greater than five, execution of the trigger ceases after the statement is rolled back, and the ad hoc error is raised. The PRINT statement is never executed because execution of the trigger ends with the ROLLBACK TRIGGER statement.

USING THE INSERTED AND DELETED TABLES IN TRIGGERS

When you write triggers for INSERT and DELETE statements, it is sometimes necessary to access the data that was just inserted into a table or the data that was deleted from a table. Transact-SQL provides two pseudotables that are used to access this information. When a trigger is fired by an INSERT statement, the data that was inserted is held in the INSERTED pseudotable while the trigger runs. Similarly, the DELETED table holds any rows deleted while a FOR DELETE trigger runs.

You can use the information in these tables to ensure that the operation that fired the trigger is valid. Generally, these tables are used with transactions. You can begin a transaction before you execute an INSERT or DELETE statement and ten verify that the operation had the expected outcome using the pseudotables. If there's something wrong with the data, you can simply roll back the transaction and continue on your way.

You can use the DELETED table in a trigger that automatically rolls back the current transaction if more than five rows are deleted from the database in a given operation. The trigger appears in Listing 16.9, and a statement that causes the trigger to fire appears in Listing 16.10.

LISTING 16.9   A TRIGGER THAT AUTOMATICALLY ROLLS BACK DELETE STATEMENTS THAT DELETE MORE THAN FIVE RECORDS

```
CREATE TRIGGER movies_delete_trigger
ON Movies
FOR DELETE
AS
IF (SELECT COUNT(*) FROM DELETED) > 5
    ROLLBACK TRIGGER
```

LISTING 16.10   A DELETE STATEMENT THAT FIRES THE TRIGGER IN LISTING 16.9

```
DELETE FROM Movies

No records deleted
```

As you can see, the trigger in Listing 16.9 is very similar to the trigger I created in Listing 16.7. Other than the fact that the trigger in Listing 16.9 is only fired when more than 5 rows are deleted, the important difference is that movies_delete_trigger utilizes the DELETED pseudotable.

You can also use these pseudotables to do some last minute checking on data that's deleted or inserted to make sure that something you don't want included in the database doesn't slip in under the radar. For example, if you want to make sure that no movies with release dates before the current date are inserted in the database, you can use a trigger such as the one in Listing 16.11.

LISTING 16.11   A TRIGGER TO ENSURE THAT NO MOVIES ARE INSERTED WITH RELEASE DATES IN THE PAST

```
CREATE TRIGGER movies_date_test_trigger
ON Movies
FOR INSERT
AS
IF EXISTS (SELECT * FROM INSERTED WHERE release_date < GETDATE())
    ROLLBACK TRIGGER
WITH RAISERROR 'Releae dates must be in the future.'
```

The EXISTS keyword in the IF statement evaluates as true if any rows are returned by the query.

IN THE REAL WORLD

One aspect of writing stored procedures in Transact-SQL that I haven't covered in this book is working with external programs and writing stored procedures in languages other than Transact-SQL. Both Sybase Adaptive Server and Microsoft SQL Server enable programmers to write programs in other languages that can be called using stored procedures and that can return data to a stored procedure.

Aside from writing special code that can be called from within the database, you can also set up tasks in Transact-SQL that simply execute applications that are external to the database. For example, if you've written a program in Perl that gets a list of email addresses from the database and sends an announcement to each of the users that is listed, you can call that program from a stored procedure, even though it's completely independent of the database.

Microsoft SQL Server comes with a scheduling feature. If you have complex processes that require database queries to run and the execution of external programs, sometimes it's easier to encapsulate them within stored procedures and then call those stored procedures than it is to write an external program that makes all the database queries and performs the external tasks as well.

The fact that Transact-SQL includes the capability to interact with extensions written in other languages and the fact that it can make calls to applications external to the database makes it much more viable as an application development environment. These capabilities enable you to do much more than just execute queries and manipulate data within the database.

Look at the two methods that can be used to deal with code external to the database. The first way that external code can be used is through extended stored procedures. These procedures are compiled as dynamic link libraries (DLLs) and are then registered with the server. After an extended stored procedure has been registered, you can call it using the EXEC command as you would any other stored procedure. The procedures can accept and return parameters the way any normal stored procedure would.

Both Microsoft SQL Server and Sybase Adaptive Server come with some extended stored procedures that you can already use. One advantage of extended stored procedures is that they make it easy for third parties to write applications that extend the functionality of a Transact-SQL database and distribute their code. Many companies might find the idea of writing stored procedures in Transact-SQL and selling them to be an economically unsound proposition because the source code to a Transact-SQL procedure would be available to the customers.

Most extended stored procedures interact with applications that are external to the database and that have interfaces that are available to the programming language used to write the extended stored procedures. For example, say that you have a fax program that has a C++ interface, and you store all your client information in a Sybase database. You can write an extended stored procedure to retrieve the fax numbers from the database and then use the C++ interface on the fax program to actually send the faxes.

Microsoft enables you to write extended stored procedures with the Open Data Services interface for C programs. You compile your programs as a DLL, and when you register them with the database server, they actually run as part of the database server's process. Because they share the memory space used by the database server, they provide excellent performance. Unfortunately, an improperly coded extended stored procedure can bring down the database server.

Sybase Adaptive Server uses a separate server, the XP Server, to manage extended stored procedures and communicate with the database. The XP Server and the database server communicate via remote procedure calls (RPCs). The advantage is that a buggy extended stored procedure won't bring down the database server; the disadvantage is that the two servers communicating via RPC are slower than simply loading the extended procedure code directly into the database server as Microsoft does.

There is a stored procedure that is used to register new extended procedures with the database, sp_addextendedproc; it accepts the name of the extended procedure and the DLL file associated with it as arguments. The syntax for sp_addextendedproc is as follows:

```
sp_addextendedproc procedure_name, DLL_name
```

The second technique, calling applications that are completely external to the database, actually uses an extended procedure, xp_cmdshell. xp_cmdshell accepts two arguments, the command line to execute and, optionally, the no_output flag, which suppresses the output of the command being executed. The syntax for the xp_cmdshell procedure is as follows:

```
xp_cmdshell 'command' [, no_output]
```

Here's a simple example of how you can use the xp_cmdshell stored procedure to call an application that requires command-line parameters. If you have a program written in Perl called show_stuff.pl and you want to execute it with the Perl interpreter in C:\perl\bin, the following procedure call is used:

```
EXEC master..xp_cmdshell 'C:\perl\bin\perl.exe show_stuff.pl'
```

By using xp_cmdshell, you can use stored procedures in your database to fire off tasks that are external to the database itself. For example, if you wrote a stored procedure that processed orders, you could use xp_cmdshell to call an external program that validates credit cards and inserts the results back into the database.

CHAPTER 17

WRITING ORACLE PL/SQL STORED PROCEDURES

In this chapter

Stored procedures for Oracle are written in PL/SQL, a procedural language that extends the standard SQL language. PL/SQL is more of a departure from standard SQL than most other stored procedure languages. For one thing, PL/SQL demands more structure than other stored procedure extensions to SQL. All PL/SQL queries must consist of three sections: the declaration section, the executable section, and the exception-handling section. PL/SQL also differs from other stored procedure languages in the way that it handles and returns data.

When you write PL/SQL code, you have the option of encapsulating it within a *procedure* and storing multiple procedures within *packages*. You can also create *anonymous blocks*, which are executed when they are entered but are not stored for future use. This chapter begins by discussing how to write PL/SQL code in anonymous blocks and then discusses how the code can be stored in procedures and packages. First, I'll cover the three sections of a PL/SQL query. All PL/SQL queries conform to the following structure:

```
DECLARE
    declaration statements
BEGIN
    executable statements
EXCEPTION
    error handling statements
END;
```

Before I begin discussing the details of how PL/SQL queries work, I'm going to provide the source code to a sample query that I will use as the basis for the discussion. Listing 17.1 contains the source code for the query, which is used to return the profits for a movie. The first version has the values for the variables set within the query; later, I'll explain how you can retrieve the values in other ways. This example inserts the profits into a new table I've created with two columns, one for the movie ID and the other for the profit.

LISTING 17.1   A QUERY THAT RETURNS THE PROFITS FOR A MOVIE

```
DECLARE
    gross NUMBER;
    budget NUMBER;
    profit NUMBER;
    movie_id INT(6);
BEGIN
    gross := 50;
    budget := 75;
    movie_id := 1;
    profit := budget - gross;
    INSERT INTO Movie_Profit VALUES (movie_id, profit);
END;
.
/

PL/SQL procedure successfully completed.
```

The . character on a line by itself indicates the end of a PL/SQL block, and / is used to execute the last block or command that was entered.

THE DECLARATION SECTION

The declaration section is used to identify the variables, constants, and cursors that will be used in the executable section of the PL/SQL block. In the example in Listing 17.1, I declared four variables, three of which were numbers; the movie_id variable is an integer. The valid data types for PL/SQL variables are the same as the data types for columns in an Oracle table. A description of the data types available in Oracle is included in Chapter 18, "Oracle."

You can also declare variables with initial values assigned to them within the declarations section of a PL/SQL query. Listing 17.2 is the same as Listing 17.1 except that the values for the variables are set in the declarations section instead of the executable section.

LISTING 17.2   A PL/SQL QUERY IN WHICH VALUES ARE ASSIGNED TO VARIABLES IN THE DECLARATIONS SECTION

```
DECLARE
    gross NUMBER := 75;
    budget NUMBER := 50;
    profit NUMBER;
    movie_id INT(6) := 1;
BEGIN
    profit := budget - gross;
    INSERT INTO Movie_Profit VALUES (movie_id, profit);
END;
.
/

PL/SQL procedure successfully completed.
```

The assignment statements were removed from the executable statements section of the block because the values are set in the declarations section. You can override values assigned in the declarations section of a query with an assignment statement within the executable section of the block, as shown in Listing 17.3.

LISTING 17.3   REPLACING DEFAULT VALUES IN VARIABLES WITH ASSIGNMENT STATEMENTS

```
DECLARE
    gross NUMBER := 75;
    budget NUMBER := 50;
    profit NUMBER;
    movie_id INT(6) := 1;
BEGIN
    gross := 77;
    budget := 56;
    movie_id := 8;
    profit := budget - gross;
    INSERT INTO Movie_Profit VALUES (movie_id, profit);
END;
.
/

PL/SQL procedure successfully completed.
```

CONSTANTS

If you want, you can declare variables as constants so that the default values that are assigned to them in the declarations section of the block cannot be overridden with assignment statements later in the executable statements section.

Tip 65 from	Use constants when there's a value that you will use more than once in the body of the query and that will not need to be changed very often. For example, if your query uses the sales tax rate for your state in a number of places, it makes sense to create a constant named `sales_tax` and to use that throughout your query. If the sales tax rate changes, you can update the query by changing a single value in the declarations section, and your code will be more readable because people will know that a formula includes the sales tax, not just some number.
Rafe Colburn	

To declare a variable as a constant, the CONSTANT keyword is inserted before the data type. To declare movie_id as a constant, the following statement is used:

```
movie_id CONSTANT INT(6) := 1;
```

DECLARING CURSORS

Any cursors that will be used within a block of code are also declared within the declaration section of the block. I explained how to declare cursors back in Chapter 14, "Transactions and Cursors," in the section titled "Using Cursors in Oracle PL/SQL," but I'd like to revisit them again briefly.

Cursors are declared using the following syntax:

```
CURSOR cursor_name IS
    SELECT statement;
```

After the cursor is declared, you can declare variables into which the data in the cursor can be fetched. You can set up a row into which all the columns from the query in the cursor can be selected using the %ROWTYPE construct. If you supply a cursor name with %ROWTYPE appended to it as the data type for a variable, that variable will use the structure of the rows fetched by the cursor. The syntax for creating a data structure using %ROWTYPE is as follows:

```
variable_name cursor_name%ROWTYPE;
```

Listing 17.4 contains the declarations section for a block of PL/SQL code that uses a cursor to retrieve the data needed to calculate movie profits.

LISTING 17.4 THE DECLARATION SECTION FOR A PL/SQL BLOCK THAT USES A CURSOR

```
DECLARE
    profit NUMBER;
    CURSOR movies_cursor IS
        SELECT movie_id, budget, gross
        FROM Movies;
    movies_rec movies_cursor%ROWTYPE;
```

THE EXECUTABLE SECTION

When all the variables, constants, and cursors that will be used in a PL/SQL block have been declared, the next step is to write the code that will do the real work. In the sample queryin Listing 17.1, the block just calculates the profit for a movie and inserts a new row into a table containing the ID and the profit for that movie. In this section, I'll talk about some more advanced tasks you can use PL/SQL to perform.

GETTING DATA OUT OF A PL/SQL BLOCK

PL/SQL is a language designed for data processing; it accepts data as input, processes that data, and then either stores or returns the new data. Before I discuss how to write code to process data within a PL/SQL block, I'd like to discuss how to get usable data out of the block.

Ultimately, PL/SQL is geared toward manipulating data stored within a database, and most PL/SQL queries are used to process data for use within INSERT, UPDATE, or DELETE statements. PL/SQL is not designed for creating advanced queries and returning tables of data or for generating reports. As you'll see in the next chapter, Oracle's SQL*Plus tool provides a number of specialized controls for formatting query results and generating reports.

PART

V

CH

17

However, data manipulation queries are not the only way to process the results of a PL/SQL block. You can store your PL/SQL code within a procedure or function, both of which can pass values back to the calling query, or you can use the DBMS_OUTPUT package to print out information to the console. Generally, DBMS_OUTPUT is used to generate debugging information. I'll discuss it in the section "Debugging PL/SQL Queries."

ASSIGNING VALUES TO VARIABLES

As you know, you can assign values to variables within the declarations section of a PL/SQL block. However, you'll need to change these values or assign values to variables that were initialized in the declarations section. In PL/SQL, the assignment operator is :=. The plain = operator is used for Boolean comparisons.

The following variable assignments were included in Listing 17.1:

```
gross := 50;
budget := 75;
movie_id := 1;
profit := budget - gross;
```

CONDITIONAL STATEMENTS

PL/SQL supports the IF, ELSIF, and ELSE statements for conditional logic. IF blocks are ended using the END IF statement. If the condition associated with an IF statement is true, the code following the IF statement is executed. If it is false, the code following the ELSE statement is executed, assuming one is present. Additional conditions can be inserted in a block of conditional statements using ELSIF. The full structure of an IF construct is as follows:

```
IF condition THEN
```

```
    statements
ELSIF condition THEN
    statements
ELSE
    statements
END IF;
```

The flow of execution through an IF construct passes from one condition to the next until a true condition is encountered. If no true conditions are found, the statements in the ELSE block are executed. If the statement contains no ELSE block, execution continues past the IF statement, and none of the statements in the IF statement are executed. An example of a complex IF statement appears in Listing 17.5.

LISTING 17.5   A BLOCK CONTAINING A COMPLEX CONDITIONAL STATEMENT

```
DECLARE
    crow INT := 10;
BEGIN
    IF crow < 10 THEN
        INSERT INTO Test
        VALUES (crow);
    ELSIF crow > 10 THEN
        INSERT INTO Test
        VALUES (crow * 2);
    ELSE
        INSERT INTO Test
        VALUES (crow / 2);
    END IF;
END;
.
/

PL/SQL procedure successfully completed.
```

In Listing 17.5, the ELSE clause winds up being executed because crow is neither greater than nor less than 10. In any case, in an IF statement, only one of the clauses will ever wind up being executed.

You can also nest IF statements if you want. An IF statement can be nested within another IF statement, in either the IF clause or the ELSE clause. An example of a nested IF statement appears in Listing 17.6.

LISTING 17.6   A NESTED IF STATEMENT

```
DECLARE
    crow INT := 10;
BEGIN
    IF crow > 5 THEN
        IF crow < 15 THEN
            INSERT INTO Test
            VALUES (crow);
        END IF;
```

```
    END IF;
END;
```

PL/SQL procedure successfully completed.

There is no limit on the depth to which you can nest IF statements. The IF statements in Listing 17.6 are just simple IF statements, but there's no reason why they couldn't both include ELSIF and ELSE clauses as well.

LOOPS

In PL/SQL, the LOOP statement is used to create a looping construct. The LOOP and END LOOP keywords are used to define the statements that make up the loop, and an EXIT WHEN statement in the body of the loop exits the loop when the condition included with it is true. An example of a LOOP statement appears in Listing 17.7.

LISTING 17.7   A PL/SQL LOOP STATEMENT

```
DECLARE
    crow INT := 1;
BEGIN
    LOOP
        INSERT INTO Test
        VALUES (crow);
        EXIT WHEN crow = 10;
        crow := crow + 1;
    END LOOP;
END;
.
/
```

PL/SQL procedure successfully completed.

The loop exits immediately when the condition in the EXIT WHEN statement is true. In this loop, the EXIT WHEN statement appears before the statement that increments the variable used in the EXIT WHEN statement. The loop is executed 10 times and exits immediately before the value of crow is incremented to 11.

LOOPING OVER A CURSOR

You can use the LOOP statement to loop over a set of rows returned by a cursor. There are special variables associated with cursors that make it easy to control the execution of your loops (or any other conditional statements, such as IF) based on the results of fetches from the cursor. These variables are listed in Table 14.1.

To write a loop that processes all the rows returned by a cursor, you can use the LOOP keyword and the %NOTFOUND attribute of the cursor in the EXIT WHEN statement.

→ For a detailed explanation of how these loops are built, **see** "Using Cursors in Oracle PL/SQL," **p. 346**

FOR LOOPS

The LOOP statement is very flexible; it sets up a loop that is executed until the condition in the EXIT WHEN statement is true. You can include any type of condition in the EXIT WHEN statement, and you can place the EXIT WHEN statement wherever you want in the body of the loop. For example, in Listing 17.7, I placed the EXIT WHEN statement after everything in the loop except for the statement that incremented the variable I was using as the loop counter.

FOR loops are more structured. When you write a FOR loop, the counter for the loop and the loop condition are specified within the FOR statement itself. Generally, FOR loops use the range operator to indicate how many times the loop will be executed. An example of a FOR loop appears in Listing 17.8.

LISTING 17.8 A FOR LOOP

```
DECLARE
    crow INT;
BEGIN
    FOR crow IN 1 .. 10 LOOP
        INSERT INTO Test
        VALUES (crow);
    END LOOP;
END;
.
/

PL/SQL procedure successfully completed.
```

As you can see, the EXIT WHEN statement does not appear in the loop in Listing 17.8. Instead, all the criteria for the loop's execution are specified directly in the FOR statement. Look at the structure of the FOR statement. The first element in the FOR statement is the variable used as the loop counter, in this case, crow. The actual values that will be assigned to the loop counter are specified after the IN keyword. In Listing 17.8, the values are generated using the range operator. The expression 1 .. 10 means "from 1 to 10." The counter is incremented by 1 for each iteration of the loop until the counter reaches 10, at which time the loop is executed once more and exits. The end of the FOR statement and the beginning of the body of the loop are signified by the LOOP keyword.

FOR LOOPS AND CURSORS

You can use a FOR loop to iterate over a cursor if you want. To use a cursor with a FOR loop, you place the name of the cursor in the IN clause of the FOR statement. Each row fetched by the cursor is assigned to the loop variable, and the loop automatically finishes when all the rows have been fetched from the cursor. The FOR loop also closes the cursor when it exits.

An example of a FOR loop that iterates over a cursor appears in Listing 17.9.

LISTING 17.9   A FOR LOOP THAT USES A CURSOR

```
DECLARE
    profit NUMBER;
    temp NUMBER;
    CURSOR movies_cursor IS
        SELECT movie_id, budget, gross
        FROM Movies;
    movies_rec movies_cursor%ROWTYPE;
BEGIN
    FOR movies_rec IN movies_cursor LOOP
        temp := movies_rec.gross - movies_rec.budget;
        INSERT INTO Movie_Profit
        VALUES (movies_rec.movie_id, temp);
    END LOOP;
END;
.
/

PL/SQL procedure successfully completed.
```

WHILE LOOPS

A WHILE loop is another type of loop; it is executed until the condition specified in the WHILE statement itself is true. Like the FOR loop, it is less flexible than the basic LOOP statement, but it is also more structured. WHILE loops are initialized using the following statement:

WHILE *condition* LOOP

As long as the condition specified in the WHILE statement is true, the execution of the loop continues. A WHILE loop is similar to a simple loop, except that instead of using the EXIT WHEN statement, the looping condition is specified at the same time the loop is initialized. Like a standard loop, the values in the loop condition must be modified within the body of the loop to ensure that at some point the exit condition for the loop will be true. Listing 17.10 contains an example of a WHILE loop.

LISTING 17.10   A WHILE LOOP

```
DECLARE
    crow INT := 1;
BEGIN
    WHILE crow <= 10 LOOP
        INSERT INTO Test
        VALUES (crow);
        crow := crow + 1;
    END LOOP;
END;
.
/

PL/SQL procedure successfully completed.
```

WHILE LOOPS AND CURSORS

You can use a WHILE loop to iterate over a cursor by using the %FOUND attribute of the cursor. As long as rows can be fetched from the cursor, the %FOUND attribute of the cursor is true. When the rows in the cursor have all been fetched, the %FOUND attribute is false, and execution of the WHILE loop ceases. An example of a cursor that uses a WHILE loop appears in Listing 17.11.

LISTING 17.11   A WHILE LOOP THAT ITERATES OVER A CURSOR

```
DECLARE
    profit NUMBER;
    CURSOR movies_crsr IS
        SELECT movie_id, budget, gross
        FROM Movies;
    movies_rec movies_crsr%ROWTYPE;
BEGIN
    OPEN movies_crsr;
    WHILE movies_crsr%FOUND LOOP
        FETCH movies_crsr INTO movies_rec;
        INSERT INTO Movie_Profit
        VALUES (movies_rec.movie_id,
(movies_rec.gross - movies_rec.budget));
    END LOOP;
END;
.
/

PL/SQL procedure successfully completed.
```

GOTO

The final statement that can be used to control the flow of execution in a PL/SQL queryis GOTO. Before you can use the GOTO statement, you have to embed labels in your code, which are used as targets for GOTO. A label is just an identifier, chosen by the querymer, enclosed in double angle brackets, like this:

```
<<label>>
```

After you've added some labels to your code, you can shift execution to that location in the queryusing the GOTO statement like this:

```
GOTO label;
```

Generally speaking, you should avoid the use of GOTO statements if possible. If you're really interested in why, you should look up the seminal paper, "Go To Considered Harmful." In brief, using GOTO is a bad idea because it makes your code difficult to maintain. There are almost no cases in which you can't write something better with a loop or an IF statement than you can with GOTO.

SELECTING VALUES INTO VARIABLES

As you learned back in Chapter 14, "Transactions and Cursors," you can use cursors to copy query results into variables and to loop over those results. If you want to use a SELECT statement that returns only a single row in a PL/SQL queryand avoid using a cursor, you can use the SELECT INTO command.

There are a couple of advantages of SELECT INTO over cursors if you are certain you're only going to be dealing with a single record. The first is that the SELECT statement does not have to be declared in the declarations section of the PL/SQL block. You can actually place the SELECT statement within the executable section, which is nice if you have multiple queries that will be called from within blocks inside conditional statements. If you're going to use a lot of such queries, it saves you from having to declare them all at the beginning of the block.

The second advantage of the SELECT INTO statement is that its use is much simpler than using cursors, as you will see. With SELECT INTO, you don't have to use the OPEN statement, fetch the row, or close the cursor. To select the number of movies in the Movies table into a variable called movie_count, the following statement is used:

```
SELECT COUNT(*) INTO movie_count
FROM Movies
```

The movie_count variable must be declared, of course, but you can see that this syntax is much simpler than using a cursor. You can also select multiple columns from a table and store the values returned in a data structure the same way you can with a cursor. You have to declare a variable that uses the %ROWTYPE construct first:

```
movie_rec Movies%ROWTYPE
```

Then, you can use SELECT INTO to push all the columns returned by a query into the data structure:

```
SELECT movie_id, movie_title, budget, gross
INTO movie_rec
FROM Movies
WHERE movie_id = 1
```

As you can see, in both the SELECT INTO statements, I ensured that the queries returned only one row. In the first case, I used an aggregate function to reduce the results to a single row, and in the second case, I used a primary key value in the WHERE clause to ensure that only one row would be returned.

EXCEPTION HANDLING

The third major section of a PL/SQL block is the exception-handling section. Unlike the other two sections, it is optional, and in fact, it appears within the executable section of the block. The exception-handling section comes into play when a user-defined or system exception occurs during the execution of the PL/SQL block. When an exception occurs, execution is transferred to the exception-handling section of the block, in search of code to handle the exception that was caught.

The exception-handling section of a block is included as the last part of the executable section of the query, before the END statement, as follows:

```
DECLARE
    declarations
BEGIN
    statements
EXCEPTION
    exception handling code
END;
```

The exception-handling section itself consists of WHEN clauses that are used to provide code to be executed when particular exceptions are encountered. You can also use the WHEN OTHERS clause, which is basically an ELSE clause for the exception-handling section of a block. Any exceptions that do not have a specific exception handler defined will be caught by the WHEN OTHERS clause.

Take a look at a simple example of an exception handler. There are a number of system exceptions that Oracle can raise; they're listed in Appendix A, "System-Defined Exceptions in PL/SQL." One exception that Oracle can raise is INVALID_NUMBER. This exception is raised when an implicit conversion to a number fails. The example appears in Listing 17.12.

LISTING 17.12 WRITING AN EXCEPTION HANDLER

```
DECLARE
    crow INT;
    bar VARCHAR2(20);
BEGIN
    crow := 5;
    bar := 'baz';
    INSERT INTO Test
    VALUES (crow + bar);
EXCEPTION
    WHEN INVALID_NUMBER THEN
        INSERT INTO Test
        VALUES ('Error');
END;
.
/

PL/SQL procedure successfully completed.

SELECT *
FROM Test;

TEST
--------------------
Error
```

As you can see, the string 'Error' was inserted into the table instead of the sum of crow and bar. When you try to add the number 5 to the value of bar, which is 'baz', the INVALID_NUMBER exception is raised by the implicit conversion. Execution immediately shifts to the exception section of the query, and the exception handler catches the error and inserts the appropriate value into the table.

OTHERS is a special exception identifier that applies to any exception that does not have an explicitly defined handler in the exception section of the query. If I replaced INVALID_NUMBER in Listing 17.12 with the OTHERS identifier, the result would be the same. The OTHERS identifier would also trap any other exceptions raised during the execution of the block.

DEFINING YOUR OWN EXCEPTIONS

In PL/SQL, you can define your own exceptions, and you can define your own error messages to be displayed when exceptions are encountered. New exceptions are defined in the declarations section of a block. The declaration looks like a variable definition with a data type of EXCEPTION, like this:

```
DECLARE new_exception EXCEPTION;
```

In the exception-handling section of your query, you need to write an exception handler for that exception. When you want to raise the exception, the RAISE command is used. The syntax is as follows:

```
RAISE new_exception;
```

You'll generally want to use the RAISE command within a conditional statement.

PL/SQL provides a built-in procedure, RAISE_APPLICATION_ERROR, which enables you to specify an error message that will be presented to the user and to exit the querywith a specific, user-defined error code. RAISE_APPLICATION_ERROR is used as the body of a WHEN clause in the exception-handing section of a query, like this:

```
WHEN new_exception THEN
    RAISE_APPLICATION_ERROR (error_code,
        'error message');
```

The error message is just a string that's displayed, and the error code is a number that must be between -20,001 and -20,999. Take a look at a PL/SQL block that applies these concepts. I'm going to define a user exception, create a handler for it, and include code in the body of the PL/SQL block that raises that exception. Listing 17.13 contains the example.

LISTING 17.13   HANDLING USER-DEFINED ERRORS IN PL/SQL

```
DECLARE
    crow INT;
    number_too_large EXCEPTION;
BEGIN
    FOR crow IN 1 .. 100 LOOP
        IF crow = 99 THEN
            RAISE number_too_large;
        END IF;
    END LOOP;
EXCEPTION
    WHEN number_too_large THEN
        RAISE_APPLICATION_ERROR (-20001,
            'The number is too large.');
```

continues

LISTING 17.13 CONTINUED

```
END;
.
/

ERROR at line 1:
ORA-20001: The number is too large.
ORA-06512: at line 12
```

WRITING STORED PROCEDURES

Now that I've discussed the basic constructs you can use to create PL/SQL blocks, I'll explain how you can turn those blocks into stored procedures.

Tip 66 from
Rafe Colburn

> Only users who have the CREATE PROCEDURE privilege or who are members of the RESOURCE role are allowed to create stored procedures. The CREATE ANY PROCEDURE privilege allows a user to create a procedure in any schema. For information on how to assign these privileges to users, see the section "Using Grant and Revoke" in Chapter 11, "The SQL Security Model."

There are three types of stored procedures that can be created in an Oracle database. The most basic type is the *procedure*. It must be explicitly called to be executed and does not return any information to the caller directly. The second type is the *function*, which is executed and returns information to the caller directly. Both procedures and functions can share data with the entity that called them using special variables declared when the procedure was defined. The third type is the *trigger*, which is executed automatically when a particular event occurs.

Oracle also provides *packages* to aid in the development of database applications. A package is a container that allows users to write multiple SQL statements, procedures, and functions that can draw from a common group of variables and cursors. Packages provide a means by which you can logically organize groups of related stored procedures into a single unit for data sharing and ease of maintenance. I'll describe how packages are created a bit further along in the chapter.

CREATING A PROCEDURE

Procedures are created using the CREATE PROCEDURE statement. If you want to create a procedure that replaces an existing procedure, you can use the CREATE OR REPLACE PROCEDURE statement. After the CREATE PROCEDURE command, the name of the new (or replacement) procedure is specified. Then, the list of input and output variables used by the procedure is included, followed by the PL/SQL code that makes up the procedure itself.

The format of a CREATE PROCEDURE command is as follows:

```
CREATE [OR REPLACE] PROCEDURE procedure_name
[(
parameter (IN ¦ OUT ¦ IN OUT] data type
[, parameter (IN ¦ OUT ¦ IN OUT] data type, ...]
)]
AS
block
```

The parameters associated with the procedure can be specified as IN, OUT, or IN OUT. IN parameters are populated with data passed to the procedure by the query that calls it. OUT parameters pass data back to the calling query. IN OUT parameters are used both to accept data as input and to return data to the calling query. Whenever you write a query that calls a stored procedure, the parameters that it sends to the procedure must map to the parameters in the procedure perfectly. In Listing 17.14, I define the query from Listing 17.1 as a stored procedure.

PART
V

CH
17

LISTING 17.14 CREATING A NEW STORED PROCEDURE

```
CREATE OR REPLACE PROCEDURE calculate_profit
    (
        gross IN NUMBER,
    budget IN NUMBER,
    profit OUT NUMBER,
    movie_id IN OUT INT(6)
        )
AS
BEGIN
    profit := budget - gross;
    INSERT INTO Movie_Profit VALUES (movie_id, profit);
END;
```

The variables used within the procedure are declared when the stored procedure is defined. The list of values in the IN clause replaces the declarations section of a standard PL/SQL block.

EXECUTING A STORED PROCEDURE

After a stored procedure has been created, you can execute it using the PL/SQL EXECUTE statement. The EXECUTE statement accepts the procedure name and the list of parameters to be passed to the stored procedure, which are enclosed within parentheses. The code to call the stored procedure I created in Listing 17.12 follows:

```
EXECUTE calculate_profit (40, 25, 1);
```

As you can see, three parameters are passed to the procedure. There are four variables defined in the CREATE PROCEDURE statement in Listing 17.12, but you only pass parameters for the IN and IN OUT variables, so it accepts three parameters. If you don't want to pass a value to a procedure for a particular parameter (assuming that parameter is not required), you can send a null as a placeholder, as follows:

```
EXECUTE calculate_profit (NULL, 25, 1);
```

This stored procedure wouldn't work with null as the value of the gross parameter, but in some cases, sending a null as a parameter is perfectly acceptable.

You can also execute procedures owned by another user. The notation for calling them is the same as the notation for using tables that belong to another user. You just prepend the name of the procedure with the username of the owner and a period. So, to call calculate_profit if it were owned by a user named patricia, you would use the following command:

```
EXECUTE patricia.calculate_profit (40, 25, 1);
```

You can also call a stored procedure in another database by prepending the database name and an at symbol (@) to the stored procedure name. So, to call the calculate_profit procedure if it were in a database called financials, the following execute statement is used:

```
EXECUTE calculate_profit@financials (40, 25, 1);
```

In either case, the user calling the stored procedure must have the proper privileges to do so. To call a stored procedure, the user must have been granted EXECUTE permission on that procedure. Permission to access any of the schema objects referenced within the stored procedure is not required. If a user does not have the necessary rights to update rows within a table but she does have EXECUTE permission for a stored procedure that updates rows within that table, she can update the table via the stored procedure. As you can see, using stored procedures and the SQL security model, you can impose even more restrictive controls on who can modify or view tables than you can with access rights and views.

Oracle synonyms, which are covered in detail in the section "Synonyms" in Chapter 18, are used to create references to objects that belong to other users or are stored in remote databases. You can create a synonym to a stored procedure that belongs to another user or exists within a remote database using the CREATE SYNONYM command. After the synonym is created, users using the current schema can call the stored procedure as though it is local to that schema. The syntax of the CREATE SYNONYM command is as follows:

```
CREATE SYNONYM calculate_profit
FOR patricia.calculate_profit
```

CREATING AND USING CUSTOM FUNCTIONS

Functions are a special type of stored procedure that can return a single value to the caller explicitly in addition to any values that are shared through OUT or IN OUT variables. The main advantage of functions is that they can be used almost anywhere the built-in functions supported by PL/SQL are used. Just as you can use the UPPER() or TRIM() functions in the select list of a query, you can use functions that you create in the select list as well.

First, create a function that accepts a movie ID as a parameter and returns the profits for that movie. The CREATE FUNCTION statement is similar to CREATE PROCEDURE, except that you must include a RETURN clause that describes the value returned by the function. The CREATE FUNCTION statement for the function get_profit appears in Listing 17.15.

LISTING 17.15   A USER-DEFINED FUNCTION

```
CREATE OR REPLACE FUNCTION get_profit
(in_movie_id IN INT)
RETURN NUMBER
IS profit NUMBER;
BEGIN
SELECT gross - budget INTO profit
WHERE movie_id = in_movie_id;
RETURN (profit);
END;
```

Look at the contents of Listing 17.15. The type of data returned by the function is indicated by the RETURN NUMBER clause, and the variable used to return the data appears in the IS clause. In the body of the function itself, I use a SELECT INTO statement to extract the profits for the movie specified through the in_movie_id parameter and store them in the variable profit. The RETURN(profit) statement actually returns the value calculated in the SELECT INTO statement to the caller.

After the function has been created, you can use it within your other queries. The most notable limitation on the usage of user-defined functions is that they can't be called from within check or default constraints. Take a look at a query that selects the title of all the movies from the database and uses get_profit to calculate the profitability of each of those movies. The query appears in Listing 17.16.

LISTING 17.16   A QUERY THAT CALLS A USER-DEFINED FUNCTION

```
SELECT movie_title, get_profit(movie_id)
FROM Movies
```

As you can see, the profit for each of the movies is returned by the function and is integrated into the query results.

BUNDLING PROCEDURES AND FUNCTIONS IN PACKAGES

One feature that Oracle has included to facilitate development of complex applications using PL/SQL is packages. Packages are groups of procedures, functions, and the attendant code that is common to those procedures and functions.

There are three significant advantages to using packages. The first is that multiple procedures and functions can share the same cursors and variables, as long as they're within the same package. The second advantage is that you can declare procedures and functions in a package as public or private. Private procedures and functions can only be called from within their package, whereas public functions and procedures are accessible from outside the package as well. Finally, procedures can include code that is executed every time any procedure or function within the package is called, preventing you from having to include the same snippet of initialization code in several procedures. Rather than doing so, you can place the initialization code in the package and then include all the procedures in that package.

Packages come in two parts: the package specification and the package body. The *package specification* is a list of all the public objects that are contained within the package; any object within the package that is not listed in the package specification can only be accessed by other members of the package. The *package body* contains the actual PL/SQL code for all the public and private members of the package, the initialization code that is executed any time the package is called, and any variables and cursors that are declared for the package. The package specification and package body are created separately, using the CREATE PACKAGE and CREATE PACKAGE BODY statements.

CREATING A PACKAGE SPECIFICATION

Say that I want to create a package that is used to handle all the queries relating to the profitability of movies. In it, I want to include the function that returns the profits for a movie given the movie ID and a procedure that logs the profitability of a given movie studio as of the current date (I might run this procedure weekly so that I can have historical data on the profitability of various studios). The first step in creating the package is to define the procedures and functions used within the package in the package specification.

There are two objects within the function right now: the get_profit function, which returns the profit for a movie given its movie ID, and a procedure called store_studio_profit, which will save historical profitability data in a table yet to be created. Just as each procedure has a name, so too does each package. In this case, I'm going to call the package movie_profit. Each object within the package is then referenced by the package name and the object name, separated by a dot.

The general syntax for CREATE PACKAGE is as follows:

```
CREATE [OR REPLACE] PACKAGE [user.]package_name
{ IS ¦ AS }
package_specification
END package_name;
```

The package specification contains a list of all the publicly accessible functions and procedures within the package. The entry in the package specification for each of the objects contains the type of object that is being created, the name of the object, and the parameters (both input and output) associated with that object. The package specification for the movie_profit package is included in Listing 17.17.

LISTING 17.17 THE PACKAGE SPECIFICATION FOR THE movie_profit PACKAGE

```
CREATE OR REPLACE PACKAGE movie_profit
AS
    FUNCTION get_profit
        (
        movie_id IN INT);
        PROCEDURE store_studio_profit
            (studio IN NUMBER,
            profit IN NUMBER);
END movie_profit;
```

The statement in Listing 17.17 creates a new package named movie_profit (or replaces movie_profit if it already exists). It consists of two objects, get_profit and store_studio_profit. As you can see, the variable specified in the package specification for get_profit corresponds to the definition of the get_profit function in Listing 17.15.

The package body contains the actual source code for the procedures, functions, and other supporting code used by the package. The package body is created with the CREATE PACKAGE BODY statement. The create statement for the package body of the movie_profit package is in Listing 17.18.

LISTING 17.18 THE PACKAGE BODY FOR movie_profit

```
CREATE OR REPLACE PACKAGE BODY movie_profit
AS
FUNCTION get_profit
(in_movie_id IN INT)
RETURN NUMBER
IS profit NUMBER;
BEGIN
SELECT gross - budget INTO profit
WHERE movie_id = in_movie_id;
RETURN (profit);
END get_profit;
PROCEDURE store_studio_profit
(studio IN NUMBER,
     profit IN NUMBER)
AS
BEGIN
INSERT INTO studio_profit
(studio_id, date_of_entry, studio_profit)
VALUES
(studio, SYSDATE, profit);
END store_studio_profit;
END movie_profit;
```

As you can see, the source code for both objects appears in the package body. The list of input and output variables for both objects corresponds exactly to the variables listed in the package specification. You can also place initialization code in your package specification that will be executed the first time any object in the package is executed. The initialization code is ordinarily used to declare cursors or variables that are used in more than one of the objects in the package.

DEBUGGING PL/SQL QUERIES

The main problem in debugging PL/SQL queries is that the language was not designed to produce output in the traditional sense. Most languages have statements built in that allow them to send output to the console, a window, or whatever environment they're running in. There are no such statements built in to PL/SQL because it is geared toward manipulating data within the database or returning values for use by the calling application. There are two aids available to help debug PL/SQL queries. The first is the SHOW ERRORS command, which prints any errors that were generated in the compilation of the query. The second is the DBMS_OUTPUT package, which enables you to include statements that print output to the console.

SHOW ERRORS

The SHOW ERRORS command prints a list of errors in a PL/SQL query. When you attempt to create a procedure, function, or package and there are errors in the code, the following message is displayed in SQL*Plus:

```
Warning: Function created with compilation errors.
```

When you see that message, you can retrieve a list of compilation errors with SHOW ERRORS. The errors in the function I tried to create follow:

```
Errors for FUNCTION GET_PROFIT:

LINE/COL ERROR
--------------------------------------------------------------------
7/1      PLS-00103: Encountered the symbol "WHERE" when expecting one of
         the following:
         . ( , % from

8/1      PLS-00103: Encountered the symbol "RETURN"
9/1      PLS-00103: Encountered the symbol "END"
```

DBMS_OUTPUT

The DBMS_OUTPUT package provides two commands that can be used to display output on the console. To see this output, you must turn on the SERVEROUTPUT option, using the following command:

```
SET SERVEROUTPUT ON
```

The DBMS_OUTPUT package prints the string argument passed to the function using PUT, or if you use PUT_LINE, it prints the argument followed by a new line. The NEW_LINE constant, when used with PUT, prints a carriage return.

Take a look at a block of PL/SQL code that iterates over a cursor and prints the values from the cursor using PUT_LINE. The PL/SQL code in Listing 17.19 retrieves a list of movies from a studio and prints the list using PUT_LINE.

LISTING 17.19   USING PUT_LINE TO GENERATE CONSOLE OUTPUT

```
DECLARE
CURSOR movies_cursor IS
    SELECT movie_title
    FROM Movies
    WHERE studio_id = 1;
movie_rec movies_cursor%ROWTYPE;
BEGIN
```

```
      WHILE movies_cursor%FOUND LOOP
          FETCH movies_cursor INTO movie_rec;
          PUT_LINE (movie_rec.movie_title);
      END LOOP;
END;
.
/

Vegetable House
Prince Kong
The Code Warrior
Bill Durham
Codependence Day
The Linux Files
SQL Strikes Back
The Programmer
Hard Code
The Rear Windows
Test Movie
```

TRIGGERS

A trigger is an event handler that executes a PL/SQL block when a specified event occurs. Oracle supports a wide variety of events that can be tied to a trigger. There are two levels of triggers, row-level and statement-level. Row-level triggers are executed once for each row in a transaction. If you run an update statement that is tied to a row-level trigger and that updates 10 rows, the trigger will run 10 times. Statement-level triggers run only once per statement that is executed. If you run the same update statement but assign a statement-level trigger to it instead, the trigger will run only once.

Triggers can be tied to the three data-modification statements, UPDATE, DELETE, and INSERT. You can also specify exactly when a particular trigger will be executed—before the event to which it is assigned, after the event, or instead of the event. All told, you're left with 14 possible types of triggers that you can create:

```
BEFORE UPDATE row
BEFORE UPDATE statement
BEFORE DELETE row
BEFORE DELETE statement
BEFORE INSERT row
BEFORE INSERT statement
AFTER UPDATE row
AFTER UPDATE statement
AFTER DELETE row
AFTER DELETE statement
AFTER INSERT row
AFTER INSERT statement
INSTEAD OF row
INSTEAD OF statement
```

Triggers are created using the following syntax:

```
CREATE [OR REPLACE] TRIGGER trigger_name
```

```
   { BEFORE ¦ AFTER ¦ INSTEAD OF }
   { DELETE ¦ INSERT ¦ UPDATE [OF column [, column] ..] }
   [OR additional event]
ON [user.]{table ¦ view}
[REFERENCING {old [AS] old ¦ new [AS] new} ...]
[FOR EACH {ROW ¦ STATEMENT}
[WHEN (condition)]
PL/SQL code
```

As you can see, the syntax for creating a trigger is rather complex. I'll go through it clause by clause. You should understand the first line of syntax; in it, the name of the trigger is specified for creation. The next section is used to specify the event or events that will cause the trigger to be executed. Every trigger can be executed by as many events as you want to assign to it.

The ON clause is used to specify the table or view to which the trigger is assigned. If the table or view is part of another user's schema, you must prepend the name of the table or view with the username and a dot. When you write a trigger that is associated with data being updated, you can use the old and new identifiers to manipulate the new data being inserted in the database, along with the old data that is being replaced. If you want to use identifiers other than new and old, you can specify them in the REFERENCING clause.

The FOR EACH clause is used to specify whether a trigger operates at the row level or the statement level. Triggers operate at the statement level by default. The default behavior is to operate at the statement level; you can specify one or the other using FOR EACH ROW and FOR EACH STATEMENT.

Finally, you can constrain the effects of row-level triggers using the WHEN clause. The WHEN clause is similar to the WHERE clause in a standard query. Any rows that are matched by the condition in the WHEN clause are processed by the trigger; rows that do not match the expression in the WHEN clause are ignored.

WRITING A TRIGGER

Take a look at a simple trigger that will prevent the insertion of movies with budgets of less than $10 million. Nearly all the code for the trigger lies in the clauses that lead up to the PL/SQL block that makes up the body of the trigger. All the body of the trigger has to do is prevent the insertion if the row does not meet the required criteria. The code for the trigger appears in Listing 17.20.

LISTING 17.20 A SAMPLE TRIGGER

```
CREATE OR REPLACE TRIGGER movies_insert
BEFORE INSERT ON Movies
FOR EACH ROW WHEN (new.budget < 10)
DECLARE
    budget_too_low EXCEPTION;
BEGIN
```

```
        RAISE budget_too_low;
EXCEPTION
    WHEN budget_too_low THEN
        RAISE_APPLICATION_ERROR (-20001,
            'Budget too low for insertion.');
END;

Trigger created.
```

Now look at some code that tests the trigger. In Listing 17.21, I try to insert a row with a budget above 10 million, and in Listing 17.22, I try to insert a row with a budget below 10 million.

LISTING 17.21 AN INSERT STATEMENT THAT WILL SUCCEED

```
INSERT INTO Movies
(movie_id, movie_title, studio_id, director_id,
budget, gross, release_date)
VALUES
(15, 'Test Movie', 1, 2, 15, 15, '21-MAY-99');

1 row created.
```

LISTING 17.22 AN INSERT STATEMENT THAT WILL FAIL

```
INSERT INTO Movies
(movie_id, movie_title, studio_id, director_id,
budget, gross, release_date)
VALUES
(16, 'Test Movie', 1, 2, 5, 5, '21-MAY-99');

ERROR at line 1:
ORA-20001: Budget too low for insertion.
ORA-06512: at "DEVELOPMENT.MOVIES_INSERT", line 7
ORA-04088: error during execution of trigger 'DEVELOPMENT.MOVIES_INSERT'
```

Now look at the trigger itself. The trigger is run before records are inserted into the Movies table and is a row-level trigger that is only executed if the new value for the budget column is less than 10. The only thing the trigger does is raise a user-defined exception if the trigger is executed.

The trigger makes use of the new qualifier. When a trigger executes, two qualifiers are made available: new and old. (They can be remained using the REFERENCING clause in the CREATE TRIGGER statement.) When you prepend new to a column name, the new value being inserted or set by the query is referenced. When you use old, the value being deleted or replaced by an update is referenced. In the trigger in Listing 21.19, I used new.budget to refer to the value of the budget being inserted.

Tip 67 from
Rafe Colburn
	When you use old and new values within the body of a trigger, you must prepend old and new with a colon. So, to reference the old value for budget in an update trigger within the trigger body, the following notation is used:
	`:old.budget`
	The new value is referenced using the following:
	`:new.budget`

INSTEAD OF TRIGGERS

`INSTEAD OF` triggers discard the statement that caused the trigger to fire and replace it with the code in the package body. This feature enables you to replace a statement that would ordinarily not work with some code that will actually do what the user intended to accomplish in the first place. For example, if you have a nonupdatable view, you can write an `INSTEAD OF` trigger that will discard statements that won't work and that will instead issue separate queries that will affect the tables making up the view.

> **Note**
>
> `INSTEAD OF` triggers can only be used on views and are only available in version 8 of Oracle.

Let me create a view to use as an example. This view lists all the roles for the movie "The Code Warrior"; the CREATE VIEW statement is in Listing 17.23.

LISTING 17.23   A NONUPDATABLE VIEW

```
CREATE VIEW Movie_Roles_Test (movie_id, title, role)
AS
SELECT Movies.movie_id, movie_title, role
FROM Movies, Cast_Movies
WHERE Movies.movie_id = 3
AND Movies.movie_id = Cast_Movies.movie_id
```

Ordinarily, this view would not be updatable because it was created with a query that uses a join. However, you can write a trigger that will enable users to update the view using INSTEAD OF. The source code for the trigger is in Listing 17.24.

LISTING 17.24   A TRIGGER THAT ENABLES USERS TO UPDATE A NONUPDATABLE VIEW

```
CREATE OR REPLACE TRIGGER movie_roles_update
INSTEAD OF UPDATE ON Movies_Roles_Test
FOR EACH ROW
BEGIN
UPDATE Movies
SET title = :new.title
WHERE movie_id = :new.movie_id;
UPDATE Cast_Movies
```

```
        SET role = :new.role
        WHERE movie_id = :new.movie_id
        AND role = :old.role;
        END;
```

When an UPDATE statement is executed against the view, the original UPDATE is not used, and the values are passed along to the trigger, where they are used to update the appropriate tables.

Tip 68 from
Rafe Colburn

INSTEAD OF triggers are an optional feature. If you want to use them, you should have your database administrator enable them.

MANIPULATING TRIGGERS

Triggers can be removed using the DROP TRIGGER command, as shown:

```
DROP TRIGGER trigger_name;
```

If you want to disable a trigger but leave it in place, you can use the ALTER TRIGGER command:

```
ALTER TRIGGER trigger_name DISABLE;
```

To turn the trigger back on, use the ENABLE setting, as follows:

```
ALTER TRIGGER trigger_name ENABLE;
```

You can also disable or enable all the triggers attached to a particular table using the ALTER TABLE command, as follows:

```
ALTER TABLE table_name DISABLE ALL TRIGGERS;
```

```
ALTER TABLE table_name ENABLE ALL TRIGGERS;
```

IN THE REAL WORLD

I'm going to use this space to further expound on the benefits of using packages, especially for large projects. As you already know, packages enable you to bundle functions and procedures in a single unit, where they can share common code. Perhaps more importantly, though, bundling your functions and procedures in packages enables you to keep your code more organized, especially for large projects.

Most large projects have a number of distinct components that in turn have individual procedures and functions associated with them. Bundling procedures and functions into packages enables you to keep them much more organized and to keep your projects more structured in general.

For example, say that you're building an electronic commerce Web site for which all the business logic will be implemented in stored procedures in the database. The site consists of a number of components: a catalog, the account-management code, the shopping cart, and the actual checkout system.

You could create packages for each of those sections of the site. The catalog package would contain procedures that do the following:

- Retrieve a list of products
- Retrieve detailed information about a product
- Retrieve availability information for the product

The checkout system would probably contain procedures that do the following:

- Create a new order with the goods in the shopping cart
- Validate payment and shipping information
- Add shipping information for the account
- Add payment information for the account
- Calculate shipping charges and tax for the account
- Submit valid order for shipping

The other packages would contain the procedures that are relevant to that functionality. Each of the packages could, in turn, be assigned to a particular querymer or team of querymers for construction. The other teams working on the site would only need to know the names of the procedures internal to each package and what parameters are associated with those procedures. This information can be found in the package specifications. As long as the querymers do their jobs correctly, people working on other sections of the site never need to look at the actual package bodies for the packages that aren't their responsibility.

Using packages also encourages code reuse. For example, all the shopping cart procedures could utilize a cursor that retrieves all the items in the user's shopping cart. If those procedures were not part of a package, that cursor would have to be initialized separately in each of the procedures. If you bundle them in a package, the cursor can be declared at the top of the package, and all the procedures in the package can use it. Procedures that share common code should be packaged together so that they can eliminate duplication of code as much as possible.

When you work on larger application-development projects that involve the use of stored procedures, the use of packages can restore sanity to the development process and make it much easier to keep your code organized. I strongly recommend their use any time you're creating more than a few stored procedures for a project.

PART **VI**

SPECIFIC DATABASES

CHAPTER 18

ORACLE

In this chapter

The first database platform I'm going to discuss in this section of the book is Oracle. I've already talked a lot about Oracle, and most of the examples in this book were written and tested in an Oracle database. Oracle has the largest market share of any database vendor, largely because it has been around for a very long time and because its database is available on a wide variety of platforms.

Oracle databases are available for everything from IBM mainframes to Windows NT. At the time of this writing, Oracle had even ported its flagship database to the Linux platform. Not only is Oracle available for many platforms, but its database software works identically on every platform that it supports. Oracle provides a layer of abstraction between the database server and the operating system so that when you communicate with the database server, the underlying platform is irrelevant.

Each distinct Oracle database is referred to as an *instance*. The instance is the actual server process running on a computer. Each instance can support multiple users, schemas, and even databases. Applications generally communicate with an Oracle database using SQL*NET, a product that allows two computers running Oracle software to communicate with one another. To use SQL*NET, a computer must have Oracle client software installed. Applications that use the Oracle database communicate with the Oracle client, which in turn communicates with the database server using SQL*NET.

Obviously, various applications are designed to communicate with an Oracle database. Enterprise resource planning applications, transaction processing systems, Web application servers, and all kinds of other applications use relational databases to store their data. In this chapter, however, I'm going to discuss some tools that are specifically designed to allow users to connect to an Oracle database and execute SQL statements.

SQL*PLUS

SQL*PLUS is a command-line utility provided by Oracle to allow users to log in to an Oracle database and build reports. SQL*PLUS provides a very simple line-based interface for entering database queries and customizing the output of the queries. Basically, users can enter SQL statements at the command prompt in SQL*PLUS and see the query results displayed line by line in the same window. Figure 18.1 shows SQL*PLUS running in a terminal window.

LAUNCHING SQL*PLUS

On UNIX systems, SQL*PLUS is launched from the shell prompt by entering the name of the program, SQL*PLUS. Before you can run SQL*PLUS, your user environment must be set up to access the Oracle libraries. Either your database administrator will provide you with the commands necessary to configure your environment to use Oracle, or you can find them in the login script of the DBA user on the system.

Figure 18.1
SQL*PLUS running in
a terminal session.

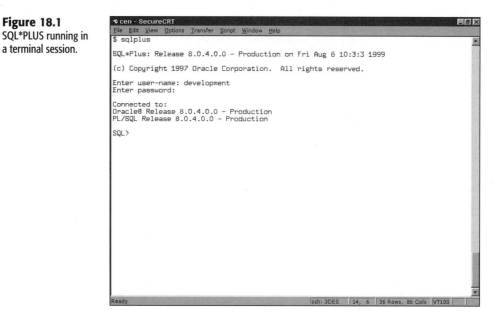

```
✦ cen - SecureCRT                                                      _ ☐ ✕
File  Edit  View  Options  Transfer  Script  Window  Help
$ sqlplus

SQL*Plus: Release 8.0.4.0.0 - Production on Fri Aug 6 10:3:3 1999

(c) Copyright 1997 Oracle Corporation.  All rights reserved.

Enter user-name: development
Enter password:

Connected to:
Oracle8 Release 8.0.4.0.0 - Production
PL/SQL Release 8.0.4.0.0 - Production

SQL>




Ready                                    ssh: 3DES   14, 6   36 Rows, 86 Cols  VT100
```

When you launch SQL*PLUS from a UNIX shell prompt, you can supply the login information on the command line to avoid entering it at the prompt when SQL*PLUS is loaded. Three command-line arguments are available for logging in: the database username, the database password, and the database name. To be able to enter a password or database name, you must supply a username on the command line. SQL*PLUS is invoked with login information as follows:

```
SQL*PLUS user/password@database
```

Thus, to log in to a database named `example` with the user name `fred` and the password `flintstone`, the following command line arguments would be used:

```
SQL*PLUS fred/flintstone@example
```

Optionally, the database name and password can be left out. All three of the following methods of launching SQL*PLUS are valid:

```
SQL*PLUS fred
```

```
SQL*PLUS fred/flintstone
```

```
SQL*PLUS fred@example
```

The database name is optional; if you don't enter it, the default database configured for the Oracle client is used. You can also enter the database name at the user prompt, as shown in Figure 18.2.

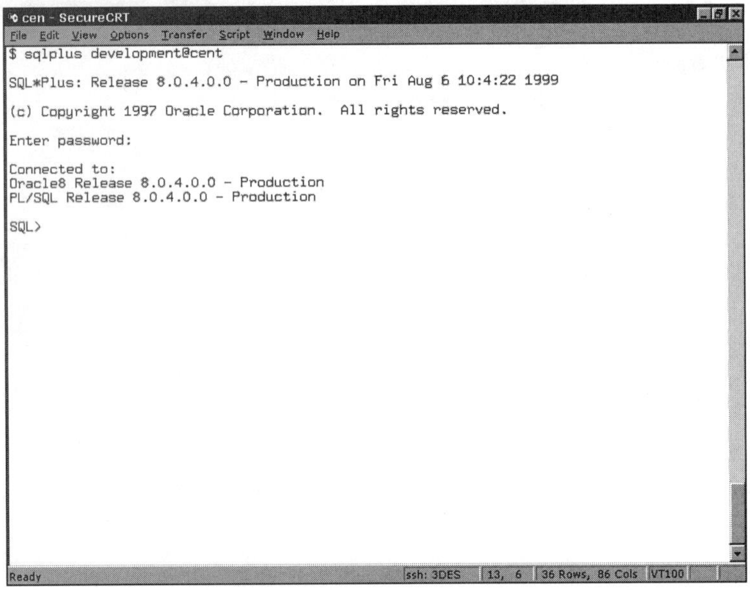

Figure 18.2
Entering a database
name of SQL*PLUS at
the user prompt.

In Figure 18.2, I'm logging in to the database rn_ipc_dev as the user rn_news. As you can see, both the username and the database name can be entered at the prompt. Figure 18.3 shows the Windows version of SQL*PLUS. As you can see, instead of providing an inline prompt for entering login information, SQL*PLUS on Windows provides a dialog box in which you can enter the username, the password, and the database name.

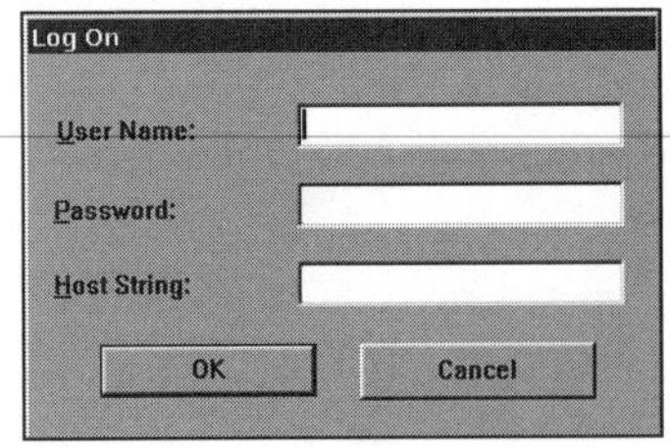

Figure 18.3
SQL*PLUS for
Windows.

USING SQL*PLUS

After launching SQL*PLUS, you can type your commands directly at the SQL> prompt. In many applications, it's not necessary to terminate your SQL statements in any way; you just type in the SQL and it is sent to the database and executed. Within SQL*PLUS, however, it's necessary to end all your SQL statements with a semicolon, as demonstrated in Listing 18.1.

LISTING 18.1 SQL COMMANDS IN SQL*PLUS MUST BE TERMINATED WITH A SEMICOLON

```
SELECT movie_title
FROM Movies
WHERE movie_id IN (1, 2, 3)
ORDER BY movie_title;

MOVIE_TITLE
--------------------
Prince Kong
The Code Warrior
Vegetable House
```

The semicolon is required because commands entered into SQL*PLUS can span multiple lines, and it is necessary to have some marker to indicate when the command ends. In Listing 18.1 several subsets of the query could all be executed as queries by themselves, so it's necessary to have some indication of when the programmer wants to end the statement. For example, both of the following two statements are valid SQL:

```
SELECT movie_title
FROM Movies

SELECT movie_title
FROM Movies
WHERE movie_id IN (1, 2, 3)
```

If the semicolon were not required, SQL*PLUS would have no way of knowing when it should execute the command. If it simply waited for a valid statement to be entered, it would have executed both of those commands before the full command was even entered.

LOADING SQL*PLUS SCRIPTS

You can store both SQL statements and SQL*PLUS commands in external files and execute those files within SQL*PLUS. For example, you can store a number of commonly run queries in an external text file and then run it whenever you want from within SQL*PLUS using the start command. The start command accepts the name of the SQL*PLUS script file that you want to run as an argument. If your file ends with .sql, you don't need to include the extension when you load the file. To load a file named commands.sql, you can use the following command in SQL*PLUS:

```
start commands
```

If the file is called commands.txt, you would need to load it like this:

```
start commands.txt
```

As an example of how SQL files are used with SQL*PLUS, Listing 18.2 contains the contents of the commands.sql file, and in Listing 18.3, I show the SQL*PLUS session in which commands.sql is loaded and executed.

LISTING 18.2 THE commands.sql FILE

```
SELECT movie_title
FROM Movies
WHERE movie_id IN (3, 5, 7);

SELECT studio_name
FROM Studios
WHERE studio_id = 1;
```

LISTING 18.3 AN SQL*PLUS SESSION IN WHICH commands.sql IS RUN

```
SQL> start commands

MOVIE_TITLE
--------------------
SQL Strikes Back
Codependence Day
The Code Warrior


STUDIO_NAME
--------------------
Giant
```

THE login.sql SCRIPT

A special SQL script—login.sql—is executed when you load SQL*PLUS. SQL*PLUS first looks for the file in the current directory; if it can't find it there, it looks in the Oracle home directory. If login.sql isn't found in either of those places, Oracle assumes that it doesn't exist.

Tip 69 from
Rafe Colburn

The behavior of login.sql is a bit different from most settings files on UNIX systems. In most cases, UNIX programs look for settings files (such as .profile, .emacs, and others) in your home directory. SQL*PLUS looks for login.sql in the current directory. You should be sure that you're in the directory where you keep your login.sql file when you start SQL*PLUS, or have the system administrator put a systemwide login.sql file in the Oracle home directory.

In any case, you can save SQL*PLUS commands (or SQL statements for that matter) in your login.sql file, and they'll be executed automatically when SQL*PLUS loads.

EDITING SQL COMMANDS

You can edit the most recent command in SQL*PLUS by entering edit at the SQL> prompt. The current SQL statement will be loaded into a text editor for revision. On UNIX systems, the editor that is used is determined by the contents of the EDITOR environment variable. For example, if EDITOR is set to /bin/vi, the SQL statement is loaded into the vi editor. If you don't have the variable EDITOR set to anything, the command is loaded into line editor, ed. On Windows systems, when you type edit, the query loads in Notepad.

Tip 70 from
Rafe Colburn

To change the editor for Windows, you can enter the following command in SQL*PLUS:

DEFINE _EDITOR="C:\ACCESS~1\PROGRA~1\WORDPAD.EXE"

That command changes the editor to Wordpad. You can enter the path to the text editor of your choice, and for the remainder of that SQL*PLUS session, that editor will be used. To make the change permanent, you have to add the command to the login.sql. As an alternative to the EDITOR environment variable on UNIX, you can use DEFINE _EDITOR to provide the path to your editor of choice.

Figure 18.4 contains an example of an SQL*PLUS edit window; in this case, the editor is vi. Note that in the editor, the SQL command is not terminated by a semicolon. In that case, the command is followed by a / on a line by itself, which executes the current statement. To run the previous SQL statement again, you can enter / at the SQL prompt. The / command is also used to run the command that is stored after you save and close your editing session.

Figure 18.4
Editing an SQL statement from within SQL*PLUS.

SAVING SQL*PLUS OUTPUT TO A FILE

The spool command in SQL*PLUS is used to save the output of a query to a file (instead of displaying it on the screen). When you open a file using the spool command, all the output from SQL*PLUS will be sent to the spooled file until you turn spooling off again. To save the output from SQL*PLUS to a file named `queries.out`, the following command is used:

```
spool queries.out
```

Then, when you're ready to stop sending output to the file, you can use `spool off` to stop writing to the file. By default, everything displayed by SQL*PLUS is saved to the spool file. Consider the commands in Listing 18.4 and the contents of the `SQL*PLUS.out` file in Listing 18.5.

LISTING 18.4 COMMANDS THAT ARE SPOOLED TO AN OUTPUT FILE

```
spool SQL*PLUS.out;
SELECT studio_name
FROM Studios;
SELECT movie_title
FROM Movies
WHERE movie_id IN (1, 3, 5);
spool off;
```

LISTING 18.5 THE CONTENTS OF SQL*PLUS.out

```
SQL> SELECT studio_name
  2  FROM Studios;

STUDIO_NAME
- - - - - - - - - - - - - - - - - - -
Giant
MPM
FKG
Delighted Artists
Metaversal Studios

SQL> SELECT movie_title
  2  FROM Movies
  3  WHERE movie_id IN (1, 3, 5);

MOVIE_TITLE
- - - - - - - - - - - - - - - - - - -
Codependence Day
The Code Warrior
Vegetable House

SQL> spool off;
```

As you can see, the entire SQL*PLUS session is captured in the output file, with the exception of the initial spool command (which makes sense because spooling doesn't begin until after the command is executed).

In some cases, you may not want to include all the information captured by default in your spool files. For example, if you're creating an output file that will be used to share data in a table with others, you probably don't want to include all the SQL prompts, SQL statements, and other extraneous information in the file.

CONTROLLING OUTPUT PRESENTATION

A number of settings affect the presentation of the output in SQL*PLUS. One of the most important features is the capability to customize the line length and lines per page that SQL*PLUS uses when formatting your output. Three settings are used to control the size of the "pages" of data generated by SQL*PLUS. The linesize setting indicates how many characters should fit on a line of output, the pagesize variable indicates how many lines of output fit on a page, and the newpage setting indicates how many lines should be skipped between pages of output.

You've seen cases in this book in which columns of output were automatically wrapped so that they would fit on a page 80 characters wide. The Movies table contains more columns of output than will fit on an 80 column line, so when you select all the columns in the table at once, the output is wrapped to fit within the 80 column limit. Listing 18.6 demonstrates the appearance of SQL*PLUS output that is automatically wrapped.

LISTING 18.6 OUTPUT OF MORE THAN 80 CHARACTERS OF DATA PER LINE

```
SELECT *
FROM Movies
WHERE movie_id IN (1, 2)

MOVIE_ID MOVIE_TITLE          STUDIO_ID DIRECTOR_ID    GROSS     BUDGET
-------- -------------------- --------- ----------- --------- ---------
RELEASE_D
---------
       2 Prince Kong                  2          10                3.25
01-MAY-79

       1 Vegetable House              1           1        30        20
01-JAN-75
```

As you can see, the contents of the release date column and the heading for that column are automatically wrapped to make room for the entire record. By default, the pagesize in SQL*PLUS is 66 lines, and the newpage setting is 3; therefore, for every 66 lines of output, 3 blank lines are printed. The commands for changing these settings are presented in Listing 18.7.

LISTING 18.7 CHANGING THE PAGE SIZE SETTINGS FOR SQL*PLUS

```
set linesize 132
set pagesize 40
set newpage 2
```

You can also control which query output is presented when you execute a query using SQL*PLUS settings. The default presentation is displayed in Listing 18.8.

LISTING 18.8   THE DEFAULT PRESENTATION OF QUERY RESULTS IN SQL*PLUS

```
SELECT movie_title
FROM Movies;

MOVIE_TITLE
--------------------
Vegetable House
Prince Kong
The Code Warrior
Bill Durham
Codependence Day
The Linux Files
SQL Strikes Back
The Programmer
Hard Code
The Rear Windows

10 rows selected.
```

The name of the column in the select list is included in the query results, as is a note indicating how many rows were returned by the query. You can turn off query headings using the `heading` setting and turn off the query comments using the `feedback` setting. To turn off both settings, the following code is used:

```
set feedback off
set heading off
```

After the headings and feedback are turned off, the query from Listing 18.8 is relieved of the extraneous information, as demonstrated in Listing 18.9.

LISTING 18.9   QUERY RESULTS AFTER HEADINGS AND FEEDBACK ARE TURNED OFF

```
Vegetable House
Prince Kong
The Code Warrior
Bill Durham
Codependence Day
The Linux Files
SQL Strikes Back
The Programmer
Hard Code
The Rear Windows
```

CREATING REPORTS IN SQL*PLUS

In addition to general database querying tasks, SQL*PLUS can also be used create formatted reports based on the output of queries. Several commands are specifically designed to allow programmers to create headers and footers for these reports and to format the actual query results for presentation.

CREATING REPORT TITLES

Several commands can be used to create headers to go along with your queries. The first is the prompt command, which simply prints all the text after the command, just like the echo command in a UNIX shell or the print statement in many other languages. It's not necessary to enclose the text to be printed in quotation marks or any other delimiters. All the text after the command is printed, as shown in Listing 18.10.

LISTING 18.10   USING THE prompt COMMAND TO PRINT TEXT

```
SQL> prompt This is printed text.
This is printed text.
```

The ttitle and btitle commands are used to create titles for the top and bottom of each page in the report. The pagesize setting determines how often these headings appear because it determines how frequently a new page is started in a report. The titles are centered based on the setting in the linesize attribute. If the text following the ttitle command is 40 characters long and the linesize is set to 80, the title will begin in column 21 of the output. Unlike the prompt command, the btitle and ttitle commands require that the headings be enclosed in single quotation marks.

If you don't want the titles to be centered, you can specify the alignment for the titles as LEFT, CENTER, or RIGHT. The alignment for the header is specified within the btitle or ttitle commands, like this:

```
btitle right 'Copyright 1999'
```

You can also specify multiple strings and alignments from within a single btitle or ttitle command by interspersing the positioning parameters and the text strings to be used as titles, like this:

```
btitle left 'Proprietary and confidential' right 'Copyright 1999'
```

The two titles will appear on the same line, aligned to the left and to the right, respectively.

ALTERING DATA DISPLAY

You can use the column command to alter how the actual data in the query results is presented. As you already know, you can rename columns using the AS command in your SELECT statements. However, when you're using SQL*PLUS, the column command provides even more options for massaging the output of your queries. Three subcommands are used with the column command: heading, format, and the wrap setting.

The heading command is used to change the heading for a column. The format is as follows:

```
column movie_title heading 'Movie Title'
```

This isn't much different from using AS "Movie Title" within your query, but some advantages exist to using the column command in SQL*PLUS. The first is that you don't have to mix presentation information in your query with the data retrieval code. You can separate all your report formatting code into SQL*PLUS commands and keep your SQL statements strictly assigned to data retrieval. The second is that using the `column heading` command is a bit more flexible than AS. For example, by using the ¦ (pipe) character, you can embed a line feed in a column heading (this also works with the `ttitle` and `btitle` commands).

Tip 71 from *Rafe Colburn*	You can change the character used to signify a line feed in column headings and titles by using the `headsep` setting. For example: `set headsep #` causes SQL*PLUS to insert a line feed where a # appears in a title or column heading.

Thus, to insert a line feed in the heading for the `movie_title` column, you would use the following command:

```
column movie_title heading 'Movie¦Title'
```

You can also alter the format of the data in the columns using the `column` command. In this case, the `column format` command is used. Basically, the `column format` command indicates how wide the column should be and which type of data the column contains. To limit the `movie_title` column to a width of 10 columns, the following command is used:

```
column movie_title format a10
```

The a indicates that the column contains alphanumeric data, and the 10 specifies the number of columns of output. You can also specify formats for numeric data by providing placeholders for all the digits that should be displayed, like this:

```
column budget format 990.00
```

A 0 indicates that a digit should always appear in that column (if no value exists for that column, a zero is inserted even though it is not significant), and a 9 is used to indicate that the digit in that place should be included. If no value exists for that column, the digit is omitted.

Finally, you can set how the characters in a column are wrapped if the value in the column is too wide to fit into a single line in the format provided. The default setting wraps any text that will not fit within the format onto the next line of output. If the format is set to a10 and the value is 13 characters long, the first 10 characters will appear on the first line, and the next three will appear on the second line. The two optional settings for word wrapping are `word_wrapped` and `truncate`. To change the setting, the following command is used:

```
column movie_title truncate
```

The `word_wrapped` setting wraps text that is too long for the field, but unlike the default setting, it breaks the text between words rather than placing the extra characters on the next line. The `truncate` setting simply drops any characters that will not fit within the specified format. If the format is a10 and the value in the `movie_title` field is `'The Code Warrior'`, then `'The Code W'` will be displayed.

You can place all the `column` settings for a particular column on a single line. For example, all the settings for the `movie_title` could be placed on one line in the following manner:

```
column movie_title heading 'Movie Title' format a10 truncate
```

At this point, you've seen enough formatting commands to create an example. When you create a report, you set up the formatting commands, and then you run the query that provides the data for the report. I'm going to place both the formatting commands and the query in a single file called `example_report.sql`. The contents of this file are in Listing 18.11, and the report itself is in Listing 18.12.

LISTING 18.11 THE `example_report.sql` FILE

```
prompt Report generated by Rafe Colburn
ttitle 'Movie Revenue Report'
btitle '(Confidential)'

column movie_title heading 'Movie|Title' format a10 truncate
column budget heading 'Budget|(in millions)' format 990.00
column gross heading 'Gross|(in millions)' format 990.00
column profit heading 'Profit|(in millions)' format 990.00

set linesize 75

SELECT movie_title, budget, gross, gross - budget AS profit
FROM Movies;
```

LISTING 18.12 THE REPORT GENERATED BY `example_report.sql`

```
SQL> start example_report
Report generated by Rafe Colburn
Input truncated to 12 characters

Thu May 20                                              page    1
                      Movie Revenue Report

Movie              Budget          Gross        Profit
Title         (in millions) (in millions) (in millions)
----------    ------------- ------------- -------------
Vegetable            20.00         30.00         10.00
Prince Kon            3.25
The Code W           10.30         17.80          7.50
Bill Durha           10.10
Codependen           15.00         30.00         15.00
The Linux            22.20         17.50         -4.70
                              (Confidential)


Thu May 20                                              page    2
                      Movie Revenue Report

Movie              Budget          Gross        Profit
Title         (in millions) (in millions) (in millions)
----------    ------------- ------------- -------------
```

continues

LISTING 18.12 CONTINUED

```
SQL Strike         5.00        10.00        5.00
The Progra        50.00        45.30       -4.70
Hard Code         77.00        30.00      -47.00
The Rear W        50.00        17.50      -32.50


                        (Confidential)


10 rows selected.
```

Next, I'll quickly go through the steps in the example_report.sql file. First, I print out the message 'Report generated by Rafe Colburn', and then I set the bottom and top titles for the report. After that, I set up the formatting for each of the columns returned by the query, including a virtual column I created using an expression and AS. Line breaks are present in all the column headings, and I've set up formats for each of the columns. The numeric columns allow three digits to the left of the decimal and always print two digits to the right of the decimal (even if they are zero). The format for the movie title is set to truncate.

After the formats are set up, I set the linesize to 75 (instead of the default of 80) and enter the query. The query selects three columns from the Movies table and creates a virtual column called profit, which contains the result of the movie's budget subtracted from the movie's gross.

OTHER DATA MANIPULATION COMMANDS

If you want to subdivide your report into sections based on the values in a particular field, you can use the break on command to do so. The break on command works in conjunction with an ORDER BY clause in the query that generates the report, and it divides the report whenever the value in the column specified in the break on command changes. This behavior enables you to clearly group items within your reports. The syntax for the break on command is

```
break on column [duplicate] skip number
```

In the break on command, you must specify a column, which corresponds to the first column specified in the ORDER BY clause in the query used with the report. The number in the query indicates how many lines should be inserted between each group created with the break on command. Optionally, you can insert the duplicate keyword in the break on command. When duplicate is present, each distinct value in the column supplied to break on will be displayed on every row of the report. By default, when you create a report that uses break on, the value in the column in the break on statement will be displayed only on the first row in which it appears.

Associated with the break on command is compute sum, which is used to add up all the values in a particular column for each group and print them. It is different than combining the GROUP BY clause and an aggregate function because the results include all the individual records in the results in addition to the subtotals. The syntax for compute sum is as follows:

compute sum of *column* on *break_on_column*

To use the `compute sum` command, you must specify two columns: the one containing the values that should be added up and the column in which the results of the query are grouped. Thus, to break down a query on `studio_id` and add up all the budgets for each studio, the following `compute sum` command is used:

compute sum of budget on studio_id

Now you'll look at a more advanced example. I'm going to extend the SQL*PLUS code in Listing 18.11 by summing the `gross` and `budget` columns as well as the `profit` virtual column. I'm also using a joining query to get the studio name for each movie, and I'm breaking the records on the studio name. Listing 18.13 contains the new report code, `new_report.sql`, and the report itself is included in Listing 18.14.

LISTING 18.13   THE new_report.sql SQL*PLUS SCRIPT

```
prompt Report generated by Rafe Colburn
ttitle 'Movie Revenue Report'
btitle '(Confidential)'

column movie_title heading 'Movie¦Title' format a10 truncate
column budget heading 'Budget¦(in millions)' format 990.00
column gross heading 'Gross¦(in millions)' format 990.00
column profit heading 'Profit¦(in millions)' format 990.00
column studio_name heading 'Studio' format a10 truncate
break on studio_name skip 2
compute sum of budget on studio_name
compute sum of gross on studio_name
compute sum of profit on studio_name

set linesize 75
set pagesize 35

SELECT studio_name, movie_title, budget, gross, gross - budget AS profit
FROM Movies, Studios
WHERE Movies.studio_id = Studios.studio_id
ORDER BY studio_name;
```

PART
VI
CH
18

LISTING 18.14   THE OUTPUT OF THE new_report.sql SCRIPT

```
Report generated by Rafe Colburn
Input truncated to 21 characters

Thu May 20                                                  page    1
                        Movie Revenue Report

           Movie            Budget         Gross        Profit
Studio     Title        (in millions) (in millions) (in millions)
---------- ---------- ------------- ------------- -------------
Delighted  Bill Durha        10.10
           SQL Strike         5.00         10.00          5.00
```

continues

LISTING 18.14   CONTINUED

```
           The Progra      50.00        45.30         -4.70
**********              ------------  ------------  ------------
sum                        65.10        55.30          0.30


FKG        The Code W      10.30        17.80          7.50
           Hard Code       77.00        30.00        -47.00
**********              ------------  ------------  ------------
sum                        87.30        47.80        -39.50


Giant      Vegetable       20.00        30.00         10.00
           Codependen      15.00        30.00         15.00
           The Rear W      50.00        17.50        -32.50
**********              ------------  ------------  ------------
sum                        85.00        77.50         -7.50


MPM        Prince Kon       3.25
           The Linux       22.20        17.50         -4.70
**********              ------------  ------------  ------------
sum                        25.45        17.50         -4.70



                      (Confidential)

10 rows selected.
```

As you can see, the sums for each studio are included in the results of the query. You can also include the grand totals for the report by including on report in your break on command, like this:

```
break on studio_name skip 2 on report
```

You can then add compute sum lines for any of the columns for which you want to compute the aggregate sum for the entire report, as follows:

```
compute sum of budget on report
compute sum of gross on report
compute sum of profit on report
```

After those lines are added, the following rows are appended to the previous report:

```
                      ------------  ------------  ------------
sum                        262.85       198.10        -51.40
```

ORACLE SYSTEM VIEWS

Like most high-end databases, Oracle stores all its configuration information within tables stored in the database. All the user information, the schema of all the tables in the databases, and all the other configuration is stored within the system tables. To provide access to all this information, several views are included with Oracle that allow you to see the contents of these tables. There's not enough room in this chapter to cover all the system tables and views provided with an Oracle database, so I'm just going to cover the ones that you're likely to use.

Tip 73 from	To get a list of the column names and datatypes for a particular table, you can use the DESC command in SQL*PLUS. For example, to retrieve the schema of the Studios table, the following command is used:
Rafe Colburn	

```
DESC Studios
```

and the results are:

```
Name                                      Null?      Type
---------------------------------------   --------   ----
STUDIO_ID                                 NOT NULL   NUMBER
STUDIO_NAME                                          VARCHAR2(20)
STUDIO_CITY                               NOT NULL   VARCHAR2(20)
STUDIO_STATE                              NOT NULL   CHAR(2)
```

As you work your way through this section of this chapter, you might find it useful to use the DESC command to view the structure of the system tables.

Basically, three major groups of system views reside in an Oracle database: ALL views, DBA views, and USER views. Other views also exist that don't fall into these groups, but the vast majority of them do. All three of the groups contain the same basic views; the only difference between them is the subset of rows from the database that they include.

DBA views contain information on all the objects that exist within the instance. For example, DBA_TABLES contains the specifications for every table in the instance. To issue queries against DBA views, the user must have the SELECT_ANY_TABLE privilege, which is generally granted only to users with DBA access. All the DBA views begin with the prefix DBA. I'm not going to discuss DBA views in this chapter because they're generally accessible only to system administrators. For programming tasks, the ALL and USER views are more interesting, anyway.

ALL views include all the objects that are accessible by the current user, including objects owned by other users, but that can be used by the current user. USER views contain only those objects that are actually owned by the current user. The ALL_TABLES view contains all the tables to which the user has access; the USER_TABLES view contains all the tables owned by the current user.

In Table 17.1, I list some of the important system views that you might find useful. I'm going to list them all with the USER prefix, but remember that they can all be used with the

DBA and ALL prefixes as well; the only thing that changes is the scope of the objects that are included.

TABLE 17.1 COMMONLY REFERENCED SYSTEM VIEWS IN ORACLE

View	Description
USER_CATALOG	Lists all the objects owned by the user: tables, views, sequences, and synonyms.
USER_CONSTRAINTS	Constraint definitions on tables owned by the user.
USER_DEPENDENCIES	Dependencies between objects owned by the user. Foreign key relationships between tables created using REFERENCES are accessible through this table.
USER_INDEXES	Indexes on tables owned by the user.
USER_LOBS	Large objects in tables owned by the user. It contains CLOBs, BLOBs, and NCLOBs, but not BFILEs because they're external to the database.
USER_ROLE_PRIVS	Roles that have been granted to the current user.
USER_SEQUENCES	Sequences owned by the current user.
USER_SOURCE	The source code to all stored procedures owned by the current user.
USER_SYNONYMS	Synonyms belonging to the current user.
USER_TABLES	Tables owned by the current user.
USER_TRIGGERS	Triggers owned by the current user.
USER_USERS	Various information about the current user, including login ID, date of creation for the account, expiration date for the account, and so on.
USER_VIEWS	Views owned by the current user.

USING SYSTEM VIEWS

Because system views are the only source of information on objects stored in the database, if you don't remember what you called a table or which views you've created, you must consult the system tables. For example, to find all the tables that belong to you, you can use the query in Listing 18.15.

LISTING 18.15 RETRIEVING THE TABLES OWNED BY THE CURRENT USER

```
SELECT DISTINCT table_name
FROM User_Tables

TABLE_NAME
------------------------------
ARTICLES
ARTICLE_KEYWORDS
CITY_STATE
EXAMPLE
KEYWORDS
```

```
LOCATIONS
MOVIES
PEOPLE
SOME_NAMES
SORTME
STOCKPRICE
STUDIOS
STUDIOS_COPY
TEMPERATURES
TEST
UNIONS
USER_KEYWORDS
```

Notice that I used the DISTINCT keyword in my query. When you're selecting a list of tables from User_Tables, this isn't necessary because one row exists per table. On the other hand, some tables include more than one row per object. For example, User_Source includes one row for every line of source code in your stored procedures. So if you just want to get a list of packages you own, the DISTINCT operator is necessary.

You can also use queries against the system tables in your programs to automatically generate SQL code. For example, I was working on a project that involved calling a number of stored procedures written in Oracle PL/SQL. I wrote a program in Perl that connected to the database, queried the ALL_SOURCE system view, and retrieved the arguments passed by the procedures. The Perl program then generated the code necessary to call those stored procedures. Over the course of the project, the program saved me a lot of manual labor.

PART

VI

CH

18

Note

> Several tools are available that will connect to an Oracle database and extract information from the system views when you're writing database applications. For example, the Tool for Oracle Application Developers, or TOAD, automatically builds a list of tables, views, and other objects belonging to the user. It also enables users to enter and run queries and view the results within the application. More information is available at http:// www.toadsoft.com. TOAD is just one of many tools that make it easier to work with Oracle; if you do a lot of Oracle development, you should investigate them.

SEQUENCES

Most databases provide some means of generating values for use as the primary key for a table. In many cases, these are called *autoincrementing fields*. Oracle handles this task a bit differently from most databases. Rather than requiring that a special datatype be assigned to a particular column and incrementing the value in that column when rows are inserted, Oracle provides *sequences*, which are just counters that are incremented whenever the next value is selected from them.

The syntax for creating a sequence is as follows:

```
CREATE SEQUENCE sequence_name
INCREMENT BY num
START WITH num
```

Each sequence is given a name, an amount by which the sequence is incremented every time the next value is selected from it, and a number where the sequence starts. Therefore, to create a sequence for the studio_id field in the Studios table, the statement in Listing 18.16 is used.

LISTING 18.16   CREATING A NEW SEQUENCE

```
CREATE SEQUENCE studio_id_seq
INCREMENT BY 1
START WITH 100
```

```
Sequence created.
```

After the sequence has been created, a new unique value from it can be extracted by using the *sequence_name*.NextVal construct. From this point forward, when we insert rows into the Studios table, the ID will be taken from the sequence, as shown in Listing 18.17. The row that was inserted is included in Listing 18.18.

LISTING 18.17   INSERTING A NEW ROW CONTAINING A VALUE FROM A SEQUENCE

```
INSERT INTO Studios
VALUES
(studio_id_seq.NextVal, 'Some Studio', 'Houston', 'TX')
```

```
1 row created.
```

LISTING 18.18   RETRIEVING A ROW WITH AN ID TAKEN FROM A SEQUENCE

```
SELECT *
FROM Studios
```

STUDIO_ID	STUDIO_NAME	STUDIO_CITY	ST
1	Giant	Los Angeles	CA
2	MPM	Burbank	CA
4	FKG	Apex	NC
3	Delighted Artists	Austin	TX
5	Metaversal Studios	Los Angeles	CA
100	Some Studio	Houston	TX

As you can see, the last row in the Studios table is the one inserted in Listing 18.17. The sequence was just created, so the ID contains the value the sequence started with. The next row inserted with studio_id_seq.NextVal as the ID will have an ID of 101, and so on. It's important to note that sequences are not bound to any particular table or column in a database. I could use the same sequence to generate the primary keys for every table in the database if I chose to do so. Anytime studio_id_seq.NextVal is referenced, the next value will be pulled from the sequence, no matter where it is used.

Tip 74 from
Rafe Colburn

Sequences yield their next value and are incremented any time their `NextVal` attribute is referenced. Thus, a query such as

```
SELECT studio_id_seq.NextVal
FROM Dual
```

will return the next value from the sequence and increment it (that ID will be lost because it wasn't assigned to a record). This is very useful if you want to know the ID for a row that you are inserting. You can select the next value from the sequence, store it in a variable, and then insert the value from that variable into the `INSERT` statement when you're ready to create the record. This is a feature that standard autoincrementing fields don't provide.

You can also retrieve the current value in a sequence using the `CurrVal` attribute, after selecting the first `NextVal` from the sequence. (You can't select the current value before a `NextVal` is retrieved because no current value exists before the first value has been retrieved.) When you use `CurrVal` (as shown in Listing 18.19), the value from the sequence generated the last time `NextVal` was used is returned, and the sequence is not incremented.

LISTING 18.19   SELECTING THE CURRENT VALUE FROM A SEQUENCE

```
SELECT studio_id_seq.NextVal
FROM Dual

NEXTVAL
----------
       101

SELECT studio_id_seq.CurrVal
FROM Dual

CURRVAL
----------
       101
```

PART

VI

CH

18

SYNONYMS

Synonyms provide a simple means by which users can use tables and views belonging to other users as though they were part of the user's own name space. For example, suppose I have two users, Peter and Paul, and they are both allowed to access all the tables belonging to either of them. If Peter has a table named `Movies` and Paul wants to execute a query against that table, he must reference it like this:

```
SELECT *
FROM Peter.Movies
```

If Paul uses Peter's `Movies` table a lot, he can create a synonym for the table in his own name space. A synonym is just a pointer to a table or a view owned by another user, and it eliminates the need to prepend the name of the user who owns the table to the table name. To create a synonym in Paul's namespace for `Peter.Movies`, the following SQL statement is used:

```
CREATE SYNONYM Movies FOR Peter.Movies;
```

After the synonym is created, Paul can query the `Movies` table in his own tables pace and retrieve rows from `Peter.Movies`. Synonyms can be created between different databases as well as between different users. Any database that can be accessed by the user can be the target of a synonym.

Users with DBA privileges can create public synonyms. A public synonym is like a normal synonym, except that the synonym belongs to the local name space of every user. If the DBA creates a public synonym to `Peter.Movies`, like this:

```
CREATE PUBLIC SYNONYM Movies FOR Peter.Movies
```

all the users in the database can access the table as though it is part of their own namespace. This is particularly useful when the DBA wants to import tables from another database into the local database for all users.

ORACLE DATA TYPES

A complete list of data types supported by Oracle is included in Table 17.2.

TABLE 17.2 ORACLE DATA TYPES

Data Type	Description
char(size)	A character field of fixed size. If the data in the field does not consume the capacity of the field, the value in the field is padded with blanks until the field is full.
date	Stores dates and times from Jan 1, 4712 BC to Dec 31, 4712 AD (in Oracle 8I, the maximum date supported is Dec 31, 9999 AD).
decimal	A synonym for the number data type, it does not allow the field size to be specified.
float	A synonym for the number data type.
integer	A numeric data type that does not support decimal values.
integer(size)	An integer *size* characters wide. It is important to remember that *size* is the physical width of the field in characters, not the number of bytes of memory the number can consume.
long	A large character object up to 2 gigabytes in size, similar to a `clob`.
long raw	A large binary object that can hold up to 2 gigabytes of data, similar to a `blob`.
long varchar	A synonym of `long`.
mlslabel	4-byte representation of a secure operating system label.

Data Type	Description
number	The base numeric data type in Oracle. Holds numbers up to 40 digits, excluding the decimal and sign.
number(*size*)	A number data type of a specified size.
number(*size*, *p*)	A number data type of a specified size and precision.
number(*)	A synonym of number.
smallint	A synonym of number. Can hold floating point data despite its name.
raw(*size*)	Stores up to *size* bytes of binary data. The maximum size is 255.
raw mlslabel	Secure operating system label in binary format.
rowid	Uniquely identifies all rows in Oracle tables. A pseudocolumn with this name and datatype is actually part of every table.
varchar2(*size*)	A basic variable-length character field that can have a size of up to 4,000 characters.
varchar(*size*)	The basic varchar type is deprecated in Oracle, having been superseded by varchar2.
blob	A binary object up to 4 gigabytes in size.
clob	A character object up to 4 gigabytes in size.
nclob	A character object that supports multibyte character sets up to 4 gigabytes in size.
bfile	A pointer to a binary file that resides in the file system.

PART

VI

CH

18

ORACLE RESOURCES ON THE WEB

When you're looking for Oracle information on the Web, the first place you should turn is the Oracle home page, at http://www.oracle.com. Like most company Web pages, the Oracle home page is designed mainly as a vehicle for disseminating marketing information, but it does have detailed information on Oracle's products and provides contact and support information for Oracle.

However, when you're looking for technical information, you'll probably have better luck if you go straight to the Oracle Technology Network home page at http://technet.oracle.com. Not only can you get downloadable versions of Oracle's software from the site, but you can also find full online versions of all the Oracle documentation and other information useful to developers. The only catch is that free registration is required.

Oracle also posts a couple of its publications online. Oracle Magazine is available at http://www.oramag.com, and Oracle Internet Developer can be found at http://www.oracle.com/ideveloper.

If you want to get past the Oracle company line, you may find some other Web sites useful. The Underground Oracle Frequently Asked Questions Web site contains tons of useful information; it can be found at http://www.orafaq.org. The site has a particularly useful set of links, which includes a list of Oracle user groups around the world and a number of Internet mailing lists for Oracle developers. The list of links is at http://www.orafaq.org/faqlink.htm.

Finally, if you need to get an Oracle-related question answered quickly, you might consider turning to one of the Oracle Usenet groups. Three main groups are related to technical discussions of Oracle:

- comp.databases.oracle.misc
- comp.databases.oracle.server
- comp.databases.oracle.tools

IN THE REAL WORLD

Oracle is the most-used relational database in the world. A Dataquest report from March 1999 put Oracle's market share on Windows NT at 46.1 percent of the market and its market share on UNIX at 60.9 percent. Because of Oracle's popularity, most database applications that are sold are built to work with Oracle, no matter which other databases they support. Nearly all "enterprise class" software has Oracle support built in, and Oracle has as good a reputation for scalability and stability as anyone in the database market.

As I said at the beginning of the chapter, one of Oracle's main advantages is that its database runs on many platforms, and more importantly, the platform on which the database is running is transparent to applications that communicate with the database server. Oracle takes care of all the data storage issues and also communicates with applications using standard protocols over a network. As long as the underlying operating system supports the appropriate protocol, Oracle is able to use it to communicate with applications running on other servers.

Oracle is known as the database industry leader in terms of capabilities, but not necessarily in terms of value. The bottom line is that Oracle is extremely expensive—at least in comparison to moderately priced products such as Microsoft SQL Server. Oracle also utilizes a Byzantine pricing structure along the lines of those that most enterprise application vendors have adopted, so it is impossible to discuss how much Oracle will cost (unless you're an Oracle sales representative, I assume).

Licenses for lower-end Oracle installations can be purchased online through Oracle's online store at

http://oraclestore.oracle.com

If your database needs are not particularly demanding, you may want to check out the offerings at the online store before negotiating with an Oracle salesperson.

After you've purchased the Oracle database server and all the required components and support, you have to get the server up and running—and keep it that way. There's a reason why Oracle database administrators are some of the highest paid people working in the computer industry. Oracle is extremely complex. Despite the fact that Oracle's database is very stable, keeping the database running at peak efficiency is not an easy job.

In some ways, it's not fair to compare Oracle to databases such as Microsoft SQL Server in terms of cost of administration because of Oracle's capability to scale to handle larger tasks. Oracle databases can be used for tasks that are far more demanding than many other databases, and thus you're faced with keeping a careful eye on an Oracle database or leaving the task undone. Oracle isn't alone at the top of the database industry in terms of scalability, but it is one member of a very small group.

Deciding which database to adopt, particularly when the requirements dictate solutions in the price range of Oracle, is generally beyond the discretion of the humble database application developer. Therefore, the vast majority of the people writing applications that work with Oracle didn't choose the database; this is true of most database platforms. The cost of switching from one relational database vendor to another is high, so the choice of which vendor to use is generally made for the long term.

CHAPTER **19**

Microsoft SQL Server and Sybase Adaptive Server

In this chapter

Microsoft SQL Server and Sybase Adaptive Server both sprang from the same roots—a technology partnership between Microsoft and Sybase that began in 1987 and yielded the Sybase DataServer product. The Microsoft-Sybase partnership ended in 1993, but the two companies had shared database technology long enough that Transact-SQL remains the query language shared by the databases from both companies. Now, even though both companies have released several versions of their products since the termination of their relationship, the two versions of Transact-SQL are still very similar.

For database programmers, this is good news. If you learn Transact-SQL, you can program both Microsoft SQL Server and Sybase Adaptive Server installations with equal facility. Transact-SQL is also supported by Sybase's lower-end database, Adaptive Server Anywhere. Because the languages are shared among all these products, you can apply your skills when you're working on workgroup databases running Adaptive Server Anywhere, Microsoft SQL Server installations running on Windows NT servers, and high-end Sybase installations running on Windows NT or UNIX. Recently, Sybase even announced a free port of Adaptive Server to Linux, which means that you can build powerful database applications free of charge.

This chapter covers some of the features that are unique to Transact-SQL and explains some of the differences that exist between Microsoft's implementation of Transact-SQL in SQL Server and Sybase's implementation in Adaptive Server.

TRANSACT-SQL DATABASE TOOLS

As you know, Transact-SQL is supported by multiple products. The two main products that use Transact-SQL as their query language are Microsoft SQL Server and Sybase Adaptive Server. Additionally, support for Transact-SQL runs through the entire line of Sybase databases. I'll briefly discuss the tools that are included with these databases.

For Windows, Microsoft provides the SQL Enterprise Manager for administering and querying SQL Server. They also provide Microsoft Query, which is used to connect to ODBC data sources and build new SQL queries.

Sybase provides an application called SQL Central for performing administrative tasks and a program called ISQL for entering queries. Also, a command-line version of ISQL is used on computers running UNIX.

SQL ENTERPRISE MANAGER

SQL Enterprise Manager is an integrated tool that enables database administrators to perform all the functions necessary to manage a database through a single interface (shown in Figure 19.1). SQL Enterprise Manager can be run on a server, including the one where the database resides, or remotely on a workstation, and it can be used to administer several SQL Server databases at once. Users simply need to register all the servers that they are going to administer.

After a server has been registered (registration involves pointing the Enterprise Manager at the location of the server running the database and supplying the appropriate user ID and password), you can view and modify all the objects associated with the database, assuming you have the appropriate privileges to do so.

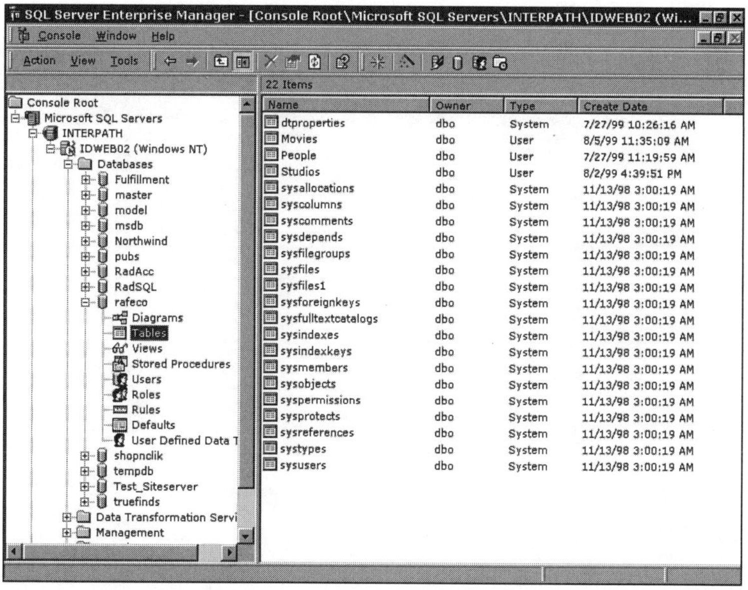

Figure 19.1
The SQL Enterprise Manager for Microsoft SQL Server.

SQL Enterprise Manager provides a hierarchical view of the database similar to the view of the file system on a computer that the Windows Explorer provides. You can drill down from the top level, which provides a list of databases on the server, to the individual object level, where the actual stored procedures, views, and tables are listed. You can then use the tools provided to modify, create, and remove those objects. For example, you can use the table editing interface (shown in Figure 19.2) to modify existing tables or to create new ones.

If you're comfortable with SQL (as you should be if you've made it this far into the book), you can use the built-in SQL query tool (called the SQL Server Query Analyzer in SQL Server 7.0) to enter queries and manipulate database objects instead of using the graphical interface.

SQL Enterprise Manager is also used to manage all the DBA-specific tasks associated with databases. It is used to manage the replication of data, data backups, and the allocation of physical drive space to the database. In this, it differs from many other database products, which split this functionality into several programs.

One nice feature of SQL Enterprise Manager is that it enables you to generate SQL scripts to perform most of the tasks that can be performed through the graphical interface. If you prefer, instead of creating a table, you can have the table generation dialog box create the

SQL to create that table instead. This enables you to save the scripts and reuse them later; thus, you can avoid using the GUI when you want to perform the tasks again or use them with a different SQL Server database. This capability is also helpful when you're learning SQL because it enables you to perform tasks through the graphical interface and then to view the SQL queries that are used to perform those tasks.

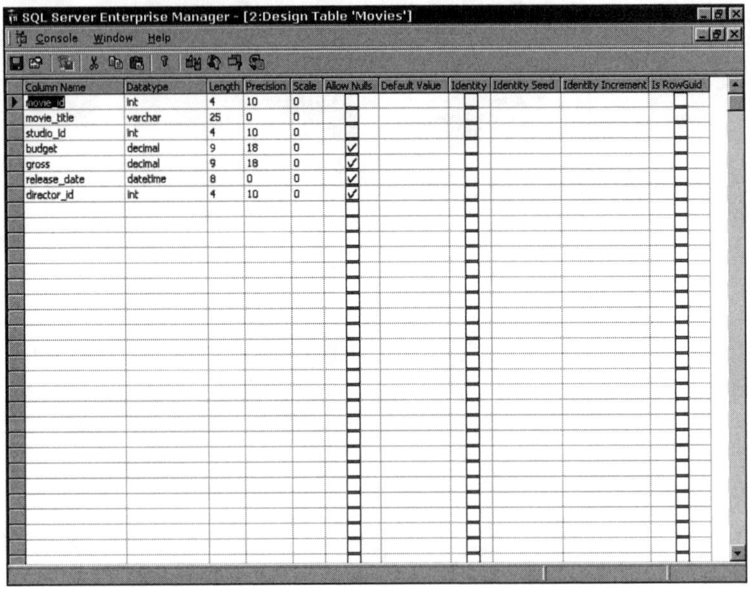

Figure 19.2
The Table Editor in
SQL Enterprise
Manager.

SQL SERVER QUERY ANALYZER

The SQL Server Query Analyzer enables database programmers to enter queries for a SQL Server database through an interactive interface and view the results. As a database programmer, chances are you'll spend most of your time in the Query Analzyer writing queries for use in your applications. Figure 19.3 shows the Query Analyzer.

You can launch the Query Analyzer from within SQL Enterprise Manager by selecting SQL Server Query Analyzer from the Tools menu. You can also launch it directly from the Start menu of a computer where the SQL Server tools are installed. The Query Analyzer connects to a particular database server; after your session begins, you need to point the analyzer to the correct database located on the server. A list of databases that reside on the server appears in a selection box in the tool; you can select the database you want to use from there. You can also use the USE command to specify which database your queries are to be directed toward, or you can specify the database explicitly within your SQL statements.

The Query Analyzer provides a split view, with one window into which you enter queries and another where results are displayed. To execute the query (or queries) entered in the Query window, you can click the Play button in the toolbar or press Control+E. All the queries in the window will be executed. If you select some subgroup of the queries entered in the Window, only those queries will be executed. As the queries are executed, the results are displayed in the Results window.

Figure 19.3
The SQL Server Query Analyzer.

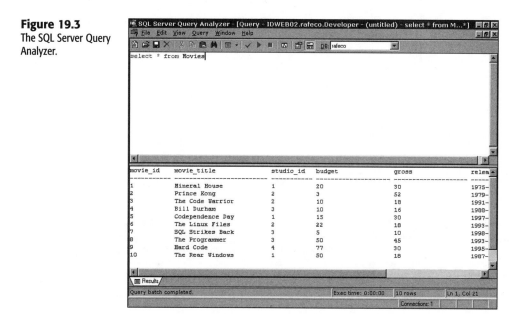

SQL CENTRAL

SQL Central is the administrative tool bundled with Sybase databases. It allows users to create and administer databases and to view all the objects in the databases. For example, Figure 19.4 shows the tree view for a SQL Anywhere database. As you can see, SQL Central provides access to all the objects native to a database from this interface.

Much like SQL Enterprise Manager, SQL Central provides a suite of tools for administering databases. In addition to creating, modifying, and deleting objects within the database that can be accessed using SQL queries, you can also use the packaged utilities to perform administrative tasks such as backing up or compressing the database, importing and exporting data, and creating or deleting entire databases. Figure 19.5 shows the utilities provided by SQL Central.

PART

VI

CH

19

Figure 19.4
The tree view of a database in SQL Central.

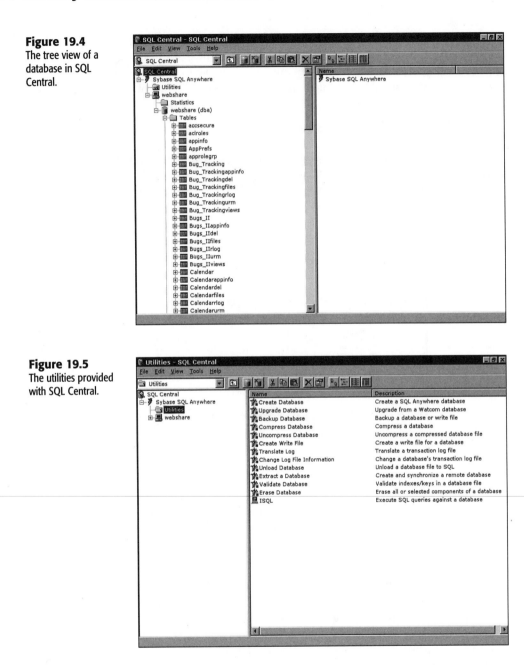

Figure 19.5
The utilities provided with SQL Central.

ISQL

ISQL is the standard query tool provided with Sybase databases. When you access databases from a computer running Windows, ISQL is a windowed application with a pane for displaying query results, a pane for entering the query, and a pane that displays execution statistics for the query. Figure 19.6 shows ISQL for Windows.

Figure 19.6
ISQL running on a
workstation running
Windows NT.

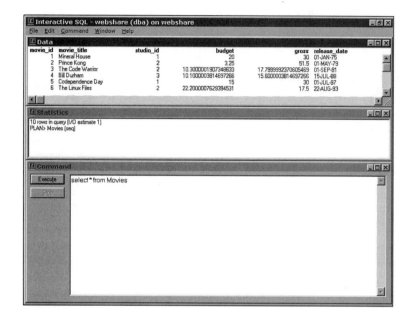

When you enter queries in the Windows version of ISQL, you can execute the queries by clicking the Execute button or by pressing the F9 key. The Data pane displays the results of the most recently executed SELECT statement, but the data is kept current. If you select all the rows from a table and then execute an UPDATE statement against the table, the data in the Data pane will be changed to reflect those changes. Similarly, if you INSERT or DELETE rows, the Data pane will be updated to reflect the results of the query. The actual outcome of the query will be displayed in the Statistics pane. For example, if an UPDATE statement affected 10 rows in a table, that will be indicated in the Statistics pane. The execution time for the query will also be displayed.

NAMING OBJECTS IN TRANSACT-SQL

Some rules govern how you can name user-created items in Microsoft and Sybase databases that support Transact-SQL. The first rule is that no items are allowed to have names more than 30 characters long; items in temporary tables should have names of 20 or fewer characters. In older databases, names of temporary items should be 12 characters or less.

You must also not use Transact-SQL reserved words as the names of objects in your database. For example, you can't call a table or column select, update, or group. The only punctuation allowed in object names in Transact-SQL is the underscore character (_).

SELECT ... INTO

SELECT ... INTO is a specialized version of the SELECT statement that is used to quickly duplicate a table. It's found only in Microsoft SQL Server. The INTO clause of the SELECT statement is used to supply the name of the new table into which the selected values will be copied. An example of a SELECT ... INTO statement appears in Listing 19.1.

LISTING 19.1   USING SELECT ... INTO TO COPY A TABLE

```
SELECT movie_title "title", budget "budget", gross "gross"
INTO New_Movies_Table
FROM Movies
```

Note

> To use SELECT ... INTO, you must make sure that the database option select into/bulkcopy is set to TRUE. You can turn on this option using the following command:
>
> EXEC sp_dboption database 'select into/bulkcopy', 'TRUE'

The example in Listing 19.1 is very simple; it retrieves some columns from one table and creates a new table consisting only of those columns. One thing you should notice about the statement is that the names of the columns in the new table follow the names of the columns in the existing table and are enclosed in double quotation marks. SELECT ... INTO does not use the AS keyword to rename columns.

After the statement in Listing 19.1 has been executed, you can issue queries against the new table. The system account can use SELECT ... INTO to create new permanent tables; other users can use only SELECT ... INTO to copy tables into tempdb.

The use of SELECT ... INTO is strongly discouraged for several reasons. In fact, the bottom line is that under no circumstances should it be used on a production database. When you use SELECT ... INTO, the statements that are executed (inserting records from the query results into the new table) are not logged in the database transaction log. Unfortunately, this brings about a number of problems. The biggest problem is that because these statements aren't logged, it corrupts the transaction log and thus requires that the database be fully backed up before transactions logged in the transaction log can be reversed. Because these statements aren't logged, users are also barred from using this statement from within a declared transaction.

The second big problem associated with SELECT ... INTO is that it creates locking issues. When you run SELECT ... INTO, the database or databases being queried are locked for the duration of the statement's execution. If you create a table in tempdb with SELECT ... INTO, both the database from which the records are being retrieved and tempdb will be locked for the duration of the operation.

SYSTEM FUNCTIONS

In other chapters, I've covered most of the functions supported by Transact-SQL. Many of the functions in Transact-SQL were covered in Chapter 12, "Handling Specific Types of Data." However, a group of system functions are used to retrieve data about the system on which the database is running. Some of them are also used for comparing data.

IDENTIFYING USERS

Several functions enable you to retrieve information about users, either the current user or a user whose name or ID is passed to the function as an argument. Functions that return the name or ID of the current user are CURRENT_USER, SESSION_USER, SYSTEM_USER, and USER; none of them require arguments. CURRENT_USER returns the username of the user executing the current command, and SESSION_USER returns the username in the current database of the user executing the command. SYSTEM_USER returns the login name of the current user as specified in the table mastersys..logins. If there is no login in the current database that is associated with the current user as created in the master database, the SESSION_USER function will return guest. USER also returns the user's name in the current database, just like SESSION_USER. The output of the four functions is demonstrated in Listing 19.2.S

LISTING 19.2 THE OUTPUT OF THE SESSION_USER, SYSTEM_USER AND CURRENT_USER, USER FUNCTIONS

```
SELECT SESSION_USER, CURRENT_USER, SYSTEM_USER, USER

-------  --------  ------------  -------
dbo      dbo       Developer     dbo

(1 row(s) affected)
```

In addition, four functions can be used to look up users in the user list for the current database or for the system database. USER_ID and SUSER_ID are used to look up a user ID given a username, and USER_NAME and SUSER_NAME are used to look up a username given a user ID. These functions are not supported by Microsoft SQL Server.

You can use the PROC_ROLE function to determine whether the current user has been assigned to a particular role. This function is only supported by Sybase because Microsoft SQL Server does not include support for roles. PROC_ROLE accepts one argument, the name of a role, and returns 1 if the current user has been assigned that role. If the user is not a member of the role, it returns 0. The syntax is as follows:

```
PROC_ROLE ("role_name")
```

IDENTIFYING A DATABASE OR SERVER

Several functions exist that are used to retrieve information about the current database or server, as well as functions used to retrieve the name or ID of a database, given the necessary identifying information.

The DB_ID and DB_NAME functions are used to return the ID and name of the current database, or if an argument is supplied, the name or ID of another database. DB_ID accepts a database name as its argument and returns the ID of that database. Likewise, DB_NAME accepts a database name and returns the ID associated with that name.

Two more general functions for identifying objects in the database (including databases themselves) are OBJECT_NAME and OBJECT_ID. Unlike DB_ID and DB_NAME, these functions will

PART
VI

CH
19

not work without arguments. The OBJECT_NAME function accepts an object ID, and optionally, a database ID (to specify which database the object ID provided resides in) as its arguments. OBJECT_ID accepts the name of the object for which the ID should be returned; the object owner can be prepended to the object name if it is necessary to identify the object. The two functions are called using the following syntax:

```
OBJECT_NAME (object_id, [database_id])
OBJECT_ID ([owner_name.]object_name)
```

An example of the usage of OBJECT_ID appears in Listing 19.3.

LISTING 19.3   USING OBJECT_ID TO RETURN THE ID FOR THE MOVIES TABLE IN THE DATABASE RAFECO

```
SELECT OBJECT_ID('rafeco..Movies')

- - - - - - - - - - -
469576711

(1 row(s) affected)
```

DATA COMPARISON FUNCTIONS

Several data comparison functions can be used within the WHERE clause or select list of a query. The values that are returned by the functions vary depending on how they were intended to be used. These functions are used to supplement the standard comparison operators that are available for use in WHERE clauses and that have specialized applications.

The first family of data comparison functions relates to null values. Three null-related functions are NULLIF, ISNULL, and COALESCE. The NULLIF function accepts two arguments, both of which can be any type of valid expression. If the two expressions are equal, it returns null; if they are not equal, the function returns the value of the first expression. Thus, a function call such as NULLIF(2 + 1, 5 - 2) returns null, and a function call such as NULLIF('a', 'b') returns a.

The ISNULL function also accepts two expressions as arguments: If the value of the first expression is null, the value of the second expression is returned; if the value of the first expression is not null, it is returned. The syntax for calling this function is as follows:

```
ISNULL (expression_to_test, value_to_return_if_null)
```

We'll look at an example of how ISNULL might be used in a query. When you write a query that returns a list of values for a report, and you don't want to leave a blank space where null values appear, it makes sense to use ISNULL to replace the null value with something that's more useful to users. For example, the query in Listing 19.4 prints 'unspecified' whenever a null value is encountered in the release_date field of the Movies table.

LISTING 19.4   USING ISNULL TO INCLUDE MESSAGES IN THE PRINTED OUTPUT OF A QUERY

```
SELECT movie_title, ISNULL(CONVERT(VARCHAR(25), release_date), 'unspecified')
FROM Movies

movie_title
-------------------------- --------------------------------------------------
Mineral House              Jan  1 1975 12:00AM
Prince Kong                May  1 1979 12:00AM
The Code Warrior           unspecified
Bill Durham                Jul 15 1988 12:00AM
Codependence Day           unspecified
The Linux Files            Aug 22 1993 12:00AM
SQL Strikes Back           unspecified
The Programmer             Apr 17 1993 12:00AM
Hard Code                  Apr 18 1995 12:00AM
The Rear Windows           Jul 11 1987 12:00AM

(10 row(s) affected)
```

Note that I used the CONVERT() function because the value used to replace null values is a string, not a date. The data type of the second argument to ISNULL must match the data type of the first argument. The third function is COALESCE, which accepts a list of expressions and returns the first non-null expression from the list. The syntax for coalesce is

```
COALESCE (expression, expression, expression, ...)
```

DATA VALIDATION FUNCTIONS

Several functions are used for data validation. They ensure that the expressions passed to them through an argument conform to a particular data type. These data validation functions are ISDATE, ISNUMERIC, and VALID_NAME.

The ISDATE function returns 1 if the expression passed to it could be converted to a DATE-TIME value, and 0 otherwise. The syntax is as follows:

```
ISDATE (expression)
```

Similarly, the ISNUMERIC function returns 1 if the expression passed to the function can be converted to a numeric data type without returning an error, and 0 otherwise. The syntax is

```
ISNUMERIC (expression)
```

The final data validation function is VALID_NAME, which tests the argument passed to it to determine whether it is a valid name for a Transact-SQL object. If the argument is indeed a valid name, the function returns 1: otherwise, it returns 0.

Tip 75 from
Rafe Colburn

For an object name to be valid in Transact-SQL, it must be less than 30 characters long and only use the characters that are permitted for names. As long as you stick with letters, numbers, and underscores in your names, you'll be fine. There is also a list of reserved words that cannot be used to name objects. For that list, consult your database documentation.

PART

VI

CH

19

CASE STATEMENTS

One flow control statement supported by Transact-SQL that is not present in other extended SQL implementations is the CASE clause. The CASE clause enables you to assign values to pseudocolumns in the select list based on the value of a particular column or expression. This is a very powerful construct because it enables you to process query results and alter the way they are displayed in real-time, as the query is processed.

For example, in Transact-SQL, Boolean values are generally stored in BIT fields, both for consistency and to conserve space. Rare is the case where you want to display the values stored in a BIT field in a report. Although the computer-savvy may understand that 1 means yes and 0 means no, the eyes of many users will glaze over when they see such notation. Without CASE, you would have to process the query results within your application to format the values in a BIT field for presentation. However, with the CASE construct, you can actually replace the value from the BIT field with one that is more suitable for the application, as shown in Listing 19.5.

LISTING 19.5 A CASE STATEMENT THAT REPLACES THE VALUE IN A BIT FIELD

```
SELECT person_fname, person_lname, person_union,
CASE person_union
WHEN 1 THEN 'Yes'
ELSE 'No'
END AS union_member
FROM People
```

person_fname	person_lname	person_union	union_member
Jeff	Price	0	No
Chuck	Peterson	1	Yes
Brandon	Brooks	0	No
Brian	Smith	0	No
Paul	Monk	0	No
Reece	Randall	1	Yes
Peter	Jong	0	No
Maggie	Davis	0	No
Becky	Orvis	1	Yes
Carol	Delano	1	Yes
Fran	Friend	0	No

```
(11 row(s) affected)
```

When the query results are displayed, the values in the person_union field are replaced by the results of the CASE construct. As you can see, the CASE is similar to a standard IF expression. If the value of person_union matches the value in the WHEN clause, 'Yes' is displayed. All other values (in the case of a BIT field, only 0) are funneled to the ELSE section of the statement. You should also note that you can add a column name to a CASE expression by placing an AS clause after the END keyword.

COMPOUND CASE STATEMENTS

The thing that makes CASE really useful is that you can include multiple WHEN clauses in your CASE constructs. For example, if the list of studios in the database is fixed, you could use a CASE expression instead of a join to insert the studio names in results selected from the Movies table, as shown in Listing 19.6.

LISTING 19.6   A COMPOUND CASE EXPRESSION

```
SELECT movie_title,
CASE studio_id
    WHEN 1 THEN 'Giant'
    WHEN 2 THEN 'MPM'
    WHEN 3 THEN 'Delighted Artists'
    WHEN 4 THEN 'FKG'
    WHEN 5 THEN 'Metaversal Studios'
    ELSE 'other studio'
    END
AS studio
FROM Movies

movie_title               studio
------------------------  -------------------
Mineral House             Giant
Prince Kong               MPM
The Code Warrior          MPM
Bill Durham               Delighted Artists
Codependence Day          Giant
The Linux Files           MPM
SQL Strikes Back          Delighted Artists
The Programmer            Delighted Artists
Hard Code                 FKG
The Rear Windows          Giant

(10 row(s) affected)
```

PART

VI

CH

19

In this case, the studio_id field for each record can match only one of the conditions in the CASE expression because all the conditions are based on equality. However, in some cases, you might want to pick up ranges of values using greater than or less than. The important thing to note in those cases is that the flow of execution of a CASE expression stops with the first matching condition. So, if the value being processed by the CASE expression matches the first of five conditions, the other four will be ignored.

Therefore, the order in which conditions are placed in a CASE statement is very important. We'll take a look at an example that uses the values in the budget column of the Movies table. Compare the query results in Listings 19.7 and 19.8.

LISTING 19.7   USING A COMPOUND CASE EXPRESSION WITH LESS THAN COMPARISONS

```
SELECT movie_title,
CASE
    WHEN budget < 50 THEN 'Pretty expensive'
    WHEN budget < 40 THEN 'Somewhat expensive'
    WHEN budget < 30 THEN 'Reasonable'
    WHEN budget < 20 THEN 'Low budget'
    WHEN budget < 10 THEN 'Dirt cheap'
    ELSE 'High dollar action movie'
    END
FROM Movies


movie_title
------------------------  ------------------------
Mineral House             Pretty expensive
Prince Kong               Pretty expensive
The Code Warrior          Pretty expensive
Bill Durham               Pretty expensive
Codependence Day          Pretty expensive
The Linux Files           Pretty expensive
SQL Strikes Back          Pretty expensive
The Programmer            High dollar action movie
Hard Code                 High dollar action movie
The Rear Windows          High dollar action movie

(10 row(s) affected)
```

LISTING 19.8   THE APPROPRIATE ORDER FOR LESS THAN COMPARISONS IN A CASE EXPRESSION

```
SELECT movie_title,
CASE
    WHEN budget < 10 THEN 'Dirt cheap'
    WHEN budget < 20 THEN 'Low budget'
    WHEN budget < 30 THEN 'Reasonable'
    WHEN budget < 40 THEN 'Somewhat expensive'
    WHEN budget < 50 THEN 'Pretty expensive'
    ELSE 'High dollar action movie'
    END
FROM Movies


movie_title
------------------------  ------------------------
Mineral House             Reasonable
Prince Kong               Dirt cheap
The Code Warrior          Low budget
Bill Durham               Low budget
Codependence Day          Low budget
The Linux Files           Reasonable
SQL Strikes Back          Dirt cheap
The Programmer            High dollar action movie
Hard Code                 High dollar action movie
The Rear Windows          High dollar action movie

(10 row(s) affected)
```

As you can see from the query results, the CASE expression in Listing 19.8 was structured correctly, and the one in Listing 19.7 was not. As soon as a matching condition is encountered in a CASE statement, the code within that condition is executed, and the remaining conditions are ignored. Therefore, if you have overlapping conditions, as we did in the example, you should place the most restrictive conditions before the less restrictive conditions.

CASE AND GROUP BY

You can use a CASE expression within the GROUP BY clause of a SELECT statement to categorize grouped values. For example, you can use the CASE expression from Listing 19.8 to categorize all the movies and use an aggregate function and the GROUP BY clause to extrapolate information from those categories. The query in Listing 19.9 calculates the average budget for each of the categories of movies created in Listing 19.8.

LISTING 19.9   USING CASE WITH GROUP BY

```
SELECT CASE
    WHEN budget < 10 THEN 'Dirt cheap'
    WHEN budget < 20 THEN 'Low budget'
    WHEN budget < 30 THEN 'Reasonable'
    WHEN budget < 40 THEN 'Somewhat expensive'
    WHEN budget < 50 THEN 'Pretty expensive'
    ELSE 'High dollar action movie'
    END,
AVG(budget)
FROM Movies
GROUP BY CASE
    WHEN budget < 10 THEN 'Dirt cheap'
    WHEN budget < 20 THEN 'Low budget'
    WHEN budget < 30 THEN 'Reasonable'
    WHEN budget < 40 THEN 'Somewhat expensive'
    WHEN budget < 50 THEN 'Pretty expensive'
    ELSE 'High dollar action movie'
    END

----------------------------  ----------------------------------------
Dirt cheap                     4.000000
High dollar action movie      59.000000
Low budget                    11.666666
Reasonable                    21.000000

(4 row(s) affected)
```

When you use CASE and GROUP BY in the same statement, the CASE statements must match exactly so that the categories created in the select list are mirrored in the GROUP BY clause.

USING CASE IN UPDATE STATEMENTS

The biggest advantage of CASE expressions is that they enable you to reduce the number of queries that you have to use for particular tasks. In cases where you might ordinarily have to write multiple queries with different WHERE clauses (and then perhaps reunite them using the

PART
VI
CH
19

UNION operator), you can use a single query and place the conditions that would ordinarily be used in the WHERE clause in a CASE expression.

Take UPDATE statements for example. If you wanted to update the gross revenues for the movies in the database to reflect the change in movie ticket prices over the years and compare them on equal footing, you need to multiply them by the factor that ticket prices have changed since the movie was released. Ticket prices might cost three times what they cost 20 years ago, and only 50 percent more than they cost five years ago. Without the CASE statement, you would need to write an UPDATE statement for every one of the date ranges to which a particular factor should be applied. Using a CASE statement, you can combine all these into a single UPDATE statement. An example of such an UPDATE statement appears in Listing 19.10.

LISTING 19.10   AN UPDATE STATEMENT THAT USES A CASE EXPRESSION

```
UPDATE Movies
SET budget = budget *
    CASE
        WHEN release_date < 'JAN 01 1970' THEN 3
        WHEN release_date < 'JAN 01 1980' THEN 2
        WHEN release_date < 'JAN 01 1985' THEN 1.5
        WHEN release_date < 'JAN 01 1990' THEN 1.25
        WHEN release_date < 'JAN 01 1995' THEN 1.1
        ELSE 1.0
    END

(10 row(s) affected)
```

SYSTEM STORED PROCEDURES

Both Sybase and Microsoft provide a library of built-in stored procedures with their databases to make life easier for programmers and database administrators. These procedures are generally used to modify data within system tables or retrieve data from them.

The stored procedures themselves fall into several categories: security-related procedures, remote-server procedures, user-defined error message procedures, data definition procedures, and system administration procedures.

This list includes some of the most commonly used system stored procedures; others are available. You can refer to your database documentation for information on the additional procedures. The arguments accepted by these stored procedures can also vary from database to database—and even from version to version. You should check your database documentation when you use these procedures to make sure that the syntax you use is up to date.

SECURITY-RELATED PROCEDURES

Security-related procedures are used to modify the access privileges for databases and users. They are used to view or modify the system tables that control the security privileges for the database.

sp_addalias

sp_addalias is used to allow one user to act as another user in the current database. For example, suppose I have a database named Movies and two users, peter and paul. peter is listed in the system database master.dbo.logins, but he does not have any access privileges to Movies. paul, on the other hand, is allowed to use the Movies database. By using the sp_addalias procedure, I can alias peter to paul, giving peter the same access rights to Movies as paul. The syntax for sp_addalias is as follows:

```
sp_addalias peter, paul
```

sp_addgroup

sp_addgroup is used to add groups to the database. Groups are used to hold a set of privileges; when a user is assigned to a group, all the privileges conferred to the group are automatically assigned to the user. After the group has been added, the GRANT and REVOKE commands can be used to assign privileges to the group or remove privileges from it. The syntax for sp_addgroup is

```
sp_addgroup group_name
```

sp_addlogin

sp_addlogin is used to create a new user account in the database. The user should be assigned a login name and a password. Optionally, you can assign the user a default language, a default database, and a full name. The syntax to call the procedure is

```
sp_addlogin login_name, password [, default_language] [, default_database] [,
full_name]
```

The syntax in SQL Server 7 for this procedure is

```
sp_addlogin [@loginame =] @login
[,[@passwd =] 'password'][sr]
[,[@defdb =] 'database']
[,[@deflanguage =] 'language'][sr]
[,[@sid =] 'sid']
[,[@encryptopt =] 'encryption_option']
```

sp_adduser

After a login has been created using sp_addlogin, you can use sp_adduser to add that login to the sysusers tables of databases. To add a user to a database, you call sp_adduser with the login name for the user, the name of the database to which they will be added, and optionally, the name of the group of which they will be a member. If a group is not specified, they will be added to the default group—public. The syntax is

```
sp_adduser login_name, database_username [, group_name]
```

sp_changedbowner

sp_changedbowner is used to change ownership of the current database to a new login name. It can use an optional argument, which is simply the word true, that indicates that all aliases and permissions for the current owner should be transferred to the new owner. The synxtax of the statement is

```
sp_changedbowner login_name [, true]
```

sp_changegroup

sp_changegroup is used to change the group to which a user is assigned. The group must first be created using the sp_addgroup procedure, of course. Because group assignments are specific to individual databases, the database username (not the login name) is used to change the user's group. The syntax is

```
sp_changegroup group_name, user_name
```

sp_dropalias

sp_dropalias is used to remove an alias created with sp_addalias. The alias for the specified login name is removed from the current database. The syntax is

```
sp_dropalias login_name
```

sp_dropgroup

sp_dropgroup is used to remove the specified group from the current database. The syntax is

```
sp_dropgroup group_name
```

> **Note**
>
> In Microsoft SQL Server 7, groups are replaced by roles, and this procedure is provided strictly for backward compatibility. The SQL Server 7 syntax is
>
> ```
> sp_dropgroup [@rolename =] 'role'
> ```

sp_droplogin

sp_droplogin is used to drop a login from the database. If the login is a user in any database, or if an alias for the login is in any databases, the user cannot be dropped. User IDs can be reused, so you might consider using sp_locklogin to disable logins instead of sp_droplogin. The syntax is

```
sp_droplogin login_name
```

sp_dropuser

sp_dropuser is used to remove a user from the current database. Users who own objects in the database cannot be dropped, nor can the owner of the database. Any aliases that point to the user being dropped are also dropped. The syntax is

```
sp_dropuser user_name
```

sp_helpgroup

sp_helpgroup is used to list all the groups in the current database or to list detailed information about a particular group. A list of groups is displayed if no argument is supplied; if a group name is supplied, the information about that group is displayed. The output of sp_helpgroup appears in Listing 19.11.

LISTING 19.11   USING sp_helpgroup

```
sp_db_owner

Group_name                Group_id Users_in_group              Userid
-----------------------   -------- -------------------------   ------
db_owner                  16384    dbo                         1

(1 row(s) affected)
```

sp_helpprotect

sp_helpprotect is used to display the permissions assigned to a particular object in the database. You can use sp_helpprotect to find out permissions for a user, a table, or for a user on a particular table. If no arguments are supplied, the permissions for the entire database are printed. The syntax is as follows:

```
sp_helpprotect [name [, username] [, "grant"
    [, "none" ¦ "granted ¦ "enabled" ¦ role]]
```

sp_helpprotect is available only in Sybase databases.

sp_helpuser

sp_helpuser returns a list of users in the current database if no argument is supplied. If a username is specified in an argument, information about that user is displayed. Listing 19.12 demonstrates both uses of sp_helpuser.

LISTING 19.12   USING sp_helpuser TO LIST USERS IN A DATABASE AND GET INFORMATION ABOUT A PARTICULAR USER

```
sp_helpuser

UserName    GroupName    LoginName               DefDBName     UserID SUserID
----------  -----------  ----------------------  ------------  ------ -------
dbo         db_owner     Developer               master        1      7
Developer   db_owner     NULL                    NULL          5      NULL
paul        public       BUILTIN\Administrators   master        7      NULL
peter       public       CARYDEV\sqlserver       master        6      6

sp_helpuser peter

UserName    GroupName    LoginName               DefDBName     UserID SUserID
----------  -----------  ----------------------  ------------  ------ -------
peter       public       CARYDEV\sqlserver       master        6      6
```

sp_password

sp_password is used to change the password for the login that calls the procedure. It accepts two arguments: the existing password for the login and the new password. The SA account can include a third parameter, a login name, to change the password for that user. If the SA user is changing the password for another login, the user's own password must be included as the first argument. The syntax for sp_password is

```
sp_password existing_password, new_password [, login_name]
```

REMOTE SERVER PROCEDURES

The remote server procedures are used to specify which remote servers are allowed to access the local server. They are also used to specify particular remote users that are allowed to access the local server. The following is a list of remote server procedures:

- sp_addremotelogin
- sp_addserver
- sp_dropremotelogin
- sp_dropserver
- sp_helpremotelogin
- sp_helpserver
- sp_remoteoption
- sp_serveroption

For more information on remote server procedures, you should consult your database documentation.

DATA DEFINITION PROCEDURES

Transact-SQL supports a large family of procedures for definition of database objects and for gathering information on objects within the database. The data definition procedures that are used to maintain referential integrity, such as sp_dropkey and sp_foreignkey, are no longer recommended in SQL Server 7. Instead, you should specify keys in the ALTER TABLE and CREATE TABLE statements that you use to create and alter tables.

sp_addtype

sp_addtype is used to add a user-defined datatype to the database. Each user-defined datatype requires a name, a physical datatype for the field, and if necessary, a length for the datatype. Numeric datatypes can also have a precision and a scale. If the datatype will contain autoincrementing numbers, the identity flag should be used. The nulltype flag is used to specify how the datatype handles null values. The three options are null, nonull, and "not null". The syntax of sp_addtype is

```
sp_addtype type_name,
physical_type [(length) ¦ (precision [, scale])]
[, "identity" ¦ nulltype]
```

sp_bindefault

sp_bindefault is used to bind a default value to a particular column or user-defined datatype. Before you can use sp_bindefault, you must create the defaults using the CREATE DEFAULT statement (discussed earlier in this chapter). The optional argument futureonly is used to indicate that only new rows inserted after the default is bound to a column will be assigned that value. Existing records will remain as they are. The syntax of sp_bindefault is

sp_bindefault default_name, object_name, futureonly

If you want to bind a default to a column, it should be specified using the table.column notation.

sp_depends

sp_depends is one of the most useful built-in stored procedures. When supplied with the name of an object, it returns a list of all the other objects that depend on it. It's particularly useful if you want to drop an object and need to know what other objects will either prevent it from being dropped or will break when it is dropped. The syntax for sp_depends is

sp_depends object_name

The object_name can refer to a table, view, stored procedure, or trigger.

sp_dropkey

sp_dropkey is used to remove a key defined using sp_commonkey, sp_foreignkey, or sp_primarykey. The syntax is

sp_dropkey keytype, table_name [, deptablename]

The keytype is primary, foreign, or common. The table_name is the table with which the key is associated, and deptablename is the name of the other table associated with a foreign or common key.

sp_droptype

sp droptype is used to remove a user-defined data type. If the user-defined data type being dropped is used within any existing objects, the data type cannot be dropped. The syntax is

sp_droptype type_name

sp_foreignkey

sp_foreignkey is used to create a foreign key relationship between two tables. It accepts as arguments the name of a table that contains the foreign key, the name of the table with the primary key that the foreign key should be linked to, and the name of the column (or columns) that are used as the primary key. The name of the primary key column (or columns) and the foreign key column (or columns) must be the same. The following is the syntax:

sp_foreignkey table_with_foreign_key, table_with_primary_key,
column [, column2]

sp_help

The `sp_help` procedure is used to gather information about an object in the database. If you use `sp_help` and specify a table name, it returns a list of columns in the table, along with other information about the table. It can also be used to get information about a view, a procedure, a trigger, or a user-defined datatype. The syntax is

```
sp_help object_name
```

sp_helpindex

`sp_helpindex` returns information about the indexes created on the specified table. The syntax for `sp_helpindex` is as follows:

```
sp_helpindex table_name
```

sp_helpjoins

`sp_helpjoins` is an interesting procedure that compares two tables or views and lists columns that are likely join candidates between the two. It checks for foreign keys, common keys, columns that share the same user-defined data type, and finally, columns with the same name and data type. Generally speaking, if you designed the database, this procedure isn't particularly useful because you already know about the columns that are good candidates for joins. Anyway, the syntax is

```
sp_helpjoins table, other_table
```

sp_helpkey

`sp_helpkey` reports information for all the keys associated with a particular table or view, or if no table or view is specified, for the entire database. The syntax is

```
sp_helpkey [table_name]
```

sp_helptext

`sp_helptext` is used to retrieve the source code for a compiled object, such as a stored procedure or trigger. The syntax is

```
sp_helptext [object_name]
```

sp_primarykey

`sp_primarykey` denotes a column (or group of columns) as the primary key for a table. The syntax is as follows:

```
sp_primarykey table_name, column [, column2 [, ...]]
```

sp_recompile

`sp_recompile` causes all stored procedures and triggers that depend on the specified table to be recompiled the next time they are executed. You would do this because when you compile a stored procedure (or other compiled object), the queries in the procedures are optimized. If you make changes to the table that could result in more efficient queries (such as adding indexes), you want to recompile the compiled objects that depend on that table to take advantage of the changes. The syntax is

```
sp_recompile table_name
```

sp_rename

sp_rename is used to change the name of a user-created object (such as a table or a stored procedure) or a user-defined data type. If you rename a column, you should prepend the old name with the table name and a dot, but not the new name. For example, to change the gross column in the Movies table to revenue, the following stored procedure call is used:

```
sp_rename Movies.gross, revenue
```

Any stored procedures that depend on a renamed object will still work until they are dropped and re-created. Unfortunately, they will still report the old name in query results. You can use sp_depends to find objects that depend on an object you are going to rename— if you want to go back and update the other objects that depend on it. The syntax for sp_rename is

```
sp_rename old_name, new_name
```

In SQL Server 7, the syntax for this procedure is

```
[@objname =] 'object_name',
[@newname =] 'new_name'
[, [@objtype =] 'object_type']
```

sp_spaceused

sp_spaceused returns the number of rows in the table specified, along with other statistics that deal with space consumption. If you do not specify a table name, the statistics for the entire database will be returned. If you include the flag 1, space information on the table's indexes will be included as well. The syntax is as follows:

```
sp_spaceused [table_name [, 1]]
```

The SQL Server syntax is:

```
[[@objname =] 'objname']
[,[@updateusage =] 'updateusage']
```

sp_unbindefault

sp_unbindefault removes a default value from a column or user_defined data type. The syntax is

```
sp_unbindefault [object_name, [futureonly]]
```

sp_unbindrule

sp_unbindrule is used to remove a rule from a column or user-defined data type. The syntax is

```
sp_unbindrule [object_name [, futureonly]]
```

PART

VI

CH

19

Other data definition procedures that I did not describe fully are

- `sp_commonkey`
- `sp_indsuspect`

TRANSACT-SQL DATA TYPES

Table 19.1 contains a complete list of data types supported by Microsoft SQL Server 6.5 and Sybase databases. Table 19.2 contains a list of data types supported by Microsoft SQL Server 7.0.

TABLE 19.1 DATA TYPES FOR MICROSOFT SQL SERVER 6.5 AND SYBASE DATABASES

Data Type	Description
`bit`	A single bit field that can hold 0 or 1.
`binary(n)`	A fixed-length field of n binary characters, with a maximum size of 255.
`char(n)`	A fixed-length character field n characters long (with a maximum length of 255).
`datetime`	A date between January 1, 1753 and December 31, 9999.
`dec (p, s)`	A floating-point number between -10^{38} and 10^{38}. p is the precision of the number: how many total digits it can hold. s is the scale: the number of digits to the right of the decimal it can hold.
`decimal`	A synonym of `dec`.
`double precision`	A floating-point number with a capacity that varies depending on the machine running the database server.
`float(precision)`	A floating-point number with a capacity that varies depending on the machine running the database server.
`int`	An integer between $-2,147,483,648$ and $2,147,483,647$ (note that `int` and `integer` are not the same data type).
`image`	A large binary field that can hold up to 2,147,483,647 bytes of binary data
`integer`	An integer between $-32,768$ and $32,767$.
`money`	A floating-point number with the range $-922,337,203,685,477.5808$ to $922,337,203,685,477.5807$.
`nchar`	A fixed-length multibyte character field n characters long (with a maximum length of 255).
`numeric`	A synonym of `dec`.
`nvarchar`	A variable-length multibyte character field up to n characters long. The maximum value of n is 255.
`real`	A floating-point number with a capacity that varies depending on the machine running the database server.
`smalldatetime`	A date between January 1, 1900 and June 6, 2079.

Data Type	Description
smallint	A synonym of integer.
smallmoney	A floating point number with the range: –214,748.3648 to 214,748.3647.
text	A large text field of up to 2,147,483,647 bytes.
tinyint	An integer between 0 and 255.
varbinary	A variable-length field of up to 255 binary characters, with a maximum length of 255.
varchar(n)	A variable-length character field up to n characters long. The maximum value of n is 255.

TABLE 19.2 DATA TYPES FOR MICROSOFT SQL SERVER 7.0

Data Type	Description
bit	A single bit field that can hold 0 or 1.
binary(n)	A fixed-length field of n binary characters, with a maximum size of 8,000 bytes.
char(n)	A fixed-length character field n characters long (with a maximum length of 8,000 characters).
cursor	A reference to a cursor.
datetime	A date between January 1, 1753 and December 31, 9999.
decimal (p, s)	A floating-point number between -10^{38} and 10^{38}. p is the precision of the number: how many digits total it can hold. s is the scale: the number of digits to the right of the decimal it can hold.
double precision	A floating-point number with a capacity that varies depending on the machine running the database server.
float(precision)	A floating-point number that ranges from –1.79E + 308 to 1.79E + 308.
int	An integer between –2,147,483,648 and 2,147,483,647 (note that int and integer are not the same data type).
image	A large binary field that can hold up to 2,147,483,647 bytes of binary data.
money	A floating-point number with the range –922,337,203,685,477.5808 to 922,337,203,685,477.5807.
nchar	A fixed-length Unicode character field n characters long (with a maximum length of 8,000 characters).
numeric	A synonym of decimal.
ntext	A Unicode text field with a capacity of 2,147,483,647 bytes.
nvarchar	A variable-length Unicode character field up to n characters long. The maximum value of n is 8,000 characters.
real	A floating point number that ranges from –3.40E + 38 to 3.40E + 38.

PART

VI

CH

19

continues

TABLE 19.2   CONTINUED

Data Type	Description
smalldatetime	A date between January 1, 1900 and June 6, 2079.
smallint	An integer between –32,768 and 32,767.
smallmoney	A floating-point number with the range –214,748.3648 to 214,748.3647.
text	A large text field of up to 2,147,483,647 bytes.
timestamp	A databasewide unique number.
tinyint	An integer between 0 and 255
uniqueidentifier	A globally unique number (GUID).
varbinary	A variable-length field of up to 8,000 bytes.
varchar(*n*)	A variable-length character field up to *n* characters long. The maximum value of *n* is 8,000 characters.

IN THE REAL WORLD

The fact that Transact-SQL is supported by two database makers provides me with the opportunity to discuss an important topic: portability versus functionality. Both Sybase and Microsoft support the same language for querying databases and writing stored procedures—Transact-SQL. Despite the fact that the languages have the same name, they are not 100 percent identical; many of the differences have been pointed out in this book.

The question you face is whether it makes sense to use all the language extensions available, regardless of whether they are supported by other databases, or whether you should stick with the basic functionality that is widely supported. For many users, this isn't an issue at all because their code will never be used with more than one database.

Many companies have standardized on not only a particular database product, but on a particular version. Some companies I have worked with use Oracle version 7.3.4 and have no plans for upgrading to Oracle 8, even though it has been released for quite some time. All their code is written to work with that version of Oracle, and it provides the capabilities that they need, so there's no reason for them to go through the painful process of upgrading all their database servers. Even if the upgrade process went without a hitch, the downtime upgrading would cause would be unacceptable.

On the other hand, in some cases your database code may need to be ported to a different database in the future, and the fewer database-specific extensions you use, the easier it will be to move to another database. This is where the advantage of Transact-SQL being supported by multiple database suppliers comes into play. If you've written an application that uses Sybase SQL Anywhere and you need a more robust database, you can move your database to Sybase's Adaptive Server or Microsoft SQL Server without rewriting any of your queries. If you moved to Oracle, chances are that you would have to rewrite some of your queries to get them to work, especially if they used built-in functions.

When you're using plain old SQL to write queries, you should stick to standard syntax as much as possible. For example, if you want to rename a column, you should use the AS syntax like this:

```
SELECT movie_title AS title
FROM Movies
```

instead of the = syntax, like this:

```
SELECT title = movie_title
FROM Movies
```

Both will work in Transact-SQL, but only the AS version works in most other databases. If you ever have to move your code to a different database, that will make one less thing that you have to change when you're porting the code.

One of the most difficult things about portability is determining whether the code you're writing is even portable. Most of the time, when you're reading documentation for a query language, you have no way of knowing whether the constructs that are being presented are specific to the product you're using or are part of the standard on which the implementation you're using is based. When you're programming, if portability is an issue, you should seek out documentation that clearly indicates which parts of the language are standardized so that you can make informed decisions about using proprietary extensions.

When it comes to writing stored procedures, writing portable code is a much trickier issue. Although the basics of SQL are pretty well standardized across databases, the extensions to SQL used to write stored procedures are not standardized between databases at all. This is an important consideration when you're developing Web applications. If the database underlying your application may change, it makes sense to avoid writing stored procedures that won't be portable to a new database. However, if the application development environment is more likely to change than the database, or you plan on accessing the database with multiple application development environments, you should write stored procedures.

CHAPTER 20

MICROSOFT ACCESS

In this chapter

Microsoft Access is a relational database that is bundled with Microsoft Office Professional Edition. However, it differs greatly from the other relational databases discussed in this book. Unlike the other databases, which are split into two components, the engine and the client, Microsoft Access is a standalone application. Most relational databases are designed to run on servers, and run all the time, starting when the server is booted. On the other hand, Microsoft Access is generally launched when it is needed, and then it is closed like a word processor, spreadsheet, or any other standard application.

Despite the differences between Access and other databases, it is a complete relational database, and it does support SQL as a query language. Because Microsoft Access is not aimed at relational database programmers, a lot of the lower-level functionality is obscured from users.

MICROSOFT DATABASE FILES

Another important difference between Access databases and what one might think of as standard relational databases is the method of storing the actual data in the database on disk. Most relational databases are allocated some disk space, either as a dedicated partition on the hard drive, or in one or more large files; that space is used for storage by the database. Generally, those files cannot be moved around or copied onto another computer and used there easily.

Microsoft Access databases are like documents generated in most other applications. They are independent of the system on which they were created, and can be used by anyone with the appropriate version of Access. All the information in the database is stored within a single file, including the data, the schema for the tables, and even stored queries and applications that can be used to access the database.

Generally speaking, Microsoft Access data files (which generally have the extension .mdb) are used within the Access application. However, one advantage of .mdb files is that they can be used with the ODBC driver (which I will discuss in the next section) to allow applications that support ODBC to connect to the database and issue SQL commands, even though Microsoft Access isn't running. In fact, as long as the appropriate ODBC driver is installed, Microsoft Access doesn't even have to be present on the machine.

ODBC

ODBC, which stands for *open database connectivity*, is an interface used by applications that communicate with relational databases on the Windows platform. Its single most important advantage is that it provides a layer of abstraction between databases and database applications. Basically, applications are written so that they can talk to any ODBC data source, and ODBC drivers are written for the databases so that they can be communicated with via ODBC.

The ODBC driver for Microsoft Access database (.mdb) files actually allows applications to communicate with the databases via ODBC, even without Microsoft Access. The ODBC driver for .mdb files already contains all the information necessary to use the .mdb files. This is nice when you develop your database using the full version of Access and you want to deploy it for something like a Web application on a server. Instead of installing Access and launching it when you want to use the database, the engine built into the ODBC driver takes care of those issues.

THE ACCESS INTERFACE

Because Microsoft Access is really a user-centric application, the interface to it differs greatly from most other databases you might have used. Unlike basic command-line applications such as SQLPLUS, Access is a graphical application that provides visual tools for creating all the elements within a database.

Unlike most relational database engines, Access also provides the capability to develop graphical database applications that are internal to the database itself. When you're using a database such as Microsoft SQL Server or Oracle, external development environments are required to build applications to access the database. For example, you can use Visual Basic or PowerBuilder to create the applications, and use the database for storage. On the other hand Access has a built-in application for building forms for database access. You can also write procedures and modules (groups of procedures) in Visual Basic for Applications and store them within the database.

In fact, there are size types of objects that can be created within an Access database. These objects are tables, queries, forms, reports, macros, and modules. A screen shot of the Access interface appears in Figure 20.1.

Figure 20.1
The Tables view in
Microsoft Access.

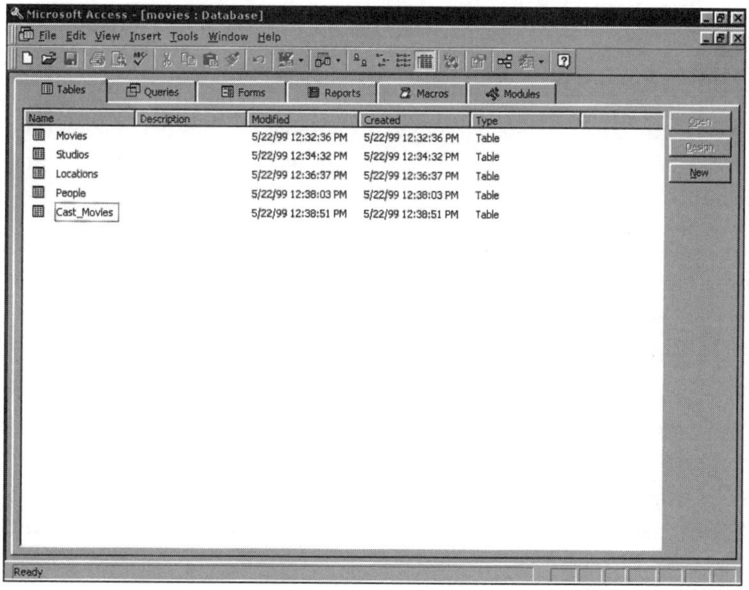

OBJECTS IN MICROSOFT ACCESS

As I noted in the previous section, there are six types of objects supported in Microsoft Access. I'm going to discuss each of these object types, and explain how they map to the objects one might (or might not) find in other traditional relational databases. One thing seasoned database developers might find frustrating about Access is that the Access paradigm is very different from other relational databases. It is designed to prevent users from having to learn or use SQL at all, so for SQL programmers, using Access can be a chore.

TABLES

Microsoft Access is a relational database; it supports tables just like every other relational database. The main difference between Microsoft Access and other relational databases is the means by which tables are created and modified. Although there are design tools available for most databases that enable users to design their tables in a graphical environment that automatically generates the CREATE statements necessary to actually build the tables, at heart most databases require a SQL statement to define tables (even if that SQL statement is never seen by the user).

Microsoft Access, on the other hand, does not rely on CREATE statements to create tables. Tables can be defined using CREATE statements, but most Access programmers avoid them and use the design tools instead. For seasoned database programmers, the view that will be most familiar is the Design view. Before I discuss the Design view, I'll cover the other database creation views briefly.

Besides the Design view, the other main view is Datasheet view. Datasheet view will be familiar to anyone who has ever used a spreadsheet. When you create a table in the Datasheet view, a tabular view is presented, and you can add new rows or columns by typing values into those rows or columns. The columns in the Datasheet view begin with the names Field1, Field2, Field3, and so on; before you save the table you should rename the columns to something meaningful by double-clicking on the column names and entering a new identifier. When you edit an existing table in Datasheet view, you can modify the values already in the table, or create new records, but you can't modify the structure of the table itself. For that, you must use Design view.

The third method that can be used to create tables is the Table Wizard. The Table Wizard has a list of sample tables, and of fields that are part of those tables. To create a new table, you just select a sample table from the list and add columns from that table to your new table. If you want, you can select one of the samples and then add all the columns from that table to the new table.

The other two options are Import Table and Link Table. These allow you to import tables from existing databases. Imported tables are created within the current database and saved there, whereas linked tables still reside in the database from which they were linked. The Design view is the most important method by which you can create and edit tables; I'll discuss it a bit later in the chapter.

QUERIES

The next category of objects that can reside in an Access database is Queries. Basically, Queries are stored SQL statements that can be executed later. Queries in some ways take the place of stored procedures and views in Access. They take the place of views in the sense that you can store a SELECT statement as a query and then run that query whenever you want to retrieve that view of the data in the database. They aren't full replacements for views, however, because you can only view the results of the query, not issue other queries against them.

Even though they're called Queries, you can actually store UPDATE and DELETE statements in them as well as SELECT statements. In Access, saved queries are particularly important because when you write Access applications, you can call the stored queries from Modules that you write.

Much like tables, queries can be created in a number of different ways. The most interesting method to us is to use the Design view; the other views involve using wizards to build the queries. There are a number of subviews that can be used within the Design view of a query. You can see the query results in the Datasheet view, but you cannot modify them. The Design view also offers a visual query designer, which allows you to define relationships between tables, and drag rows from the E-R diagram at the top of the window into the list of columns returned by the query in the lower half of the window, as shown in Figure 20.2.

Figure 20.2
Design mode for queries in Access.

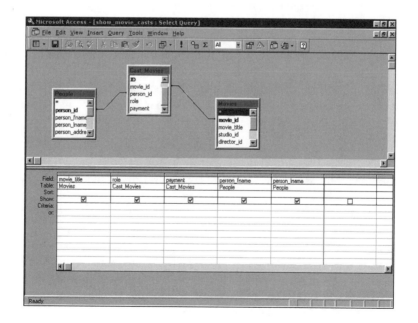

You can also alternate between the visual query designer and SQL mode, which allows you to create and edit queries by typing simply typing them in. Figure 20.3 shows the same query that appears in Figure 20.2 in SQL mode.

Figure 20.3
A view of an Access
query in SQL mode.

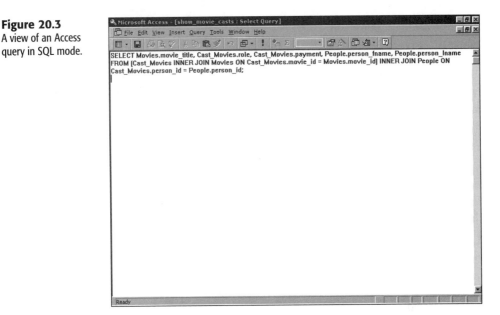

```
SELECT Movies.movie_title, Cast_Movies.role, Cast_Movies.payment, People.person_fname, People.person_lname
FROM [Cast_Movies INNER JOIN Movies ON Cast_Movies.movie_id = Movies.movie_id] INNER JOIN People ON
Cast_Movies.person_id = People.person_id;
```

FORMS

Forms are used in the creation of Microsoft Access applications. Basically, forms are used to provide an interface to some data stored in the database. When you write Microsoft Access applications, you create forms to allow users to enter and modify data in the database, and write modules in VBA (Visual Basic for Applications) to provide the functionality behind the form. At their simplest, forms are used without VBA code, and just have fields on them that are tied directly to columns within the database. The items on forms that interface with the database are referred to as controls. When you alter or enter data using controls, the corresponding fields in the database are updated (or a new record is inserted, as appropriate). This chapter mainly discusses the aspects of Microsoft Access that relate directly to relational databases, so I won't be discussing how forms are created here.

Like other objects in Access, you can create forms through a Design view, or using wizards. Basically, the wizards provide a number of templates that encompass common tasks one might want to perform with an Access application. Instead of forcing the user to build these forms from scratch, users can rough them out using the wizards, and then modify the forms produced by the wizards to meet the requirements of their application. The Design view consists of a canvas and palette of tools that you can use to lay out controls and static elements on a form. After a control has been placed on the form you're creating, you can tie it to particular events or fields to add functionality. Figure 20.4 contains the Design view of a simple form used to modify the Studios table.

Figure 20.4
Form Design view in
Microsoft Access.

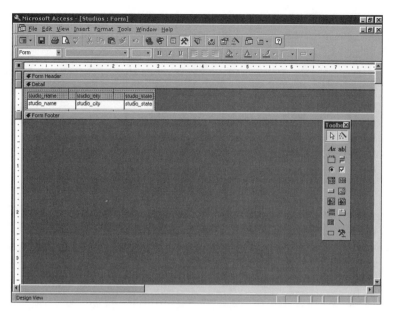

REPORTS

Reports are similar to forms, except that they are used to present data from the database rather than allow users to modify or enter data. Like forms, reports are made up of a combination of static elements and controls. The controls are fields or queries that retrieve the data needed for the report from the database and present it. Using the built-in report designer, you can include graphical elements on your reports and format the text any way you like. Again, because this chapter (and this book) are focused on programming relational databases with SQL, I won't be discussing the report designer in Access in any detail.

MACROS

Macros provide a simpler method for programming Access than modules written in VBA. Basically, macros consist of one or more individual actions that are performed any time the macro is executed. For example, you can create a macro that executes a group of queries, or opens a form, or exports data from the database into a file. You can add conditional constructs to your macros if you want, so that certain actions in the macro are taken only if the specified conditions are met.

Unlike the other objects in Access, there are no wizards for creating macros. You must create macros in Design mode. There is also no macro recorder in Access, as there are in some other applications that support macros. However, you can easily add some actions to your macros by dragging database objects that you want to open from a macro into the list of actions in the Design view of the macro. A pointless macro that opens a form, some tables, and a query and closes the form is shown in Figure 20.5.

PART

VI

CH

20

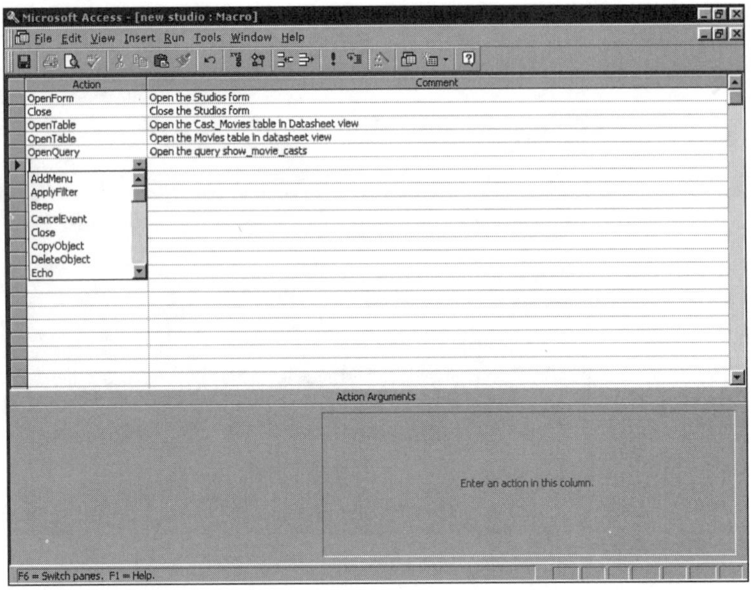

Figure 20.5
Macro Design view in Access.

MODULES

Modules are repositories for VBA code used in Access applications. Unlike macros, which are simple sets of actions that can potentially be triggered based on a condition, modules are written in a full programming environment. The modules accessible through the Modules tab in Access are standard modules; they contain code that can be used anywhere in the database of which they are a part. There are also form and report modules that contain code specific to a particular form or report. Inside these modules are event procedures, which are executed when the event to which they correspond occurs in the form or report to which they are assigned. For example, you can create a button on a form that is tied to an event procedure. Whenever the button is clicked, the code in the event procedure will be executed.

There are two types of procedures that can be written, function procedures and sub procedures. The difference between them is that function procedures return a value and subs do not. For example, if you have a function called IsValidMovieTitle that returns an integer, you can use the function call within an expression, like this:

```
if IsValidMovieTitle("The Code Warrior") = 1 then
```

Subroutines do not return a value; when a subroutine is called, the code in the subroutine is executed, and then execution resumes at the statement after the subroutine call.

CREATING TABLES

One of the tasks that differs most greatly from standard SQL in Microsoft Access is creating tables. As you know, in databases that support some standard version of SQL, the CREATE

TABLE statement is used to create new tables. There are several methods that can be used to create tables, I'm going to discuss three of them in this chapter. The first method is to create the tables in the Datasheet view, which is similar to a spreadsheet. The second method is to create tables in the Design view, which will be the most familiar to database programmers. The third method is to create a data definition query in the Queries tab, and then run the query.

CREATING TABLES IN THE DATASHEET VIEW

The Datasheet view is most similar to a spreadsheet like Microsoft Excel. It isn't particularly useful to database programmers because it doesn't offer fine control over the datatypes included in the table. However, users who don't understand the relational model may find the Datasheet view easy to approach when creating new databases. They simply enter their data and name the columns, and the tables are created automatically. When you create a table in the Datasheet view, a spreadsheet appears with generic column headings. At that point, you can begin to define the table.

Unlike most databases, Access allows you to add rows to the database and define the actual columns that make up the table simultaneously. When you're editing the table initially in the Datasheet view, you can enter values in any columns you want, and double-click on the column names to change them. At the time of creation, the actual datatypes for the columns are unimportant. When you save the new table, Access will automatically set the datatypes based on the values that you typed into the columns you were defining.

If you're used to carefully designing your databases to fit the information you'll be storing exactly, the free form approach offered by the Datasheet view will not be for you. Let's look at an example. In Figure 20.6, I'm creating a new table in the Datasheet view.

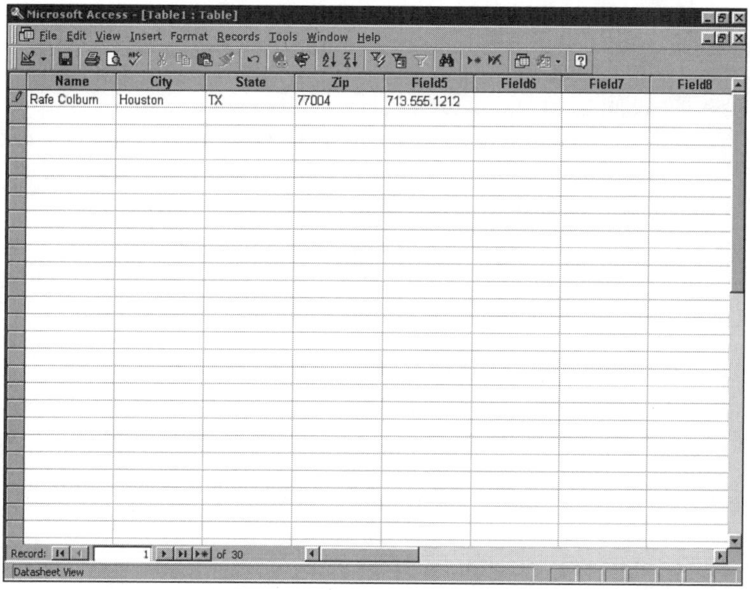

Figure 20.6
Creating a table in the Datasheet view.

As you can see, I've changed the headings of the first four columns, and I've entered data in the first five columns. Figure 20.7 shows the table that I just created in the Design view.

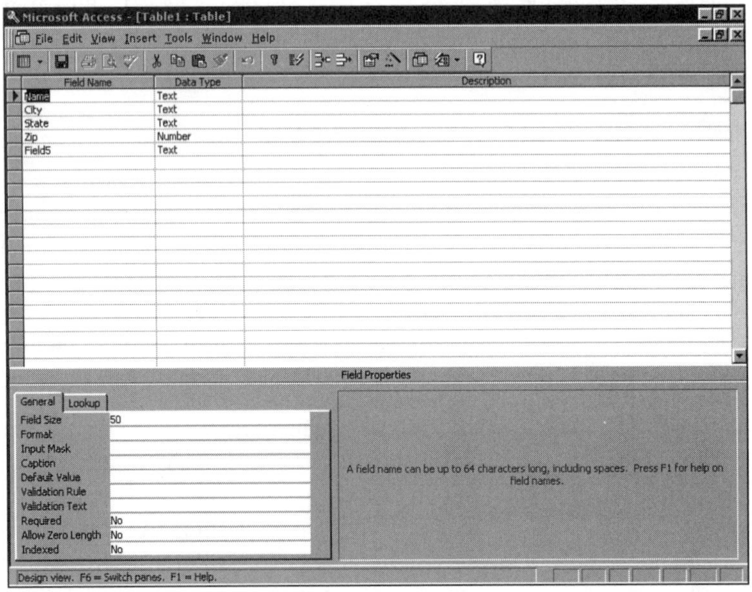

Figure 20.7
Editing a table in Design view that was created in Datasheet view.

As you can see from the Design view, all five columns into which I entered data are captured in the table layout, including the column that I didn't assign a name to. It appears in the table with the default column heading, Field5. It also sets the field sizes automatically when you close the table. For text fields (which are the equivalent of varchar fields in other databases), the default size is 50. If you enter more than 50 characters in the Datasheet view, the field will be expanded to the maximum size, 255.

The two columns that contain numbers rather than text are specified as number fields. Any column that contains only numbers in the Datasheet view is defined as a numeric field.

CREATING TABLES IN THE DESIGN VIEW

The Design view for creating and modifying tables will probably be the easiest method of creating tables for SQL programmers to adjust to. To create a new table in the Design view, you need to follow these steps:

1. Click on the Tables tab to view a list of tables in the database.
2. Click on the New button on the right side of the dialog box to create the new table.
3. At that point, you'll be confronted with a list of methods that you can use to create the table. You'll want to click on Design View and then click on the OK button.

4. Next you'll need to enter the column names, datatypes, and, optionally, comments in the lines of the table creation form. One thing you'll notice right away when you start creating tables is that the datatypes available in the Access Design view are significantly different than the standard SQL datatypes.

5. After you have entered all the field names and datatypes into the new table, you can create the table by clicking on the Save button on the toolbar. You will be prompted to enter the name of the table, and then it will be created in the database.

Creating the actual columns in the Design view is easy. You just enter the name of the column, and select the datatype from the pull-down menu, as shown in Figure 20.8.

Figure 20.8
The datatype pull-down menu in Access.

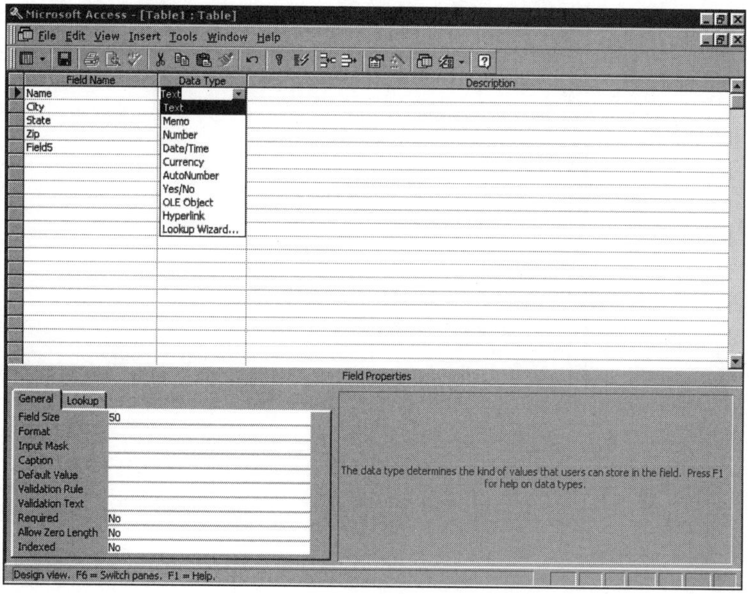

There are a number of other options for each field that can be set in the Design view, as well as a few options that are not standard in relational databases. The options available for each field vary on the datatype. For example, you can set the field size for text fields, but not for Date/Time fields.

The input mask allows you to define a format that is required for data entered in the field. For example, you could create a mask for phone numbers that prevents users from entering phone numbers in a nonstandard format. You can also specify whether characters that are part of the input mask are stored in the database along with the data that the user enters. If you created an input mask for phone numbers, you could set up the mask so that the parentheses around the area code and hyphen between the exchange and extension are discarded before the telephone number is entered in the database. The input mask is used when you create forms to allow users to enter data.

PART
VI
CH
20

The data you enter in the Caption field is used when the field appears on a form. The Default Value field is used to enter a value for the field that will be inserted if no other value is entered when the record is inserted in the table.

The Validation Rule field is used to create a constraint on the values allowed in a field. It differs from the Input Mask in that it is used to validate the actual value in the field, rather than verify that the value fits within a particular format. It is similar to a check constraint in standard SQL. You can enter expressions just like those that would appear in the WHERE clause of a SELECT statement, as shown in Figure 20.9.

Figure 20.9
Validation Rule and
Validation Text fields.

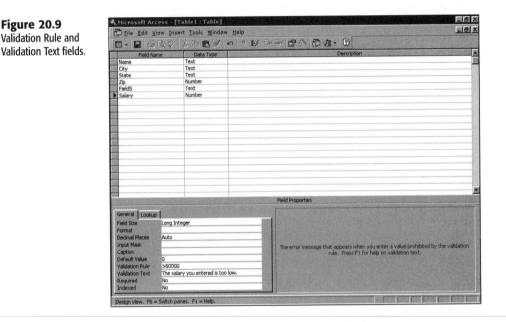

When you enter a value in a field that does not satisfy the conditions of the Validation Rule, the Validation Text you entered will be displayed.

The last two fields are the Required field and the Index field. The Required field is equivalent to the NOT NULL constraint in SQL. When Required is set to yes, a value must be inserted in that field when a new record is added to the table, or the insertion will fail. The Indexed setting allows you to create an index on the column. There are three settings: yes, no, and yes with no duplicates. These correspond to the indexing options provided by standard SQL.

If you create a table with no primary key field defined, Access will ask you if you want to create one automatically when you save the table. If you allow it to create a primary key, it will add a new column to the table called ID with the Autonumber datatype. If there's already a column with the name ID, it will call the column ID1 and so on. To set a column as the primary key for a table when you create it, highlight the column's entry in the Design view and select Primary Key from the Edit menu, or click on the primary key button on the toolbar.

WRITING DATA DEFINITION QUERIES

Building queries for data definition (like CREATE and ALTER) statements is a bit different than writing SELECT statements. Data definition statements are created as Query objects, just like data selection statements, but the steps taken to create such a statement are different. Let's take a look at how you create a data definition statement in Access.

1. Open the Queries tab in Access.
2. Create a new query.
3. In the New Query dialog box, select Design View.
4. In the Show Table dialog box, just click the Close button without selecting any tables.
5. From the Query menu, select the Data Definition option in the SQL Specific submenu. At that point, the Data Definition Query will open, as shown in Figure 20.10.

Figure 20.10
The Data Definition
Query window.

In the Data Definition Query window, you can type your SQL statement. In the next section of the chapter, I'm going to cover the datatypes supported by Access. Access supports the use of the CONSTRAINT clause to place constraints on the columns in the table, as shown in Listing 20.1.

PART

VI

CH

20

LISTING 20.1   A CREATE TABLE STATEMENT FOR ACCESS

```
CREATE TABLE Example
(field1 TEXT(25) CONSTRAINT example_pkey PRIMARY KEY,
field2 YESNO,
field3 OLEOBJECT)
```

You can also use the ALTER TABLE and CREATE INDEX statements in the Data Definition Query window. To run the query you created, simply double-click on the query in the Query view.

DATATYPES

Let's take a look at the datatypes supported by Access. The datatypes in Access differ from those supported by other databases because Access is designed to be friendly to users of Microsoft Office, rather than to be a database for programmers who are well versed with SQL and relational database design. So, instead of datatypes like VARCHAR and CHAR, it has datatypes that are more comprehensible to non-expert users. A list of datatypes and their capabilities appear in Table 20.1.

TABLE 20.1 DATATYPES SUPPORTED BY MICROSOFT ACCESS

Name	Details	Size
Text	Text fields are equivalent to VARCHAR fields in other databases; they only consume the amount of space utilized by the data in the field. They can hold up to 255 characters.	1 byte per character
Memo	The Memo datatype is designed to be used in situations where more than 255 characters need to be stored in a particular field. It has a capacity of up to 65,535 characters. Unlike the Text datatype, you cannot specify the size of a field created with the Memo datatype.	1 byte per character
Number	The Number datatype is, of course, used to hold numbers. The type of number that can be stored in a Number field is specified using the Field Size pull-down menu. The list of numeric types is included in Table 20.2.	Varies depending on subtype
Date/Time	A Date/Time field can hold any valid date and time between the years 100 and 9999.	8 bytes
Currency	A Currency field is just a numeric field that is precise out to four digits to the right of the decimal. It can store up to 15 digits on the left of the decimal.	8 bytes
AutoNumber	AutoNumber is a 4- or 16-byte field (depending on the Field Size setting) that is incremented by 1 whenever a new row is inserted in the table. The behavior of these fields can be changed using the NewValue property, so that a random value is included when a new row is inserted in place of an incremented value.	4 bytes
Yes/No	Yes/No is a 1-bit field that can be formatted in one of three different ways, as specified in the Format setting. The three formats are Yes/No, On/Off, and True/False.	1 bit

Name	Details	Size
OLE Object	The OLE Object datatype is like a large object field in other databases. It can hold a pointer to an OLE object, or the object itself can be embedded in the database. The objects themselves can be up to 1 gigabyte. OLE objects include documents created in other Office applications, sounds, and images.	Up to 1GB
Hyperlink	A specialized datatype designed to hold Web addresses. It has three components, the link display text, the URL associated with the link, and the anchor in the page associated with the link. Each component can be up to 2048 characters.	Up to 2048 bytes
Lookup Wizard	The Lookup Wizard datatype creates a link from a column in the current table to the contents of a column in another table. It is used so that you can build form elements dynamically from the values stored in another column.	Varies

As I noted previously, the Number datatype actually encompasses a number of different datatypes. The real datatype of a Number field is set using the Field Size pull-down menu in the Design view. Using the pull-down menu, you can specify whether a field can hold integer or floating point numbers, and how large the numbers can be. Table 20.2 contains a list of the field sizes supported by the Number datatype.

TABLE 20.2   FIELD SIZES SUPPORTED BY THE Number DATATYPE.

Field Size	Description
Byte	Stores positive numbers between 0 and 255. It supports only integers.
Integer	Supports integers between $-32,768$ and $32,767$. It's a 2-byte signed integer.
Long Integer	The default field size for number fields. Supports integers between $-2,147,483,648$ and $2,147,483,647$. It's a 4-byte signed integer.
Single	A 4-byte floating point number. It supports positive values from $1.401298E45$ to $3.402823E38$, and negative values from $-3.402823E38$ to $-1.401298E45$.
Double	A 6-byte floating point number. It supports positive numbers from $1.79769313486231E308$ to $4.94065645841247E324$ and negative numbers from $-1.79769313486231E308$ to $-4.94065645841247E324$.
Replication ID	Holds 16-byte global unique identifiers.

PART
VI

CH
20

CREATING AND RUNNING QUERIES

One feature that database programmers using Microsoft Access will miss is the capability to simply type SQL queries into a window and instantly view the results, or to insert, update, and delete records quickly by entering SQL queries. In Access, queries are treated as objects to be stored within the database. This fits in with the application development paradigm for which Access was designed. Access is designed as a platform for deploying database applications rather than as a simple repository for data that is designed to work with other development environments.

There are a number of methods that can be used to create queries; the two most interesting options are to use SQL mode or Design mode to build them. The other options involve using wizards that will probably be frustrating for most database programmers. Let's take a look at the other two methods of building queries.

BUILDING QUERIES IN DESIGN VIEW

Access provides a visual query designer that is actually very useful. When you create a new query and select the Design view as the means you will use to create it, a dialog box appears (shown in Figure 20.11) that allows you to choose which tables will be used in the query.

Figure 20.11
The Show Table dialog box.

You can select as many tables as you like from the list of tables in the database, and those tables will appear in the FROM clause of the query automatically. When you add multiple tables to a query, Access tries to infer the relationships between the tables for you, based on the column names. Unfortunately, sometimes it doesn't get these relationships right. If I create a query and include the Movies, Cast_Members, and Locations tables in it, the database concludes that the relationships are structured as shown in Figure 20.12.

Access is correct to guess that the movie_id column in Movies is also the foreign key in Cast_Movies. Unfortunately, it has also created an invalid relationship between the ID columns in Cast_Movies and Locations, and missed the foreign key relationship between Movies and Locations. The only reason the ID column appears in those tables is that Access suggested that I create it when I finished designing the tables. There is no relationship between them. Interestingly, the order in which you select tables for the query does have an effect on which relationships are identified. You should be prepared to create the proper relationships between the tables in your query after Access chooses what it thinks the relationships are.

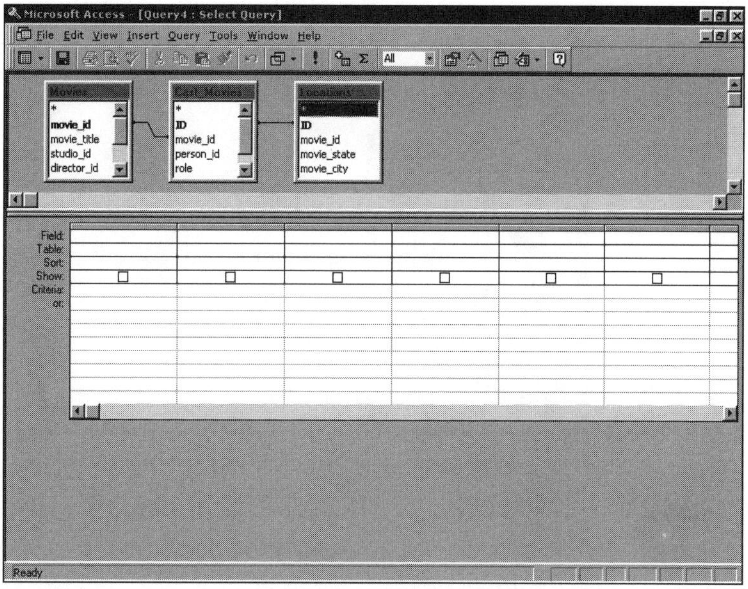

Figure 20.12 Relationships that are defined automatically by Access.

Tip 76 from *Rafe Colburn*

Sometimes, in Access, you should create a new ID column for your tables even if you already have candidate keys within the data that already exists. Access does not support compound primary keys, and dealing with the ID field created by Access as the primary key can be easier at times.

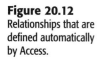

In order to create a valid query, you need to remove the relationship between the two ID fields. Doing so is as easy as clicking on the line that signifies the relationship, and pressing the Delete button on your keyboard. The new diagram, without the ID relationship, appears in Figure 20.13.

When you've got the correct tables included in the query, and you've cleaned up the relationships between them, you can select columns to be included in the query results. Adding a column to the query results or to the WHERE clause is simple. You just double-click on its name in the list of columns in the table, or drag its name into the lower area of the window.

To use an item in the WHERE clause, you must enter a condition in the Criteria field on the design form. To include the column in the list of values returned by the query, select the check box in the Show field. Compare the Design view of the query in Figure 20.14 with the SQL version of the same query in Listing 20.2.

LISTING 20.2 THE SQL VERSION OF THE QUERY IN FIGURE 20.13

```
SELECT Movies.movie_title
FROM (Locations INNER JOIN Movies ON Locations.movie_id = Movies.movie_id)
INNER JOIN Cast_Movies ON Movies.movie_id = Cast_Movies.movie_id
WHERE (((Cast_Movies.movie_id)>5));
```

Figure 20.13
A set of tables in the query Design view with the correct relationships.

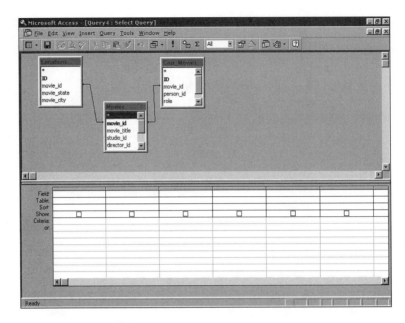

Figure 20.14
The Design view of a SELECT statement.

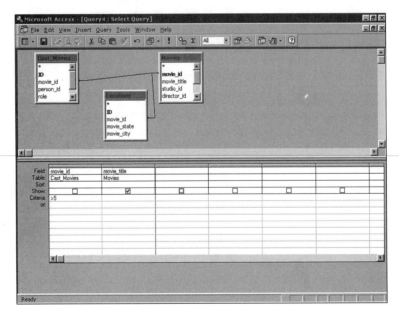

As you can see, the `movie_title` field is the only field included in the query results, and there are no criteria associated with it in the WHERE clause. On the other hand, the `movie_id` field from the `Cast_Movies` table is included in the select list, but not in the WHERE clause.

In the Design view, you can also use outer joins by altering the relationships between the tables in the upper part of the window. By right-clicking on the relationship and selecting Join Properties, you can open a dialog box that allows you to change the type of join used with the two tables, as demonstrated in Figure 20.15.

Figure 20.15
Changing the type of join in Access.

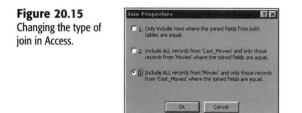

WRITING QUERIES IN THE SQL VIEW

The other option I'd like to discuss is the creation of queries directly in the SQL view. One nice feature of Access is that you can switch between the SQL view and the Design view freely, and any changes you make in one view will be applied to the query in the other view as well. So you can rough out your queries in the Design view, and then switch over to the SQL view to make sure they're exactly right. Often, this is much faster than typing in the queries by hand, particularly if they're complicated. Another advantage of using the Design view is that you're less likely to make typos when you're not actually typing in all the table and column names.

In any case, you can switch to SQL view from Design view by selecting SQL View from the View menu. You can switch back to Design view if you want by selecting Design View from the View menu.

Tip 77 from
Rafe Colburn

You can test the syntax of your query and view the results at any time by selecting Datasheet View from the View menu. It will execute the query and bring up the results in a spreadsheet format. If there are any errors in your code, it will report them before the query is executed.

SQL view in Access will be familiar to any database programmer. It is just a simple text-editing Window in which you can enter SQL code or modify an existing query. A screen shot of a query being edited in the SQL view appears in Figure 20.16.

Figure 20.16
Editing a query in the
SQL view.

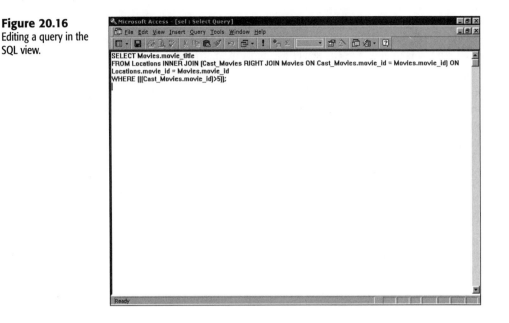

CREATING AN ODBC DATASOURCE

If you plan on using a Microsoft Access database as a means of storage for data from other applications, you will, more than likely, be communicating with it via ODBC. As I mentioned earlier in the chapter, ODBC provides a generic interface for connecting applications to relational databases. As long as the application includes ODBC support, and there is an ODBC driver available for the database, the two can communicate through ODBC.

In order to connect to a database through ODBC, the database must be configured as an ODBC datasource. ODBC maintains a registry of datasources that applications can use to find out which databases are available on the machine. The databases tied to each datasource do not necessarily have to be local to the machine. ODBC can be used to connect to remote databases as well. There are three scopes for ODBC datasources: File, System, and User.

User datasources allow only applications run by the current user to access them. System datasources are visible to all the users of the system, as well as any services that are running. File datasources can be shared among all the users who have the drivers installed for that datasource. The ODBC Data Source Administrator appears in Figure 20.17.

To create a datasource, click on the tab that corresponds to the type of DSN you want to create, and click on the Add button. The Create New Data Source dialog box will appear. Select the driver for the database associated with the new datasource, and click on the Finish button.

Figure 20.17
The ODBC Data
Source Administrator.

Tip 78 from
Rafe Colburn

If the driver for your database does not appear in the list of available drivers, you probably need to obtain it from the company that provided the database. Generally, the ODBC drivers for a database can be found on the installation media for the database, or can be downloaded from the Web site of the company who wrote the database.

After you select a driver, the configuration dialog associated with that driver will appear. The configuration dialog for Access appears in Figure 20.18. After you enter the configuration settings necessary for the database, just click on OK to create it. In Access, all you need to enter is a name for the DSN, and the location of the database file with which the DSN should be associated.

Figure 20.18
Configuring an Access
datasource.

MICROSOFT ACCESS RESOURCES

Microsoft Access is part of Microsoft Office Professional, so it's installed on the desktop computers of millions of users. For most people, it's the only database development environment that they've been exposed to. There are a lot of Microsoft Access resources available, in terms of books and Web sites. The first place you should stop is the official

Microsoft Access Web site, at `http://www.microsoft.com/access`. There's a Web page specifically targeted to Microsoft Access developers at `http://www.microsoft.com/accessdev/`.

You might also want to check out the Microsoft Office Update Web site (`http://officeupdate.microsoft.com`) to download free add-ons to Access, and to make sure that you've downloaded any patches for the product that might be available.

Other Web sites that have information about Microsoft Access that you might find interesting include

- Inside Microsoft Access (`http://www.zdjournals.com/ima/`)
- Microsoft Access Webring (`http://www.webring.org/cgi-bin/webring?ring=accessring;list`)

If you have questions about Access, you might find Usenet newsgroups to be useful:

- `comp.databases.ms-access`
- `microsoft.public.access.*`

IN THE REAL WORLD

Despite the fact that Access is very feature-rich and easy to use, many Access users find it necessary to upgrade their database to something more robust when the use of their application increases. Not only is Access not as scalable as other high-end database packages, but it also has some inherent limitations by which other databases are not bound.

For example, the size constraints on the string datatypes in Access are pretty limiting. The text datatype, which is equivalent to the varchar type in most databases, has a limit of 255 characters. Oracle's limit for varchar fields is 4000 characters. Similarly, the large object field for strings in Access, memo, cannot hold more than 65,535 characters of data. Compare this to Oracle's CLOB field, which can hold up to 4 gigabytes of data.

In any case, the size limits on data in Microsoft SQL Server 7 are similar to those of Oracle databases. Varchar fields in SQL Server 7 can hold a whopping 8000 characters of data. Fortunately, Microsoft has anticipated the need of Access developers to move to SQL Server, and has provided some useful tools for "upsizing" Access databases to SQL Server.

Microsoft provides two tools at their Web site (which come packaged together) for migrating Access applications into SQL Server 7.0. One tool, the Upsizing Wizard, allows you to migrate the data in your Access database to a SQL Server database. The other, SQL Server Browser, enables you to control a SQL Server database through Microsoft Access. The tools are available through the Microsoft Developer Network at

`http://msdn.microsoft.com`

The first step in upsizing a database is to install the upsizing package from Microsoft. The upsizing package actually comes with two tools, the Upsizing Wizard, and the SQL Server Browser tool. Both of them can be accessed through the Add-ins Menu in the Tools menu in Microsoft Access.

The Upsizing Wizard enables you to import your Access data into a SQL Server database via ODBC. If you don't already have the SQL Server database set up as an ODBC datasource on your computer, you must configure it first. After it's configured, you can select it as the database to which you will export the tables from your Access database.

When you upsize your database, you have two choices; you can either create a new SQL Server database with the tables from your Access database, or you can move your tables into an existing SQL Server database. After you decide how you want to move the tables, the next step is to select the ODBC datasource for the SQL Server database that you'll be exporting to. If a login and password are required for the database, you'll be prompted to enter them before you move on.

The next step is to choose the tables you want to export into the SQL Server database. After you select some tables, you'll be asked to specify which attributes of those tables to export (the default is to move all the attributes), and whether you want to create links to the tables that have been exported in your existing Access database. At that point, the tables will be exported into the SQL Server database.

Unfortunately, that probably won't be where your work ends. Depending on the complexity of your database, you may find that you have some cleanup work and refining ahead of you once you've exported your data from Access to SQL Server.

CHAPTER 21

MSQL AND MySQL

In this chapter

Mini-SQL (referred to from here on as MSQL) and MySQL are lightweight relational data-bases that are available inexpensively. MySQL is designed to be compatible with the MSQL database, and both of the databases are very popular, particularly among users of free operating systems such as Linux and FreeBSD. The reason for the popularity of these databases is that they're quite powerful, they're inexpensive, and the source code is available for both of them.

These databases are not designed to compete with the likes of Oracle and Microsoft SQL Server. Indeed, they are missing several features that many DBAs would consider to be absolutely essential. (For more information on the features that are missing from MSQL and MySQL, see the section titled "MySQL Limitations" later in the chapter.) Both MSQL and MySQL are perfectly sufficient for many database-related tasks. These database servers are widely used by developers who create database-backed Web sites, particularly for Web sites that use relational databases to store content rather than transactional information.

One of the main reasons MSQL and MySQL have become popular is that they are very inexpensive to use. In fact, for most users, MySQL is free (Windows users must pay a licensing fee after an evaluation period). Programmers looking for a low-cost relational database solution have been able to turn to MySQL and MSQL. Both of them are very stable and offer good performance, and there is no comparison between them and products such as Sybase Adaptive Server Enterprise and Oracle in terms of price.

In this chapter, the examples provided have been generated in MySQL. MySQL was designed from the outset to be a drop-in replacement for MSQL; both the implementation of SQL and the programming API for MySQL are designed to be as similar as possible to those of MSQL. MySQL also provides some functionality that is not available in MSQL. I'm going to compare the two databases later in this chapter.

OBTAINING MYSQL AND MSQL

Generally, MSQL and MySQL are downloaded over the Internet, rather than being pur-chased in a store. If you're interested in downloading a copy of MySQL, you should check out the MySQL home page at `http://www.mysql.net`. If you prefer MSQL, you can find it at `http://www.hughes.com.au`. If you don't know which you prefer, I'll explain the differences between the two in the next section of the chapter. Before you can download MSQL, you must register on the Hughes Technologies site. (Hughes Technologies is the creator of MSQL.) On the other hand, you can download MySQL by going to the download page and choosing the appropriate package from the list.

Both MySQL and MSQL are available in source code form, which can be compiled on almost every version of UNIX. To make life easier for people who want to install these data-bases on supported systems, precompiled versions of MySQL are distributed as well.

For most users, downloading a precompiled and installable version of the database is the right option. Many varieties of the UNIX operating system don't even come with the neces-sary tools to build the software, and even if they do, compiling the software yourself adds extra steps to the installation process that just aren't necessary for most users. The bottom line here is that if you're accustomed to downloading all your software as source code and building it yourself, you might want to download the source for MSQL or MySQL and compile it. Otherwise, it's easier to use one of the existing MySQL packages.

MSQL is distributed as a single gzipped tar file containing the source code for the database. It is up to the user to extract the source code from the tar file, compile it, and install it. The source code is written in a very portable manner, and will compile and run on most versions of UNIX.

In addition to being available in source code form, MySQL is also packaged for easy installation on a number of platforms. For example, you can download MySQL in an RPM package, for installation on computers running Red Hat Linux. There is also a version of MySQL available for computers running Windows 95, 98, and NT.

CONTRASTING MySQL AND MSQL

MSQL was developed before MySQL; in fact, MySQL was developed because MSQL did not meet the requirements of MySQL's developers. The similarity lies in the fact that MySQL was designed with the goal of making it easy for software written to use MSQL to be adapted to use MySQL as well. Because the two databases were developed independently of one another, they grow more different with each successive release. Both of them are lightweight relational databases that run on UNIX and UNIX-like operating systems. Both of them support a subset of SQL as a query language (I'll talk about the limitations of these databases in terms of SQL support later in the chapter). Unlike most higher end databases, they both run well on free UNIX-like operating systems such as Linux and FreeBSD.

Some of the differences between MSQL and MySQL are included in the following list. These differences should also give you an idea of where MySQL and MSQL lack capabilities that are found in most other databases. This list is adapted from the MySQL Reference Manual, which can be found on the Web at

`http://www.mysql.net/Manual_chapter/doc.html`

- With MySQL, you can create indexes at the time the table is created from within the `CREATE TABLE` statement, or afterward using `CREATE INDEX`. With MSQL, you can only create indexes after the table has been created, using `CREATE INDEX`.
- MySQL allows default values to be specified for columns, whereas MSQL does not.
- MySQL allows auto-incrementing columns; MSQL uses Oracle-style sequences.
- MSQL does not support `GROUP BY` with aggregate functions; MySQL does.
- MSQL evaluates Boolean expressions in left to right order, rather than in mathematical order. MySQL uses mathematical precedence for Boolean operators.
- MSQL requires that column names be qualified with the table name whenever multiple tables are used in a query.
- MSQL only supports table aliases; MySQL supports column aliases and table aliases.

PART
VI
CH
21

- MSQL does not support the use of functions in SELECT statements.

- MySQL supports the use of the HAVING clause with columns that appear in the select list. MSQL does not support the HAVING clause.

- Neither of the databases supports the SQL security model using GRANT and REVOKE. MySQL privileges are manipulated through the user table; MSQL uses the mSQL.acl file.

USING MYSQL

I'm going to discuss using MySQL specifically, and then I'm going to move on and discuss using MSQL. MySQL has two components, the database server and the database client. MySQL provides other applications with a number of methods to communicate with the database server. There is a native MySQL API that applications can use to communicate with the server, and MySQL also provides support for two common database interfaces, ODBC and JDBC.

Because of MySQL's popularity among free software users, most free software products that work with relational databases can communicate with MySQL. For example, the following popular application development packages all include support for MySQL:

- Perl, through DBI/DBD

- Python, through MySQLdb

- TCL, through tcl-sql

- PHP, native support

In this chapter, I'm going to talk about the client component that ships with MySQL; it's conveniently named mysql. If you're familiar with Oracle's SQL*PLUS, it's similar to that utility, in that it allows you to connect to a MySQL database as a particular user and type queries that are executed against the database.

THE MYSQL CLIENT

The MySQL client is invoked by typing mysql at a shell prompt. You can specify the login parameters using the following command line flags:

```
mysql [-h hostname] [-u username] [-p] [database]
```

All the command line parameters are optional. The -h parameter is used to provide the hostname for the server on which the MySQL database you wish to connect to resides. If you leave out the -h parameter, MySQL assumes that you want to connect to the database on the local machine. The -u parameter allows you to specify the database login of the user you want to connect as. If this parameter is left out, MySQL assumes you want to log in under the UNIX ID with which you're currently logged into the server. The -p flag is used to indicate that you will provide a password while logging in. If you prefer, you can enter the password on the command line as well, by appending it to the -p flag without a space.

Unfortunately, this isn't very secure. It's preferable to just indicate that you're going to use a password with -p and then enter the password separately when prompted, as shown in Listing 21.1.

LISTING 21.1 LOGGING IN TO MySQL

```
$ mysql -u movies -p movies
Enter password:
Welcome to the MySQL monitor.  Commands end with ; or \g.
Your MySQL connection id is 3 to server version: 3.22.16a-gamma

Type 'help' for help.

mysql>
```

Take a look at the command I entered at the shell prompt. I indicated that I wanted to log in to the database with the username movies; that I was going to supply a password when prompted, and that I wanted to use the database movies as well. When prompted for the password, I entered it, and was granted access to the database.

Tip 79 from
Rafe Colburn

> If you forget the root password for your computers, you need not despair. You can stop MySQL by killing the mysqld daemon, and then restart the database with the --skip-grant flag, which eliminates all access controls on items within the database. This is secure because only the root user should have the necessary privileges to start and stop the MySQL daemon. After the daemon has been restarted with access control turned off, you can log in as anyone you like and change the password for the root user with a command like
>
> ```
> SET PASSWORD FOR root@localhost = PASSWORD('secret');
> ```

Entering queries in MySQL is just as you would suspect. You simply type in the query at the mysql> prompt, and the results are returned. The only rule is that you must end your commands with a semicolon or \g. For example, you can retrieve the contents of the Movies table using the query in Listing 21.2.

LISTING 21.2 A SQL QUERY IN MySQL

```
mysql> SELECT movie_title, gross, budget
    -> FROM Movies;

+-----------------+-------+--------+
| movie_title     | gross | budget |
+-----------------+-------+--------+
| Mineral House   | 30.00 |  20.00 |
| Mineral House   | 30.00 |  20.00 |
| Prince Kong     | 51.50 |   3.25 |
| The Code Warrior | 17.80 |  10.30 |
| Bill Durham     | 15.60 |  10.10 |
| Codependence Day | 30.00 |  15.00 |
```

PART

VI

CH

21

continues

LISTING 21.2   CONTINUED

```
| The Linux Files  | 17.50 |  22.20 |
| SQL Strikes Back | 10.00 |   5.00 |
+------------------+-------+--------+
8 rows in set (0.01 sec)
```

You should be able to make a couple of interesting observations based on the contents of the query results. The first is that the number of rows returned by the query, and the time it took for the query to run, are presented with the query results. This information is available no matter which query you run.

Note

When you write queries in MySQL, the case sensitivity of database objects varies depending on the operating system MySQL is running on. If filenames in the underlying operating system are case sensitive, database and table names will be case sensitive. If the operating system does not support case-sensitive file naming, table names in your queries will not be case sensitive. For column names and SQL commands, MySQL is never case sensitive.

Tip 80 from
Rafe Colburn

MySQL keeps a history of the queries and commands that have been used previously. You can recall queries you entered in the past by pressing the up arrow key, or Ctrl+P in the MySQL client. Each time you press the "previous command" key, MySQL will move backward one command in the history. The commands appear in the history from most recent to furthest in the past. If you want to move back downward through the list, you can use the down arrow or Ctrl+N.

MySQL FEATURES

MySQL supports a number of features that distinguish it from other databases. MySQL provides a somewhat unique underlying architecture that makes it difficult for the authors of MySQL to add some common functionality to their database, but it makes up for it in speed, stability, and portability of the data. Unlike most databases, which store all their data in large common files, or even in a separate file system, MySQL stores each table in a set of three files. The table files are organized based on which database they're a part of; each database consists of a directory unto itself, and all the files associated with tables in that database are stored in that directory.

A really nice feature of that architecture is that you can easily move database files from one MySQL server to another, and they can be easily backed up. To move them, you can just copy them into the new database directory where they will reside. For example, if your MySQL database files were stored in the directory /usr/local/var and you wanted to move the Movies table from the mysql database to a new database you created called Film, you could use the following shell commands (assuming you were logged in as the root user):

```
cd /usr/local/var
cp mysql/Movies.* Film/
```

All the files that begin with `Movies.` would be copied from the directory associated with the `mysql` database to the directory associated with the `Film` database. The other large advantage of MySQL relating to this architecture is that you can perform file operations on table files that aren't currently being used. Most databases are difficult to back up because they store all their data in one or a few monolithic data files. If the database server is using any data in the data files, they generally can't be copied. On the other hand, because the storage of MySQL data is broken down by table, only the actual tables being used by MySQL at any given time are locked. You're free to perform any operations you like on the other table files.

MySQL also provides some interesting commands that aren't supported by other databases. For example, you can use the `REPLACE` statement to automatically replace rows in a table if the new record you're inserting has the same primary key as an existing record. Take a look at the queries in Listing 21.3 to see how `REPLACE` is used.

LISTING 21.3   USING THE REPLACE STATEMENT

```
SELECT movie_id, movie_title
FROM Movies
WHERE movie_id IN (1, 8);

+----------+---------------+
¦ movie_id ¦ movie_title   ¦
+----------+---------------+
¦        1 ¦ Mineral House ¦
+----------+---------------+
1 row in set (0.00 sec)

REPLACE Movies
(movie_id, movie_title, studio_id, budget, gross,
release_date, director_id)
VALUES
( 1, 'Another Movie', 1, 25, 35, '1987-12-01', 1);

Query OK, 2 rows affected (0.00 sec)

REPLACE Movies
(movie_id, movie_title, studio_id, budget, gross,
release_date, director_id)
VALUES
( 8, 'The Programmer', 3, 50, 45.3, '17-APR-93', 1);

Query OK, 1 row affected (0.01 sec)

SELECT movie_id, movie_title
FROM Movies
WHERE movie_id IN (1, 8);

+----------+---------------+
¦ movie_id ¦ movie_title   ¦
+----------+---------------+
¦        1 ¦ Another Movie ¦
```

PART

VI

CH

21

continues

LISTING 21.3 CONTINUED

```
|        8 | The Programmer |
+----------+----------------+
2 rows in set (0.00 sec)
```

The first query simply selects movies with a `movie_id` of 1 or 8 from the database to show that only the row with the `movie_id` 1 exists. Then you issue two REPLACE commands, one which has the same primary key value as an existing row, and one which does not. The first of the two REPLACE statements replaces the row with a `movie_id` of 1. MySQL reports that the query affected two rows because it deletes the existing row before it inserts the new record in its place. The second query simply inserts the record because there are no existing movies with a `movie_id` of 8. Finally, run the SELECT statement again to show that the row with a `movie_id` of 1 has been replaced, and that the new movie has been inserted.

MySQL also provides two interesting commands for extracting information internal to the database. The DESCRIBE command is used to retrieve the specifications for a table, and the SHOW command is used to extract all sorts of general information about objects in the database. The DESCRIBE (or DESC) command provides a list of columns from a table, along with their data types, default values, indexes, and other information. The description of the Movies table appears in Listing 21.4.

LISTING 21.4 A TABLE DESCRIPTION FROM MYSQL

```
SHOW Movies;
```

```
+--------------+-------------+------+-----+---------+-------+
| Field        | Type        | Null | Key | Default | Extra |
+--------------+-------------+------+-----+---------+-------+
| movie_id     | int(11)     |      | PRI | 0       |       |
| movie_title  | varchar(25) | YES  |     | NULL    |       |
| studio_id    | int(11)     | YES  |     | NULL    |       |
| budget       | float(10,2) | YES  |     | NULL    |       |
| gross        | float(10,2) | YES  |     | NULL    |       |
| release_date | date        | YES  |     | NULL    |       |
| director_id  | int(11)     | YES  |     | NULL    |       |
+--------------+-------------+------+-----+---------+-------+
7 rows in set (0.00 sec)
```

The columns in the results of a DESCRIBE are the column name, the data type for the column, whether the column can be null, whether the column is a key, the default value for the column, and any extra information about the column. For example, if a column is auto-incrementing, the Extra column contains `auto_increment`. The DESCRIBE command is actually a synonym for the SHOW COLUMNS command. There are a number of other SHOW commands used to gather internal information from a database. For example, you can get a list of tables for a particular database by using the SHOW TABLES command, as shown in Listing 21.5.

LISTING 21.5   RETRIEVING A LIST OF TABLES FROM A DATABASE

```
SHOW TABLES FROM movies;

+------------------+
¦ Tables in movies ¦
+------------------+
¦ Movies           ¦
¦ Studios          ¦
+------------------+
2 rows in set (0.01 sec)
```

MySQL Limitations

One important fact to remember about MySQL is that it doesn't support the entire SQL-92 specification. In fact, there are a number of features that are found in most relational databases that are not found in MySQL. Some of these features have been left out by design; others are on the to-do list, but hadn't been added at the time of writing.

LACK OF SUBQUERIES

One important SQL construct not supported by MySQL is subqueries. In MySQL, you cannot use queries like

```
SELECT movie_title
FROM Movies
WHERE studio_id IN
        (SELECT studio_id
         FROM Studios
         WHERE studio_state = 'CA')
```

Support for subqueries is planned for a future version of MySQL; they just aren't available yet. As I discussed throughout Chapter 9, "Subqueries," in most cases where a subquery can be used, a join can be used as well. For example, you can duplicate the functionality of the subquery I just entered using the joining query in Listing 21.6.

LISTING 21.6   A JOINING QUERY THAT REPLACES A SUBQUERY

```
SELECT movie_title
FROM Movies, Studios
WHERE Movies.studio_id = Studios.studio_id
AND studio_state = 'CA'

+------------------+
¦ movie_title      ¦
+------------------+
¦ Another Movie    ¦
¦ Codependence Day ¦
¦ Prince Kong      ¦
¦ The Code Warrior ¦
¦ The Linux Files  ¦
+------------------+
5 rows in set (0.01 sec)
```

NO TRANSACTIONS

MySQL does not include support for transactions. All statements that modify the database are committed as soon as they are executed, and no means for rolling back changes is provided. Implementing a transactional system involves storing all the changes made to the database, so that those changes can be undone in the future, if required. MySQL is not equipped to store changes in that manner.

The second major advantage of transactions, other than the ability to roll back any changes you have made, is the ability to prevent users of the database from viewing or altering data that is currently being modified by another user. MySQL allows users to manually lock tables using the LOCK TABLES and UNLOCK TABLES statements. You can simulate a transaction by locking a table, making all of the modifications required, and then unlocking the table. The locks prevent other users from accessing the table (or tables) while you're doing your work. Of course, overuse of locks can degrade the performance of your database significantly if there are lots of concurrent users all trying to use and lock the same table.

STORED PROCEDURES, TRIGGERS, AND CURSORS

Currently, there is no support in MySQL for stored procedures, triggers, or cursors. Support for stored procedures and cursors is planned for a future version. There are no plans to include support for triggers in MySQL because of the performance implications of using triggers. MySQL is pretty tightly focused on providing high performance, and the developers generally do not support features that are detrimental to overall database performance.

FOREIGN KEY RELATIONSHIPS

MySQL does not support foreign key relationships, like those created with the REFERENCES clause in other databases. As the developers of MySQL point out in their manual, and as has been mentioned elsewhere in this book, foreign key relationships are used to maintain referential integrity, not to allow joins between tables. Joins can occur between any join-compatible columns.

MySQL does not support foreign key relationships for reasons of performance. When you create a foreign key relationship, any time you issue an insert, update, or delete, that relationship must be checked to ensure that integrity exists between the record being inserted and the referenced values in other tables. There is some performance penalty for this verification.

There are also locking issues involved with foreign key relationships. You can create foreign keys that cascade changes from one table to other tables as well. Whenever one of these statements is executed, all the tables to which the change applies must be locked. For multi-user databases, this can also hamper performance.

MySQL Data Types

MySQL provides a wide variety of data types that you can use when you define tables. They fall into the four standard categories available in most databases; numeric data, character data, temporal data, and large objects. Table 21.1 contains a list of the data types supported by MySQL, and the amount of data that they can hold. You can specify integers as being unsigned if you prefer.

TABLE 21.1   DATA TYPES SUPPORTED BY MySQL

Datatype	Description
TINYINT	A 1-byte integer field, which supports unsigned integers from 0 to 255, or signed integers from –127 to 127.
SMALLINT	A 2-byte integer. It has an unsigned range from 0 to 65,535, and a signed range from –32,768 to 32,768.
MEDIUMINT	A 3-byte integer. Unsigned range from 0 to 16,777,215, signed range from –8,388,608 to 8,388,607.
INT	A 4-byte integer. Ranges from –2,147,483,648 to 2,147,483,647, or 0 to 4,294,967,295 as an unsigned integer. INTEGER is a synonym for INT.
BIGINT	An 8-byte integer. Calculations are performed using BIGINT values, so if you're going to use a BIGINT field in your database, make sure that the values in it are not so large that they will overflow the database when used in calculations.
FLOAT (*precision*)	A float field with the precision expressed in terms of the number of bytes consumed. The two accepted values for precision are 4 and 8. Using 4 creates a single precision floating point number, and 8 creates a double precision floating point number. The details of these two types will be described in terms of the FLOAT and DOUBLE data types.
FLOAT	A 4-byte floating point number, which can range from –3.402823466E+38 to –1.175494351E-38, 0 and –1.175494351E-38 to 3.402823466E+38.
DOUBLE	An 8-byte double precision floating point number, which can hold the following range of values: –1.7976931348623157E+308 to –2.2250738585072014E-308, 0 and 2.2250738585072014E-308 to 1.7976931348623157E+308. The DOUBLE PRECISION and REAL datatypes are synonyms for DOUBLE.
DECIMAL	A floating point field with the same capacity as DOUBLE. The number is stored within the field in a character format instead of being reduced to its hexadecimal equivalent for storage. The NUMERIC datatype is a synonym for DECIMAL.

PART

VI

CH

21

continues

TABLE 21.1   CONTINUED

Datatype	Description
DATE	A date (without a time). It prints dates in YYYY-MM-DD format, and can accept dates in a number of formats. Supports dates from 1000-01-01 to 9999-12-31.
DATETIME	A date and time field. It displays values in this format: YYYY-MM-DD HH:MM:SS. It supports values from 1000-01-01 00:00:00 to 9999-12-31 23:59:59.
TIMESTAMP	A date and time ranging from the beginning of the UNIX epoch, 1970-01-01 00:00:00, until the 32-bit field containing the number of seconds since the epoch overflows in the year 2037. If no value is assigned to this field in an INSERT or UPDATE statement, the current date and time are inserted.
TIME	A time value ranging from –838:59:59 to 838:59:59.
YEAR	A year. The allowable values are 1901 to 2155, and 0000. MySQL displays YEAR values in YYYY format, but allows you to assign values to YEAR columns using either strings or numbers. (The YEAR type is new in MySQL 3.22.)
CHAR	A fixed length character field that can range from 1 to 255 bytes in length. CHAR fields are right padded with spaces to consume excess capacity left after a value is inserted in them.
VARCHAR	A variable length character field from 1 to 255 bytes. It only consumes as much space as the data in the field occupies.
TINYBLOB, TINYTEXT	A binary or text column up to 255 characters in size.
BLOB, TEXT	A binary or text column up to 65,535 bytes in size.
MEDIUMBLOB, MEDIUMTEXT	A binary or text column up to 16,777,215 bytes in size.
LONGBLOB, LONGTEXT	A binary or text column up to 4,294,967,295 bytes in size.
ENUM ('item1', 'item2', ...)	A string column that can consist of one of the values specified in the list of values in the column definition.
SET ('item1', 'item2', ...)	A string column that can contain any number of members of the list of values specified when the column is defined.

Integer types in MySQL can be defined with the UNSIGNED keyword to indicate that all values in the field must be positive numbers. This doubles the capacity of the field in terms of the size of number it can hold by shifting all the capacity into positive numbers. MySQL also provides the optional ZEROFILL flag, which left pads numbers with zeros up to their capacity when they are displayed. All floating point fields can also be entered with optional display sizes and levels of precision after the decimal point. The display size includes all of the digits in the number, and the decimal and sign if necessary. So, if you define a column as FLOAT (5,2), any of the following numbers will fit: –9.99, 99.99, 1.00, –1.00, 11.00. Because three spaces in the number are used by the two mandatory digits after the decimal and the decimal itself, this particular field won't hold any more than a two digit number.

MySQL Syntax

MySQL supports standard SQL syntax for nearly all statements; however, like all databases, it does provide its own wrinkles with regard to the SQL language. Like most databases, MySQL has its own distinct join syntax. In fact, MySQL supports perhaps the widest variety of methods for joining tables of any database.

It supports the standard join syntax supported by most relational databases; placing multiple tables in the FROM clause of a SELECT statement, and joining them with a condition in the WHERE clause. Listing 21.7 contains an example of this type of join that I'll use as the baseline for discussing the other forms of joins you can use. I'm only including one movie in the query results in order to conserve space.

LISTING 21.7   A STANDARD SQL JOIN

```
SELECT movie_title, studio_name
FROM Movies, Studios
WHERE Movies.studio_id = Studios.studio_id
AND Movies.movie_id = 1

+---------------+--------------+
| movie_title   | studio_name  |
+---------------+--------------+
| Another Movie | Giant        |
+---------------+--------------+
1 row in set (0.01 sec)
```

If you prefer, you can replace the comma in the FROM clause with the keyword JOIN in your queries. A query written this way is included in Listing 21.8. The only difference between a query using this syntax and the standard syntax is that the comma is replaced with JOIN; the join comparison in the WHERE clause is still required.

LISTING 21.8   USING THE JOIN KEYWORD IN A QUERY

```
SELECT movie_title, studio_name
FROM Movies JOIN Studios
WHERE Movies.studio_id = Studios.studio_id
AND Movies.movie_id = 1

+---------------+--------------+
| movie_title   | studio_name  |
+---------------+--------------+
| Another Movie | Giant        |
+---------------+--------------+
1 row in set (0.00 sec)
```

In place of the JOIN keyword in Listing 21.8, you can use the STRAIGHT_JOIN keyword, or the CROSS JOIN keywords; all have the same effect. MySQL also supports the SQL-92 syntax used by Microsoft Access and some other databases. In fact, for outer joins, the SQL-92 syntax is the only syntax supported by MySQL. When you use this syntax, the joining

PART

VI

CH

21

comparison is included in the ON clause, and the other limiting comparisons stay in the WHERE clause. The LEFT JOIN syntax is demonstrated in Listing 21.9.

```
SELECT movie_title, studio_name
FROM Movies LEFT JOIN Studios
ON Movies.studio_id = Studios.studio_id
WHERE Movies.movie_id = 1

+---------------+-------------+
| movie_title   | studio_name |
+---------------+-------------+
| Another Movie | Giant       |
+---------------+-------------+
1 row in set (0.01 sec)
```

You can turn the query into an outer join by inserting the OUTER keyword between LEFT and JOIN in the query. Interestingly, MySQL does not support the equivalent RIGHT JOIN syntax. If you wanted to write the query in such a way that all the rows from the Studios table would be included in an outer join, you would need to swap the order of the tables in the query, placing the Studios table on the left of the LEFT OUTER JOIN keywords.

There's another method available for creating joins using the SQL-92 syntax. Rather than including a join comparison in the ON clause, you can specify columns with USING to create an equijoin. For example, in Listing 21.10, I rewrite the query from Listing 21.7 with USING.

LISTING 21.10   WRITING A JOIN QUERY WITH THE USING CONSTRUCT

```
SELECT movie_title, studio_name
FROM Movies LEFT JOIN Studios
USING (studio_id)
WHERE Movies.movie_id = 1

+---------------+-------------+
| movie_title   | studio_name |
+---------------+-------------+
| Another Movie | Giant       |
+---------------+-------------+
1 row in set (0.00 sec)
```

The columns listed in the USING clause must appear in all the tables being joined. It is similar to the final join syntax that I'm going to cover, the natural join. A natural join does not require a joining comparison, as it simply matches all the columns with the same name between the tables in the join, as shown in Listing 21.11.

LISTING 21.11   USING A NATURAL JOIN

```
SELECT movie_title, studio_name
FROM Movies NATURAL LEFT JOIN Studios
WHERE Movies.movie_id = 1
```

```
+----------------+---------------+
| movie_title    | studio_name   |
+----------------+---------------+
| Another Movie  | Giant         |
+----------------+---------------+
1 row in set (0.01 sec)
```

COMMENTS

MySQL supports two comment styles. It supports C-style block level comments, which begin with /* and end with */, so if you wanted to remove the WHERE clause from a query, you could do so using the following comments:

```
SELECT studio_name
FROM Studios
/*
WHERE studio_city = 'Orange'
AND studio_state = 'TX'
*/
```

It also supports the use of the # character to comment out the characters from the point where it is used to the end of the current line of code. It's useful if you want to remove a single line from your code, or you want to include comments beside existing code, like this:

```
# Get a list of studios in Orange, Texas
SELECT studio_name             # Select only the studio name
FROM Studios
WHERE studio_city = 'Orange'   # Orange is a small town in east Texas
AND studio_state = 'TX'
```

MySQL does not support the standard ANSI single line comment marker, --.

Tip 81 from
Rafe Colburn

> Despite the fact that the MySQL database server does not support -- to begin an inline comment, the mysql client application automatically strips out any input that follows a --. So if you paste queries from other databases into mysql, they'll work with the standard ANSI comments; you just can't use them in programs that call a MySQL database.

MSQL

MSQL, or Mini-SQL, is the predecessor to MySQL. MSQL provides users with an even smaller subset of SQL commands than does MySQL. Like MySQL, MSQL is very light-weight, easy to install, and easy to administer. It is also supported by the same array of application development tools that support MySQL.

Like MySQL, MSQL ships with its own command tool, conveniently named msql. To start the msql command-line tool, you can type the following command at the UNIX shell prompt:

```
msql [-h host] database
```

However, before you can use msql to run queries, you must create a database (and tables within that database), and create tables within that database. Databases are created using the msqladmin program. To create a database, you simply run the following command:

```
msqladmin database_name
```

To create the movies database in MSQL, the following command is used (you must be logged in as a user with write access to the database directories):

```
msqladmin movies
```

After the database is created, you can log in to the database with the msql program:

```
msql movies
```

RUNNING QUERIES IN MSQL

MSQL supports a very limited subset of the SQL standard. It supports SELECT, UPDATE, INSERT, and DELETE statements, and allows users to CREATE and DROP objects within the database. However, it doesn't provide a lot of the advanced functionality found in other databases, including aggregate functions, such as GROUP BY, or HAVING.

When you use the MSQL command-line tool, commands other than SQL statements begin with a \ (backslash) character. For example, to execute a query after it has been entered, you must use the command \g. The MSQL backslash commands are

- \h for help
- \g to execute the current query
- \e to edit the previous query
- \q to quit the MSQL tool

CREATING DATABASE OBJECTS IN MSQL

MSQL supports the creation of tables, indexes, and sequences using the CREATE statement. The CREATE TABLE command supports the NOT NULL constraint, but does not provide a facility for setting the default value for columns, primary keys, foreign key relationships, or other constraints on the data that can appear in a column. An example of a CREATE TABLE statement for MSQL appears in Listing 21.12.

LISTING 21.12   A CREATE TABLE STATEMENT FOR MSQL

```
CREATE TABLE Movies
(movie_id INT NOT NULL,
movie_title CHAR(25),
studio_id INT,
budget REAL,
gross REAL,
release_date DATE.
director_id INT)

Query OK.  1 row(s) modified or retrieved.
```

The data types supported by MSQL are very primitive. As you can see from the CREATE TABLE statement in Listing 21.12, three data types are used in the table; int, char, and real. In fact, the entire set of MSQL datatypes comprises only those three types, along with the text type. These datatypes are described in Table 21.2.

TABLE 21.2   MSQL DATATYPES

Datatype	Description
CHAR(*size*)	A standard character field, right padded out to *size* if the data entered in the field does not occupy all the space allocated to it.
TEXT(*size*)	A text field that is resized dynamically to fit the text inserted in it. Neither indexes nor LIKE comparisons work with TEXT fields.
DATE	Stores dates in DD-Mon-YYYY format.
MONEY	Numeric datatype accurate to two decimal places.
INT	Numeric datatype for integers.
UINT	Numeric datatype for unsigned integers.
REAL	Numeric datatype for floating point numbers.

MSQL supports the use of both indexes and unique indexes. The CREATE INDEX statement in MSQL hews to the SQL standard, as shown in Listing 21.13.

LISTING 21.13   A CREATE INDEX STATEMENT IN MSQL

```
CREATE UNIQUE INDEX movie_id_index
ON Movies (movie_id)

Query OK.  1 row(s) modified or retrieved.
```

For creating unique IDs for use as primary keys, MSQL uses sequences rather than autoincrementing fields. I believe that sequences are actually preferable to autoincrementing fields because they allow you to find the primary key for a field before you actually insert the row. Listing 21.14 contains the code necessary to create a sequence for the movie_id field in the table Movies.

LISTING 21.14   CREATING A SEQUENCE IN MSQL

```
CREATE SEQUENCE ON Movies STEP 1 VALUE 1
\g

Query OK.  1 row(s) modified or retrieved.
```

PART
VI
CH
21

The VALUE keyword indicates where the sequence should begin, and the STEP keyword indicates how much to increment the sequence by each time a value is selected from it. After a sequence is created, you can retrieve the next value from it (and increment it) by selecting the column _seq from the table on which the sequence was created, as shown in Listing 21.15.

LISTING 21.15   RETRIEVING THE NEXT VALUE FROM AN MSQL SEQUENCE

```
SELECT _seq
FROM Movies
\g

Query OK.  1 row(s) modified or retrieved.

    +----------+
    | _seq     |
    +----------+
    | 2        |
    +----------+
```

DROPPING OBJECTS IN MSQL

Just as you can create items in MSQL, you can also drop them. There are three DROP state-ments, one for each of the objects that can be created. To drop a sequence, you use the DROP SEQUENCE command, as shown in Listing 21.16.

LISTING 21.16   DROPPING A SEQUENCE

```
DROP SEQUENCE FROM Movies
\g

Query OK.  1 row(s) modified or retrieved.
```

The code for dropping an index appears in Listing 21.17.

LISTING 21.17   DROPPING AN INDEX

```
DROP INDEX movie_id_index FROM Movies
\g

Query OK.  1 row(s) modified or retrieved.
```

Finally, MSQL uses the standard SQL syntax for dropping tables, as shown in Listing 21.18.

LISTING 21.18   DROPPING A TABLE IN MSQL

```
DROP TABLE Movies
\g

Query OK.  1 row(s) modified or retrieved.
```

OTHER MSQL QUERIES

SELECT, UPDATE, INSERT, and DELETE all conform to the standards described in the earlier chapters in this book. As I already explained earlier in the chapter, there is a significant amount of functionality in the SQL standard that is supported by many databases, but is not supported by MSQL (or MySQL, in some cases). When you're designing applications, you should be mindful of those limitations.

MSQL supports the standard syntax for joining queries; specifying multiple tables in the FROM clause and including a joining comparison in the WHERE clause of the query.

STRING COMPARISONS IN MSQL AND MYSQL

Both MSQL and MySQL support some advanced functionality for use with the LIKE comparison in SQL. Naturally, both of them support the basic LIKE comparison, which uses % to match any group of characters and _ to match any single character. (Use of the LIKE comparison is described in Chapter 6, "Using the WHERE Clause.")

However, they also offer some advanced versions of LIKE. Both MSQL and MySQL support the use of RLIKE, which is similar to LIKE, except that instead of supporting two basic wildcard characters, it supports the full suite of UNIX regular expressions. MSQL also includes support for CLIKE, a non–case-sensitive LIKE comparison, and SLIKE, which compares the Soundex values for two strings (described in Chapter 12).

There are two differences in the way LIKE works in MSQL and MySQL. The first is that MySQL supports the ESCAPE clause, which allows programmers to specify an escape character for the wildcards in LIKE. MSQL supports only the use of \ (backslash) as the escape character in strings used in LIKE comparisons. The second is that MSQL LIKE comparisons are case sensitive; if you want to use LIKE in a non–case-sensitive manner, you must use CLIKE. MySQL matches strings with the LIKE clause without regard for case.

USING RLIKE

The RLIKE comparison takes advantage of one of the most powerful features of the UNIX operating system, regular expressions. *Regular expressions* are really a language unto themselves for creating patterns to match specific strings. Regular expressions are much more powerful than the basic wildcard characters available in the ANSI SQL standard. Before I explain how to use regular expressions, take a look at the regular expression tokens available, listed in Table 21.3.

TABLE 21.3 REGULAR EXPRESSION TOKENS IN MSQL AND MYSQL

Token	Function
^	Match beginning of string. ^abc matches 'abc', but not '123abc'
$	Match end of string. abc$ matches '123abc' but not 'abc123'
*	Match 0 or more characters. X* matches 0 or more occurrences of X
+	Match 1 or more characters. X+ matches 1 or more occurrences of X.
?	Match 0 or 1 character. X? matches 0 or 1 occurrences of X.

PART

VI

CH

21

continues

TABLE 21.3   CONTINUED

Token	Function
.	Match any character. . matches any character; .* matches any group of characters, including an empty string
¦	Match either substring, for example (foo¦bar) matches either foo or bar
()	Group characters or substrings. (foo)* matches 0 or more occurrences of the string foo, for example 'foofoofoo'
[]	Match any one of the characters enclosed within. [abc]? matches a, b, or c
[^abc]	Match any character not enclosed within. [^abc]? matches any character other than a, b, or c.

The thing about the regular expression tokens is that they are meant to be used together as building blocks for single regular expressions. For example, a regular expression like .* just matches everything. Not very useful. However, a regular expression like '.*(foo¦bar).*' matches every string containing either foo or bar. That's more useful.

The ?, +, and * tokens can only be used with other characters or tokens; they have no meaning unto themselves. They just tell how many occurrences of the token that precedes them should be matched. The distinction between + and * is important. Consider the following comparison:

```
'foo' RLIKE '.+foo.+'
```

That comparison does not match, because .+ matches any one or more characters. Because there are no characters in the string before or after foo, the comparison fails. If the expression were written as follows, the match would be successful:

```
'foo' RLIKE '.*foo.*'
```

The .* construct matches 0 or more occurrences of any character, so the fact that there are no characters on either side of foo does not prevent the query from matching. The square braces construct is also important. It treats the characters within it as individuals, rather than grouping them together. Consider the following two comparisons:

```
'bacabc' RLIKE '[abc]*'
'bacabc' RLIKE '(abc)*'
```

The first comparison will match; the second will not. The second comparison will match any number of occurrences of the string abc, so it will match the following strings:

```
''
'abc'
'abcabc'
'abcabcabc'
```

It will not match any strings that contain anything other than occurrences of 'abc'. The first of the two RLIKE comparisons will match any number of occurrences of the characters a, b, or c. Because the string being evaluated against the regular expression contains only a's, b's, and c's, the regular expression matches it.

Regular expressions may seem a bit esoteric at first, but they're incredibly powerful. The key is to learn the basic pattern matching tokens, and then experiment with them. Find a column with a variety of strings to match, and practice writing regular expressions that match particular subsets of those strings. Eventually, you'll get the hang of it.

IN THE REAL WORLD

Before you decide to use any software product, it's important to determine whether it's really suited to the task you're planning to use it to accomplish. Just because a product can be used to take on a particular task, doesn't mean you should use it for that task. I could have written this entire book in Notepad (or in ed, if I wanted to write it on a computer running UNIX), but there were better tools available for doing so.

While MySQL and MSQL provide a lot of nice features, their real strength is in the fact that they are very lightweight, fast, and easy to maintain. The other advantage that they provide is that they are extremely inexpensive. The problem is that they don't provide a number of capabilities that many other databases do offer.

The most significant barrier to widespread adoption of MSQL and MySQL is the lack of transactions. Because neither of the databases keep transaction logs or allow transactions to be rolled back, it is difficult to use them in an environment where lost transactions are absolutely unacceptable. Other missing features, such as the lack of views and the lack of support for subqueries, can make the development process a bit more difficult, but they don't jeopardize the ability of the database to provide bulletproof reliability.

Lack of support for transactions pretty much eliminates MSQL and MySQL from contention as data repositories for transaction processing systems. Not many enterprises can afford to bank on using a database that presents a real chance of catastrophic loss of data if the database fails between backups. However, MySQL and MSQL are still very useful for plenty of other data storage and retrieval tasks.

MSQL and MySQL have seen wide adoption as the data repositories for Web sites. More and more Web sites are publishing their content dynamically from relational databases, and the availability of MySQL and MSQL for common Web server platforms such as Linux and FreeBSD, as well as easy connectivity with common Web publishing tools such as PHP and Perl, has made them the natural choice for Web application programmers.

Many Web sites are being built that store all of their content in relational databases, and publish pages by retrieving data from the database and presenting it using templates. In these types of scenarios, the weaknesses of MySQL and MSQL are not particularly important. In these cases, relational databases simply provide a more convenient form of storage than flat text files, and thus the integrity features that are integral to some applications are not required. The high performance and cost savings provided by MySQL and MSQL can outweigh the high-end features that are the major selling points of most commercial databases.

PUBLISHING DATABASES ON THE WEB

CHAPTER 22

WEB PROGRAMMING FUNDAMENTALS

In this chapter

Relational databases and the World Wide Web are, in many ways, a match made in heaven. The Web is based on the idea of a universal client for data access, and relational databases are, file systems excluded, the dominant technology for the storage and retrieval of data. By creating interfaces from relational databases to Web browsers, you can provide quick and easy access to your data to an incredibly wide audience without forcing them to learn SQL or installing a special application on their own computer.

The key component when deploying Web-based database applications is a *middleware* piece that allows the Web server to communicate with the relational database. Because this software component is so important, there are many, many products that provide this functionality. No matter what application development paradigm you're used to, there's a Web *application server* that will enable you to apply that paradigm to Web application development.

Before I discuss individual application servers and how they are used, I'd like to first explain, in a basic sense, how communications between Web browsers and Web servers are accomplished, how the Web works overall, and, more importantly, how these relate to writing database-backed applications. I'd also like to cover some preliminary topics such as the basic HTML you need to know and how Web applications in general work.

BASIC WEB ARCHITECTURE

A detailed discussion of how the Web works is beyond the scope of this book, but I would like to cover at least the basics of how the Web works. You're probably already aware that the Web is just a single Internet application. The Web is a client/server system; the Web browser serves as the client, and the Web server is, well, the server.

When relational databases are integrated into a Web application, an application server is generally tossed into the mix as well. The application server processes requests sent to it by the Web server, and it creates the response that the Web server sends to the Web client. The communication between the Web client and server is accomplished using HTTP, the Hypertext Transfer Protocol.

The details of how this communication occurs are documented in RFC 1945, which describes version 1.0 of the protocol, and RFC 2068, which describes version 1.1 of the protocol. You can find more information about how the HTTP protocol works at the following URLs:

- http://www.cis.ohio-state.edu/htbin/rfc/rfc1945.html
- http://www.cis.ohio-state.edu/htbin/rfc/rfc2068.html

HTML

In this chapter, I don't plan on discussing HTML in detail because it's a topic that can, and has, filled entire books. HTML is a markup language; tags are inserted into standard text to describe how that text should be presented. It has been extended since its creation to enable

Web developers to create forms-based application interfaces. Most Web browsers also support JavaScript, a simple scripting language designed to enable application developers to include interactive features in their applications that don't require communication with the server.

HTML forms are very important to Web application developers and are described in this chapter. Another HTML feature that is important for database programmers is support for presenting data in a tabular format. When you retrieve query results from a database, in many cases, it's useful to present the data within a table (especially because relational data takes the form of tables within the database).

There is plenty of reference material available for learning HTML, both on the Web and in printed form. You might find the following Web sites useful if you're interested in learning HTML:

- http://www.htmlhelp.com
- http://www.wdvl.com
- http://www.webreference.com

You might also want to look at the following books. There are many HTML books available, and these are just some of the most popular or best regarded:

- *Teach Yourself Web Publishing with HTML 4 in a Week*, Laura Lemay and Arman Danesh
- *HTML 4 for the World Wide Web: Visual Quickstart Guide*, Liz Castro
- *HTML: The Definitive Guide*, Chuck Musciano, Bill Kennedy, and Mike Loukides

CREATING HTML FORMS

HTML forms are created using HTML tags. There are a number of different standard user interface elements that can be used within HTML forms. Text fields, radio buttons, check boxes, and pull-down select lists can all be incorporated into the design of a Web page. Form elements are assigned names and are returned to the Web server as name/value pairs when the form is submitted.

Generally speaking, HTML forms will map directly to queries that will be submitted to the database used by the application. For example, the fields in a search form might be used to populate the WHERE or ORDER BY clauses of a SELECT statement. A user registration form would be used to specify the values for an INSERT statement. As I discuss the various fields available for forms, you should consider how they would map to the schema of a database.

When you create pages that use forms, it's important to remember that the form elements take the appearance of the standard user interface widgets on the platform on which the application is being viewed. So, on a Macintosh, the form fields look like other Macintosh input widgets, and on Windows, they look like Windows widgets. At present, you can't make many changes to the appearance of form elements through a Web page; the appearance is standard. This isn't altogether a bad thing because the common appearance of the form elements helps users distinguish them from the rest of an HTML page.

Before you can start creating the fields in a form, you have to create the form itself. Forms are created using the opening and closing <form> tags, as shown in this example:

```
<form>
... insert form fields here ...
</form>
```

The <form> tag has a number of attributes. First, let me discuss the default behavior of a form. If you specify no attributes in the <form> tag, the following assumptions are made:

- The form is submitted to itself. If the form appears on a static HTML page, nothing will happen. However, if the same program is used to generate the page and process the form input, this makes sense. This is often useful if the form validates the user's input and returns the form to the user with her input intact if she made a mistake when she entered data.

- The form uses the get method. The name and value pairs from the form will be encoded and appended to the URL when the form is submitted, where they can be accessed using the QUERY_STRING environment variable.

- The default encoding scheme to escape special characters in the form input is application/x-www-form-urlencoded. This is perfectly fine as long as the form does not include a file upload field.

Now look at the attributes that can be used to modify the default behavior of forms. To change the URL to which the form will be submitted, the action attribute is used. For example, to submit a form to a CGI program called form_proc.cgi, the following tag is used:

```
<form action="/cgi-bin/form_proc.cgi">
```

When the form is submitted, it will call the form_proc.cgi script in the cgi-bin directory on the Web server. You can even submit forms to programs on different Web servers by including the full URL to the form-processing program in the action attribute of your form.

For form submission, there are two methods available, get and post. The get method submits all the values in the form through the query string, which is appended to the URL in the action attribute. The get method is the default. In some cases, you might prefer to use the post method, which submits the form data in the body of the request sent to the Web server. The two methods are processed differently when they arrive at the Web server.

Choosing Between get and post

Under what circumstances should you use the get and post methods? There are some particular cases under which the get method is very useful, but most of the time, you can use the post method.

Basically, the get method should be used when you want to be able to access the results of the query without resubmitting the form. For example, say that you have a page that enables users to enter their zip code into a form field and to retrieve a weather forecast for their area. If you use the `get` method, the user can bookmark the results page and come back any time because his zip code will be captured as part of the URL for the results page. The URL would look something like this:

```
http://www.example.com/cgi-bin/weather.cgi?zip=27511
```

On the other hand, if you used the `post` method, the zip code would be stored in the body of the request, and the URL would be as follows:

```
http://www.example.com/cgi-bin/weather.cgi
```

If a user wanted to come back and see his weather report again later, he'd be forced to enter his zip code in the form again and resubmit it.

Sometimes, you'll want to call programs that accept arguments without using a form at all. In those cases, the `get` method is more or less mandatory. A program that uses the `post` method must be called through a form; on the other hand, you can call a program that uses the `get` method from a normal link such as this one:

```
<a href="view.cgi?view=all">View all records.</a>
```

When the user clicks the link, the `view.cgi` script will be called, and the `view=all` name and value pair will be sent to the script through the query string.

On the other hand, if your form has many fields, the URL can get very long if you use the `get` method. In those cases, it often makes more sense to go ahead and use the `post` method.

To change the encoding scheme for a form, the `enctype` attribute is used. The default setting for `enctype` is fine unless you have a file upload field in your form, which I'll describe a bit later.

There are some other form attributes that are mainly used in JavaScript programming. For example, you can enter a name for your forms using the `name` attribute, but the form name is only used if you want to reference the form using JavaScript.

Of course, a form with no input fields isn't very useful. Now that you know how to create a form, let me review the form elements supported by HTML individually.

FORM FIELDS CREATED USING THE `<input>` TAG

Most form fields are created using the `<input>` tag. You can change the appearance and functionality of an input field by changing the value of the `type` attribute. The main thing that input fields have in common is that they need a name, which is assigned using the `name` attribute, to identify the data in that field when it is sent back to the server. A value can be assigned to them using the `value` attribute.

Consider briefly how a form field in an HTML form would map to an `UPDATE` statement for a database. HTML form fields have a `name` attribute and a `value` attribute. The `value` attribute just specifies the default value in the form; it is replaced by whatever the user enters in the form. The `name` attribute identifies the field. So, if you had a form that provided the front end to an `UPDATE` statement for the `Movies` table, you'd probably have a text field that enabled you to update the movie's title. First, the form would be populated using a `SELECT` statement before it was presented. The existing contents of the row being updated would be placed in the `value` attributes of the form to let the user know what she is updating. The field names would map to the names of the fields in the Movies table to enable the programmer to map the form input to fields used in the UPDATE statement. When the form is submitted, all the values from the form would be placed in an UPDATE statement, which would be executed to update the record.

Text Fields

Text fields are the most commonly used and most flexible form fields because they provide a space into which users can simply enter characters. The display size and maximum number of characters can be specified when the field is created. Generally speaking, the capacity of the form field should match the size of the field in the database with which the text field corresponds. Text fields are the staple of most forms for an obvious reason: They can accept nearly any type of data. An example of a text field is provided in Figure 22.1.

Figure 22.1
An HTML form.

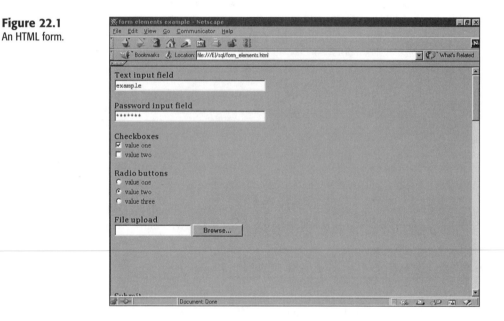

The code for creating a text field is as follows:

```
<input type="text" name="textfield" value="example"
size="40" maxlength ="100">
```

The <input> tag itself enables you to create several types of form elements, the type attribute is used to specify what type of element will be created. As you can see in the sample code, the type for this field is text. The value attribute is optional. If it is included, the text associated with the value attribute will be included in the text field when the page loads. The size attribute specifies how many characters wide the field will be, and the maxlength attribute specifies how many characters can be entered in the field.

Truth be told, every one of the attributes is optional. In Netscape Communicator 4.5, if you leave out all the attributes, leaving the tag <input>, a text field 20 characters wide with no name or value will appear. However, because the field has no name, the value entered in the field will not be included with the form when it is submitted. Also, leaving out attributes such as type and size is highly uncertain; you're far better off specifying exactly how the form should look rather than letting the browser do it for you.

PASSWORD FIELDS

Password fields are identical to text fields, except that all the characters entered in the field are masked so that the characters that the person enters can't be read on the screen. The field is designed so that people can't read private information over the shoulder of the person entering the value. All the attributes of the password type are identical to those of the text type. Figure 22.1 contains a password field, and the code that was used to create it is displayed here:

```
<input type="password" name="passwordfield" value="example"
size="40" maxlength="100">
```

> **Note**
>
> No special care is taken to protect the contents of a password field when they are sent to the Web server; they're sent as plain text. The mask on the field is really only useful to prevent snooping. When you store passwords in your database, you might want to consider encrypting them in some way or making sure that the permissions on your database don't allow unauthorized users to view the contents of that field.

CHECK BOXES

Check boxes are fields with only two states, on and off. Two check box fields are displayed in Figure 22.1. The code to create a check box field is as follows:

```
<input type="checkbox" value="yes" name="test" checked>
```

As you can see, the type for a check box field is checkbox. Also, like the password and text fields, there are both name and value attributes associated with a check box. As you know, a check box field has two states, on and off. There is only one value associated with the field. To get around this potential problem, the name and value pair is only returned to the Web server when the form is submitted if the check box is checked. If it is not checked, nothing corresponding to that field is sent back to the server. In that sense, the value associated with the check box field is meaningless. In your programs, you just need to check whether the field is defined in the request. If it is not, you know the check box was not checked. The checked attribute simply causes the default state of the field to be on. If the checked attribute is left out, the field will be unchecked when the form loads.

Tip 82 from
Rafe Colburn

> Check boxes generally correspond to fields that contain Boolean values in your database. If you have a BIT field in a table, the HTML form field that is best suited to correspond to it is the check box.

RADIO BUTTONS

Radio buttons enable users to select one of a group of options. Radio buttons usually appear as a group of <input> tags, rather than as a single <input> tag. When one button in the group is selected, the button that is currently selected is deselected. You can see an example of a radio button in Figure 22.1. The code used to create the three radio buttons is as follows:

```
<input type="radio" value="a" name="radio_button"> value one<br>
<input type="radio" value="b" name="radio_button" checked> value two<br>
<input type="radio" value="c" name="radio_button"> value three<br>
```

Buttons are grouped by the field name. All the radio buttons in a form that share the same name are considered to be members of a single group. When you click any of the three buttons, if one of the other buttons is selected, it will automatically be deselected. The checked attribute causes the button to be selected when the form loads. If you want, you can specify that more than one of the buttons is selected, but there's no reason to do so. You can leave out the checked attribute altogether, and the form will load with none of the buttons selected. If the user submits the form without one of the buttons in the group selected, that name and value will be left out of the form submission, as if it were a check box.

FILE UPLOADS

The file input type enables users to upload files through a form. The field itself appears as a text area and a Browse button. The user can either enter the path to the file she wants to upload in the field, or she can click the button to open a file selection box and specify the file that way. An example of a file field appears in Figure 22.1, and the <input> tag that creates it follows:

```
<input type="file" name="file_field">
```

> **Note**
>
> There are several means by which form submissions can be encoded. The default encoding type is as follows:
>
> `application/x-www-form-urlencoded`
>
> However, if you want to successfully upload files through an HTML form interface, you must use a different encoding scheme:
>
> `multipart/form-data`
>
> The encoding scheme is specified using the enctype attribute of the <form> tag. I'll discuss the encoding types more when I explain how form data is processed.

When a file is specified through a file field, the entire file is uploaded when the user submits the form. It is up to the program that receives the form submission to process the file.

There are a number of ways to handle files uploaded through one of these fields on the server side. Perhaps the easiest way to handle them is to just save the file to disk and store the path to the file in some sort of character field in the database. Another alternative is to create some sort of large object field in which to store the files and then just store the files themselves in the database.

HIDDEN FIELDS

Another type of form field that is created using the `<input>` tag is the hidden form field. Hidden fields are created by specifying the value `hidden` for the `type` attribute. There is no figure for this form field because hidden fields are not displayed in the browser. The `value` attribute is not required when you create hidden fields, but because users cannot see (or change) the values in hidden fields, a hidden field with no value is not very useful. A hidden field is created using the following tag:

```
<input type="hidden" name="user" value="rafeco">
```

When the form is submitted, the `user=rafeco` name and value pair is submitted along with the values of the rest of the fields in the form.

Caution

Hidden fields are not displayed in the browser window, but users can easily view the contents of a hidden field by viewing the source code of the page in which the field appears. Furthermore, users can actually change the values in hidden fields by saving the source code of the page, modifying the value in the field, and then submitting the data through the form they created rather than through your form on the Web. You should never try to hide confidential data in a hidden form field or rely on the fact that users can't edit the values in a hidden form field in your applications. HTML forms are inherently insecure. You should not make any assumptions about the data you receive through them.

Hidden fields generally aren't used to populate queries on the back end; rather, they're used to maintain application state. For example, say that you are writing a Web application to insert a new record in a table with 30 columns. One option is to present the user with a form with 30 fields on it, which takes a long time to fill out. Another option is to break the form up into two parts and to allow the user to fill both of them out before the actual record is inserted into the database. To accomplish this task, you break the form into two separate forms. When the first form is submitted, the second form presents the user with all the fields that were excluded from the first form, as well as all the information from the first form in hidden fields. Then, when the user submits the second form, all the information for the new record is included. You can use that information to populate an `INSERT` statement.

SUBMIT BUTTONS

After a form is filled out, it must be sent to a Web server for processing. If a form contains one text field, no more and no less, the form can be submitted by hitting the Enter key while the cursor is in that field. If the form contains either no text fields or more than one text field, a submit button is required to send the form to the server.

Note

You can also submit forms using JavaScript, but for the most part, you'll want to include submit buttons on your forms. Submit buttons make the forms understandable to users and enable users with browsers that don't support JavaScript to use the form.

To create a submit button on a form, an `<input>` tag with the attribute `type="submit"` is required. The submit button in Figure 22.2 is created using this tag:

```
<input type="submit">
```

Figure 22.2
Submit and reset buttons.

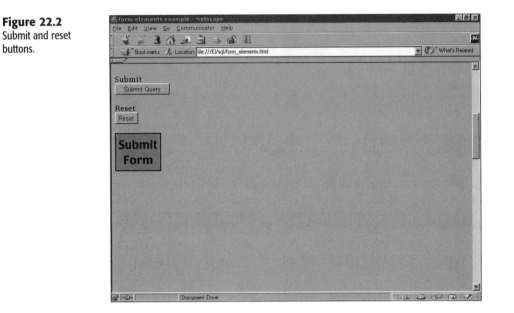

The basic functionality of a submit button is to send the contents of a form to the URL specified in the action attribute of the `<form>` tag itself. To change the label on a submit button, the `value` attribute is used. The text assigned to the `value` attribute is used as the label on the button; if no value is specified, the Web browser's default is used instead. As you can see from Figure 22.2, `Submit Query` is the default for Netscape Communicator 4.5. If the `name` attribute is specified, the `name` and `value` for the submit button are submitted along with the rest of the values in the form. This is useful if you want to create a form that has multiple submit buttons that provide different results. You can either assign different names to the buttons and check for the presence of those fields in your program or assign the same names and different values to the buttons. Only the name and value pair for the button that is clicked will be returned to the server.

RESET BUTTONS

Reset buttons, which are created using the `<input>` tag and a `type` attribute of `reset`, return a form to the state that it was in when the page loaded. It is important to remember that this button does not empty all the fields on a form. If there are default values in the form fields or the `checked` attribute is included for a field, that is the state to which the form will be returned. To create a reset button, the following code is used:

```
<input type="reset">
```

To change the label on a reset button, the value attribute is used, just as it is with submit buttons. No information is returned to the Web server from a reset button, even if a name is specified. There is an example of a reset button in Figure 22.2.

USING IMAGES AS SUBMIT BUTTONS

For some applications, the standard appearance of a submit button might not be appropriate to the interface design. Using the image input type, you can use images as submit buttons on your forms. This input type is really a hybrid of the <img> tag, which is used to include inline images in Web pages, and the <input> tag. The image with the text "Submit Form" in Figure 22.2 is an input field of type image. The HTML tag used to create the button in Figure 22.2 is as follows:

```
<input type="image" src="sbtn.gif" border=0>
```

All the attributes associated with the <img> tag can also be used with an image input button. Take a look at the following code, which contains all the attributes available for an image button.

```
<input type="image" src="sbtn.gif" border=0 height=80 width=100
hspace=5 vspace=5 alt="submit">
```

Most of the attributes used with the image input type are related to the image rather than to the form field. The height and width attributes are used to specify the size of the image, and the hspace and vspace attributes are used to create margins around the image. The alt attribute is used to enter a text message to be displayed if the image does not load, and the border attribute specifies the width, in pixels, of the border drawn around the image.

If a name attribute is assigned to an image input field, the x and y coordinates of the spot where the user clicked the image are sent to the server as values.

SELECT LISTS

Select lists are another common type of input field. There are really two distinct types of select list, as shown in Figure 22.3. Both are created using the <select> tag, and the difference is the value of the size attribute, which is used to specify the number of lines in the select list. Look at a single-line select list first. The following code is used to create the single-line select list in Figure 22.3:

```
<select name="select_list" size=1>
    <option value="1">Alaska
    <option value="2">California
    <option value="3">Pennsylvania
    <option value="4">Texas
</select>
```

Unlike input fields, select lists require both opening and closing <select> tags. The items in a select list are created using the <option> tag. All the <option> tags inside a set of <select> tags become individual items in the select list. The value attribute in each <option> tag specifies the value that is sent to the server if that item is selected, and the text that follows the <option> tag appears in the select list.

Figure 22.3
Select fields.

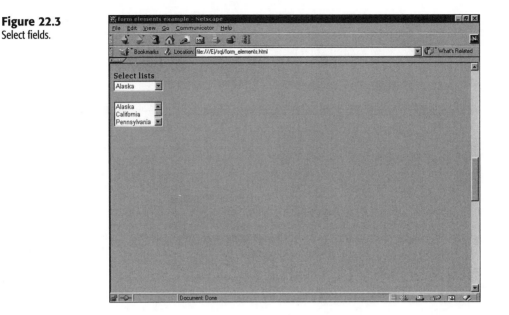

By default, the first item in the select list will be selected when the page containing the form loads. However, the `selected` attribute can be used to specify that a particular item is selected by default. For example, to cause the item `Pennsylvania` to be selected by default in the single-line select field in Figure 22.2, the following code would be used:

```
<select name="select_list" size=1>
    <option value="1">Alaska
    <option value="2">California
    <option value="3" selected>Pennsylvania
    <option value="4">Texas
</select>
```

For a single-line select box, a single name and value pair containing the name specified in the `<select>` tag and the value of the currently selected option is sent back to the server.

You can also create multi-line select lists that support the selection of more than one item. An example of a multi-line select list appears in Figure 22.3. It can be created using the following HTML:

```
<select name="multi_select" size=3>
    <option value="1">Alaska
    <option value="2">California
    <option value="3">Pennsylvania
    <option value="4">Texas
</select>
```

The preceding code creates a select list that displays three items from the list at a time. The `size` attribute of the `<select>` tag is used to specify the number of items that appear at a time.

Optionally, you can enable users to select more than one item at a time in a multi-item select list. To turn on this option, the `multiple` attribute is used. Here's the code used to create such a field:

```
<select name="multi_select" size=3 multiple>
    <option value="1">Alaska
    <option value="2">California
    <option value="3">Pennsylvania
    <option value="4">Texas
</select>
```

In Figure 22.4, you can see that both the items `Alaska` and `Pennsylvania` are selected. When the request is sent to the server, the items are sent as separate name and value pairs with the same name. Various application servers handle this scenario in different ways.

Figure 22.4
A select list that enables you to select multiple items.

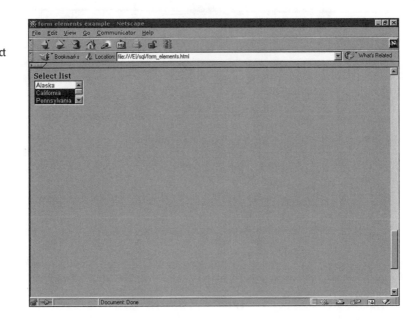

Select lists generally have an important role to play in database-backed Web applications. More often than not, they're populated by a query. For example, if you were writing a form to update records in the `Movies` table, you might enable the user to choose a studio for the movie from a select box. You would retrieve a list of all the studio names and IDs using a `SELECT` statement. The values in the select box would contain the studio IDs, and the studio names would be displayed. The `selected` attribute would be assigned based on the results of the query used to retrieve the record to be updated. The programmer is then assured that a valid studio is selected by the user and placed in the updated record.

TEXT AREAS

In some situations, you might require a larger input area than a single text-input field provides. You can create a multi-line text-input field using the <textarea> tag. There is an example of a text area in Figure 22.5, and the code to create that field is as follows:

```
<textarea name="text_area" rows=5 cols=60 wrap="virtual">
text goes here.
</textarea>
```

Figure 22.5
A multi-line
text-entry field.

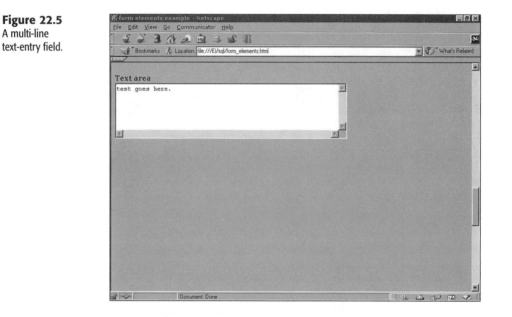

As you can see from the sample code, the <textarea> tag has a complementary closing tag. The text enclosed by the tag is placed in the text entry field when the form loads. Take a look at the attributes of the <textarea> tag. The rows and cols attributes are used to specify the size of the text input box.

The wrap attribute indicates how text should be formatted within the box and in the request when it is sent to the server. The default value for this attribute is none, which does not wrap the text within the box, nor does it add line feeds when the data is sent to the server. When the wrap attribute is set to none, you can type as many characters on a line as you want, and you will have to use the horizontal scrollbar in the text area to access the complete line of text. The only line feeds sent to the server will be those that the user enters manually.

The virtual setting causes the text entered in a text box to wrap automatically when you reach the right side of the box, but those line feeds are removed when the text is actually sent to the server. The virtual setting is useful if you want to want the text within a text box to be readable to users without forcing them to enter line feeds manually. Just as with the none setting, only line feeds that the user enters will be sent to the server.

The physical setting automatically wraps the text at the right side of the text entry box, and preserves those line wraps when the text is sent to the server. Basically, you can think of the virtual setting as soft-wrapping the text, and the physical setting as hard-wrapping the text.

Tip 83 from *Rafe Colburn*	When using textarea fields in a database-backed application, you need to keep in mind that there is no official size limit for these fields (although generally speaking, Web browsers have a limit on the amount of text that can be placed in such a field). So, you need to make sure that you allow enough space in the tables in your database to accommodate input from these types of fields, and that you check the user input before inserting it into the database to make sure that it isn't too large.

THE COMMON GATEWAY INTERFACE

To process data submitted through a form, the Web server usually has to provide the data to an external program and send that output of that program back to the user. An interface to external programs called the *Common Gateway Interface* (CGI) was included in the NCSA Web server, one of the first Web servers available. CGI provided a simple means by which external programs could be called by the Web server. Because it was the first such interface available, CGI has seen wide adoption and is now implemented by almost every Web server available. Because of its simplicity and the fact that it is almost universal, I'm going to discuss it here.

Many Web servers provide other interfaces to external programs that work differently. There are some problems with CGI, mainly related to performance, and these alternative interfaces avoid those problems. However, these interfaces are more often used by software developers than by Web programmers. For example, most application servers are written to take advantage of these higher performance interfaces instead of CGI. For now, I'd like to discuss how Web requests are handled through the CGI interface.

PROCESSING FORM DATA

After you have created a form, you have to process the data that is sent to the server when a user submits the form. Fortunately, there are a number of application server solutions available that eliminate the necessity of writing code to process form data. Even if you're writing a CGI script, there are libraries available for nearly every programming language that will automatically process data submitted through a form and place it in variables so that you can access it from within your program. That said, I'd still like to explain briefly how this is accomplished.

Remember that there are two methods that can be used for Web requests, get and post, and that the get method sends the form data as part of the URL. The post method sends the data as the body of the request. These two methods are processed by the Web server differently. I'm going to describe how data is passed from the Web server to an external program through CGI.

When a request is sent to the Web server using the get method, the form data is placed in the QUERY_STRING environment variable. Programs that process this data must read the data from the environment variable and process it from there.

On the other hand, when data is submitted using the post method, the Web server passes the data to the CGI program through standard input. Instead of reading the QUERY_STRING variable, your program should simply read and process the input stream delivered through standard input. You should also note that a request submitted using the post method can also include data passed to the server through the URL, and it will still be found in the QUERY_STRING environment variable.

As I said before, these days it's rarely necessary to even think about dealing with the data in the raw form in which it is delivered by the Web server. This task is so common that there are existing libraries that perform this task and provide the data in a more usable form.

RETURNING DATA TO A WEB BROWSER

After your CGI program has processed a request, it must send the results back to the user who sent the request. At this point, I'm not going to talk about how that request is processed internally by a CGI program. Instead, I'm going to focus on the form in which data must be sent back to the Web server.

When a Web server calls a CGI program, it captures the output of the program and sends it back to the server. The first thing sent back to the server by a CGI program must be the Content-type: HTTP header. In most cases, the Web server will create all the other headers necessary to complete the response, but the Web server has no way to tell what type of data is being generated by the CGI program. So, for the Web server to accept the output of the program, you must specify the type of content that will be sent back to the user.

If you're sending HTML to the user (which is most often the case), your program should send the following header to the Web server:

```
Content-type: text/html
```

This line should be followed by two line feeds. Just as a Web browser lets the Web server know that it is done sending headers and is sending content by sending a blank line, your CGI program must indicate to the server that it is finished sending its header and is sending content by sending a blank line as well. So, a full response might look something like this:

```
Content-type: text/html

<html><head><title>Response</title></head>
<body>This is a minimal response.</body></html>
```

Now look at an extremely simple CGI program that would generate this response. Note that this CGI program ignores all the content in the request and sends the same response no matter what. The CGI program is in Listing 22.1.

LISTING 22.1   A SIMPLE CGI PROGRAM

```
#!/bin/sh
echo "Content-type: text/html";
echo;
echo "<html><head><title>Response</title></head>";
echo "<body>This is a minimal response.</body></html>";
```

As I mentioned indirectly before, one advantage of CGI is that you can write CGI programs in almost any programming language. The sample CGI program in Listing 22.1 is written as a Bourne shell script. It could just as easily be written in Perl, C, or pretty much any other language that can produce text output.

The output of the program is the HTTP header and HTML code that is provided as the sample output of a CGI script. When the output of the script is received by a Web browser, the results are rendered as shown in Figure 22.6.

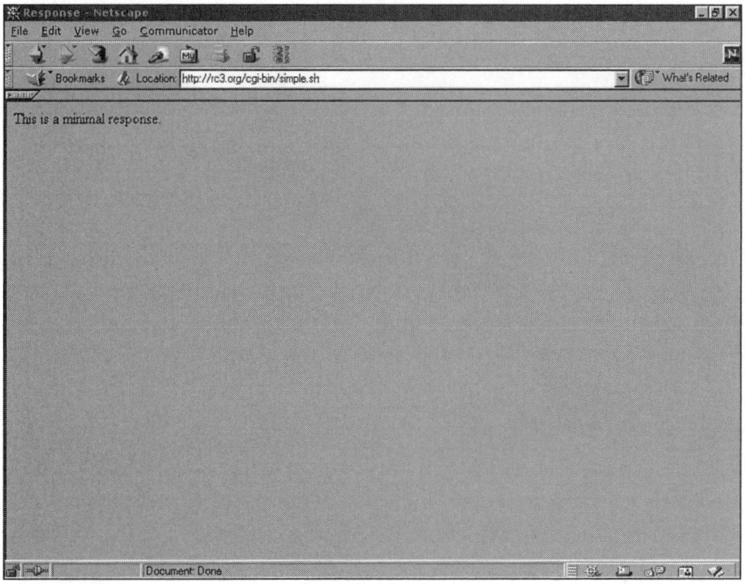

Figure 22.6
The results of a call to the sample CGI script.

The meat of CGI programs is outside the two areas I've just covered. Processing input from forms and writing output to the Web server are the easy parts. The potentially more complex part is processing the input from the form and returning the results desired by the user.

XML

At this point, I'm going to shift from where you are to where you're headed. XML, or the Extensible Markup Language, is by most accounts where the future of the Web lies. XML is a markup language that is designed to describe the actual structure of the data, not just the way it should be presented. It is designed to address some of the flaws in the way HTML was designed and, more importantly, in the way browsers interpret HTML and how it has been applied.

When HTML was designed, it was originally envisioned that the tags would be used to describe the structure of documents. For example, the <H1> tag would be used to indicate that the text within the tag was the top level heading for the document. Unfortunately, when Web browsers were created and developers began applying HTML, they used the <H1> tag, for the most part, to indicate that the text within it should appear boldfaced in a large font, no matter what it signified in the document. As this type of usage became common and more widespread, the value of HTML as a means of describing document structure was eliminated.

XML was formulated to address this problem. The main advantage of XML is that rather than providing a set of tags for marking up documents, it is a framework that enables users to create their own sets of tags that are appropriate for their data. These groups of tags are documented in a formalized manner in what's called a DTD, or Document Type Definition. These document types can be standardized across companies, industries, or other common sets of users so that data can be shared in a format known to all parties involved.

Obviously, XML is not required to create data interchange formats. The advantage of XML is that it is interpreted by a program called a parser. No matter what DTD is being used or what type of data that DTD describes, the XML parser can read the file and determine whether it complies with the DTD.

Because XML provides such a robust means of describing data structure, it meshes very well with relational data. You can export data from a relational database into an XML file and then share that data with any application that includes an XML parser and has a use for that data.

XML AND WEB PUBLISHING

XML is also interesting to Web publishers when it is combined with other Web technologies, such as CSS (Cascading Style Sheets), and XSL, the Extensible Style Language. Both of these technologies enable developers to apply style information to structured data that is stored using XSL.

Let me explain how this works using a simple example. A newspaper that publishes online could build an XML DTD to describe news stories. The DTD would include elements for the story's headline, byline, dateline, and body paragraphs. If the newspaper published syndicated articles as well, the DTD could also contain syndication information and all sorts of other meta-information about the articles that would not necessarily have to be presented to users.

The actual stories could even be stored within a relational database, with each story represented by a row in a table of stories. Chances are that there would be some many-to-many and one-to-many relationships in the newspaper data model, so the data would have to be normalized, but even so, this data can be represented in a relational manner.

The information could then be extracted from the relational database and stored in an XML file. That file can then be used in many more ways than a file that is formatted using HTML. Unlike HTML, XML is easily parsed by machines, so the XML file could be used to syndicate the article to other news organizations. At the same time, the XML file could be distributed with a CSS file that describes the formatting for the elements in the XML file. Browsers that support both XML and CSS would be capable of applying the styles in the CSS file to the XML and presenting users with a nicely formatted version of the structured document. Finally, on the server side, a program that understands both XSL and XML could apply XSL transformations to the XML document, turn it into an HTML document, and then present that to users with browsers that only support HTML.

As you can see, XML presents Web publishers with a lot more options than HTML, which is creaky and has been chronically misapplied.

XML AND RELATIONAL DATABASES

Because XML facilitates the representation of data in a structured manner, it is an effective tool for extracting and presenting data stored in relational databases. In fact, the World Wide Web Consortium has a document that describes exactly how data from a relational database would be represented in XML, at the following URL:

```
http://www.w3.org/XML/RDB.html
```

IN THE REAL WORLD

One problem often faced by people designing Web-based applications is the intersection of visual design and programming. In most cases, the people who are writing the business logic that drives an application and the code necessary to connect to the database aren't the same people who are designing the graphics, choosing the colors for the page, or laying out the interface elements.

With that fact in mind, when you are programming Web applications, you should try to design your applications internally so that you can separate the programming tasks from the visual design tasks. For example, many people writing CGI programs simply generate all their HTML using print statements from within the program. Although this approach certainly works, visual designers almost have to know how to write programs in the language used by the CGI script to make changes to the look and feel of the program's output.

A better approach is to create templates with tokens in them that will be replaced by output of a CGI program when it runs. The CGI program reads the template, replaces the tokens with the appropriate output, and then sends the filled template to the server. Take a look at a small example of a template. If I were going to put the movie database online, I'd want to create a detail page for each of the movies in the database. Listing 22.2 contains an example of what the template code would look like.

LISTING 22.2   A TEMPLATE FOR PRODUCING A MOVIE DETAIL PAGE

```
<html>
<head>
<title>#MOVIE_TITLE#</title>
</head>
<body>
<h1>#MOVIE_TITLE#</h1>
<p><b>#DIRECTOR_NAME#</b></p>
<p>#STUDIO_NAME#</p>
</body>
</html>
```

As you can see, included in the HTML file are tokens such as #MOVIE_TITLE#, which would have to be detected and replaced by your CGI program. You could give this template to the visual designer, who could then apply the appropriate look and feel to the document.

Creating your Web applications in such a way that look and feel are segregated from the inner workings of the applications can make life easier for both the programmer and the visual designer.

CHAPTER **23**

WEB APPLICATION SERVERS

In this chapter

In the preceding chapter, I talked in general terms about how the Web operates and how Web applications are created. In this chapter, I'm going to discuss the categories of products that are used to develop Web applications, and I'm also going to cover some of the specific products that are available for this purpose.

I have discussed some of the details of how a Web server interacts with an external program through the CGI interface. The Web application servers discussed in this chapter eliminate the need to worry about such issues. Generally, the engine that runs the application server takes care of those details and enables you to concentrate on building the application logic itself.

There are an incredible number of Web application servers available today, and more are released all the time. Some focus on tight integration with existing systems, whereas others are more concerned with providing easy-to-use, rapid application-development environments for Web programmers. Before you begin to develop a Web application, you must first determine which application server is right for you. I'm going to kick off this chapter with a discussion of the various types of application servers available.

A SURVEY OF WEB APPLICATION SERVER CATEGORIES

I'd like to arbitrarily assign Web application servers to a set of categories. The authors of these products might disagree with their characterization, but I feel that for the purposes of the application developer, these categories will make sense.

The first, and oldest, is the standard program category. The most famous member of this category is the venerable CGI program. Java servlets are also a member of this category. In this category, I place all technologies that are written using standard programming languages that generate HTML as output instead of plain text or graphics. The differentiation of this category from the others will make more sense when I describe the other categories.

The second category contains application servers that work with HTML documents that have actual program statements embedded within them. For example, a ColdFusion document has conditional statements and loops intermingled with standard HTML. Before the document is sent to the Web browser, the application server searches the document for code, evaluates the embedded statements, and replaces the code with the output of the statements. Other popular Web application servers in this category are Microsoft's Active Server Pages and PHP.

The third category, which is generally inhabited by high-end Web application servers, combines HTML documents and programs. The HTML documents used by servers in this category contain tokens that are parsed by the Web application server and are used to call external programs. Generally, the tokens are then replaced with the data returned by those calls. This enables application developers to write their code in the structured or object-oriented manner that they prefer, without forcing them to embed the code within HTML documents or write statements that generate HTML code. Products in this category include NetDynamics and Apple's WebObjects.

The fourth category consists of products that are designed to serve some specific purpose and happen to use a relational database as their storage medium. For example, Vignette Storyserver is not designed to serve as a tool for interfacing with databases, but it does use a relational database to store all its content. Obviously, these types of products are not of particular interest to the database developer, but you should be aware of them because you might have to design the databases for them or administer them someday.

GENERAL TRUTHS ABOUT WEB APPLICATION SERVERS

Most Web application servers work in a similar fashion. Generally speaking, Web application servers run as distinct processes on the same computer on which the Web server application itself runs. These application servers run constantly, listening for requests from the Web server. These requests can be passed from the Web server to the application server in a number of ways.

Many application servers provide a basic CGI interface between the Web server and the application server. When the user wants to request information from the application server, she calls the CGI script, which runs, accepts the request from the Web server, and passes the request on to the application server. The application server then fulfills the request and passes the results on the CGI application, which then, in turn, sends the response to the Web server, from where it is sent back to the client. The CGI interface is usually provided for compatibility reasons. Because most Web servers implement CGI, creators of application servers can write a CGI program that accepts request from the server and then work with almost every Web server on the market. Unfortunately, the problem with CGI is that it is somewhat slow, at least when compared to other technologies. In this sense, CGI can be thought of as the least common denominator between application servers and Web servers.

Most application servers offer interfaces to one or more of the proprietary interfaces available with specific Web servers. For example, Netscape's Web servers provide the NSAPI for connecting to external applications, Microsoft's IIS Web server has an interface known as ISAPI, and the dominant Web server, Apache, can be extended using modules. Depending on the platforms for which they are available, most application servers support one or all of these interfaces for communications. The most significant advantage of these interfaces is that they enable the application servers to communicate directly with the Web server without running a CGI application to pass the messages along.

Another feature common to most Web application servers is that they provide a layer of abstraction between the database and the user. The Web application server takes care of establishing and maintaining connections with the database, and the developer is free to issue SQL queries against the database without worrying about those details.

STANDALONE PROGRAMS

The first type of database-publishing mechanism I'd like to look at is database publishing through stand-alone programs. These programs can't really be referred to as application servers because they actually take care of all phases of communicating with both the database and the Web server. Application servers generally perform all the underlying tasks, and the user only needs to implement the actual logic that adds functionality to the application.

For example, a Perl program that runs as a CGI script must parse the data submitted by the user and passed to the program, connect to the relational database and make the required SQL calls, and perform all the processing necessary to return the appropriate results to the user. On the other hand, an application server such as ColdFusion takes care of communicating with the database and the Web server. All the user needs to do is process the request, which has already been moved into variables accessible to the script, perform the necessary database operations, and then generate the HTML. The response is sent back to the Web server by the application server. Now take a look at some examples of stand-alone programming technologies.

PERL/CGI

The most venerable technology for deploying Web applications is the combination of Perl and CGI. I described CGI in detail in the previous chapter, but I didn't get around to talking about Perl. Perl is a scripting language that originated on the UNIX platform and has a rich set of features for manipulating text. Somehow, it became the most popular language for writing CGI applications and is considered by many to be the default language for writing Web-based applications.

One of the nicest benefits of using Perl is that there is an enormous body of freely available code that can be downloaded and used within your applications. This code enables you to extend the functionality of Perl and to save time by using this code instead of creating the functionality yourself.

There have been more books written on Perl than I can count on both hands, and if you're interested in learning the language, you can find one of them and go from there. However, I'd like to briefly introduce how Perl can be used to create CGI scripts and how it can be used to connect to relational databases.

Modules are bundles of Perl code that have been packaged so that they can easily be utilized from within another Perl program. Most of the Perl code that has been created for public use is distributed via modules. In fact, there are a number of modules that are distributed with the Perl interpreter; one of these is CGI.pm, which is used to make CGI programming easy.

CGI.pm has many capabilities; in fact, there is a book available that simply covers writing CGI programs with CGI.pm. Most often, CGI.pm is used to parse a CGI request and to move the name and value pairs submitted through forms into a more usable format. Take a look at a very simple CGI program written in Perl using CGI.pm. First, look at the HTML form used to generate the CGI script, which is included in Listing 23.1. Figure 23.1 shows what the form looks like in a browser window.

LISTING 23.1 A SAMPLE HTML FORM

```
<html><head><title>Sample Form</title></head>
<body>
<form action="/cgi-bin/sample.cgi">
Name: <input type="text" name="name" size="40"><br>
Rank: <input type="text" name="rank" size="40"><br>
Serial number: <input type="text" name="serial_num" size="40"><br>
<input type="submit">
</form>
</body></html>
```

Figure 23.1
A sample form.

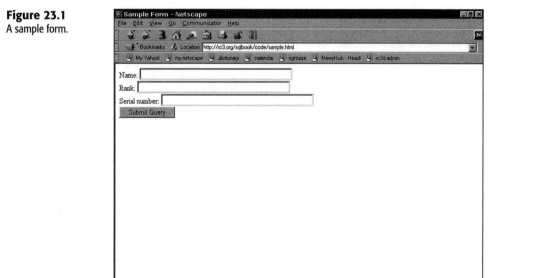

After the form has been created, you can write the CGI program to process the form. Take a look at a CGI program that simply processes the request and returns all the parameters to the user. Listing 23.2 contains a Perl CGI program that performs this task.

LISTING 23.2 A PERL PROGRAM THAT PROCESSES DATA FROM A FORM

```
#!/usr/bin/perl
use CGI;
$query = new CGI;
$name = $query->param('name');
$rank = $query->param('rank');
$serial_num = $query->param('serial_num');
print $query->header;
print "<html><head><title>Welcome</title></head>\n";
print "<body>\n<p>Hello $name.</p>\n";
print "<p>I see that your rank is $rank, and that your \n";
print "serial number is $serial_num.</p>\n";
```

Take a quick look at how this program works. The first line of the program, called the she-bang line, is a pointer to the Perl executable on the system. (This line isn't required if the CGI program is running on Windows NT.) Basically, it lets the system know which program should be used to interpret and execute the code that follows. This is standard on UNIX; for example, most shell scripts begin with the following shebang line:

```
#!/bin/sh
```

The next line is used to tell the program that the CGI.pm library needs to be imported. The program assumes that the module has the pm extension, so only the name of the module, CGI, is needed. After the module is imported, I create a CGI object named $query. In Perl, $query is a scalar variable, and in this case, the variable holds a reference to the CGI object so that you can access it.

When the CGI object is created, all the parameters passed to the program by the request are loaded into a hash called param. In the next three lines of the program, I copy the values passed to the program by the form into normal scalar variables, using this code:

```
$name = $query->param('name');
$rank = $query->param('rank');
$serial_num = $query->param('serial_num');
```

Copying values out of param and into scalar variables isn't necessary. I'm just doing it here for purposes of readability. Notice that the names in the param hash correlate with the field names in the HTML form in Listing 23.1.

The final step is to generate the output to send back to the browser. As I explained in the preceding chapter, before you start generating HTML, you need to send the Content-type: HTTP header to the server. CGI.pm provides a method that does this for us, so I just used the following code to generate the header:

```
print $query->header;
```

The next step is to print the HTML output. To include the form data in the output, I simply include the variable names in the strings being printed. Perl automatically substitutes the values associated with variables for their names if the strings being printed are enclosed in double quotes. The output of the CGI script appears in Figure 23.2.

Tip 84 from
Rafe Colburn

Another popular library for CGI programming is cgi-lib.pl. However, CGI.pm has become the de facto standard for CGI programming in Perl, if for no other reason than because it is now bundled with the standard Perl distribution. Many programmers are more comfortable with cgi-lib.pl, which is what they're used to using, mainly because it was available before CGI.pm. Fortunately, you can use CGI.pm in cgi-lib.pl compatibility mode; if you're more familiar with cgi-lib.pl, use the following line of code to import CGI.pm:

```
use CGI qw(:cgi-lib);
```

You can then use the ReadParse() function as you would with cgi-lib.pl. If you're learning CGI programming for the first time, I recommend using native CGI.pm methods.

Figure 23.2
The output of the
name, rank, and serial
number program.

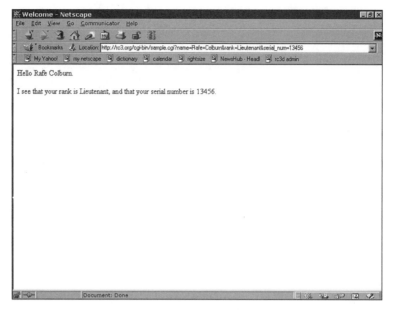

Debugging CGI Programs

There are a few very common problems that tend to plague CGI programs. Any time you try to access a CGI program and it doesn't work, you should investigate these problems first.

One of the most common problems is improper file permissions. If your Web server is running UNIX, the Web server must have permission to execute the CGI program. Generally, this means that the permissions setting for your CGI program should be 755.

You should also make sure that your program is in the cgi-bin directory of your Web server or that your Web server is set up to allow CGI programs to run from the directory where the program lives. If your program is not in the cgi-bin directory, you should also make sure that it has the appropriate filename extension. If your Web server is set up to recognize only programs with the .cgi extension as CGI programs, a program with the extension .pl will not be treated as a CGI program when it is called.

Another extremely common problem is the failure to generate the appropriate header in your CGI programs. One way to avoid this is to use the header method in CGI.pm, as I explained earlier.

If the error log for your Web server says that this is the problem, it could mean that your CGI program didn't run for some other reason. For example, if your program fails to compile, it will send an error message to the Web server instead of the Content-type: header. This confuses the Web server and causes it to report that your CGI program failed because the header was malformed.

Make sure that your program runs from the command line. CGI.pm has an interactive mode that enables you to run CGI programs from the command line and make sure that they work before you try them out over the Web. Even if you're writing your CGI program in another language or you're not using CGI.pm, you can still make sure that your CGI program compiles and executes by running it from the command line.

STORING FORM DATA IN A DATABASE

If the only thing you could do with CGI programs was return the data to the user in a new format, they wouldn't be very useful. Because CGI programs are standard applications, you can store and process the data they receive in any way that you prefer. You can store the data in flat text files, in a UNIX DBM file, or, as luck would have it, in a relational database. Because this book is about SQL, I'm going to explain at this point how you can access a relational database from a Perl CGI program.

First, of course, I need to create a table in a database to store the information gathered using the form. For this example, I'm creating a table in a MySQL database to store the name, rank, and serial number data. The CREATE statement for the table is provided in Listing 23.3.

LISTING 23.3   THE Soldier_Data TABLE

```
CREATE TABLE Soldier_Data
(serial_num VARCHAR(40) PRIMARY KEY,
name VARCHAR(40),
rank VARCHAR(40))
```

After the table is created, I need to add the code to the CGI program that will insert the code into the database. To communicate with my MySQL database, additional libraries are required. One nice advantage of Perl is that there is a standard library used for communicating with relational databases, called DBI (which stands for Database Interface). No matter which database you're using, you can use the same calls provided by DBI. The back-end communications are handled by the appropriate DBD module. The combination of the two provides a layer of abstraction between your programs and relational databases.

Take a look at the code after it has been modified so that it inserts the form data into the Soldier_Data table in addition to sending a response to the browser. The complete listing appears in Listing 23.4.

LISTING 23.4   THE sample.cgi SCRIPT AFTER IT HAS BEEN MODIFIED TO COMMUNICATE WITH A DATABASE

```
#!/usr/bin/perl
use DBI;
use CGI;
$query = new CGI;
$name = $query->param('name');
$rank = $query->param('rank');
$serial_num = $query->param('serial_num');

$dbh = DBI->connect('DBI:mysql:rc3', 'rc3', 'donkey');
$statement = qq{
        INSERT INTO Soldier_Data
        (name, rank, serial_num)
        VALUES
        ('$name', '$rank', '$serial_num')
};
$sth = $dbh->prepare($statement);
```

```
$rc = $sth->execute;

print $query->header;
print "<html><head><title>Welcome</title></head>\n";
print "<body>\n<p>Hello $name.</p>\n";
print "<p>I see that your rank is $rank, and that your \n";
print "serial number is $serial_num.</p>\n";
```

The code I added uses the DBI module to connect to the MySQL database and insert the record into the Soldier_Data table. Just as I had to import the CGI module to use its functionality, I had to include the use DBI; line to import the code that connects to the MySQL database.

After the database interface has been imported, I need to connect to the database. The connect method of the DBI package is used to create a database connection and is used in the program as follows:

```
$dbh = DBI->connect('DBI:mysql:rc3', 'rc3', 'donkey');
```

I assign the database connection to the variable $dbh. The arguments to connect define the type and name of the database I'm connecting to and the username and password of the database user. In this case, the database driver is DBI:mysql, the database name is rc3, the username is rc3, and the password is donkey. After the database connection has been established, the next step is to define the SQL statement that will be executed.

One nice feature of Perl is that you can use the qq construct to quote a string inside the delimiters you choose instead of standard quotation marks. So, to store a SQL statement with like feeds inside a single string, I use qq{} to place everything within the braces in a scalar variable, $statement. The statement itself inserts the data from the form into the Soldier_Data table in the database. After the statement has been assigned to a variable, the prepare method is used to ready the statement to be executed. The prepared statement is assigned to the $sth variable so that it can be executed. The next line of the program does just that, calling the execute method for the prepared statement in $sth and assigning the result code for the query to $rc. After the statement has been executed, the row is inserted in the database, and I proceed to print the HTML.

PART
VII

CH
23

Tip 85 from
Rafe Colburn

The program in Listing 23.4 does not contain any error-checking code. It does not verify that the input takes any particular format, nor does it verify that the program connected successfully to the database or that the SQL statement executed properly. If this program were a real application designed for a production environment, all these tests would need to be included in the program.

Tip 86 from
Rafe Colburn

DBI also provides a disconnect method that can be used to close the connection to the database. However, I didn't call this method within my program because the connection to the database closes automatically when the CGI program finishes executing. Because CGI programs start when the CGI request is made and exit after the response has been sent,

> you generally don't need to clean things up by closing open file handles or database con-
> nections. If you're running your CGI scripts in some sort of persistent fashion (through
> FastCGI or something like it), performing these types of cleanup tasks is generally prudent.
> In any case, cleaning things up before you exit is always the right thing to do if you want to
> be safe.

Take a look at a typical transaction that uses the application I just designed. The first step is
to fill out the form, as shown in Figure 23.3. After the form is submitted, the information
you entered is stored in the `Soldier_Data` table and is displayed in the browser in the format
shown in Figure 23.4. In Listing 23.5, you can see where the information you enter in the
form is stored within the `Soldier_Data` table.

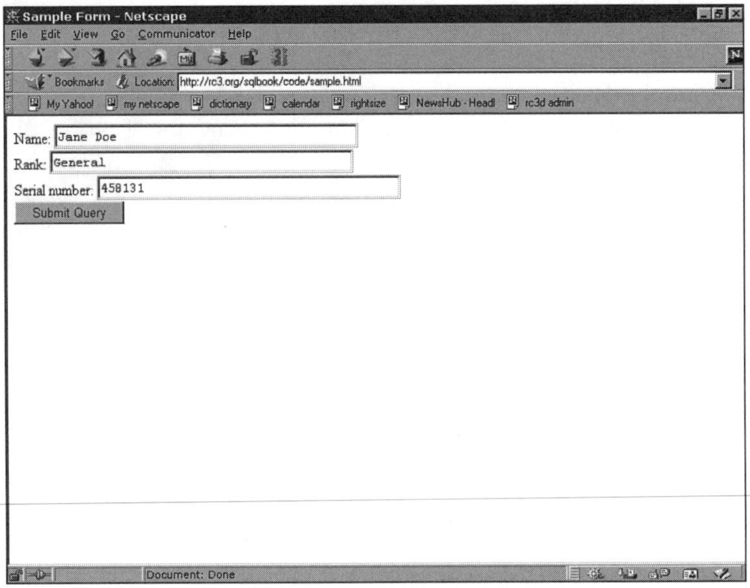

Figure 23.3
The soldier informa-
tion input form.

LISTING 23.5   THE CONTENTS OF THE Soldier_Data TABLE

```
SELECT *
FROM Soldier_Data

+-----------+----------------+---------+
| serial_num | name           | rank    |
+-----------+----------------+---------+
| 123456789 | Rafe Colburn   | General |
| 83813319  | John Doe       | Private |
| 83819311  | Jane Doe       | Major   |
+-----------+----------------+---------+
3 rows in set (0.00 sec)
```

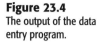

Figure 23.4
The output of the data entry program.

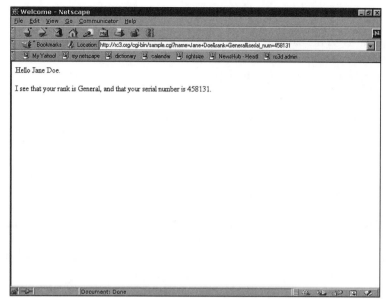

QUERYING A DATABASE FROM A CGI PROGRAM

Most applications involve data entry and data retrieval. The previous script demonstrated how data can be inserted into a relational database from a Perl CGI script. Now, I'm going to explain how to write a script that retrieves data from a database and generates HTML output.

Basically, this script retrieves data from the database, iterates over the records retrieved by the query, and formats them using HTML. Listing 23.6 contains the source code to the program used to retrieve the data from the Soldier_Data table and render it in HTML.

LISTING 23.6   A PROGRAM THAT DISPLAYS DATABASE CONTENTS IN HTML

```perl
#!/usr/bin/perl
use CGI;
use DBI;
$query = new CGI;
$dbh = DBI->connect('DBI:mysql:rc3', 'rc3', 'donkey');
$statement = "SELECT * FROM Soldier_Data";
$sth = $dbh->prepare($statement);
$rc = $sth->execute;
print $query->header;
print "<html><head><title>Soldier List</title></head>\n";
print "<body><h1>Soldier List</h1>\n";
while (($serial_num, $name, $rank) = $sth->fetchrow) {
    print "$name, $rank, $serial_num<br>\n";
}
print "</body></html>\n";
```

Now examine the code in Listing 23.6 closely. A lot of it is similar to the code in Listing 23.4. In this program, I import the CGI and DBI libraries, create a new CGI object, and connect to the database just as I did in Listing 23.4. In this program, I create a SQL statement that simply retrieves all the rows in the Soldier_Data table, and I assign it to the $statement variable. I then prepare and execute the statement.

The only time I use the CGI library in this program is to generate the HTTP header. I could have just as easily left out the use CGI; line and generated the content-type line manually. However, using the library makes the program easier to extend later if I do want to use additional features of the library.

At this point, this program differs from the input program. In the input program, after I insert the row, I'm finished interacting with the database. In this case, I actually have to process the output of the query. However, I'll need to do that in the body of the page, so first, I print the heading information for the HTML document that I'm generating. After the HTML page header information is created and I add a title to the page using the h1 tag, I process the actual output of the query. The operative block of code here is the following:

```
while (($serial_num, $name, $rank) = $sth->fetchrow) {
    print "$name, $rank, $serial_num<br>\n";
}
```

This compact block of code does several things at once. The first thing it does is create a while loop. A while loop in Perl processes as long as the expression within the parentheses evaluates as true. Take a look at the expression and see what it does. In some languages, only a condition could be placed within a loop expression, such as 5 > 2. In Perl, you can do real work in this expression. In this case, I use the fetchrow method of the statement handle ($sth) to retrieve rows from the result set one at a time. When there are no more rows left to retrieve, the fetchrow method returns the value undefined, which causes the loop expression to evaluate as false. Thus, when there are no more rows of data left to process, the loop exits.

fetchrow returns the fields in each row of the query results as an array. Because there are three columns in the Soldier_Data table, each row is returned as an array of three elements. I could decide to read those results into another array, using a construct such as the following:

```
@current_row = $sth_fetchrow;
```

However, I decide to make the program more readable by reading the results into three scalar variables, which are specified in the list context, using this code:

```
($serial_num, $name, $rank) = $sth->fetchrow
```

This assigns the first three values returned by the fetchrow method to the three variables specified in parentheses. If more than three values were returned, they would be discarded. However, in this case, because I know how the query is structured, I know that the resulting array will always consist of three values.

So, to review quickly, the `while` loop is executed once for every row in the result set and assigns the values in each row to the three variables specified. The body of the loop consists of a single statement in this case. All it does is print out the current values of the `$serial_num`, `$rank`, and `$name` variables along with an HTML line break:

```
print "$name, $rank, $serial_num<br>\n";
```

After the loop is finished executing, the script prints the closing `<body>` and `<html>` tags and then exits. Figure 23.5 contains a browser window displaying the output of the `listsoldiers.cgi`.

Figure 23.5
The output of the
`listsoldiers.cgi`
script.

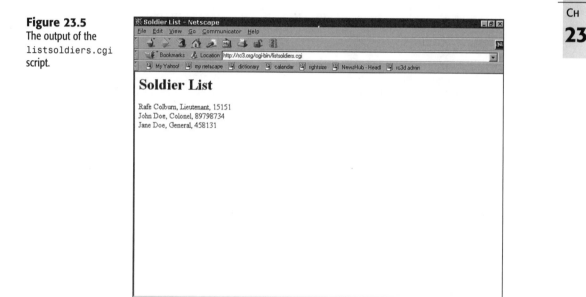

Tip 87 from
Rafe Colburn

If there were a lot of entries in the database, it would make sense to enable users to filter the results. In that case, you would need to call the `listsoldiers.cgi` script using a form and to somehow create the WHERE clause of the query on-the-fly to retrieve only the results in which the user is interested. Any time your scripts are going to return large result sets, you should either group the results so that too many aren't displayed on the screen at once, or you should provide a search interface so that users can filter the results themselves.

HTML-EMBEDDED CODE

The HTML-embedded code category of application servers is already very popular, and it seems to be growing the most quickly, mainly because it seems that this category is the easiest to approach for nonprogrammers. Basically, these technologies either have special tags that operate as program instructions, rather than markup controls, or they enable you to embed code within delimiters inside your HTML.

These programs work by processing your HTML documents before they are sent to the user and by interpreting and executing any code they find within the document before it is sent. As I said before, there are two different paradigms that are used within this category. The first uses tags that work as program instructions. The most common example of this type is Allaire's ColdFusion.

The second type of program uses delimiters to encapsulate code within HTML documents. With these types of technologies, entire blocks of code can be enclosed within a single set of delimiters. Examples of this type of application server include PHP and Microsoft's Active Server Pages.

The main advantage of these technologies is that they require programmers to write less code than they might otherwise have to if they wrote CGI programs. Because the code is embedded inside HTML, the programmer is forced to write a lot less output-related code. Another advantage is that these languages usually provide very high-level instructions for writing code. Common tasks are encapsulated into single commands, which makes application development very fast and easy to learn.

I'm going to cover a few of these technologies individually because of their popularity in the marketplace and because they are representative of the larger body of products in this category.

ALLAIRE'S COLDFUSION

ColdFusion was one of the first HTML-based Web application servers available. At the time of its release, most Web applications were written as CGI scripts in Perl or some other scripting language. ColdFusion in some ways revolutionized Web programming because it made Web application development accessible to a much larger audience than CGI programming did.

The secret behind ColdFusion's success was its use of a tag-based programming language. People who write HTML already understand tag-based markup; learning to use programming instructions that are encapsulated in tags is a small step forward. Take a quick look at some ColdFusion code to demonstrate what I mean. The code in Listing 23.7 contains a conditional statement that checks the value in a variable and displays text based on that value.

LISTING 23.7   AN EXAMPLE OF COLDFUSION CODE

```
<cfset temp="blue">
<cfif temp is "blue">
    The value of temp is blue.
<cfelse>
    The value of temp is not blue.
</cfif>
```

As you can see from the example, the syntax of the code is very straightforward and adheres closely to the conventions established with HTML. Instead of using brackets of some kind to denote the beginning and end of code blocks, ColdFusion uses a closing tag. You should also note that tags that are specific to ColdFusion all begin with cf. This makes it easy to differentiate ColdFusion code from standard HTML code.

Another advantage, demonstrated in the <cfset> tag used in the preceding listing, is that ColdFusion accepts parameters for its tags in the same way that attributes are used with HTML tags. Now take a look at some other elements of ColdFusion. To print values stored in variables or retrieved through queries into HTML pages with ColdFusion, the <cfoutput> tag is used. The text enclosed within opening and closing <cfoutput> tags is parsed for delimiters that indicate that the identifier inside them is a token that should be replaced by the value associated with that identifier. There's an example in Listing 23.8.

LISTING 23.8   VALUE SUBSTITUTION IN COLDFUSION

```
<cfset temp="blue">
<cfoutput>The value of temp is #temp#.</cfoutput>
<cfoutput>Here's an example of a function call: #Now()#</cfoutput>
```

The # characters are used to indicate that the item inside them is an identifier that should be parsed by the ColdFusion interpreter. Inside the first of the two <cfoutput> tags, I use a callout to the variable temp to return the value blue. The second case calls a function, Now(), which returns the current date and time and inserts that value in the output. Variable names and function calls can be intermingled within # delimiters to generate output.

QUERYING DATABASES WITH COLDFUSION

One of the fundamental purposes of ColdFusion was to make it easy for users to query relational databases and to publish the output of those queries on the Web. It was this functionality that set ColdFusion apart from other products as a CGI replacement. Allaire had the vision to realize that database publishing would swiftly become one of the dominant uses of Internet applications.

The fact is that ColdFusion is designed around the idea of querying databases and processing and displaying the results of those queries. ColdFusion is also designed so that you don't need to know SQL to be able to query databases. I'm not going to cover the aspects of ColdFusion that enable you to write your queries using ColdFusion tags instead of SQL statements, mainly because you haven't bought this book to get around writing queries in SQL. In fact, you probably prefer writing in SQL because of the added power that SQL provides.

If you are going to write SQL yourself, ColdFusion provides an all-purpose tag for sending SQL queries to a relational database: <cfquery>. The <cfquery> tag simply passes the text enclosed in the tag to the relational database server and awaits results. There are a number of attributes associated with <cfquery> that enable the database to be queried. The most important attribute is datasource, which specifies which ODBC data source the query should be sent to. The `name` attribute is used to identify the query so that you can access the results later in your document. ColdFusion enables you to specify data sources with an administration application and enter login information there, but if you haven't done so, you can specify the username and password for the data source as attributes as well. Listing 23.9 contains an example of a query issued from within ColdFusion.

LISTING 23.9   A DATABASE QUERY IN COLDFUSION

```
<cfquery datasource="some_db" name="some_query">
    SELECT *
    FROM Movies
</cfquery>
```

After the query results have been retrieved, the `<cfoutput>` tag can be used to display them. I've already explained how the substitution delimiters and `<cfoutput>` tag can be used to insert values into the HTML in a document. The `<cfoutput>` tag has a special parameter that enables it to iterate over the results of a query. Instead of substituting a single value, all the text within the `<cfoutput>` tag is displayed once for each row in the query results, and the substitutions are processed each time. An example of how `<cfoutput>` can be used with a query is provided in Listing 23.10.

LISTING 23.10   CODE THAT USES THE `<cfoutput>` TAG TO DISPLAY THE RESULTS OF A QUERY

```
<cfoutput query="some_query">
#title#, #gross#, #budget#<br>
</cfoutput>
```

The code in Listing 23.10 is very simple. It simply prints out the title, budget, and gross for all the movies retrieved with the query in Listing 23.9. When the query attribute is specified within a `<cfoutput>` tag, the `<cfoutput>` tag automatically creates a loop that runs once for each row retrieved by the query identified by the name in the attribute. Within a `<cfoutput>` tag for which a query is specified, the column names in the query results are automatically made available as variable names that can be used within expressions. The full code for a page that retrieves and prints the title, budget, and gross for all the movies in the database is included in Listing 23.11, and the output of the page is shown in Figure 23.6.

LISTING 23.11   A SAMPLE COLDFUSION DATABASE QUERY PAGE

```
<html>
<head><title>Movie Listing</title></head>
<body>
<h1>Movie Listing</h1>
<cfquery datasource="some_db" name="some_query">
    SELECT *
    FROM Movies
</cfquery>
```

```
<cfoutput query="some_query">
#movie_title#, #gross#, #budget#<br>
</cfoutput>
</body></html>
```

Figure 23.6
The output of
list_movies.cfm.

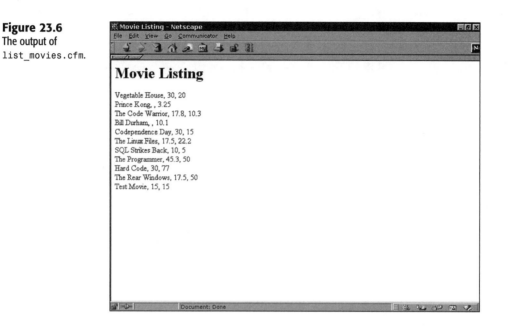

You can also iterate over the results of a query using the `<cfloop>` tag. The main difference between `<cfloop>` and `<cfoutput>` is that other ColdFusion tags can be used within a `<cfloop>` block. When you use the `<cfoutput>` tag, expression parsing is turned on, and restrictions are placed on the types of ColdFusion tags that can be placed within the `<cfoutput>` tag. The `<cfloop>` tag does not place these types of restrictions on the tags that can be used. If you use a `<cfloop>` to process the results of a query, you must use a `<cfoutput>` tag within the `<cfloop>` to print data retrieved by the query. In these cases, you shouldn't include the query attribute in the `<cfoutput>` tag because the `<cfloop>` tag is already iterating over the result set. Listings 23.12 and 23.13 demonstrate the right and wrong ways to use `<cfloop>` and `<cfoutput>` together. In Figure 23.7, you can see the results of the broken `<cfloop>`/`<cfoutput>` combination.

LISTING 23.12   CODE THAT USES `<cfloop>` TO PROCESS QUERY RESULTS

```
<cfloop query="some_query">
    <cfoutput>#some_query.movie_title<br></cfoutput>
</cfloop>
```

> **LISTING 23.13   CODE THAT MISTAKENLY ITERATES OVER THE QUERY RESULTS 10 TIMES**
>
> ```
> <cfloop query="some_query">
>     <cfoutput query="some_query">#movie_title#<br></cfoutput>
> </cfloop>
> ```

Figure 23.7
The output of an improperly formed loop/output combination.

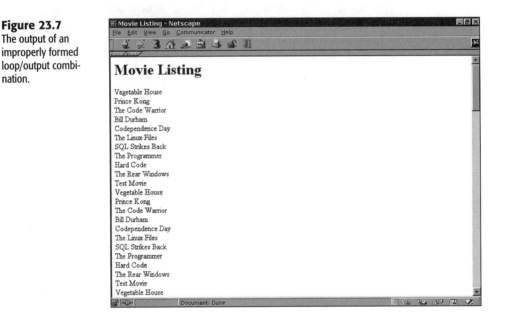

The code in Listing 23.11 prints the title of each of the movies returned by some_query. The most important thing to notice here is that because the query to be used by the <cfoutput> tag is not specified, it's necessary to indicate which query the movie_title column came from in the expression. ColdFusion uses dot notation to tie columns to queries, so some_query.movie_title indicates that the value of movie_title in the current row of some_query should be printed.

ACTIVE SERVER PAGES

Microsoft's offering in the Web application server arena is Active Server Pages, a technology that enables programmers to embed VBScript (a scripting language based on Visual Basic) or JavaScript code in HTML pages. Much like ColdFusion, these scripts are interpreted by the server and the output of the scripts is inserted into the HTML document where they reside.

There are a number of advantages that make Active Server Pages a nice technology for developing Web applications. The first is that it supports standard programming languages. Microsoft claims that more programmers use Visual Basic than any other language, and

VBScript is basically a scaled down version of Visual Basic. JavaScript has become extremely popular among Web developers because it is the only language that is supported by all the major Web browsers. Microsoft has also enabled application developers to extend Active Server Pages to support other programming languages, such as ActiveState's Perl derivative, PerlScript.

Another advantage of Active Server Pages is that they enable developers to create server-side components that can interact with ASP scripts. These components are libraries that provide advanced functionality that the author might not want to write in an ASP-compatible scripting language. For example, database connectivity is not actually native to ASP. It is provided by the ActiveX Database component (ADO), which is bundled with the ASP libraries themselves.

Unlike ColdFusion, which places each instruction within a discrete tag, ASP code is placed within an HTML document, but it is separated from the rest of the document using the <% and %> delimiters. Any text that is contained within those delimiters is treated as ASP code by the server. For example, take a look at the simple ASP code in Listing 23.14.

LISTING 23.14   A WEB PAGE CONTAINING ASP CODE

```
<%@ Language=VBScript %>
<html>
<head><title>Test ASP Page</title></head>
<body>
It is currently <%  = Time %> on <% = Date %>.
</body>
</html>
```

The code in the script inserts the current date and time in the HTML document. The Time and Date functions are used to obtain the date, and an expression with data only to the right of the = sign indicates that the value returned by the expression should be printed. So, = Time means "print the current time in the output." Using the expression = "Rafe" would print the word Rafe in the output.

One interesting characteristic of Active Server Pages is that when you use the <% and %> delimiters to intersperse scripting instructions within your document, the document itself is basically treated as one large program in which everything is assumed to be in a print statement if it isn't enclosed in the ASP delimiters. For example, you can create conditional statements that display undelimited HTML, depending on the condition, as follows:

```
<% If 1 > 2 Then %>
    1 is greater than 2.
<% Else %>
    1 is not greater than 2.
<% End If %>
```

Conditional statements in ASP (and in ColdFusion) control the rendering of the HTML in the document, so when they are encountered, only the HTML that appears within the section of the flow control construct that evaluates as true is displayed.

QUERYING A DATABASE USING ASP

Obviously, the aspect of ASP that is most interesting concerning SQL is its capabilities with regard to querying databases. All database connections in ASP are handled by the Active Database Object, which provides the functionality necessary for connecting to relational databases through ODBC, issuing queries, and retrieving the results of those queries. Here's an example of a typical SQL query issued through ASP:

```
<%
Set someConnection = Server.CreateObject("ADODB.Connection")
someConnection.Open "Movies"
someConnection.Execute "DELETE FROM Movies WHERE studio_id = 1"
%>
```

Take a look at the code line by line. The first line creates a new ADO connection object, which will be used to open a connection to a particular database and retrieve the query results. The second line uses the Open method of the database object to open the connection to the database tied to the DSN Movies. Then, the next line uses the Execute method to issue a SQL statement against the database, which in this case would delete all the movies in the database from the studio with an ID of 1.

Now take a look at a query that retrieves rows from a database and processes them:

```
<%
Set someConnection = Server.CreateObject("ADODB.Connection")
someConnection.Open "Movies"
Set someResults = someConnection.Execute("SELECT * FROM Movies")
Do While Not someResults.EOF
    = someResults.Fields.Item("movie_title")
    = "<BR>"
    someResults.MoveNext
Loop
%>
```

That's one way that you can you can retrieve records from a database using ASP and print the results of the query in your HTML document. Here's how the code works. First, I create the connection object and establish the connection to the Movies database. In the next step, I execute the SELECT statement and assign the results to a recordset called someResults. The cursor for the recordset starts out set at the BOF position (before the first record), so I use the MoveFirst method of the someResults object to move to the first item in the results.

To display the results, I create a Do While loop, which executes until the EOF position in someResults is reached. EOF is the position after the last row in the query results. Inside the loop, I print the contents of the movie_title field and a line break, and I then move forward one record in the recordset. Listing 23.15 contains the full source code to an HTML page that incorporates the query I just explained.

LISTING 23.15 AN ACTIVE SERVER PAGE THAT QUERIES A DATABASE

```
<html>
<head><title>Movie Listing</title></head>
<body>
```

```
<h1>Movie Listing</h1>
<%
Set someConnection = Server.CreateObject("ADODB.Connection")
someConnection.Open "Movies"
Set someResults = someConnection.Execute("SELECT * FROM Movies")
someResults.MoveFirst
Do While Not someResults.EOF
    = someResults.Fields.Item("movie_title")
    = "<BR>"
    someResults.MoveNext
Loop
%>
</body></html>
```

JAVA SERVLETS

Another platform for writing Web applications that is growing in popularity is Java servlets. Java servlets are Java applications that are designed to run from within a Web server and to accept and respond to HTTP requests. In many ways, Java servlets are similar to CGI scripts. They are just programs with built-in handlers for parsing HTTP headers, and they send all the output that they produce back to the Web server.

However, there are some important differences between Java servlets and CGI scripts. The most significant difference is that even though Java servlets are independent programs, they can only run within the context of a Web server. Generally speaking, either the Web server itself or the servlet engine, which is tied to the Web server, includes a Java virtual machine. The servlets are run using that virtual machine. This is important because it enables servlets to be executed in a persistent fashion.

Most CGI scripts exit when they have responded to the request that caused them to be launched, and the programmer must deal with the overhead of relaunching the CGI program for every request. On the other hand, servlets are started when the servlet engine is started, and they persist as long as the engine is up and running. They wait for a request to be sent to them, respond to the request, and then go back into their waiting state until the next request is received. This can save a significant amount of overhead because the code does not need to be compiled and executed for every request.

Another significant advantage of servlets is that they are built using Java, which is already very robust and is growing in popularity with time. Because Java provides an object-oriented architecture for building applications and has strong support for building software in a componentized manner, there are a wide variety of prebuilt components and APIs that can be used to connect to all sorts of applications and services. For example, there is a standardized API for connecting to relational databases that is supported by most relational database vendors called JDBC. When you write a Java application that will communicate with a relational database, you can simply use the JDBC API instead of using an API-specific to the vendor.

For more information about Java servlets, you can check out Sun's servlet page, which includes the development kit for creating servlets, and a list of products that support Java servlets:

```
http://www.javasoft.com/products/servlet
```

You can also find more information on JDBC at the JavaSoft Web site. The URL follows:

```
http://www.javasoft.com/products/jdbc
```

TEMPLATING SYSTEMS

Most high-end Web application servers use templates to deliver dynamic pages to users. These types of systems have the advantage of storing the actual program code in separate files from the pages that are used to deliver the output of that code. When you build applications that use this type of system, you can have programmers work on writing the actual application code while the visual designers work on the interface. Also, it improves the readability and reusability of your code by separating the dynamic functionality from the way it is presented.

For example, if you were writing a commerce application that displayed the user's current account balance on every page using a system like this, you would write one function that retrieved the current user's account balance from a database and display it, and you would then call that function everywhere it was needed. The advantage of such a development paradigm really becomes obvious when you consider that many of the output functions might actually use the same internal code to communicate with the database, to format the output, or to perform other tasks internal to the application. All these functions can be bundled into components or libraries and can then be utilized internally by the application to reuse as much code as possible.

Performing such tasks is more difficult when all the code you use is embedded within the Web pages themselves. The same sort of advantages can be obtained in systems that consist entirely of programs, such as CGI-based applications, but then, unless the CGI program is designed properly, you lose the advantage of creating all your HTML code in templates instead of entering it in print statements within the program.

Unfortunately, most of these systems are too complex to demonstrate adequately within the context of this chapter. However, I would like to discuss some of the more popular offerings in this product segment. Most of the solutions in this area enable programmers to develop applications using Java or C++, although some also provide support for other programming languages as well.

One venerable offering in this area is Apple's WebObjects. WebObjects is based on the programming model for NextStep, which provided an object-oriented programming environment in Objective C and, later, Java. Apple has continued to update WebObjects after acquiring Next as part of their enterprise software division.

Another technology very similar to WebObjects is NetDynamics, which enables programmers to develop Web applications using C++ or Java. NetDynamics was acquired by Sun, and their application server is now touted as the linchpin of Sun's Web application strategy.

Kiva Application Server, now Netscape Application Server, was another high-end application server offering from a small company that was eventually acquired. Like both WebObjects and NetDynamics, Kiva provided support for both C++ and Java programs.

HOW TEMPLATING APPLICATION SERVERS WORK

I mentioned earlier that templating systems work by separating the application code from the HTML pages that are used to present that code to users. These systems work by enabling designers to create HTML pages with tokens that are parsed by the application server before the page is sent to the user. When the application server parses these pages, it examines the tokens that are returned and then calls the actual program associated with that token.

For example, if you wanted to personalize a Web site so that it printed the user's real name on the home page every time she visits with one of these servers, you would have a token in the home page like the following:

```
[SHOW realname]
```

Then, the application server would find the token as it parsed the page, call the routine that looks up the user's real name (probably based on the value in a cookie returned by the user), and then insert the output of that routine into the page where the token was encountered.

The designers just have to know the relatively simple syntax associated with inserting the tokens in the page, and the programmers are charged with writing the actual logic associated with the tokens.

IN THE REAL WORLD

When you're designing a Web application, the first step you'll face is deciding which application server you want to use. There are already a number of options out there for would-be Web application developers, and that number seems to be growing every day. Choosing from among these products is a tough decision, and it will shape the direction that your project takes, so making the right decision up front will definitely be a key to your success.

Ultimately, one of the key deciding factors in your decision should be which languages and development environments the programmers working on the project are most familiar with. There are so many application servers on the market at this point that you're certain to be able to find one that matches well with the programming skills that you already possess.

Seasoned Visual Basic programmers will probably prefer a technology such as Active Server Pages or any of the other application servers that enable you to take advantage of knowledge of Visual Basic, such as Haht's HahtSite. On the other hand, UNIX programmers will probably prefer a solution such as Perl for Web application programming. Java programmers will have a heyday in the Web application arena because there are many offerings that are either Java-based or support programs written in Java.

Less well-known is the fact that most of the companies that provide development environments for client/server applications have expanded their offerings to provide support for Web applications as well. For example, one of the most popular client/server development tools, Sybase's PowerBuilder, supports the creation of Web applications as well as client/server applications. Oracle has also expanded its line of application-server products to support Web-based applications as well.

After you've narrowed down the list of application servers that you're considering based on the skills you have available, there are a number of other factors you might want to take into account before committing to a particular product. Surprisingly, one area that is less a factor than you might think is database support. The database support for most products is wide, and interfaces such as ODBC for Windows and JDBC for Java provide a layer of abstraction that makes it easy for application servers and databases to communicate with one another. Naturally, you should always confirm that the tool you want to use will work with your existing database, but this is rarely a stumbling block in choosing a Web application server.

An issue that does crop up frequently is product maturity. Almost all the products written for the Web are fairly new because the Web itself has only been around since 1993 and didn't really explode in popularity until 1996. Unfortunately, this means that many of the products designed to work on the Web are immature; they either lack in promised features or are unstable. You should always talk to people who are using a particular product in a real-world situation before betting on it for use in your own Web applications. Prototyping is also especially important when it comes to creating Web applications. It's far better to get a feel for a product's limitations on a project of small scope before committing to it for a long-term project.

Everything else held equal, my experience is that an application server designed for general application development is often a better choice than one designed for a single purpose. Most projects are complex enough that application servers designed for specific tasks fail to provide all the functionality that is required. Because these application servers don't provide the flexibility of general purpose application servers, often you are forced to turn to other tools to create the additional functionality that you need.

Another problem that plagues application servers designed for specific purposes, such as commerce, publishing, or group discussion, is that they usually are designed to work with a particular database schema. Rather than enabling you to create your own database schema or to use existing tables within a database, the application server forces you to map your data to the schema it expects.

On the other hand, if you need to get an application up and running quickly and you're flexible with regard to the project requirements, specialized solutions can offer significant time savings. They can also provide you with functionality that you could not otherwise develop in-house. In some cases, you can base your application on a general application development tool such as Active Server Pages or Perl/CGI and then acquire a third-party application based on that technology, which in some ways provides you with the best of both worlds. The functionality that you needed is already written, but at the same time, you can extend the application in the ways that you require because the application is built using a standard Web application server.

CHAPTER **24**

A SAMPLE WEB APPLICATION

In this chapter

In the previous two chapters, I've explained the principles of Web application development and covered some of the programming languages and application servers that can be used to create Web applications. You've seen enough information to get you started developing Web applications, but I'd like to tie it all together by providing a single, detailed example of a working Web application.

This application provides an interface to the movie database that I began discussing in the first chapter of this book. It will allow users to enter new movies into the database, edit existing movies, and view detailed information on all the movies in the database. This example will take the form of a Web-based application, but it could just as easily be written as a client/server application—or even as a mainframe application.

One tough question I faced as I planned this chapter was, "Which Web application server should I use to write the application?" As you learned in Chapter 23, "Web Application Servers," a number of fine offerings exist in this segment of the market. Choosing one for this example was tough. Ultimately, I decided to use ColdFusion, for a couple of reasons. One is that ColdFusion is one of the highest-level programming languages available, so I don't have to spend a lot of time explaining the meaning of low-level functions, and my code listings will be shorter. The second reason is that ColdFusion is so simple that it is nearly as readable as pseudo-code (or SQL). It's very easy to read ColdFusion source code, so you should be able to take the concepts from this chapter and apply them to other projects, even if you opt not to use ColdFusion to develop those projects.

A final advantage of ColdFusion is that it is available both for Windows NT and Solaris, and a free evaluation version is available at `http://www.allaire.com`. You can download it, save the scripts in this chapter, and get the sample application up and running quickly and easily.

MOVIE APPLICATION ARCHITECTURE

An alarmingly high percentage of Web applications have the same basic architecture. For the most part, they're simple data entry and retrieval systems, which require interfaces that allow users to browse, edit, enter, and delete records from a database. The applications vary largely in how the data is presented and which users have access to which functionality. For example, a newspaper Web site allows writers who work for the newspaper to enter content into a database and allows everyone who visits to retrieve those stories and read them. On the other hand, a customer comment application on a Web site probably allows all visitors to enter a comment, but allows only people who work for the company to view the comments.

In this case, I'm going to assume that all the application's users are allowed to edit and view all the information in the database. This is rarely the case in the real world, but making this assumption enables me to explain more important concepts in the space that I have. The application itself consists of several "screens," which include

- A page that lists movies
- A movie detail page

- A page that allows users to enter new movies
- A page that allows users to edit an existing movie
- A page that allows users to edit the cast of a movie
- A page that allows users to edit the locations for an existing movie
- A page that allows users to remove an existing movie

This is merely the tip of the iceberg. I could create any number of other screens that make the application more robust, but these provide the baseline functionality that I require. The remainder of this chapter is devoted to discussing how each of these pages is constructed. I'm going to excerpt the interesting parts of the code for each page as I discuss them, and then provide the full source code for the pages at the end of each section. You may find it helpful to skip ahead to the full listing as you read through each section to get an idea of how all the code fits together.

THE MOVIE LISTING PAGE

The first page users see when they enter the site is an interface to the movie listing page. Chances are that eventually enough movies will be in the database to make listing them all on the first page impractical. I decided to split the movies among multiple pages, 10 per page, and sort them in descending order by release date. The page automatically makes links to the Next 10 Movies Page, and if the user is not on the first page of the listing, a link back to the previous 10 movies is included as well.

The script that creates the movie listing first determines whether the page was called with the begin variable specified. If it was, the page lists 10 movies starting with the value of the begin variable. If the begin variable is missing, the script assumes that the first 10 movies in the database should be listed. The code that figures this out follows:

```
<cfif IsDefined("URL.begin")>
    <cfset first_item=URL.begin>
<cfelse>
    <cfset first_item="1">
</cfif>
```

In ColdFusion, the url object contains all the name and value pairs sent to the server through the query string. This if statement checks to see whether the begin variable exists using the IsDefined function. If begin does not exist, the value of the first_item variable, which is local to the page, is set to 1. If the begin parameter was passed to the script through the query string, first_item is set equal to the value of begin.

Tip 88 from
Rafe Colburn

If this script was part of a real Web application, this section of the page would probably need to contain more error-checking code. For example, it should test to make sure that the parameter passed to the page via the begin variable is actually a number, and that the number is within the bounds of the records in the database.

After the `first_item` variable has been set, the page prints the HTML header and the "Movie Listing" heading. The next step is to retrieve the list of movies from the database, as shown:

```
<cfquery name="get_movie_list"
    datasource="development">
    SELECT movie_id, movie_title, release_date
    FROM Movies
    ORDER BY release_date DESC
</cfquery>
```

The `cfquery` tag is used to execute a query; the results are then assigned to the object indicated by the `name` parameter of the tag. The `datasource` parameter indicates which database is to be queried. The SQL statement itself is supplied in the body of the `cfquery` tag. Even though the page is going to list only 10 movies, all the movies in the table are retrieved by this query. The only way to write a query that does not retrieve all the results indicated by the `WHERE` clause is to use a cursor, and the result set for the sample database does not necessitate retrieving partial results. Note that the `ORDER BY` clause indicates that the results should be sorted in descending order by release date.

After the list of movies has been assigned to the `get_movie_list` object, the next step is to print the movies on the screen in a table and provide links to the detail pages for each movie. The following code prints a table with a row for each movie in the database:

```
<center>
<table border=1 cellpadding=4 cellspacing=0>
    <tr>
        <th>title</th>
        <th>release date</th>
    </tr>
<cfoutput query="get_movie_list" maxrows=10 startrow=#first_item#>
    <tr>
        <td><a href="detail.cfm?movie=#movie_id#">
            #movie_title#</a></td>
        <td>#DateFormat(release_date, "mmm d, yyyy")#</td>
    </tr>
</cfoutput>
</table>
</center>
```

The table itself will be centered on the page (using the `center` tag). The table is generated using the HTML `table` tag. The `table` tag contains `tr` tags, which create rows in the table, and the `tr` tags contain `td` tags, which define the cells on each row. After the table has been created, a row is created to hold the column headings for the table. Inside that row, two cells are defined using `th` tags. The `th` tag stands for table heading; it creates a cell just like a `td` tag except that the contents of the cell are automatically displayed in a bold font and centered.

After the heading has been created, the next step is to create a row for the 10 movies that should be displayed on this page. The `cfoutput` tag is used to loop over the results of the query `get_movie_list`. The `maxrows` attribute of the `cfoutput` tag is used to specify the maximum number of times the cfoutput code should be executed, and the startrow attribute indicates where in the result set the cfoutput tag should begin. In this case, I decided that no more than 10 rows should ever be displayed on a single page, and the first_item variable contains the starting point for the table of results. Therefore, if the begin parameter in the query string were set to 21, the first_item variable would be set to 21, and the cfoutput tag would display records 21 through 30 from the query.

Inside the cfoutput tag is the code that actually prints each row in the table. There are two cells per row: The first contains the title of the movie (which is linked to the detail page for the movie) and the second contains the release date of the movie. The detail page is a script that expects to receive the movie ID for the movie to be displayed as an input parameter. Thus, I create the link using the following code:

```
<a href="detail.cfm?movie=#movie_id#">#movie_title#</a>
```

Because this is being executed within a cfoutput tag, the # characters indicate that the value between them should be replaced by the value associated with it. In this case, the movie ID for the movie is inserted in the URL referenced by the link, and the movie title is the link itself.

After the table has been generated, the next step is to generate the navigational elements on the page. In addition to the link to the new movie creation page, links to other pages in the movie listing can exist. If further results are available, a link to the next set of movies is provided; if this page is not the first page in the result set, a link is also provided to the previous 10 movies. The code used to create these links follows:

```
<cfif first_item gt 10>
    <center><p>
    <a href="list.cfm?begin=<cfoutput>#evaluate(first_item - 10)#</cfoutput>">
    Previous 10 movies ...</a>
    </p></center>
</cfif>
<cfset first_item=first_item + 10>
<cfset movies_left=(get_movie_list.RecordCount - (first_item - 1))>
<cfif movies_left gt 0>
    <cfif movies_left gt 10>
        <cfset movies_left=10>
    </cfif>
    <center><p>
    <a href="list.cfm?begin=<cfoutput>#first_item#</cfoutput>">
    Next <cfoutput>#movies_left#</cfoutput> movies ...</a>
    </p></center>
</cfif>
```

This code first checks to see whether it needs to link to the previous page of movies. If the first_item variable is greater than 10, the user is not viewing the first page of results. In that case, a link back to the previous page is created. This link simply points to the list.cfm page (the current page) with a different value specified in the begin parameter.

The code to generate the link to the next page of results is a bit more complex. The first_item variable is incremented by 10, then the value of first_item (minus one) is subtracted from the total number of records retrieved by the `get_movie_list` query. This value is assigned to the variable `movies_left`, and indicates how many movies remain that have not been displayed.

Tip 89 from	Most SQL databases do not provide an easy method that can be used to determine how
Rafe Colburn	many records are returned by a particular query (in some cases, you have to use the `COUNT` aggregate function to get that value). ColdFusion provides the `RecordCount` method for each query to indicate how many records are in the query results.

If the `movies_left` variable contains a positive number, indicating that movies are still left in the result set that haven't been displayed, a link to the next page of results is displayed. This link is built in the same way as the link to the previous page, except that the number of movies that appears on the next page of results must be calculated. For example, if 25 movies are in the database, the third and final page of results will contain 5 movies. If more than 10 movies are left, the value of `movies_left` is set to 10 because I only show 10 movies per page of results.

To complete the rendering of the page, a link to the Add a Movie page is inserted, and the body and HTML tags are closed. The full code for this page is included in Listing 24.1, and Figure 24.1 shows the output of this script.

Figure 24.1
The Movie Listing page.

LISTING 24.1   THE FULL LISTING OF list.cfm

```
<cfif IsDefined("url.begin")>
    <cfset first_item=url.begin>
<cfelse>
    <cfset first_item=1>
</cfif>

<html>
<head><title>Movie Listing</title></head>
<body>
<h1 align="center">Movie Listing</h1>
<cfquery name="get_movie_list"
    datasource="development">
    SELECT movie_id, movie_title, release_date
    FROM Movies
    ORDER BY release_date DESC
</cfquery>
<center>
<table border=1 cellpadding=4 cellspacing=0>
    <tr>
        <th>title</th>
        <th>release date</th>
    </tr>
<cfoutput query="get_movie_list" maxrows=10 startrow=#first_item#>
    <tr>
        <td><a href="detail.cfm?movie=#movie_id#">
            #movie_title#</a></td>
        <td>#DateFormat(release_date, "mmm d, yyyy")#</td>
    </tr>
</cfoutput>
</table>
</center>

<cfif first_item gt 10>
    <center><p>
    <a href="list.cfm?begin=<cfoutput>#evaluate(first_item - 10)#</cfoutput>">
    Previous 10 movies ...</a>
    </p></center>
</cfif>
<cfset first_item=first_item + 10>
<cfset movies_left=(get_movie_list.RecordCount - (first_item - 1))>
<cfif movies_left gt 0>
    <cfif movies_left gt 10>
        <cfset movies_left=10>
    </cfif>
    <center><p>
    <a href="list.cfm?begin=<cfoutput>#first_item#</cfoutput>">
    Next <cfoutput>#movies_left#</cfoutput> movies ...</a>
    </p></center>
</cfif>

<center><p><a href="add.cfm">add new movie</a></p></center>
</body>
</html>
```

THE MOVIE DETAIL PAGE

The movie detail page is reached by clicking one of the links in the movie list on the movie listing page. All the movies are presented in the same template, and the `movie` parameter in the URL indicates which movie should be presented when the page is called. The page presents a detailed view of the movie, including details from the main `Movies` table, the cast of the movie, and a list of shooting locations for the movie. Links on this page also enable you to edit the information associated with the movie.

First, the page checks for the presence of the `movie` parameter. If that parameter is not specified, the `cflocation` tag is used to send the users back to the listing page so that they can select a movie. This validation is insufficient for a real application, but it is suitable here. The following code verifies the existence of the `movies` parameter:

```
<cfif not IsDefined("url.movie")>
    <cflocation url="list.cfm">
</cfif>
```

Next, the page retrieves from the database the records that will be displayed on the page. The first query retrieves the basic information about the movie from the `Movies` table; it also fetches the name of the director from the `People` table and the name of the studio from the `Studios` table:

```
<cfquery name="get_movie_detail" datasource="development">
    SELECT M.movie_id, M.movie_title, M.budget, M.gross,
    M.release_date, S.studio_name, P.person_fname,
        P.person_lname
    FROM Movies M, Studios S, People P
    WHERE M.movie_id = #url.movie#
    AND M.studio_id = S.studio_id
    AND P.person_id = M.director_id
</cfquery>
```

As you can see, this query is a three table join. It retrieves the `studio_name` column from the `Studios` table and the `person_fname` and `person_lname` columns from the `People` table; the remaining columns are from the `Movies` table. Only one row is returned because `movie_id`, `person_id`, and `studio_id` are all primary keys. The next query is used to retrieve the cast of the movie:

```
<cfquery name="get_cast" datasource="development">
    SELECT CM.role, CM.payment, P.person_fname, P.person_lname
    FROM Cast_Movies CM, People P
    WHERE CM.movie_id = #url.movie#
    AND CM.person_id = P.person_id
</cfquery>
```

This query joins the `Cast_Movies` and `People` tables to retrieve the names, roles, and the amount of payment for each person who appeared in the movie referenced by the `movie` parameter. The final query retrieves the locations where the movie was shot:

```
<cfquery name="get_locations" datasource="development">
    SELECT city, state
    FROM Locations
```

```
    WHERE movie_id = #url.movie#
</cfquery>
```

This query retrieves all the rows in the table that are associated with the movie ID included in the query string. After all the data used on the page has been retrieved, the movie detail itself is printed. The queries that are used to gather the data for the page are included in the page before any HTML is printed because the title of the page contains the title of the movie retrieved in the get_movie_detail query. The title is printed using the following code:

```
<title><cfoutput>#get_movie_detail.movie_title#</cfoutput></title>
```

The detail information is printed in a table, but this table is used only for formatting. Unlike the table on the movie listing page, this table does not contain one record per row. The following code creates the table:

```
<table>
<tr>
    <td align="right"><b>title</b></td>
    <td><cfoutput>#get_movie_detail.movie_title#</cfoutput></td>
</tr>
<tr>
    <td align="right"><b>studio</b></td>
    <td><cfoutput>#get_movie_detail.studio_name#</cfoutput></td>
</tr>
<tr>
    <td align="right"><b>director</b></td>
    <td><cfoutput>#get_movie_detail.person_fname#
    #get_movie_detail.person_lname#</cfoutput></td>
</tr>
<tr>
    <td align="right"><b>budget</b></td>
    <td><cfoutput>#get_movie_detail.budget#</cfoutput></td>
</tr>
<tr>
    <td align="right"><b>gross</b></td>
    <td><cfoutput>#get_movie_detail.gross#</cfoutput></td>
</tr>
</table>
```

Instead of using a cfoutput tag with the query attribute to iterate over the results of a query, I use individual cfoutput tags where I need to insert a piece of data retrieved from the database. This works because only one row is returned by the query get_movie_detail. Each row in the table displayed in the browser (shown in Figure 24.2) contains one name and value pair.

In addition to the basic detail information from the Movies table, the page also displays the list of locations and cast members for the movie. As you saw earlier, the locations and cast members were retrieved using different queries from the main query. First, I print the cast members for the movie. Cast member information has not been entered for all the movies in the database, so before the heading for the cast section of the page is displayed, the script checks to make sure that cast members are actually available to be printed. The following code presents the list of cast members:

```
<cfif get_cast.RecordCount gt 0>
    <h3 align="center">cast</h3>
    <p><center>
    <cfoutput query="get_cast">
        #role# - #person_fname# #person_lname#<br>
    </cfoutput>
    </center></p>
</cfif>
```

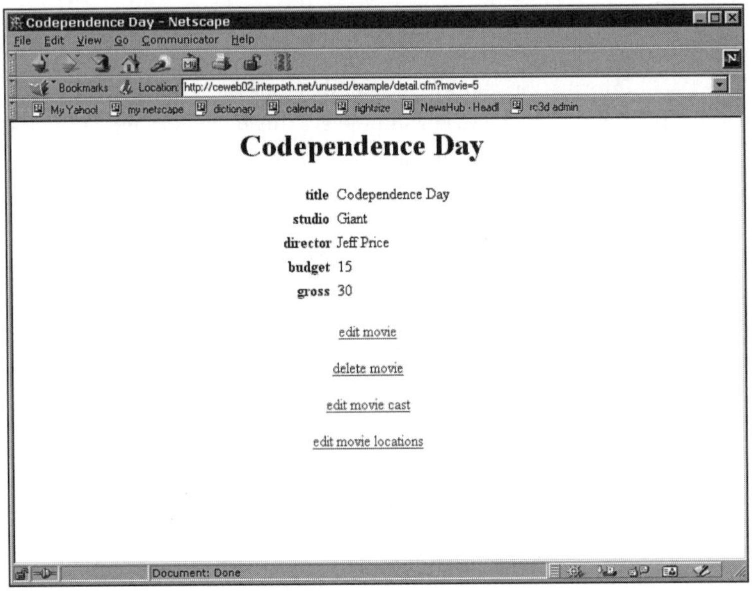

Figure 24.2
A movie detail page.

First, the cfif tag prints only the cast member list if records were returned by the get_cast query. If the query returned no results, this section of the script is skipped. If rows were returned, a heading is displayed along with a list of cast members and the roles that they played, as shown in Figure 24.3.

The next step is to print a list of locations where the movie was shot. This section of the page is nearly identical to the cast section. If any locations are retrieved for a movie, this section of the page is displayed. If no locations were retrieved, this section is ignored. Here's the code:

```
<cfif get_locations.RecordCount gt 0>
    <h3 align="center">locations</h3>
    <p><center>
    <cfoutput query="get_locations">
        #city#, #state#<br>
    </cfoutput>
    </center></p>
</cfif>
```

Figure 24.3
The list of cast members on a movie detail page.

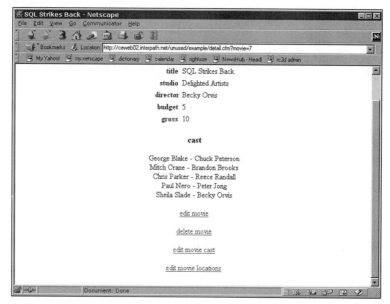

The final task performed by the detail.cfm script is to print links to pages that allow users to edit the data associated with the movie: to add or remove locations and cast members and to delete the movie altogether. The code that creates these links is as follows:

```
<p><a href="edit.cfm?movie=<cfoutput>#current_movie#</cfoutput>">
edit movie</a></p>

<p><a href="delete.cfm?movie=<cfoutput>#current_movie#</cfoutput>">
delete movie</a></p>

<p><a href="add_cast.cfm?movie=<cfoutput>#current_movie#</cfoutput>">
edit movie cast</a></p>

<p><a href="add_location.cfm?movie=<cfoutput>#current_movie#</cfoutput>">
edit movie locations</a></p>
```

As you can see, the current_movie variable, which was set to the movie ID of the movie that is currently being displayed after the movie detail was retrieved from the database, is included in the links to other pages. The full code to the detail.cfm page is included in Listing 24.2.

LISTING 24.2   THE CODE FOR THE detail.cfm PAGE

```
<cfif not IsDefined("url.movie")>
    <cflocation url="list.cfm">
</cfif>
<cfquery name="get_movie_detail" datasource="development">
    SELECT M.movie_id, M.movie_title, M.budget, M.gross,
```

continues

LISTING 24.2 CONTINUED

```
        M.release_date, S.studio_name, P.person_fname,
            P.person_lname
    FROM Movies M, Studios S, People P
    WHERE M.movie_id = #url.movie#
    AND M.studio_id = S.studio_id
    AND P.person_id = M.director_id
</cfquery>
<cfset current_movie=get_movie_detail.movie_id>
<cfquery name="get_cast" datasource="development">
    SELECT CM.role, CM.payment, P.person_fname, P.person_lname
    FROM Cast_Movies CM, People P
    WHERE CM.movie_id = #url.movie#
    AND CM.person_id = P.person_id
</cfquery>
<cfquery name="get_locations" datasource="development">
    SELECT city, state
    FROM Locations
    WHERE movie_id = #url.movie#
</cfquery>
<html>
<head>
    <title><cfoutput>#get_movie_detail.movie_title#</cfoutput></title>
</head>
<body>

<h1 align="center">
<cfoutput>#get_movie_detail.movie_title#</cfoutput>
</h1>

<center>
<table>
<tr>
    <td align="right"><b>title</b></td>
    <td><cfoutput>#get_movie_detail.movie_title#</cfoutput></td>
</tr>
<tr>
    <td align="right"><b>studio</b></td>
    <td><cfoutput>#get_movie_detail.studio_name#</cfoutput></td>
</tr>
<tr>
    <td align="right"><b>director</b></td>
    <td><cfoutput>#get_movie_detail.person_fname#
    #get_movie_detail.person_lname#</cfoutput></td>
</tr>
<tr>
    <td align="right"><b>budget</b></td>
    <td><cfoutput>#get_movie_detail.budget#</cfoutput></td>
</tr>
<tr>
    <td align="right"><b>gross</b></td>
    <td><cfoutput>#get_movie_detail.gross#</cfoutput></td>
</tr>
</table>
```

```
<cfif get_cast.RecordCount gt 0>
    <h3 align="center">cast</h3>
    <p><center>
    <cfoutput query="get_cast">
        #role# - #person_fname# #person_lname#<br>
    </cfoutput>
    </center></p>
</cfif>

<cfif get_locations.RecordCount gt 0>
    <h3 align="center">locations</h3>
    <p><center>
    <cfoutput query="get_locations">
        #city#, #state#<br>
    </cfoutput>
    </center></p>
</cfif>

<p><a href="edit.cfm?movie=<cfoutput>#current_movie#</cfoutput>">
edit movie</a></p>

<p><a href="delete.cfm?movie=<cfoutput>#current_movie#</cfoutput>">
delete movie</a></p>

<p><a href="add_cast.cfm?movie=<cfoutput>#current_movie#</cfoutput>">
edit movie cast</a></p>

<p><a href="add_location.cfm?movie=<cfoutput>#current_movie#</cfoutput>">
edit movie locations</a></p>

</center>

</body>
</html>
```

ENTERING A NEW MOVIE

The add.cfm page is used to create a new movie. It provides a form in which users can enter the information associated with a new movie. It validates the data entered in the form, and then inserts the data into the Movies table. This form is not used to add cast members or specify locations where a movie was shot. To add cast members or locations, the movie must be created, and then the user most go back and add this data for the movie.

The movie creation page and movie update page have a lot in common; basically, they differ only in that the creation page uses an INSERT statement, whereas the movie update page uses an UPDATE statement, and the update form is populated with the existing values for the movie.

To save coding time and keep everything consistent, I created two components that are used with both the creation and update pages. One component generates the HTML form that allows users to enter or update content; the second component validates the data entered in the form and determines whether the record should be inserted or updated. Before I discuss these components, I'll discuss the structure of the movie creation page, and then I'll explain the contents of the components.

The first line of code in the page simply defines the error_message variable. The validation component adds error messages to this variable if problems occur with the form input. If errors exist, the contents of this variable are displayed so that the user can fix them. Here's the code:

```
<cfset error_message="">
```

The next major section of the page is a cfif construct that is executed only if the form has already been submitted. This page consists of a form that is submitted to itself, so it must contain some decision logic that determines whether the form is being printed for the first time or has already been submitted. The decision logic is implemented in the code that follows:

```
<cfif IsDefined("form.movie_title")>
    <cfinclude template="validate.cfm">

    <cfif error_message is "">
        <cfquery name="add_movie" datasource="development">
            INSERT INTO Movies
            (movie_id, movie_title, studio_id, director_id,
            budget, gross, release_date)
            VALUES
            (movie_id_seq.NEXTVAL,
            '#form.movie_title#',
            #form.studio_id#,
            #director_id#,
            #budget#,
            #gross#,
            '#DateFormat(release_date, "dd-mmm-yy")#')
        </cfquery>
        <cflocation url="list.cfm">
    </cfif>
</cfif>
```

Note

The INSERT statement in the previous script is specific to Oracle databases because it assigns the ID to the movie by retrieving the next value from the sequence movie_id_seq. If you were writing this script for an Access database or Microsoft SQL Server, the ID field would either be an autoincrementing field—in which case it would be left out of the INSERT statement—or a standard numeric field, in which case you'd need to specify the value for the ID field yourself.

Tip 90 from
Rafe Colburn

Two advantages exist to using a single script that generates an HTML form and submits the form to itself for action. The first is that you can use the same code to present the initial form and a form containing the data the user entered if any input exists that is not valid. The second advantage is that you are not forced to separate your code into more than one file. In many cases, scripts that have the form in an HTML file and process the input in a separate program require users to click the Back button or go back to make revisions to the data that they entered. Bundling the form and validation into a single script enables the developer to easily respond to invalid data with a prefilled form and a request for a correction.

The form generated by this script uses the post method to send data to the server when it is submitted; therefore, the form object is used to access the data submitted through the form. In this case, the page checks to see whether the form.movie_title parameter exists. This parameter corresponds to a text field in the form. If this parameter does exist, the code within this cfif tag is executed.

The validate.cfm script is loaded and executed using the cfinclude tag as the template is compiled. When a template is processed, all the cfinclude tags are evaluated first, and the code is read into the template. Then the template is compiled and executed. This script looks at all the data submitted through the form and determines whether it is valid. For each field that contains an invalid value, an error is added to the error_message variable. If the validate.cfm script is executed and no errors are generated, the new row is inserted into the Movies table. You might want to note quickly that the movie_id is generated using an Oracle sequence. After the row is inserted, the cflocation tag is used to return the user to the list of movies.

After the page header and title have been printed, the page checks to see whether the error_message variable contains any errors, as shown:

```
<cfif error_message is not "">
    <ul>
        <cfoutput>#error_message#</cfoutput>
    </ul>
</cfif>
```

This is why I have to set the error_message variable before calling the validate.cfm script. If the page loads and the form.movie_title field is absent, the validate.cfm script will never be called, and this cfif tag would return an error because the error_message variable was not defined. As you'll see later, each error message generated by validate.cfm is inserted in error_message as a list item. If error messages are present, the opening and closing unordered list tags are inserted around the value in the error_message variable to create a list. The next step is to set the values that will appear in the form:

```
<cfif IsDefined("form.movie_title")>
    <cfset movie_title=form.movie_title>
    <cfset director_id=form.director_id>
    <cfset budget=form.budget>
    <cfset gross=form.gross>
    <cfset release_date=form.release_date>
    <cfset director_id=form.director_id>
    <cfset studio_id=form.studio_id>
<cfelse>
    <cfset movie_title="">
    <cfset director_id="">
```

```
    <cfset budget="">
    <cfset gross="">
    <cfset release_date="">
    <cfset director_id="none">
    <cfset studio_id="none">
</cfif>
```

This is another cfif construct, which sets up the form values depending on whether the form has already been submitted. Basically, on the add.cfm page, two conditions exist under which the form can be printed. The first option is that the page is called from a link on another page, in which case all the fields should contain the default value or should be empty. The second option is that the form has been submitted, and errors were found in the form input by the validate.cfm script. In this case, the form should be populated with the values that the user entered when they submitted the form. These variables are set to cover both of these situations.

The final bit of processing the page does reads in the movie_form.cfm template, using the following code:

```
<center>
<cfinclude template="movie_form.cfm">
</center>
```

The form is created and populated with the values in the variables that I just set. The entire add.cfm script is included in Listing 24.3. Figure 24.4 contains a browser window displaying the form. When the form has been successfully filled out, submitted, validated, and inserted into the database, the execution of this page is finished. Before I go on to the next script, I'll explain how the two components used in this page, validate.cfm and movie_form.cfm, work.

Figure 24.4
The add.cfm form.

LISTING 24.3 THE add.cfm SCRIPT

```
<cfset error_message="">
<cfif IsDefined("form.movie_title")>
    <cfinclude template="validate.cfm">

    <cfif error_message is "">
        <cfquery name="add_movie" datasource="development">
            INSERT INTO Movies
            (movie_id, movie_title, studio_id, director_id,
            budget, gross, release_date)
            VALUES
            (movie_id_seq.NEXTVAL,
            '#form.movie_title#',
            #form.studio_id#,
            #director_id#,
            #budget#,
            #gross#,
            '#DateFormat(release_date, "dd-mmm-yy")#')
        </cfquery>
        <cflocation url="list.cfm">
    </cfif>
</cfif>

<html>
<head>
    <title>Add New Movie</title>
</head>
<body>

<h1 align="center">Add New Movie</h1>

<cfif error_message is not "">
    <ul>
        <cfoutput>#error_message#</cfoutput>
    </ul>
</cfif>

<cfif IsDefined("form.movie_title")>
    <cfset movie_title=form.movie_title>
    <cfset director_id=form.director_id>
    <cfset budget=form.budget>
    <cfset gross=form.gross>
    <cfset release_date=form.release_date>
    <cfset director_id=form.director_id>
    <cfset studio_id=form.studio_id>
<cfelse>
    <cfset movie_title="">
    <cfset director_id="">
    <cfset budget="">
    <cfset gross="">
    <cfset release_date="">
    <cfset director_id="none">
    <cfset studio_id="none">
</cfif>
```

PART
VII
CH
24

continues

LISTING 24.3   CONTINUED

```
<center>
<cfinclude template="movie_form.cfm">
</center>

</body>
</html>
```

THE VALIDATION COMPONENT

The validation component is very simple for this application, but it could be as complex as I choose. In this case, it consists of a number of cfif tags that verify that all the required fields are filled out and that some of the fields contain the appropriate type of data. The validation code is included in Listing 24.4.

LISTING 24.4   THE validate.cfm COMPONENT

```
<cfset crlf=Chr(13) & Chr(10)>
<cfset error_message="">
<cfif form.movie_title is "">
    <cfset error_message=error_message &
    "<li>You must enter a movie title." & crlf>
</cfif>
<cfif not IsNumeric(form.budget)>
    <cfset error_message=error_message &
    "<li>The budget must be a number." & crlf>
</cfif>
<cfif not IsNumeric(form.gross)>
    <cfset error_message=error_message &
    "<li>The gross must be a number." & crlf>
</cfif>
<cfif not IsDate(form.release_date)>
    <cfset error_message=error_message &
    "<li>Release date must be a valid date." & crlf>
</cfif>
<cfif form.director_id is "none">
    <cfset error_message=error_message &
    "<li>You must choose a director." & crlf>
</cfif>
<cfif form.studio_id is "none">
    <cfset error_message=error_message &
    "<li>You must choose a studio." & crlf>
</cfif>
```

Tip 91 from
Rafe Colburn

One advantage of bundling all the validation code into a single component is that it is a "black box." It performs all the required validation and simply adds any errors to the error_message variable. I could add any validation code I wanted to this component, and it wouldn't affect the way the rest of the script works.

First, the validation code sets a couple of preliminary variables. It creates a variable called `crlf` that contains the line ending characters, which I use to embed carriage returns into the `error_message` string. I also set the `error_message` variable to an empty string in case the calling page failed to do so. At that point, I test each of the values from the form to ensure that they contain valid data. The following are the actions taken for each of the fields:

- I check to make sure that something was entered in the `movie_title` field.
- I check to make sure that a number was entered in the `budget` field.
- I verify that a number was entered in the `gross` field.
- I use the `IsDate` function to make sure that a valid date was entered in the `release_date` field.
- I make sure that a value other than the default value of `"none"` was selected in the `director_id` field.
- I make sure that a value other than `"none"` was selected for `studio_id`.

PART

VII

CH

24

An example of a form that was submitted with invalid values is included in Figure 24.5.

Figure 24.5
A form submitted with invalid data.

THE FORM COMPONENT

The `movie_form.cfm` component creates the form through which movies are added or updated. It includes the values set before the component is loaded to populate the `value` attributes for each of the fields in the form. First, the component retrieves the values for the `director_id`, and `studio_id` select lists from the `People` and `Studios` tables, respectively:

```
<cfquery name="get_studios" datasource="development">
    SELECT studio_name, studio_id
```

```
      FROM Studios
      ORDER BY studio_name
</cfquery>

<cfquery name="get_people" datasource="development">
      SELECT person_lname, person_fname, person_id
      FROM People
      ORDER BY person_lname, person_fname
</cfquery>
```

The select lists are populated with the names from each of these two queries, and the values are set to the corresponding IDs. The next step is to create the form itself. The form is formatted using a table, and the form tag contains only the method attribute because it is being submitted to itself (removing the need for the action attribute). Submitting the form to itself makes it easier to use a form component because I don't have to worry about setting a variable in the calling page to indicate which script the form should be submitted to.

We'll go through the individual form fields. The first is the movie_title field:

```
<tr>
    <td align="right"><b>title</b></td>
    <td><input type="text" name="movie_title" size=20 maxlength=20
    value="<cfoutput>#movie_title#</cfoutput>"></td>
</tr>
```

The movie_title field is a text field that has both a size and a maxlength of 20. This is because the movie_title field itself in the Movies table is a varchar field of size 20. In a production application, I would want to confirm that the value entered here was 20 characters or less despite the presence of the maxlength attribute because forms can be spoofed.

The next field in the form is the studio_id field, which is a select list.

```
<tr>
    <td align="right"><b>studio</b></td>
    <td>
    <select size=1 name="studio_id">
        <option value="none">
    <cfset temp_studio_id=studio_id>
    <cfloop query="get_studios">
        <cfif get_studios.studio_id is temp_studio_id>
            <cfoutput>
            <option value="#get_studios.studio_id#"
            selected>#get_studios.studio_name#
            </cfoutput>
        <cfelse>
            <cfoutput>
            <option value="#get_studios.studio_id#">#get_studios.studio_name#
            </cfoutput>
        </cfif>
    </cfloop>
    </select>
      </td>
</tr>
```

Creating a select list is a bit more complicated than creating a simple text field. This form field contains an option for each row retrieved by the get_studios query. When the form loads, one of the items in the select list must actually be selected. In this case, I've already set the studio_id variable before calling the movie_form.cfm component. I create a new variable, temp_studio_id, to store the current studio ID within the loop to prevent the cfloop tag from overwriting the value in the real studio_id variable. This is a variable scope issue. Because the variable name studio_id corresponds to the name of a field in the query being processed by the cfloop tag, the studio_id value from the query overwrites my variable.

The selected attribute is used to indicate which item in a select list should be selected when the form loads initially. If none of the form options have the selected attribute, the first item in the form is selected automatically. In this case, a cfif tag within the loop compares the current studio_id retrieved by the query with the value of the temp_studio_id variable, which contains the default studio_id for the form. When the two values match, the selected attribute is inserted for that item. For all the other options, the selected attribute is left out. The code to create the director_id list is identical except for the query and name of the form field:

```
<tr>
    <td align="right"><b>director</b></td>
    <td>
<select size=1 name="director_id">
    <option value="none">
    <cfloop query="get_people">
        <cfif get_people.person_id is director_id>
            <cfoutput>
            <option value="#get_people.person_id#"
            selected>#get_people.person_fname# #get_people.person_lname#
            </cfoutput>
        <cfelse>
            <cfoutput>
            <option value="#get_people.person_id#">#get_people.person_fname#
#get_people.person_lname#
            </cfoutput>
        </cfif>
    </cfloop>
    </select>
      </td>
</tr>
```

The next two fields are the budget and gross fields; both of them are text input fields, as is the release_date field. After all the input fields have been created, the submit and reset buttons are inserted in the last row of the table. The full source code to the movie_form component appears in Listing 24.5. The most important thing to notice about this form is that all the values for the fields are drawn from data set in the calling page. This allows the form to be used in any type of application that allows a movie to be created or updated.

LISTING 24.5 THE movie_form.cfm COMPONENT

```
<cfquery name="get_studios" datasource="development">
    SELECT studio_name, studio_id
    FROM Studios
```

continues

LISTING 24.5 CONTINUED

```
    ORDER BY studio_name
</cfquery>

<cfquery name="get_people" datasource="development">
    SELECT person_lname, person_fname, person_id
    FROM People
    ORDER BY person_lname, person_fname
</cfquery>

<form method="post">
<table border=1 cellspacing=0 cellpadding=4>
    <tr>
        <td align="right"><b>title</b></td>
        <td><input type="text" name="movie_title" size=20 maxlength=20
        value="<cfoutput>#movie_title#</cfoutput>"></td>
    </tr>
    <tr>
        <td align="right"><b>studio</b></td>
        <td>
        <select size=1 name="studio_id">
            <option value="none">
        <cfset temp_studio_id=studio_id>
        <cfloop query="get_studios">
            <cfif get_studios.studio_id is temp_studio_id>
                <cfoutput>
                <option value="#get_studios.studio_id#"
                selected>#get_studios.studio_name#
                </cfoutput>
            <cfelse>
                <cfoutput>
                <option value="#get_studios.studio_id#">#get_studios.studio_name#
                </cfoutput>
            </cfif>
        </cfloop>
        </select>
        </td>
    </tr>
    <tr>
        <td align="right"><b>director</b></td>
        <td>
        <select size=1 name="director_id">
            <option value="none">
        <cfloop query="get_people">
            <cfif get_people.person_id is director_id>
                <cfoutput>
                <option value="#get_people.person_id#"
                selected>#get_people.person_fname# #get_people.person_lname#
                </cfoutput>
            <cfelse>
                <cfoutput>
                <option value="#get_people.person_id#">#get_people.person_fname#
#get_people.person_lname#
                </cfoutput>
            </cfif>
        </cfloop>
        </select>
```

```
          </td>
      </tr>
      <tr>
          <td align="right"><b>budget</b></td>
          <td><input type="text" name="budget" size=10 maxlength=10
          value="<cfoutput>#budget#</cfoutput>">
      </tr>
      <tr>
          <td align="right"><b>gross</b></td>
          <td><input type="text" name="gross" size=10 maxlength=10
          value="<cfoutput>#gross#</cfoutput>">
      </tr>
      <tr>
          <td align="right"><b>release date</b></td>
          <td><input type="text" name="release_date" size=20
          value="<cfoutput>#release_date#</cfoutput>">
      </tr>
      <tr>
          <td><br></td>
          <td><input type="submit"> <input type="reset"></td>
      </tr>
  </table>
  </form>
```

PART

VII

CH

24

UPDATING AN EXISTING MOVIE

The page for updating existing movies, edit.cfm, is remarkably similar to the add.cfm page. As I said when I discussed add.cfm, the only difference is that when edit.cfm is called initially, the form is populated with the values from the database that are associated with the movie being updated. A prepopulated update form is shown in Figure 24.6.

Figure 24.6
An update form containing values from the database.

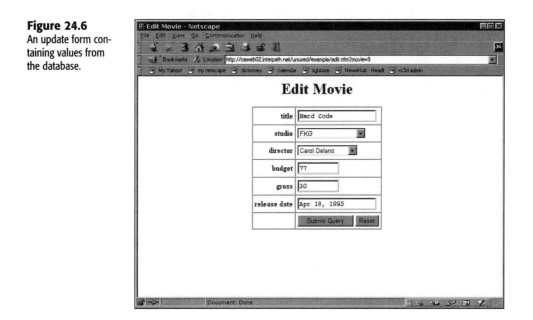

The first code in the edit.cfm page is like that in the detail.cfm page; it checks to make sure that a movie ID was passed as a parameter. If that parameter does not exist, the user is returned to the list.cfm page:

```
<cfif not IsDefined("url.movie")>
    <cflocation url="list.cfm">
</cfif>
```

Then, the script determines whether the form has been submitted or is being rendered for the first time. If the form has been submitted, and the results of the form submission are being processed, the validate.cfm component is called to check for errors. If no errors are present (which is indicated by the error_message variable being empty), the record is updated in the database using an UPDATE statement, and the user is returned to the list.cfm page.

However, if the form is being called for the first time and has not been submitted, the cfelse retrieves the data associated with the movie specified through the query string using the get_movie_detail query. The following is the decision code that determines whether the form has been submitted:

```
<cfset error_message="">
<cfif IsDefined("form.movie_title")>
    <cfinclude template="validate.cfm">

    <cfif error_message is "">
        <cfquery name="add_movie" datasource="development">
            UPDATE Movies
            SET movie_title = '#form.movie_title#',
            director_id = #form.director_id#,
            studio_id = #form.studio_id#,
            budget = #form.budget#,
            gross = #form.gross#,
            release_date = '#DateFormat(release_date, "dd-mmm-yy")#'
            WHERE movie_id = #url.movie#
        </cfquery>
        <cflocation url="list.cfm">
    </cfif>
<cfelse>
    <cfquery name="get_movie_detail" datasource="development">
        SELECT movie_id, movie_title, budget, gross,
        release_date, director_id, studio_id
        FROM Movies
        WHERE Movies.movie_id = #url.movie#
    </cfquery>
</cfif>
```

After the database operations have been performed, the page header is printed. If the form was submitted and errors were found, the contents of error_message are displayed. Just as in the add.cfm page, the next step is to set the variables that will be inserted as values in the form on the page. In this case, however, the choice is between adding the values from the form that has already been submitted and the values pulled from the database. In the case of the add.cfm script, the choice was between values from the submitted form and empty default values for a new movie. Here is the code:

```
<cfif IsDefined("form.movie_title")>
    <cfset movie_title=form.movie_title>
    <cfset director_id=form.director_id>
    <cfset budget=form.budget>
    <cfset gross=form.gross>
    <cfset release_date=form.release_date>
    <cfset director_id=form.director_id>
    <cfset studio_id=form.studio_id>
<cfelse>
    <cfset movie_title=get_movie_detail.movie_title>
    <cfset director_id=get_movie_detail.director_id>
    <cfset budget=get_movie_detail.budget>
    <cfset gross=get_movie_detail.gross>
    <cfset release_date=DateFormat(get_movie_detail.release_date, "mmm d, yyyy")>
    <cfset director_id=get_movie_detail.director_id>
    <cfset studio_id=get_movie_detail.studio_id>
</cfif>
```

After the values for the form have been set up, the `movie_form.cfm` component is loaded, and the page is complete. The full source code for `edit.cfm` appears in Listing 24.6.

LISTING 24.6   THE FULL SOURCE CODE FOR `edit.cfm`

```
<cfif not IsDefined("url.movie")>
    <cflocation url="list.cfm">
</cfif>

<cfset error_message="">
<cfif IsDefined("form.movie_title")>
    <cfinclude template="validate.cfm">

    <cfif error_message is "">
        <cfquery name="add_movie" datasource="development">
            UPDATE Movies
            SET movie_title = '#form.movie_title#',
            director_id = #form.director_id#,
            studio_id = #form.studio_id#,
            budget = #form.budget#,
            gross = #form.gross#,
            release_date =
            '#DateFormat(release_date, "dd-mmm-yy")#'
            WHERE movie_id = #url.movie#
        </cfquery>
        <cflocation url="list.cfm">
    </cfif>
<cfelse>
    <cfquery name="get_movie_detail" datasource="development">
        SELECT movie_id, movie_title, budget, gross,
        release_date, director_id, studio_id
        FROM Movies
        WHERE Movies.movie_id = #url.movie#
    </cfquery>
</cfif>

<html>
```

continues

LISTING 24.6   CONTINUED

```
<head>
    <title>Edit Movie</title>
</head>
<body>

<h1 align="center">Edit Movie</h1>

<cfif error_message is not "">
    <ul>
        <cfoutput>#error_message#</cfoutput>
    </ul>
</cfif>

<cfif IsDefined("form.movie_title")>
    <cfset movie_title=form.movie_title>
    <cfset director_id=form.director_id>
    <cfset budget=form.budget>
    <cfset gross=form.gross>
    <cfset release_date=form.release_date>
    <cfset director_id=form.director_id>
    <cfset studio_id=form.studio_id>
<cfelse>
    <cfset movie_title=get_movie_detail.movie_title>
    <cfset director_id=get_movie_detail.director_id>
    <cfset budget=get_movie_detail.budget>
    <cfset gross=get_movie_detail.gross>
    <cfset release_date=DateFormat(get_movie_detail.release_date, "mmm d, yyyy")>
    <cfset director_id=get_movie_detail.director_id>
    <cfset studio_id=get_movie_detail.studio_id>
</cfif>

<center>
<cfinclude template="movie_form.cfm">
</center>

</body>
</html>
```

EDITING THE CAST OF A MOVIE

As I discussed in Chapter 2, "Database Design," two relationships exist between the Movies table and the People table. The first is a one-to-many relationship between People and Movies expressed through the director_id field in the Movies table. Each person can direct many movies, but movies can have only one director. This relationship can be edited through the movie update form. The other relationship is a many-to-many relationship, which is used to specify the cast for each movie. Each movie can have many cast members, and each person can appear in many movies. This relationship is expressed through the Cast_Movies joining table. Because each movie can be associated with multiple records in Cast_Movies, this data cannot be edited through the standard movie update form.

Instead, I created a special form that allows users to view, add, and remove cast members from a movie. The add_cast.cfm script enables users to make changes to the cast of a movie. As you saw earlier, it is accessible through the detail page of a movie. This script is somewhat interesting because unlike the other scripts in the system, it provides several functions. Decision logic is built into the script, which enables the script to determine which action the user wants to take and process the data accordingly.

Because this script is designed to act on a particular movie, it requires that the ID of the movie be specified in the query string. If the ID of the movie is not specified, the user is returned to the list.cfm page. Three variables are set at the beginning of the script: the error validation message, the end of line string, and the current movie ID:

```
<cfset crlf=Chr(13) & Chr(10)>
<cfset error_message = "">
<cfse movie=url.movie>
```

When the page is initially called, no action is specified. In that case, the script assumes that you want a listing of the movie's cast. If no action is specified, the page goes ahead and prints the cast list without first performing any actions on the list. The IsDefined() function is used to determine whether the action attribute exists:

```
<cfif IsDefined("url.action")>
```

If the action parameter does exist, the script determines which action is specified. The first option is delete, which indicates that the specified cast member should be removed. In this case, a DELETE query is used to remove that cast member:

```
<cfif url.action is "delete">
    <cfquery name="delete_cast_member" datasource="development">
            DELETE FROM Cast_Movies
        WHERE movie_id = #url.movie#
        AND person_id = #url.cast#
    </cfquery>
```

To delete an item, both the cast and the movie URL parameters are required in the query string that calls the page. If either of these elements are left out, the query will fail to delete the record because both of them are used to specify a primary key value in the Cast_Movies table. As you will see soon, both of these elements are hard coded into the links on this page; therefore, the user would have to manually edit the URL to cause the action to fail.

The add action is used to insert a new row into the Cast_Movies table. The following code is executed if the action attribute contains the value add:

```
<cfelseif url.action is "add">
    <cfif Trim(url.role) is "">
        <cfset error_message = error_message &
        "<li>You must specify the role the actor played."
        & crlf>
    </cfif>
    <cfif not IsNumeric(url.payment)>
        <cfset error_message = error_message &
        "<li>The actor's payment must be entered."
        & crlf>
    </cfif>
```

```
    <cfif url.cast is "none">
        <cfset error_message= error_message &
        "<li>You must select an actor for this role."
        & crlf>
    </cfif>
    <cfif error_message is "">
        <cfquery name="add_cast_member"
        datasource="development">
            INSERT INTO Cast_Movies
            (movie_id, person_id, role, payment)
            VALUES
            (#url.movie#, #url.cast#,
            '#url.role#', #url.payment#)
        </cfquery>
    </cfif>
</cfif>
```

This code uses the `error_message` code that you've seen in the other scripts in this application. If the user fails to enter a value in the `payment` or `role` fields, or if the user does not select an actor from the list, the page is sent back to the user with the error message displayed. If the form input is valid, the new row is inserted into the database. As you can see, four values are passed to the script through the query string. These values make up the new record in the database. Because so few fields are in the table, users are not allowed to modify existing cast members. If they want to make a change, they must remove the existing cast member entry and add a new entry with the correct information.

When the action segment of the page is finished executing, the information is gathered from the database so that it can be presented on the page. The database queries are as follows:

```
<cfquery name="get_movie_title" datasource="development">
    SELECT movie_title
    FROM Movies
    WHERE movie_id = #url.movie#
</cfquery>

<cfquery name="get_movie_cast" datasource="development">
    SELECT payment, role, person_fname, person_lname,
    Cast_Movies.person_id AS person_id
    FROM Cast_Movies, People
    WHERE movie_id = #url.movie#
    AND Cast_Movies.person_id = People.person_id
</cfquery>

<cfquery name="get_people" datasource="development">
    SELECT person_id, person_fname, person_lname
    FROM People
    ORDER BY person_fname, person_lname
</cfquery>
```

The first query just gets the title of the movie from the database. This page doesn't present any other data from the `Movies` table, so a separate query is required to grab and present the movie title. The next query retrieves the cast of the movie using a joining query that retrieves the first and last names of each cast member from the `People` table and the role and payment from the `Cast_Movies` table. The final query retrieves a full list of people from the

People database, which is used to populate the pull-down box in the "add new cast member" form.

After the heading for the page is printed, the table containing the list of cast members is displayed:

```
<table cellpadding=4 cellspacing=0 border=1>
<cfoutput query="get_movie_cast">
    <tr>
        <td>#person_fname# #person_lname#</td>
        <td>#role#</td>
        <td>#payment#</td>
        <td><a
➥href="add_cast.cfm?action=delete&movie=#url.movie#&cast=#person_id#">
        delete</a></td>
    </tr>
</cfoutput>
</table>
```

Again, I use the table and cfoutput tags to create a table containing the records returned by a query. Each row contains the actor's name, the role played, and the payment received. I also generate a link that is used to delete the cast member in that row. The action, movie, and cast parameters are inserted into the command line within the link. The table containing the cast members appears in Figure 24.7.

Figure 24.7
A table containing the cast members in a movie.

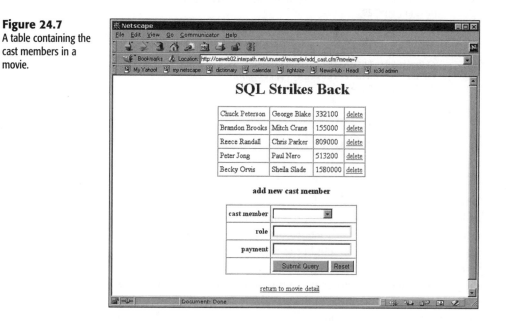

After the table containing the cast for the movie is displayed, the next step is to create the form used to add new cast members to the table. Like the movie creation/update form, this form is formatted within a table for readability:

```
<form action="add_cast.cfm" method="get">
<input type="hidden" name="action" value="add">
<input type="hidden" name="movie" value="<cfoutput>#movie#</cfoutput>">
<table border=1 cellspacing=0 cellpadding=4>
    <tr>
        <td align="right"><b>cast member</b></td>
        <td>
        <select size=1 name="cast">
            <option value="none">
        <cfloop query="get_people">
            <cfif get_people.person_id is cast>
                <cfoutput><option
                value="#get_people.person_id#"
                selected>#get_people.person_fname# #get_people.person_lname#
                </cfoutput>
            <cfelse>
                <cfoutput><option
                value="#get_people.person_id#">#get_people.person_fname#
#get_people.person_lname#</cfoutput>
            </cfif>
        </cfloop>
        </select>
    </tr>
    <tr>
        <td align="right"><b>role</b></td>
        <td><input type="text" name="role"
        value="<cfoutput>#role#</cfoutput>" size="20"
        maxlength="20"></td>
    </tr>
    <tr>
        <td align="right"><b>payment</b></td>
        <td><input type="text" name="payment"
        value="<cfoutput>#payment#</cfoutput>" size="20"
        maxlength="20"></td>
    </tr>
    <tr>
        <td><br></td>
        <td><input type="submit"> <input type="reset"></td>
    </tr>
</table>
</form>
```

This form contains two hidden fields: action and movie. Because this form is used only to add new cast members to a movie, the hidden field can be used to pass the action attribute to the server. This page also contains cast members for only this movie; therefore, we can safely hard code the movie field in the page as well. This form is similar in most ways to the form in the movie_form.cfm script, so I won't cover the gory details here. The script creates the pull-down menu of actors by looping over the results of the get_people query and adding the selected attribute to the actor that was selected when the form was submitted, if the form is being rendered along with an error message. The "add new cast member" form is included in Figure 24.8. The full source code listing for add_cast.cfm appears in Listing 24.7.

Figure 24.8
The "add new cast member" form.

PART

VII

CH

24

LISTING 24.7 THE FULL SOURCE CODE FOR THE add_cast.cfm SCRIPT

```
<CFSET crlf=CHR(13) & CHR(10)>
<CFSET error_message = "">
<CFSET movie=URL.MOVIE>

<CFIF IsDefined("url.action")>

    <CFIF URL.action IS "delete">
        <CFQUERY NAME="delete_cast_member" DATASOURCE="development">
        DELETE FROM Cast_Movies
            WHERE movie_id = #URL.movie#
            AND person_id = #URL.cast#
        </CFQUERY>
    <CFELSEIF URL.action IS "add">
        <CFIF TRIM(URL.role) IS "">
            <CFSET error_message = error_message &
            "<li>You must specify the role the actor played."
            & crlf>
        </CFIF>
        <CFIF NOT IsNumeric(URL.payment)>
            <CFSET error_message = error_message &
            "<li>The actor's payment must be entered."
            & crlf>
        </CFIF>
        <CFIF URL.cast IS "none">
            <CFSET error_message= error_message &
            "<li>You must select an actor for this role."
            & crlf>
```

continues

LISTING 24.7 CONTINUED

```
        </CFIF>
        <CFIF error_message IS "">
            <CFQUERY NAME="add_cast_member"
            DATASOURCE="development">
                INSERT INTO Cast_Movies
                (movie_id, person_id, role, payment)
                VALUES
                (#url.movie#, #URL.cast#,
                '#url.role#', #URL.payment#)
            </CFQUERY>
        </CFIF>
    </CFIF>
</CFIF>

<CFIF NOT IsDefined("cast")>
    <CFSET cast="0">
</CFIF>
<CFIF NOT IsDefined("role")>
    <CFSET role="">
</CFIF>
<CFIF NOT IsDefined("payment")>
    <CFSET payment="">
</CFIF>
<CFQUERY NAME="get_movie_title" DATASOURCE="development">
    SELECT movie_title
    FROM Movies
    WHERE movie_id = #URL.movie#
</CFQUERY>

<CFQUERY NAME="get_movie_cast" DATASOURCE="development">
    SELECT payment, role, person_fname, person_lname,
    Cast_Movies.person_id AS person_id
    FROM Cast_Movies, People
    WHERE movie_id = #URL.movie#
    AND Cast_Movies.person_id = People.person_id
</CFQUERY>

<CFQUERY NAME="get_people" DATASOURCE="development">
    SELECT person_id, person_fname, person_lname
    FROM People
    ORDER BY person_fname, person_lname
</CFQUERY>


<TABLE CELLPADDING=4 CELLSPACING=0 BORDER=1>
<CFOUTPUT QUERY="get_movie_cast">
    <TR>
        <TD>#person_fname# #person_lname#</TD>
        <TD>#role#</TD>
        <TD>#payment#</TD>
        <TD><A
HREF="add_cast.cfm?action=delete&movie=#URL.movie#&cast=#person_id#">
        delete</A></TD>
    </TR>
</CFOUTPUT>
```

```
</TABLE>


<CFIF ERROR_MESSAGE IS NOT "">
    <UL>
    <CFOUTPUT>#error_message#</CFOUTPUT>
    </UL>
</CFIF>

<CENTER>
</CENTER>
<FORM ACTION="add_cast.cfm">
<INPUT TYPE="hidden" NAME="action" VALUE="add">
<INPUT TYPE="hidden" NAME="movie" VALUE="<CFOUTPUT>#movie#</CFOUTPUT>">
<TABLE BORDER=1 CELLSPACING=0 CELLPADDING=4>
    <TR>
        <TD ALIGN="right"><B>cast member</B></TD>
        <TD>
        <SELECT SIZE=1 NAME="cast">
            <OPTION VALUE="none">
        <CFLOOP QUERY="get_people">
            <CFIF GET_PEOPLE.PERSON_ID IS CAST>
                <CFOUTPUT><OPTION
                VALUE="#get_people.person_id#"
                SELECTED>#get_people.person_fname#
#get_people.person_lname#</CFOUTPUT>
        <CFELSE>
                <CFOUTPUT><OPTION
                VALUE="#get_people.person_id#">#get_people.person_fname#
#get_people.person_lname#</CFOUTPUT>
            </CFIF>
        </CFLOOP>
        </SELECT>
    </TR>
    <TR>
        <TD ALIGN="right"><B>role</B></TD>
        <TD><INPUT TYPE="text" NAME="role"
        VALUE="<CFOUTPUT>#role#</CFOUTPUT>" size="20"
        maxlength="20"></TD>
    </TR>
    <TR>
        <TD ALIGN="right"><B>payment</B></TD>
        <TD><INPUT TYPE="text" NAME="payment"
        VALUE="<CFOUTPUT>#payment#</CFOUTPUT>" size="20"
        maxlength="20"></TD>
    </TR>
    <TR>
        <TD><BR></TD>
        <TD><INPUT TYPE="submit"> <INPUT TYPE="reset"></TD>
    </TR>
</TABLE>
</FORM>

<CENTER>
<P>
```

PART

VII

Cʜ

24

continues

LISTING 24.7   CONTINUED

```
    <A HREF="detail.cfm?movie=<CFOUTPUT>#movie#</CFOUTPUT>">return
to movie detail</A>
</P>
</CENTER>

</BODY>
</HTML>

<cfif not IsDefined("url.movie")>
        <cflocation url="list.cfm">
</cfif>

<cfset crlf=Chr(13) & Chr(10)>
<cfset error_message = "">
<cfset movie=url.movie>

<cfif IsDefined("url.action")>
        <cfif url.action is "delete">
                <cfquery name="delete_cast_member" datasource="development">
                        DELETE FROM Cast_Movies
                        WHERE movie_id = #url.movie#
                        AND person_id = #url.cast#
                </cfquery>
        <cfelseif url.action is "add">
                <cfif Trim(url.role) is "">
                        <cfset error_message = error_message & "<li>You must
specify the role the actor played." & crlf>
                </cfif>
                <cfif not IsNumeric(url.payment)>
                        <cfset error_message = error_message & "<li>The actor's
payment must be entered." & crlf>
                </cfif>
                <cfif url.cast is "none">
                        <cfset error_message= error_message & "<li>You must
select an actor for this role." & crlf>
                </cfif>
                <cfif error_message is "">
                        <cfquery name="add_cast_member" datasource="development"
>
                                INSERT INTO Cast_Movies
                                (movie_id, person_id, role, payment)
                                VALUES
                                (#url.movie#, #url.cast#, '#url.role#',
#url.payment#)
                        </cfquery>
                </cfif>
        </cfif>
</cfif>

<cfif error_message is not "">
        <cfset cast=url.cast>
        <cfset role=url.role>
        <cfset payment=url.payment>
<cfelse>
        <cfset cast="none">
        <cfset role="">
```

```
        <cfset payment="">
</cfif>

<cfquery name="get_movie_title" datasource="development">
        SELECT movie_title
        FROM Movies
        WHERE movie_id = #url.movie#
</cfquery>

<cfquery name="get_movie_cast" datasource="development">
        SELECT payment, role, person_fname, person_lname, Cast_Movies.person_id
AS person_id
        FROM Cast_Movies, People
        WHERE movie_id = #url.movie#
        AND Cast_Movies.person_id = People.person_id
</cfquery>

<cfquery name="get_people" datasource="development">
        SELECT person_id, person_fname, person_lname
        FROM People
        ORDER BY person_fname, person_lname
</cfquery>

<h1 align="center"><cfoutput>#get_movie_title.movie_title#</cfoutput></h1>

<center>
<table cellpadding=4 cellspacing=0 border=1>
<cfoutput query="get_movie_cast">
        <tr>
                <td>#person_fname# #person_lname#</td>
                <td>#role#</td>
                <td>#payment#</td>
                <td><a href="add_cast.cfm?action=delete&movie=#url.movie#&cast=#
person_id#">delete</a></td>
        </tr>
</cfoutput>
</table>
</center>

<h3 align="center">add new cast member</h3>

<cfif error_message is not "">
        <ul>
        <cfoutput>#error_message#</cfoutput>
        </ul>
</cfif>

<center>
<form action="add_cast.cfm" method="get">
<input type="hidden" name="action" value="add">
<input type="hidden" name="movie" value="<cfoutput>#movie#</cfoutput>">
<table border=1 cellspacing=0 cellpadding=4>
        <tr>
                <td align="right"><b>cast member</b></td>
                <td>
```

LISTING 24.7 CONTINUED

```
                    <select size=1 name="cast">
                            <option value="none">
                    <cfloop query="get_people">
                            <cfif get_people.person_id is cast>
                                    <cfoutput><option value="#get_people.person_id#"
 selected>#get_people.person_fname# #get_people.person_lname#</cfoutput>
                            <cfelse>
                                    <cfoutput><option value="#get_people.person_id#"
 >#get_people.person_fname# #get_people.person_lname#</cfoutput>
                            </cfif>
                    </cfloop>
                    </select>
        </tr>
        <tr>
                    <td align="right"><b>role</b></td>
                    <td><input type="text" name="role" value="<cfoutput>#role#
</cfoutput>" size="20" maxlength="20"></td>
        </tr>
        <tr>
                    <td align="right"><b>payment</b></td>
                    <td><input type="text" name="payment" value="<cfoutput>#payment#
</cfoutput>" size="20" maxlength="20"></td>
        </tr>
        <tr>
                    <td><br></td>
                    <td><input type="submit"> <input type="reset"></td>
        </tr>
</table>
</form>
</center>

<center>
<p>
        <a href="detail.cfm?movie=<cfoutput>#movie#</cfoutput>">return to movie
detail</a>
</p>
</center>

</body>
</html>
```

MODIFYING A MOVIE'S LOCATIONS

The script used to modify movie locations is very similar to the add_cast.cfm script. The only real difference is that this script retrieves and modifies records in the Locations table instead of the Cast_Movies table. I won't spend much time covering this script because it is so similar to the cast script. I would like to point out a couple of interesting points in this script, however.

Remember that the primary key of Locations actually comprises all three columns in the table. Thus, in the query used to remove a record from the table, all three columns must be referenced, as you can see from the following code:

```
<cfquery name="delete_location" datasource="development">
    DELETE FROM Locations
    WHERE movie_id = #url.movie#
        AND city = '#url.city#'
    AND state = '#url.state#'
</cfquery>
```

This script doesn't verify that the state the user enters is valid. If you were going to deploy this script in a production environment, you would want to include code in it that verified that the state the user enters actually exists. You could either hard code all the states into the script, or you could create a table in your database consisting of records that contain the abbreviations for all 50 states. You could then query the database to determine whether the state entered is valid.

The full source code to the add_location.cfm script appears in Listing 24.8, and the page is shown in Figure 24.9.

PART
VII

CH
24

Figure 24.9
The
add_location.cfm
page.

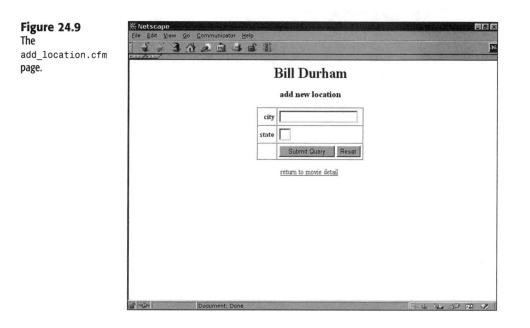

LISTING 24.8   THE SOURCE CODE TO THE add_location.cfm SCRIPT

```
<cfif not IsDefined("url.movie")>
    <cflocation url="list.cfm">
</cfif>
```

continues

LISTING 24.8   CONTINUED

```coldfusion
<cfset crlf=Chr(13) & Chr(10)>
<cfset error_message = "">
<cfset movie=url.movie>

<cfif IsDefined("url.action")>
    <cfif url.action is "delete">
        <cfquery name="delete_location" datasource="development">
            DELETE FROM Locations
            WHERE movie_id = #url.movie#
            AND city = '#url.city#'
            AND state = '#url.state#'
        </cfquery>
    <cfelseif url.action is "add">
        <cfif Trim(url.city) is "">
            <cfset error_message = error_message
            & "<li>You must enter the name of a city." & crlf>
        </cfif>
        <cfif Len(url.state) is not 2>
            <cfset error_message = error_message
            & "<li>You must enter a state." & crlf>
        </cfif>
        <cfif error_message is "">
            <cfquery name="add_location" datasource="development">
                INSERT INTO Locations
                (movie_id, city, state)
                VALUES
                (#url.movie#, '#url.city#', '#url.state#')
            </cfquery>
        </cfif>
    </cfif>
</cfif>

<cfif error_message is not "">
    <cfset city=url.city>
    <cfset state=url.state>
<cfelse>
    <cfset city="">
    <cfset state="">
</cfif>

<cfquery name="get_movie_title" datasource="development">
    SELECT movie_title
    FROM Movies
    WHERE movie_id = #url.movie#
</cfquery>

<cfquery name="get_movie_locations" datasource="development">
    SELECT city, state
    FROM Locations
    WHERE movie_id = #url.movie#
</cfquery>

<h1 align="center"><cfoutput>#get_movie_title.movie_title#</cfoutput></h1>
```

```
<center>
<table cellpadding=4 cellspacing=0 border=1>
<cfoutput query="get_movie_locations">
    <tr>
        <td>#city#, #state#</td>
        <td><a
href="add_location.cfm?action=delete&movie=#url.movie#&city=#city#&state=#state#">
delete</a></td>
    </tr>
</cfoutput>
</table>
</center>

<h3 align="center">add new location</h3>

<cfif error_message is not "">
    <ul>
    <cfoutput>#error_message#</cfoutput>
    </ul>
</cfif>

<center>
<form action="add_location.cfm" method="get">
<input type="hidden" name="action" value="add">
<input type="hidden" name="movie" value="<cfoutput>#movie#</cfoutput>">
<table border=1 cellspacing=0 cellpadding=4>
    <tr>
        <td align="right"><b>city</b></td>
        <td><input type="text" name="city"
        value="<cfoutput>#city#</cfoutput>" size="20"
        maxlength="20"></td>
    </tr>
    <tr>
        <td align="right"><b>state</b></td>
        <td><input type="text" name="state"
        value="<cfoutput>#state#</cfoutput>" size="2"
        maxlength="2"></td>
    </tr>
    <tr>
        <td><br></td>
        <td><input type="submit"> <input type="reset"></td>
    </tr>
</table>
</form>
</center>

<center>
<p>
    <a href="detail.cfm?movie=<cfoutput>#movie#</cfoutput>">
    return to movie detail</a>
</p>
</center>

</body>
</html>
```

DELETING AN ITEM

The `delete.cfm` script is very simple. Basically, the script executes the queries that delete the specified movie and then redirects the user to the `list.cfm` page to view the remaining movies. First, the page verifies that the `movie` parameter is present, and it either redirects the user to `list.cfm` or executes the queries depending on whether the parameter is set.

The queries delete the entries corresponding to the specified movie in both the `Cast_Movies` and `Locations` tables, along with the entry for the movie in the `Movies` table itself. It does not delete items from the `People` or `Studios` tables because they are independent of the `Movies` table. The source code for the `delete.cfm` script is provided in Listing 24.9.

LISTING 24.9   THE SOURCE CODE FOR `delete.cfm`

```
<cfif not IsDefined("url.movie")>
    <cflocation url="list.cfm">
</cfif>

<cfquery name="delete_locations" datasource="development">
    DELETE FROM Locations
    WHERE movie_id = #url.movie#
</cfquery>

<cfquery name="delete_cast" datasource="development">
    DELETE FROM Cast_Movies
    WHERE movie_id = #url.movie#
</cfquery>

<cfquery name="delete_movie" datasource="development">
    DELETE FROM Movies
    WHERE movie_id = #url.movie#
</cfquery>

<cflocation url="list.cfm">
```

IN THE REAL WORLD

This book concluded with a discussion of how you might write a real-world database-backed Web application. Through the course of this book, I've explained database design, basic SQL queries, joins, subqueries, and views. I've also covered stored procedures, database security, and a number of specific databases.

At this point, you should be well equipped to apply your SQL programming skills in any real-world situation that might arise. So I wish you good luck and send you on your way.

A

SYSTEM-DEFINED EXCEPTIONS IN PL/SQL

In this chapter

In Chapter 17, "Writing Oracle PL/SQL Stored Procedures," I discussed the creation of stored procedures in Oracle PL/SQL. In that chapter, I explained that there are a number of exceptions that can be raised while a stored procedure is executing, and they can be trapped in the exception-handling section of the program. This appendix contains a list of those exceptions.

Exception	Error Code	Description
ACCESS_INTO_NULL	-6530	The program attempted to assign values to an uninitiated object.
COLLECTION_IS_NULL	-6531	The program attempted to apply collection methods other than EXISTS to an uninitiated nested table or array, or it attempted to assign values to an uninitiated nested table or array.
CURSOR_ALREADY_OPEN	-6511	The program attempted to open a cursor that had already been opened.
DUP_VAL_ON_INDEX	-1	An INSERT or UPDATE statement was executed that would have created a duplicate value in a unique index.
INVALID_CURSOR	-1001	The program attempted to open an undeclared cursor, close a cursor that had already been closed, fetch from an unopened cursor, or caused any other general cursor-related failure.
INVALID_NUMBER	-1722	This occurs when the conversion of character data to a number fails.
LOGIN_DENIED	-1017	The login/password supplied for a particular database was not valid.
NO_DATA_FOUND	+100	A SELECT statement (not a cursor fetch) returned no rows. This is a non-fatal error.

continues

continued

Exception	Error Code	Description
NOT_LOGGED_ON	-1012	This is raised whenever a user attempts to execute a SQL statement or any PL/SQL code before she has logged on.
PROGRAM_ERROR	-6501	This error is raised if PL/SQL is unable to execute the code that is currently being attempted.
SELF_IS_NULL	-30625	The program attempted to call a MEMBER method on a null instance.
STORAGE_ERROR	-6500	This is raised whenever the PL/SQL code that is currently executing requires more memory than is available.
SUBSCRIPT_BEYOND_COUNT	-6533	The program attempted to reference an element in a nested table or array with an index number larger than the number of elements in the collection.
SUBSCRIPT_OUTSIDE_LIMIT	-6532	The program attempted to reference a nested table or array with an index number outside the legal limit.
SYS_INVALID_ROWID	-1410	The conversion of a character string to a row ID failed.
TIMEOUT_ON_RESOURCE	-51	This error is raised when an attempt to access a resource takes too long.
TOO_MANY_ROWS	-1427	This is raised when a SELECT statement that is supposed to return a single row returns multiple rows. For example, if you use a subquery in the WHERE clause of a query and compare the results of the subquery to the value, that subquery must return only one row. If it returns more than one, this error will be raised.
TRANSACTION_BACKED_OUT	-61	This is raised when the remote part of a transaction is rolled back.
VALUE_ERROR	-6502	This is raised when a value is corrupted by some operation. Examples include truncation, mathematical operations that violate the precision specified for the field, data conversion errors, and the like.
ZERO_DIVIDE	-1476	This is raised when a program tries to divide a number by zero.
OTHERS	none	This is raised whenever an error that is not covered by any of the other system exceptions occurs.

INDEX

32JOINS/JOIN QUERIES